CCNA 200-301 Official Cert Guide, Volume 2, Second Edition

Companion Website and Pearson Test Prep Access Code

Access interactive study tools on this book's companion website, including practice test software, review exercises, Key Term flash card application, a study planner, and more!

To access the companion website, simply follow these steps:

1. Go to www.ciscopress.com/register.

2. Enter the **print book ISBN**: 9780138214951.

3. Answer the security question to validate your purchase.

4. Go to your account page.

5. Click on the **Registered Products** tab.

6. Under the book listing, click on the **Access Bonus Content** link.

When you register your book, your Pearson Test Prep practice test access code will automatically be populated with the book listing under the Registered Products tab. You will need this code to access the practice test that comes with this book. You can redeem the code at **PearsonTestPrep.com**. Simply choose Pearson IT Certification as your product group and log into the site with the same credentials you used to register your book. Click the **Activate New Product** button and enter the access code. More detailed instructions on how to redeem your access code for both the online and desktop versions can be found on the companion website.

If you have any issues accessing the companion website or obtaining your Pearson Test Prep practice test access code, you can contact our support team by going to **ciscopress.com/support**.

T0293441

CCNA
200-301

Official Cert Guide
Volume 2

Second Edition

WENDELL ODOM, CCIE No. 1624

JASON GOOLEY, CCIEx2 (RS, SP) No. 38759

DAVID HUCABY, CCIE No. 4594

Cisco Press

CCNA 200-301 Official Cert Guide, Volume 2, Second Edition

Wendell Odom
Jason Gooley
David Hucaby

Copyright© 2025 Pearson Education, Inc.

Published by:
Cisco Press
Hoboken, New Jersey

1 2024

Library of Congress Control Number: 2024934307

ISBN-13: 978-0-13-821495-1

ISBN-10: 0-13-821495-6

Warning and Disclaimer

This book is designed to provide information about the Cisco CCNA 200-301 exam. Every effort has been made to make this book as complete and as accurate as possible, but no warranty or fitness is implied.

The information is provided on an "as is" basis. The author, Cisco Press, and Cisco Systems, Inc. shall have neither liability nor responsibility to any person or entity with respect to any loss or damages arising from the information contained in this book or from the use of the discs or programs that may accompany it.

The opinions expressed in this book belong to the author and are not necessarily those of Cisco Systems, Inc.

Trademark Acknowledgments

All terms mentioned in this book that are known to be trademarks or service marks have been appropriately capitalized. Cisco Press or Cisco Systems, Inc., cannot attest to the accuracy of this information. Use of a term in this book should not be regarded as affecting the validity of any trademark or service mark.

Special Sales

For information about buying this title in bulk quantities, or for special sales opportunities (which may include electronic versions; custom cover designs; and content particular to your business, training goals, marketing focus, or branding interests), please contact our corporate sales department at corpsales@pearsoned.com or (800) 382-3419.

For government sales inquiries, please contact governmentsales@pearsoned.com.

For questions about sales outside the U.S., please contact intlcs@pearson.com.

Feedback Information

At Cisco Press, our goal is to create in-depth technical books of the highest quality and value. Each book is crafted with care and precision, undergoing rigorous development that involves the unique expertise of members from the professional technical community.

Readers' feedback is a natural continuation of this process. If you have any comments regarding how we could improve the quality of this book, or otherwise alter it to better suit your needs, you can contact us through email at feedback@ciscopress.com. Please make sure to include the book title and ISBN in your message.

We greatly appreciate your assistance.

Please contact us with concerns about any potential bias at https://www.pearson.com/report-bias.html.

GM K12, Early Career and Professional Learning: Soo Kang

Alliances Manager, Cisco Press: Caroline Antonio

Director, ITP Product Management: Brett Bartow

Managing Editor: Sandra Schroeder

Development Editor: Christopher Cleveland

Senior Project Editor: Tonya Simpson

Copy Editor: Chuck Hutchinson

Technical Editor: Denise Donohue

Editorial Assistant: Cindy Teeters

Cover Designer: Chuti Prasertsith

Composition: codeMantra

Indexer: Timothy Wright

Proofreader: Donna E. Mulder

Americas Headquarters
Cisco Systems, Inc.
San Jose, CA

Asia Pacific Headquarters
Cisco Systems (USA) Pte. Ltd.
Singapore

Europe Headquarters
Cisco Systems International BV
Amsterdam, The Netherlands

Cisco has more than 200 offices worldwide. Addresses, phone numbers, and fax numbers are listed on the Cisco Website at **www.cisco.com/go/offices**.

CCDE, CCENT, Cisco Eos, Cisco HealthPresence, the Cisco logo, Cisco Lumin, Cisco Nexus, Cisco StadiumVision, Cisco TelePresence, Cisco WebEx, DCE, and Welcome to the Human Network are trademarks; Changing the Way We Work, Live, Play, and Learn and Cisco Store are service marks; and Access Registrar, Aironet, AsyncOS, Bringing the Meeting To You, Catalyst, CCDA, CCDP, CCIE, CCIP, CCNA, CCNP, CCSP, CCVP, Cisco, the Cisco Certified Internetwork Expert logo, Cisco IOS, Cisco Press, Cisco Systems, Cisco Systems Capital, the Cisco Systems logo, Cisco Unity, Collaboration Without Limitation, EtherFast, EtherSwitch, Event Center, Fast Step, Follow Me Browsing, FormShare, GigaDrive, HomeLink, Internet Quotient, IOS, iPhone, iQuick Study, IronPort, the IronPort logo, LightStream, Linksys, MediaTone, MeetingPlace, MeetingPlace Chime Sound, MGX, Networkers, Networking Academy, Network Registrar, PCNow, PIX, PowerPanels, ProConnect, ScriptShare, SenderBase, SMARTnet, Spectrum Expert, StackWise, The Fastest Way to Increase Your Internet Quotient, TransPath, WebEx, and the WebEx logo are registered trademarks of Cisco Systems, Inc. and/or its affiliates in the United States and certain other countries.

All other trademarks mentioned in this document or website are the property of their respective owners. The use of the word partner does not imply a partnership relationship between Cisco and any other company. (0812R)

About the Authors

Wendell Odom, CCIE Enterprise No. 1624, was the first Cisco Press author for Cisco certification guides. He wrote all prior editions of this book, along with books on topics ranging from introductory networking to CCENT, CCNA R&S, CCNA DC, CCNP ROUTE, CCNP QoS, and CCIE R&S. In his four decades as a networker, he has worked as a network engineer, consultant, systems engineer, instructor, and course developer. He now spends his time focused on updating the CCNA books, his blog (www.certskills.com), building his new CCNA YouTube channel (www.youtube.com/@NetworkUpskill), and teaching online (www.certskills.com/courses). You can find him at www.LinkedIn.com/in/WendellOdom, Twitter (@WendellOdom), and at his blog, which provides a variety of free CCNA learning resources.

Jason Gooley, CCIEx2 (RS, SP) No. 38759, is a very enthusiastic and engaging speaker who focuses on teaching others. Jason has more than 30 years of experience in the industry and currently works as the technical evangelist for the Worldwide Enterprise Networking and Software Sales team at Cisco. Jason is very passionate about helping others in the industry succeed. In addition to being a public speaker, Jason has authored numerous Cisco Press books, is a CiscoLive Distinguished Speaker, and is a developer of CCIE exams, training, and blogs for Learning@Cisco. Jason is also a co-founder and member of the Program Committee Board for the Chicago Network Operators Group (CHI-NOG). Jason is the founder and host of @MetalDevOps, which is a YouTube video show about the intersection of metal music and technology. Jason has earned the nickname of "The Godfather of Programmability" from his students and peers and continues to help drive the industry forward around topics such as network programmability and automation.

David Hucaby, CCIE No. 4594, CWNE No. 292, is a technical education content engineer for Cisco Meraki. Previously, he worked as a wireless escalation engineer in a large healthcare environment for more than 20 years. David holds bachelor's and master's degrees in electrical engineering. He has been authoring Cisco Press titles for 25 years. David lives in Kentucky.

About the Technical Reviewer

Denise Donohue, CCIE No. 9566 (Routing and Switching), has worked with information systems since the mid-1990s and network architecture since 2004. During that time, she has worked with a wide range of networks, private and public, of all sizes, across most industries. Her focus is on aligning business and technology. Denise has authored several Cisco Press books and frequently shares her knowledge in webinars and seminars, and at conferences.

Dedications

Wendell Odom:

For Raymond Lanier Odom, still the best dad ever.

Jason Gooley:

To my family: Mother, thank you for always being my guiding light from up above. To my wife, Jamie, your love and support mean the world to me. To my children, Kaleigh and Jaxon, always believe in yourself and go for your dreams, no matter how lofty they may seem. To my father, thanks for believing in that stubborn kid so many years ago! To my brother, thanks for always having my back broham. Thank you, God—without you none of this would be possible!

Acknowledgments

Wendell Odom:

Brett Bartow and I have been a team for a few decades. He has had more to do with the successes of the Cisco Press product line than anyone else. More than ever, his insights and wisdom have been a key to navigating Cisco's big changes to certifications back in 2020. With Cisco's 2023 pivot to a lean development model for certifications, with the possibility of new exam content annually, Brett's leadership matters more than ever. (See "Your Study Plan" for more about what that new lean development cycle means.) He's always a great partner in working through big-picture direction as well as features to make the books the best they can be for our readers. It is always appreciated, but not voiced every time—so thanks, Brett, for your consistent leadership and wisdom!

Chris Cleveland did the development editing for the very first Cisco Press exam certification guide way back in 1998, and he still can't seem to get away from us! Seriously, when Brett and I first discuss any new book, my first priority is to ask whether Chris has time to develop the book—and lobby if there are any barriers! It's always a pleasure working with you, Chris.

The technical editors also have a meaningful positive impact on the books. And we got Denise to do it! Denise and I teamed up to write the *CCIE R&S Official Cert Guide* for two editions, and she has written extensively herself—which is why I wondered if we could get her help. Her deep technical skills to go along with her unique insights into the book authoring process have been a great help to both weed out the mistakes and get good advice on how to improve the chapters.

Cisco's move to an annual exam update cadence (they at least consider updating each exam once per year) has more impact on the production side of our publishing process than it does on the authoring side. Knowing early that both Sandra and Tonya are back at it, finding ways to continue the high quality while being creative with the new publication cycle, sets me more at ease. When writing, I could rest knowing that the second half of the process, which happens after I've finished 99 percent of my work, will be done well!

Thanks to all the production team for making the magic happen. I usually do not interact with you directly beyond Sandra and Tonya, but I see your work, and the books truly improve through the process! From fixing all my grammar and passive-voice sentences to pulling the design and layout together, they do it all; thanks for putting it all together and making it look easy.

A special thank you to you readers who write in with suggestions and possible errors, and especially those of you who post online at the Cisco Learning Network and at my blog (www.certskills.com). More so than any edition I can remember, reader comments have had more to do with changes I made to improve existing content in these editions. The comments I received directly and those I overheard by participating at CLN made this edition a better book. (See the heading "Feedback Information" just a page or so back to see how to get in touch with us!)

My wonderful wife Kris and I reached our 25th anniversary while working on the early draft of this edition. She makes this challenging work lifestyle a breeze—even happily scheduling our 25th anniversary vacation around the book schedule! Thanks to my daughter Hannah for perspectives on how 20-somethings think about learning and studying. And thanks to Jesus Christ, Lord of everything in my life.

Jason Gooley:

I would like to thank Wendell for trusting me and having me on this amazing journey. Looking forward to our future work together!

Thank you to everyone at Pearson and Cisco Press for always making sure our products are of the best quality!

Thank you to my wife, Jamie, and my children, Kaleigh and Jaxon, for putting up with your father's crazy projects!!!

Contents at a Glance

Reader Services

To access additional content for this book, simply register your product. To start the registration process, go to www.ciscopress.com/register and log in or create an account.* Enter the product ISBN 9780138214951 and click **Submit**. After the process is complete, you will find any available bonus content under Registered Products.

*Be sure to check the box that you would like to hear from us to receive exclusive discounts on future editions of this product.

Contents

Online Appendixes

Icons Used in This Book

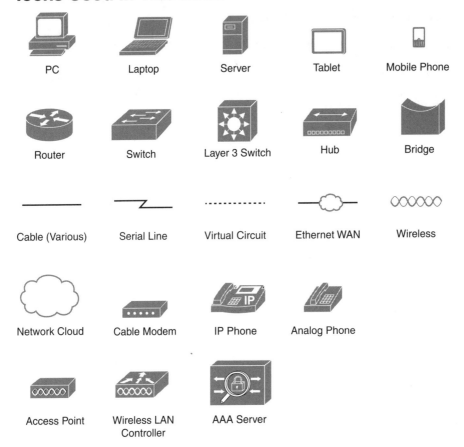

Command Syntax Conventions

The conventions used to present command syntax in this book are the same conventions used in the IOS Command Reference. The Command Reference describes these conventions as follows:

- **Boldface** indicates commands and keywords that are entered literally as shown. In actual configuration examples and output (not general command syntax), boldface indicates commands that are manually input by the user (such as a **show** command).

- *Italic* indicates arguments for which you supply actual values.

- Vertical bars (|) separate alternative, mutually exclusive elements.

- Square brackets ([ ]) indicate an optional element.

- Braces ({ }) indicate a required choice.

- Braces within brackets ([{ }]) indicate a required choice within an optional element.

Introduction

You are setting out on a journey to achieve your CCNA certification. For many, that step happens at the beginning of a new career path. For others, CCNA validates their knowledge and skills already learned on the job.

Surprisingly for an entry-level exam, the CCNA 200-301 exam includes more content by volume than many of the CCNP-level exams. As a result, Cisco Press publishes the Certification Guide for CCNA as two volumes. You can refer to the books as Volume 1 and Volume 2, but more formally, the books are

- *CCNA 200-301 Official Cert Guide, Volume 1*, Second Edition
- *CCNA 200-301 Official Cert Guide, Volume 2*, Second Edition (this book)

If you have already used the Volume 1 book and read or skimmed its Introduction, you do not need to read the entire Introduction to this book. This book has the same features and style as Volume 1. However, you might be interested to review the section titled "Book Organization, Chapters, and Appendixes," for information specific to this book.

Regardless of your path to CCNA, the journey takes some time and effort. I encourage you to spend some time in the Introduction to learn more about CCNA and the books so you can have the best experience preparing for CCNA! To that end, this introduction discusses these main points:

Cisco Certifications and the CCNA

Book Features

Book Elements (Reference)

About Getting Hands-on Skills

About IP Subnetting

Cisco Certifications and the CCNA

Congratulations! If you're reading far enough to look at this book's Introduction, you've probably already decided to go for your Cisco certification. Cisco has been the dominant vendor in networking for decades. If you want to be taken seriously as a network engineer, building your Cisco skills using Cisco certifications makes perfect sense. Where to start? CCNA.

Cisco Certifications as of 2024

CCNA acts as the entry point to a hierarchy of Cisco certifications. CCNA includes the foundational topics, with CCNP as the next higher challenge level, followed by CCIE. Figure I-1 shows the hierarchy, with more detail about each in the list that follows.

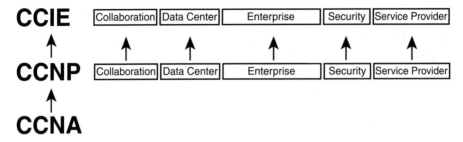

Figure I-1   *Cisco CCNA, CCNP, and CCIE Certifications*

CCNA – Cisco Certified Network Associate: Cisco began CCNA with a single CCNA certification back in 1998. They later expanded CCNA to include ten different CCNA certifications about different technology areas. Cisco retired all the varieties of CCNA back in 2020, leaving us again with a single CCNA certification, now referred to as simply "CCNA."

CCNP – Cisco Certified Network Professional: Cisco followed the same progression with different CCNP certifications over time, starting with one in 1998. The big changes in 2020 consolidated the lineup to five CCNP certifications, all of which benefit from having knowledge of CCNA before moving on to CCNP.

CCIE – Cisco Certified Internetwork Expert: First introduced in 1993, these expert-level certifications require both a written exam plus a one-day practical exam with extensive hands-on lab challenges.

Beyond the CCNA, CCNP, and CCIE certifications, Cisco offers two other certification tracks—one for network automation and another for cybersecurity. The CCNA certification can be helpful as a foundation for those tracks as well. They are

DevNet Certifications: The DevNet Associate, DevNet Professional, and DevNet Expert certifications mirror the progression of CCNA/CCNP/CCIE, just without using those specific acronyms. The DevNet certifications focus on software development and APIs that matter to managing networks.

CyberOps Certifications: The CyberOps Associate and CyberOps Professional certifications mirror the progression of CCNA/CCNP. These security exams focus on security concepts, security monitoring, host-based analysis, network intrusion analysis, and security policies and procedures.

How to Get Your CCNA Certification

As you saw in Figure I-1, all career certification paths now begin with CCNA. So how do you get the CCNA certification? Today, you have one and only one option to achieve CCNA certification:

Take and pass one exam: the Cisco 200-301 CCNA exam.

To take the 200-301 exam, or any Cisco exam, you will use the services of Pearson VUE. The process works something like this:

1. Establish a login at https://vue.com/cisco (or use your existing login).

2. Register for, schedule a time and place, and pay for the Cisco 200-301 exam, all from the VUE website.

3. Take the exam at the VUE testing center or from home with a video proctor watching to prevent cheating.

4. You will receive a notice of your score, and whether you passed, before you leave the testing center.

Content in the CCNA 200-301 Exam

We've all thought it, wondered, for almost every important test we ever took, and maybe even asked the teacher: "What's on the test?" For the CCNA exam, and for all Cisco certification exams, Cisco tells us.

Cisco publishes an exam blueprint for every Cisco exam, with the blueprint listing the exam topics for the exam. To find them, browse www.cisco.com/go/certifications, look for the CCNA page, and navigate until you see the exam topics. And if you haven't already done so, create a bookmark folder for CCNA content in your web browser and bookmark a link to this page.

The exam blueprint organizes the exam topics into groups called domains. The document also tells us the percentage of points on the exam that come from each domain. For instance, every CCNA exam should score 25 percent of your points from the exam topics in the IP Connectivity domain. The exam does not tell you the domain associated with each question, but the percentages give us a better idea of the importance of the domains for the exam. Figure I-2 shows the domains of the CCNA 200-301 Version 1.1 blueprint, the percentages, and the number of primary exam topics in each.

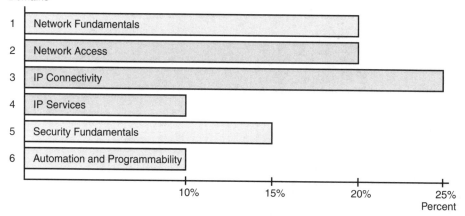

Figure I-2   *CCNA 200-301 Domains and Percentage of Exam Score*

Within each domain, the exam topic document lists exam topics that follow two different styles of wording. The main exam topics use a verb in the phrase that tells you the level of mastery required; I call those primary exam topics. The exam topics document shows subtopics that I refer to as secondary exam topics. Those do not have a verb, but list more technology details (nouns), and assume the verb from the primary exam topic.

For instance, the following excerpt from the exam topics document lists one primary exam topic with the *describe* verb, with more detail added by two secondary exam topics.

1.11 Describe wireless principles

1.11.a Nonoverlapping Wi-Fi channels

1.11.b SSID

Exam Topic Verbs (Depth) and Nouns (Breadth)

Understanding an exam topic requires that you think about each exam topic wording, focusing on the verbs and nouns. The nouns identify the technical topics, such as LAN switching, IP routing, protocols like OSPF, and so on. The verbs in each primary exam topic inform us about the type and depth of knowledge and skill tested per the exam topics.

For example, consider the following primary exam topic:

Describe IPsec remote access and site-to-site VPNs

I'm sure you know what the word *describe* means in the normal use of the term. But for people who build exams, the verb has special meaning as to what the exam questions should and should not require of the test taker. For instance, you should be ready to describe whatever "IPsec remote access and site-to-site VPNs" are. But the exam should not ask you to perform higher performance verbs, like *analyze* or *configure*.

Figure I-3 shows a pyramid with verbs found in Cisco exam blueprints. It shows the lower-skill verbs at the bottom and higher skills at the top. An exam topic with a lower verb should not be tested with questions from higher knowledge and skill levels. For instance, with the exam topic "describe...first hop redundancy protocols," you should not expect to need to configure, verify, or troubleshoot the feature.

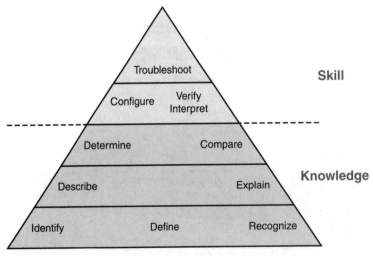

Figure I-3 *Cisco Exam Topic Verbs*

Knowing that, how should you study? Well, instead of a many-layer pyramid, think of it as two layers: Knowledge and Skill. When learning content whose exam topics use verbs from the lower three rows of the pyramid, study the same way no matter which of those verbs the exam topic uses. Learn the topic well. Be ready to describe it, explain it, and interpret the meaning. For content with exam topics with the verbs *configure* and *verify*, think of those as including the first level of knowledge, plus also requiring configuration and verification skills Also, think about the common configuration mistakes so you can troubleshoot those mistakes.

Comparing the Exam and Exam Topics

To understand what Cisco tells us about the exam versus the exam topics, return to cs.co/go/certifications or cisco.com/go/ccna. Find the CCNA exam topics and open the PDF version (the text we need to consider is currently only in the PDF version). Open the PDF and spend 10–15 seconds scanning it.

Did you read the first two paragraphs, the ones before the list of exam topics? Or did you skip those and move straight to the long list of exam topics? Many people skip those paragraphs. One of those tells us much about the exam versus the exam topics, so I've copied it here, with emphasis added:

> The following topics are *general guidelines* for the content likely to be included on the exam. However, *other related topics may also appear on any specific delivery of the exam.* To better reflect the contents of the exam and for clarity purposes, the *guidelines below may change at any time without notice.*

The first bold phrase mentions the most obvious point about the exam topics: They make a general statement. They do not detail every concept, fact, configuration option, and fact hidden in verification command output. Instead, anyone who cares about a Cisco exam like CCNA has to make a judgment about exactly what details the exam topic includes and excludes—and those judgements are subjective.

Our interpretation and expansion of the exam topics dictate what we choose to include and omit from the books. But we know from long experience that narrow interpretation can cover a large amount of CCNA content, but leave out too much. To cover as much as possible, we use a broad and deep interpretation. That has worked well throughout the 25 plus years for this book and its predecessors. It also matches the overwhelming feedback from reader surveys. In short, we shoot for the middle box in the concept drawing in Figure I-4.

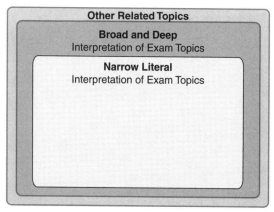

Figure I-4 *Scope Concept: Exam Versus Exam Topics*

Cisco tells us the exam can ask questions about topics outside the exam topics. Look back again to the copy of the text that begins the exam blueprint PDF, to the bold phrase with the term "other related topics." Yes, the exam might ask things outside even a broad interpretation of the exam topics, as implied by the outer ring in Figure I-4.

When choosing book content, I also make some predictions as to what those other related topics might be. Given the policies, we cannot possibly predict and include everything you might see on your exam. What we do promise is to cover each exam topic based on a broad and deep interpretation.

How to Prepare for the Generalized Exam Topics

Given the general nature of Cisco exam topics, plus the possibility of topic areas not listed in the exam topics, how should you go about preparing for the CCNA exam? Most importantly, strive to master all information and skills implied by the exam topics. On exam day, you may still see a few questions about topics you have not studied—but you should know far more than enough to pass the exam.

So, how do you master the topics listed in the exam blueprint? Let me give you a few suggestions.

1. Follow the suggestions in Volume 1's section "Your Study Plan" just before Chapter 1 of that book.

2. Practice hands-on CLI skills. The later section of the Introduction titled "About Building Hands-On Skills" discusses some ways to practice.

3. Pay close attention to troubleshooting topics in the book.

4. Practice all math-related skills, over time, until you master them.

5. Ensure you know all exam topic content as listed in the exam topics. Read the exam topics, consider your own literal interpretation, and when uncertain or confused, dig in and study further.

6. Trust that the book uses its broad interpretation of the exam topics to help you learn as much as possible that might be on the exam.

Types of Questions on the CCNA 200-301 Exam

You can expect the following kinds of questions on the exam; just be aware that the style of questions may change over time.

- Multiple-choice, single-answer

- Multiple-choice, multiple-answer

- Drag-and-drop

- Lab

For the multichoice questions, the exam software gives us a few important advantages:

■ There is no penalty for guessing.

■ Multichoice questions with a single correct answer require you to answer and allow only one answer.

■ Multichoice questions with multiple correct answers tell you the number of correct answers and warn you if you have not selected that many answers.

For instance, if a question tells you there are two correct answers, and you select only one and then try to move to the next question, the app reminds you that you should choose another answer before moving on.

As for drag-and-drop, some questions use simple text blocks that you move from one list to another. However, you might see questions where you move items in a network diagram or some other creative use of drag-and-drop.

Finally, Cisco introduced lab questions (formally called performance-based questions) in 2022. Lab questions present you with a lab scenario with a lab pod of virtual routers and switches running in the background; you get console access to a few devices. Your job: find the missing or broken configuration and reconfigure the devices so that the lab scenario works. The best way to practice for these questions is to practice in lab; more on that in the section titled "About Building Hands-On Skills."

As an aside, prior Cisco exams had Sim questions instead of lab questions. Sim questions required the same from us: read the scenario and fix the configuration. However, Sim questions used simulated Cisco devices with limited command support, which frustrated some test takers. The lab questions use real Cisco operating systems running in a virtual environment, so they provide a much more realistic experience compared to old Sim questions.

Book Features

This book includes many study features beyond the core explanations and examples in each chapter. This section acts as a reference to the various features in the book.

The CCNA Books: Volume 1 and Volume 2

The CCNA exam covers a large amount of content, and it does not fit in a single volume. As a result, Cisco Press has long published books for the CCNA exam as a two-book set. Volume 1 covers about half of the content, and Volume 2 covers the rest, as shown in Figure I-5. To best use both books, start in Volume 1 and work through the book in order, and then do the same with Volume 2.

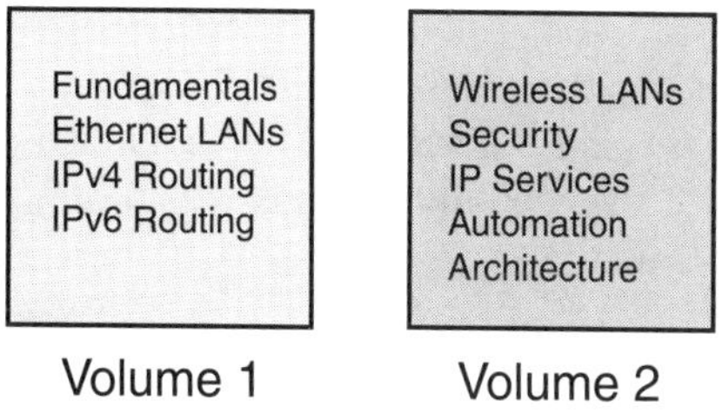

Fundamentals	Wireless LANs
Ethernet LANs	Security
IPv4 Routing	IP Services
IPv6 Routing	Automation
	Architecture

Volume 1   Volume 2

Figure I-5   *Two Books for CCNA 200-301*

When you start each new chapter, review the list of exam topics that begins the chapter. The book does not follow the same order of exam topics in the blueprint, but instead follows a more effective order for learning the topics. For reference, look to Appendix B, "Exam Topics Cross-Reference," in the back of the book. The appendix includes:

- A list of exam topics and the chapter(s) covering each topic
- A list of chapters and the exam topics covered in each chapter

Exam Blueprint Versions and Book Editions

Cisco made minor changes to the CCNA exam blueprint in 2024, the first change to the CCNA 200-301 exam since the year 2020. The much more important change (announced in 2023) had to do with the entire Cisco certification program about how Cisco announces and releases new exams and exam blueprints. Before 2023, when Cisco changed any CCNA or CCNP exam, they also changed the exam number, and the announcement was sudden. Those days are gone.

You should read and understand Cisco's long-term strategy for being more forthright about exam plans as detailed at www.cisco.com/go/certroadmap. Summarizing some key points, when Cisco changes an exam in the future, Cisco will keep the same exam number. To identify the changes, they will use a major.minor version numbering plan for every exam blueprint. More importantly, Cisco tells us when they will consider changing CCNA each year, but we know when Cisco will announce changes and when the new exam will be released, within a few months' timing.

The exam blueprint version changes based on two determinations: 1) whether Cisco will change the exam that year at all, and 2) if so, whether Cisco considers the changes to be major or minor. For instance, Cisco considered making a change to CCNA during February–April 2023 but chose not to change it, announcing that fact in the May–July 2023 timeframe. In 2024, Cisco chose to make minor changes to the CCNA blueprint. As a result, the former CCNA blueprint version 1.0 (major version 1, minor version 0) changed to version 1.1, increasing the minor version by 1.

Looking forward, if the next three future CCNA blueprint changes are also minor, they would be blueprint versions 1.2, 1.3, and 1.4. However, if any of them are major, that version would move to the next major version (2.0), with subsequent minor version changes as 2.1, 2.2, and so on.

Cisco also tells us that each year, internally, Cisco considers what to do with CCNA in the February–April timeframe. They will announce their plans to us all between May–July, and they will release the new exam (if changes are being made) sometime in the six months or so following the announcement.

As for the publishing plans to support that new update cycle, you should read and monitor the publisher's web page at www.ciscopress.com/newcerts. Also, opt in for communications on that page so the publisher will email you about future plans and updates.

Summarizing a few key points about the publisher's plans, this book, the second edition, was written for version 1.1 of the CCNA 200-301 blueprint, but it should be the book used for CCNA for subsequent blueprint versions as well. During the life of this second edition book, Cisco may update the CCNA 200-301 exam blueprint a few times, while this book (plus the Volume 1 Second Edition book) may remain unchanged. New exam content may be made available as electronic downloads. At some point, a new edition will be appropriate. (Figure I-6 shows one example of what might happen over time, with downloadable PDFs between editions.)

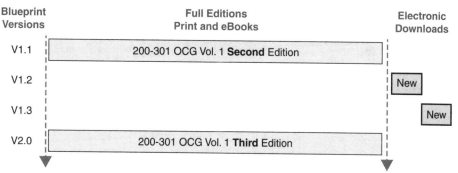

Figure I-6   *Possible Progression of Book Editions, New Content Release, Versus Exams*

NOTE   I cannot stress enough: monitor both the Cisco Press and Cisco pages linked in the preceding paragraphs, and opt in for communications at those pages, to stay aware of any exam and publishing plans. Also, consider watching my blog (www.certskills.com), where I expect to post about changes.

When you finish the technology chapters in this book (Chapters 1–24), make sure to also read Chapter 25, "Exam Updates." We post updated versions of that chapter online. We use that chapter to deliver small content updates to you as well as to inform you about future content updates. Make sure to read through that chapter and learn how to download the latest version of the chapter, discovering if new content has been posted after this book was published.

Also, just to reduce confusion about the book titles, note that the prior edition of this book is nearly identical to this book's title. Comparing the titles:

- *CCNA 200-301 Official Cert Guide, Volume 2* (the prior edition, published in 2019 for 200-301 exam blueprint version 1.0)

- *CCNA 200-301 Official Cert Guide, Volume 2*, Second Edition (this edition, published in 2024 for 200-301 exam blueprint version 1.1 and beyond)

Comparing This Edition to the Previous

This book replaces a similar book that applied to the former CCNA 200-301 exam blueprint 1.0. Some of you may buy this book but have already begun studying with the prior edition. The following list of major changes to this book versus the previous may help you avoid rereading identical or similar content in this book.

Chapter 4: (Formerly Volume 1, Chapter 29) Added examples and GUI screenshots for wireless LAN configuration using a WLC with IOS XE.

Chapter 7: (Formerly Chapter 3) Significant rewrite; added more about rules for ACL editing, and noted differences with ACLs between IOS and IOS XE.

Chapter 8: New chapter about matching different protocols using ACLs.

Chapter 10: (Formerly Chapter 5) Revised password type discussion and added IOS versus IOS XE details.

Chapter 13: (Formerly Chapter 9) Added CDP/LLDP timers and LLDP-MED with TLVs.

Chapter 14: (Formerly Chapter 10) Revised NAT chapter to simplify and strengthen the examples.

Chapter 16: (Formerly Chapter 12) Split FHRP into a separate chapter, expanding discussions to give more detail on VRRP and GLBP.

Chapter 17: (Formerly Chapter 12) Split SNMP, FTP, and TFTP from FHRP into a separate chapter. Expanded the SNMP section and revised the IFS topic with IOS XE examples.

Chapter 18: (Formerly Chapter 13) Added topics for UTP cabling, multigig Ethernet, multimode Ethernet for campus LANs, and improved PoE descriptions.

Chapter 19: (Formerly Chapter 14) Updated notes about 5G WAN, and added detail on IPsec.

Chapter 20: (Formerly Chapter 15) Added concepts of containers and VRFs, and adds cloud management topics including Meraki.

Chapters 21–22: (Formerly Chapters 16 and 17) Updated for various software version updates and product rebranding, and adds the AI/ML topic.

Chapter 23: (Formerly Chapter 18) Updated for exam topic change to include API authentication.

Chapter 24: (Formerly Chapter 19) Updated for exam topic change to replace the descriptions of Puppet and Chef with new information about Terraform.

If you find the preceding information useful, consider looking in two other places that allow us to provide ongoing updates and to answer questions. First, I expect to post blog posts about the new CCNA exam changes, as always, at my blog (www.certskills.com). Look there for posts in the News section (click the General menu item and then News), for posts made mid-year 2024 when Cisco should announce their plans.

Second, look to the companion website for this book for details about future exam revisions and publishing plans. The companion website gives the publisher a place to list details about changes moving forward. See this Introduction's later section titled "The Companion Website for Online Content" for the instructions for finding the site.

Chapter Features

Beginning to study CCNA can be overwhelming at first due to the volume. The best way to overcome that reaction requires a change in mindset: *treat each chapter as a separate study task*. Breaking your study into manageable tasks helps a lot.

Each chapter of this book is a self-contained short course about one small topic area, organized for reading and study. I create chapters so they average about 20 pages to cover the technology so that no one chapter takes too long to complete. Each chapter breaks down as follows:

"Do I Know This Already?" quizzes: Each chapter begins with a pre-chapter quiz so you can self-assess how much you know coming into the chapter.

Foundation Topics: This is the heading for the core content section of the chapter, with average length of 20 pages.

Chapter Review: This section includes a list of study tasks useful to help you remember concepts, connect ideas, and practice skills-based content in the chapter.

Do not read the "Foundation Topics" section of chapter after chapter without pausing to review and study. Each "Chapter Review" section uses a variety of other book features to help you study and internalize that chapter's content, including the following:

■ **Review Key Topics:** All the content in the books matters, but some matters more. Cisco Press certification guides use a Key Topic icon next to those items in the "Foundation Topics" section. The "Chapter Review" section lists the key topics in a table. You can scan the chapter to review them or review the Key Topics more conveniently using the companion website.

■ **Complete Tables from Memory:** We convert some tables in the book to interactive study tables called memory tables. You access memory tables from the companion website. Memory tables repeat the table, but with parts of the table removed. You can then fill in the table to exercise your memory and click to check your work.

■ **Key Terms You Should Know:** The "Chapter Review" section lists the key terminology from the chapter. For a manual process with the book, think about each term and use the Glossary to cross-check your own mental definitions. Alternately, review the key terms with the "Key Terms Flashcards" app on the companion website.

■ **Labs:** You should practice hands-on skills for any exam topics with the *configure* and *verify* verbs. The upcoming section titled "About Building Hands-On Skills" discusses your lab options. Also, the Chapter and Part Reviews refer you to lab exercises specific to the chapter or part.

■ **Command References:** Some book chapters discuss the configure and verify exam topics, so they list various router and switch commands. The "Chapter Review" section of those chapters includes command reference tables, useful both for reference and for study. Just cover one column of the table and see how much you can remember and complete mentally.

■ **Review DIKTA Questions:** Even if you used the DIKTA questions to begin the chapter, re-answering those questions can prove a useful way to review facts.

By design, I do not mention the DIKTA questions in the "Chapter Review" sections but do suggest using them again for all chapters in a part during Part Review. Use the Pearson Test Prep (PTP) web app to easily use those questions any time you have a few minutes, a device, and Internet access.

Part Features

Your second mindset change: Use the book parts as major milestones in your study journey. Each part groups a small number of related chapters together. Take the time at the end of each part to review all topics in the part, effectively rewarding yourself with a chance to deepen your knowledge and internalize more of the content before moving to the next part. Figure I-7 shows the concept.

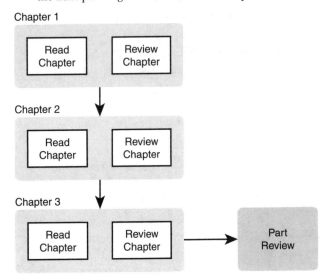

Figure I-7 *Part Review: The Second Review of Most Content*

The Part Review element at the end of each part suggests review and study activities. Spaced reviews—that is, reviewing content several times over the course of your study— help improve retention. Using the Chapter and Part Review process, the Part Review serves as your second review of the content in each chapter. The Part Review repeats some Chapter Review activities and offers some new ones, including a reminder to use practice questions set aside specifically for Part Review.

The Companion Website for Online Content

Some Chapter and Part Review tasks can be done from the book. However, several of them work better as an interactive online tool. For instance, you can take a "Do I Know This Already?" quiz by reading the pages of the book, but you can also use the PTP testing software. As another example, when you want to review the key terms from a chapter, you can find all those in electronic flashcards.

This book's companion website hosts all the electronic components of the book. The companion website gives you a big advantage: you can do most of your Chapter and

Part Review work from anywhere using the interactive tools on the site. The advantages include

- **Easier to use:** Instead of having to print out copies of the appendixes and do the work on paper, you can use these new apps, which provide you with an easy-to-use, interactive experience that you can easily run over and over.

- **Convenient:** When you have a spare 5–10 minutes, go to the book's website and review content from one of your recently finished chapters.

- **Good break from reading:** Sometimes looking at a static page after reading a chapter lets your mind wander. Breaking up your reading with some review from the keyboard can help keep you focused on the activity.

The interactive Chapter Review elements should improve your chances of passing as well. Our in-depth reader surveys over the years show that those who do the Chapter and Part Reviews learn more. Those who use the interactive review elements tend to do the review tasks more often. So, take advantage of the tools and maybe you will be more successful as well. Table I-1 summarizes these interactive applications and the traditional book features that cover the same content.

Table I-1 Book Features with Both Traditional and App Options

Feature	Traditional	App
Key Topic	The "Chapter Review" section lists the key topics. To review, flip pages in the chapter.	Key Topics Table app with links to view each key topic
Config Checklist	This list of steps, in text, describes how to configure a feature.	Config Checklist app, where you complete the checklist by adding commands
Key Terms	Terms are listed in each "Chapter Review" section; review using the end-of-book Glossary.	Key Terms Flash Cards app
Appendixes: ACL Practice	Appendix E provides static text practice problems and answers in the PDF appendixes.	Apps with the same practice problems, found in the "Memory Tables and Practice Exercises" section

The companion website also includes links to download, navigate, or stream for these types of content:

- Pearson Sim Lite Desktop App

- Pearson Test Prep (PTP) Desktop App

- Pearson Test Prep (PTP) Web App

- Videos

How to Access the Companion Website

To access the companion website, which gives you access to the electronic content with this book, start by establishing a login at www.ciscopress.com and register your book. To do so, simply go to www.ciscopress.com/register and enter the ISBN of the print book: 9780138214951. After you have registered your book, go to your account page and click the **Registered Products** tab. From there, click the **Access Bonus Content** link to get access to the book's companion website.

Note that if you buy the *Premium Edition eBook and Practice Test* version of this book from Cisco Press, your book will automatically be registered on your account page. Simply go to your account page, click the **Registered Products** tab, and select **Access Bonus Content** to access the book's companion website.

How to Access the Pearson Test Prep (PTP) App

You have two options for installing and using the Pearson Test Prep application: a web app and a desktop app. To use the Pearson Test Prep application, start by finding the registration code that comes with the book. You can find the code in these ways:

- You can get your access code by registering the print ISBN 9780138214951 on ciscopress.com/register. Make sure to use the print book ISBN, regardless of whether you purchased an eBook or the print book. After you register the book, your access code will be populated on your account page under the Registered Products tab. Instructions for how to redeem the code are available on the book's companion website by clicking the Access Bonus Content link.

- If you purchase the Premium Edition eBook and Practice Test directly from the Cisco Press website, the code will be populated on your account page after purchase. Just log in at ciscopress.com, click Account to see details of your account, and click the digital purchases tab.

NOTE   After you register your book, your code can always be found in your account under the Registered Products tab.

Once you have the access code, to find instructions about both the PTP web app and the desktop app, follow these steps:

Step 1.   Open this book's companion website as shown earlier in this Introduction under the heading, "How to Access the Companion Website."

Step 2.   Click the **Practice Exams** button.

Step 3.   Follow the instructions listed there for both installing the desktop app and using the web app.

Note that if you want to use the web app only at this point, just navigate to pearsontestprep.com, log in using the same credentials used to register your book or purchase the Premium Edition, and register this book's practice tests using the registration code you just found. The process should take only a couple of minutes.

Feature Reference

The following list provides an easy reference to get the basic idea behind each book feature:

- **Practice exam:** The book gives you the rights to the Pearson Test Prep (PTP) testing software, available as a web app and a desktop app. Use the access code on a piece of cardboard in the sleeve in the back of the book, and use the companion website to download the desktop app or navigate to the web app (or just go to www.pearsontestprep.com).

- **eBook:** Pearson offers an eBook version of this book that includes extra practice tests as compared to the print book. The product includes two versions of the eBook: PDF (for reading on your computer) and EPUB (for reading on your tablet, mobile device, or Kindle, Nook, or other e-reader). It also includes additional practice test questions and enhanced practice test features, including links from each question to the specific heading in the eBook file.

- **Mentoring videos:** The companion website also includes a number of videos about other topics as mentioned in individual chapters. Some of the videos explain common mistakes made with CCNA topics, whereas others provide sample CCNA questions with explanations.

- **CCNA 200-301 Network Simulator Lite:** This Lite version of the best-selling CCNA Network Simulator from Pearson provides you with a means, right now, to experience the Cisco command-line interface (CLI). No need to go buy real gear or buy a full simulator to start learning the CLI. Just install it from the companion website.

- **CCNA Simulator:** If you are looking for more hands-on practice, you might want to consider purchasing the CCNA Network Simulator. You can purchase a copy of this software from Pearson at http://pearsonitcertification.com/networksimulator or other retail outlets. To help you with your studies, Pearson has created a mapping guide that maps each of the labs in the simulator to the specific sections in each volume of the CCNA Cert Guide. You can get this mapping guide free on the Extras tab on the book product page: www.ciscopress.com/title/9780138214951.

- **Author's website and blogs:** The author maintains a website that hosts tools and links useful when studying for CCNA. In particular, the site has a large number of free lab exercises about CCNA content, additional sample questions, and other exercises. Additionally, the site indexes all content so you can study based on the book chapters and parts. To find it, navigate to www.certskills.com. Additionally, look for CCNA activities and lectures at his YouTube channel (www.youtube.com/@networkupskill).

Book Organization, Chapters, and Appendixes

This book contains 24 chapters about CCNA topics organized into seven parts. The core chapters cover the following topics:

- **Part I: Wireless LANs**

  - **Chapter 1, "Fundamentals of Wireless Networks,"** includes the foundational concepts of wireless 802.11 LANs, including wireless topologies and basic wireless radio communications protocols.

- Chapter 2, "**Analyzing Cisco Wireless Architectures**," turns your attention to the questions related to the systematic and architectural issues surrounding how to build wireless LANs and explains the primary options available for use.

- Chapter 3, "**Securing Wireless Networks**," explains the unique security challenges that exist in a wireless LAN and the protocols and standards used to prevent different kinds of attacks.

- Chapter 4, "**Building a Wireless LAN**," shows how to configure and secure a wireless LAN using a Wireless LAN Controller (WLC).

- **Part II: IP Access Control Lists**

  - Chapter 5, "**Introduction to TCP/IP Transport and Applications**," completes most of the detailed discussion of the upper two layers of the TCP/IP model (transport and application), focusing on TCP and applications.

  - Chapter 6, "**Basic IPv4 Access Control Lists**," examines how standard IP ACLs can filter packets based on the source IP address so that a router will not forward the packet.

  - Chapter 7, "**Named and Extended IP ACLs**," examines both named and numbered ACLs, and both standard and extended IP ACLs.

  - Chapter 8, "**Applied IP ACLs**," shows how to match overhead protocols like DNS, DHCP, and OSPF with ACLs.

- **Part III: Security Services**

  - Chapter 9, "**Security Architectures**," discusses a wide range of fundamental concepts in network security.

  - Chapter 10, "**Securing Network Devices**," shows how to secure the router and switch CLI and introduces the concepts behind firewalls and intrusion prevention systems (IPSs).

  - Chapter 11, "**Implementing Switch Port Security**," explains the concepts as well as how to configure and verify switch port security, a switch feature that does basic MAC-based monitoring of the devices that send data into a switch.

  - Chapter 12, "**DHCP Snooping and ARP Inspection**," shows how to implement two related switch security features, with one focusing on reacting to suspicious DHCP messages and the other reacting to suspicious ARP messages.

- **Part IV: IP Services**

  - Chapter 13, "**Device Management Protocols**," discusses the concepts and configuration of some common network management tools: syslog, NTP, CDP, and LLDP.

  - Chapter 14, "**Network Address Translation**," works through the complete concept, configuration, verification, and troubleshooting sequence for the router NAT feature, including how it helps conserve public IPv4 addresses.

- Chapter 15, "**Quality of Service (QoS),**" discusses a wide variety of concepts all related to the broad topic of QoS.

- Chapter 16, "**First Hop Redundancy Protocols,**" explains the purpose, functions, and concepts of FHRPs, including HSRP, VRRP, and GLBP.

- Chapter 17, "**SNMP, FTP, and TFTP,**" discusses three protocols often used for managing network devices: SNMP, TFTP, and FTP.

- **Part V: Network Architecture**

  - Chapter 18, "**LAN Architecture,**" examines various ways to design Ethernet LANs, discussing the pros and cons, and explains common design terminology, including Power over Ethernet (PoE).

  - Chapter 19, "**WAN Architecture,**" discusses the concepts behind three WAN alternatives: Metro Ethernet, MPLS VPNs, and Internet VPNs.

  - Chapter 20, "**Cloud Architecture,**" explains the basic concepts and then generally discusses the impact that cloud computing has on a typical enterprise network, including the foundational concepts of server virtualization.

- **Part VI: Network Automation**

  - Chapter 21, "**Introduction to Controller-Based Networking,**" discusses many concepts and terms related to how Software-Defined Networking (SDN) and network programmability are impacting typical enterprise networks.

  - Chapter 22, "**Cisco Software-Defined Access (Cisco SD-Access),**" discusses Cisco's Software-Defined Networking (SDN) offering for the enterprise, including the Cisco Catalyst Center (formerly Cisco DNA Center) controller.

  - Chapter 23, "**Understanding REST and JSON,**" explains the foundational concepts of REST APIs, data structures, and how JSON can be useful for exchanging data using APIs.

  - Chapter 24, "**Understanding Ansible and Terraform,**" discusses the need for configuration management software and introduces the basics of each of these configuration management tools.

- **Part VII: Exam Updates and Final Review**

  - Chapter 25, "***CCNA 200-301 Official Cert Guide, Volume 2*, Second Edition, Exam Updates,**" is a place for the author to add book content mid-edition. Always check online for the latest PDF version of this appendix; the appendix lists download instructions.

  - Chapter 26, "**Final Review,**" suggests a plan for final preparation after you have finished the core parts of the book, in particular explaining the many study options available in the book.

- **Part VIII: Print Appendixes**

  - Appendix A, "**Numeric Reference Tables,**" lists several tables of numeric information, including a binary-to-decimal conversion table and a list of powers of 2.

- **Appendix B, "Exam Topics Cross-Reference,"** provides some tables to help you find where each exam objective is covered in the book.

- **Appendix C, "Answers to the 'Do I Know This Already?' Quizzes,"** includes the explanations to all the "Do I Know This Already" quizzes.

- The **Glossary** contains definitions for many of the terms used in the book, including the terms listed in the "Key Terms You Should Know" sections at the conclusion of the chapters.

- **Part IX: Online Appendixes**

  - **Appendix D, "Topics from Previous Editions"**

  - **Appendix E, "Practice for Chapter 6: Basic IPv4 Access Control Lists"**

  - **Appendix F, "Study Planner,"** is a spreadsheet with major study milestones, where you can track your progress through your study.

About Building Hands-On Skills

To do well on the CCNA exam, you need skills in using Cisco routers and switches, specifically the Cisco command-line interface (CLI). The Cisco CLI is a text-based command-and-response user interface; you type a command, and the device (a router or switch) displays messages in response.

For the exam, CLI skills help you in a couple of ways. First, lab questions require CLI skills. Each lab question can take 7–8 minutes if you know the topic, so poor CLI skills can cost several minutes per lab question. Additionally, any question type can ask about CLI commands, so the more comfortable you are remembering commands, parameters, and what they do, the more points you will pick up on the exam.

This next section walks through the options of what is included in the book, with a brief description of lab options outside the book.

Config Lab Exercises

I created some lab exercises called Config Labs and put them on my blog. Each Config Lab details a straightforward lab exercise. It begins with a scenario, a topology, and an existing configuration. You choose the configuration to add to each device to meet the goals of the scenario.

To make the labs accessible to all, the blog has no login requirements and no cost. You can do each lab just by viewing the page, reading, and writing your answer on paper or typing it in an editor. Optionally, you can attempt most labs in the Cisco Packet Tracer Simulator. In either case, the Config Lab page lists the intended answer, so you can check your work.

To find the Config Labs, first go to www.certskills.com. Navigate from the top menus for "Labs." Alternatively, use the advanced search link, from which you can combine search parameters to choose a book chapter or part, and to search for Config Lab posts.

Note that the blog organizes these Config Lab posts by book chapter, so you can easily use them at both Chapter Review and Part Review. See the "Your Study Plan" element that follows the Introduction for more details about those review sections.

A Quick Start with Pearson Network Simulator Lite

The decision of how to get hands-on skills can be a little scary at first. The good news: You have a free and simple first step to experience the CLI—install a desktop simulator app called Pearson Network Simulator Lite (or NetSim Lite) that comes with this book.

Pearson builds a CCNA Simulator app designed to help you learn most of the CCNA configure and verify exam topics. They also make a free Lite version of the simulator, included with this book. The Lite version gives you the means to experience the Cisco CLI just after a 5–10-minute installation process. No need to go buy real gear or buy a full simulator to start learning the CLI. Just install the Sim Lite from the companion website.

This latest version of NetSim Lite for Volume 2 (which differs from the NetSim Lite that comes with Volume 1) includes labs about IP ACLs.

The Pearson Network Simulator

The Config Labs and the Pearson Network Simulator Lite both fill specific needs, and they both come with the book. However, you need more than those two tools.

The single best option for lab work to do along with this book is the paid version of the Pearson Network Simulator. This simulator product simulates Cisco routers and switches so that you can learn for CCNA certification. But more importantly, it focuses on learning for the exam by providing a large number of useful lab exercises. Reader surveys tell us that those people who use the simulator along with the book love the learning process and rave about how the book and simulator work well together.

Of course, you need to make a decision for yourself and consider all the options. Thankfully, you can get a great idea of how the full simulator product works by using the Pearson Network Simulator Lite product included with the book. Both have the same base code, same user interface, and same types of labs. Try the Lite version to decide if you want to buy the full product.

On a practical note, when you want to do labs when reading a chapter or doing Part Review, the Simulator organizes the labs to match the book. Just look for the Sort by Chapter tab in the Simulator's user interface.

At the time this book was published, Pearson had no plan to update its CCNA Simulator product to a new version, as the current edition covers the latest exam topics. A software update will be issued that maps the labs to the organization of the new Cert Guide chapter structure by the summer of 2024.

More Lab Options

Many other lab options exist. For instance, you can use real Cisco routers and switches. You can buy them, new or used, or borrow them at work. For example, you can buy routers and switches that are useful for CCNA learning, but are two or three product generations old. You can also find sites from which you can rent time on real devices or virtual devices.

Cisco also makes a free simulator that works very well as a learning tool: Cisco Packet Tracer. Unlike the Pearson Network Simulator, it does not include lab exercises that direct you as to how to go about learning each topic. However, you can usually find lab exercises that rely on Packet Tracer, like the Config Labs at my blog. If interested in more information about Packet Tracer, check out www.certskills.com/ptinstall.

Cisco offers a virtualization product that lets you run router and switch operating system (OS) images in a virtual environment on your PC. This tool, the Cisco Modeling Labs–Personal Edition (CML PE), lets you create a lab topology, start the operating system for each device, and connect to the CLI of these real router and switch OS images. There is a fee, and you may need a PC hardware upgrade to use it effectively. Check out www.cisco.com/go/cml for more information, and inquire for more information at the Cisco Learning Network's CML community (learningnetwork.cisco.com).

The next two options work somewhat like CML PE, but with free software but no Cisco operating systems supplied. GNS3 (gns3.com) and EVE-NG (eve-ng.net) support creating topologies of virtual routers and switches that run real Cisco operating systems. Both have free options. However, both require that you provide the OS images. Also, as with CML PE, you may need to buy a small server or at least upgrade your personal computer to run more than a few routers and switches in a lab topology.

This book does not tell you what option to use, but you should plan on getting some hands-on practice somehow. For people starting with CCNA, many use some simulator like Pearson Sim Lite and the free Cisco Packet Tracer simulator. If you go far in your Cisco certification journey, you will likely try at least one of the virtualization options and also use real gear. The important thing to know is that most people need to practice using the Cisco CLI to be ready to pass these exams.

For More Information

If you have any comments about the book, submit them via www.ciscopress.com. Just go to the website, select **Contact Us**, and type your message.

Cisco might make changes that affect the CCNA certification from time to time. You should always check www.cisco.com/go/ccna for the latest details.

The *CCNA 200-301 Official Cert Guide*, *Volume 2*, Second Edition, helps you attain CCNA certification. This is the CCNA certification book from the only Cisco-authorized publisher. We at Cisco Press believe that this book certainly can help you achieve CCNA certification, but the real work is up to you! I trust that your time will be well spent.

Figure Credits

Figure 17.10: FileZilla

Figure 20.11: Amazon Web Services, Inc.

Figure 23.8: Postman, Inc.

Figure 24.3: GitHub, Inc.

Figures 26.3, 26.4: Pearson Education, Inc.

CCNA 200-301 Official Cert Guide, Volume 2, Second Edition, moves through a wide variety of topic areas, with major transitions occurring with each book part. The book works through wireless LANs, network security, network services, network architecture, and finally, network automation.

In this first part of this volume, we turn our attention to the LAN...not to wired Ethernet LANs, but to IEEE 802.11 wireless LANs—in other words, Wi-Fi. The four chapters in this part of the book lay down the foundations of how wireless LANs work and then show how to implement wireless LANs using Cisco devices.

Building wireless LANs requires some thought because the endpoints that use the LAN do not sit in one place and connect via a known cable and known switch port. To explain those details, Chapter 1 begins with the basics of how a wireless client can connect to the wireless network through a wireless access point (AP). After you learn the foundations in Chapter 1, Chapter 2 takes an architectural view of wireless LANs to discuss how you might build a wireless LAN for an enterprise, which requires much different thinking than, for instance, building a wireless LAN for your home.

Chapter 3 completes the three concepts-focused wireless LAN chapters by working through the alphabet soup that is wireless LAN security. The fact that wireless LAN clients come and go means that the LAN may be under constant attack as an easy place for attackers to gain access to the network, so wireless LANs must use effective security. Finally, Chapter 4 closes by showing how to configure an enterprise wireless LAN using Cisco APs and the Cisco Wireless LAN Controller (WLC) from the WLC's graphical interface.

Part I

Wireless LANs

CHAPTER 1

Fundamentals of Wireless Networks

This chapter covers the following exam topics:

> **1.0 Network Fundamentals**
>
> > **1.1 Explain the role and function of network components**
> >
> > > **1.1.d Access Points**
> >
> > **1.11 Describe wireless principles**
> >
> > > **1.11.a Non-overlapping Wi-Fi Channels**
> > >
> > > **1.11.b SSID**
> > >
> > > **1.11.c RF**

Wireless communication usually involves a data exchange between two devices. A wireless LAN goes even further; many devices can participate in sharing the medium for data exchanges. Wireless LANs must transmit a signal over radio frequencies (RF) to move data from one device to another. Transmitters and receivers can be fixed in consistent locations, or they can be mobile and free to move around. This chapter explains the topologies that can be used to control access to the wireless medium and provide data exchange between devices.

"Do I Know This Already?" Quiz

Take the quiz (either here or use the PTP software) if you want to use the score to help you decide how much time to spend on this chapter. The letter answers are listed at the bottom of the page following the quiz. Appendix C, found both at the end of the book as well as on the companion website, includes both the answers and explanations. You can also find both answers and explanations in the PTP testing software.

Table 1-1   "Do I Know This Already?" Foundation Topics Section-to-Question Mapping

Foundation Topics Section	Questions
Comparing Wired and Wireless Networks	1
Wireless LAN Topologies	2–4
Other Wireless Topologies	5, 6
Wireless Bands and Channels	7, 8

1. Wired Ethernet and Wi-Fi are based on which two IEEE standards, respectively?

    a. 802.1, 802.3

    b. 802.3, 802.1

    c. 802.3, 802.11

    d. 802.11, 802.3

2. Devices using a wireless LAN must operate in which one of the following modes?

   a. Round-robin access
   b. Half duplex
   c. Full duplex
   d. None of these answers are correct

3. An access point is set up to offer wireless coverage in an office. Which one of the following is the correct 802.11 term for the resulting standalone network?

   a. BSA
   b. BSD
   c. BSS
   d. IBSS

4. Which one of the following is used to uniquely identify an AP and the basic service set it maintains with its associated wireless clients?

   a. SSID
   b. BSSID
   c. Ethernet MAC address
   d. Radio MAC address

5. Which one of the following can be used to provide wireless connectivity to a nonwireless device?

   a. Wireless repeater
   b. Workgroup bridge
   c. Transparent bridge
   d. Adaptive bridge

6. Which one of the following is not needed in a Cisco outdoor mesh network?

   a. A BSS function
   b. Ethernet cabling to each AP
   c. A workgroup bridge
   d. A backhaul network

7. Which of the following are frequency bands commonly used for Wi-Fi? (Choose two answers.)

   a. 2.5 KHz
   b. 2.5 MHz
   c. 5 MHz
   d. 2.5 GHz
   e. 5 GHz

8. Which of the following are considered to be nonoverlapping channels? (Choose two answers.)

   a. Channels 1, 2, and 3 in the 2.4-GHz band
   b. Channels 1, 5, and 10 in the 2.4-GHz band
   c. Channels 1, 6, and 11 in the 2.4-GHz band
   d. Channels 40, 44, and 48 in the 5-GHz band

Foundation Topics

Comparing Wired and Wireless Networks

In a wired network, any two devices that need to communicate with each other must be connected by a wire. (That was obvious!) The "wire" might contain strands of metal or fiber-optic material that run continuously from one end to the other. Data that passes over the wire is bounded by the physical properties of the wire. In fact, the IEEE 802.3 set of standards defines strict guidelines for the Ethernet wire itself, in addition to how devices may connect, send, and receive data over the wire.

Wired connections have been engineered with tight constraints and have few variables that might prevent successful communication. Even the type and size of the wire strands, the number of twists the strands must make around each other over a distance, and the maximum length of the wire must adhere to the standard.

Therefore, a wired network is essentially a bounded medium; data must travel over whatever path the wire or cable takes between two devices. If the cable goes around a corner or lies in a coil, the electrical signals used to carry the data must also go around a corner or around a coil. Because only two devices may connect to a wire, only those two devices may send or transmit data. Even better: the two devices may transmit data to each other simultaneously because they each have a private, direct path to each other—assuming there are enough wires dedicated to each direction within the cable.

Wired networks also have some shortcomings. When a device is connected by a wire, it cannot move around very easily or very far. Before a device can connect to a wired network, it must have a connector that is compatible with the one on the end of the wire. As devices get smaller and more mobile, it just is not practical to connect them to a wire.

As its name implies, a wireless network removes the need to be tethered to a wire or cable. Convenience and mobility become paramount, enabling users to move around at will while staying connected to the network. A user can (and often does) bring along many different wireless devices that can all connect to the network easily and seamlessly.

Wireless data must travel through free space, without the constraints and protection of a wire. In the free space environment, many variables can affect the data and its delivery. To minimize the variables, wireless engineering efforts must focus on two things:

- Wireless devices must adhere to a common standard (IEEE 802.11).

- Wireless coverage must exist in the area where devices are expected to use it.

Answers to the "Do I Know This Already?" quiz:

1 C **2** B **3** C **4** B **5** B **6** B **7** D, E **8** C, D

As you study for the CCNA 200-301 exam, keep in mind that the exam is geared more toward a functional view of wireless technology. More detailed topics like RF characteristics, antenna performance, and so on are reserved for the Implementing Cisco Enterprise Network Core Technologies ENCOR 300-401 exam.

Wireless LAN Topologies

Wireless communication takes place over free space through the use of RF signals. The signals are sent by one device, the transmitter, to another device, the receiver. As Figure 1-1 shows, the transmitter can contact the receiver at any and all times, as long as both devices are tuned to the same frequency (or channel) and use the same scheme to carry the data between them. That all sounds simple, except that it is not really practical.

Figure 1-1 *Unidirectional Communication*

To fully leverage wireless communication, data should travel in *both* directions, as shown in Figure 1-2. Sometimes Device A needs to send data to Device B, while Device B would like to take a turn to send at other times.

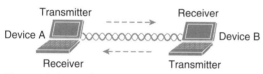

Figure 1-2 *Bidirectional Communication*

Because the two devices are using the same channel, two phrases in the preceding sentence become vitally important: *take a turn* and *send at other times*. With wireless communication, if multiple signals are received at the same time, they can interfere with each other. The likelihood of interference increases as the number of wireless devices grows. For example, Figure 1-3 shows four devices tuned to the same channel and what might happen if some or all of them transmit at the same time.

Figure 1-3 *Interference from Simultaneous Transmissions*

All this talk about waiting turns and avoiding interference might remind you of a traditional (nonswitched) Ethernet LAN, where multiple hosts can connect to a shared media and share a common bandwidth. To use the media effectively, all the hosts must operate in half-duplex mode so that they try to avoid colliding with other transmissions already in progress. The side effect is that no host can transmit and receive at the same time on a shared medium.

A wireless LAN is similar. Because multiple hosts can share the same channel, they also share the "airtime" or access to that channel at any given time. Therefore, to keep everything clean, only one device should transmit at any given time. To contend for use of the channel, devices based on the 802.11 standard have to determine whether the channel is clear and available before transmitting anything.

NOTE   IEEE 802.11 WLANs are always half duplex because transmissions between stations use the same frequency or channel. Only one station can transmit at any time; otherwise, collisions occur. To achieve full-duplex mode, one station's transmission would have to occur on one frequency while it receives over a different frequency—much like full-duplex Ethernet links work. Although this operation is certainly possible and practical, the 802.11 standard does not permit full-duplex operation. Some amendments to the standard do provide a means for multiple devices to transmit on the same channel at the same time, but this is beyond the scope of this book.

At the most basic level, there is no inherent organization to a wireless medium or any inherent control over the number of devices that can transmit and receive frames. Any device that has a wireless network adapter can power up at any time and try to communicate. At a minimum, a wireless network should have a way to make sure that every device using a channel can support a common set of parameters. Beyond that, there should be a way to control which devices (and users) are allowed to use the wireless medium and the methods that are used to secure the wireless transmissions.

Basic Service Set

The solution is to make every wireless service area a closed group of mobile devices that forms around a fixed device; before a device can participate, it must advertise its capabilities and then be granted permission to join. The 802.11 standard calls this a **basic service set (BSS)**. At the heart of every BSS is a wireless **access point (AP)**, as shown in Figure 1-4. The AP operates in **infrastructure mode**, which means it offers the services that are necessary to form the infrastructure of a wireless network. The AP also establishes its BSS over a single wireless channel. The AP and the members of the BSS must all use the same channel to communicate properly.

Because the operation of a BSS hinges on the AP, the BSS is bounded by the area where the AP's signal is usable. This is known as the *basic service area* (BSA) or **cell**. In Figure 1-4, the cell is shown as a simple shaded circular area that centers around the AP itself. Cells can have other shapes too, depending on the antenna that is connected to the AP and on the physical surroundings that might affect the AP's signals.

The AP serves as a single point of contact for every device that wants to use the BSS. It advertises the existence of the BSS by periodically transmitting an 802.11 **beacon** frame so that devices can find it and try to join. Beacon frames contain a text string called a **Service Set Identifier (SSID)**, which identifies the BSS. Beacons are normally broadcast about ten times per second (100-ms intervals), and also contain information about the data rates to be used within the BSS and any vendor-specific information needed. If the AP supports multiple SSIDs, a different beacon is broadcast for each SSID.

Recall that wired Ethernet devices each have a unique MAC address to send frames from a source to a destination over a Layer 2 network. Wireless devices must also have unique MAC addresses to send wireless frames at Layer 2 over the air. When the AP transmits wireless frames, it uses a **Basic Service Set Identifier (BSSID)** that is based on the AP's own radio MAC address.

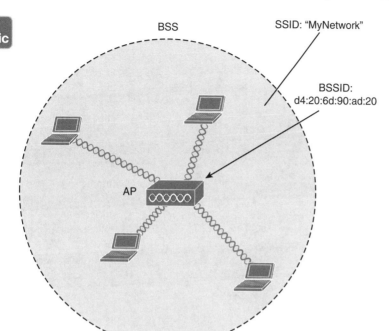

Figure 1-4 *802.11 Basic Service Set*

TIP Think of the BSSID as a machine-readable name tag that uniquely identifies the BSS ambassador (the AP), and the SSID as a nonunique, human-readable name tag that identifies the wireless service.

A wireless device can learn about BSSs within range by listening to the beacons that are received. This operation is known as **passive scanning**. Devices can also actively discover SSIDs that are within range by transmitting 802.11 **probe request** frames. APs can answer the request by sending a probe response frame that contains most of the beacon information.

Membership with the BSS is called an *association*. A wireless device must send an 802.11 **association request** frame to the AP, and the AP must either grant or deny the request by sending an *association response* frame. Once associated, a device becomes a client, or an 802.11 **station (STA)**, of the BSS.

What then? As long as a wireless client remains associated with a BSS, most communications to and from the client must pass *through* the AP, as indicated in Figure 1-5. When the BSSID is used as a source or destination address, data frames can be relayed to or from the AP.

You might be wondering why all client traffic has to traverse the AP at all. Why can two clients not simply transmit data frames directly to each other and bypass the middleman? If clients are allowed to communicate directly, then the whole idea of organizing and managing a BSS is moot. By sending data through the AP first, the BSS remains stable and under control.

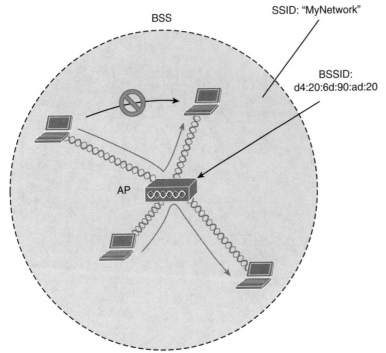

Figure 1-5 *Traffic Flows Within a BSS*

> **TIP** Even though data frames are meant to pass through an AP, keep in mind that other devices in the same general area that are listening on the same channel can overhear the transmissions. After all, wireless frames are not contained within a wire that connects a device to an AP. Instead, the frames are freely available over the air to anyone that is within range to receive them. If the frames are unencrypted, then anyone may inspect their contents. Only the BSSID value contained within the frames indicates that the intended sender or recipient is the AP.

Distribution System

Notice that a BSS involves a single AP and no explicit connection into a regular Ethernet network. In that setting, the AP and its associated clients make up a standalone network. But the AP's role at the center of the BSS does not just stop with managing the BSS; sooner or later, wireless clients will need to communicate with other devices that are not members of the BSS. Fortunately, an AP can also uplink into an Ethernet network because it has both wireless and wired capabilities. The 802.11 standard refers to the upstream wired Ethernet as the **distribution system (DS)** for the wireless BSS, as shown in Figure 1-6.

You can think of an AP as a translational bridge, where frames from two dissimilar media (802.11 wireless and 802.3 wired) are translated and then bridged at Layer 2. In simple terms, the AP is in charge of mapping a virtual local-area network (VLAN) to an SSID. In Figure 1-6, the AP maps VLAN 10 to the wireless LAN using SSID "MyNetwork." Clients associated with the "MyNetwork" SSID will appear to be connected to VLAN 10.

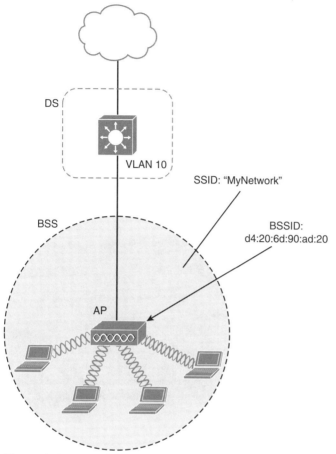

Figure 1-6   *Distribution System Supporting a BSS*

This concept can be extended so that multiple VLANs are mapped to multiple SSIDs. To do this, the AP must be connected to the switch by a trunk link that carries the VLANs. In Figure 1-7, VLANs 10, 20, and 30 are trunked to the AP over the DS. The AP uses the 802.1Q tag to map the VLAN numbers to the appropriate SSIDs. For example, VLAN 10 is mapped to SSID "MyNetwork," VLAN 20 is mapped to SSID "YourNetwork," and VLAN 30 to SSID "Guest."

In effect, when an AP uses multiple SSIDs, it is trunking VLANs over the air, and over the same channel, to wireless clients. The clients must use the appropriate SSID that has been mapped to the respective VLAN when the AP was configured. The AP then appears as multiple logical APs—one per BSS—with a unique BSSID for each. With Cisco APs, this is usually accomplished by incrementing the last digit of the radio's MAC address for each SSID.

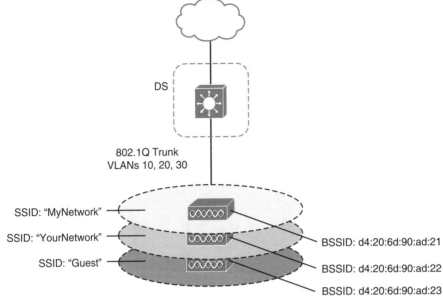

Figure 1-7 *Supporting Multiple SSIDs on One AP*

Even though an AP can advertise and support multiple logical wireless networks, each of the SSIDs covers the same geographic area. The reason is that the AP uses the same transmitter, receiver, antennas, and channel for every SSID that it supports. Beware of one misconception though: multiple SSIDs can give an illusion of scale. Even though wireless clients can be distributed across many SSIDs, all of those clients must share the same AP's hardware and must contend for airtime on the same channel.

Extended Service Set

Normally, one AP cannot cover the entire area where clients might be located. For example, you might need wireless coverage throughout an entire floor of a business, hotel, hospital, or other large building. To cover more area than a single AP's cell can cover, you simply need to add more APs and spread them out geographically.

When APs are placed at different geographic locations, they can all be interconnected by a switched infrastructure. The 802.11 standard calls this an **extended service set (ESS)**, as shown in Figure 1-8.

The idea is to make multiple APs cooperate so that the wireless service is consistent and seamless from the client's perspective. Ideally, any SSIDs that are defined on one AP should be defined on all the APs in an ESS; otherwise, it would be very cumbersome and inconvenient for a client to be reconfigured each time it moves into a different AP's cell.

Notice that each cell in Figure 1-8 has a unique BSSID, but both cells share one common SSID. Regardless of a client's location within the ESS, the SSID will remain the same, but the client can always distinguish one AP from another. Having a consistent SSID through the ESS is called an **Extended Service Set Identifier (ESSID)**.

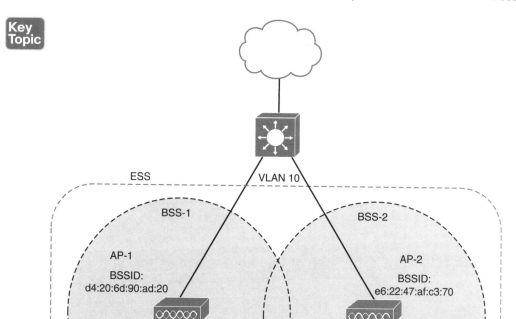

Figure 1-8 *Scaling Wireless Coverage with an 802.11 Extended Service Set*

In an ESS, a wireless client can associate with only one AP while it is physically located near that AP. If the client later moves to a different location, it can move its association to a different nearby AP by sending a **reassociation request** frame to the new AP. That AP sends a reassociation response frame in return.

Passing from one AP to another is called **roaming**. Keep in mind that each AP offers its own BSS on its own channel, to prevent interference between the APs. As a client device roams from one AP to another, it must scan the available channels to find a new AP (and BSS) to roam toward. In effect, the client is roaming from BSS to BSS, and from channel to channel.

Independent Basic Service Set

Usually, a wireless network leverages APs for organization, control, and scalability. Sometimes that is not possible or convenient in an impromptu situation. For example, two people who want to exchange electronic documents at a meeting might not be able to find a BSS available or might want to avoid having to authenticate to a production network. In addition, many personal printers have the capability to print documents wirelessly, without relying on a regular BSS or AP.

The 802.11 standard allows two or more wireless clients to communicate directly with each other, with no other means of network connectivity. This is known as an **ad hoc wireless network**, or an **independent basic service set (IBSS)**, as shown in Figure 1-9. For this connection to work, one of the devices must take the lead and begin advertising a network name and the necessary radio parameters, much like an AP would do. Any other device can then join as needed. IBSSs are meant to be organized in an impromptu, distributed fashion; therefore, they do not scale well beyond eight to ten devices.

IBSS

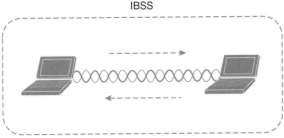

Figure 1-9   *802.11 Independent Basic Service Set*

Other Wireless Topologies

Wireless APs can be configured to operate in noninfrastructure modes when a normal BSS cannot provide the functionality that is needed. The following sections cover the most common modes.

Repeater

Normally, each AP in a wireless network has a wired connection back to the DS or switched infrastructure. To extend wireless coverage beyond a normal AP's cell footprint, additional APs and their wired connections can be added. In some scenarios, it is not possible to run a wired connection to a new AP because the cable distance is too great to support Ethernet communication.

In that case, you can add an additional AP that is configured for *repeater mode*. A wireless **repeater** takes the signal it receives and repeats or retransmits it in a new cell area around the repeater. The idea is to move the repeater out away from the AP so that it is still within range of both the AP and the distant client, as shown in Figure 1-10.

If the repeater has a single transmitter and receiver, it must operate on the same channel that the AP is using. That can create the possibility that the AP's signal will be received and retransmitted by the repeater, only to be received again by the AP—halving the effective throughput because the channel will be kept busy twice as long as before. As a remedy, some repeaters can use two transmitters and receivers to keep the original and repeated signals isolated on different channels. One transmitter and receiver pair is dedicated to signals in the AP's cell, while the other pair is dedicated to signals in the repeater's own cell.

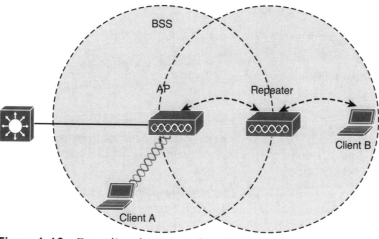

Figure 1-10 *Extending the Range of an AP with a Wireless Repeater*

Workgroup Bridge

Suppose you have a device that supports a wired Ethernet link but is not capable of having a wireless connection. For example, some mobile medical devices might be designed with only a wired connection. While it is possible to plug the device into an Ethernet connection when needed, a wireless connection would be much more practical. You can use a **workgroup bridge (WGB)** to connect the device's wired network adapter to a wireless network.

Rather than providing a BSS for wireless service, a WGB becomes a wireless client of a BSS. In effect, the WGB acts as an external wireless network adapter for a device that has none. In Figure 1-11, an AP provides a BSS; Client A is a regular wireless client, while Client B is associated with the AP through a WGB.

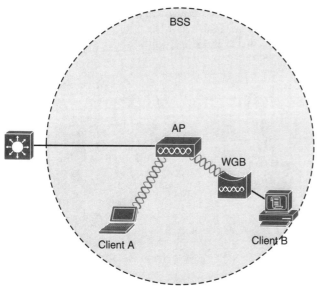

Figure 1-11 *Nonwireless Device Connecting Through a Workgroup Bridge*

You might encounter two types of *workgroup bridges*:

- **Universal workgroup bridge (uWGB):** A single wired device can be bridged to a wireless network.

- **Workgroup bridge (WGB):** A Cisco-proprietary implementation that allows multiple wired devices to be bridged to a wireless network.

Outdoor Bridge

An AP can be configured to act as a bridge to form a single wireless link from one LAN to another over a long distance. Outdoor bridged links are commonly used for connectivity between buildings or between cities.

If the LANs at two locations need to be bridged, a **point-to-point bridged** link can be used. One AP configured in bridge mode is needed on each end of the wireless link. Special-purpose antennas are normally used with the bridges to focus their signals in one direction—toward the antenna of the AP at the far end of the link. This configuration maximizes the link distance, as shown in Figure 1-12.

Figure 1-12 *Point-to-Point Outdoor Bridge*

Sometimes the LANs at multiple sites need to be bridged together. A point-to-multipoint bridged link allows a central site to be bridged to several other sites. The central site bridge is connected to an omnidirectional antenna, such that its signal is transmitted equally in all directions so that it can reach the other sites simultaneously. The bridges at each of the other sites can be connected to a directional antenna aimed at the central site. Figure 1-13 shows the point-to-multipoint scenario.

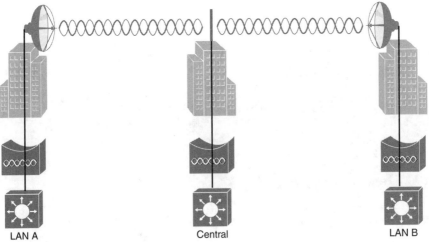

Figure 1-13 *Point-to-Multipoint Outdoor Bridge*

Mesh Network

To provide wireless coverage over a very large area, it is not always practical to run Ethernet cabling to every AP that would be needed. Instead, you could use multiple APs configured in mesh mode. In a mesh topology, wireless traffic is bridged from AP to AP, in a daisy-chain fashion, using another wireless channel.

Mesh APs can leverage dual radios—one using a channel in one range of frequencies and one a different range. Each mesh AP usually maintains a BSS on one channel, with which wireless clients can associate. Client traffic is then usually bridged from AP to AP over other channels as a backhaul network. At the edge of the **mesh network**, the backhaul traffic is bridged to the wired LAN infrastructure. Figure 1-14 shows a typical mesh network. With Cisco APs, you can build a mesh network indoors or outdoors. The mesh network runs its own dynamic routing protocol to work out the best path for backhaul traffic to take across the mesh APs.

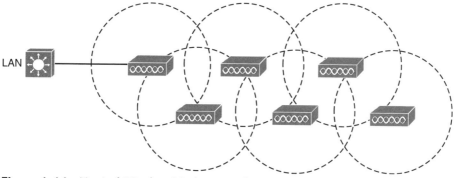

Figure 1-14 *Typical Wireless Mesh Network*

Wireless Bands and Channels

The electromagnetic waves involved in a wireless signal can be measured and described in several ways. One fundamental property is the frequency of the wave, or the number of times the signal oscillates or makes one complete positive and negative cycle in one second. One complete cycle within one second is known as one hertz (Hz). Wi-Fi signals use frequencies that oscillate more than one billion times per second, or one gigahertz (GHz).

One of the three main frequency ranges used for wireless LAN communication lies between 2.400 and 2.4835 GHz. This is usually called the *2.4-GHz* **band**, even though it does not encompass the entire range between 2.4 and 2.5 GHz. It is much more convenient to refer to the band name instead of the specific range of frequencies included. Another wireless LAN range is usually called the *5-GHz band* because it lies between 5.150 and 5.825 GHz. The 5-GHz band actually contains four smaller separate and distinct bands, with the possibility of more small bands being added in the future. The 6-GHz band lies between 5.925 and 7.125 GHz. It is broken up into four smaller bands too.

To keep everything orderly and compatible, bands are usually divided into a number of distinct **channels**. Each channel is known by a channel number and is assigned to a specific frequency. As long as the channels are defined by a national or international standards body, they can be used consistently in all locations. Figures 1-15 and 1-16 show the channel layout for the 2.4- and 5-GHz bands, respectively.

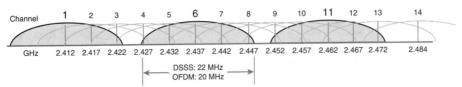

Figure 1-15 *Channel Layout in the 2.4-GHz Band*

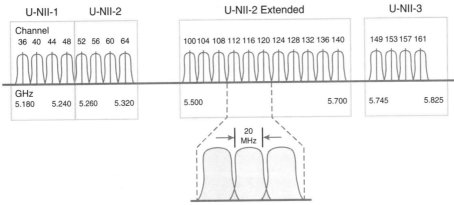

Figure 1-16 *Channel Layout in the 5-GHz Band*

You might assume that an AP can use any channel number without affecting any APs that use other channel numbers. In the 5-GHz band, this is the case because each channel is allocated a frequency range that does not encroach on or overlap the frequencies allocated for any other channel. In other words, the 5-GHz band consists of **nonoverlapping channels**. In Figure 1-16 notice that the valid channel numbers are not incremental; instead, they increase by four. That means channel numbers in between, such as channels 37, 38, and 39, are not valid or used. Channels in the 6-GHz band are numbered in a similar fashion.

The same is *not* true of the 2.4-GHz band. Each of its channels is much too wide to avoid overlapping the next lower or upper channel number. In fact, each channel covers the frequency range that is allocated to more than four consecutive channels! Notice the width of the channel spacing in Figure 1-15 as compared to the width of one of the shaded signals centered on channels 1, 6, and 11. The only way to avoid any overlap between adjacent channels is to configure APs to use only channels 1, 6, and 11. Even though there are 14 channels available to use, you should always strive for nonoverlapping channels in your network.

It might be obvious that wireless devices and APs should all be capable of operating on the same band. For example, a 5-GHz wireless phone can communicate only with an AP that offers Wi-Fi service on 5-GHz channels. In addition, the devices and APs must also share a compatibility with the parts of the 802.11 standard they support.

As the IEEE 802.11 Wi-Fi standard evolves and develops, new amendments with new functionality get proposed. These amendments are known by "802.11" followed by a one- or two-letter suffix until they are accepted and rolled up into the next generation of the complete 802.11 standard. Even then, it is common to see the amendment suffixes still used to distinguish specific functions.

You should be aware of several amendments that define important characteristics such as data rates, methods used to transmit and receive data, and so on. For the CCNA 200-301 exam, you should know which band each of the amendments listed in Table 1-2 uses. The ENCOR 300-401 exam goes further into the data rates and modulation and coding schemes used by each.

Table 1-2   Basic Characteristics of Some IEEE 802.11 Amendments

Amendment	2.4 GHz	5 GHz	6 GHz	Max Data Rate	Notes
802.11-1997	Yes	No	No	2 Mbps	The original 802.11 standard ratified in 1997
802.11b	Yes	No	No	11 Mbps	Introduced in 1999
802.11g	Yes	No	No	54 Mbps	Introduced in 2003
802.11a	No	Yes	No	54 Mbps	Introduced in 1999
802.11n	Yes	Yes	No	600 Mbps	HT (high throughput), introduced in 2009
802.11ac	No	Yes	No	6.93 Gbps	VHT (very high throughput), introduced in 2013
802.11ax	Yes	Yes	Yes	4x 802.11ac	High Efficiency Wireless

The 802.11 amendments are not mutually exclusive. Wireless client devices and APs can be compatible with one or more amendments; however, a client and an AP can communicate only if they both support and agree to use the same amendment.

When you look at the specifications for a wireless device, you may find supported amendments listed in a single string, separated by slashes. For example, a device that supports 802.11b/g will support both 802.11b and 802.11g. One that supports b/g/a/n/ac will support 802.11b, 802.11g, 802.11a, 802.11n, and 802.11ac. You should become familiar with Table 1-2 so that you can know which bands a device can use based on its 802.11 amendment support.

If a device can operate on both bands, how does it decide which band to use? APs can usually operate on both bands simultaneously to support any clients that might be present on each band. However, wireless clients typically associate with an AP on one band at a time, while scanning for potential APs on both bands. The band used to connect to an AP is chosen according to the operating system, wireless adapter driver, and other internal configuration. A wireless client can initiate an association with an AP on one band and then switch to the other band if the signal conditions are better there.

NOTE   Cisco APs can have multiple radios (sets of transmitters and receivers) to support a BSS on each supported band. Some models have two 5-GHz radios that can be configured to operate BSSs on two different channels at the same time, providing wireless coverage to higher densities of users that are located in the same vicinity.

You can configure a Cisco AP to operate on a specific channel number. As the number of APs grows, manual channel assignment can become a difficult task. Fortunately, Cisco wireless architectures can automatically and dynamically assign each AP to an appropriate channel. The architecture is covered in Chapter 2, "Analyzing Cisco Wireless Architectures," while dynamic channel assignment is covered on the ENCOR 300-401 exam.

In open space, usable RF signals can propagate or reach further on the 2.4-GHz band than on the 5-GHz or 6-GHz band. They also tend to penetrate indoor walls and objects more easily at 2.4 GHz than 5 or 6 GHz. However, the 2.4-GHz band is commonly more crowded with wireless devices. Remember that only three nonoverlapping channels are available, so the chances of other neighboring APs using the same channels are greater. In contrast, the 5- and 6-GHz bands have many more channels available to use, making channels less crowded and experiencing less interference.

As Wi-Fi has evolved, the 802.11 standard has grown and new amendments have been introduced, making it difficult to keep track. The Wi-Fi Alliance introduced a set of simplified names to identify each Wi-Fi generation, as listed in Table 1-3. Wi-Fi 0 denotes the original 802.11 standard in its earliest form, followed by each generation, the supported bands, and the prominent 802.11 amendment used. Wireless products are often named or described by these generational names. For example, you might see APs or clients listed as "Wi-Fi 6E," which simply means they can operate in all three bands using IEEE 802.11ax.

Table 1-3 Wi-Fi Alliance Generational Names

Wi-Fi Alliance Designation	Bands Supported	IEEE 802.11 Amendments Supported
Wi-Fi 0	2.4	802.11 (the original)
Wi-Fi 1	2.4	802.11b
Wi-Fi 2	5	802.11a
Wi-Fi 3	2.4	802.11g
Wi-Fi 4	2.4, 5	802.11n
Wi-Fi 5	5	802.11ac
Wi-Fi 6	2.4, 5	802.11ax
Wi-Fi 6E	2.4, 5, 6	802.11ax
Wi-Fi 7	2.4, 5, 6	802.11be

Chapter Review

Review this chapter's material using either the tools in the book or the interactive tools for the same material found on the book's companion website. Table 1-4 outlines the key review elements and where you can find them. To better track your study progress, record when you completed these activities in the second column.

Table 1-4 Chapter Review Tracking

Review Element	Review Date(s)	Resource Used
Review key topics		Book, website
Review key terms		Book, website
Answer DIKTA questions		Book, PTP
Review memory tables		Website

Review All the Key Topics

Table 1-5   Key Topics for Chapter 1

Key Topic Element	Description	Page Number
Figure 1-4	Basic service set	9
Figure 1-7	Multiple SSIDs	12
Figure 1-8	Extended service set	13
Paragraph	Nonoverlapping channels and bands	18
Table 1-2	Basic Characteristics of Some 802.11 Amendments	19

Key Terms You Should Know

access point (AP), ad hoc wireless network, association request, band, basic service set (BSS), Basic Service Set Identifier (BSSID), beacon, cell, channel, distribution system (DS), extended service set (ESS), Extended Service Set Identifier (ESSID), independent basic service set (IBSS), infrastructure mode, mesh network, nonoverlapping channels, passive scanning, point-to-point bridge, probe request, reassociation request, repeater, roaming, Service Set Identifier (SSID), station (STA), workgroup bridge (WGB)

CHAPTER 2

Analyzing Cisco Wireless Architectures

This chapter covers the following exam topics:

2.0 Network Access

2.6 Compare Cisco Wireless Architectures and AP modes

In Chapter 1, "Fundamentals of Wireless Networks," you learned how a single access point (AP) can provide a basic service set (BSS) for a cell area and how multiple APs can be connected to form an extended service set (ESS) for a larger network. In this chapter, you learn more about different approaches or architectures that allow APs to be networked together for an enterprise. You also learn how some architectures are more scalable than others and how to manage each type of wireless network architecture.

As you work through this chapter, think about how each architecture can be applied to specific environments—how easy it would be to manage, deploy, and troubleshoot the network, how the APs can be controlled, and how data would move through the network.

"Do I Know This Already?" Quiz

Take the quiz (either here or use the PTP software) if you want to use the score to help you decide how much time to spend on this chapter. The letter answers are listed at the bottom of the page following the quiz. Appendix C, found both at the end of the book as well as on the companion website, includes both the answers and explanations. You can also find both answers and explanations in the PTP testing software.

Table 2-1 "Do I Know This Already?" Section-to-Question Mapping

Foundation Topics Section	Questions
Autonomous AP Architecture	1
Cloud-based AP Architecture	2
Split-MAC Architectures	3–5
Comparing Cisco Wireless LAN Controller Deployments	6
Cisco AP Modes	7, 8

1. Which one of the following terms best describes a Cisco wireless access point that operates in a standalone, independent manner?

    a. Autonomous AP

    b. Independent AP

    c. Lightweight AP

    d. Embedded AP

2. The Cisco Meraki cloud-based APs are most accurately described by which one of the following statements?

    a. Autonomous APs joined to a WLC

    b. Autonomous APs centrally managed

    c. Lightweight APs joined to a WLC

    d. Lightweight APs centrally managed

3. A "lightweight" access point is said to participate in which one of the following architectures?

    a. Light-MAC

    b. Tunnel-MAC

    c. Split-MAC

    d. Big-MAC

4. How does an access point communicate with a wireless LAN controller?

    a. Through an IPsec tunnel

    b. Through a CAPWAP tunnel

    c. Through a GRE tunnel

    d. Directly over Layer 2

5. Which one of the following is not needed for a Cisco AP in default local mode to be able to support three SSIDs that are bound to three VLANs?

    a. A trunk link carrying three VLANs

    b. An access link bound to a single VLAN

    c. A WLC connected to three VLANs

    d. A CAPWAP tunnel to a WLC

6. Which one of the following WLC deployment models would be best for a large enterprise with around 3000 APs?

    a. Cisco Mobility Express

    b. Embedded

    c. Centralized

    d. Cloud-based

7. If a Cisco AP provides at least one BSS for wireless clients, which one of the following modes does it use?

    a. Local

    b. Normal

    c. Monitor

    d. Client

8. Regarding Cisco AP modes, which one of the following is true?

    a. An AP can operate in multiple modes at the same time.

    b. An AP has only one possible mode of operation.

    c. The Run mode is the default mode.

    d. The SE-Connect mode is used for spectrum analysis.

Foundation Topics

Autonomous AP Architecture

An access point's primary function is to bridge wireless data from the air to a normal wired network. An AP can accept "connections" from a number of wireless clients so that they become members of the LAN, as if the same clients were using wired connections.

APs act as the central point of access (hence the AP name), controlling client access to the wireless LAN. An **autonomous AP** is self-contained; it is equipped with both wired and wireless hardware so that the wireless client associations can be terminated onto a wired connection locally at the AP. The APs and their data connections must be distributed across the coverage area and across the network.

Autonomous APs offer one or more fully functional, standalone basic service sets (BSSs). They are also a natural extension of a switched network, connecting wireless Service Set Identifiers (SSIDs) to wired virtual LANs (VLANs) at the access layer. Figure 2-1 shows the basic architecture; even though only four APs are shown across the bottom, a typical enterprise network could consist of hundreds or thousands of APs.

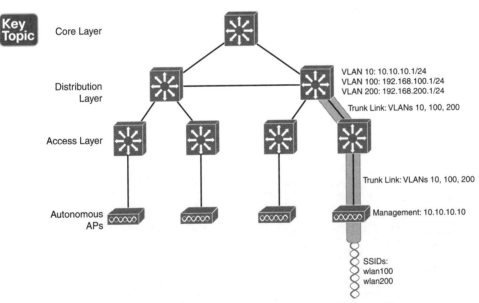

Figure 2-1   *Wireless Network Architecture with Autonomous APs*

What exactly does an autonomous AP need to become a part of the network? The wireless network in Figure 2-1 consists of two SSIDs: wlan100 and wlan200. They correspond to wired VLANs 100 and 200, respectively. As shown by the shaded links, the VLANs must be trunked from the distribution layer switch (where routing commonly takes place) to the access layer, where they are extended further over a trunk link to the AP.

An autonomous AP offers a short and simple path for data to travel between the wireless and wired networks. Data has to travel only through the AP to reach the network on the other side. Two wireless users that are associated to the same autonomous AP can reach each other through the AP without having to pass up into the wired network. As you work through the wireless architectures discussed in the rest of the chapter, notice the data path that is required for each.

An autonomous AP must also be configured with a management IP address (10.10.10.10 in Figure 2-1) so that you can remotely manage it. After all, you will want to configure SSIDs, VLANs, and many RF parameters like the channel and transmit power to be used. The management address is not normally part of any of the data VLANs, so a dedicated management VLAN (i.e., VLAN 10) must be added to the trunk links to reach the AP. Each AP must be configured and maintained individually unless you leverage a management platform such as Cisco Prime Infrastructure or Cisco Catalyst Center.

Because the data and management VLANs may need to reach every autonomous AP, the network configuration and efficiency can become cumbersome as the network scales. For example, you will likely want to offer the same SSID on many APs so that wireless clients can associate with that SSID in most any location or while roaming between any two APs. You might also want to extend the corresponding VLAN (and IP subnet) to each and every AP so that clients do not have to request a new IP address for each new association.

Because SSIDs and their VLANs must be extended at Layer 2, you should consider how they are extended throughout the switched network. The shaded links in Figure 2-2 show an example of a single VLAN's extent in the data plane. Working top to bottom, follow VLAN 100 as it reaches through the network. VLAN 100 is routed within the distribution layer and must be carried over trunk links to the access layer switches and then to each autonomous AP. In effect, VLAN 100 must extend end to end across the whole infrastructure—something that is usually considered to be a bad practice.

That approach might sound straightforward until you have to add a new VLAN and configure every switch and AP in your network to carry and support it. Even worse, suppose your network has redundant links between each layer of switches. The Spanning Tree Protocol (STP) running on each switch becomes a vital ingredient to prevent bridging loops from forming and corrupting the network. For these reasons, client roaming across autonomous APs is typically limited to the Layer 2 domain, or the extent of a single VLAN. As the wireless network expands, the infrastructure becomes more difficult to configure correctly and becomes less efficient.

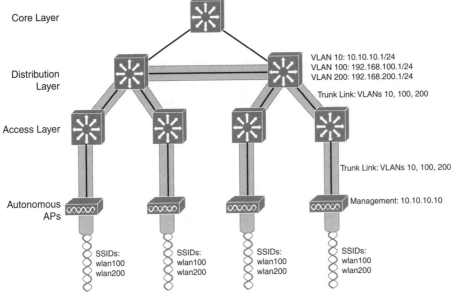

Figure 2-2   *Extent of a Data VLAN in a Network of Autonomous APs*

Cloud-based AP Architecture

Recall that an autonomous AP needs quite a bit of configuration and management. To help manage more and more autonomous APs as the wireless network grows, you could place an AP management platform such Cisco Catalyst Center (also known as DNA Center) in a central location within the enterprise. The management platform would need to be purchased, configured, and maintained too.

A simpler approach is a **cloud-based AP** architecture, where the AP management function is pushed out of the enterprise and into the Internet cloud. Cisco Meraki is cloud-based and offers centralized management of wireless, switched, and security networks built from Meraki products. For example, through the cloud networking service, you can configure and manage APs, monitor wireless performance and activity, generate reports, and so on.

Cisco Meraki APs can be deployed automatically, after you register with the Meraki cloud. Each AP will contact the cloud when it powers up and will self-configure. From that point on, you can manage the AP through the Meraki cloud dashboard.

Figure 2-3 illustrates the basic cloud-based architecture. Notice that the network is arranged identically to that of the autonomous AP network. The reason is that the APs in a cloud-based network are all autonomous too. The most visible difference is that all of the APs are managed, controlled, and monitored centrally from the cloud.

Answers to the "Do I Know This Already?" quiz:

1 A **2** B **3** C **4** B **5** A **6** C **7** A **8** D

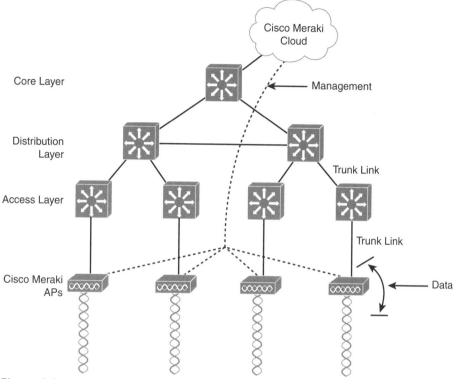

Figure 2-3 *Cisco Meraki Cloud-Based Wireless Network Architecture*

From the cloud, you can push out code upgrades and configuration changes to the APs in the enterprise. The Cisco Meraki cloud also adds the intelligence needed to automatically instruct each AP on which channel and transmit power level to use. It can also collect information from all of the APs about things such as RF interference, rogue or unexpected wireless devices that were overheard, and wireless usage statistics.

Finally, there are a couple of things you should observe about the cloud-based architecture. The data path from the wireless network to the wired network is very short; the autonomous AP directly links the two networks. Data to and from wireless clients does not have to travel up into the cloud and back; the cloud is used only to bring management functions into the data plane.

Also, notice that the network in Figure 2-3 consists of two distinct paths—one for data traffic and another for management traffic, corresponding to the following two functions:

- **A control plane:** Traffic used to control, configure, manage, and monitor the AP itself

- **A data plane:** End-user traffic passing through the AP

This division will become important in the following sections as other types of architecture are discussed.

Split-MAC Architectures

Because autonomous APs are...well, autonomous, managing their RF operation can be quite difficult. As a network administrator, you are in charge of selecting and configuring the channel used by each AP and detecting and dealing with any rogue APs that might be interfering. You must also manage things such as the transmit power level to make sure that the wireless coverage is sufficient, it does not overlap too much, and there aren't any coverage holes—even when an AP's radio fails.

Managing wireless network security can also be difficult. Each autonomous AP handles its own security policies, with no central point of entry between the wireless and wired networks. That means there is no convenient place to monitor traffic for things such as intrusion detection and prevention, quality of service, bandwidth policing, and so on.

To overcome the limitations of distributed autonomous APs, many of the functions found within autonomous APs have to be shifted toward some central location. In Figure 2-4, most of the activities performed by an autonomous AP on the left are broken up into two groups—management functions on the top and real-time processes on the bottom.

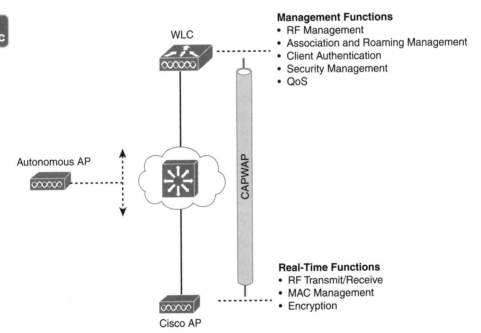

Figure 2-4 *Autonomous Versus Cisco Access Point*

The real-time processes involve sending and receiving 802.11 frames, beacons, and probe messages. The 802.11 data encryption is also handled in real time, on a per-packet basis. The AP must interact with wireless clients on some low level, known as the **Media Access Control (MAC) layer**. These functions must stay with the AP hardware, closest to the clients.

The management functions are not integral to handling frames over the RF channels, but are things that should be centrally administered. Therefore, those functions can be moved to a centrally located platform away from the AP.

When the functions of an autonomous AP are divided, the Cisco AP hardware performs only the real-time 802.11 operation. Its code image and local intelligence are stripped down, or lightweight, compared to the traditional autonomous AP.

The management functions are usually performed on a **wireless LAN controller (WLC)**, which controls many Cisco APs. This is shown in the bottom right portion of Figure 2-4. Notice that the AP is left with duties in Layers 1 and 2, where frames are moved into and out of the RF domain. The AP becomes totally dependent on the WLC for every other WLAN function, such as authenticating users, managing security policies, and even selecting RF channels and output power.

NOTE   Remember that a Cisco AP cannot normally operate on its own; it is very dependent on a WLC somewhere in the network. That means the AP will become nonfunctional if it loses connectivity to its WLC. The only exception is the FlexConnect AP mode, which is discussed later in this chapter.

The AP-WLC division of labor is known as a **split-MAC architecture**, where the normal MAC operations are pulled apart into two distinct locations. This occurs for every AP in the network; each one must boot and bind itself to a WLC to support wireless clients. The WLC becomes the central hub that supports a number of APs scattered about in the network.

How does an AP bind with a WLC to form a complete working access point? The two devices must use a tunneling protocol between them, to carry 802.11-related messages and also client data. Remember that the AP and WLC can be located on the same VLAN or IP subnet, but they do not have to be. Instead, they can be located on two entirely different IP subnets in two entirely different locations.

The Control and Provisioning of Wireless Access Points (**CAPWAP**) tunneling protocol makes this all possible by encapsulating the data between the LAP and WLC within new IP packets. The tunneled data can then be switched or routed across the campus network. As Figure 2-5 shows, the CAPWAP relationship actually consists of two separate tunnels, as follows:

- **CAPWAP control messages:** Carry exchanges that are used to configure the AP and manage its operation. The control messages are authenticated and encrypted, so the AP is securely controlled by only the appropriate WLC, then transported over the control tunnel.

- **CAPWAP data:** Used for packets traveling to and from wireless clients that are associated with the AP. Data packets are transported over the data tunnel but are not encrypted by default. When data encryption is enabled for an AP, packets are protected with Datagram Transport Layer Security (DTLS).

NOTE   CAPWAP is defined in RFCs 5415, 5416, 5417, and 5418. CAPWAP is based on the Lightweight Access Point Protocol (LWAPP), which was a legacy Cisco proprietary solution.

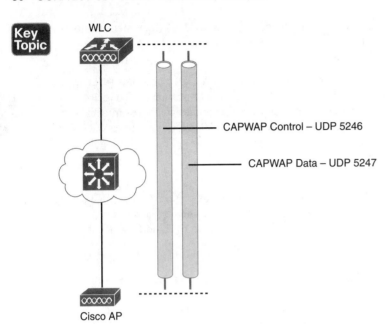

Figure 2-5 *Linking an AP and WLC with CAPWAP*

Every AP and WLC must also authenticate each other with digital certificates. An X.509 certificate is preinstalled in each device when it is purchased. By using certificates behind the scenes, every device is properly authenticated before becoming part of the wireless network. This process helps assure that no one can add an unauthorized AP to your network.

The CAPWAP tunneling allows the AP and WLC to be separated geographically and logically. It also breaks the dependence on Layer 2 connectivity between them. For example, Figure 2-6 uses shaded areas to show the extent of VLAN 100. Notice how VLAN 100 exists at the WLC and in the air as SSID 100, near the wireless clients—but not in between the AP and the WLC. Instead, traffic to and from clients associated with SSID 100 is transported across the network infrastructure encapsulated inside the CAPWAP data tunnel. The tunnel exists between the IP address of the WLC and the IP address of the AP, which allows all of the tunneled packets to be routed at Layer 3.

Also, notice how the AP is known by only a single IP address: 10.10.10.10. Because the AP sits on the access layer where its CAPWAP tunnels terminate, it can use one IP address for both management and tunneling. No trunk link is needed because all of the VLANs it supports are encapsulated and tunneled as Layer 3 IP packets, rather than individual Layer 2 VLANs.

As the wireless network grows, the WLC simply builds more CAPWAP tunnels to reach more APs. Figure 2-7 depicts a network with four APs. Each AP has a control and a data tunnel back to the centralized WLC. SSID 100 can exist on every AP, and VLAN 100 can reach every AP through the network of tunnels.

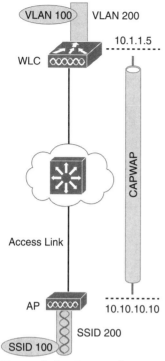

Figure 2-6   *Extent of VLAN 100 in a Cisco Wireless Network*

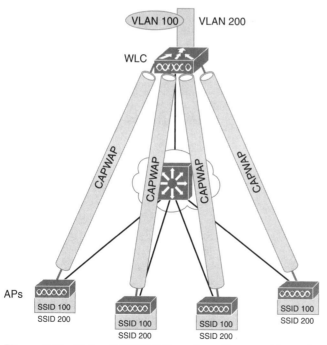

Figure 2-7   *Using CAPWAP Tunnels to Connect APs to One Central WLC*

After CAPWAP tunnels are built from a WLC to one or more lightweight APs, the WLC can begin offering a variety of additional functions. Think of all the puzzles and shortcomings that were discussed for the traditional autonomous WLAN architecture as you read over the following list of WLC activities:

- **Dynamic channel assignment:** The WLC can automatically choose and configure the RF channel used by each AP, based on other active access points in the area.

- **Transmit power optimization:** The WLC can automatically set the transmit power of each AP based on the coverage area needed.

- **Self-healing wireless coverage:** If an AP radio dies, the coverage hole can be "healed" by turning up the transmit power of surrounding APs automatically.

- **Flexible client roaming:** Clients can roam between APs with very fast roaming times.

- **Dynamic client load balancing:** If two or more APs are positioned to cover the same geographic area, the WLC can associate clients with the least used AP. This approach distributes the client load across the APs.

- **RF monitoring:** The WLC manages each AP so that it scans channels to monitor the RF usage. By listening to a channel, the WLC can remotely gather information about RF interference, noise, signals from neighboring APs, and signals from rogue APs or ad hoc clients.

- **Security management:** The WLC can authenticate clients from a central service and can require wireless clients to obtain an IP address from a trusted DHCP server before allowing them to associate and access the WLAN.

- **Wireless intrusion prevention (or protection) system:** Leveraging its central location, the WLC can monitor client data to detect and prevent malicious activity.

Comparing Cisco Wireless LAN Controller Deployments

Suppose you want to deploy a WLC to support multiple lightweight APs in your network. Where should you put the WLC? The split-MAC concept can be applied to several different network architectures. Each architecture places the WLC in a different location within the network—a choice that also affects how many WLCs might be needed to support the number of APs required.

One approach is to locate the WLC in a central location so that you can maximize the number of APs joined to it. This is usually called a **centralized WLC deployment** or *unified WLC deployment*, which tends to follow the concept that most of the resources users need to reach are located in a central location such as a data center or the Internet. Traffic to and from wireless users would travel over CAPWAP tunnels that reach into the center of the network, near the core, as shown in Figure 2-8. A centralized WLC also provides a convenient place to enforce security policies that affect all wireless users.

Figure 2-8 shows four APs joined to a single WLC. Your network might have more APs—many, many more. A large enterprise network might have thousands of APs connected to its access layer. Scalability then becomes an important factor in the centralized design. Typical centralized WLCs can support a maximum of around 6000 APs. If you have more APs than the maximum, you will need to add more WLCs to the design, each located centrally.

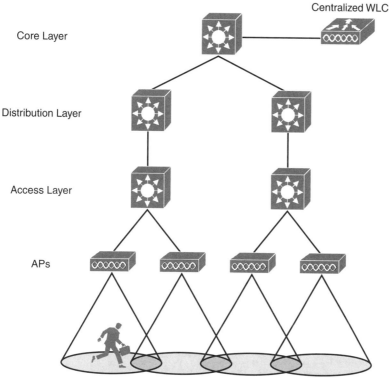

Figure 2-8 *WLC Location in a Centralized Deployment*

When a WLC is centrally located inside a public or private cloud, it is known as a **cloud-based WLC deployment**. Because a private cloud is usually part of the enterprise network, the WLC can stay relatively close to its APs and minimize the length of the data path between them. However, locating the WLC in a public cloud brings an interesting twist—the controller can be quite a distance from the APs that join to it. The APs can maintain a CAPWAP control tunnel to the controller, but all wireless data passing through the APs must be locally switched in and out of the VLANs directly connected to the APs. Therefore, the APs must operate only in **FlexConnect mode**, which is described later in this chapter in the section titled "FlexConnect Mode." Cloud-based controllers can typically support up to 6000 APs, as of this writing.

For small campuses or distributed branch locations, where the number of APs is relatively small in each, WLCs can be located further down in the network, as shown in Figure 2-9. This is known as a **distributed WLC deployment** because multiple controllers are distributed within the network. Typical distributed WLCs can support up to 250 APs. As the number of APs grows, additional WLCs can be added by locating them in other strategic areas of the network.

Finally, in small-scale environments, such as small, midsize, or multisite branch locations, you might not want to invest in dedicated WLCs at all. In this case, the WLC function can be co-located with an AP that is installed at the branch site. This is known as an **embedded wireless controller (EWC) deployment**, as shown in Figure 2-10. It is also called a **controller-less wireless deployment** because it does not involve a discrete physical controller at all. The AP that hosts the WLC forms a CAPWAP tunnel with the WLC, along with any other APs at the same location. An EWC can support up to 100 APs.

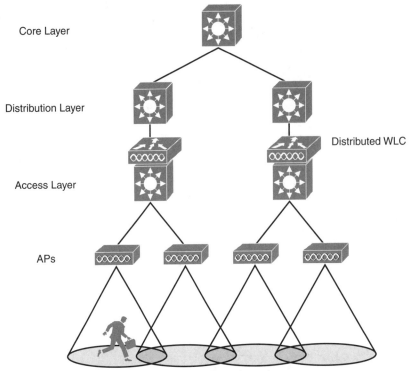

Figure 2-9   *WLC Location in a Distributed Deployment*

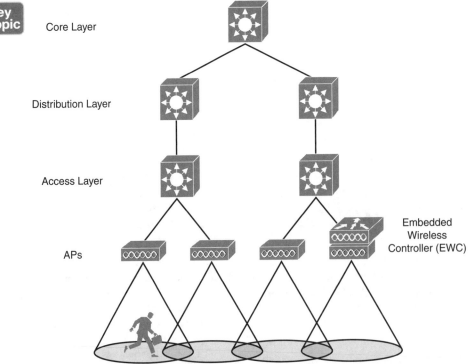

Figure 2-10   *WLC Location in an Embedded Wireless Deployment*

Refer to Table 2-2 for a summary of WLC deployment models, WLC locations, and a typical maximum number of APs and clients that each one supports.

Table 2-2   Summary of WLC Deployment Models

Deployment Model	WLC Location	APs Supported	Clients Supported	Typical Use
Centralized	Central	6000	64,000	Large enterprise
Cloud-based	Public or private cloud	6000	64,000	Large enterprise
Distributed	Access	250	5000	Small campus
Embedded	Other	100	2000	Branch location
Autonomous	N/A	N/A	N/A	N/A

Cisco AP Modes

Cisco APs can operate in one of the following modes, depending on how they are configured:

- **Local:** This default lightweight mode offers one or more functioning BSSs on a specific channel. During times that it is not transmitting, the AP will scan the other channels to measure the level of noise, measure interference, discover rogue devices, and match against wireless intrusion detection system (WIDS) events.

- **Monitor:** The AP does not transmit at all, but its receiver is enabled to act as a dedicated sensor. The AP checks for IDS events, detects rogue access points, and determines the position of stations through location-based services.

- **FlexConnect:** An AP at a remote site can locally switch traffic between an SSID and a VLAN if its CAPWAP tunnel to the WLC is down and if it is configured to do so.

- **Sniffer:** An AP dedicates its radios to receiving 802.11 traffic from other sources, much like a sniffer or packet capture device. The captured traffic is then forwarded to a PC running network analyzer software such as WireShark, where it can be analyzed further.

- **Rogue detector:** An AP dedicates itself to detecting rogue devices by correlating MAC addresses heard on the wired network with those heard over the air. Rogue devices are those that appear on both networks.

- **Bridge:** An AP becomes a dedicated bridge (point-to-point or point-to-multipoint) between two networks. Two APs in bridge mode can be used to link two locations separated by a distance. Multiple APs in bridge mode can form an indoor or outdoor mesh network.

- **Flex+Bridge:** FlexConnect operation is enabled on a mesh AP.

■ **SE-Connect:** The AP dedicates its radios to spectrum analysis on all wireless channels. You can remotely connect a PC running software such as MetaGeek Chanalyzer or Cisco Spectrum Expert to the AP to collect and analyze the spectrum analysis data to discover sources of interference.

> **NOTE**   Remember that a Cisco AP is normally in **local mode** when it is providing BSSs and allowing client devices to associate to wireless LANs. When an AP is configured to operate in one of the other modes, local mode is disabled.

FlexConnect Mode

In a switched campus infrastructure, the split-MAC traffic pattern is efficient because the WLC can be located reasonably close to the APs. That pattern tends to minimize latency and maximize bandwidth between them. Suppose that the network grows to include some remote branch sites. APs are placed at the branch sites, but the only WLC is located back at the main site. This scenario forces wireless traffic to traverse the CAPWAP tunnel between the branch and main sites to reach centralized resources, as shown in the left portion of Figure 2-11. Even traffic between two wireless users has to follow the tunnel to the controller and back, which might not be ideal.

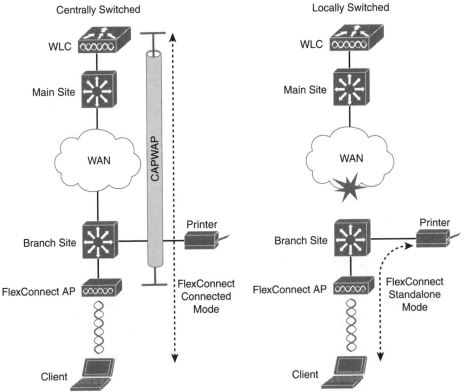

Figure 2-11   *FlexConnect AP Operating in Centrally and Locally Switched Modes*

Now consider the importance of the WAN link connecting the remote site. An AP at the branch site is normally completely dependent on the WLC to form the split-MAC relationship. If the WAN link goes down, and the WLC is unreachable, as shown in the right portion of Figure 2-11, then the AP ceases to operate.

The FlexConnect AP mode can make the most of each situation, whether the WAN link is up or down. In **connected mode**, the AP joins the WLC, and all wireless traffic flows over the CAPWAP tunnel. However, if the WAN link is down, the AP can use its **standalone mode** to keep operating independently from the WLC, supporting wireless users locally and allowing them to communicate with other local devices.

Switching between connected and standalone modes is automatic, based on connectivity to the WLC. Even better, you can configure FlexConnect APs to locally switch traffic that needs to stay within the remote site on a per-wireless LAN basis, even if the controller is still reachable. That approach avoids the long and unnecessary hairpin path to and from the controller for local traffic, while maintaining the CAPWAP tunnel for traffic that needs to be centrally switched at the main site.

Cisco OfficeExtend is another solution for connecting remote sites to a main location but is meant to be used at teleworkers' homes. Like FlexConnect, OfficeExtend can present the same corporate wireless LANs at the remote site. However, the two solutions are very different in terms of scale. A FlexConnect AP is meant to support a large number of wireless users and can co-exist with other FlexConnect APs, allowing wireless users to roam between APs. An OfficeExtend AP is meant to exist as a single AP at the teleworker's home, so roaming is not supported.

The two solutions also differ in the way that user data traffic is protected between the AP and the WLC. FlexConnect protects and encrypts only control traffic by default; user data is not protected. Because OfficeExtend is designed to handle a small number of users on a single AP, both the control and data traffic are always encrypted with DTLS. Table 2-3 summarizes the differences between the two solutions.

Table 2-3   Comparing FlexConnect and OfficeExtend APs

	FlexConnect	OfficeExtend
Does AP join a WLC?	Yes	Yes
Is data traffic protected?	Optional	Yes, with DTLS
Typical number of APs at remote site	No limit	One
Is roaming supported?	Yes	No

Chapter Review

Review this chapter's material using either the tools in the book or the interactive tools for the same material found on the book's companion website. Table 2-4 outlines the key review elements and where you can find them. To better track your study progress, record when you completed these activities in the second column.

Table 2-4 Chapter Review Tracking

Review Element	Review Date(s)	Resource Used
Review key topics		Book, website
Review key terms		Book, website
Answer DIKTA questions		Book, PTP
Review memory tables		Website

Review All the Key Topics

Review the most important topics in this chapter, noted with the Key Topic icon in the outer margin of the page. Table 2-5 lists a reference of these key topics and the page numbers on which each is found.

Table 2-5 Key Topics for Chapter 2

Key Topic Element	Description	Page Number
Figure 2-1	Autonomous AP architecture	24
Figure 2-3	Cloud-based AP architecture	27
Figure 2-4	Split-MAC architecture	28
Figure 2-5	CAPWAP tunnels	30
Figure 2-8	Centralized WLC deployment	33
Figure 2-9	Distributed WLC deployment	34
Figure 2-10	Embedded WLC deployment	34
List	Cisco AP modes	35

Key Terms You Should Know

autonomous AP, CAPWAP, centralized WLC deployment, cloud-based AP, cloud-based WLC deployment, connected mode, controller-less wireless deployment, distributed WLC deployment, embedded wireless controller (EWC) deployment, FlexConnect mode, local mode, Media Access Control (MAC) layer, split-MAC architecture, standalone mode, wireless LAN controller (WLC)

CHAPTER 3

Securing Wireless Networks

This chapter covers the following exam topics:

1.0 Network Fundamentals

    1.11 Describe Wireless Principles

        1.11.d Encryption

5.0 Security Fundamentals

    5.9 Describe wireless security protocols (WPA, WPA2, and WPA3)

As you know by now, wireless networks are complex. Many technologies and protocols work behind the scenes to give end users a stable, yet mobile, connection to a wired network infrastructure. From the user's perspective, a wireless connection should seem no different than a wired connection. A wired connection can give users a sense of security; data traveling over a wire is probably not going to be overheard by others. A wireless connection is inherently different; data traveling over the air can be overheard by anyone within range.

Therefore, securing a wireless network becomes just as important as any other aspect. A comprehensive approach to wireless security focuses on the following areas:

- Identifying the endpoints of a wireless connection
- Identifying the end user
- Protecting the wireless data from eavesdroppers
- Protecting the wireless data from tampering

The identification process is performed through various authentication schemes. Protecting wireless data involves security functions like encryption and frame authentication.

This chapter covers many of the methods you can use to secure a wireless network. Be warned: wireless security can be a confusing topic because it is filled with many acronyms. Some of the acronyms rhyme like words from a children's book. In fact, this chapter is a story about WEP, PSK, TKIP, MIC, AES, EAP, EAP-FAST, EAP-TLS, LEAP, PEAP, WPA, WPA2, WPA3, CCMP, GCMP, and on and on it goes. When you finish with this chapter, though, you will come away with a clearer view of what these terms mean and how they all fit together. You might even be ready to configure a wireless LAN with effective security.

"Do I Know This Already?" Quiz

Take the quiz (either here or use the PTP software) if you want to use the score to help you decide how much time to spend on this chapter. The letter answers are listed at the bottom of the page following the quiz. Appendix C, found both at the end of the book as well as on the companion website, includes both the answers and explanations. You can also find both answers and explanations in the PTP testing software.

Table 3-1 "Do I Know This Already?" Foundation Topics Section-to-Question Mapping

Foundation Topics Section	Questions
Anatomy of a Secure Connection	1, 2
Wireless Client Authentication Methods	3, 4
Wireless Privacy and Integrity Methods	5, 6
WPA, WPA2, and WPA3	7, 8

1. Which of the following are necessary components of a secure wireless connection? (Choose all that apply.)

    a. Encryption

    b. MIC

    c. Authentication

    d. All of these answers are correct.

2. Which one of the following is used to protect the integrity of data in a wireless frame?

    a. WIPS

    b. WEP

    c. MIC

    d. EAP

3. Which one of the following is a wireless encryption method that has been found to be vulnerable and is not recommended for use?

    a. AES

    b. WPA

    c. EAP

    d. WEP

4. Which one of the following is used as the authentication framework when 802.1x is used on a WLAN?

    a. Open authentication

    b. WEP

    c. EAP

    d. WPA

5. Suppose you would like to select a method to protect the privacy and integrity of wireless data. Which one of the following methods should you avoid because it has been deprecated ?

    a. TKIP

    b. CCMP

    c. GCMP

    d. EAP

6. Which one of the following is the data encryption and integrity method used by WPA2?

   a. WEP

   b. TKIP

   c. CCMP

   d. WPA

7. The Wi-Fi Alliance offers which of the following certifications for wireless devices that correctly implement security standards? (Choose all that apply.)

   a. WEP

   b. WPA2

   c. 802.11

   d. AES

8. A pre-shared key is used in which of the following wireless security configurations? (Choose all that apply.)

   a. WPA2 personal mode

   b. WPA2 enterprise mode

   c. WPA3 personal mode

   d. WPA3 enterprise mode

Foundation Topics

Anatomy of a Secure Connection

In the previous chapters of this book, you learned about wireless clients forming associations with wireless access points (APs) and passing data back and forth across the air.

As long as all clients and APs conform to the 802.11 standard, they can all coexist—even on the same channel. Not every 802.11 device is friendly and trustworthy, however. Sometimes it is easy to forget that transmitted frames do not just go directly from the sender to the receiver, as in a wired or switched connection. Instead, they travel according to the transmitter's antenna pattern, potentially reaching any receiver that is within range.

Consider the scenario in Figure 3-1. The wireless client opens a session with some remote entity and shares a confidential password. Because two untrusted users are also located within range of the client's signal, they may also learn the password by capturing frames that have been sent on the channel. The convenience of wireless communication also makes it easy for transmissions to be overheard and exploited by malicious users.

If data is sent through open space, how can it be secured so that it stays private and intact? The 802.11 standard offers a framework of wireless security mechanisms that can be used to add trust, privacy, and integrity to a wireless network. The following sections give an overview of the wireless security framework.

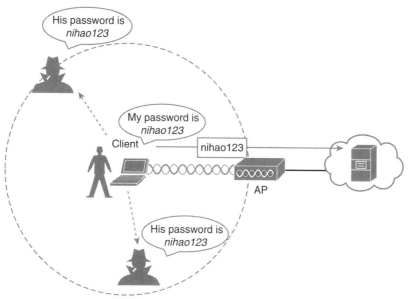

Figure 3-1 *Wireless Transmissions Reaching Unintended Recipients*

Authentication

To use a wireless network, clients must first discover a basic service set (BSS) and then request permission to associate with it. Clients should be authenticated by some means before they can become functioning members of the wireless LAN. Why?

Suppose that your wireless network connects to corporate resources where confidential information can be accessed. In that case, only devices known to be trusted and expected should be given access. Guest users, if they are permitted at all, should be allowed to join a different guest WLAN where they can access nonconfidential or public resources. Rogue clients, which are not expected or welcomed, should not be permitted to associate at all. After all, they are not affiliated with the corporate network and are likely to be unknown devices that happen to be within range of your network.

To control access, wireless networks can authenticate the client devices before they are allowed to associate. Potential clients must identify themselves by presenting some form of credentials to the APs. Figure 3-2 shows the basic client authentication process.

Figure 3-2 *Authenticating a Wireless Client*

Wireless authentication can take many forms. Some methods require only a static text string that is common across all trusted clients and APs. The text string is stored on the client device and presented directly to the AP when needed. What might happen if the device was stolen or lost? Most likely, any user who possessed the device could still authenticate to the network. Other more stringent authentication methods require interaction with a corporate user database. In those cases, the end user must enter a valid username and password—something that would not be known to a thief or an imposter.

If you have ever joined a wireless network, you might have focused on authenticating your device or yourself, while implicitly trusting the nearest AP. For example, if you turn on your wireless device and find a wireless network that is available at your workplace, you probably join it without hesitating. The same is true for wireless networks in an airport, a hotel, a hot spot, or in your home—you expect the AP that is advertising the SSID to be owned and operated by the entity where you are located. But how can you be sure?

Normally, the only piece of information you have is the SSID being broadcast or advertised by an AP. If the SSID looks familiar, you will likely choose to join it. Perhaps your computer is configured to automatically connect to a known SSID so that it associates without your intervention. Either way, you might unwittingly join the same SSID even if it was being advertised by an imposter.

Some common attacks focus on a malicious user pretending to be an AP. The fake AP can send beacons, answer probes, and associate clients just like the real AP it is impersonating. Once a client associates with the fake AP, the attacker can easily intercept all communication to and from the client from its central position. A fake AP could also send spoofed management frames to disassociate or deauthenticate legitimate and active clients, just to disrupt normal network operation.

To prevent this type of man-in-the-middle attack, the client should authenticate the AP before the client itself is authenticated. Figure 3-3 shows a simple scenario. Even further, any management frames received by a client should be authenticated too, as proof that they were sent by a legitimate and expected AP.

Figure 3-3   *Authenticating a Wireless AP*

Message Privacy

Suppose that the client in Figure 3-3 must authenticate before joining the wireless network. It might also authenticate the AP and its management frames after it associates but before it is itself authenticated. The client's relationship with the AP might become much more trusted, but data passing to and from the client is still available to eavesdroppers on the same channel.

To protect data privacy on a wireless network, the data should be encrypted for its journey through free space. This task is accomplished by encrypting the data payload in each wireless frame just prior to being transmitted, then decrypting it as it is received. The idea is to use an encryption method that the transmitter and receiver share, so the data can be encrypted and decrypted successfully by them and nobody else.

In wireless networks, each WLAN may support only one authentication and encryption scheme, so all clients must use the same encryption method when they associate. You might think that having one encryption method in common would allow every client to eavesdrop on every other client. That is not necessarily the case because the AP should securely negotiate a unique encryption key to use for each associated client.

Ideally, the AP and a client are the only two devices that have the encryption keys in common so that they can understand each other's data. No other device should know about or be able to use the same keys to eavesdrop and decrypt the data. In Figure 3-4, the client's confidential password information has been encrypted before being transmitted. The AP can decrypt it successfully before forwarding it onto the wired network, but other wireless devices and users cannot.

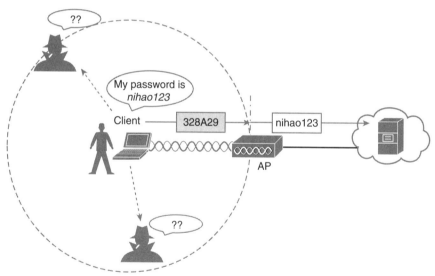

Figure 3-4 *Encrypting Wireless Data to Protect Data Privacy*

The AP also maintains a "group key" that it uses when it needs to send encrypted data to all clients in its cell at one time. Each of the associated clients uses the same group key to decrypt the data.

Message Integrity

Encrypting data obscures it from view while it is traveling over a public or untrusted network. The intended recipient should be able to decrypt the message and recover the original contents, but what if someone managed to alter the contents along the way? The recipient would have a very difficult time discovering that the original data had been modified.

A **message integrity check (MIC)** is a security tool that can protect against data tampering. You can think of a MIC as a way for the sender to add a secret stamp inside the encrypted data frame. The stamp is based on the contents of the data bits to be transmitted. After the recipient decrypts the frame, it can compare the secret stamp to its own idea of what the stamp should be, based on the data bits that were received. If the two stamps are identical, the recipient can safely assume that the data has not been tampered with. Figure 3-5 shows the MIC process.

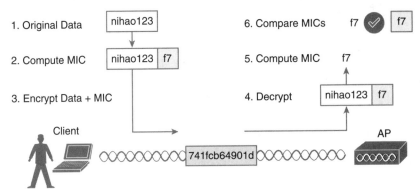

Figure 3-5   *Checking Message Integrity over a Wireless Network*

Wireless Client Authentication Methods

You can use many different methods to authenticate wireless clients as they try to associate with the network. The methods have been introduced over time and have evolved as security weaknesses have been exposed and wireless hardware has advanced. This section covers the most common authentication methods you might encounter.

Open Authentication

The original 802.11 standard offered only two choices to authenticate a client: open authentication and WEP.

Open authentication is true to its name; it offers open access to a WLAN. The only requirement is that a client must use an 802.11 authentication request before it attempts to associate with an AP. No other credentials are needed.

When would you want to use open authentication? After all, it does not sound very secure because it is not. With no challenge, any 802.11 client may authenticate to access the network. That is, in fact, the whole purpose of open authentication—to validate that a client is a valid 802.11 device by authenticating the wireless hardware and the protocol. Authenticating the user's identity is handled as a true security process through other means.

You have probably seen a WLAN with open authentication when you have visited a public location. If any client screening is used at all, it comes in the form of web authentication. A client can associate right away but must open a web browser to see and accept the terms for use and enter basic credentials. From that point, network access is opened up for the client. Most client operating systems flag such networks to warn you that your wireless data will not be secured in any way if you join.

WEP

As you might expect, open authentication offers nothing that can obscure or encrypt the data being sent between a client and an AP. As an alternative, the 802.11 standard has traditionally defined **Wired Equivalent Privacy (WEP)** as a method to make a wireless link more like or equivalent to a wired connection.

WEP uses the RC4 cipher algorithm to make every wireless data frame private and hidden from eavesdroppers. The same algorithm encrypts data at the sender and decrypts it at the receiver. The algorithm uses a string of bits as a key, commonly called a WEP key, to derive other encryption keys—one per wireless frame. As long as the sender and receiver have an identical key, one can decrypt what the other encrypts.

WEP is known as a shared-key security method. The same key must be shared between the sender and receiver ahead of time so that each can derive other mutually agreeable encryption keys. In fact, every potential client and AP must share the same key ahead of time so that any client can associate with the AP.

The WEP key can also be used as an optional authentication method as well as an encryption tool. Unless a client can use the correct WEP key, it cannot associate with an AP. The AP tests the client's knowledge of the WEP key by sending it a random challenge phrase. The client encrypts the challenge phrase with WEP and returns the result to the AP. The AP can compare the client's encryption with its own to see whether the two WEP keys yield identical results.

WEP keys can be either 40 or 104 bits long, represented by a string of 10 or 26 hex digits. As a rule of thumb, longer keys offer more unique bits for the algorithm, resulting in more robust encryption. Except in WEP's case, that is. Because WEP was defined in the original 802.11 standard in 1999, every wireless adapter was built with encryption hardware specific to WEP. In 2001, a number of weaknesses were discovered and revealed, so work began to find better wireless security methods. By 2004, the 802.11i amendment was ratified, and WEP was officially deprecated. Both WEP encryption and WEP shared-key authentication are widely considered to be weak methods to secure a wireless LAN.

802.1x/EAP

With only open authentication and WEP available in the original 802.11 standard, a more secure authentication method was needed. Client authentication generally involves some sort of challenge, a response, and then a decision to grant access. Behind the scenes, it can also involve an exchange of session or encryption keys, in addition to other parameters needed for client access. Each authentication method might have unique requirements as a unique way to pass information between the client and the AP.

Rather than build additional authentication methods into the 802.11 standard, a more flexible and scalable authentication framework, the **Extensible Authentication Protocol (EAP)**, was chosen. As its name implies, EAP is extensible and does not consist of any one authentication method. Instead, EAP defines a set of common functions that actual authentication methods can use to authenticate users. As you read through this section, notice how many authentication methods have EAP in their names. Each method is unique and different, but each one follows the EAP framework.

EAP has another interesting quality: it can integrate with the IEEE **802.1x** port-based access control standard. When 802.1x is enabled, it limits access to network media until a client authenticates. This means that a wireless client might be able to associate with an AP but will not be able to pass data to any other part of the network until it successfully authenticates.

With open and WEP authentication, wireless clients are authenticated locally at the AP without further intervention. The scenario changes with 802.1x; the client uses open authentication to associate with the AP, and then the actual client authentication process occurs at a dedicated authentication server. Figure 3-6 shows the three-party 802.1x arrangement that consists of the following entities:

- **Supplicant:** The client device that is requesting access

- **Authenticator:** The network device that provides access to the network (usually a wireless LAN controller [WLC])

- **Authentication server (AS):** The device that takes user or client credentials and permits or denies network access based on a user database and policies (usually a **RADIUS server**)

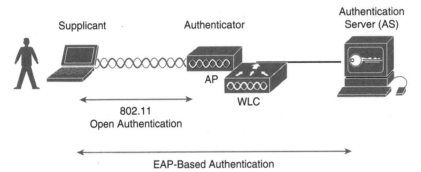

Figure 3-6 *802.1x Client Authentication Roles*

The wireless LAN controller becomes a middleman in the client authentication process, controlling user access with 802.1x and communicating with the authentication server using the EAP framework.

The following sections provide an overview of several common EAP-based authentication methods. The goal here is to become aware of the many methods without trying to memorize them all. In fact, even when you configure user authentication on a wireless LAN, you will not have to select a specific method. Instead, you select "802.1x" on the WLC so that it is ready to handle a variety of EAP methods. It is then up to the client and the authentication server to use a compatible method. You will learn more about configuring security on a wireless LAN in Chapter 4, "Building a Wireless LAN."

LEAP

As an early attempt to address the weaknesses in WEP, Cisco developed a proprietary wireless authentication method called **Lightweight EAP (LEAP).** To authenticate, the client must supply username and password credentials. Both the authentication server and the client exchange challenge messages that are then encrypted and returned. This process provides mutual authentication; as long as the messages can be decrypted successfully, the client and the AS have essentially authenticated each other.

At the time, WEP-based hardware was still widely used. Therefore, LEAP attempted to overcome WEP weaknesses by using dynamic WEP keys that changed frequently. Nevertheless, the method used to encrypt the challenge messages was found to be vulnerable, so LEAP has since been deprecated. Even though wireless clients and controllers still offer LEAP, you should not use it.

EAP-FAST

Cisco developed a more secure method called **EAP Flexible Authentication by Secure Tunneling (EAP-FAST)**. Authentication credentials are protected by passing a **protected access credential (PAC)** between the AS and the supplicant. The PAC is a form of shared secret that is generated by the AS and used for mutual authentication. EAP-FAST is a sequence of three phases:

- **Phase 0:** The PAC is generated or provisioned and installed on the client.

- **Phase 1:** After the supplicant and AS have authenticated each other, they negotiate a Transport Layer Security (TLS) tunnel.

- **Phase 2:** The end user can then be authenticated through the TLS tunnel for additional security.

Notice that two separate authentication processes occur in EAP-FAST: one between the AS and the supplicant and another with the end user. These occur in a nested fashion, as an outer authentication (outside the TLS tunnel) and an inner authentication (inside the TLS tunnel).

As with other EAP-based methods, a RADIUS server is required. However, the RADIUS server must also operate as an EAP-FAST server to be able to generate PACs, one per user.

PEAP

Like EAP-FAST, the **Protected EAP (PEAP)** method uses an inner and outer authentication; however, the AS presents a digital certificate to authenticate itself with the supplicant in the outer authentication. If the supplicant is satisfied with the identity of the AS, the two will build a TLS tunnel to be used for the inner client authentication and encryption key exchange.

The digital certificate of the AS consists of data in a standard format that identifies the owner and is "signed" or validated by a third party. The third party is known as a **certificate authority (CA)** and is known and trusted by both the AS and the supplicants. The supplicant must also possess the CA certificate just so that it can validate the one it receives from the AS. The certificate is also used to pass a public key, in plain view, which can be used to help decrypt messages from the AS.

Notice that only the AS has a certificate for PEAP. That means the supplicant can readily authenticate the AS. The client does not have or use a certificate of its own, so it must be authenticated within the TLS tunnel using one of the following two methods:

- **MSCHAPv2:** Microsoft Challenge Authentication Protocol version 2

- **GTC:** Generic Token Card; a hardware device that generates one-time passwords for the user or a manually generated password

EAP-TLS

PEAP leverages a digital certificate on the AS as a robust method to authenticate the RADIUS server. It is easy to obtain and install a certificate on a single server, but the clients are left to identify themselves through other means. **EAP Transport Layer Security (EAP-TLS)** goes one step further by requiring certificates on the AS and on every client device.

With EAP-TLS, the AS and the supplicant exchange certificates and can authenticate each other. A TLS tunnel is built afterward so that encryption key material can be securely exchanged.

EAP-TLS is considered to be the most secure wireless authentication method available; however, implementing it can sometimes be complex. Along with the AS, each wireless client must obtain and install a certificate. Manually installing certificates on hundreds or thousands of clients can be impractical. Instead, you would need to implement a **Public Key Infrastructure (PKI)** that could supply certificates securely and efficiently and revoke them when a client or user should no longer have access to the network. This usually involves setting up your own CA or building a trust relationship with a third-party CA that can supply certificates to your clients.

NOTE   EAP-TLS is practical only if the wireless clients can accept and use digital certificates. Many wireless devices, such as communicators, medical devices, and RFID tags, have an underlying operating system that cannot interface with a CA or use certificates.

Wireless Privacy and Integrity Methods

The original 802.11 standard supported only one method to secure wireless data from eavesdroppers: WEP. As you have learned in this chapter, WEP has been compromised, deprecated, and can no longer be recommended. What other options are available to encrypt data and protect its integrity as it travels through free space?

TKIP

During the time when WEP was embedded in wireless client and AP hardware, yet was known to be vulnerable, the **Temporal Key Integrity Protocol (TKIP)** was developed.

TKIP adds the following security features using legacy hardware and the underlying WEP encryption:

- **MIC:** This efficient algorithm adds a hash value to each frame as a message integrity check to prevent tampering; commonly called "Michael" as an informal reference to MIC.

- **Time stamp:** A time stamp is added into the MIC to prevent replay attacks that attempt to reuse or replay frames that have already been sent.

- **Sender's MAC address:** The MIC also includes the sender's MAC address as evidence of the frame source.

- **TKIP sequence counter:** This feature provides a record of frames sent by a unique MAC address, to prevent frames from being replayed as an attack.

- **Key mixing algorithm:** This algorithm computes a unique 128-bit WEP key for each frame.

- **Longer initialization vector (IV):** The IV size is doubled from 24 to 48 bits, making it virtually impossible to exhaust all WEP keys by brute-force calculation.

TKIP became a reasonably secure stopgap security method, buying time until the 802.11i standard could be ratified. Some attacks have been created against TKIP, so it, too, should be avoided if a better method is available. In fact, TKIP was deprecated in the 802.11-2012 standard.

CCMP

The **Counter/CBC-MAC Protocol (CCMP)** is considered to be more secure than TKIP. CCMP consists of two algorithms:

- AES counter mode encryption
- Cipher Block Chaining Message Authentication Code (CBC-MAC) used as a message integrity check (MIC)

The Advanced Encryption Standard (AES) is the current encryption algorithm adopted by the U.S. National Institute of Standards and Technology (NIST) and the U.S. government, and widely used around the world. In other words, AES is open, publicly accessible, and represents the most secure encryption method available today.

Before CCMP can be used to secure a wireless network, the client devices and APs must support the AES counter mode and CBC-MAC in hardware. CCMP cannot be used on legacy devices that support only WEP or TKIP. How can you know if a device supports CCMP? Look for the WPA2 designation, which is described in the following section.

GCMP

The **Galois/Counter Mode Protocol (GCMP)** is a robust authenticated encryption suite that is more secure and more efficient than CCMP. GCMP consists of two algorithms:

- AES counter mode encryption
- Galois Message Authentication Code (GMAC) used as a message integrity check (MIC)

GCMP is used in WPA3, which is described in the following section.

WPA, WPA2, and WPA3

This chapter covers a variety of authentication methods and encryption and message integrity algorithms. When it comes time to configure a WLAN with wireless security, should you try to select some combination of schemes based on which one is best or which one is not deprecated? Which authentication methods are compatible with which encryption algorithms?

The Wi-Fi Alliance (http://wi-fi.org), a nonprofit wireless industry association, has worked out straightforward ways to do that through its **Wi-Fi Protected Access (WPA)** industry certifications. To date, there are three different versions: WPA, WPA2, and WPA3. Wireless products are tested in authorized testing labs against stringent criteria that represent correct implementation of a standard. As long as the Wi-Fi Alliance has certified a wireless client device and an AP and its associated WLC for the same WPA version, they should be compatible and offer the same security components.

The Wi-Fi Alliance introduced its first generation WPA certification (known simply as WPA and not WPA1) while the IEEE 802.11i amendment for best practice security methods was still being developed. WPA was based on parts of 802.11i and included 802.1x authentication, TKIP, and a method for dynamic encryption key management.

After 802.11i was ratified and published, the Wi-Fi Alliance included it in full in its **WPA Version 2 (WPA2)** certification. WPA2 is based around the superior AES CCMP algorithms, rather than the deprecated TKIP from WPA. It should be obvious that WPA2 was meant as a replacement for WPA.

In 2018, the Wi-Fi Alliance introduced **WPA Version 3 (WPA3)** as a future replacement for WPA2, adding several important and superior security mechanisms. WPA3 leverages stronger encryption by AES with the Galois/Counter Mode Protocol (GCMP). It also uses **Protected Management Frames (PMF)** to secure important 802.11 management frames between APs and clients, to prevent malicious activity that might spoof or tamper with a BSS's operation.

Table 3-2 summarizes the basic differences between WPA, WPA2, and WPA3. Each successive version is meant to replace prior versions by offering better security features. You should use WPA3 if it is widely available on all the wireless client devices, APs, and WLCs in your network; otherwise, use WPA2 and avoid WPA.

Table 3-2   Comparing WPA, WPA2, and WPA3

Authentication and Encryption Feature Support	WPA	WPA2	WPA3*
Authentication with **pre-shared keys**?	Yes	Yes	Yes
Authentication with **802.1x**?	Yes	Yes	Yes
Encryption and MIC with **TKIP**?	Yes	No	No
Encryption and MIC with **AES and CCMP**?	Yes	Yes	No
Encryption and MIC with **AES and GCMP**?	No	No	Yes

* WPA3 includes other features beyond WPA and WPA2, such as Simultaneous Authentication of Equals (SAE), forward secrecy, and Protected Management Frames (PMF).

Notice that all three WPA versions support two client authentication modes: a pre-shared key (PSK) or 802.1x, based on the scale of the deployment. These are also known as **personal mode** and **enterprise mode**, respectively.

With personal mode, a key string must be shared or configured on every client and AP before the clients can connect to the wireless network. The pre-shared key is normally kept confidential so that unauthorized users have no knowledge of it. The key string is never sent over the air. Instead, clients and APs work through a four-way handshake procedure that uses the pre-shared key string to construct and exchange encryption key material that can be openly exchanged. When that process is successful, the AP can authenticate the client, and the two can secure data frames that are sent over the air.

With WPA-Personal and WPA2-Personal modes, a malicious user can eavesdrop and capture the four-way handshake between a client and an AP. That user can then use a dictionary attack to automate guessing the pre-shared key. If successful, that user can then decrypt the wireless data or even join the network posing as a legitimate user.

WPA3-Personal avoids such an attack by strengthening the key exchange between clients and APs through a method known as **Simultaneous Authentication of Equals (SAE)**. Rather than a client authenticating against a server or AP, the client and AP can initiate the authentication process equally and even simultaneously.

Even if a password or key is compromised, WPA3-Personal offers **forward secrecy**, which prevents attackers from being able to use a key to unencrypt data that has already been transmitted over the air.

TIP   The Personal mode of any WPA version is usually easy to deploy in a small environment or with clients that are embedded in certain devices because a simple text key string is all that is needed to authenticate the clients. Be aware that every device using the WLAN must be configured with an identical pre-shared key. If you ever need to update or change the key, you must touch every device to do so. As well, the pre-shared key should remain a well-kept secret; you should never divulge the pre-shared key to any unauthorized person.

Notice from Table 3-2 that WPA, WPA2, and WPA3 also support 802.1x or enterprise authentication. This support implies EAP-based authentication, but the WPA versions do not require any specific EAP method. Instead, the Wi-Fi Alliance certifies interoperability with well-known EAP methods like EAP-TLS, PEAP, EAP-TTLS, and EAP-SIM. Enterprise authentication is more complex to deploy than personal mode because authentication servers must be set up and configured as a critical enterprise resource.

TIP   The Wi-Fi Alliance has made wireless security configuration straightforward and consistent through its WPA, WPA2, and WPA3 certifications. Each version is meant to replace its predecessors because of improved security mechanisms. You should always select the highest WPA version that the clients and wireless infrastructure in your environment will support.

Chapter Review

At this point in the chapter, you might still be a little overwhelmed with the number of acronyms and security terms to learn and keep straight in your mind. Spend some time reviewing Table 3-3, which lists all of the topics described in this chapter. The table is organized in a way that should help you remember how the acronyms and functions are grouped together. Remember that an effective wireless security strategy includes a method to authenticate clients and a method to provide data privacy and integrity. These two types of methods are listed in the leftmost column. Work your way to the right to remember what types of authentication and privacy/integrity are available. The table also expands the name of each acronym as a memory tool.

Also remember that WPA, WPA2, and WPA3 simplify wireless network configuration and compatibility because they limit which authentication and privacy/integrity methods can be used.

Table 3-3   Review of Wireless Security Mechanisms and Options

Security Mechanism	Type		Type Expansion	Credentials Used
Authentication Methods	Open		Open Authentication	None, other than 802.11 protocol
	WEP		Wired Equivalent Privacy	Static WEP keys
	802.1x/EAP (Extensible Authentication Protocol)	LEAP	Lightweight EAP	Deprecated; uses dynamic WEP keys
		EAP-FAST	EAP Flexible Authentication by Secure Tunneling	Uses protected access credential (PAC)
		PEAP	Protected EAP	AS authenticated by digital certificate
		EAP-TLS	EAP Transport Layer Security	Client and AS authenticated by digital certificate
Privacy & Integrity Methods	TKIP		Temporal Key Integrity Protocol	N/A
	CCMP		Counter/CBC-MAC Protocol	N/A
	GCMP		Galois/Counter Mode Protocol	N/A

You should also review this chapter's material using either the tools in the book or the interactive tools for the same material found on the book's companion website. Table 3-4 outlines the key review elements and where you can find them. To better track your study progress, record when you completed these activities in the second column.

Table 3-4   Chapter Review Tracking

Review Element	Review Date(s)	Resource Used
Review key topics		Book, website
Review key terms		Book, website
Answer DIKTA questions		Book, PTP
Review memory tables		Website

Review All the Key Topics

Review the most important topics in this chapter, noted with the Key Topic icon in the outer margin of the page. Table 3-5 lists a reference of these key topics and the page numbers on which each is found.

Table 3-5   Key Topics for Chapter 3

Key Topic Element	Description	Page Number
List	802.1x entities	48
Table 3-2	WPA, WPA2, and WPA3 comparison	52
Table 3-3	Wireless security mechanism review	54

Key Terms You Should Know

802.1x, authentication server (AS), authenticator, certificate authority (CA), Counter/ CBC-MAC Protocol (CCMP), EAP Flexible Authentication by Secure Tunneling (EAP-FAST), EAP Transport Layer Security (EAP-TLS), enterprise mode, Extensible Authentication Protocol (EAP), forward secrecy, Galois/Counter Mode Protocol (GCMP), Lightweight EAP (LEAP), message integrity check (MIC), open authentication, personal mode, protected access credential (PAC), Protected EAP (PEAP), Protected Management Frame (PMF), Public Key Infrastructure (PKI), RADIUS server, Simultaneous Authentication of Equals (SAE), supplicant, Temporal Key Integrity Protocol (TKIP), Wi-Fi Protected Access (WPA), Wired Equivalent Privacy (WEP), WPA Version 2 (WPA2), WPA Version 3 (WPA3)

3

CHAPTER 4

Building a Wireless LAN

This chapter covers the following exam topics:

1.0 Network Fundamentals

> **1.1 Explain the role and function of network components**

>> **1.1.e Controllers**

2.0 Network Access

>> **2.7 Describe physical infrastructure connections of WLAN components (AP, WLC, access/trunk ports, and LAG)**

>> **2.8 Describe network device management access (Telnet, SSH, HTTP, HTTPS, console, and TACACS+/RADIUS)**

>> **2.9 Interpret the wireless LAN GUI configuration for client connectivity, such as WLAN creation, security settings, QoS profiles, and advanced settings**

5.0 Security Fundamentals

> **5.10 Configure and verify WLAN within the GUI using WPA2 PSK**

In Chapters 1 through 3, you learned about the fundamentals of wireless networks. As a CCNA, you will also need to know how to apply that knowledge toward building a functioning network with APs and a WLC.

In addition, based on the concepts you learned in Chapter 3, "Securing Wireless Networks," you will be able to configure the WLAN to use WPA2-Personal (WPA2-PSK).

Before getting into the chapter, be aware that Cisco no longer uses the original WLC operating system, AireOS. Instead, WLCs run IOS XE. Newer WLCs with IOS XE have a CLI, as do many enterprise-class Cisco routers, but you configure WLANs from the WLC GUI. However, the AireOS and IOS XE GUIs differ, both in the GUI pages' styling and configuration elements. This chapter moves back and forth through examples of each so you can learn the ideas and compare the differences and similarities.

For the exam, exam topics 2.9 and 5.10 refer to details visible from the WLC—but they do not mention for which operating system. You should be ready for both, so we include both.

"Do I Know This Already?" Quiz

Take the quiz (either here or use the PTP software) if you want to use the score to help you decide how much time to spend on this chapter. The letter answers are listed at the bottom of the page following the quiz. Appendix C, found both at the end of the book as well as on the companion website, includes both the answers and explanations. You can also find both answers and explanations in the PTP testing software.

Table 4-1 "Do I Know This Already?" Foundation Topics Section-to-Question Mapping

Foundation Topics Section	Questions
Connecting a Cisco AP	1, 2
Accessing a Cisco WLC	3
Connecting a Cisco WLC	4, 5
Configuring a WLAN	6–8

1. Suppose you need to connect a Cisco AP to a network. Which one of the following link types would be necessary?

   a. Access mode link

   b. Trunk mode link

   c. LAG mode link

   d. EtherChannel link

2. An autonomous AP will be configured to support three WLANs that correspond to three VLANs. The AP will connect to the network over which one of the following?

   a. Access mode link

   b. Trunk mode link

   c. LAG mode link

   d. EtherChannel link

3. Suppose you would like to connect to a WLC to configure a new WLAN on it. Which one of the following protocols can be used to access the WLC?

   a. SSH

   b. HTTPS

   c. HTTP

   d. All of these answers are correct.

4. Which one of the following correctly describes the single logical link formed by bundling all of a controller's distribution system ports together?

   a. PHY

   b. DSP

   c. LAG

   d. GEC

5. Which one of the following controller interfaces is used on an AireOS controller to map a WLAN to a VLAN?

   a. Bridge interface

   b. Virtual interface

   c. WLAN interface

   d. Dynamic interface

6. Which of the following things are bound together when a new WLAN is created? (Choose two answers.)

    a. VLAN

    b. AP

    c. CAPWAP tunnel

    d. SSID

7. What is the maximum number of WLANs you can configure on a Cisco wireless controller?

    a. 8

    b. 16

    c. 512

    d. 1024

8. Which of the following parameters are necessary when creating a new WLAN on an IOS-XE controller? (Choose all that apply.)

    a. WLAN profile

    b. Channel number

    c. Policy profile

    d. BSSID

    e. IP subnet

Foundation Topics

Connecting a Cisco AP

A Cisco wireless network consists of APs that are coupled with one or more wireless LAN controllers. An AP's most basic function is to connect wireless devices to a wired network. Therefore, you should understand how to connect the wired side of an AP so that it can pass traffic between the appropriate WLANs and VLANs.

Recall that an autonomous AP is a standalone device; nothing else is needed to forward Ethernet frames from a wired VLAN to a wireless LAN, and vice versa. In effect, the AP maps each VLAN to a WLAN and BSS. The autonomous AP has a single wired Ethernet interface, as shown in the left portion of Figure 4-1, which means that multiple VLANs must be brought to it over a trunk link.

> **TIP** A switch port providing a wired connection to an AP must be configured to support either access or trunk mode. In trunk mode, 802.1Q encapsulation tags each frame according to the VLAN number it came from. The wireless side of an AP inherently trunks 802.11 frames by marking them with the BSSID of the WLAN where they belong.

A Cisco AP also has a single wired Ethernet interface; however, it must be paired with a WLC to be fully functional. Wired VLANs that terminate at the WLC can be mapped to WLANs that emerge at the AP. Even though multiple VLANs are being extended from the

WLC to the AP, they are all carried over the CAPWAP tunnel between the two. That means the AP needs only an access link to connect to the network infrastructure and terminate its end of the tunnel, as shown in the right portion of Figure 4-1.

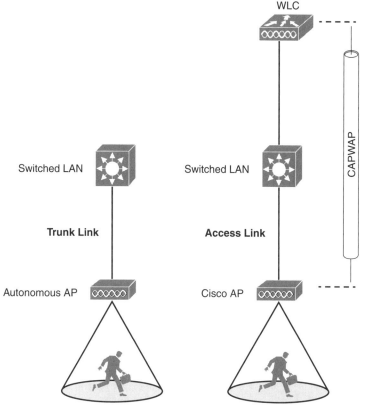

Figure 4-1 *Comparing Connections to Autonomous and Cisco APs*

Cisco APs are normally and most efficiently managed via a browser session to the WLC; however, you can directly connect a serial console cable from your PC to the console port on the AP to monitor its bootup process or to make some basic configuration changes if needed. When the AP is operational and has an IP address, you can also use Telnet or SSH to connect to its CLI over the wired network.

Accessing a Cisco WLC

To connect and configure a WLC, you need to open a web browser to the WLC's management address using either HTTP or HTTPS. You can do this only after the WLC has an initial configuration, a management IP address assigned to its management interface, and has built a valid SSL certificate for HTTPS use. The web-based GUI provides an effective way to monitor, configure, and troubleshoot a wireless network. You can also connect to a WLC with an SSH session, where you can use its CLI to monitor, configure, and debug activity.

Both the web-based GUI and the CLI require management users to log in. Users can be authenticated against an internal list of local usernames or against an authentication, authorization, and accounting (AAA) server, such as TACACS+ or RADIUS.

When you first open a web browser to the management address, you will see the initial login screen. Click the **Login** button, as shown in Figure 4-2 (IOS-XE controller) and Figure 4-3 (AireOS controller); then enter your user credentials as you are prompted for them.

Figure 4-2   *Accessing an IOS-XE WLC with a Web Browser*

Figure 4-3   *Accessing an AireOS WLC with a Web Browser*

Answers to the "Do I Know This Already?" quiz:

1 A **2** B **3** D **4** C **5** D **6** A, D **7** C **8** A, C

NOTE The CCNA exam objectives focus on using the WLC GUI to configure a WLAN and a security suite. Therefore, the examples in this section assume that someone has already entered an initial configuration to give the WLC a working IP address for management.

When you are successfully logged in, the WLC will display a monitoring dashboard similar to the one shown in Figure 4-4 (IOS-XE) and Figure 4-5 (AireOS). You will not be able to make any configuration changes there, so you must select **Configuration** in the left column (IOS-XE) or click on the **Advanced** link in the upper-right corner (AireOS).

Figure 4-4 *Accessing the IOS-XE WLC Configuration Menus*

Figure 4-5 *Accessing the AireOS WLC Advanced Configuration Interface*

On an IOS-XE WLC, you can select from a large list of configuration categories, as shown in Figure 4-6. In contrast, an AireOS WLC displays tabs across the top of the screen, as shown in Figure 4-7, which presents a list of functions on the left side of the screen. You will get a feel for which menu and list items you should use on both types of controller as you work through the remainder of the chapter.

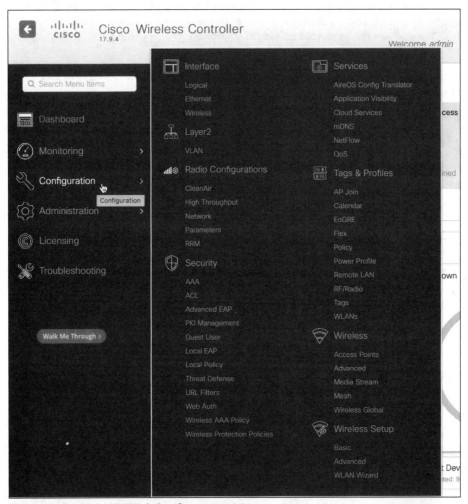

Figure 4-6 *IOS-XE WLC Configuration Menus*

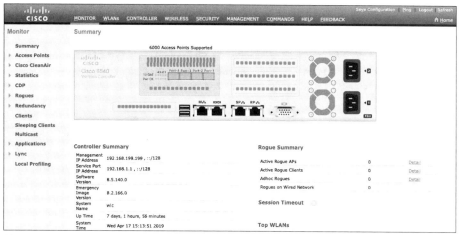

Figure 4-7   *AireOS WLC Advanced Configuration Categories*

Connecting a Cisco WLC

Cisco wireless LAN controllers (WLCs) offer several different types of ports and connections. The sections that follow explain each connection type in more detail. You learn more about configuring WLC ports in the "Configuring a WLAN" for IOS-XE and AireOS sections later in the chapter.

WLC Physical Ports

A WLC has several different types of physical ports you can connect to your network, as shown in Figure 4-8. For example, you can connect to a serial *console port* for initial boot functions and system recovery. An Ethernet *service port* is used for out-of-band management via SSH or a web browser. This is sometimes called the *device management interface*. A *redundancy port* connects to a peer controller for high availability (HA) operation.

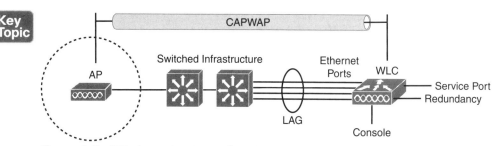

Figure 4-8   *Wireless LAN Controller Physical Ports*

Controllers also have multiple Ethernet ports that you must connect to the network. These ports carry most of the data coming to and going from the controller. For example, both control and data CAPWAP tunnels that extend to each of a controller's APs pass across these ports. In addition, any management traffic using a web browser, SSH, Simple Network Management Protocol (SNMP), Trivial File Transfer Protocol (TFTP), and so on, normally reaches the controller in-band through the ports.

NOTE   The Ethernet ports on an AireOS controller are called *distribution system ports*. You might be thinking that is an odd name for what appear to be regular data ports. Recall from the section titled "Wireless LAN Topologies" in Chapter 1, "Fundamentals of Wireless Networks," that the wired network that connects APs together is called the distribution system (DS). With the split MAC architecture, the point where APs touch the DS is moved upstream to the WLC instead.

Because the Ethernet ports must carry data that is associated with many different VLANs, VLAN tags and numbers become very important. Later in this chapter, you learn how the controller maps VLANs to wireless LANs. The Ethernet ports on an IOS-XE controller should always be configured to operate in 802.1Q trunking mode. AireOS controller ports can operate only in trunking mode and cannot be configured otherwise. When you connect the controller ports to a switch, you should also configure the switch ports for unconditional 802.1Q trunk mode to match.

The controller's Ethernet ports can operate independently, each one transporting multiple VLANs to a unique group of internal controller interfaces. For resiliency, the ports can be configured as a link aggregation group (LAG) such that they are bundled together to act as one larger link, much like an EtherChannel or port channel on a switch. In fact, the switch ports where the controller ports connect must also be configured as a port channel. With a LAG configuration, traffic can be load-balanced across the individual ports that make up the LAG. In addition, LAG offers resiliency; if one or more individual ports fail, traffic will be redirected to the remaining working ports instead.

Cisco wireless controllers must provide the necessary connectivity between wireless LANs and wired VLANs. The controller can touch VLANs through its physical Ethernet ports, but WLANs are carried over CAPWAP tunnels and terminate internally. Therefore, the controller must use internal dynamic interfaces that map between VLANs and WLANs, as shown in Figure 4-9.

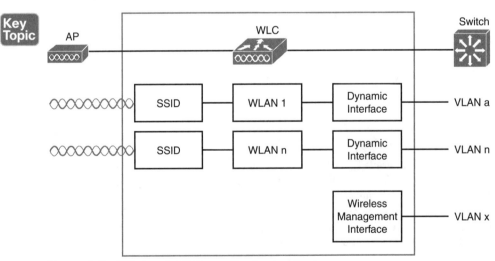

Figure 4-9   *Wireless LAN Controller Logical Ports*

The dynamic interfaces on an IOS-XE controller work at Layer 2, so the controller doesn't need a Layer 3 IP address on each VLAN. In contrast, an AireOS controller must have an IP address, subnet mask, default gateway, and a Dynamic Host Configuration Protocol (DHCP) server configured on each of its dynamic interfaces that touch a VLAN.

Both IOS-XE and AireOS controller platforms require a wireless management interface (WMI) for all in-band management traffic. The interface is used for normal management traffic, such as RADIUS user authentication, WLC-to-WLC communication, web-based and SSH sessions, SNMP, Network Time Protocol (NTP), syslog, and so on. The management interface is also used to terminate CAPWAP tunnels between the controller and its APs.

The WMI uses an IP address, subnet mask, and default gateway to allow the controller to communicate on the network. The WMI is usually connected to a management VLAN on an upstream switch. On IOS-XE controllers, the WMI is actually a switched virtual interface (SVI) and has the only configured IP address on the entire controller.

The virtual interface is used for only certain client-facing operations. For example, when a wireless client issues a request to obtain an IP address, the controller can relay the request on to an actual DHCP server that can provide the appropriate IP address. From the client's perspective, the DHCP server appears to be the controller's virtual interface address. Clients may see the virtual interface's address, but that address is never used when the controller communicates with other devices on the switched network. You should configure the virtual interface with a unique, nonroutable address such as 10.1.1.1 that is within a private address space defined in RFC 1918.

The virtual interface address is also used to support client mobility. For that reason, every controller that exists in the same mobility group should be configured with a virtual address that is identical to the others. By using one common virtual address, all the controllers will appear to operate as a cluster as clients roam from controller to controller.

Configuring a WLAN

A wireless LAN controller and an access point work in concert to provide network connectivity to wireless clients. From a wireless perspective, the AP advertises a Service Set Identifier (SSID) for wireless clients to join. From a wired perspective, the controller connects to a virtual LAN (VLAN) through one of its dynamic interfaces. To complete the path between the SSID and the VLAN, as illustrated in Figure 4-10, you must first define a WLAN on the controller.

NOTE Two of the CCNA exam objectives involve configuring a WLAN for client connectivity with WPA2 and a PSK using only the controller GUI. As you work through this section, you will find that it presents a complete WLAN example that is based on the topology shown in Figure 4-10 using the WPA2-Personal (PSK) security model.

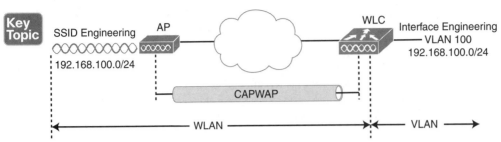

Figure 4-10 *Connecting Wired and Wireless Networks with a WLAN*

The controller will bind the WLAN to one of its dynamic interfaces and then push the WLAN configuration out to all of its APs by default. From that point on, wireless clients will be able to learn about the new WLAN by receiving its beacons and will be able to probe and join the new BSS.

You can use WLANs, like VLANs, to segregate wireless users and their traffic into logical networks. Users associated with one WLAN cannot cross over into another one unless their traffic is bridged or routed from one VLAN to another through the wired network infrastructure.

Before you begin to create new WLANs, it is usually wise to plan your wireless network first. In a large enterprise, you might have to support a wide variety of wireless devices, user communities, security policies, and so on. You might be tempted to create a new WLAN for every occasion, just to keep groups of users isolated from each other or to support different types of devices. Although that is an appealing strategy, you should be aware of two limitations:

■ Cisco controllers support a maximum of 512 WLANs, but only 16 of them can be actively configured on an AP.

■ Advertising each WLAN to potential wireless clients uses up valuable airtime.

Every AP must broadcast beacon management frames at regular intervals to advertise the existence of a BSS. Because each WLAN is bound to a BSS, each WLAN must be advertised with its own beacons. Beacons are normally sent 10 times per second, or once every 100 ms, at the lowest mandatory data rate. The more WLANs you have created, the more beacons you will need to announce them.

Even further, the lower the mandatory data rate, the more time each beacon will take to be transmitted. The end result is this: if you create too many WLANs, a channel can be starved of its usable airtime. Clients will have a hard time transmitting their own data because the channel is overly busy with beacon transmissions coming from the AP. As a rule of thumb, always limit the number of WLANs to five or fewer; a maximum of three WLANs is best.

By default, a controller has a limited initial configuration, so no WLANs are defined. Before you create a new WLAN, think about the following parameters it will need to have:

■ SSID string

■ Controller interface and VLAN number

■ Type of wireless security needed

The sections that follow demonstrate how to create a WLAN on an IOS-XE controller and then an AireOS controller. Each configuration step is performed using a web browser session that is connected to the WLC's management IP address.

Configuring a WLAN on an IOS-XE WLC

The IOS-XE wireless controller platform is very versatile and powerful, giving you granular control over every part of the wireless network configuration. You can configure all of the network's APs the same, in a global fashion, or you can tailor their configurations depending on their location or some other common requirements. For example, your enterprise might consist of many buildings. You might want the APs in one building to offer WLANs on only one band. Perhaps you want a group of APs to offer only a subset of the entire list of WLANs. In other buildings, you might need to support a different set of constraints.

With an IOS-XE controller, you can configure and apply the parameters that define AP operation in three general categories:

- **Policy:** Things that define each wireless LAN and security policies

- **Site:** Things that affect the AP-controller and CAPWAP relationship and FlexConnect behavior on a per-site basis

- **RF:** Things that define the RF operation on each wireless band

Each of these three categories is applied to each AP in the network through configuration *profiles* and *tags*. You can define policy, site, and RF profiles that contain the desired customizations. Then each AP is tagged to identify which policy, site, and RF profiles it should use. Figure 4-11 illustrates this concept, along with a list of the relevant parameters you can customize in each profile type.

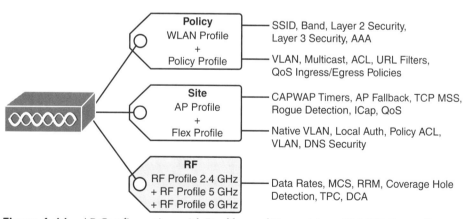

Figure 4-11 *AP Configuration with Profiles and Tags with an IOS-XE Controller*

NOTE Although it's possible to fine-tune a wide variety of AP options, the CCNA exam is focused only on the WLAN profile and Policy profile that you can map to APs with the policy tag. In other words, you should be concerned with only the things that pertain to the topmost tag in Figure 4-11. The CCNP ENCOR exam goes into further detail about the other tags and profiles.

The policy tag maps two different profiles: a WLAN profile that defines a list of SSIDs and WLAN security that an AP will offer, and a policy profile that defines how the AP will handle various types of traffic.

You can begin configuring a new WLAN by navigating to **Configuration > Wireless Setup > WLANs,** then selecting the **Start Now** button. The controller will display a "timeline," or the full sequence of all profiles and tags that you can configure, as shown in Figure 4-12. For the purposes of CCNA study, only the highlighted items are discussed in this chapter.

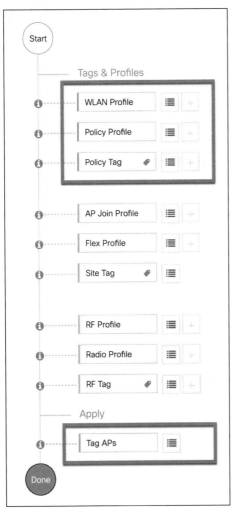

Figure 4-12 *IOS-XE Tags and Profiles Configuration Sequence*

As you might guess from the figure, configuring a new WLAN requires the following four steps:

Step 1. Configure a WLAN profile.

Step 2. Configure a policy profile.

Step 3. Map the WLAN and policy profiles to a policy tag.

Step 4. Apply the policy tag to some APs.

As you work through the WLAN configuration steps that follow, be aware that you can select the small "list" icons in the Tags & Profiles task sequence (see Figure 4-12) to display a list of related profiles or tags that already exist on the controller. You can then select one from the list to edit, or select the **Add** button to add a new one. Otherwise, you can immediately begin creating a new profile or tag by selecting the small + (plus) icon to the right of the profile or tag item.

Step 1: Configure a WLAN Profile

Select the **+** icon to the right of WLAN Profile. Beginning with the Add WLAN > General tab, as shown in Figure 4-13, you will be prompted to enter text strings for the WLAN profile name and the SSID (1–32 characters). By default, the WLAN profile name will be copied into the SSID field, but you can edit it if needed. The WLAN ID is simply a number that indexes the various WLANs that are configured on the controller.

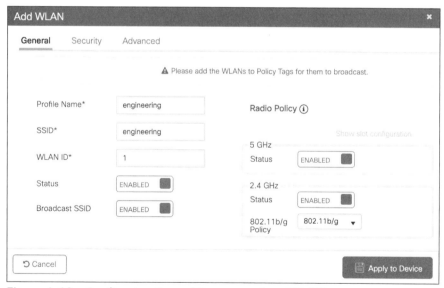

Figure 4-13 *Configuring General Parameters for a WLAN*

You can change the WLAN Status to Enabled so that it will be put into active use. You should also enable Broadcast SSID to allow APs to advertise the SSID to potential wireless clients.

The General tab also provides you with the opportunity to select which frequency bands to use for the WLAN. By default, all supported bands are enabled, allowing wireless clients to choose the band according to their internal algorithms.

Because the 2.4-GHz band is often crowded with nearby unrelated networks, you could disable it on your own APs and use only the higher frequency bands instead. The 5- and 6-GHz bands (6-GHz band not pictured in Figure 4-13) are much less crowded with competing APs and offer much better performance—desirable qualities for wireless applications like voice and video. In the 2.4-GHz band, you can also select the 802.11 policy to use. By default, both the 802.11b and g amendments are supported. You can select **802.11g-only** to completely disable the slower legacy data rates used by 802.11b devices.

Next, select the **Security** tab to configure WLAN security parameters. Figure 4-14 shows the Layer2 tab contents. Notice that there are options running across the screen for WPA+WPA2, WPA2+WPA3, WPA3, Static WEP, and None. The options relevant for the sample scenario in this chapter (and the CCNA exam) are highlighted in the figure. The scenario uses WPA2 with a PSK, so you could select either WPA+WPA2 or WPA2+WPA3, then move to the WPA Parameters section and uncheck the box next to the WPA version you do not want to use.

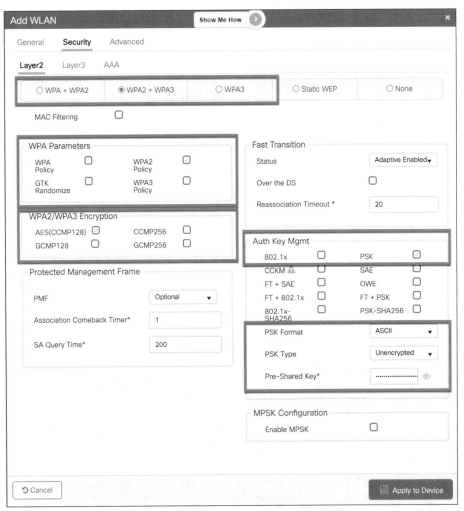

Figure 4-14   *Configuring Security Parameters for a WLAN*

With the WPA2 policy, you can select **AES(CCMP128)** encryption (the default), plus **PSK**, then enter the pre-shared key text string (8–63 ASCII characters). You can also enter the PSK as a hexadecimal string (exactly 64 digits), if desired.

In Figure 4-14, in the Auth Key Mgmt section, notice that PSK is checked but 802.1x is not. If you want the WLAN to use WPA2 Enterprise instead, then 802.1x would be necessary to support user authentication and the EAPOL four-way handshake for encryption key material exchange. You would also have to define a RADIUS, ISE, or LDAP server under the Security > AAA tab.

You might want to allow 802.11r, also known as Fast Transition (FT), to streamline wireless client roaming and reauthentication as clients move throughout the WLAN. FT options are displayed in the Fast Transition section. By default, the FT adaptive mode is enabled, which allows a mix of clients that are 802.11r-capable and clients that are not.

The Security > Layer3 tab, as shown in Figure 4-15, contains a few parameters related to Web authentication (webauth). Figure 4-16 shows the Security > AAA tab, where you can apply an authentication list that contains AAA servers that will authenticate users. You can also enable Local EAP Authentication to have the controller perform the RADIUS function instead of a dedicated external server.

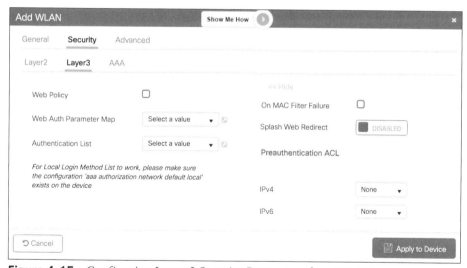

Figure 4-15 *Configuring Layer 3 Security Parameters for a WLAN*

The Add WLAN > Advanced tab contains a large collection of options that affect many different controller and AP operations. Figure 4-17 shows the first half of the options.

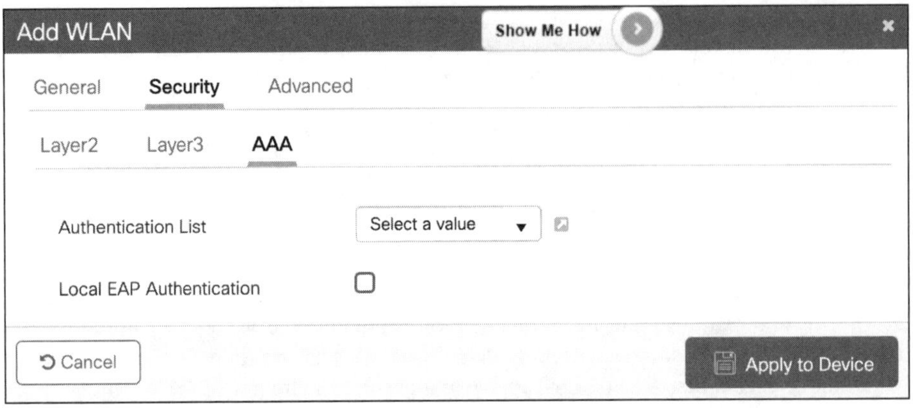

Figure 4-16   *Configuring AAA Parameters for a WLAN*

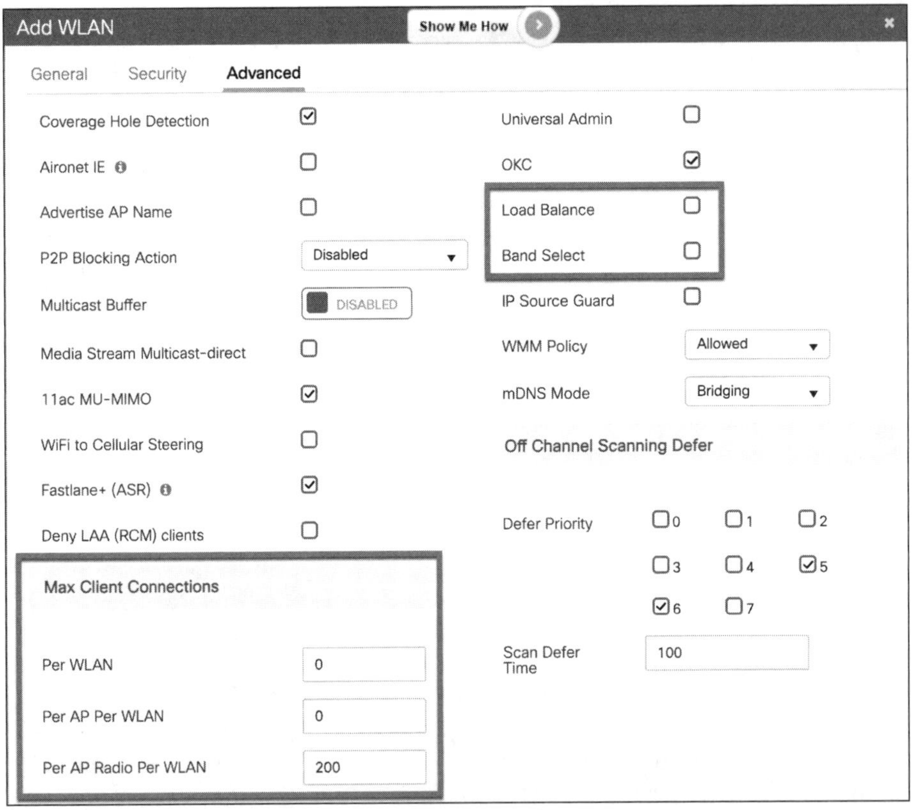

Figure 4-17   *Configuring Advanced Parameters for a WLAN*

You can set limits on the client connection load in the Max Client Connections section. By default, the controller will allow an unlimited (designated by zero) number of connections per WLAN, an unlimited number per AP per WLAN, and 200 per AP radio per WLAN.

Notice the subtle difference between them: "per WLAN" means across all APs that carry the WLAN, "per AP" limits connections on any one AP and all of its radios, and "per AP radio" limits connections on each radio independently.

You might also want to let the controller decide how it accepts wireless clients onto an AP radio. For example, you can use the Load Balance option to let the controller distribute clients across neighboring APs as they probe and associate. The Band Select option lets the controller actively influence clients to join a more efficient frequency band if they try to associate on a lower, less efficient band. For instance, Band Select can attempt to prevent clients from joining a 2.4-GHz channel if a 5-GHz channel is also available nearby.

Figure 4-18 shows the lower half of the Advanced tab options. While most of them are more advanced than the CCNA exam covers, you should know that the Enable 11ax option (enabled by default) can be used to control 802.11ax use on the WLAN.

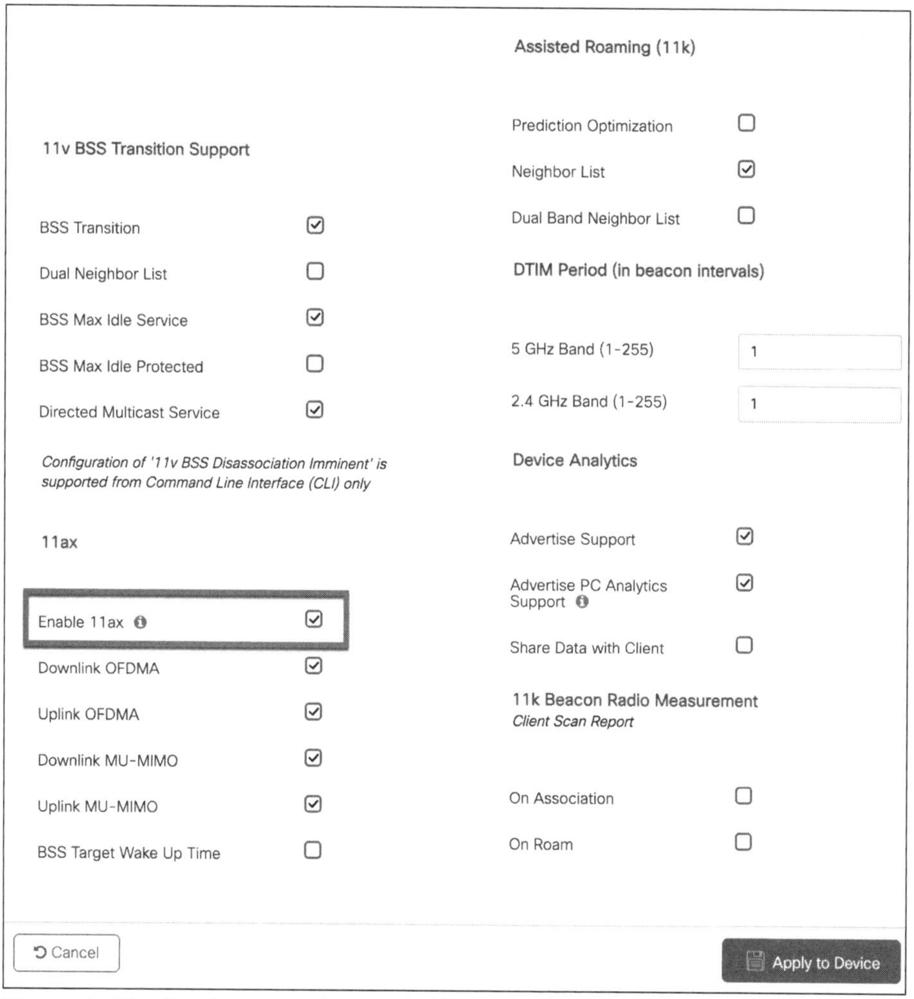

Figure 4-18 *Configuring Additional Advanced Parameters for a WLAN*

After you have configured and verified all of the desired parameters, be sure to click the **Apply to Device** button to commit the changes to the controller's WLAN configuration. When the controller returns to display the list of WLANs again, as shown in Figure 4-19, you should verify that the new WLAN is enabled (shown by a green up arrow in the browser page), the SSID is correct, and the security settings are accurate. You can verify from the figure that the "engineering" SSID is up and is configured for WPA2-PSK with AES.

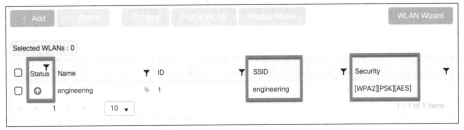

Figure 4-19 *Verifying the WLAN Configuration*

Step 2: Configure a Policy Profile

Next, you will need to configure a policy profile to define how the controller should handle the WLAN profile. From the Tags & Profiles task sequence (refer to Figure 4-12), select the + icon next to Policy Profile to create a new one. As shown in Figure 4-20, the General tab lets you name the profile and set its status as Enabled.

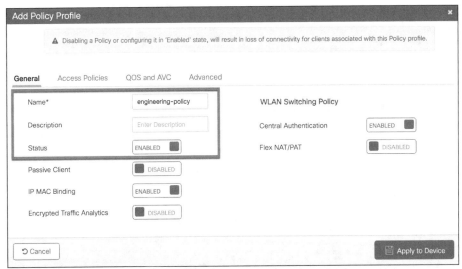

Figure 4-20 *Configuring General Parameters for a Policy Profile*

Select the **Access Policies** tab to configure a VLAN that the controller will map to your new WLAN. In Figure 4-21, the WLAN will be mapped to VLAN 100.

You can select the **QOS and AVC** tab to configure ingress and egress quality of service (QoS) policies, as well as other voice call and traffic flow monitoring features. Figure 4-22 shows the default settings.

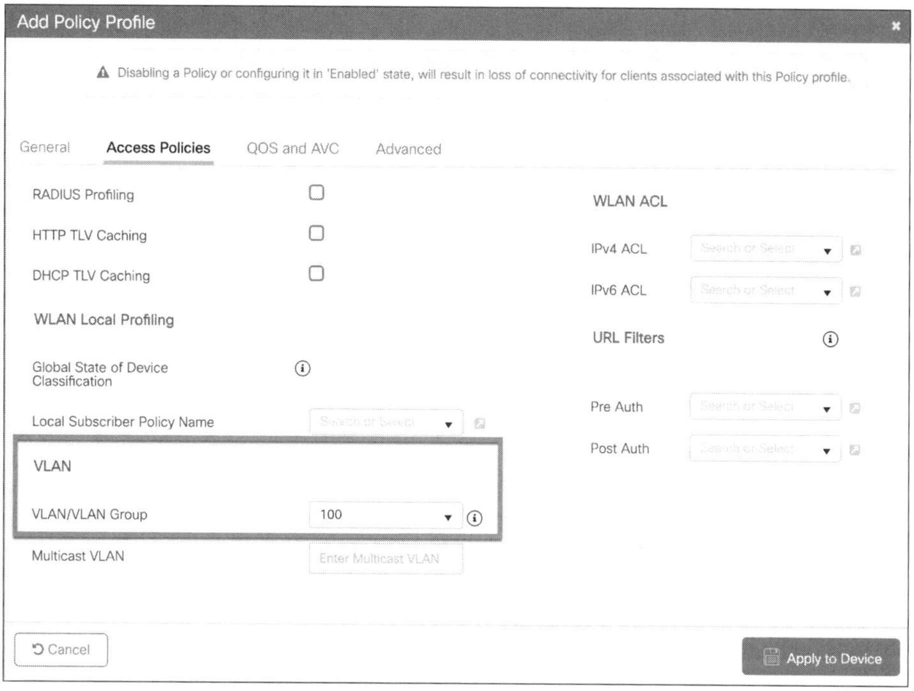

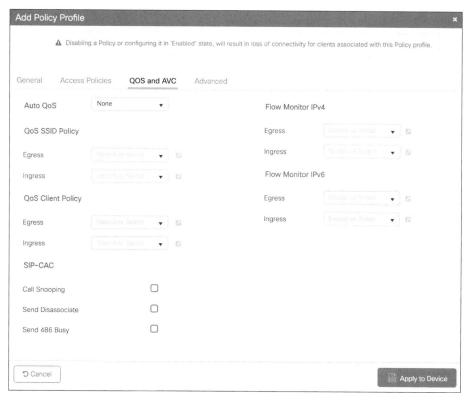

Figure 4-21 *Configuring Access Policies Parameters for a Policy Profile*

Figure 4-22 *Configuring QoS and AVC Parameters for a Policy Profile*

Next, select the **Advanced** tab to display many more parameters related to the WLAN operation, as shown in Figure 4-23. The highlighted WLAN Timeout section contains several limits related to wireless client activity.

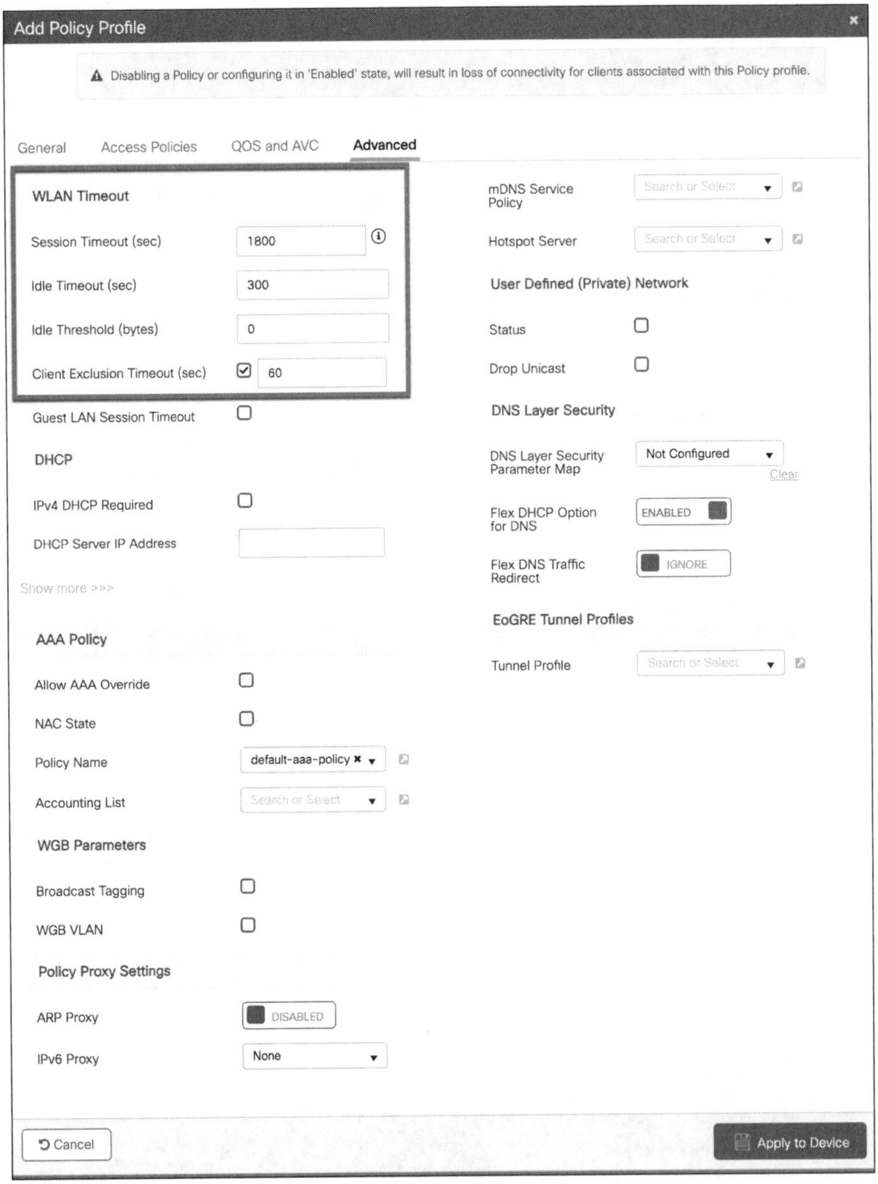

Figure 4-23 *Configuring Advanced Parameters for a Policy Profile*

You can configure the Session Timeout to set the amount of time client sessions are allowed to continue before forcing them to reauthenticate. By default, sessions will be timed out after 1800 seconds (30 minutes). If 802.1x is used in the WLAN, you can set the session timeout value within the range 300 to 86,400 seconds; if not, the range is 0 to 86,400, where 0 means no timeout.

Use the Idle Timeout and Idle Threshold values to limit the amount of time (15 to 100,000 seconds, default 300) and number of traffic bytes (0 to 4,294,967,295 bytes) elapsed before a client is considered to be idle and dropped.

If the Client Exclusion box is checked, the controller will use its wireless intrusion prevention system (IPS) to evaluate client activity against a database of signatures. If it detects that some suspicious activity is occurring, the controller will put the client into an exclusion list and will isolate it from the wireless network for a default of 60 seconds.

After you have configured and verified all of the desired parameters, be sure to click the **Apply to Device** button to commit the changes to the policy profile configuration.

Step 3: Map the WLAN and Policy Profiles to a Policy Tag

From the Tags & Profiles task sequence (refer to Figure 4-12), select the **+** icon next to Policy Tag. Enter a name for the policy tag and an optional description, as shown in Figure 4-24. Select the WLAN profile of the WLAN to be advertised, along with the policy profile that defines the VLAN to be used. Select the checkmark icon to add the profile combination to the policy tag.

Figure 4-24   *Mapping WLAN and Policy Profiles to a Policy Tag*

If you want APs to advertise more WLANs, you can click the **Add** button to add more WLAN and policy profile entries to the policy tag. Click the **Apply to Device** button to save your configuration changes to the controller.

Step 4: Apply the Policy Tag to Some APs

Recall that each AP in the network must have three different tags mapped to it: Policy, Site, and RF. To do so, go to the bottom of the Tags & Profiles task sequence (refer to Figure 4-12); then select the list icon next to Tag APs.

The Tag APs window, as shown in Figure 4-25, consists of two parts: a list of available APs in the background and tags configuration in the foreground. You must first select the APs that will receive the tag mapping either by checking the boxes next to the desired AP entries or by filtering the APs according to the attribute columns. Next, use the **Policy Tag** drop-down menu to select the policy tag with the correct WLAN and Policy profile mappings.

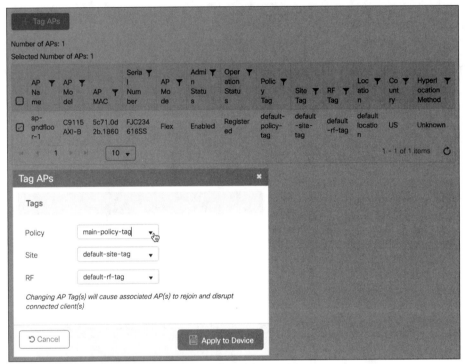

Figure 4-25 *Applying Policy, Site, and RF Tags to APs*

You will also have to identify a site tag and an RF tag to be used, even though this chapter has not covered those because they are beyond the scope of the CCNA exam. Fortunately, the controller has a set of predefined default tags that contain mappings to corresponding default profiles:

- *default-site-tag*: Maps to default profiles named default-ap-profile and default-flex-profile

- *default-rf-tag*: Maps to the controller's global RF configuration

- *default-policy-tag*: Does not map to anything by default, because there is no default WLAN and SSID configuration for any network

The default profiles are preconfigured with commonly used parameters that can offer a fully functional wireless network. You can always use the default tags and profiles if you do not need to change anything in them.

NOTE   You could avoid creating your own profiles and tags by making all of your custom changes to the controller's default profiles and tags; however, that would affect all APs globally unless they have been assigned other nondefault tags and profiles. Ideally, you should create your own set of custom profiles and tags to take full advantage of the granularity and to set the stage for future policy adjustments and custom tuning.

Configuring a WLAN on an AireOS WLC

Legacy AireOS controllers do not use the same profile and tag concept as IOS-XE controllers. Instead, you can configure WLANs directly in the GUI, with much less granular control over AP configuration.

Creating a new WLAN involves the following three steps:

Step 1.   Create a dynamic interface; then assign an interface name and a VLAN ID.

Step 2.   Create a WLAN; then assign a WLAN profile name and SSID, along with a unique WLAN ID.

Step 3.   Configure the WLAN parameters, enable it, and allow it to broadcast the SSID.

Each of these steps is discussed more fully in the sections that follow.

Step 1: Create a Dynamic Interface

On an AireOS controller, a dynamic interface is used to connect the controller to a VLAN on the wired network. When you create a WLAN, you will bind the dynamic interface (and VLAN) to a wireless network.

To create a new dynamic interface, navigate to **Controller > Interfaces**. You should see a list of all the controller interfaces that are currently configured. In Figure 4-26, two interfaces named "management" and "virtual" already exist. Click the **New** button to define a new interface. Enter a name for the interface and the VLAN number it will be bound to. In Figure 4-27, the interface named Engineering is mapped to wired VLAN 100. Click the **Apply** button.

Figure 4-26   *Displaying a List of Dynamic Interfaces*

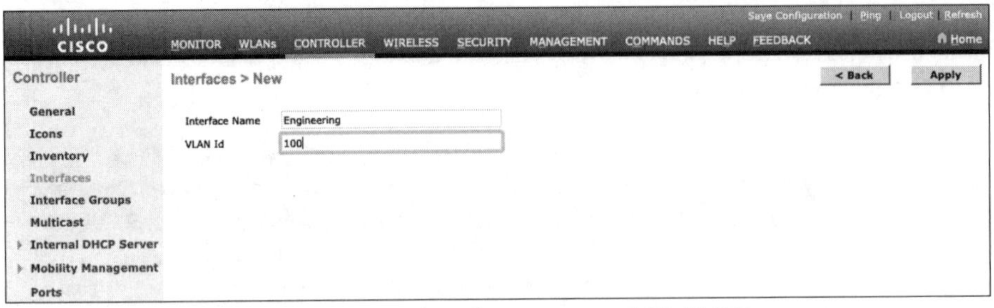

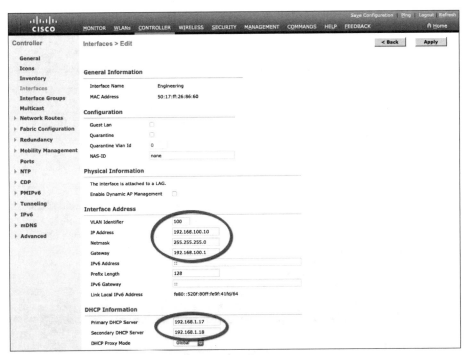

Figure 4-27 *Defining a Dynamic Interface Name and VLAN ID*

Next, enter the IP address, subnet mask, and gateway address for the interface. You should also define primary and secondary DHCP server addresses that the controller will use when it relays DHCP requests from clients that are bound to the interface.

Figure 4-28 shows how the interface named Engineering has been configured with IP address 192.168.100.10, subnet mask 255.255.255.0, gateway 192.168.100.1, and DHCP servers 192.168.1.17 and 192.168.1.18. Click the **Apply** button to complete the interface configuration and return to the list of interfaces.

Figure 4-28 *Editing the Dynamic Interface Parameters*

Step 2: Create a New WLAN

You can display a list of the currently defined WLANs by selecting **WLANs** from the top menu bar. In Figure 4-29, the controller does not have any WLANs already defined. You can create a new WLAN by selecting **Create New** from the drop-down menu and then clicking the **Go** button.

Figure 4-29 *Displaying a List of WLANs*

Next, enter a descriptive name as the profile name and the SSID text string. In Figure 4-30, the profile name and SSID are identical, just to keep things straightforward. The ID number is used as an index into the list of WLANs that are defined on the controller. The ID number becomes useful when you use templates in Prime Infrastructure (PI) to configure WLANs on multiple controllers at the same time.

NOTE WLAN templates are applied to specific WLAN ID numbers on controllers. The WLAN ID is only locally significant and is not passed between controllers. As a rule, you should keep the sequence of WLAN names and IDs consistent across multiple controllers so that any configuration templates you use in the future will be applied to the same WLANs on each controller.

Figure 4-30 *Creating a New WLAN*

Click the **Apply** button to create the new WLAN.

Step 3: Configure the WLAN

The next page will allow you to edit four categories of parameters, corresponding to the tabs across the top, as shown in Figure 4-31. By default, the General tab is selected.

You should enable the new WLAN by checking the **Status** check box. Even though the General page shows a specific security policy for the WLAN (the default WPA2 with 802.1x), you can make changes in a later step through the Security tab. Remember that 802.1x is used for "enterprise" authentication models that use RADIUS servers and digital certificates—not for pre-shared key authentication.

Figure 4-31 *Configuring the General WLAN Parameters*

Under Radio Policy, select the type of radio that will offer the WLAN. By default, the WLAN will be offered on all radios that are joined with the controller. You can select a more specific policy with options like 802.11a only, 802.11a/g only, 802.11g only, or 802.11b/g only. For example, if you are creating a new WLAN for devices that have only a 2.4-GHz radio, it probably does not make sense to advertise the WLAN on both 2.4- and 5-GHz AP radios.

Next, select which of the controller's dynamic interfaces will be bound to the WLAN. By default, the management interface is selected. The drop-down list contains all the dynamic interface names that are available. In Figure 4-31, the new engineering WLAN will be bound to the Engineering interface.

Finally, use the Broadcast SSID check box to select whether the APs should broadcast the SSID name in the beacons they transmit. Broadcasting SSIDs is usually more convenient for users because their devices can learn and display the SSID names automatically. In fact, most devices actually need the SSID in the beacons to understand that the AP is still available for that SSID. Hiding the SSID name, by not broadcasting it, does not really provide any worthwhile security. Instead, it just prevents user devices from discovering an SSID and trying to use it as a default network.

For reference and study, Table 4-2 lists some of the values used in the past few configuration panels on the WLC, with data formats and lengths. The table also lists some values shown in the upcoming figures as well.

Table 4-2 WLAN Configuration Fields and Formats

Field	Length	Data Format	Other Rules
Profile name	1–32	ASCII	
SSID	1–32	ASCII	Alphanumeric, space, and printable special characters allowed; some special values reserved
VLAN ID	2–4094	Decimal	

Field	Length	Data Format	Other Rules
WLAN ID	1–512	Decimal	
Pre-shared key (PSK)	8–63 Exactly 64	ASCII or Hexadecimal	

Configuring WLAN Security

Select the **Security** tab to configure the security settings. By default, the Layer 2 Security tab is selected. From the Layer 2 Security drop-down menu, select the appropriate security scheme to use. Table 4-3 lists the types that are available.

Table 4-3   Layer 2 WLAN Security Type

Option	Description
None	Open authentication
WPA+WPA2	Wi-Fi protected access WPA or WPA2
802.1x	EAP authentication with dynamic WEP
Static WEP	WEP key security
Static WEP + 802.1x	EAP authentication or static WEP
CKIP	Cisco Key Integrity Protocol
None + EAP Passthrough	Open authentication with remote EAP authentication

As you select a security type, be sure to remember which choices are types that have been deprecated or proven to be weak, and avoid them if possible. Further down the screen, you can select which specific WPA, WPA2, and WPA3 methods to support on the WLAN. You can select more than one, if you need to support different types of wireless clients that require several security methods.

In Figure 4-32, WPA+WPA2 has been selected from the pull-down menu so that WPA2 will be a valid option. If you want to support efficient client roaming between APs, you can leverage the 802.11r amendment, also known as Fast Transition. In the Fast Transition section, notice that it is enabled by default with the Adaptive mode, which permits clients that do and do not support 802.11r.

In the WPA+WPA2 Parameters section, WPA2 Policy and AES encryption have been selected. The WPA and TKIP check boxes have been unchecked, so the methods are avoided because they are legacy and have been deprecated.

Under the Authentication Key Management section, you can select the authentication methods the WLAN will use. Only PSK has been selected in the figure, so the WLAN will allow only WPA2-Personal with pre-shared key authentication.

Suppose you need to use WPA2-Enterprise instead of WPA2-Personal or PSK. Client authentication could be performed by RADIUS servers, Cisco ISE, LDAP, and so on. You would select the 802.1X option rather than PSK. In that case, 802.1x and EAP would be used to authenticate wireless clients against one or more RADIUS servers. The controller would use servers from a global list that you define under **Security > AAA > RADIUS > Authentication**. To specify which servers the WLAN should use, you would select the **Security** tab and then the **AAA Servers** tab in the WLAN edit screen. You can identify up to six specific RADIUS servers in the WLAN configuration.

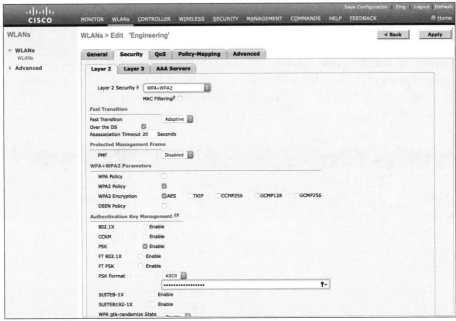

Figure 4-32 *Configuring Layer 2 WLAN Security*

Beside each server, select a specific server IP address from the drop-down menu of globally defined servers. The servers are tried in sequential order until one of them responds. Although the CCNA exam objective specifies WPA2-Personal, Figure 4-33 shows what a WLAN configured for WPA2-Enterprise might look like, with servers 1 through 3 being set to 192.168.200.28, 192.168.200.29, and 192.168.200.30, respectively.

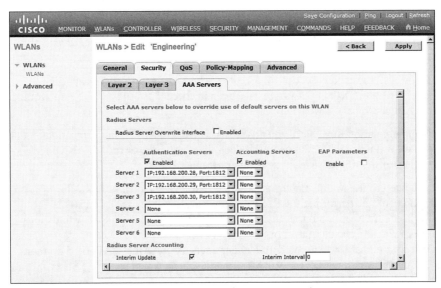

Figure 4-33 *Selecting RADIUS Servers for WLAN Authentication*

Configuring WLAN QoS

Select the **QoS** tab to configure quality of service settings for the WLAN, as shown in Figure 4-34. By default, the controller will consider all frames in the WLAN to be normal data, to be handled in a "best effort" manner. You can set the Quality of Service (QoS) drop-down menu to classify all frames in one of the following ways:

- Platinum (voice)

- Gold (video)

- Silver (best effort)

- Bronze (background)

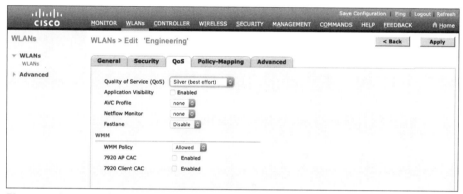

Figure 4-34   *Configuring QoS Settings*

You can also set the Wi-Fi Multimedia (WMM) policy, call admission control (CAC) policies, and bandwidth parameters on the QoS page. You can learn more about QoS later in Chapter 15, "Quality of Service (QoS)."

Configuring Advanced WLAN Settings

Finally, you can select the **Advanced** tab to configure a variety of advanced WLAN settings. From the page shown in Figure 4-35, you can configure many features—most of them are beyond the scope of the CCNA objectives and are not shown; however, you should be aware of a few parameters and defaults that might affect your wireless clients.

You can configure the Session Timeout to set the amount of time client sessions are allowed to continue before forcing them to reauthenticate. By default, sessions will be timed out after 1800 seconds (30 minutes). If 802.1x is used in the WLAN, you can set the session timeout value within the range 300 to 86,400 seconds; if not, the range is 0 to 86,400, where 0 means no timeout.

If the Client Exclusion box is enabled, the controller will use its wireless intrusion prevention system (IPS) to evaluate client activity against a database of signatures. If it detects that some suspicious activity is occurring, the controller will put the client into an exclusion list and will isolate it from the wireless network for a default of 180 seconds.

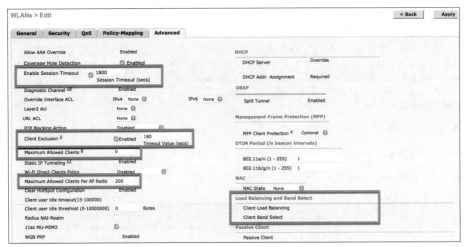

Figure 4-35   *Configuring Advanced WLAN Settings*

You can set limits on the number of concurrent clients by setting the Maximum Allowed Clients value. By default, the controller will allow an unlimited (designated by zero) number of clients per WLAN. You can also limit the number of clients permitted to connect to each AP radio in the WLAN, which defaults to 200.

You might also want to let the controller decide how it accepts wireless clients onto an AP radio. For example, you can use the Client Load Balancing option to let the controller distribute clients across neighboring APs as they probe and associate. The Client Band Select option lets the controller actively influence clients to join a more efficient frequency band if they try to associate on a lower, less efficient band. For instance, Client Band Select can attempt to prevent clients from joining a 2.4-GHz channel if a 5-GHz channel is also available nearby.

> **TIP**   Is 180 seconds really enough time to deter an attack coming from a wireless client? In the case of a brute-force attack, where passwords are guessed from a dictionary of possibilities, 180 seconds is enough to disrupt and delay an attacker's progress. What might have taken 3 minutes to find a matching password without an exclusion policy would take 15 years with one.

Finalizing WLAN Configuration

When you are satisfied with the settings in each of the WLAN configuration tabs, click the **Apply** button in the upper-right corner of the WLAN Edit screen. The WLAN will be created and added to the controller configuration. In Figure 4-36, the Engineering WLAN has been added as WLAN ID 1 and is enabled for use.

Figure 4-36 *Displaying WLANs Configured on a Controller*

Don't forget to verify the new WLAN's configuration. From the information shown in Figure 4-36, you can confirm that the SSID is correct, the Admin Status is enabled, and the security settings are accurate for WPA2-PSK.

Chapter Review

Review this chapter's material using either the tools in the book or the interactive tools for the same material found on the book's companion website. Table 4-4 outlines the key review elements and where you can find them. To better track your study progress, record when you completed these activities in the second column.

Table 4-4   Chapter Review Tracking

Review Element	Review Date(s)	Resource Used
Review key topics		Book, website
Review key terms		Book, website
Answer DIKTA questions		Book, PTP

Review All the Key Topics

Table 4-5   Key Topics for Chapter 4

Key Topic Element	Description	Page Number
Figure 4-1	Physical connections to an AP	59
Figure 4-8	Wireless LAN controller physical ports	63
Figure 4-9	Wireless LAN controller logical interfaces	64
Figure 4-10	Planning a WLAN	66
Figure 4-11	AP configuration with an IOS-XE controller	67
Table 4-2	WLAN Configuration Fields and Formats	82
Table 4-3	Configuring WLAN security	83

Part I Review

Keep track of your part review progress with the checklist in Table P1-1. Details on each task follow the table.

Table P1-1   Part I Part Review Checklist

Activity	1st Date Completed	2nd Date Completed
Repeat All DIKTA Questions		
Answer Part Review Questions		
Review Key Topics		
Watch Video		
Use Per-Chapter Interactive Review		

Repeat All DIKTA Questions

For this task, answer the "Do I Know This Already?" questions again for the chapters in this part of the book, using the PTP software.

Answer Part Review Questions

For this task, answer the Part Review questions for this part of the book, using the PTP software.

Review Key Topics

Review all key topics in all chapters in this part, either by browsing the chapters or by using the Key Topics application on the companion website.

Watch Video

The companion website includes a variety of common mistake and Q&A videos organized by part and chapter. Use these videos to challenge your thinking, dig deeper, review topics, and better prepare for the exam. Make sure to bookmark a link to the companion website and use the videos for review whenever you have a few extra minutes.

Use Per-Chapter Interactive Review

Using the companion website, browse through the interactive review elements, like memory tables and key term flashcards, to review the content from each chapter.

The *CCNA 200-301 Official Cert Guide, Volume 2*, Second Edition, includes the topics that help you build an enterprise network so all devices can communicate with all other devices. Parts II and III of this book focus on how to secure that enterprise network so that only the appropriate devices and users can communicate.

Part II focuses on IP Version 4 (IPv4) access control lists (ACLs). ACLs are IPv4 packet filters that can be programmed to look at IPv4 packet headers, make choices, and either allow a packet through or discard the packet. Because you can implement IPv4 ACLs on any router, a network engineer has many options of where to use ACLs, without adding additional hardware or software, making ACLs a very flexible and useful tool.

Chapter 5 begins this part with an introduction to the TCP/IP Transport layer protocols TCP and UDP, along with an introduction to several TCP/IP applications. This chapter provides the necessary background to understand the ACL chapters.

Chapters 6, 7, and 8 get into details about ACLs. Chapter 6 discusses ACL basics, avoiding advanced topics to ensure that you master the basics. Chapter 7 explores named ACLs, which allow easier configuration and editing, and extended ACLs, which provide more options to match packets. Chapter 8 completes the ACL discussion by examining specific implementation issues, first regarding several overhead protocols, and then discussing some improved ACL features introduced by IOS XE.

Part II

IP Access Control Lists

Introduction to TCP/IP Transport and Applications

This chapter covers the following exam topics:

1.0 Network Fundamentals

    1.5 Compare TCP to UDP

4.0 IP Services

    4.3 Explain the role of DHCP and DNS in the network

The CCNA exam focuses mostly on functions at the lower layers of TCP/IP, which define how IP networks can send IP packets from host to host using LANs and WANs. This chapter explains the basics of a few topics that receive less attention on the exams: the TCP/IP transport layer and the TCP/IP application layer. The functions of these higher layers play a big role in real TCP/IP networks. Additionally, many of the security topics in Parts I and II of this book and some of the IP services topics in Part III require you to know the basics of how the transport and application layers of TCP/IP work. This chapter serves as that introduction.

This chapter begins by examining the functions of two transport layer protocols: Transmission Control Protocol (TCP) and User Datagram Protocol (UDP). The second major section of the chapter examines the TCP/IP application layer, including some discussion of how Domain Name System (DNS) name resolution works.

"Do I Know This Already?" Quiz

Take the quiz (either here or use the PTP software) if you want to use the score to help you decide how much time to spend on this chapter. The letter answers are listed at the bottom of the page following the quiz. Appendix C, found both at the end of the book as well as on the companion website, includes both the answers and explanations. You can also find both answers and explanations in the PTP testing software.

Table 5-1 "Do I Know This Already?" Foundation Topics Section-to-Question Mapping

Foundation Topics Section	Questions
TCP/IP Layer 4 Protocols: TCP and UDP	1–4
TCP/IP Applications	5, 6

1. Which of the following header fields identify which TCP/IP application gets data received by the computer? (Choose two answers.)

    a. Ethernet Type

    b. SNAP Protocol Type

    c. IP Protocol

  d. TCP Port Number

  e. UDP Port Number

2. Which of the following are typical functions of TCP? (Choose four answers.)

  a. Flow control (windowing)

  b. Error recovery

  c. Multiplexing using port numbers

  d. Routing

  e. Encryption

  f. Ordered data transfer

3. Which of the following functions is performed by both TCP and UDP?

  a. Windowing

  b. Error recovery

  c. Multiplexing using port numbers

  d. Routing

  e. Encryption

  f. Ordered data transfer

4. What do you call data that includes the Layer 4 protocol header, and data given to Layer 4 by the upper layers, not including any headers and trailers from Layers 1 to 3? (Choose two answers.)

  a. L3PDU

  b. Chunk

  c. Segment

  d. Packet

  e. Frame

  f. L4PDU

5. In the URI http://www.certskills.com/config-labs, which part identifies the web server?

  a. http

  b. www.certskills.com

  c. certskills.com

  d. http://www.certskills.com

  e. The file name.html includes the hostname.

6. Fred opens a web browser and connects to the www.certskills.com website. Which of the following are typically true about what happens between Fred's web browser and the web server? (Choose two answers.)

  a. Messages flowing toward the server use UDP destination port 80.

  b. Messages flowing from the server typically use RTP.

  c. Messages flowing to the client typically use a source TCP port number of 80.

  d. Messages flowing to the server typically use TCP.

Foundation Topics

TCP/IP Layer 4 Protocols: TCP and UDP

The OSI transport layer (Layer 4) defines several functions, the most important of which are error recovery and flow control. Likewise, the TCP/IP transport layer protocols also implement these same types of features. Note that both the OSI model and the TCP/IP model call this layer the transport layer. But as usual, when referring to the TCP/IP model, the layer name and number are based on OSI, so any TCP/IP transport layer protocols are considered Layer 4 protocols.

The key difference between TCP and UDP is that TCP provides a wide variety of services to applications, whereas UDP does not. For example, routers discard packets for many reasons, including bit errors, congestion, and instances in which no correct routes are known. As you have read already, most data-link protocols notice errors (a process called **error detection**) but then discard frames that have errors. TCP provides retransmission (**error recovery**) and helps to avoid congestion (**flow control**), whereas UDP does not. As a result, many application protocols choose to use TCP.

However, do not let UDP's lack of services make you think that UDP is worse than TCP. By providing fewer services, UDP needs fewer bytes in its header compared to TCP, resulting in fewer bytes of overhead in the network. UDP software does not slow down data transfer in cases where TCP can purposefully slow down. Also, some applications, notably today voice over IP (VoIP) and video over IP, do not need error recovery, so they use UDP. So, UDP also has an important place in TCP/IP networks today.

Table 5-2 lists the main features supported by TCP/UDP. Note that only the first item listed in the table is supported by UDP, whereas all items in the table are supported by TCP.

Table 5-2 TCP/IP Transport Layer Features

Function	Description
Multiplexing using **ports**	Function that allows receiving hosts to choose the correct application for which the data is destined, based on the port number
Error recovery (reliability)	Process of numbering and acknowledging data with Sequence and Acknowledgment header fields
Flow control using windowing	Process that uses window sizes to protect buffer space and routing devices from being overloaded with traffic
Connection establishment and termination	Process used to initialize port numbers and Sequence and Acknowledgment fields
Ordered data transfer and data segmentation	Continuous stream of bytes from an upper-layer process that is "segmented" for transmission and delivered to upper-layer processes at the receiving device, with the bytes in the same order

Next, this section describes the features of TCP, followed by a brief comparison to UDP.

Answers to the "Do I Know This Already?" quiz:

1 D, E **2** A, B, C, F **3** C **4** C, F **5** B **6** C, D

Transmission Control Protocol

Each TCP/IP application typically chooses to use either TCP or UDP based on the application's requirements. For example, TCP provides error recovery, but to do so, it consumes more bandwidth and uses more processing cycles. UDP does not perform error recovery, but it takes less bandwidth and uses fewer processing cycles. Regardless of which of these two TCP/IP transport layer protocols the application chooses to use, you should understand the basics of how each of these transport layer protocols works.

TCP, as defined in Request For Comments (RFC) 9293, accomplishes the functions listed in Table 5-2 through mechanisms at the endpoint computers. TCP relies on IP for end-to-end delivery of the data, including routing issues. In other words, TCP performs only part of the functions necessary to deliver the data between applications. Also, the role that it plays is directed toward providing services for the applications that sit at the endpoint computers. Regardless of whether two computers are on the same Ethernet, or are separated by the entire Internet, TCP performs its functions the same way.

Figure 5-1 shows the fields in the TCP header. Although you don't need to memorize the names of the fields or their locations, the rest of this section refers to several of the fields, so the entire header is included here for reference.

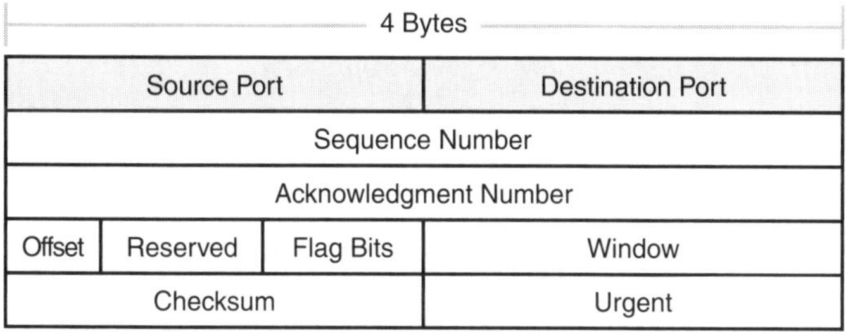

5

4 Bytes	
Source Port	Destination Port
Sequence Number	
Acknowledgment Number	

Offset	Reserved	Flag Bits	Window

Checksum	Urgent

Figure 5-1 *TCP Header Fields*

The message created by TCP that begins with the TCP header, followed by any application data, is called a TCP **segment**. Alternatively, the more generic term *Layer 4 PDU*, or *L4PDU*, can also be used.

Multiplexing Using TCP Port Numbers

TCP and UDP both use a concept called *multiplexing*. Therefore, this section begins with an explanation of multiplexing with TCP and UDP. Afterward, the unique features of TCP are explored.

Multiplexing by TCP and UDP involves the process of how a computer thinks when receiving data. The computer might be running many applications, such as a web browser, an email package, or an Internet VoIP application (for example, Skype). TCP and UDP multiplexing tells the receiving computer to which application to give the received data.

Some examples will help make the need for multiplexing obvious. The sample network consists of two PCs, labeled Hannah and George. Hannah uses an application that she wrote to send advertisements that appear on George's screen. The application sends a new ad to George every 10 seconds. Hannah uses a second application, a wire-transfer application, to send George some money. Finally, Hannah uses a web browser to access the web server that runs on George's PC. The ad application and wire-transfer application are imaginary, just for this example. The web application works just like it would in real life.

Figure 5-2 shows the sample network, with George running three applications:

■ A UDP-based advertisement application

■ A TCP-based wire-transfer application

■ A TCP web server application

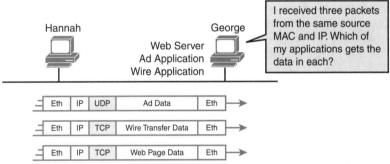

Figure 5-2   *Hannah Sending Packets to George, with Three Applications*

George needs to know which application to give the data to, but *all three packets are from the same Ethernet and IP address.* You might think that George could look at whether the packet contains a UDP or TCP header, but as you see in the figure, two applications (wire transfer and web) are using TCP.

TCP and UDP solve this problem by using a port number field in the TCP or UDP header, respectively. Each of Hannah's TCP and UDP segments uses a different *destination port number* so that George knows which application to give the data to. Figure 5-3 shows an example.

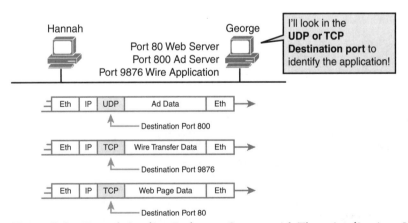

Figure 5-3   *Hannah Sending Packets to George, with Three Applications Using Port Numbers to Multiplex*

Multiplexing relies on a concept called a *socket*. A socket consists of three things:

- An IP address

- A transport protocol

- A port number

So, for a web server application on George, the socket would be (10.1.1.2, TCP, port 80) because, by default, web servers use the well-known port 80. When Hannah's web browser connects to the web server, Hannah uses a socket as well—possibly one like this: (10.1.1.1, TCP, 49160). Why 49160? Well, Hannah just needs a port number that is unique on Hannah, so Hannah sees that port 49160.

The Internet Assigned Numbers Authority (IANA), the same organization that manages IP address allocation worldwide, subdivides the port number ranges into three main ranges. The first two ranges reserve numbers that IANA can then allocate to specific application protocols through an application and review process, with the third category reserving ports to be dynamically allocated as used for clients, as with the port 49160 example in the previous paragraph. The names and ranges of port numbers (as detailed in RFC 6335) are

- **Well Known (System) Ports:** Numbers from 0 to 1023, assigned by IANA, with a stricter review process to assign new ports than user ports.

- **User (Registered) Ports:** Numbers from 1024 to 49151, assigned by IANA with a less strict process to assign new ports compared to well-known ports.

- **Ephemeral (Dynamic, Private) Ports:** Numbers from 49152 to 65535, not assigned and intended to be dynamically allocated and used temporarily for a client application while the app is running.

Figure 5-4 shows an example that uses three ephemeral ports on the user device on the left, with the server on the right using two well-known ports and one user port. The computers use three applications at the same time; hence, three socket connections are open. Because a socket on a single computer should be unique, a connection between two sockets should identify a unique connection between two computers. This uniqueness means that you can use multiple applications at the same time, talking to applications running on the same or different computers. Multiplexing, based on sockets, ensures that the data is delivered to the correct applications.

Port numbers are a vital part of the socket concept. Servers use well-known ports (or user ports), whereas clients use dynamic ports. Applications that provide a service, such as FTP, Telnet, and web servers, open a socket using a well-known port and listen for connection requests. Because these connection requests from clients are required to include both the source and destination port numbers, the port numbers used by the servers must be known beforehand. Therefore, each service uses a specific well-known port number or user port number. Both well-known and user ports are listed at www.iana.org/assignments/service-names-port-numbers/service-names-port-numbers.txt.

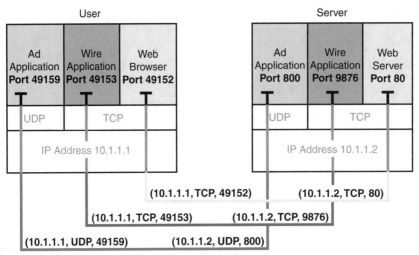

Figure 5-4 *Connections Between Sockets*

On client machines, where the requests originate, any locally unused port number can be allocated. The result is that each client on the same host uses a different port number, but a server uses the same port number for all connections. For example, 100 web browsers on the same host computer could each connect to a web server, but the web server with 100 clients connected to it would have only one socket and, therefore, only one port number (port 80, in this case). The server can tell which packets are sent from which of the 100 clients by looking at the source port of received TCP segments. The server can send data to the correct web client (browser) by sending data to that same port number listed as a destination port. The combination of source and destination sockets allows all participating hosts to distinguish between the data's source and destination. Although the example explains the concept using 100 TCP connections, the same port-numbering concept applies to UDP sessions in the same way.

NOTE   You can find all RFCs online at www.rfc-editor.org/rfc/rfc*xxxx*.txt, where *xxxx* is the number of the RFC. If you do not know the number of the RFC, you can try searching by topic at www.rfc-editor.org.

Popular TCP/IP Applications

Throughout your preparation for the CCNA exam, you will come across a variety of TCP/IP applications. You should at least be aware of some of the applications that can be used to help manage and control a network.

The World Wide Web (WWW) application exists through web browsers accessing the content available on web servers. Although it is often thought of as an end-user application, you can actually use WWW to manage a router or switch. You enable a web server function in the router or switch and use a browser to access the router or switch.

The Domain Name System (DNS) allows users to use names to refer to computers, with DNS being used to find the corresponding IP addresses. DNS also uses a client/server model, with **DNS servers** being controlled by networking personnel and DNS client functions being part of most any device that uses TCP/IP today. The client simply asks the DNS server to supply the IP address that corresponds to a given name.

Simple Network Management Protocol (SNMP) is an application layer protocol used specifically for network device management. For example, Cisco supplies a large variety of network management products, many of them in the Cisco Prime network management software product family. They can be used to query, compile, store, and display information about a network's operation. To query the network devices, Cisco Prime software mainly uses SNMP protocols.

Traditionally, to move files to and from a router or switch, Cisco used Trivial File Transfer Protocol (TFTP). TFTP defines a protocol for basic file transfer—hence the word *trivial*. Alternatively, routers and switches can use File Transfer Protocol (FTP), which is a much more functional protocol, to transfer files. Both work well for moving files into and out of Cisco devices. FTP allows many more features, making it a good choice for the general end-user population. TFTP client and server applications are very simple, making them good tools as embedded parts of networking devices.

Some of these applications use TCP, and some use UDP. For example, Simple Mail Transfer Protocol (SMTP) and Post Office Protocol version 3 (POP3), both used for transferring mail, require guaranteed delivery, so they use TCP.

Regardless of which transport layer protocol is used, applications use a well-known port number so that clients know which port to attempt to connect to. Table 5-3 lists several popular applications and their well-known port numbers.

Table 5-3   Popular Applications and Their Well-Known Port Numbers

Port Number	Protocol	Application
20	TCP	FTP data
21	TCP	FTP control
22	TCP	SSH
23	TCP	Telnet
25	TCP	SMTP
53	UDP, TCP*	DNS
67	UDP	DHCP Server
68	UDP	DHCP Client
69	UDP	TFTP
80	TCP	HTTP (WWW)
110	TCP	POP3
161	UDP	SNMP
443	TCP, UDP	HTTPS
514	UDP	Syslog

* DNS uses both UDP and TCP in different instances. It uses port 53 for both TCP and UDP.

Connection Establishment and Termination

TCP **connection establishment** occurs before any of the other TCP features can begin their work. Connection establishment refers to the process of initializing Sequence and Acknowledgment fields and agreeing on the port numbers used. Figure 5-5 shows an example of connection establishment flow.

Figure 5-5   *TCP Connection Establishment*

This three-way connection establishment flow (also called a three-way handshake) must complete before data transfer can begin. The connection exists between the two sockets, although the TCP header has no single socket field. Of the three parts of a socket, the IP addresses are implied based on the source and destination IP addresses in the IP header. TCP is implied because a TCP header is in use, as specified by the protocol field value in the IP header. Therefore, the only parts of the socket that need to be encoded in the TCP header are the port numbers.

TCP signals connection establishment using 2 bits inside the flag fields of the TCP header. Called the SYN and ACK flags, these bits have a particularly interesting meaning. SYN means "synchronize the sequence numbers," which is one necessary component in initialization for TCP.

Figure 5-6 shows TCP connection termination. This four-way termination sequence is straightforward and uses an additional flag, called the *FIN bit*. (FIN is short for "finished," as you might guess.) One interesting note: Before the device on the right sends the third TCP segment in the sequence, it notifies the application that the connection is coming down. It then waits on an acknowledgment from the application before sending the third segment in the figure. Just in case the application takes some time to reply, the PC on the right sends the second flow in the figure, acknowledging that the other PC wants to take down the connection. Otherwise, the PC on the left might resend the first segment repeatedly.

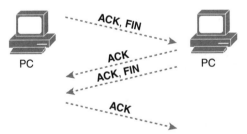

Figure 5-6   *TCP Connection Termination*

TCP establishes and terminates connections between the endpoints, whereas UDP does not. Many protocols operate under these same concepts, so the terms *connection-oriented* and *connectionless* are used to refer to the general idea of each. More formally, these terms can be defined as follows:

■ **Connection-oriented protocol:** A protocol that requires an exchange of messages before data transfer begins, or that has a required pre-established correlation between two endpoints.

■ **Connectionless protocol:** A protocol that does not require an exchange of messages and that does not require a pre-established correlation between two endpoints.

Error Recovery and Reliability

TCP provides for reliable data transfer, which is also called *reliability* or *error recovery*, depending on what document you read. To accomplish reliability, TCP numbers data bytes using the Sequence and Acknowledgment fields in the TCP header. TCP achieves reliability in both directions, using the Sequence Number field of one direction combined with the Acknowledgment field in the opposite direction.

Figure 5-7 shows an example of how the TCP Sequence and Acknowledgment fields allow the PC to send 3000 bytes of data to the server, with the server acknowledging receipt of the data. The TCP segments in the figure occur in order, from top to bottom. For simplicity's sake, all messages happen to have 1000 bytes of data in the data portion of the TCP segment. The first Sequence number is a nice round number (1000), again for simplicity's sake. The top of the figure shows three segments, with each sequence number being 1000 more than the previous, identifying the first of the 1000 bytes in the message. (That is, in this example, the first segment holds bytes 1000–1999; the second holds bytes 2000–2999; and the third holds bytes 3000–3999.)

Figure 5-7   *TCP Acknowledgment Without Errors*

The fourth TCP segment in the figure—the only one flowing back from the server to the web browser—acknowledges the receipt of all three segments. How? The acknowledgment value of 4000 means "I received all data with sequence numbers up through one less than 4000, so I am ready to receive your byte 4000 next." (Note that this convention of acknowledging by listing the next expected byte, rather than the number of the last byte received, is called **forward acknowledgment**.)

This first example does not recover from any errors, however; it simply shows the basics of how the sending host uses the sequence number field to identify the data, with the receiving host using forward acknowledgments to acknowledge the data. The more interesting discussion revolves around how to use these same tools to do error recovery. TCP uses the Sequence and Acknowledgment fields so that the receiving host can notice lost data, ask the sending host to resend, and then acknowledge that the re-sent data arrived.

Many variations exist for how TCP does error recovery. Figure 5-8 shows just one such example, with similar details compared to the previous figure. The web browser again sends three TCP segments, again 1000 bytes each, again with easy-to-remember sequence numbers. However, in this example, the second TCP segment fails to cross the network.

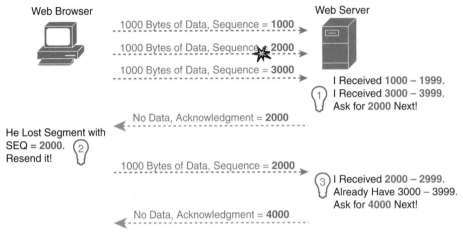

Figure 5-8   *TCP Acknowledgment with Errors*

The figure points out three sets of ideas behind how the two hosts think. First, on the right, the server realizes that it did not receive all the data. The two received TCP segments contain bytes numbered 1000–1999 and 3000–3999. Clearly, the server did not receive the bytes numbered in between. The server then decides to acknowledge all the data up to the lost data—that is, to send back a segment with the Acknowledgment field equal to 2000.

The receipt of an acknowledgment that does not acknowledge all the data sent so far tells the sending host to resend the data. The PC on the left may wait a few moments to make sure no other acknowledgments arrive (using a timer called the retransmission timer), but will soon decide that the server means "I really do need 2000 next—resend it." The PC on the left does so, as shown in the fifth of the six TCP segments in the figure.

Finally, note that the server can acknowledge not only the re-sent data but also any earlier data that had been received correctly. In this case, the server received the re-sent second TCP segment (the data with sequence numbers 2000–2999), but the server had already received the third TCP segment (the data numbered 3000–3999). The server's next Acknowledgment field acknowledges the data in both of those segments, with an Acknowledgment field of 4000.

Flow Control Using Windowing

TCP implements flow control by using a window concept that is applied to the amount of data that can be outstanding and awaiting acknowledgment at any one point in time. The window concept lets the receiving host tell the sender how much data it can receive right now, giving the receiving host a way to make the sending host slow down or speed up. The receiver can slide the window size up and down—called a **sliding window** or *dynamic window*—to change how much data the sending host can send.

The sliding window mechanism makes much more sense with an example. The example, shown in Figure 5-9, uses the same basic rules as the examples in the previous few figures. In this case, none of the TCP segments have errors, and the discussion begins one TCP segment earlier than in the previous two figures.

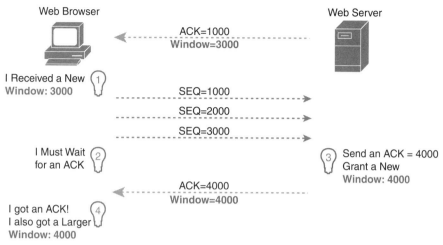

Figure 5-9 *TCP Windowing*

Begin with the first segment, sent by the server to the PC. The Acknowledgment field should be familiar by now: it tells the PC that the server expects a segment with sequence number 1000 next. The new field, the window field, is set to 3000. Because the segment flows to the PC, this value tells the PC that the PC can send no more than 3000 bytes over this connection before receiving an acknowledgment. So, as shown on the left, the PC realizes it can send only 3000 bytes, and it stops sending, waiting on an acknowledgment, after sending three 1000-byte TCP segments.

Continuing the example, the server not only acknowledges receiving the data (without any loss) but also decides to slide the window size a little higher. Note that second message flowing right to left in the figure, this time with a window of 4000. When the PC receives this TCP segment, the PC realizes it can send another 4000 bytes (a slightly larger window than the previous value).

Note that while the last few figures show examples for the purpose of explaining how the mechanisms work, the examples might give you the impression that TCP makes the hosts sit there and wait for acknowledgments a lot. TCP does not want to make the sending host have to wait to send data. For instance, if an acknowledgment is received before the window is exhausted, a new window begins, and the sender continues sending data until the current window is exhausted. Often, in a network that has few problems, few lost segments, and little congestion, the TCP windows stay relatively large with hosts seldom waiting to send.

User Datagram Protocol

UDP provides a service for applications to exchange messages. Unlike TCP, UDP is connectionless and provides no reliability, no windowing, no reordering of the received data, and no segmentation of large chunks of data into the right size for transmission. However, UDP provides some functions of TCP, such as data transfer and multiplexing using port numbers, and it does so with fewer bytes of overhead and less processing required than TCP.

UDP data transfer differs from TCP data transfer in that no reordering or recovery is accomplished. Applications that use UDP are tolerant of the lost data, or they have some application mechanism to recover lost data. For example, VoIP uses UDP because if a voice packet is lost, by the time the loss could be noticed and the packet retransmitted, too much delay would have occurred, and the voice would be unintelligible. Also, DNS requests may use UDP because the user will retry an operation if the DNS resolution fails. As another example, the Network File System (NFS), a remote file system application, performs recovery with application layer code, so UDP features are acceptable to NFS.

Figure 5-10 shows the UDP header format. Most importantly, note that the header includes source and destination port fields, for the same purpose as TCP. However, the UDP has only 8 bytes, in comparison to the 20-byte TCP header shown in Figure 5-1. UDP needs a shorter header than TCP simply because UDP has less work to do.

4 Bytes	
Source Port	Destination Port
Length	Checksum

Figure 5-10   *UDP Header*

TCP/IP Applications

The whole goal of building an enterprise network, or connecting a small home or office network to the Internet, is to use applications such as web browsing, text messaging, email, file downloads, voice, and video. This section examines one particular application—web browsing using Hypertext Transfer Protocol (**HTTP**).

The World Wide Web (WWW) consists of all the Internet-connected web servers in the world, plus all Internet-connected hosts with web browsers. **Web servers**, which consist of web server software running on a computer, store information (in the form of *web pages*) that might be useful to different people. A *web browser*, which is software installed on an end user's computer, provides the means to connect to a web server and display the web pages stored on the web server.

> **NOTE**   Although most people use the term *web browser*, or simply *browser*, web browsers are also called *web clients*, because they obtain a service from a web server.

For this process to work, several specific application layer functions must occur. The user must somehow identify the server, the specific web page, and the protocol used to get the data from the server. The client must find the server's IP address, based on the server's name, typically using DNS. The client must request the web page, which actually consists of multiple separate files, and the server must send the files to the web browser. Finally, for electronic commerce (e-commerce) applications, the transfer of data, particularly sensitive financial data, needs to be secure. The following sections address each of these functions.

Uniform Resource Identifiers

For a browser to display a web page, the browser must identify the server that has the web page, plus other information that identifies the particular web page. Most web servers have many web pages. For example, if you use a web browser to browse www.cisco.com and you click around that web page, you'll see another web page. Click again, and you'll see another web page. In each case, the clicking action identifies the server's IP address as well as the specific web page, with the details mostly hidden from you. (These clickable items on a web page, which in turn bring you to another web page, are called *links*.)

The browser user can identify a web page when you click something on a web page or when you enter a Uniform Resource Identifier (**URI**) in the browser's address area. Both options—clicking a link and typing a URI—refer to a URI, because when you click a link on a web page, that link actually refers to a URI.

NOTE   Most browsers support some way to view the hidden URI referenced by a link. In several browsers, hover the mouse pointer over a link, right-click, and select **Properties**. The pop-up window should display the URI to which the browser would be directed if you clicked that link.

In common speech, many people use the terms *web address* or the similar related terms *Universal Resource Locator* (or Uniform Resource Locator; URL) instead of URI, but URI is indeed the correct formal term. In fact, URL had been more commonly used than URI for more than a few years. However, the Internet Engineering Task Force, or IETF (the group that defines TCP/IP), along with the W3C consortium (W3.org, a consortium that develops web standards) has made a concerted effort to standardize the use of URI as the general term. See RFC 7595 for some commentary to that effect.

From a practical perspective, the URIs used to connect to a web server include three key components, as noted in Figure 5-11. The figure shows the formal names of the URI fields. More importantly to this discussion, note that the text before the :// identifies the protocol used to connect to the server, the text between the // and / identifies the server by name, and the text after the / identifies the web page.

Figure 5-11   *Structure of a URI Used to Retrieve a Web Page*

In this case, the protocol is Hypertext Transfer Protocol (HTTP), the hostname is www.certskills.com, and the name of the web page is config-labs.

Finding the Web Server Using DNS

A host can use DNS to discover the IP address that corresponds to a particular hostname. URIs typically list the name of the server—a name that can be used to dynamically learn the IP address used by that same server. The web browser cannot send an IP packet to a destination name, but it can send a packet to a destination IP address. So, before the browser can send a packet to the web server, the browser typically needs to resolve the name inside the URI to that name's corresponding IP address.

To pull together several concepts, Figure 5-12 shows the DNS process as initiated by a web browser, as well as some other related information. From a basic perspective, the user enters the URI (in this case, http://www.cisco.com/go/learningnetwork), resolves the www.cisco.com name into the correct IP address, and starts sending packets to the web server.

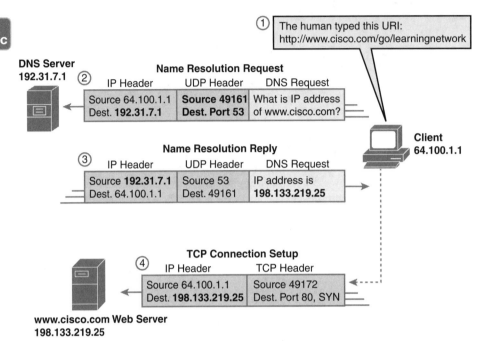

Figure 5-12   *DNS Resolution and Requesting a Web Page*

The steps shown in the figure are as follows:

1. The user enters the URI, http://www.cisco.com/go/learningnetwork, into the browser's address area.

2. The client sends a DNS request to the DNS server. Typically, the client learns the DNS server's IP address through DHCP. DNS supports using either TCP or UDP, with UDP in this example. In either case, the protocol uses the well-known port 53. (See Table 5-3, earlier in this chapter, for a list of popular well-known ports.)

3. The DNS server sends a reply, listing IP address 198.133.219.25 as www.cisco.com's IP address. Note also that the reply shows a destination IP address of 64.100.1.1, the client's IP address. It also shows a UDP header, with source port 53; the source port is 53 because the data is sourced, or sent by, the DNS server.

4. The client begins the process of establishing a new TCP connection to the web server. Note that the destination IP address is the just-learned IP address of the web server. The packet includes a TCP header, because HTTP uses TCP. Also note that the destination TCP port is 80, the well-known port for HTTP. Finally, the SYN bit is shown, as a reminder that the TCP connection establishment process begins with a TCP segment with the SYN bit turned on (binary 1).

The example in Figure 5-12 shows what happens when the client host does not know the IP address associated with the hostname but the enterprise does know the address. However, hosts can cache the results of DNS requests so that for a time the client does not need to ask the DNS to resolve the name. Also, the DNS server can cache the results of previous DNS requests; for instance, the enterprise DNS server in Figure 5-12 would not normally have configured information about hostnames in domains outside that enterprise, so that example relied on the DNS having cached the address associated with hostname www.cisco.com.

When the local DNS does not know the address associated with a hostname, it needs to ask for help. Figure 5-13 shows an example with the same client as in Figure 5-12. In this case, the enterprise DNS acts as a **recursive DNS server**, sending repeated DNS messages in an effort to identify the authoritative DNS server.

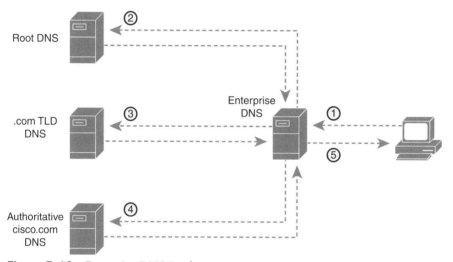

Figure 5-13   *Recursive DNS Lookup*

The steps shown in the figure are as follows:

1. The client sends a DNS request for www.cisco.com to the DNS server it knows, which is the enterprise DNS server.

2. The (recursive) enterprise DNS server does not know the answer yet, but it does not reject the client's DNS request. Instead, it follows a repetitive (recursive) process (shown as steps 2, 3, and 4), beginning with the DNS request sent to a root DNS server. The root does not supply the address either, but it supplies the IP address of another DNS server, one responsible for the .com top-level domain.

3. The recursive enterprise DNS sends the next DNS request to the DNS server learned at the previous step—this time the TLD DNS server for the .com domain. This DNS also does not know the address, but it knows the DNS server that should be the authoritative DNS server for domain cisco.com, so it supplies that DNS server's address.

4. The enterprise DNS sends another DNS request, to the DNS server whose address was learned in the previous step, again asking for resolution of the name www.cisco.com. This DNS server, the authoritative server for cisco.com, supplies the address.

5.   The enterprise DNS server returns a DNS reply back to the client, supplying the IP
     address requested at step 1.

Transferring Files with HTTP

After a web client (browser) has created a TCP connection to a web server, the client can
begin requesting the web page from the server. Most often, the protocol used to transfer the
web page is HTTP. The HTTP application layer protocol, defined in RFC 7230, defines how
files can be transferred between two computers. HTTP was specifically created for the purpose of transferring files between web servers and web clients.

HTTP defines several commands and responses, with the most frequently used being the
HTTP GET request. To get a file from a web server, the client sends an HTTP GET request
to the server, listing the filename. If the server decides to send the file, the server sends an
HTTP GET response, with a return code of 200 (meaning OK), along with the file's contents.

> **NOTE**   Many return codes exist for HTTP requests. For example, when the server does not
> have the requested file, it issues a return code of 404, which means "file not found." Most
> web browsers do not show the specific numeric HTTP return codes, instead displaying a
> response such as "page not found" in reaction to receiving a return code of 404.

Web pages typically consist of multiple files, called *objects*. Most web pages contain text
as well as several graphical images, animated advertisements, and possibly voice or video.
Each of these components is stored as a different object (file) on the web server. To get them
all, the web browser gets the first file. This file can (and typically does) include references to
other URIs, so the browser then also requests the other objects. Figure 5-14 shows the
general idea, with the browser getting the first file and then two others.

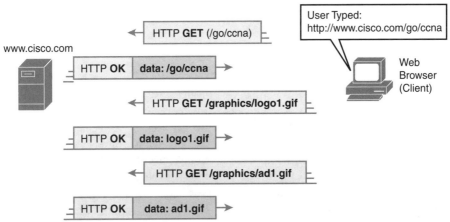

Figure 5-14   *Multiple HTTP GET Requests/Responses*

In this case, after the web browser gets the first file—the one called "/go/ccna" in the URI—
the browser reads and interprets that file. Besides containing parts of the web page, the file
refers to two other files, so the browser issues two additional HTTP GET requests. Note
that, even though it isn't shown in the figure, all these commands flow over one (or possibly

more) TCP connection between the client and the server. This means that TCP would provide error recovery, ensuring that the data was delivered.

How the Receiving Host Identifies the Correct Receiving Application

This chapter closes with a discussion of the process by which a host, when receiving any message over any network, can decide which of its many application programs should process the received data.

As an example, consider host A shown on the left side of Figure 5-15. The host happens to have three different web browser windows open, each using a unique TCP port. Host A also has an email client and a chat window open, both of which use TCP. Both the email and chat applications use a unique TCP port number on host A as shown in the figure.

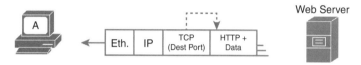

Browser: TCP port 49124
Browser: TCP port 49125
Browser: TCP port 49126
Email: TCP port 49127
Chat: TCP port 49128

Figure 5-15   *Dilemma: How Host A Chooses the App That Should Receive This Data*

This chapter has shown several examples of how transport layer protocols use the destination port number field in the TCP or UDP header to identify the receiving application. For instance, if the destination TCP port value in Figure 5-15 is 49124, host A will know that the data is meant for the first of the three web browser windows.

Before a receiving host can even examine the TCP or UDP header, and find the destination port field, it must first process the outer headers in the message. If the incoming message is an Ethernet frame that encapsulates an IPv4 packet, the headers look like the details in Figure 5-16.

 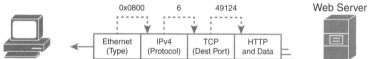

Figure 5-16   *Three Key Fields with Which to Identify the Next Header*

The receiving host needs to look at multiple fields, one per header, to identify the next header or field in the received message. For instance, host A uses an Ethernet NIC to connect to the network, so the received message is an Ethernet frame. The Ethernet Type field identifies the type of header that follows the Ethernet header—in this case, with a value of hex 0800, an IPv4 header.

The IPv4 header has a similar field called the IP Protocol field. The IPv4 Protocol field has a standard list of values that identify the next header, with decimal 6 used for TCP and decimal 17 used for UDP. In this case, the value of 6 identifies the TCP header that follows the IPv4 header. Once the receiving host realizes a TCP header exists, it can process the destination port field to determine which local application process should receive the data.

HTTP Versions

For much of the history of CCNA since its inception in 1998, you could ignore the details of HTTP versions and version differences. With the introduction of HTTP/3 around 2020, you need to be more aware of HTTP protocol versions. This section works through the versions and the differences that matter for CCNA.

HTTP 1.0 and 1.1

Web browsers and servers first came into existence in the early 1990s. Eventually, the IETF took ownership of the Hypertext Transfer Protocol (HTTP), used by web browsers and servers to transfer objects. In those early years, the IETF published HTTP RFCs for HTTP 0.9, **HTTP 1.0**, and **HTTP 1.1**, with various improvements at each version. However, differences exist in how the application protocol works, with the details unimportant to building the network infrastructure. For instance, they all use HTTP and TCP, with the same HTTP GET Request and Response methods discussed in the last several pages of this chapter.

These early HTTP versions use common networking features. They all use TCP for the transport protocol, with IANA reserving well-known TCP port 80 for the server. HTTP defines URLs with a scheme (protocol) of http, with URLs like http://www.example.com. The URL can specify a nondefault server port number, but if omitted (as is typical), the URL implies the default well-known port. Also, the http scheme means no additional security features, such as authentication or encryption, are used.

From using web browsers, you might notice that URLs do not typically reference any kind of version number. Instead, the web browser and web servers support many or most versions. They connect using details of one version and can then use application-layer headers to signal a change to use a different version. As a user, you do not notice the difference. As a network engineer, with these earlier versions, you did not need to be concerned about which was used.

HTTP/2 and TLS

Independent from the specific HTTP protocol versions, additional RFCs defined how to add security features to HTTP using Transport Layer Security (TLS). An RFC from the late 1990s defined **Secure HTTP**, also called HTTP over TLS. Because it added security to existing protocols, Secure HTTP uses the initial sequence like any other browser session, beginning with a TCP connection between the client and server. However, before sending HTTP messages, the endpoints create a TLS connection per the TLS protocol, implementing security features such as server authentication and encryption. Only then do the HTTP messages flow.

To signal that the connection uses Secure HTTP, the RFC defines a new URI scheme (protocol) of https, with URLs like https://www.example.com. (Almost all URLs you use daily begin with *https* and use Secure HTTP.)

From a networking perspective, two differences exist with HTTP 1.1 without TLS. The URLs differ, as just noted. Also, IANA reserves well-known TCP port 443 for Secure HTTP, so a URL that begins *https* implies TCP port 443 as the server's well-known port.

> **NOTE**   You might see references to HTTP versions as HTTP 1.1 or with a /, such as HTTP/1.1.

HTTP 1.1 and Secure HTTP/1.1 became the norm for many years, particularly into the 2000s and into the 2010s, with more and more traffic using the secure option over time. However, as time passed, many stakeholders saw issues with website performance with HTTP/1.1—particularly when transferring many objects with each web page. HTTP/2 and HTTP/3 attempt to address the performance issues with different approaches.

HTTP/2, which reached RFC status in the mid-2010s, improves the inner workings of the HTTP application layer protocol while keeping the same URL schemes, TCP transport, well-known ports, and the same use of HTTP over TLS. The changes impact the details of the HTTP application layer protocol but not the networking or security details. So, while important in IT, the introduction of HTTP/2 did not introduce new complexities for most network engineering projects because HTTP/2 uses the same TCP transport protocol and well-known ports as the earlier HTTP versions.

HTTP 3.0

HTTP/3 significantly shifts in HTTP performance with an approach that makes additional fundamental changes, including using UDP instead of TCP.

Google developed what has become HTTP/3 during the 2010s. While useful, Google's work found that TCP's error recovery and flow control features slowed performance for HTTP. To solve that problem, Google built a new transport protocol based on UDP called **QUIC** (not an acronym, just the name), now published in RFC 9369. QUIC also has some TCP-like features (error recovery, flow control), and it integrates the TLS work at the same time, reducing overhead flows. So, some HTTP/3 performance improvements come from migrating away from TCP plus TLS running independently to an approach that integrates UDP, QUIC, and TLS functions.

HTTP itself also changed. The IETF split some parts of the protocol into different RFCs in 2022 (RFCs 9110, 9111, and 9114), with HTTP/3 specifically in RFC 9114.

In the real world, HTTP/2 adoption showed slow growth, but HTTP/3 and its QUIC transport protocol have grown tremendously. According to some statistics from Cisco, Internet HTTP/3 traffic now exceeds HTTP/2 traffic. Many major Internet services, like Google, Facebook, YouTube, and Instagram, have embraced HTTP/3. Most of us have been using HTTP/3 without even being aware of it.

HTTP/3 changes several networking details compared to the other versions, most notably the headers. As discussed in the following few chapters, those changes impact what you can match with IP ACLs. While its RFC bills QUIC as a transport protocol, from a header perspective, it looks like another header that follows a UDP header. So, QUIC is an additional protocol that rides on UDP, as shown in Figure 5-17.

5

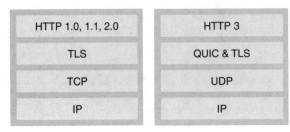

HTTP 1.0, 1.1, 2.0
TLS
TCP
IP

HTTP/2 & Earlier w/ TLS

HTTP 3
QUIC & TLS
UDP
IP

HTTP/3

Figure 5-17 *Comparing HTTP/3 with Earlier Versions*

NOTE HTTP/3 always uses TLS, partly because QUIC integrates TLS features but partly because the security features of TLS make sense for web connections. IANA reserves UDP port 443 as the well-known port for web servers when using HTTP/3.

To summarize, as a user, you do not choose what HTTP version to use. The browser and server will begin using a version and optionally change to another version based on the information exchanged between the two. As a network engineer, you should be aware of the versions, aware that HTTP messages in your network today include traditional TCP-based HTTP/1.0, HTTP/1.1, and HTTP/2 traffic to well-known TCP ports 80 and 443, but they also include messages with UDP headers using UDP port 443.

NOTE Web servers and most other server applications can use a port number other than their well-known reserved port. This chapter shows the predictable well-known ports.

Chapter Review

One key to doing well on the exams is to perform repetitive spaced review sessions. Review this chapter's material using either the tools in the book or interactive tools for the same material found on the book's companion website. Refer to the "Your Study Plan" element for more details. Table 5-4 outlines the key review elements and where you can find them. To better track your study progress, record when you completed these activities in the second column.

Table 5-4 Chapter Review Tracking

Review Element	Review Date(s)	Resource Used
Review key topics		Book, website
Review key terms		Book, website
Answer DIKTA questions		Book, PTP
Review memory tables		Book, website

Review All the Key Topics

Table 5-5   Key Topics for Chapter 5

Key Topic Element	Description	Page Number
Table 5-2	Functions of TCP and UDP	94
Table 5-3	Well-known TCP and UDP port numbers	99
Figure 5-5	Example of TCP connection establishment	100
List	Definitions of connection-oriented and connectionless	101
Figure 5-12	DNS name resolution	106
Figure 5-16	Header fields that identify the next header	109

Key Terms You Should Know

connection establishment, DNS server, error detection, error recovery, flow control, forward acknowledgment, HTTP, HTTP/1.0, HTTP/1.1, HTTP/2, HTTP/3, ordered data transfer, port, QUIC, recursive DNS server, Secure HTTP, segment, sliding windows, URI, web server

5

CHAPTER 6

Basic IPv4 Access Control Lists

This chapter covers the following exam topics:

5.0 Security Fundamentals

5.6 Configure and verify access control lists

IPv4 access control lists (ACLs) allow network engineers to program a filter into a router. Each router, on each interface, for both the inbound and outbound direction, can enable a different IP ACL with different rules. Each IP ACL's rules tell the router which packets to discard and which to allow through.

This chapter discusses the basics of IPv4 ACLs, specifically a type by the name *standard numbered IP ACLs* or simply **standard access lists**. Standard numbered ACLs use simple logic, matching on the source IP address field only, and use a configuration style that references the ACL using a number. This chapter sets out to help you learn this simpler type of ACL first. The next chapter, titled "Named and Extended IP ACLs," discusses other variations of IP ACLs that use names (named ACLs) and that have more advanced matching logic than standard ACLs (extended ACLs).

"Do I Know This Already?" Quiz

Take the quiz (either here or use the PTP software) if you want to use the score to help you decide how much time to spend on this chapter. The letter answers are listed at the bottom of the page following the quiz. Appendix C, found both at the end of the book as well as on the companion website, includes both the answers and explanations. You can also find both answers and explanations in the PTP testing software.

Table 6-1 "Do I Know This Already?" Foundation Topics Section-to-Question Mapping

Foundation Topics Section	Questions
IPv4 Access Control List Basics	1
Standard Numbered IPv4 ACLs	2–6

1. Barney is a host with IP address 10.1.1.1 in subnet 10.1.1.0/24. Which of the following things could a standard IP ACL be configured to do? (Choose two answers.)

   a. Match the exact source IP address.

   b. Match IP addresses 10.1.1.1 through 10.1.1.4 with one **access-list** command without matching other IP addresses.

   c. Match all IP addresses in Barney's subnet with one **access-list** command without matching other IP addresses.

   d. Match only the packet's destination IP address.

2. Which of the following answers list a valid number that standard numbered IP ACLs can use? (Choose two answers.)

   a. 1987

   b. 2187

   c. 187

   d. 87

3. Which of the following wildcard masks is most useful for matching all IP packets in subnet 10.1.128.0, mask 255.255.255.0?

   a. 0.0.0.0

   b. 0.0.0.31

   c. 0.0.0.240

   d. 0.0.0.255

   e. 0.0.15.0

   f. 0.0.248.255

4. Which of the following wildcard masks is most useful for matching all IP packets in subnet 10.1.128.0, mask 255.255.240.0?

   a. 0.0.0.0

   b. 0.0.0.31

   c. 0.0.0.240

   d. 0.0.0.255

   e. 0.0.15.255

   f. 0.0.248.255

5. ACL 1 has three statements, in the following order, with address and wildcard mask values as follows: 1.0.0.0 0.255.255.255, 1.1.0.0 0.0.255.255, and 1.1.1.0 0.0.0.255. If a router tried to match a packet sourced from IP address 1.1.1.1 using this ACL, which ACL statement does a router consider the packet to have matched?

   a. First

   b. Second

   c. Third

   d. Implied deny at the end of the ACL

6. Which of the following **access-list** commands, taken from a router's running-config file, match all packets sent from hosts in subnet 172.16.4.0/23?

   a. **access-list 1 permit 172.16.0.5 0.0.255.0**

   b. **access-list 1 permit 172.16.4.0 0.0.1.255**

   c. **access-list 1 permit 172.16.5.0**

   d. **access-list 1 permit 172.16.5.0 0.0.0.127**

Foundation Topics

IPv4 Access Control List Basics

IPv4 **access control lists (IP ACLs)** allow network engineers to identify different types of packets. To do so, the ACL configuration lists values that the router can see in the IP, TCP, UDP, and other headers. For example, an ACL can match packets whose source IP address is 1.1.1.1, or packets whose destination IP address is some address in subnet 10.1.1.0/24, or packets with a destination port of TCP port 23 (Telnet).

IPv4 ACLs perform many functions in Cisco routers, with the most common use as a packet filter. Engineers can enable ACLs on a router so that the ACL sits in the forwarding path of packets as they pass through the router. After enabling it, the router considers whether each IP packet will either be discarded or allowed to continue as if the ACL did not exist.

However, ACLs can be used for many other IOS features as well. As an example, ACLs can be used to match packets for applying quality of service (QoS) features. QoS allows a router to give some packets better service and other packets worse service. For example, packets that hold digitized voice need to have very low delay, so ACLs can match voice packets, with QoS logic in turn forwarding voice packets more quickly than data packets.

This first section introduces IP ACLs as used for packet filtering. To better understand ACLs, the text first discusses the implications of the choice of the location and direction of the enabled ACL. Following that, the text examines the packet matching logic allowed in the configuration commands. The final section summarizes the actions to take when filtering packets: to deny (discard) the packet or permit the packet to continue along its original path.

ACL Location and Direction

Cisco routers can apply ACL logic to packets at the point at which the IP packets enter an interface, or the point at which they exit an interface. In other words, the ACL can be applied inbound to the router, before the router makes its forwarding (routing) decision, or outbound, after the router makes its forwarding decision and has determined the exit interface to use.

The arrows in Figure 6-1 show where you could filter packets flowing left to right in the topology. For example, imagine that you wanted to allow packets sent by host A to server S1, but to discard packets sent by host B to server S1. Each arrowed line represents a location and direction at which a router could apply an ACL, filtering the packets sent by hosts A and B.

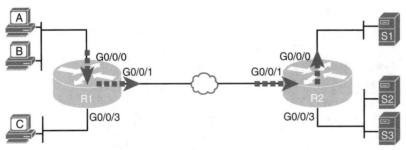

Figure 6-1 *Locations to Filter Packets from Hosts A and B Going Toward Server S1*

Answers to the "Do I Know This Already?" quiz:

1 A, C **2** A, D **3** D **4** E **5** A **6** B

The four arrowed lines in the figure point out the location and direction for the router interfaces used to forward the packet from host B to server S1. In this particular example, those interfaces and direction are inbound on R1's G0/0/0 interface, outbound on R1's G0/0/1 interface, inbound on R2's G0/0/1 interface, and outbound on R2's G0/0/0 interface.

To filter a packet, the ACL must be in the path that the packet travels. For example, if you enabled an ACL on R2's G0/0/3 interface, in either direction, that ACL could not possibly filter the packet sent from host B to server S1, because R2's G0/0/3 interface is not part of the route from host B to server S1. To summarize the logic:

> To filter a packet with an ACL, identify the inbound and outbound interfaces that the packet uses when passing through the router, and enable the ACL on one of those interfaces in that same direction.

When enabled, the router then processes every inbound or outbound IP packet using that ACL. For example, if enabled on R1 for packets inbound on interface G0/0/0, R1 would compare every inbound IP packet on G0/0/0 to the ACL to decide that packet's fate: to continue unchanged or to be discarded.

> **NOTE**   This book shows figures and examples of IP ACLs on routers. Multilayer switches configured to router IP packets also support IP ACLs using the same concepts and configuration.

Matching Packets

When you think about the location and direction for an ACL, you must already be thinking about what packets you plan to filter (discard) and which ones you want to allow through. To tell the router those same ideas, you must configure the router with an IP ACL that matches packets. *Matching packets* refers to how to configure the ACL commands to look at each packet, listing how to identify which packets should be discarded and which should be allowed through.

Each IP ACL consists of one or more configuration commands, with each command listing details about values to look for inside a packet's headers. Generally, an ACL command uses logic like "look for these values in the packet header, and if found, discard the packet." (The action could instead be to allow the packet rather than discard.) Specifically, the ACL looks for header fields you should already know well, including the source and destination IP addresses, plus TCP and UDP port numbers.

For example, consider an example with Figure 6-2, in which you want to allow packets from host A to server S1, but to discard packets from host B going to that same server. The hosts all now have IP addresses, and the figure shows pseudocode for an ACL on R2. Figure 6-2 also shows the chosen location to enable the ACL: inbound on R2's G0/0/1 interface.

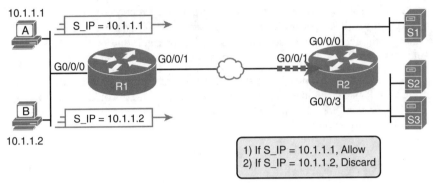

Figure 6-2   *Pseudocode to Demonstrate ACL Command-Matching Logic*

Figure 6-2 shows a two-line ACL in a rectangle at the bottom, with simple matching logic: both statements just look to match the source IP address in the packet. When enabled, R2 looks at every inbound IP packet on that interface and compares each packet to those two ACL commands. Packets sent by host A (source IP address 10.1.1.1) are allowed through, and those sourced by host B (source IP address 10.1.1.2) are discarded.

Taking Action When a Match Occurs

When IP ACLs are used to filter packets, only one of two actions can be chosen. The configuration commands use the keywords **deny** and **permit**, and they mean (respectively) to discard the packet or to allow it to keep going as if the ACL did not exist.

This book focuses on using ACLs to filter packets, but IOS uses ACLs for many more features. Those features typically use the same matching logic. However, in other cases, the **deny** or **permit** keywords imply some other action.

Types of IP ACLs

Cisco IOS has supported IP ACLs since the early days of Cisco routers. Beginning with the original standard numbered IP ACLs in the early days of IOS, which could enable the logic shown earlier around Figure 6-2, Cisco has added many ACL features, including the following:

- Standard numbered ACLs (1–99)

- Extended numbered ACLs (100–199)

- Additional ACL numbers (1300–1999 standard, 2000–2699 extended)

- Named ACLs

- Improved editing with sequence numbers

This chapter focuses solely on standard numbered IP ACLs, while the next chapter discusses the other three primary categories of IP ACLs. Briefly, IP ACLs will be either numbered or named in that the configuration identifies the ACL either using a number or a name. ACLs will also be either standard or extended, with extended ACLs having much more robust abilities in matching packets. Figure 6-3 summarizes the big ideas related to categories of IP ACLs.

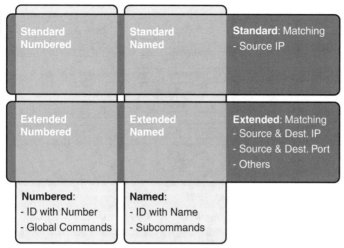

Figure 6-3 *Comparisons of IP ACL Types*

Standard Numbered IPv4 ACLs

The title of this section serves as a great introduction, if you can decode what Cisco means by each specific word. This section is about a type of Cisco filter (*ACL*) that matches only the source IP address of the packet (*standard*), is configured to identify the ACL using numbers rather than names (*numbered*), and looks at IPv4 packets.

This section first examines the idea that one ACL contains a list of commands, each containing matching and action logic. Following that, the text closely looks at how to match the source IP address field in the packet header, including the syntax of the commands. This section ends with a complete look at the configuration and verification commands to implement standard ACLs.

List Logic with IP ACLs

A single ACL is both a single entity and, at the same time, a list of one or more configuration commands. As a single entity, the configuration enables the entire ACL on an interface, in a specific direction, as shown earlier in Figure 6-1. As a list of commands, each command has different matching logic that the router must apply to each packet when filtering using that ACL.

When doing ACL processing, the router processes the packet, compared to the ACL, as follows:

ACLs use first-match logic. Once a packet matches one line in the ACL, the router takes the action listed in that line of the ACL and stops looking further in the ACL.

To see exactly what that means, consider the example built around Figure 6-4. The figure shows a sample ACL 1 with three lines of pseudocode. This example applies ACL 1 on R2's G0/0/1 interface, inbound (the same location as in Figure 6-2).

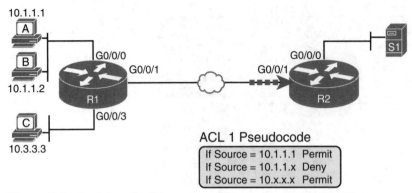

Figure 6-4   *Backdrop for Discussion of List Process with IP ACLs*

Consider the first-match ACL logic for a packet sent by host A to server S1. The source IP address will be 10.1.1.1 and routed so that it enters R2's G0/0/1 interface, driving R2's ACL 1 logic. R2 compares this packet to the ACL, matching the first item in the list with a permit action. This packet should be allowed through, as shown in Figure 6-5, on the left.

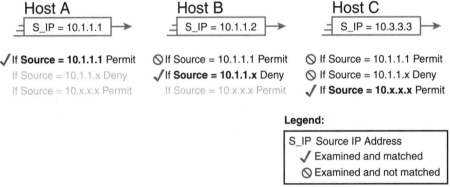

Figure 6-5   *ACL Items Compared for Packets from Hosts A, B, and C in Figure 6-4*

Next, consider a packet sent by host B, source IP address 10.1.1.2. When the packet enters R2's G0/0/1 interface, R2 compares the packet to ACL 1's first statement and does not make a match (10.1.1.1 is not equal to 10.1.1.2). R2 then moves to the second statement, which requires some clarification. The ACL pseudocode, back in Figure 6-4, shows 10.1.1.x, which is meant to be shorthand that any value can exist in the last octet. Comparing only the first three octets, R2 decides that this latest packet does have a source IP address that begins with the first three octets 10.1.1, so R2 considers that to be a match on the second statement. R2 takes the listed action (deny), discarding the packet. R2 also stops ACL processing on the packet, ignoring the third line in the ACL.

Finally, consider a packet sent by host C, again sent to server S1. The packet has source IP address 10.3.3.3, so when it enters R2's G0/0/1 interface and drives ACL processing on R2, R2 looks at the first command in ACL 1. R2 does not match the first ACL command (10.1.1.1 in the command is not equal to the packet's 10.3.3.3). R2 looks at the second command, compares the first three octets (10.1.1) to the packet source IP address (10.3.3), and still finds no match. R2 then looks at the third command. In this case, the wildcard means ignore the last three octets and just compare the first octet (10), so the packet matches. R2 then takes the listed action (permit), allowing the packet to keep going.

All Cisco IOS ACLs use this first-match logic: IP ACLs, IPv6 ACLs, standard or extended, named or numbered.

Finally, every ACL ends with *deny any* logic, the equivalent of an **access-list** *number* **deny any** command. It does not exist in the configuration, but if a router keeps searching the list, making no match by the end of the list, IOS considers the packet to have matched the implied deny any, with the router discarding the packet.

Matching Logic and Command Syntax

Standard numbered IP ACLs use the following global command:

```
access-list {1-99 | 1300-1999} {permit | deny} matching-parameters
```

Each standard numbered ACL has one or more **access-list** commands with the same number, any number from the ranges shown in the preceding line of syntax. One number is no better than the other. IOS refers to each line in an ACL as an **access control entry (ACE)**, but many engineers just call them ACL statements.

After the ACL number, the **access-list** global command lists the action (**permit** or **deny**) and then the matching logic. The next few pages focus on configuring the source address's matching parameters.

Matching the Exact IP Address

To match a specific source IP address, configure that IP address at the end of the command. For example, the previous example uses pseudocode for "permit if source = 10.1.1.1." The following command configures that logic with correct syntax using ACL number 1:

```
access-list 1 permit 10.1.1.1
```

For historical reasons, IOS (and IOS XE) support two alternative syntax options for standard ACLs to match a single address. You could use either of the following two options to configure the same logic as the previous command:

```
access-list 1 permit host 10.1.1.1
access-list 1 permit 10.1.1.1 0.0.0.0
```

The first of the alternate options uses a **host** keyword before the single address, with the other listing the address followed by a value called a **wildcard mask** (in this case, 0.0.0.0). Although IOS accepts both additional formats, it stores the command with the first syntax (the version with neither the **host** keyword nor 0.0.0.0 wildcard mask). (The text defines the wildcard mask and its use in the next topic.) Table 6-2 summarizes the options for easier study and review.

Table 6-2   Summary of Standard ACL Syntax Supported to Match One IP Address

	address **0.0.0.0**	**host** *address*	*address*
Standard ACLs	Yes	Yes	Yes*

*IOS stores the command with this syntax no matter the configuration style.

Matching a Subset of the Address with Wildcard Masks

You often need to match a range of IP addresses rather than a single one. Maybe you want to match all IP addresses in a subnet. Maybe you want to match all IP addresses in a range of subnets. Regardless, you want to check for more than one IP address in a range of addresses.

IOS allows standard ACLs to match a range of addresses using a tool called a *wildcard mask*. Note that this is not a subnet mask. The wildcard mask (which this book abbreviates as *WC mask*) gives the engineer a way to tell IOS to ignore parts of the address when making comparisons, essentially treating those parts as wildcards, as if they already matched.

You can think about WC masks in decimal and in binary, and both have their uses. To begin, think about WC masks in decimal, using these rules:

Decimal 0: The router must compare this octet as normal.

Decimal 255: The router ignores this octet, considering it to match already.

Keeping these two rules in mind, consider Figure 6-6, which demonstrates this logic using three different but popular WC masks: one that tells the router to ignore the last octet, one that tells the router to ignore the last two octets, and one that tells the router to ignore the last three octets.

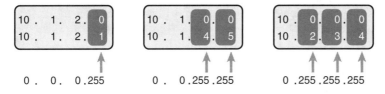

255 = Ignore

Figure 6-6   *Logic for WC Masks 0.0.0.255, 0.0.255.255, and 0.255.255.255*

All three examples in the boxes of Figure 6-6 show clearly different numbers. The WC mask causes IOS to compare only some of the octets, while ignoring other octets. All three examples result in a match, because each wildcard mask tells IOS to ignore some octets. The example on the left shows WC mask 0.0.0.255, which tells the router to treat the last octet as a wildcard, essentially ignoring that octet for the comparison. Similarly, the middle example shows WC mask 0.0.255.255, which tells the router to ignore the two octets on the right. The rightmost case shows WC mask 0.255.255.255, telling the router to ignore the last three octets when comparing values.

To see the WC mask in action, think back to the earlier examples related to Figures 6-4 and 6-5. The pseudocode ACL in those two figures used logic that can be created using a WC mask. As a reminder, the logic in the pseudocode ACL in those two figures included the following:

Line 1: Match and permit the packets with a source address of exactly 10.1.1.1.

Line 2: Match and deny the packets with source addresses with first three octets 10.1.1.

Line 3: Match and permit the packets with addresses with a first octet value of 10.

The **access-list** command matches a range of addresses by listing two parameters: the first number in the range plus a wildcard mask. As an example, Figure 6-7 shows the updated version of Figure 6-4, but with the completed, correct ACL syntax, including the WC masks. In particular, note the use of WC mask 0.0.0.255 in the second ACE, telling R2 to ignore the last octet of the number 10.1.1.0, and the WC mask 0.255.255.255 in the third ACE, telling R2 to ignore the last three octets in the value 10.0.0.0.

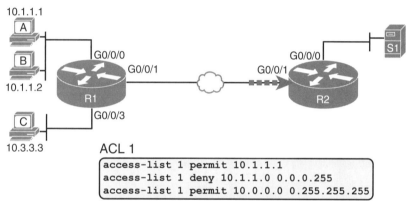

ACL 1
```
access-list 1 permit 10.1.1.1
access-list 1 deny 10.1.1.0 0.0.0.255
access-list 1 permit 10.0.0.0 0.255.255.255
```

Figure 6-7 *Syntactically Correct ACL Replaces Pseudocode from Figure 6-4*

The generic syntax of the command, **access-list** *number action source* [*wildcard-mask*], refers to the matching parameters as source and wildcard mask. When using a wildcard mask, the source value defines the first number in the range of addresses.

Binary Wildcard Masks

Wildcard masks, as dotted-decimal number (DDN) values, represent a 32-bit binary number. As a 32-bit number, the WC mask directs the router's logic bit-by-bit rather than octet-by-octet. In short, compare the two numbers bit-by-bit when the WC mask bit equals 0, but ignore the bits when the WC mask bit in the same relative position is a binary 1.

Thankfully, for CCNA study, and for most real-world applications, you can ignore the binary WC mask. Why? Well, we generally want to match a range of addresses that can be easily identified by a subnet number and mask, whether it be a real subnet or a summary route that groups subnets together. If you can describe the range of addresses with a subnet number and mask, you can find the numbers to use in your ACL with some simple decimal math, as discussed next.

NOTE If you really want to know the binary mask logic, take the two DDN numbers the ACL will compare (one from the **access-list** command and the other from the packet header) and convert both to binary. Then, also convert the WC mask to binary, so you now have three 32-bit numbers. Ignore the bit for any bits in which the wildcard mask bit is a 1, but for wildcard mask bits of 0, compare that bit in the two addresses. If all the bits you checked are equal, it's a match!

Finding the Right Wildcard Mask to Match a Subnet

To match a subnet with an ACL, you can use the following shortcut:

- Use the subnet number as the source value in the **access-list** command.

- Use a wildcard mask found by subtracting the subnet mask from 255.255.255.255.

For example, for subnet 172.16.8.0 255.255.252.0, use the subnet number (172.16.8.0) as the source parameter, and then do the following math to find the wildcard mask:

255.255.255.255
– 255.255.252.0
0. 0. 3.255

Continuing this example, a completed command for this same subnet would be as follows:

```
access-list 1 permit 172.16.8.0 0.0.3.255
```

The section "Practice Applying Standard IP ACLs" gives you a chance to practice matching subnets when configuring ACLs.

Matching Any/All Addresses

In some cases, you will want one ACL command to match any and all packets that reach that point in the ACL. First, you have to know the (simple) way to match all packets using the **any** keyword. More importantly, you need to think about when to match any and all packets.

First, to match any and all packets with an ACL command, just use the **any** keyword for the address. For example, to permit all packets:

```
access-list 1 permit any
```

So, when and where should you use such a command? Remember, all Cisco IP ACLs end with an implicit **deny any** concept at the end of each ACL. That is, if a router compares a packet to the ACL, and the packet matches none of the configured ACEs, the router discards the packet. Want to override that default behavior? Configure a **permit any** at the end of the ACL.

You might also want to explicitly configure a command to deny all traffic (for example, **access-list 1 deny any**) at the end of an ACL. Why, when the same logic already sits at the end of the ACL anyway? Well, the ACL **show** commands list counters for the number of packets matched by each command in the ACL, but there is no counter for that implicit **deny any** concept at the end of the ACL. So, configure an explicit deny any if you want to see counters for how many packets are matched by the logic at the end of the ACL.

Implementing Standard IP ACLs

This chapter has already introduced all the configuration steps in bits and pieces. This section summarizes those pieces as a configuration process. The process also refers to the **access-list** command, whose generic syntax is repeated here for reference:

```
access-list access-list-number {deny | permit} source [source-wildcard]
```

Step 1. Plan the location (router and interface) and direction (in or out) on that interface:

  a. Standard ACLs should be placed near the packet's destination so that they do not unintentionally discard packets that should not be discarded.

  b. Because standard ACLs can only match a packet's source IP address, identify the source IP addresses of packets as they go in the direction that the ACL is examining.

Step 2. Configure one or more **access-list** global configuration commands to create the ACL, keeping the following in mind:

  a. The list is searched sequentially, using first-match logic.

  b. The default action, if a packet does not match any of the **access-list** commands, is to **deny** (discard) the packet.

Step 3. Enable the ACL on the chosen router interface, in the correct direction, using the **ip access-group** *number* {**in** | **out**} interface subcommand.

Note that the **ip access-group** interface subcommand works on interfaces enabled for IP routing. That is, the interface has an IP address configured. The examples in this chapter use physical interfaces on routers; however, in other cases, a router or multilayer switch enables IP routing on subinterfaces or VLAN interfaces. In those cases, you can enable an ACL on those interfaces. For a reminder of some of the various types of interfaces a router or switch might enable IP, refer to *CCNA 200-301 Official Cert Guide, Volume 1*, Second Edition, Chapter 18, "IP Routing in the LAN."

Standard Numbered ACL Scenario 1

The first ACL scenario shows the configuration for the same requirements demonstrated with Figures 6-4 and 6-5. Restated, the requirements for this ACL are as follows:

  1. Enable the ACL inbound on router R2's G0/0/1 interface.

  2. Permit packets coming from host A.

  3. Deny packets coming from other hosts in host A's subnet.

  4. Permit packets coming from any other address in Class A network 10.0.0.0.

  5. The original example made no comment about what to do by default, so simply deny all other traffic.

Example 6-1 shows a completed correct configuration, starting with the configuration process, followed by output from the **show running-config** command.

Example 6-1 *Standard Numbered ACL Example 1 Configuration*

```
R2# configure terminal
Enter configuration commands, one per line. End with CNTL/Z.
R2(config)# access-list 1 permit 10.1.1.1
R2(config)# access-list 1 deny 10.1.1.0 0.0.0.255
R2(config)# access-list 1 permit 10.0.0.0 0.255.255.255
R2(config)# interface gigabitethernet 0/0/1
R2(config-if)# ip access-group 1 in
R2(config-if)# ^Z
R2# show running-config
! Lines omitted for brevity

access-list 1 permit 10.1.1.1
access-list 1 deny 10.1.1.0 0.0.0.255
access-list 1 permit 10.0.0.0 0.255.255.255
```

First, pay close attention to the configuration process at the top of Example 6-1. Note that the **access-list** command does not change the command prompt from the global configuration mode prompt because the **access-list** command is a global configuration command. Then, compare that to the output of the **show running-config** command: the details are identical to the commands added in configuration mode. Finally, make sure to note the **ip access-group 1 in** command, under R2's G0/0/1 interface, which enables the ACL logic (both location and direction).

Example 6-2 lists some output from router R2 that shows information about this ACL. The **show ip access-lists** command lists details about IPv4 ACLs only, while the **show access-lists** command lists details about IPv4 ACLs plus any other types of ACLs that are currently configured—for example, IPv6 ACLs. These commands list the same output in the same format.

Example 6-2 *ACL* show *Commands on R2*

```
R2# show ip access-lists
Standard IP access list 1
    10 permit 10.1.1.1 (107 matches)
    20 deny    10.1.1.0, wildcard bits 0.0.0.255 (4 matches)
    30 permit 10.0.0.0, wildcard bits 0.255.255.255 (10 matches)
R2# show access-lists
Standard IP access list 1
    10 permit 10.1.1.1 (107 matches)
    20 deny    10.1.1.0, wildcard bits 0.0.0.255 (4 matches)
    30 permit 10.0.0.0, wildcard bits 0.255.255.255 (10 matches)
R2# show ip interface g0/0/1
GigabitEthernet0/0/1 is up, line protocol is up
  Internet address is 10.1.2.2/24
  Broadcast address is 255.255.255.255
```

```
  Address determined by non-volatile memory
  MTU is 1500 bytes
  Helper address is not set
  Directed broadcast forwarding is disabled
  Multicast reserved groups joined: 224.0.0.9
  Outgoing access list is not set
  Inbound access list is 1
! Lines omitted for brevity
```

The output of both the **show ip access-lists** and **show access-lists** commands show two items of note. The first line of output notes the type (standard) and the number. If more than one ACL existed, you would see multiple stanzas of output, one per ACL, each with a heading line like this one. Next, these commands list packet counts for the number of packets that the router has matched with each ACE. For example, 107 packets so far have matched the ACE. (When troubleshooting, you can use the **clear ip access-list counters** command to reset all these counters to 0.)

The end of Example 6-2 also lists the **show ip interface** command output. This command lists, among many other items, the number or name of any IP ACL enabled on the interface per the **ip access-group** interface subcommand.

Standard Numbered ACL Scenario 2

For the second ACL scenario, use Figure 6-8, and imagine your boss gives you some requirements hurriedly in the hall. At first, he tells you he wants to filter packets going from the servers on the right toward the clients on the left. Then, he says he wants you to allow access for hosts A, B, and other hosts in their same subnet to server S1, but deny access to that server to the hosts in host C's subnet. Then, he tells you that, additionally, hosts in host A's subnet should be denied access to server S2, but hosts in host C's subnet should be allowed access to server S2—all by filtering packets going right to left only. He then tells you to put the ACL inbound on R2's G0/0/0 interface.

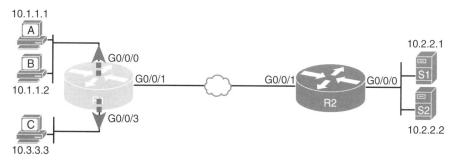

Figure 6-8 *Standard Numbered ACL Scenario 2*

If you cull through all the boss's comments, the requirements might be reduced to the following:

1. Enable the ACL inbound on R2's G0/0/0 interface.

2. Permit packets from server S1 going to hosts in A's subnet.

3. Deny packets from server S1 going to hosts in C's subnet.

4. Permit packets from server S2 going to hosts in C's subnet.

5. Deny packets from server S2 going to hosts in A's subnet.

6. (There was no comment about what to do by default; use the implied **deny any** default.)

As it turns out, you cannot do everything your boss asked with a standard ACL. For example, consider the obvious command for requirement number 2: **access-list 2 permit 10.2.2.1**. That permits all traffic whose source IP is 10.2.2.1 (server S1). The next requirement asks you to filter (deny) packets sourced from that same IP address! Even if you added another command that checked for source IP address 10.2.2.1, the router would never get to it because routers use first-match logic when searching the ACL. You cannot check both the destination and source IP address because standard ACLs cannot check the destination IP address.

To solve this problem, you should get a new boss! No, seriously, you should rethink the problem and change the rules. In real life, you would probably use an extended ACL instead, which lets you check both the source and destination IP address.

For the sake of practicing another standard ACL, imagine your boss lets you change the requirements. The logic will still consider packets moving right to left in the figure; however, the design uses two outbound ACLs, both on router R1. Each ACL will permit traffic from a single server to be forwarded onto that connected LAN, with the following modified requirements:

1. Using an outbound ACL on R1's G0/0/0 interface, permit packets from server S1, and deny all other packets.

2. Using an outbound ACL on R1's G0/0/3 interface, permit packets from server S2, and deny all other packets.

Example 6-3 shows the configuration that completes these requirements.

Example 6-3 *Alternative Configuration in Router R1*

```
access-list 2 remark This ACL permits server S1 traffic to host A's subnet
access-list 2 permit 10.2.2.1
!
access-list 3 remark This ACL permits server S2 traffic to host C's subnet
access-list 3 permit 10.2.2.2
!
interface G0/0/0
 ip access-group 2 out
!
interface G0/0/3
 ip access-group 3 out
```

As highlighted in the example, the solution with ACL number 2 permits all traffic from server S1, with that logic enabled for packets exiting R1's G0/0/0 interface. All other traffic will be discarded because of the implied **deny any** at the end of the ACL. In addition, ACL 3 permits traffic from server S2, which is then permitted to exit R1's G0/0/3 interface.

Finally, make sure to notice the **access-list remark** parameter, which allows you to leave text documentation that stays with the ACL. You can add as many remarks as you like into a single ACL.

NOTE   Routers treat self-created packets differently than packets routed (received and then forwarded) by the router. A router applies any outbound ACL logic to routed packets but bypasses the ACL for self-created packets. Examples of those packets include routing protocol messages and packets sent by the **ping** and **traceroute** commands on that router.

Troubleshooting and Verification Tips

Troubleshooting IPv4 ACLs requires some attention to detail. In particular, you have to be ready to look at the address and wildcard mask and confidently predict the addresses matched by those two combined parameters. The upcoming practice problems a little later in this chapter can help prepare you for that part of the work. But a few other tips can help you verify and troubleshoot ACL problems on the exams as well.

First, you can tell whether the router matches packets with a couple of tools. Example 6-2 already showed that IOS keeps statistics about the packets matched by each line of an ACL. In addition, if you add the **log** keyword to the end of an **access-list** command, IOS then issues log messages with occasional statistics about matches of that particular line of the ACL. Both the statistics and the log messages can be helpful in deciding which line in the ACL is being matched by a packet.

For example, Example 6-4 shows an updated ACL 2 from Example 6-3, with the **log** keyword added. The bottom of the example then shows a typical log message, showing the resulting match based on a packet with source IP address 10.2.2.1 (as matched with the ACL) to destination address 10.1.1.1.

Example 6-4   *Creating Log Messages for ACL Statistics*

```
R1# show running-config
! lines removed for brevity
access-list 2 remark This ACL permits server S1 traffic to host A's subnet
access-list 2 permit 10.2.2.1 log
!
interface G0/0/0
 ip access-group 2 out

R1#
Feb 4 18:30:24.082: %SEC-6-IPACCESSLOGNP: list 2 permitted 0 10.2.2.1 -> 10.1.1.1,
1 packet
```

Also, when you troubleshoot an ACL for the first time, begin by thinking about both the interface on which the ACL is enabled and the direction of packet flow. Ignore the matching logic at first. Sometimes, the matching logic is perfect—but the ACL has been enabled on the wrong interface, or for the wrong direction, to match the packets as configured for the ACL.

For example, Figure 6-9 repeats the same ACL shown earlier in Figure 6-7. The first line of that ACL matches the specific host address 10.1.1.1. If that ACL exists on router R2, placing that ACL as an inbound ACL on R2's G0/0/1 interface can work because packets sent by host 10.1.1.1—on the left side of the figure—can enter R2's G0/0/1 interface. However, if R2 enables ACL 1 on its G0/0/0 interface, for inbound packets, the ACL will never match a packet with source IP address 10.1.1.1 because packets sent by host 10.1.1.1 will never enter that interface. Packets sent by 10.1.1.1 will exit R2's G0/0/0 interface, but never enter it, just because of the network topology.

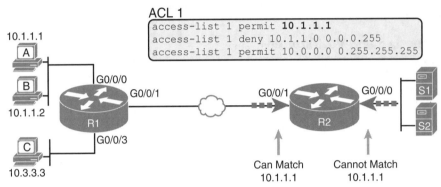

Figure 6-9   *Example of Checking the Interface and Direction for an ACL*

Practice Applying Standard IP ACLs

Some CCNA topics, like ACLs, simply require more drills and practice than others. ACLs require you to think of parameters to match ranges of numbers, and that of course requires some use of math and some use of processes.

This section provides some practice problems and tips, from two perspectives. First, this section asks you to build one-line standard ACLs to match some packets. Second, this section asks you to interpret existing ACL commands to describe what packets the ACL will match. Both skills are useful for the exam.

Practice Building access-list Commands

In this section, practice getting comfortable with the syntax of the **access-list** command, particularly with choosing the correct matching logic. These skills will be helpful when reading about extended and named ACLs in the next chapter.

First, the following list summarizes some important tips to consider when choosing matching parameters to any **access-list** command:

- To match a specific address, just list the address.

- To match any and all addresses, use the **any** keyword.

- To match based only on the first one, two, or three octets of an address, use the 0.255.255.255, 0.0.255.255, and 0.0.0.255 WC masks, respectively. Also, make the source (address) parameter have 0s in the wildcard octets (those octets with 255 in the wildcard mask).

■ To match a subnet, use the subnet ID as the source, and find the WC mask by subtracting the DDN subnet mask from 255.255.255.255.

Table 6-3 lists the criteria for several practice problems. Your job: Create a standard ACL ACE that matches the packets. The answers are listed in the section "Answers to Earlier Practice Problems," later in this chapter.

Table 6-3   Building One-Line Standard ACLs: Practice

Problem	Criteria
1	Packets from 172.16.5.4
2	Packets from hosts with 192.168.6 as the first three octets
3	Packets from hosts with 192.168 as the first two octets
4	Packets from any host
5	Packets from subnet 10.1.200.0/21
6	Packets from subnet 10.1.200.0/27
7	Packets from subnet 172.20.112.0/23
8	Packets from subnet 172.20.112.0/26
9	Packets from subnet 192.168.9.64/28
10	Packets from subnet 192.168.9.64/30

Reverse Engineering from ACL to Address Range

In some cases, you may not be creating your own ACL. Instead, you may need to interpret some existing **access-list** commands. To answer these types of questions on the exams, you need to determine the range of IP addresses matched by a particular address/wildcard mask combination in each ACL statement.

Under certain assumptions that are reasonable for CCNA certifications, calculating the range of addresses matched by an ACL can be relatively simple. Basically, the range of addresses begins with the source parameter configured in the ACL command. The range of addresses ends with the sum of the source parameter and the wildcard mask. That's it.

For example, with the command **access-list 1 permit 172.16.200.0 0.0.7.255**, the low end of the range is simply 172.16.200.0, taken directly from the command itself. Then, to find the high end of the range, just add this number to the WC mask, as follows:

172.16.200.0
+ 0. 0.   7.255
172.16.207.255

For this last bit of practice, look at the existing **access-list** commands in Table 6-4. In each case, make a notation about the exact IP address, or range of IP addresses, matched by the command.

Table 6-4   Finding IP Addresses/Ranges Matching by Existing ACLs

Problem	Commands for Which to Predict the Source Address Range
1	access-list 1 permit 10.7.6.5
2	access-list 2 permit 192.168.4.0 0.0.0.127
3	access-list 3 permit 192.168.6.0 0.0.0.31
4	access-list 4 permit 172.30.96.0 0.0.3.255
5	access-list 5 permit 172.30.96.0 0.0.0.63
6	access-list 6 permit 10.1.192.0 0.0.0.31
7	access-list 7 permit 10.1.192.0 0.0.1.255
8	access-list 8 permit 10.1.192.0 0.0.63.255

Interestingly, IOS lets the CLI user type an **access-list** command in configuration mode, and IOS will potentially change the source parameter before placing the command into the running-config file. This process of just finding the range of addresses matched by the **access-list** command expects that the **access-list** command came from the router, so that any such changes were complete.

The change IOS can make with an **access-list** command is to convert to 0 any octet of an address for which the wildcard mask's octet is 255. For example, with a wildcard mask of 0.0.255.255, IOS ignores the last two octets. IOS expects the source parameter to end with two 0s. If not, IOS still accepts the **access-list** command, but IOS changes the last two octets of the address to 0s. Example 6-5 shows an example, where the configuration shows source 10.1.1.1, but wildcard mask 0.0.255.255.

Example 6-5   *IOS Changing the Address Field in an* **access-list** *Command*

```
R2# configure terminal
Enter configuration commands, one per line. End with CNTL/Z.
R2(config)# access-list 21 permit 10.1.1.1 0.0.255.255
R2(config)# ^Z
R2#
R2# show ip access-lists
Standard IP access list 21
    10 permit 10.1.0.0, wildcard bits 0.0.255.255
```

The math to find the range of addresses relies on whether the command is fully correct or whether IOS has already set these address octets to 0, as shown in the example.

NOTE   The most useful WC masks, in binary, do not interleave 0s and 1s. This book assumes the use of only these types of WC masks. However, Cisco IOS allows WC masks that interleave 0s and 1s, but using these WC masks breaks the simple method of calculating the range of addresses. As you progress through to CCIE studies, be ready to dig deeper to learn how to determine what an ACL matches.

Chapter Review

One key to doing well on the exams is to perform repetitive spaced review sessions. Review this chapter's material using either the tools in the book or interactive tools for the same material found on the book's companion website. Refer to the "Your Study Plan" element for more details. Table 6-5 outlines the key review elements and where you can find them. To better track your study progress, record when you completed these activities in the second column.

Table 6-5   Chapter Review Tracking

Review Element	Review Date(s)	Resource Used
Review key topics		Book, website
Review key terms		Book, website
Answer DIKTA questions		Book, PTP
Review command tables		Book

Review All the Key Topics

Table 6-6   Key Topics for Chapter 6

Key Topic Element	Description	Page Number
Paragraph	Summary of the general rule of the location and direction for an ACL	117
Figure 6-3	Summary of four main categories of IPv4 ACLs in Cisco IOS	119
Paragraph	Summary of first-match logic used by all ACLs	119
Table 6-2	Standard ACL configuration options to match a single IP address	122
List	Wildcard mask logic for decimals 0 and 255	122
List	Wildcard mask logic to match a subnet	124
List	Steps to plan and implement a standard IP ACL	125
List	Tips for creating matching logic for the source address field in the **access-list** command	130

Key Terms You Should Know

access control entry, access control list, standard access list, wildcard mask

Additional Practice for This Chapter's Processes

For additional practice with analyzing subnets, you may do the same set of practice problems using your choice of tools:

Application: Use the two ACL practice exercise applications listed on the companion website.

PDF: Alternatively, practice the same problems found in these apps using online Appendix E, "Practice for Chapter 6: Basic IPv4 Access Control Lists."

Command References

Tables 6-7 and 6-8 list configuration and verification commands used in this chapter. As an easy review exercise, cover the left column in a table, read the right column, and try to recall the command without looking. Then repeat the exercise, covering the right column, and try to recall what the command does.

Table 6-7   Chapter 6 Configuration Command Reference

Command	Description
access-list *access-list-number* {**deny** | **permit**} *source* [*source-wildcard*] [**log**]	Global command for standard numbered access lists. Use a number between 1 and 99 or 1300 and 1999, inclusive.
access-list *access-list-number* **remark** *text*	Command that defines a remark to help you remember what the ACL is supposed to do.
ip access-group *number* {**in** | **out**}	Interface subcommand to enable access lists.

Table 6-8   Chapter 6 EXEC Command Reference

Command	Description
show ip interface [*type number*]	Includes a reference to the access lists enabled on the interface
show access-lists [*access-list-number* | *access-list-name*]	Shows details of configured access lists for all protocols
show ip access-lists [*access-list-number* | *access-list-name*]	Shows IP access lists with identical output format as **show access-lists** for IP ACLs
clear ip access-list counters	Resets the statistical counter of ACE matches for all IPv4 ACLs

Answers to Earlier Practice Problems

Table 6-9 lists the answers to the problems listed earlier in Table 6-3.

Table 6-9   Building One-Line Standard ACLs: Answers

Problem	Answers
1	access-list 1 permit 172.16.5.4
2	access-list 2 permit 192.168.6.0 0.0.0.255
3	access-list 3 permit 192.168.0.0 0.0.255.255
4	access-list 4 permit any
5	access-list 5 permit 10.1.200.0 0.0.7.255
6	access-list 6 permit 10.1.200.0 0.0.0.31
7	access-list 7 permit 172.20.112.0 0.0.1.255
8	access-list 8 permit 172.20.112.0 0.0.0.63
9	access-list 9 permit 192.168.9.64 0.0.0.15
10	access-list 10 permit 192.168.9.64 0.0.0.3

Table 6-10 lists the answers to the problems listed earlier in Table 6-4.

Table 6-10   Address Ranges for Problems in Table 6-4: Answers

Problem	Address Range
1	One address: 10.7.6.5
2	192.168.4.0–192.168.4.127
3	192.168.6.0–192.168.6.31
4	172.30.96.0–172.30.99.255
5	172.30.96.0–172.30.96.63
6	10.1.192.0–10.1.192.31
7	10.1.192.0–10.1.193.255
8	10.1.192.0–10.1.255.255

6

Named and Extended IP ACLs

This chapter covers the following exam topics:

5.0 Security Fundamentals

    5.6 Configure and verify access control lists

The previous chapter introduced basic IP ACL concepts and configuration using numbered standard IP ACLs. While understanding numbered standard IP ACLs is useful and important, most networks need the greater matching abilities of extended ACLs. Extended ACLs allow you to match various header fields in each line of the ACL (each access control entry, or ACE), making them more powerful.

Additionally, most networks use named ACLs instead of numbered ones. Identifying ACLs using names makes it easy to add information in the name that reminds all as to the purpose of the ACL. Additionally, from the first introduction of named ACLs into IOS decades ago, named ACLs used ACL configuration mode, with **permit** and **deny** subcommands, making the configuration clearer and easier to change over time.

This chapter begins by discussing named ACLs, using only standard ACL examples for simplicity. That first section also shows how to edit named ACLs and why that capability improves on the older editing features for numbered ACLs. The second major section then examines extended ACLs in detail, using named extended ACLs for the most part.

"Do I Know This Already?" Quiz

Take the quiz (either here or use the PTP software) if you want to use the score to help you decide how much time to spend on this chapter. The letter answers are listed at the bottom of the page following the quiz. Appendix C, found both at the end of the book as well as on the companion website, includes both the answers and explanations. You can also find both answers and explanations in the PTP testing software.

Table 7-1 "Do I Know This Already?" Foundation Topics Section-to-Question Mapping

Foundation Topics Section	Questions
Named ACLs and ACL Editing	1, 2
Extended IP Access Control Lists	3–6

1. Which answer best compares named standard IP ACLs with numbered standard IP ACLs?

    a. Uses a name instead of a number, but with no other configuration changes

    b. Adds additional fields to match beyond standard numbered IP ACLs

    c. Enables you to configure matching parameters and permit/deny action in ACL mode

    d. Enables you to configure matching parameters and permit/deny action in interface mode

2. You just configured standard named ACL WAN_ACL with commands that did not use sequence numbers. Which command, if typed in ACL configuration mode for this ACL, would become the third ACE in the ACL?

   a. 15 permit 172.16.0.0 0.0.255.255

   b. permit 16 172.16.0.0 0.0.255.255

   c. 21 permit 172.16.0.0 0.0.255.255

   d. permit 29 172.16.0.0 0.0.255.255

3. Which answers list a field that cannot be matched by an extended IP ACL? (Choose two answers.)

   a. Protocol

   b. Source IP address

   c. Destination IP address

   d. TCP source port

   e. URL

   f. Filename for FTP transfers

4. Which **access-list** commands permit packets from host 10.1.1.1 to all web servers whose IP addresses begin with 172.16.5? (Choose two answers.)

   a. access-list 101 permit tcp host 10.1.1.1 172.16.5.0 0.0.0.255 eq www

   b. access-list 1951 permit ip host 10.1.1.1 172.16.5.0 0.0.0.255 eq www

   c. access-list 2523 permit ip host 10.1.1.1 eq www 172.16.5.0 0.0.0.255

   d. access-list 2523 permit tcp host 10.1.1.1 eq www 172.16.5.0 0.0.0.255

   e. access-list 2523 permit tcp host 10.1.1.1 172.16.5.0 0.0.0.255 eq www

5. Which of the following **access-list** commands permits packets going to any web client from all web servers whose IP addresses begin with 172.16.5?

   a. access-list 101 permit tcp host 10.1.1.1 172.16.5.0 0.0.0.255 eq www

   b. access-list 1951 permit ip host 10.1.1.1 172.16.5.0 0.0.0.255 eq www

   c. access-list 2523 permit tcp any eq www 172.16.5.0 0.0.0.255

   d. access-list 2523 permit tcp 172.16.5.0 0.0.0.255 eq www 172.16.5.0 0.0.0.255

   e. access-list 2523 permit tcp 172.16.5.0 0.0.0.255 eq www any

6. Consider the following output from a **show access-list** command. Which ACEs match packets from 10.22.33.99 to 10.33.22.22 destined to any SSH server?

```
ip access-list extended sample
   10 permit tcp 10.22.33.0 0.0.0.63 10.33.22.0 0.0.0.127 eq 22
   20 permit tcp 10.22.33.0 0.0.0.127 eq 24 10.33.22.0 0.0.0.63
   30 permit tcp 10.22.33.0 0.0.0.127 10.33.22.0 0.0.0.127 eq 22
   40 permit tcp 10.22.33.0 0.0.0.255 10.33.22.0 0.0.0.31 eq 24
```

   a. Line 10

   b. Line 20

   c. Line 30

   d. Line 40

Foundation Topics

Named ACLs and ACL Editing

From the earliest days of Cisco, IOS supported numbered ACLs. Over time, Cisco added support for **named access lists**. This section details how to configure and use named ACLs, along with one of the key features enabled by named ACLs: ACL editing.

Named IP Access Lists

Named IP ACLs have many similarities with numbered IP ACLs. They function as packet filters but other IOS features use them for matching packets and taking other actions. They can also match the same fields: standard numbered ACLs can match the same fields as a standard named ACL, and extended numbered ACLs can match the same fields as an extended named ACL.

Of course, there are differences between named and numbered ACLs. Named ACLs originally had three significant differences compared to numbered ACLs:

- Using names instead of numbers to identify the ACL, making it easier to remember the reason for the ACL

- Using ACL mode subcommands, not global commands, to define the action and matching parameters

- Using ACL editing features that allow the CLI user to delete individual lines from the ACL and insert new lines

You can easily learn named ACL configuration by just converting numbered ACLs to use the equivalent named ACL configuration. Figure 7-1 shows just such a conversion, using a simple three-line standard ACL number 1. To create the three **permit** subcommands for the named ACL, you copy parts of the three numbered ACL commands, beginning with the **permit** keyword.

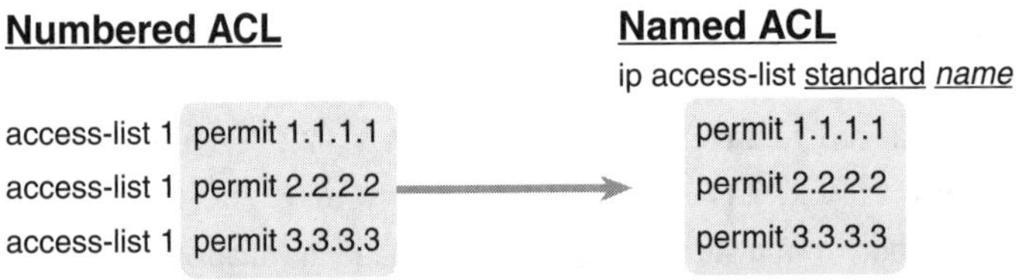

Numbered ACL

access-list 1   permit 1.1.1.1
access-list 1   permit 2.2.2.2 ⟶
access-list 1   permit 3.3.3.3

Named ACL

ip access-list standard *name*

permit 1.1.1.1
permit 2.2.2.2
permit 3.3.3.3

Figure 7-1 *Named ACL Versus Numbered ACL Configuration*

The **ip access-list {standard | extended}** *name* global configuration command creates the ACL, defines its type, and defines its name. It also moves the user to ACL configuration mode, as shown in upcoming Example 7-1. Once in ACL configuration mode, you configure **permit**, **deny**, and **remark** commands that mirror the syntax of numbered **access-list** global commands. If you're configuring a standard named ACL, these commands match the syntax of standard numbered ACLs; if you're configuring extended named ACLs, they match the syntax of extended numbered ACLs.

Answers to the "Do I Know This Already?" quiz:

1 C **2** C **3** E, F **4** A, E **5** E **6** C

Example 7-1 shows the configuration of a named standard ACL. Pay particular attention to the configuration mode prompts, which show standard named ACL configuration mode.

Example 7-1 *Named Access List Configuration*

```
R2# configure terminal
Enter configuration commands, one per line. End with CNTL/Z.
R2(config)# ip access-list standard Hannah
R2(config-std-nacl)# remark A sample ACL, originally five lines
R2(config-std-nacl)# permit 10.1.1.2
R2(config-std-nacl)# deny 10.1.1.1
R2(config-std-nacl)# deny 10.1.3.0 0.0.0.255
R2(config-std-nacl)# deny 10.1.2.0 0.0.0.255
R2(config-std-nacl)# permit any
R2(config-std-nacl)# interface GigabitEthernet0/0/1
R2(config-if)# ip access-group Hannah out
R2(config-if)# ^Z
R2#
```

Reviewing the configuration, the **ip access-list standard Hannah** command creates the ACL, naming it Hannah, and placing the user in ACL configuration mode. This command also defines the ACL as a standard ACL. Next, five different **permit** and **deny** statements define the matching logic and resulting action when matched.

The names in named ACLs must follow these rules:

- They must begin with an alphabetic character.

- They cannot use spaces and quotation marks.

- The names are case sensitive.

Example 7-2 shows the named ACL that results from the configuration in Example 7-1. Both the **show running-config** and **show access-lists** commands list the ACEs from Example 7-1 in the same order. The output also shows the automatically added sequence numbers on the **permit** and **deny** subcommands. When ignoring them during configuration, IOS adds sequence numbers, using 10 for the first ACE and incrementing by 10 for each successive ACE.

Example 7-2 *Named Access List Verification (IOS XE)*

```
R2# show running-config
Building configuration...

Current configuration:
! lines omitted for brevity
interface GigabitEthernet0/0/1
 ip access-group Hannah out
!
```

7

```
ip access-list standard Hannah
 10 permit 10.1.1.2
 20 deny   10.1.1.1
 30 deny   10.1.3.0 0.0.0.255
 40 deny   10.1.2.0 0.0.0.255
 50 permit any


R2# show access-list
Standard IP access list Hannah
    10 permit 10.1.1.2 (3 matches)
    20 deny   10.1.1.1 (5 matches)
    30 deny   10.1.3.0, wildcard bits 0.0.0.255 (10 matches)
    40 deny   10.1.2.0, wildcard bits 0.0.0.255 (15 matches)
    50 permit any (1256 matches)
```

NOTE   The **show access-lists** and **show ip access-lists** commands list sequence numbers on both IOS and IOS XE. The **show running-config** and **show startup-config** commands reveal the sequence numbers only in IOS XE but not in IOS. The output in Example 7-2 comes from a router running IOS XE.

For both exam preparation and real networking jobs, prepare so that you understand both numbered and named ACL syntax. Given a choice, most network engineers choose to use named ACLs. However, you may still find numbered ACLs used in production routers in enterprises, and the CCNA exam may ask about both styles. As shown in Figure 7-1, when you see a numbered ACL, you can mentally create the equivalent named ACL's subcommands by removing the **access-list** *number* prefix in the numbered global commands.

Editing ACLs

For CCNA exam preparation, you need to know some of the intricacies of ACL editing with both the old global commands and newer ACL mode commands. This section starts with named ACLs using ACL mode. Following that, the text describes the differences compared to numbered ACLs and some minor differences when using IOS versus IOS XE.

Editing Named ACLs

When Cisco created ACL mode and named ACLs, they created the ability to add and remove single ACEs from an ACL easily. IOS supports deleting individual ACEs, adding new ACEs to the end of the ACL, and even adding ACEs anywhere in the ACL using **ACL sequence numbers**.

To delete one ACE, you first get into ACL configuration mode using the **ip access-list** {**standard** | **extended**} *name* global command. For any existing ACE, you have two options to delete specific subcommands:

- Repeat the entire **permit, deny,** or **remark** ACL subcommand without a line number but preceded with the **no** command.

- Use the **no** *sequence-number* command, without the rest of the command, to delete the ACE that uses the listed sequence number.

Example 7-3 shows an example based on the five-line ACL Hannah in Example 7-2. One deletes the fourth ACE in the ACL with the full command after the **no** command, and the other deletes the second ACE with the **no 20** subcommand.

Example 7-3 *Demonstrating Both Methods to Remove an ACE from a Named ACL*

```
R2# configure terminal
Enter configuration commands, one per line. End with CNTL/Z.
R2(config)# ip access-list extended Hannah
R2(config-std-nacl)# no deny 10.1.2.0 0.0.0.255
R2(config-std-nacl)# no 20
R2(config-std-nacl)# ^Z
R2# show access-lists

Standard IP access list Hannah
    10 permit 10.1.1.2
    30 deny   10.1.3.0, wildcard bits 0.0.0.255
    50 permit any
```

The example also shows some important detail about the sequence numbers. The remaining ACEs have the same relative order as before—even though the sequence numbers of those lines did not change. The absolute values of the sequence numbers do not matter—only their relative values matter, as they confirm the order of the ACEs in the ACL. (The section, "Resequencing ACL Sequence Numbers" in Chapter 8, "Applied IP ACLs," discusses how to renumber ACL sequence numbers to clean up the numbering.)

To add one ACE to an ACL, again from ACL configuration mode, use these options:

- To insert the ACE between lines, configure the **permit** or **deny** command preceded by a sequence number. The number dictates the new ACE's location in the ACL.

- To insert the ACE at the end of the ACL, configure the **permit** or **deny** command without a sequence number, and IOS will automatically add a sequence number to place the ACE at the end of the ACL.

For example, imagine you wanted to add the two ACEs you deleted to the same ACL (Hannah). Example 7-4 shows the classic mistake of ignoring the sequence numbers, which results in the two new ACEs to the end of the ACL. As a reminder, ACL Hannah, at the end of Example 7-3, has three ACEs numbered 10, 30, and 50.

7

Example 7-4 *Demonstrating Adding ACEs to the End of the ACL*

```
R2# configure terminal
Enter configuration commands, one per line. End with CNTL/Z.
R2(config)# ip access-list extended Hannah
R2(config-std-nacl)# deny 10.1.2.0 0.0.0.255
R2(config-std-nacl)# deny 10.1.1.1
R2(config-std-nacl)# ^Z
R2# show access-lists

Standard IP access list Hannah
    10 permit 10.1.1.2
    30 deny   10.1.3.0, wildcard bits 0.0.0.255
    50 permit any
    60 deny 10.1.2.0 0.0.0.255
    70 deny 10.1.1.1
```

Forgetting about the sequence numbers—and adding ACEs to the end of the ACL—is seldom what you want to accomplish. In this case, adding those lines has no benefit. The two ACEs added in Example 7-4 reside behind the explicit **permit any** command at line 50, so the ACL would never use the two lines added in the example.

To reinsert the two ACEs in their original locations, as the second and fourth ACEs, use sequence numbers to begin the commands. Example 7-5 does that, again starting with the state at the end of Example 7-3, with ACEs 10, 30, and 50 in the ACL. Example 7-5 shows the two **deny** commands with sequence numbers 20 and 40.

Example 7-5 *Demonstrating Inserting ACEs in Different ACL Positions*

```
R2# configure terminal
Enter configuration commands, one per line. End with CNTL/Z.
R2(config)# ip access-list extended Hannah
R2(config-std-nacl)# 40 deny 10.1.2.0 0.0.0.255
R2(config-std-nacl)# 20 deny 10.1.1.1
R2(config-std-nacl)# ^Z
R2# show access-lists

Standard IP access list Hannah
    10 permit 10.1.1.2
    20 deny   10.1.1.1
    30 deny   10.1.3.0, wildcard bits 0.0.0.255
    40 deny   10.1.2.0, wildcard bits 0.0.0.255
    50 permit any
```

NOTE   While Example 7-5 used sequence numbers 20 and 40 for the configuration commands, any sequence number between the two existing ACEs would have worked. For instance, the **20 deny 10.1.1.1** ACL subcommand could have been either **11 deny 10.1.1.1** or **29 deny 10.1.1.1**, as the neighboring ACEs currently use sequence numbers 10 and 30.

Editing Numbered ACLs

In the history of IOS and its features, numbered ACLs came early in Cisco's history. They added named ACLs around the year 2000, so both styles have been around for a long time. When creating named ACLs, Cisco set about to improve some shortcomings with numbered ACLs—one of which was poor ACL editing features for numbered ACLs. The solution to that problem as it exists today is to allow the editing of numbered ACLs as if they were named ACLs by using ACL mode configuration commands.

To discuss numbered ACLs, Example 7-6 provides a sample standard ACL 8 equivalent to ACL Hannah in the previous examples. The configuration uses **access-list** global commands (note the command prompts). As usual with numbered ACLs, the commands do not identify it as a standard ACL; instead, the number (8) implies it is a standard ACL per the number ranges for standard ACLs (1–99, 1300–1999).

Example 7-6 *Numbered Access List Configuration with Global Commands*

```
R2# configure terminal
Enter configuration commands, one per line. End with CNTL/Z.
R2(config)# access-list 8 permit 10.1.1.2
R2(config)# access-list 8 deny 10.1.1.1
R2(config)# access-list 8 deny 10.1.3.0 0.0.0.255
R2(config)# access-list 8 deny 10.1.2.0 0.0.0.255
R2(config)# access-list 8 permit any
R2(config)# interface GigabitEthernet0/0/1
R2(config-if)# ip access-group 8 out
R2(config-if)# ^Z
R2#
```

Originally, most edits to a numbered ACL required deleting the ACL and reconfiguring the entire ACL. Those rules still apply today if you use the **access-list** global command:

- You cannot delete an individual ACE; any command that begins **no access-list** *acl-number* deletes the entire ACL.

- You cannot add an ACE to an existing ACL other than to the end of the ACL.

On the first point, the **no access-list** *number* global command deletes the entire ACL. But if you type that command with additional parameters, IOS ignores the additional parameters and deletes the whole ACL. For instance, if you issued the **no access-list 8 deny 10.1.1.1** global command for the ACL in Example 7-6, to attempt to delete the second line in ACL 8, IOS would instead treat the command as the **no access-list 8** command and delete ACL 8.

As for adding ACEs, the global **access-list** command has no option for sequence numbers. You could add lines to the end of the ACL by typing additional **access-list** global commands. To insert a line anywhere other than the end of the ACL, you delete the ACL and reconfigure it.

NOTE When you're editing any ACL, Cisco recommends disabling it from any interfaces before editing and re-enabling it after it is finished.

Today, you can overcome the old numbered ACL editing difficulties by instead editing them using the ACL mode. IOS allows you to configure and edit numbered ACLs using the ACL mode commands. As you have read over the last few pages, you can easily remove and add single ACEs using ACL mode. Example 7-7 shows an example using the following sequence:

Step 1.   The **show access-lists** command reveals the line numbers that IOS automatically added to each line in the numbered ACL as configured in Example 7-6.

Step 2.   Two **no** commands in ACL mode delete the second and fourth ACEs.

Step 3.   The **show access-lists** command confirms the single-ACE deletions.

Step 4.   The excerpt from the **show running-config** command reveals that even though the configuration process used ACL mode commands, IOS still stores the numbered ACL as **access-list** global commands.

Example 7-7   *Removing ACEs from a Numbered ACL (IOS)*

```
R2# show access-lists 8
Standard IP access list 8
    10 permit 10.1.1.2
    20 deny   10.1.1.1
    30 deny   10.1.3.0, wildcard bits 0.0.0.255
    40 deny   10.1.2.0, wildcard bits 0.0.0.255
    50 permit any
R2# configure terminal
Enter configuration commands, one per line. End with CNTL/Z.
R2(config)# ip access-list standard 8
R2(config-std-nacl)# no deny 10.1.2.0 0.0.0.255
R2(config-std-nacl)# no 20
R2(config-std-nacl)# ^Z
R2# show access-lists 8
Standard IP access list 8
    10 permit 10.1.1.2
    30 deny   10.1.3.0, wildcard bits 0.0.0.255
    50 permit any


R2# show running-config
! Lines omitted for brevity
access-list 8 permit 10.1.1.2
access-list 8 deny   10.1.3.0 0.0.0.255
access-list 8 permit any
```

Extended IP Access Control Lists

Extended IP ACLs work just like standard IP ACLs, except they can match multiple header fields in a single ACE. Just like standard IP ACLs, extended ACLs must be enabled on interfaces for a direction (in or out). IOS searches the list sequentially, using first-match logic, taking the permit or deny action per the first-matched ACE. The differences reduce to the variety and complexity of the matching logic.

One extended ACE (ACL statement) can examine multiple parts of the packet headers so that all matching parameters must match the packet for IOS to consider the ACE to match the packet. Each ACE must list matching parameters for a protocol, source address, and destination address, with additional optional fields. The powerful matching logic makes **extended access lists** more valuable and complex than standard IP ACLs. This major section of the chapter examines extended ACLs in some detail.

IOS and IOS XE support both numbered and named extended ACLs. The comparisons between numbered extended IP ACLs and named extended IP ACLs are the same as with standard ACLs.

Matching the Protocol, Source IP, and Destination IP

Like standard numbered IP ACLs, extended numbered IP ACLs also use the **access-list** global command. IOS identifies an ACL as extended by the number range, with extended ACL numbers being 100–199 or 2000–2699. Both support **permit** and **deny** actions. The big difference comes in the matching parameters, with the rest of this chapter and some of the next devoted to discussing extended ACL matching options.

As for extended named IP ACLs, the **permit** and **deny** subcommands follow the same syntax as the extended numbered IP ACLs.

The first matching parameter for extended ACLs refers to the protocol. The protocol keyword can be **ip**, referring to all IP packets. It can also refer to a subset of IP packets based on the protocol of the header that follows the IP header, as defined by the IP header's protocol type field. Figure 7-2 shows the location of the IP Protocol field, the concept of it pointing to the type of header that follows, along with some details of the IP header for reference.

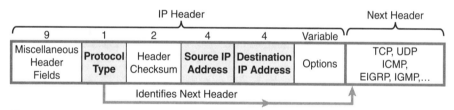

Figure 7-2 *IP Header, with Focus on Required Fields in Extended IP ACLs*

To match the protocol type, you simply use a keyword, such as **tcp**, **udp**, or **icmp**, matching IP packets that also happen to have a TCP, UDP, or ICMP header, respectively, following the IP header. Or you can use the keyword **ip**, which means "all IPv4 packets."

You also must configure parameters for the source and destination IP address fields that follow; these fields use the same syntax and options for matching the IP addresses as discussed in Chapter 6, "Basic IPv4 Access Control Lists." Figure 7-3 shows the syntax.

Extended ACLs support two syntax options to match a single address, while standard ACLs support three. (The section "Matching the Exact IP Address" in the preceding chapter discussed the three options.) Table 7-2 summarizes the options supported. Of note, no matter the syntax you choose to use when configuring, IOS stores the command with a preferred syntax, as noted in the table.

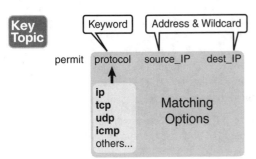

Figure 7-3   *Extended ACL Syntax, with Required Fields*

Table 7-2   Summary of Syntax Supported to Match One IP Address

Syntax Options	*address* 0.0.0.0	host *address*	*address*
Standard ACLs	Yes	Yes	Yes*
Extended ACLs	Yes	Yes*	No

* IOS stores the command with this syntax no matter the configuration style.

Table 7-3 lists several sample **access-list** commands that use only the required matching parameters. As an exercise, hide the right column and predict the logic of the command in the left column. Then review the answer in the right column. Or just review the explanations on the right column to get an idea for the logic in some sample commands. Note that the table shows ACL mode subcommand for named ACLs, but the same syntax exists in the global commands used by numbered ACLs.

Table 7-3   Extended **access-list** Commands and Logic Explanations

access-list Statement	What It Matches
deny tcp any any	Any IP packet that has a TCP header
deny udp any any	Any IP packet that has a UDP header
deny icmp any any	Any IP packet that has an ICMP header
deny ip host 1.1.1.1 host 2.2.2.2	All IP packets from host 1.1.1.1 going to host 2.2.2.2, for all IP packets
deny udp 1.1.1.0 0.0.0.255 any	All IP packets that also have a UDP header, from subnet 1.1.1.0/24, and going to any destination

The last entries in Table 7-3 help make an important point about how IOS processes extended ACLs:

In an extended ACL **access-list** command, all the matching parameters must match the packet for the packet to match the command.

For example, in that last example from Table 7-3, the command checks for UDP, a source IP address from subnet 1.1.1.0/24, and any destination IP address. If a router processed a packet with source IP address 1.1.1.1, it would match the source IP address check. However, if the packet also had a TCP header following the IP header, the router would fail to match the packet with that ACE. All parameters in an ACE must match the packet.

Matching TCP and UDP Port Numbers

Extended ACLs can also examine parts of the TCP and UDP headers, particularly the source and destination port number fields. The port numbers identify the application that sends or receives the data.

The most useful ports to check are the well-known ports used by servers. For example, web servers use well-known port 80 by default. Figure 7-4 shows the location of the port numbers in the TCP header, following the IP header.

Key Topic

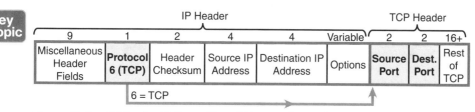

Figure 7-4   *IP Header, Followed by a TCP Header and Port Number Fields*

When an extended ACL command includes either the **tcp** or **udp** keyword, that command can optionally reference the source and/or destination port. To make these comparisons, the syntax uses keywords for equal, not equal, less than, greater than, and for a range of port numbers. In addition, the command can use either the literal decimal port numbers or more convenient keywords for some well-known application ports. Figure 7-5 shows the positions of the source and destination port fields in the **access-list** command and these port number keywords.

Key Topic

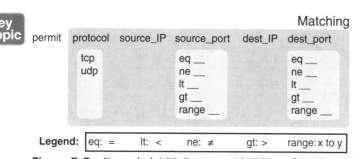

Figure 7-5   *Extended ACL Syntax with TCP and UDP Port Numbers Enabled*

For example, consider the simple network shown in Figure 7-6. The FTP server sits on the right, with the client on the left. The figure shows the syntax of an ACL that matches the following:

- Packets that include a TCP header

- Packets sent from the client subnet

- Packets sent to the server subnet

- Packets with TCP destination port 21 (FTP server control port)

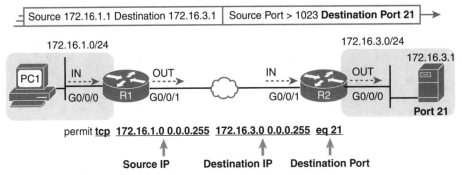

Figure 7-6 *Filtering Packets Based on Destination Port*

To fully appreciate the matching of the destination port with the **eq 21** parameters, consider packets moving from left to right, from PC1 to the server. Assuming the server uses well-known port 21 (FTP control port), the packet's TCP header has a destination port value of 21. The ACL syntax includes the **eq 21** parameters after the destination IP address. The position after the destination address parameters is important: that position identifies the fact that the **eq 21** parameters should be compared to the packet's destination port. As a result, the ACL statement shown in Figure 7-6 would match this packet and the destination port of 21 if used in any of the four locations implied by the four dashed arrowed lines in the figure.

Conversely, Figure 7-7 shows the reverse flow, with a packet sent by the server back toward PC1. In this case, the packet's TCP header has a source port of 21, so the ACL must check the source port value of 21, and the ACL must be located on different interfaces. In this case, the **eq 21** parameters follow the source address field but come before the destination address field.

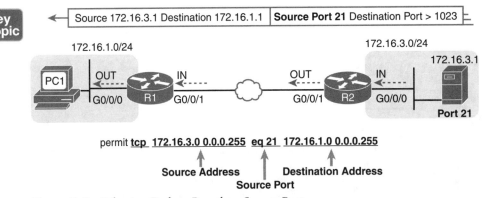

Figure 7-7 *Filtering Packets Based on Source Port*

When examining ACLs that match port numbers, first consider the location and direction to apply the ACL. That direction determines whether the packet is being sent to the server or from the server. You can then decide whether you need to check the source or destination port in the packet. For reference, Tables 7-4 and 7-5 list many of the popular port numbers and their transport layer protocols and applications.

NOTE   You will likely want to memorize the ACL command keywords for the port numbers as well. Whether you use the keyword or a port number when configuring, IOS stores the keyword rather than the number when IOS has a defined keyword for that port.

Table 7-4   IT Services Their Well-Known Port Numbers

Port Number(s)	Protocol	Application	access-list and permit | deny Command Keywords
20	TCP	FTP data	**ftp-data**
21	TCP	FTP control	**ftp**
22	TCP	SSH	—
23	TCP	Telnet	**telnet**
49	UDP, TCP	TACACS+	—
53	UDP, TCP	DNS	**domain**
67	UDP	DHCP Server	**bootps**
68	UDP	DHCP Client	**bootpc**
69	UDP	TFTP	**tftp**
161	UDP	SNMP	**snmp**
514	UDP	Syslog	—
1645, 1646	UDP	Radius (original)	—
1812, 1813	UDP	Radius (current)	—

Table 7-5   User Applications and Their Well-Known Port Numbers

Port Number(s)	Protocol	Application	access-list and permit | deny Command Keywords
25	TCP	SMTP	**smtp**
80	TCP	HTTP (WWW)	**www**
443	TCP	HTTPS (w/ TLS)	—
110	TCP	POP3 (no TLS)	**pop3**
995	TCP	POP3 w/ TLS	—
143	TCP	IMAP (no TLS)	—
993	TCP	IMAP w/ TLS	—
16,384–32,767	UDP	RTP (voice, video)	—

7

IOS has some surprising conventions when configuring well-known port numbers. First, you can always configure the port number. However, IOS supports a small set of well-known port keywords, as shown in the far-right column of Table 7-4. In the command you enter, you can type either the number or the keyword; for instance, you could use **80** or **www** to refer to well-known port 80.

However, be aware that if a text keyword exists, IOS stores the ACL command using that keyword. For example, a command typed with **permit tcp any any eq 80** becomes **permit tcp any any eq www** in the running-config.

Table 7-6 lists several sample **access-list** commands that match based on port numbers. Again, use the table as an exercise by covering the right column and analyzing the contents of the left column. Then check the right side of the table to see if you agree. As with Tables 7-4 and 7-5, the table uses ACL mode subcommands used by named ACLs, but the same syntax exists within extended ACL global commands.

Table 7-6   Extended **access-list** Command Examples and Logic Explanations

access-list Statement	What It Matches
deny tcp any gt **49151** host **10.1.1.1** eq **23**	Packets with a TCP header, any source IP address, with a source port greater than (**gt**) 49151, a destination IP address of exactly 10.1.1.1, and a destination port equal to (**eq**) 23.
deny tcp any host **10.1.1.1** eq **23**	The same as the preceding example, but any source port matches because the command omits the source port parameters.
deny tcp any host **10.1.1.1** eq **telnet**	The same as the preceding example. The **telnet** keyword is used instead of port 23.
deny udp **1.0.0.0 0.255.255.255** lt **1023** any	A packet with a source in network 1.0.0.0/8, using UDP with a source port less than (**lt**) 1023, with any destination IP address.

Extended IP ACL Configuration

Extended ACLs support far too many options to allow a single generic representation of the command syntax. However, the commands in Table 7-7 summarize the syntax options covered in this book. The first two rows show numbered ACL commands, with the final two rows showing the same syntax in the ACL mode **permit** and **deny** commands.

Table 7-7   Extended IP Access List Configuration Commands

Command	Configuration Mode and Description
access-list *access-list-number* {deny | permit} *protocol source source-wildcard destination destination-wildcard* [log]	Global command for extended numbered access lists. Use a number between 100 and 199 or 2000 and 2699, inclusive.
access-list *access-list-number* {deny | permit} {tcp | udp} *source source-wildcard* [*operator* [*port*]] *destination destination-wildcard* [*operator* [*port*]] [log]	A version of the **access-list** command with parameters specific to TCP and UDP.
ip access-group *number/name* in|out	Interface subcommand to enable an IP ACL on an interface for a direction. Used for numbered and named ACLs.
ip access-list extended *name*	A global command to create an extended ACL and move the user into ACL configuration mode.

Command	Configuration Mode and Description
{deny | permit} *protocol source source-wildcard destination destination-wildcard* [log]	ACL subcommand with the syntax to match the required parameters: protocol, plus source and destination IP address.
{deny | permit} {tcp | udp} *source source-wildcard* [*operator* [*port*]] *destination destination-wildcard* [*operator* [*port*]] [log]	ACL subcommand with parameters to match parameters specific to TCP and UDP.

The configuration process for extended ACLs mostly matches the same process used for standard ACLs. You must choose the location and direction to enable the ACL so that you can characterize whether specific addresses and ports will be either the source or destination. Configure the ACL using **access-list** commands, and when complete, then enable the ACL using the same **ip access-group** command used with standard ACLs. All these steps mirror what you do with standard ACLs; however, when configuring, keep the following differences in mind:

- Place extended ACLs as close as possible to the source of the packets that the ACL needs to filter. Filtering close to the source of the packets saves some bandwidth.

- Remember that all fields in one ACE must match a packet for the router to consider the packet to match that ACE.

- For numbered ACLs, use numbers 100–199 and 2000–2699 on the **access-list** commands; no one number is inherently better than another.

Extended IP ACL Example 1: Packets to Web Servers

The two examples to close the first major section of the chapter focus on matching packets to web servers (in the first example) and from web servers (in the second example.) Both use the same topology and web servers, with a different direction in each case. Figure 7-8 shows the topology, IP subnets, and specific IP addresses as needed.

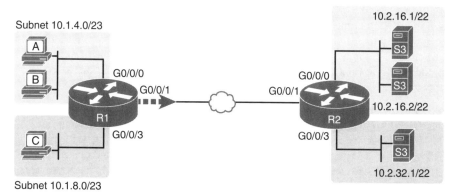

Figure 7-8 *Network Diagram for Extended Access List: Example 1*

Treat both examples as an exercise to understand the mechanics of extended ACLs. For that purpose, consider how to create an ACL for router R1, where users sit at a branch office. The

ACL will be applied outbound on router R1's WAN link, that is, toward the servers. The matching requirements are

1. Permit traffic *sent by* the upper user subnet on the left (10.1.4.0/23) and *going to* the web servers in the subnet in the upper right of the drawing (at an internal data center.)

2. Permit traffic *sent by* the upper user subnet on the left (10.1.4.0/23) and *going to* the single web server 10.2.32.1 in the lower right of the figure.

3. In both cases, allow both HTTP and HTTPS protocols.

4. Deny all other traffic.

Example 7-8 shows an extended named ACL that does just that. It has two pairs of **permit** statements. In each pair, the first matches the port number for HTTP (80) while the second matches the port number for HTTPS (443). The first pair matches packets to the upper-right subnet 10.2.16.0/22, while the second pair matches packets to host 10.2.32.1.

Example 7-8 *R1's Extended Access List: Example 1*

```
R1# configure terminal
Enter configuration commands, one per line.  End with CNTL/Z.
R1(config)# ip access-list extended branch_WAN
R1(config-ext-nacl)# remark Example ACL to match HTTP/S
R1(config-ext-nacl)# permit tcp 10.1.4.0 0.0.1.255 10.2.16.0 0.0.3.255 eq 80
R1(config-ext-nacl)# permit tcp 10.1.4.0 0.0.1.255 10.2.16.0 0.0.3.255 eq 443
R1(config-ext-nacl)# permit tcp 10.1.4.0 0.0.1.255 host 10.2.32.1 eq 80
R1(config-ext-nacl)# permit tcp 10.1.4.0 0.0.1.255 host 10.2.32.1 eq 443
R1(config-ext-nacl)# interface gigabitethernet0/0/1
R1(config-if)# ip access-group branch_WAN out
R1(config-if)# ^Z
R1#
```

To emphasize some key points from earlier in this chapter, note that all four permit statements use **tcp** as the protocol type. HTTP and HTTPS both use TCP, and to match port numbers in the ACL, you must specify **tcp** or **udp** in the command. Also, in each command, take time to identify the parameters that define the address(es) for the source and destination address matching. Then note that the port number matching at the end of the **permit** commands all follow the destination address matching parameters—meaning that the statements all attempt to match the destination port number.

To complete the review, note that the configuration enables the ACL outbound on R1's G0/0/1 interface. Also, the ACL ends with an implied **deny any**, in effect, an implied final command of **deny ip any any**. Given the explicit lines in the ACL, the ACL permits only HTTP/HTTPS traffic, with limited source and destination address ranges, and denies all other traffic. (This ACL would be far too restrictive in a production network, but it provides enough detail to learn the syntax and logic.)

Example 7-9 confirms that the ACL has been enabled, with statistics showing some usage of the first two lines in the ACL.

Example 7-9   *Verifying the Extended ACL*

```
R1# show ip interface gigabitethernet0/0/1
GigabitEthernet0/0/1 is up, line protocol is up
  Internet address is 10.1.12.1/24
  Broadcast address is 255.255.255.255
  Address determined by non-volatile memory
  MTU is 1500 bytes
  Helper address is not set
  Directed broadcast forwarding is disabled
  Multicast reserved groups joined: 224.0.0.5 224.0.0.10 224.0.0.6
  Outgoing access list is branch_WAN
  Inbound access list is not set
! Lines omitted for brevity

R1# show access-list
Extended IP access list branch_WAN
    10 permit tcp 10.1.4.0 0.0.1.255 10.2.16.0 0.0.3.255 eq www (18 matches)
    20 permit tcp 10.1.4.0 0.0.1.255 10.2.16.0 0.0.3.255 eq 443 (416 matches)
    30 permit tcp 10.1.4.0 0.0.1.255 host 10.2.32.1 eq www
    40 permit tcp 10.1.4.0 0.0.1.255 host 10.2.32.1 eq 443
```

This example also demonstrates IOS's surprising habit of changing some numeric port numbers into text keywords, as discussed earlier in the text just before Tables 7-4 and 7-5. Those tables list some of the more common TCP and UDP port numbers and the ACL keywords IOS supports. IOS uses keyword **www** for port 80, so it replaced the configured numeric 80 with the **www** keyword. However, IOS left port 443 as is because it has no ACL keyword for that port number.

Extended IP ACL Example 2: Packets from Web Servers

One of the most common mistakes when learning about extended ACLs relates to matching TCP and UDP ports. The syntax and the underlying concepts can be confusing. The earlier section "Matching TCP and UDP Port Numbers" explained the details, with this next example giving you a chance to think through the problem.

As an exercise, plan to create an ACL on router R2 instead of router R1 as in the previous example. You will achieve the same goals, but place the ACL on router R2, outgoing on its WAN link, as shown in Figure 7-9. Most importantly, note that this change means that the ACL matches the opposite direction versus the previous example.

Think about this example for yourself first, and even try creating the ACL in a text editor before reading further.

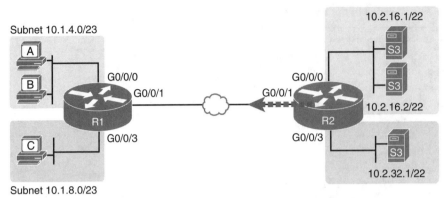

Figure 7-9 *Network Diagram for Extended Access List: Example 2*

The list that follows details a revised version of the ACL requirements listed just before Example 7-8, for the previous example. The list reverses the logic so it matches packets flowing in the opposite direction: right to left in the figure.

1. Reversing original requirement 1, permit traffic *going to* the upper user subnet on the left (10.1.4.0/23) and *sent by* the web servers in the subnet in the upper right of the drawing (at an internal data center).

2. Reversing original requirement 2, permit traffic *going to* the upper user subnet on the left (10.1.4.0/23) and *sent by* the single web server 10.2.32.1 in the lower right of the figure.

3. As before, allow both HTTP and HTTPS protocols.

4. As before, deny all other traffic.

Example 7-10 shows the resulting ACL on router R2. Note the highlighted matching fields for the port numbers that reside just after the source address parameters.

Example 7-10 *Extended ACL on Router R2 to Match Packets Sent by the Web Servers*

```
R2# show running-config | section access-list
ip access-list extended DC_WAN
 10 permit tcp 10.2.16.0 0.0.3.255 eq www 10.1.4.0 0.0.1.255
 20 permit tcp 10.2.16.0 0.0.3.255 eq 443 10.1.4.0 0.0.1.255
 30 permit tcp host 10.2.32.1 eq www 10.1.4.0 0.0.1.255
 40 permit tcp host 10.2.32.1 eq 443 10.1.4.0 0.0.1.255
```

Adjusting ACLs for HTTP/3

In Chapter 5, "Introduction to TCP/IP Transport and Applications," the section titled "HTTP 3.0" details how a relatively new version of HTTP, HTTP/3 (or HTTP 3.0), moves away from using TCP. Instead, it uses QUIC as the transport protocol, which itself uses a UDP header as the next header after the IP header. IANA reserves UDP port 443 as the well-known port for web servers using HTTP/3. So, not only can you match HTTP/3 traffic, but also consider updating existing ACLs to match HTTP/3 traffic as needed.

To show a specific example, reconsider the previous scenario, with ACL DC_WAN as shown in Example 7-10, but add this requirement:

5. Ensure the ACL matches not only TCP-based HTTP versions but also HTTP/3, which uses UDP and QUIC.

As a reminder, the previous ACL matches the source well-known port. The revised version in Example 7-11 highlights the new lines that match UDP messages with well-known port 443. Note that you do not need to match UDP 80 as a well-known port because HTTP/3 always uses TLS (HTTPS) and defines well-known UDP port 443.

Example 7-11 *Revised ACL from Example 7-10 Now Matches HTTP/3*

```
R2# show running-config | section access-list
ip access-list extended DC_WAN
 10 permit tcp 10.2.16.0 0.0.3.255 eq www 10.1.4.0 0.0.1.255
 20 permit tcp 10.2.16.0 0.0.3.255 eq 443 10.1.4.0 0.0.1.255
 25 permit udp 10.2.16.0 0.0.3.255 eq 443 10.1.4.0 0.0.1.255
 30 permit tcp host 10.2.32.1 eq www 10.1.4.0 0.0.1.255
 40 permit tcp host 10.2.32.1 eq 443 10.1.4.0 0.0.1.255
 45 permit udp host 10.2.32.1 eq 443 10.1.4.0 0.0.1.255
```

Practice Building access-list Commands

Table 7-8 supplies a practice exercise to help you get comfortable with the syntax of extended ACL commands, particularly choosing the correct matching logic. Your job: create a one-line extended ACL that matches the packets and uses a permit action. You can use the syntax for a global **access-list** command or an ACL mode **permit** command. The answers are shown in the section "Answers to Earlier Practice Problems" at the end of this chapter. Note that if the criteria mention a particular application protocol, for example, "web client," that means to match for that application protocol specifically.

Table 7-8 Building One-Line Extended ACLs: Practice

Problem	Criteria
1	From web client 10.1.1.1, sent to a web server in subnet 10.1.2.0/24.
2	From Telnet client 172.16.4.3/25, sent to a Telnet server in subnet 172.16.3.0/25. Match all hosts in the client's subnet as well.
3	ICMP messages from the subnet in which 192.168.7.200/26 resides to all hosts in the subnet where 192.168.7.14/29 resides.
4	From web server 10.2.3.4/23's subnet to clients in the same subnet as host 10.4.5.6/22.
5	From Telnet server 172.20.1.0/24's subnet, sent to any host in the same subnet as host 172.20.44.1/23.
6	From web client 192.168.99.99/28, sent to a web server in subnet 192.168.176.0/28. Match all hosts in the client's subnet as well.
7	ICMP messages from the subnet in which 10.55.66.77/25 resides to all hosts in the subnet where 10.66.55.44/26 resides.
8	Any and every IPv4 packet.

7

ACL Implementation Considerations

ACLs can be a great tool to enhance the security of a network, but engineers should think about some broader issues before simply configuring an ACL to fix a problem. To help, Cisco makes the following general recommendations:

- Place extended ACLs as close as possible to the packet's source. This strategy allows ACLs to discard the packets early.

- Place standard ACLs as close as possible to the packet's destination. This strategy avoids the mistake with standard ACLs (which match the source IPv4 address only) of unintentionally discarding packets.

- Place more specific statements early in the ACL and less specific statements later in the ACL.

- Disable an ACL from its interface (using the **no ip access-group** interface subcommand) before editing the ACL.

- Ensure the **ip access-group** interface refers to the ACL number or name you intended; take care to spell named ACLs correctly, using the correct case.

The first point deals with the concept of where to locate your ACLs. If you intend to filter a packet, filtering closer to the packet's source means that the packet takes up less bandwidth in the network, which seems to be more efficient—and it is. Therefore, Cisco suggests locating extended ACLs as close to the source as possible.

However, the second point seems to contradict the first point, at least for standard ACLs, to locate them close to the destination. Why? Because standard ACLs look only at the source IP address, they tend to filter more than you want filtered when placed close to the source. For instance, in Figures 7-8 and 7-9, imagine an inbound ACL on router R1's LAN interface (G0/0/0) that discards packets from host A (10.1.4.1). That may be exactly what you need. However, if you want that host to be able to send packets to server S1 but not to S3, then that standard ACL cannot create that logic in that location in the network.

For the third item in the list, placing more specific matching parameters early in each list makes you less likely to make mistakes in the ACL. For example, imagine that the ACL first listed a command that permitted traffic coming from subnet 10.1.4.0/23, and the second command denied traffic coming from host 10.1.4.1. Packets sent by host 10.1.4.1 would match the first ACE and never match the more specific second command. Note that later IOS versions prevent this mistake during configuration in some cases.

You avoid issues with ACL in an interim state by disabling ACLs on the interfaces before you edit them. First, IOS does not filter any packets if you delete an entire ACL and leave the IP ACL enabled on an interface. However, as soon as you add one ACE to that enabled ACL, IOS starts filtering packets based on that ACL. Those interim ACL configurations could cause problems.

Finally, IOS does not complain if you configure the **ip access-group** interface subcommand with the number or name of an undefined ACL. IOS considers the ACL to have no ACEs (a null ACL), and IOS does not filter packets with a null ACL enabled on an interface. However, double-check your spelling of ACL names between the commands that define the ACL and the **ip access-group** command. It is easy to make a spelling mistake or use difference case. (ACL names are case sensitive.)

Chapter Review

One key to doing well on the exams is to perform repetitive spaced review sessions. Review this chapter's material using either the tools in the book or interactive tools for the same material found on the book's companion website. Refer to the "Your Study Plan" element for more details. Table 7-9 outlines the key review elements and where you can find them. To better track your study progress, record when you completed these activities in the second column.

Table 7-9   Chapter Review Tracking

Review Element	Review Date(s)	Resource Used
Review key topics		Book, website
Review key terms		Book, website
Answer DIKTA questions		Book, PTP
Review memory tables		Book, website
Review command tables		Book

Review All the Key Topics

Table 7-10   Key Topics for Chapter 7

Key Topic Element	Description	Page Number
List	Differences between named and numbered ACLs	138
List	Naming conventions for named ACL names	139
List	Rules for deleting individual ACEs in ACL mode	141
List	Rules for adding individual ACEs in ACL mode	141
Figure 7-3	Syntax and notes about the three required matching fields in the extended ACL **access-list** command	146
Table 7-2	Options for matching a single IP address in an ACE	146
Paragraph	Summary of extended ACL logic that all parameters must match in a single **access-list** statement for a match to occur	146
Figure 7-4	Drawing of the IP header followed by a TCP header	147
Figure 7-5	Syntax and notes about matching TCP and UDP ports with extended ACL **access-list** commands	147
Figure 7-7	Logic and syntax to match TCP source ports	148
Table 7-4	Popular IT services and their well-known ports	149
Table 7-5	Popular user applications and their well-known ports	149
List	Guidelines for using extended numbered IP ACLs	151
List	ACL implementation recommendations	156

Key Terms You Should Know

ACL sequence number, extended access list, named access list

Command References

Tables 7-11 and 7-12 list configuration and verification commands used in this chapter. As an easy review exercise, cover the left column in a table, read the right column, and try to recall the command without looking. Then repeat the exercise, covering the right column, and try to recall what the command does.

Table 7-11 Chapter 7 ACL Configuration Command Reference

Command	Description
access-list *access-list-number* {deny | permit} *protocol source source-wildcard destination destination-wildcard* [log]	Global command for extended numbered access lists. Use a number between 100 and 199 or 2000 and 2699, inclusive.
access-list *access-list-number* {deny | permit} tcp *source source-wildcard* [*operator* [*port*]] *destination destination-wildcard* [*operator* [*port*]] [log]	A version of the access-list command with TCP-specific parameters.
access-list *access-list-number* remark *text*	Command that defines a remark to help you remember what the ACL is supposed to do.
ip access-group {*number* | *name* [in | out]}	Interface subcommand to enable access lists.
ip access-list {standard | extended} *name*	Global command to configure a named standard or extended ACL and enter ACL configuration mode.
{deny | permit} *source* [*source wildcard*] [log]	ACL mode subcommand to configure the matching details and action for a standard named ACL.
{deny | permit} *protocol source source-wildcard destination destination-wildcard* [log]	ACL mode subcommand to configure the matching details and action for an extended named ACL.
{deny | permit} tcp|udp *source source-wildcard* [*operator* [*port*]] *destination destination-wildcard* [*operator* [*port*]] [log]	ACL mode subcommand to configure the matching details and action for a named ACL that matches TCP or UDP messages.
remark *text*	ACL mode subcommand to configure a description of a named ACL.
no {deny | permit} *protocol source source-wildcard destination destination-wildcard*	ACL mode subcommand to delete a single ACE if an ACE exists with the exact same detail as in the no command.
no *sequence-number*	ACL mode subcommand to delete a single ACE if an ACE with that sequence number exists.

Table 7-12 Chapter 7 EXEC Command Reference

Command	Description
show ip *interface* [*type number*]	Includes a reference to the access lists enabled on the interface
show access-lists [*access-list-number* | *access-list-name*]	Shows details of configured access lists for all protocols
show ip access-lists [*access-list-number* | *access-list-name*]	Shows IP access lists, with the same information and format as the show access-lists command

Answers to Earlier Practice Problems

Table 7-13 lists the answers to the practice problems listed in Table 7-8. Note that for any question that references a client, you might have chosen to match port numbers greater than 49151, matching all dynamic ports. The answers in this table mostly ignore that option, but just to show one sample, the answer to the first problem lists one with reference to client ports greater than 49151 and one without. The remaining answers simply omit this part of the logic.

Table 7-13   Building One-Line Extended ACLs: Answers

	Criteria
1	permit tcp host 10.1.1.1 10.1.2.0 0.0.0.255 eq www or permit tcp host 10.1.1.1 gt 49151 10.1.2.0 0.0.0.255 eq www
2	permit tcp 172.16.4.0 0.0.0.127 172.16.3.0 0.0.0.127 eq telnet
3	permit icmp 192.168.7.192 0.0.0.63 192.168.7.8 0.0.0.7
4	permit tcp 10.2.2.0 0.0.1.255 eq www 10.4.4.0 0.0.3.255
5	permit tcp 172.20.1.0 0.0.0.255 eq 23 172.20.44.0 0.0.1.255
6	permit tcp 192.168.99.96 0.0.0.15 192.168.176.0 0.0.0.15 eq www
7	permit icmp 10.55.66.0 0.0.0.127 10.66.55.0 0.0.0.63
8	permit ip any any

7

CHAPTER 8

Applied IP ACLs

This chapter covers the following exam topics:

5.0 Security Fundamentals

5.6 Configure and verify access control lists

When you plan a real IP ACL to enable in a production network, the task often becomes large and complex. For instance, imagine you rely on the implied **deny any** logic at the end of the ACL. In doing so, your ACL must include permit commands matching all traffic you want to allow; otherwise, the ACL denies (discards) those packets. If you add a **permit ip any any** command to the end of your extended ACL, making the default to permit traffic, you have the opposite problem: you need to work hard to identify everything you want to deny and match that in your ACL. The complexities increase with multiple network engineers, competing IT interests, and a changing business environment.

This chapter gives you a glimpse into some of the issues you will need to consider when taking that next step. The first section of the chapter examines how to ensure you permit several essential protocols in the network so that later deny ACEs in an ACL do not discard the traffic. For instance, if your ACL matched much of the end-user traffic correctly but forgot about DNS, DHCP, ICMP, and OSPF, discarding those, the network would fail miserably. The first section works through some practical examples that may be useful in your network engineering job and give you deeper skills for the CCNA exam.

The final (short) section discusses some differences between Cisco IOS and IOS XE operating systems regarding IP ACLs. The CCNA exam does not imply any need to know such differences; however, knowing the minor differences can help. Also, that section discusses two features not yet discussed in the ACL chapters—how to use ACL resequencing and how to add a second ACL to an interface—so take the time to read through the final section.

"Do I Know This Already?" Quiz

Take the quiz (either here or use the PTP software) if you want to use the score to help you decide how much time to spend on this chapter. The letter answers are listed at the bottom of the page following the quiz. Appendix C, found both at the end of the book as well as on the companion website, includes both the answers and explanations. You can also find both answers and explanations in the PTP testing software.

Table 8-1 "Do I Know This Already?" Foundation Topics Section-to-Question Mapping

Foundation Topics Section	Questions
ACLs and Network Infrastructure Protocols	1–4
Comparing ACLs in IOS and IOS XE	5, 6

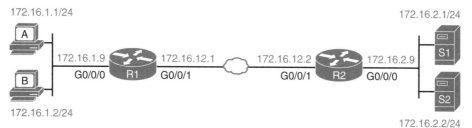

172.16.1.1/24

A

172.16.1.9
G0/0/0   R1   G0/0/1
172.16.12.1

172.16.12.2
G0/0/1   R2   G0/0/0
172.16.2.9

172.16.2.1/24

S1

S2

B

172.16.1.2/24

172.16.2.2/24

Refer to This Figure for Questions 1–4

1. Router R1 in the figure uses the ACL below, with the **ip access-group QA_01 out** interface subcommand added to interface G0/0/1. The router has no other ACL-related configuration. In the output of the **show access-lists** command, which ACL line's counter should increment each time router R1 sends an OSPF Hello?

   ```
   ip access-list extended QA_01
      10 permit tcp host 172.16.12.1 any eq 520
      20 permit tcp host 172.16.12.1 any
      30 permit ospf host 224.0.0.5 any
      40 permit ospf host 172.16.12.1 any
   ```

   a. Line 10

   b. Line 20

   c. Line 30

   d. Line 40

   e. None of the other answers are correct

2. In the figure, router R2 enables an ACL inbound on its G0/0/0 interface. Hosts A and B need to lease IP addresses from DHCP server S1. Router R1 provides the IP helper feature with the **ip helper-address 172.16.2.1** subcommand on its G0/0/0 interface. Which answers list an ACE that, if part of the ACL, would match DHCP messages between the server and clients? (Choose two answers.)

   a. permit ip host 172.16.2.1 any

   b. permit ip any host 172.16.2.1

   c. permit udp any eq bootps host 0.0.0.0

   d. permit udp host 172.16.2.1 eq bootpc any

   e. permit udp host 172.16.2.1 eq bootps any

3. In the figure, router R1 uses standard ACL QA_03. The ACL has one ACE; the ACE permits packets sourced from subnet 172.16.1.0/24. An engineer wants to filter SSH traffic, so only hosts from subnet 172.16.1.0/24 can SSH into a router. Which answer best describes how the engineer should proceed?

   a. Enable the ACL in vty mode with the **access-class QA_01 in** subcommand.

   b. Enable the ACL in vty mode with the **access-class QA_01 out** subcommand.

   c. Enable the ACL in vty mode with the **ip access-group QA_01 in** subcommand.

   d. Enable the ACL in vty mode with the **ip access-group QA_01 out** subcommand.

4. In the figure, an engineer enables ACL QA_04 inbound on router R1's G0/0/0 interface. Imagine host A attempts to SSH to address 172.16.12.1. Which line in the ACL will the packets match in this scenario?

```
ip access-list extended QA_04
    10 permit udp 172.16.1.0 0.0.0.255 any eq 22
    20 permit tcp 172.16.1.0 0.0.0.255 any eq 22
    30 deny udp any any eq 22
    40 deny tcp any any eq 22
```

   a. Line 10

   b. Line 20

   c. Line 30

   d. Line 40

   e. The implied **deny ip any any**

5. Before the introduction of the "Common" ACL in IOS XE, which answer is most accurate regarding how many IP ACLs can be enabled on one router?

   a. One per router

   b. One per router interface

   c. One per router interface per direction

   d. Two per router interface per direction

   e. Many per router interface per direction

6. Named ACL QA_06 has four lines with sequence numbers 10, 20, 30, and 40. As an exercise during a job interview, you are asked to edit the ACL so that the ACEs keep the same relative order but instead use sequence numbers 50, 70, 90, and 110. Which answer lists the method to effect this change with the fewest commands from the CLI?

   a. Issue the **ip access-list resequence QA_06 50 20** command in privileged EXEC mode.

   b. Issue the **ip access-list resequence QA_06 50 20** command in global configuration mode.

   c. Delete the entire ACL with the **no ip access-list...** global command and then reconfigure the entire ACL.

   d. From ACL mode, delete each **permit** or **deny** command and then reconfigure each.

   e. From ACL mode, issue the **resequence 50 20** subcommand.

Foundation Topics

ACLs and Network Infrastructure Protocols

Chapter 7, "Named and Extended IP ACLs," completes the discussion of most of the core ACL configuration features. However, the complexity of ACLs comes not from the configuration but from applying the tool to the large variety of networking protocols whose packets run through routers. This first major section of the chapter considers how to match some of those protocols in an ACL. This section discusses how to create ACEs for some of those overhead networking protocols. The topics include

- DNS

- ICMP Echos and Time Exceeded

- Routing Protocols and OSPF

- DHCP

- SSH and Telnet into routers and switches

Filtering DNS

DNS messages flow through almost every router interface in an enterprise, so a production-ready IP ACL needs to permit it. The question becomes how permissive to be: to permit all of it, with no restrictions, or be more selective.

First, consider an enterprise with many branches. Figure 8-1 shows an example, with one branch router (B1), on the left, but many more branches exist. The figure shows two DNS servers and the DHCP server used in the upcoming discussions of ACLs and DHCP.

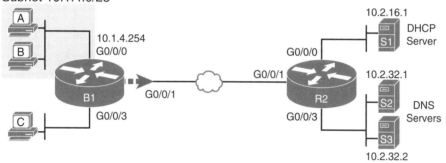

Figure 8-1 *Enterprise Branches with DHCP and DNS Servers*

Next, think about planning an ACL so every branch router could use the same ACEs to match DNS traffic. You could begin by choosing the location and direction of each branch router's WAN interface in the outbound direction. As a result, the branch ACLs process packets sent toward the DNS servers.

Example 8-1 shows one approach. It ignores all IP addresses, matching source and destination addresses with the **any** keyword. The ACEs match based on these DNS facts:

- DNS uses both UDP and TCP.

- DNS uses well-known server port 53 (ACL keyword **domain**).

Example 8-1 *Permitting All DHCP Traffic to DNS Servers*

```
R1# show running-config | section access-list
! ACEs below are part of extended ACL Branch_Common
 50 permit udp any any eq domain
 60 permit tcp any any eq domain
```

> **NOTE** The ACLs in the many examples in this section focus on a few ACEs related to each topic. Those ACEs would be part of a much larger ACL.

Assuming no other earlier ACEs matched the DNS packets, the ACEs in the example permit all packets destined to any DNS server, regardless of source and destination address.

Example 8-2 shows a more secure alternative using the same location and direction. However, because IT controls the only legitimate DNS servers, the permit ACEs match the legitimate DNS servers' IP addresses (lines 110–140). ACEs 150 and 160 then deny all other traffic to other DNS servers. This two-phase approach strikes a balance of being more restrictive while allowing all legitimate DNS traffic.

Example 8-2 *Permitting All DHCP Traffic to DHCP and DNS Servers*

```
R1# show running-config | section access-list
! Excerpt from extended ACL Branch_Common, replacing previous example's ACEs
 110 permit udp any host 10.2.32.1 eq domain
 120 permit udp any host 10.2.32.2 eq domain
 130 permit tcp any host 10.2.32.1 eq domain
 140 permit tcp any host 10.2.32.2 eq domain
! The next lines mimic example 8-1's ACEs, denying DNS (UDP and TCP)
 150 deny udp any any eq domain
 160 deny tcp any any eq domain
```

Filtering ICMP

For another interesting networking feature impacted by ACLs, consider the **ping** command detailed in *CCNA 200-301 Official Cert Guide, Volume 1*, Chapter 20, "Troubleshooting IPv4 Routing." The **ping** command generates ICMP Echo Request messages. A host that responds to those messages generates ICMP Echo Reply messages. Want ping to work? The ACLs must permit all ICMP, or message types for Echo Request and Reply.

For example, consider the case with the branch office router B1 in Figure 8-1, again with an outbound ACL on router B1's G0/0/1 interface. But how much to permit and deny? The following list details three scenarios for ICMP with increasing restrictions. Example 8-3, which follows, shows ACEs for the first two scenarios.

1. Taking a one-stage approach: Permitting all ICMP messages

2. Taking a two-stage approach:

    a. Permitting all ICMP messages with source and destination from within the enterprise's private network 10.0.0.0

    b. Denying all other ICMP

3. The same as scenario 2 but permitting ICMP Echo Request and Reply only

---

Answers to the "Do I Know This Already?" quiz:

1 E **2** A, E **3** A **4** B **5** C **6** B

Key Topic

Example 8-3 *ACLs That Implement Two Alternative Approaches*

```
! The following single ACE achieves scenario 1 above
210 permit icmp any any


! Alternately, the following two ACEs achieve scenario 2 above
220 permit icmp 10.0.0.0 0.255.255.255 10.0.0.0 0.255.255.255
230 deny icmp any any
```

The first ACE, line number 210, matches all ICMP messages. As for the syntax, to match ICMP messages, you do not use the TCP or UDP protocol types. Instead, you use the keyword **icmp**. (ICMP does not use TCP or UDP. Instead, the ICMP header follows directly after the IP header.)

The two-ACE alternative at the end of Example 8-3 matches all ICMP but with the added checks for both source and destination addresses. If the enterprise uses private class A network 10.0.0.0, this additional check means only packets sent from and to addresses in that private network match the **permit** statement. ICMP packets with a source or destination outside network 10.0.0.0, such as hosts in the Internet, fail to match line 220 but match line 230, with the router discarding those packets.

Example 8-4 shows the ACEs to achieve the third scenario. To match specific ICMP message types, use a keyword after the destination address field, as seen in lines 250 and 260. (The ICMP message type appears after the destination address in the ACE syntax.) Lines 250 and 260 together permit all ICMP Echo Request and Reply messages to/from hosts inside the enterprise's private network 10.0.0.0. The final line discards any other ICMP traffic, not relying on the default **deny any** to discard those packets.

Example 8-4 *Permitting Internal ICMP Echos, Denying All Other ICMP*

```
! ACEs for the third ICMP scenario
ip access-list extended icmp_Echo_network_10
 250 permit icmp 10.0.0.0 0.255.255.255 10.0.0.0 0.255.255.255 echo
 260 permit icmp 10.0.0.0 0.255.255.255 10.0.0.0 0.255.255.255 echo-reply
 270 deny icmp any any
```

Example 8-4 probably discards too much traffic. One of the significant dangers with ACLs is filtering too much and preventing proper network operation. ICMP defines many message subtypes, with over 50 shown in CLI help in configuration mode. The ACE at line 270 in Example 8-4 discards all other ICMP message types, which likely prevents other useful ICMP functions. For example, those ACEs would filter ICMP Time Exceeded messages used by the **traceroute** command so that **traceroute** commands would not complete. The scenario 2 option, configured at the end of Example 8-3, might be the better compromise.

Filtering OSPF

IP ACLs may discard OSPF messages, but there is no benefit to discarding them. So when you think about OSPF and ACLs, think about matching and permitting all OSPF packets. In particular, avoid unfortunate cases of matching OSPF packets with a deny action—for instance, by matching them with the implied **deny any** at the end of the ACL.

The scope of routing protocol packets impacts what packets an IP ACL might filter. As typical of routing protocol messages, OSPF packets have a short trip through a network. For example, in Figure 8-2, no OSPF packets flow past the dashed lines, and no routers forward any OSPF messages.

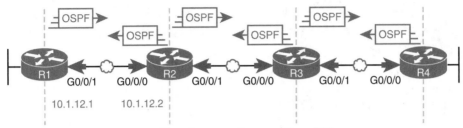

Figure 8-2 *OSPF Message Flow Between Routers R1 and R2*

The last new concept when thinking about ACLs and routing protocols has to do with the default IOS behavior without outbound ACLs:

Routers bypass outbound ACLs for local packets (packets generated by the router), including OSPF messages.

Combine that fact with the fact that routers do not forward OSPF packets, and the only ACLs that could discard OSPF messages are inbound ACLs. The arrow lines on the interfaces in Figure 8-2 show ACLs' locations and directions (inbound only) that could match OSPF messages.

> **NOTE** IOS XE (but not IOS) allows you to change the behavior of bypassing outbound ACLs for router-generated packets by issuing the **ip access-list match-local-packets** global command.

ACLs should permit OSPF packets. You need to match the packets but not to filter a subset: instead, permit all OSPF messages. To match OSPF packets, use the **ospf** protocol keyword. OSPF does not use UDP or TCP but exists as a protocol whose header follows just after the IP header, so IOS supplies a keyword to match the OSPF protocol.

Example 8-5 shows ACEs for two scenarios, both of which expect an inbound ACL on router R1's G0/0/1 WAN interface from Figure 8-2. The example again shows two approaches: permitting all OSPF, or permitting OSPF messages from known neighbors while discarding all other OSPF messages. Summarizing the two scenarios:

1. Taking a one-stage approach: Permitting all OSPF messages

2. Taking a two-stage approach:

   a. Permitting all OSPF messages from router R2's WAN IP address (10.1.12.2)

   b. Denying all other OSPF messages

Key Topic

Example 8-5 *Two OSPF Scenarios*

```
! Line 310 for OSPF scenario 1
 310 permit ospf any any
! Alternately, lines 320 and 330 for OSPF scenario 2.
 320 permit ospf host 10.1.12.2 any
 330 deny ospf any any
```

NOTE Appendix D, "Topics from Previous Editions," contains some older ACL content beyond the current CCNA exam topics. Some content discusses troubleshooting ACLs, with the rest discussing unexpected behavior with ACLs and router-generated packets. If you want to learn more, refer to the "Troubleshooting with IPv4 ACLs" section in Appendix D.

Filtering DHCP

At first glance, you might expect to treat DHCP much the same as DNS regarding ACLs. Most companies use a single DHCP server (with high availability features), or maybe a few, but all have identifiable IP addresses. DHCP messages flow end to end through the network over most network links. DHCP uses a well-known server port (67). Matching DHCP messages on some routers follows the same straightforward logic you learned for web servers and DNS earlier in the chapter. However, applying ACLs for DHCP packets on the same router that performs the IP helper function has some unexpected rules.

For context, consider Figure 8-3, with DHCP clients on the left and a DHCP server on the right. The figure highlights four possible locations to consider for ACLs that would match packets headed toward the DHCP server. (You could also filter in the other direction; I just chose the left-to-right flow for the examples.) At all ACL locations and directions shown in the figure, the packets have a destination UDP port number of 67. However, the addresses differ based on the location in the network due to the IP helper feature on router R1.

Key Topic

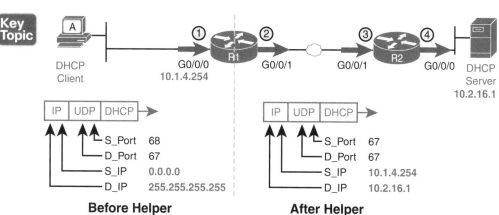

Figure 8-3 *ACL Locations to Consider: Packets to DHCP Server*

Now consider the straightforward case, on router R2, with ACL locations three and four in the figure. R2 does not perform the helper function, so you can match based on the well-known DHCP server port and the server's IP address. You can also use the same options discussed earlier for DNS servers with Examples 8-1 and 8-2. Example 8-6 shows similar

ACEs as seen in Example 8-2 for DNS. The ACL would be useful on router R2 in location three or four per Figure 8-3:

- **One-stage:** Permit all DHCP messages going toward a DHCP server (port 67).

- **Two-stage:** First, permit all DHCP messages to the legitimate DHCP server and then filter (deny) all other messages to DHCP servers.

Example 8-6 *Permitting All DHCP Traffic to DNS Servers on Router Main*

```
R2# show running-config section access-list
! Option 1: Allow all packets destined to DHCP server port (bootps 67)
 240 permit udp any any eq bootps
! Option 2: permit DHCP to known server and discard other messages sent to DHCP 67
 250 permit udp any host 10.2.16.1 eq bootps
 260 deny udp any any eq bootps
```

However, the ACL matching logic for DHCP differs on the router that performs the helper function. In particular:

1. By default, packets changed by a router due to the **ip helper-address** command bypass any outgoing ACL.
2. On a router interface with both an inbound ACL and the helper function, the router performs the ACL function first, before the helper function changes the IP addresses in DHCP messages.

For the first of those rules, consider ACL location two in Figure 8-3, the outbound ACL on R1's WAN interface. Per the first rule here, that ACL has not considered DHCP messages processed by router R1's IP helper function. R1 uses that function for DHCP clients like host A on the left side of Figure 8-3. Router R1 processes those incoming DHCP messages with the helper function, changes the source and destination address, and bypasses the outbound ACL.

Note that this default behavior on the IP helper router works well. You probably want to permit DHCP messages sent to the legitimate DHCP server you configured in the **ip helper-address** command, and those messages bypass any outbound ACL you enable there.

For the second rule about inbound ACLs, consider Example 8-7's configuration for router R1's LAN interface. It shows the **ip helper-address** command along with an enabled inbound ACL.

Example 8-7 *Router R1 LAN Interface: Interactions with Inbound ACL and Helper*

```
R1# show running-config
(Lists relevant excerpts…)
interface GigabitEthernet0/0/0
  ip address 10.1.4.254 255.255.254.0
  ip helper-address 10.2.16.1
  ip access-group R1_Common in
!
! ACL excerpt: permit packets with unusual source/destination addresses to DHCP server
 250 permit udp host 0.0.0.0 host 255.255.255.255 eq bootps
 260 deny udp any any eq bootps
```

As noted in the second rule, IOS applies the inbound ACL logic before performing the helper function, as depicted by the ACL at location one in Figure 8-4. Because of that, any matching based on IP address must match the unusual IP addresses shown on the left side of Figure 8-4. (You could always choose to match the addresses with the **any** keyword, ignoring the addresses.) Just be aware that if you attempt to match based on IP address, you must match the addresses that exist before the router applies the helper function.

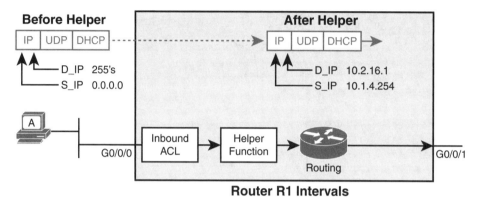

Figure 8-4   *Order of Operations: Inbound ACL and IP Helper*

Filtering SSH and Telnet

SSH and Telnet both give users a way to connect to the command-line interface of different operating systems. Telnet, the older of the two, is much less secure, which is why most people prefer SSH today.

When thinking about ACLs and the SSH and Telnet protocols, you should consider them for the usual interface ACLs just as with the other protocols discussed so far in this chapter. Additionally, routers and switches support Telnet and SSH, with IOS providing another method to enable an ACL to protect that specific function. First, this topic examines SSH/Telnet for packets passing through the router, matched with interface ACLs, and then it examines the **vty ACL** feature that filters router SSH/Telnet access.

Filtering for End User SSH/Telnet

IT staff, and possibly some end users, may need to use SSH and Telnet to connect to a command line (shell) prompt on servers in the network. So if you plan to add an ACL on an interface, it will need to consider the Telnet and SSH protocols.

SSH and Telnet use TCP, with well-known ports 22 and 23, respectively. As a result, you can easily match both ports in one ACE using the **range 22 23** parameters in a **permit** command. (Note that IOS, as usual, changes some numeric port numbers to keywords—in this case, changing 23 to **telnet**.)

Example 8-8 shows two sets of ACEs, similar to a few other examples. The first shows a more general permit of SSH and Telnet traffic, while the second adds more restrictions.

1. One-stage: Permitting all SSH and Telnet messages going toward a server

2. Two-stage:

   a. Permitting all SSH and Telnet messages moving toward a server, with source and destination addresses from within the enterprise's private network 10.0.0.0

   b. Denying all other SSH and Telnet

Example 8-8 *ACEs for the Two SSH and Telnet Scenarios for Host-Based Servers*

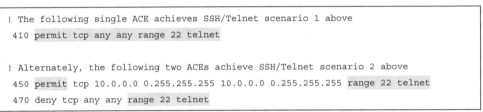
```
! The following single ACE achieves SSH/Telnet scenario 1 above
 410 permit tcp any any range 22 telnet


! Alternately, the following two ACEs achieve SSH/Telnet scenario 2 above
 450 permit tcp 10.0.0.0 0.255.255.255 10.0.0.0 0.255.255.255 range 22 telnet
 470 deny tcp any any range 22 telnet
```

The sample ACEs in Example 8-8 work to permit SSH and Telnet traffic when you know where all servers are. If you plan an ACL that matches packets moving toward the servers, you can then rely on matching the destination port. Conversely, if the plan enables the ACL for packets sent from the server to the client, you can check the well-known source ports.

However, with Telnet and SSH, you can seldom know where all SSH servers reside. All the routers and switches and many other IT devices support SSH or Telnet (or both). For instance, consider Figure 8-5. Host A uses SSH to connect to server S1, and host C connects to the switch SW2 SSH server. An outbound ACL on router R1's WAN interface (G0/0/1) would examine packets destined to SSH server S1 and also packets sourced from the SSH server in switch SW2. Packets flowing from the SW2 SSH server back to SSH client C will have a well-known source port of 22.

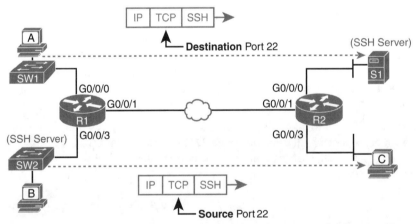

Figure 8-5 *The Need to Match Both Directions for SSH and Telnet Traffic*

As a result, the choice to match SSH and Telnet by port number probably means you should match for both directions—that is, check for the source or destination port. Example 8-9 shows expanded sets of ACEs versus Example 8-8. The original ACEs checked for the SSH and Telnet destination ports, while the new lines also check for the SSH and Telnet source ports. In the new (highlighted) lines, pay close attention to the location of the **range 22 telnet** parameters.

Example 8-9   *Updated SSH/Telnet ACEs to Add Checks for Both Directions*

```
! SSH/Telnet scenario 1, revised for packets both to and from the server
410 permit tcp any any range 22 telnet
420 permit tcp any range 22 telnet any

! SSH/Telnet scenario 2, revised for packets both to and from the server
450 permit tcp 10.0.0.0 0.255.255.255 10.0.0.0 0.255.255.255 range 22 telnet
460 permit tcp 10.0.0.0 0.255.255.255 range 22 telnet 10.0.0.0 0.255.255.255
470 deny tcp any any range 22 telnet
480 deny tcp any range 22 telnet any
```

Filtering for Router VTY Access

IOS provides another feature to protect CLI access further by using a vty ACL enabled by the **access-class** command in vty configuration mode. When a user connects to a router or switch using Telnet or SSH, IOS associates a vty line with that user connection. IOS can apply an ACL to the vty lines, filtering the addresses that can telnet or SSH into the router or switch. Figure 8-6 shows the concept, with a network engineer at host A logging in to router R1 using SSH. The box above the router R1 icon represents the router's internal logic.

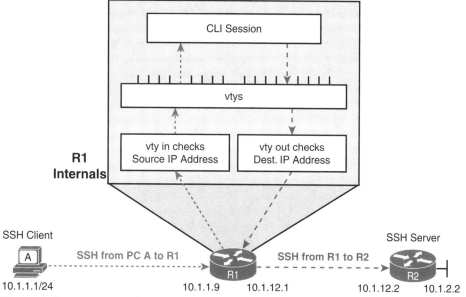

Figure 8-6   *IP ACLs and the Router's Internal SSH/Telnet Servers*

First, consider a vty ACL enabled for the inbound direction, which examines packets for SSH/Telnet clients attempting to log in to a router. You can use either a standard or extended

ACL for a vty ACL, but a standard ACL works well. A vty ACL is not an interface ACL. Independent of the ACL matching logic, IOS applies these rules to vty ACLs:

■ Consider only packets sent to the router's IP addresses on working interfaces.

■ Consider only packets destined for the SSH (port 22) or Telnet (port 23) servers.

Beginning with those limits, the only other helpful match to make is the SSH/Telnet clients' IP addresses. A standard ACL works well for that.

For example, imagine all networking staff have IP addresses in subnet 10.1.1.0/24. As an extra precaution, you configure a vty ACL to permit SSH/Telnet from clients in that subnet but deny all other source addresses. Example 8-10 shows the configuration of the complete ACL on router R1 in Figure 8-6 and how to enable it in vty mode using the **access-class** command.

Example 8-10   *vty Access Control Using the* access-class in *Command*

```
line vty 0 15
 transport input all
 access-class IT_only in
!
ip access-list standard IT_only
 10 remark matches packets sourced from subnet 10.1.1.0/24 only; implied deny any
 10 permit 10.1.1.0 0.0.0.255
```

IOS uses the **access-class** *acl* **in** vty subcommand to enable the function. The keyword **in** refers to Telnet and SSH connections into this router. As configured, ACL **IT_only** permits packets with source addresses from the IT subnet and denies all others due to the implied **deny any** at the end of the list. Note that the command to enable the ACL, **access-class**, used in vty mode, is a different command and mode than is used to enable ACLs on interfaces.

Inbound vty ACLs are popular, but IOS also supports the less common outbound vty ACL. The outbound option works in cases for which a current SSH/Telnet user at the CLI uses the **ssh** or **telnet** EXEC command to connect to the CLI of another device. For instance, in Figure 8-6, the user at host A could SSH to router R1. Once logged in, if that user then used the **ssh** or **telnet** EXEC command to attempt to connect to router R2, IOS would apply the outbound vty ACL to that connection request.

To use an outbound vty ACL, create an ACL and enable it with the **access-class** *acl* **out** command in vty configuration mode. As with inbound vty ACLs, IOS processes limited packets (those sourced from router IP addresses) and destined for the SSH or Telnet well-known ports.

Standard ACLs often work well for outbound vty ACLs, but with a surprising twist. When used as an outbound vty ACL, IOS compares the standard IP ACL address parameters to the *destination IP address of the packet* rather than the source address. That is, it filters based on the device to which the **telnet** or **ssh** command tries to connect. Example 8-11 demonstrates with an outbound vty ACL that permits only address 10.1.12.1, but not 10.1.2.2. The example shows the failed SSH attempt and IOS error message, followed by the successful attempt.

Example 8-11   *vty Access Control Outbound on Router R1*

```
! Configuration excerpt first
line vty 0 15
 transport input all
 access-class R2_WAN out
!
ip access-list standard R2_WAN
  10 permit host 10.1.12.1
!
! An attempt denied by the ACL to router R2's far-side LAN IP address
R1# ssh -l wendell 10.1.12.2
% Connections to that host not permitted from this terminal

! An attempt permitted by the ACL, resulting in password prompt from router R2.
R2# ssh -l wendell 10.1.12.1
Password:

R2>
```

On a final note, outbound vty ACLs also support extended ACLs, but with the logic you would expect. It matches the source address parameters to the packet source address and the destination address parameters to the destination address.

Comparing ACLs in IOS and IOS XE

Cisco added ACLs to IOS in the early days of the company. Over many decades, Cisco has added ACL features and commands over many IOS versions. Cisco has added some features and command options to IOS XE that differ from IOS over time.

This final section of the chapter summarizes some of the current differences between the recent versions of IOS and IOS XE in early 2023 when I most recently revised this chapter. I did not choose to add this section because of any exam topic. More generally, the exam topics do not mention any need to compare ACLs on IOS versus IOS XE. Cisco historically avoids asking anything to do with IOS software versions. However, you may practice ACLs with IOS, but then an exam question may use output from IOS XE, or vice versa. This short section summarizes some of the differences to prepare you. The goal is for you to be comfortable if you see minor differences in an ACL exam question versus what you see during your study time.

This section first summarizes the differences and then discusses two ACL features that behave differently on IOS than on IOS XE: sequence number resequencing and the common ACL.

Configuration Syntax and Show Commands

The original numbered IP ACLs used global commands, specifically the **access-list** global command. Later, IOS added support for ACL mode, which can be reached with the **ip access-list** command, with subcommands to define the detail. Informally, consider those two options as global mode and ACL mode.

Table 8-2 lists some of the differences between ACL support in IOS versus IOS XE. The ACL chapters in this book have mentioned several of these similarities and differences in context, but the table organizes them for easy reference. Note that the table also lists a few similarities to provide more context.

Table 8-2 ACL Differences with IOS and IOS XE

Feature	IOS	IOS XE
Numbered ACLs: Allows configuration with global commands	Yes	Yes
Numbered ACLs: Allows configuration with ACL mode commands for easy ACL editing	Yes	Yes
Numbered ACLs: **running-config** shows ACL as global commands*	Yes	No
Named ACLs: Configured and stored as ACL mode commands	Yes	Yes
Named ACLs: **show running-config** lists sequence numbers	No	Yes
Named ACLs: **show access-lists** lists sequence numbers	Yes	Yes
Resequences ACL sequence numbers on reload by default**	Yes	No
Supports second (common) ACL per interface/direction	No	Yes
Allows matching multiple nonconsecutive ports with **eq**	No	Yes

* IOS stores the commands as global commands, while IOS XE stores them as ACL mode commands, regardless of configuration style.

** XE can be configured to resequence ACLs on reload, but by default, it does not.

Working through the table, the first two rows confirm that IOS and IOS XE allow configuring numbered ACLs with the original-style global commands or ACL mode subcommands. The third line shows the difference: IOS stores the configuration as globals, but IOS XE stores them as ACL mode subcommands—no matter how you configured them.

The next three rows (unhighlighted) reveal similar features for named ACLs. The one difference: IOS XE reveals ACL sequence numbers in **show running-config** command output, while IOS does not. IOS requires the **show access-lists** or **show ip access-lists** commands to see the sequence numbers.

The final topics of this chapter discuss the remaining rows in the table, which list features that differ between IOS and IOS XE.

Resequencing ACL Sequence Numbers

You have seen many examples of ACL sequence numbers in this chapter and the preceding chapter. For instance, if you ignore them when configuring, IOS (and IOS XE) adds them for you, beginning at 10. IOS (and IOS XE) assigns sequence numbers to each successive **permit** or **deny** command in increments of 10. Alternatively, you can choose your sequence numbers with commands that begin the sequence number before the **permit** or **deny** command. You can also delete lines and add new ones using sequence numbers.

At one point in the history of IOS, Cisco decided to add **ACL resequencing** features. First and foremost, IOS will resequence ACL sequence numbers automatically at reload and that behavior continues today for IOS. So, for IOS, when you reload the router, IOS changes the sequence numbers of all ACEs in each ACL. It gives the first ACE sequence number 10, the next 20, and so on, with an increment of 10. For instance, an ACL with ACEs numbered 10,

30, and 60 before the reload would have the same ACEs in the same order after reload but with sequence numbers 10, 20, and 30.

Additionally, IOS supports manual ACL resequencing. The **ip access-list resequence** *name/number first increment* global configuration command performs the task, for one specific ACL, with the listed initial sequence number and increment. For instance, imagine the ACL named acl_01 had three **permit** commands with line numbers 10, 30, and 60 again. Example 8-12 shows the results of the **ip access-list resequence acl_01 100 20** global command. The last two parameters define the first sequence number as 100 with increments of 20. (Both IOS and IOS XE support resequencing, as shown in the example.)

Example 8-12   *Resequencing ACLs with the* **ip access-list resequence** *Global Command*

```
R1# configure terminal
R1(config)# ip access-list resequence acl_01 100 20
R1(config)# do show access-list acl_01
Extended IP access list acl_01
    100 permit ip 10.1.4.0 0.0.1.255 any
    120 permit ip 10.2.4.0 0.0.1.255 any
    140 permit ip 10.0.0.0 0.255.255.255 10.0.0.0 0.255.255.255
```

IOS and IOS XE differ with automatic resequencing. IOS always resequences at any restart (the **reload** command or power off/on), while IOS XE does not resequence at restart. IOS XE calls its approach **ACL persistence**, configured by the (default) global command **ip access-list persistent**. IOS XE allows the same resequencing behavior as IOS by disabling ACL persistence with the **no ip access-list persistent** global command.

ACL sequence number persistence, the default with IOS XE, makes sense. You can choose to renumber your ACLs only when desired and use different numbering plans other than starting at 10 and incrementing by 10.

Using a Second (Common) Interface ACL

For the long history of ACL support in Cisco IOS, the following rule dictates how many router ACLs you can enable on an interface:

One ACL per layer three protocol, per direction, per interface.

For instance, today, the most common Layer 3 protocols in enterprise routers are IPv4 and IPv6. On any router interface, the router supports one IPv4 ACL inbound, one IPv4 ACL outbound, one IPv6 ACL inbound, and one IPv6 ACL outbound. Do you need all those at once? Seldom. More importantly, you cannot configure logic with multiple ACLs enabled on one interface in one direction to be processed one after the other. Instead, you have to put all the ACEs into one ACL.

IOS XE breaks that mold allowing two IPv4 ACLs on an interface in the same direction. Cisco refers to the first ACL as the **common ACL**, with the second as the *regular ACL*. However, both ACLs still use the same syntax and logic as before. The router optimizes internal processing, but the result is that it matches packets as if it first matched the common ACL and then the regular ACL, as shown in Figure 8-7.

8

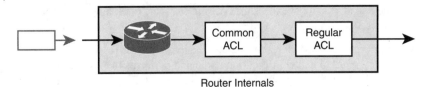

Router Internals

Figure 8-7 *Two ACLs per Interface per Direction with a Common ACL*

You still use the **ip access-group** command to enable the two ACLs, but with different syntax. Example 8-13 shows how to enable two ACLs outbound on some router's G0/0/1 interface and confirms the enabled ACLs with the **show ip interface** command. You may want to compare this output to the same command's output in Example 6-2 from Chapter 6, "Basic IPv4 Access Control Lists," taken from IOS, so it does not mention a common ACL. The output here confirms an outgoing common and regular ACL but no incoming ACLs.

Example 8-13 *Enabling Two IP ACLs, Outbound*

```
R1# configure terminal
R1(config-if)# interface gigabitEthernet 0/0/1
R1(config-if)# ip access-group common common_all unique_01 out
R1(config-if)# do show ip interface g0/0/1
GigabitEthernet0/0/1 is up, line protocol is up
  Internet address is 10.1.12.1/24
  Broadcast address is 255.255.255.255
  Address determined by non-volatile memory
  MTU is 1500 bytes
  Helper address is not set
  Directed broadcast forwarding is disabled
  Multicast reserved groups joined: 224.0.0.5 224.0.0.10 224.0.0.6
  Outgoing Common access list is common_all
  Outgoing access list is unique_01
  Inbound Common access list is not set
  Inbound access list is not set
```

Note that the addition of the common ACL feature does not improve what you can match with an ACL; instead, Cisco's motivation for this feature stems from a need to conserve entries in tables used by hardware ASICs in multilayer switches and in some routers. The first **ip access-group** command that enables a common ACL requires table entries for the common ACL's ACEs. But the router or switch can reuse those. So, any repeated **ip access-group** command that enables the same common ACL does not require additional ASIC table entries, reducing the consumption of that resource.

> **NOTE** IOS allows one **ip access-group** subcommand for each direction, but no more— regardless of whether the commands refer to a common ACL. For example, with an existing **ip access-group fred out** interface subcommand, configuring the **ip access-group common wilma betty out** subcommand on the interface replaces the existing command.

Matching Multiple Nonconsecutive Ports with eq

When matching TCP and UDP port numbers, Cisco ACLs have long supported matching a single port with the **eq** *number* parameters or a range of consecutive ports with the **range** *first-last* parameters. However, to match multiple nonconsecutive ports, the syntax required multiple ACEs.

IOS XE adds syntax and logic to match up to ten port numbers after the **eq** keyword in a single ACE. For instance, the command **permit tcp any any eq 10 12 14 16 18 20** matches all IP packets that have a TCP header, with any of the port numbers. In other words, IOS XE uses a logical OR between the port numbers, so it would match port 10, or 12, or 14, and so on.

Chapter Review

One key to doing well on the exams is to perform repetitive spaced review sessions. Review this chapter's material using either the tools in the book or interactive tools for the same material found on the book's companion website. Refer to the "Your Study Plan" element for more details. Table 8-3 outlines the key review elements and where you can find them. To better track your study progress, record when you completed these activities in the second column.

Table 8-3   Chapter Review Tracking

Review Element	Review Date(s)	Resource Used
Review key topics		Book, website
Review key terms		Book, website
Repeat DIKTA questions		Book, PTP
Review memory tables		Book, website
Review command tables		Book

Review All the Key Topics

Table 8-4   Key Topics for Chapter 8

Key Topic Element	Description	Page Number
Example 8-3	Two alternative approaches for permitting some ICMP traffic	165
Paragraph	Router logic for outbound ACL bypass for local packets	166
Example 8-5	Two alternative approaches for permitting OSPF traffic	167
Figure 8-3	Addresses and port numbers in DHCP, before and after the DHCP helper function	167
Example 8-6	Two alternative approaches for permitting DHCP traffic	168
List	Special rules that affect ACL processing for DHCP on a router using the **ip helper-address** command	168
Example 8-8	Two alternative approaches for permitting SSH traffic routed by a router	170

Key Topic Element	Description	Page Number
Figure 8-6	Vty ACL concepts	171
Example 8-10	Inbound vty ACL	172
Example 8-12	Demonstrating ACL resequencing by command	175

Key Terms You Should Know

ACL persistence, ACL resequencing, Common ACL, vty ACL

Command References

Tables 8-5 and 8-6 list configuration and verification commands used in this chapter. As an easy review exercise, cover the left column in a table, read the right column, and try to recall the command without looking. Then repeat the exercise, covering the right column, and try to recall what the command does.

The tables list commands introduced in this chapter; refer to Chapters 6 and 7 for more documentation on commands related to IP ACLs.

Table 8-5 Chapter 8 ACL Configuration Command Reference

Command	Description
access-list *access-list-number* {deny | permit} ospf *source source-wildcard destination destination-wildcard* [log]	A version of the access-list command that matches all OSPF messages.
[sequence-number] {deny | permit} ospf *source source-wildcard destination destination-wildcard* [log]	The equivalent of the previous row's command but in ACL mode.
access-list *access-list-number* {deny | permit} icmp *source source-wildcard destination destination-wildcard* [*icmp-message*]	A version of the access-list command that matches ICMP with the option to list the specific ICMP message type.
[sequence-number] {deny | permit} icmp *source source-wildcard destination destination-wildcard* [*icmp-message*]	The equivalent of the previous row's command but in ACL mode.
ip access-list resequence *name/number initial increment*	Global command to resequence ACL sequence numbers, beginning with the initial value, and adding the increment to get each successive sequence number.
[no] ip access-list persistent	Global command to toggle on (without the no; default) or off (with the no) ACL sequence number persistence. IOS XE only.
ip access-group common *common_acl regular_acl* {[in | out]}	Interface subcommand, which allows two ACLs to be enabled simultaneously on one interface and direction. IOS XE only.

Table 8-6   Chapter 8 EXEC Command Reference

Command	Description
ssh -l *username address*/*hostname*	Initiates an SSH client connection from the CLI to another device at the listed address or hostname, using the listed username to log in
telnet *address*/*hostname*	Initiates a Telnet client connection from the CLI to another device at the listed address or hostname
show ip access-lists [*access-list-number* | *access-list-name*]	Shows IP access lists

8

Part II Review

Keep track of your part review progress with the checklist in Table P2-1. Details about each task follow the table.

Table P2-1 Part II Part Review Checklist

Activity	1st Date Completed	2nd Date Completed
Repeat All DIKTA Questions		
Answer Part Review Questions		
Review Key Topics		
Do Labs		

Repeat All DIKTA Questions

For this task, use the PTP software to answer the "Do I Know This Already?" questions again for the chapters in this part of the book.

Answer Part Review Questions

For this task, use PTP to answer the Part Review questions for this part of the book.

Review Key Topics

Review all key topics in all chapters in this part, either by browsing the chapters or by using the Key Topics application on the companion website.

Do Labs

Depending on your chosen lab tool, here are some suggestions for what to do in lab:

Pearson Network Simulator: If you use the full Pearson CCNA simulator, focus more on the configuration scenario and troubleshooting scenario labs associated with the topics in this part of the book. These types of labs include a larger set of topics and work well as Part Review activities. (See the Introduction for some details about how to find which labs are about topics in this part of the book.)

Config Labs: The author's blog (https://www.certskills.com) includes a series of configuration-focused labs that you can do on paper, each in 10–15 minutes. Review and perform labs for this part of the book by using the menus to navigate to the per-chapter content and then finding all config labs related to that chapter. (You can see more detailed instructions at https://www.certskills.com/config-labs).

Other: If you are using other lab tools, here are a few suggestions: when building ACL labs, you can test with Telnet (port 23), SSH (port 22), ping (ICMP), and traceroute (UDP) traffic as generated from an extra router. So, do not just configure the ACL; make an ACL that can match these types of traffic, denying some and permitting others, and then test.

Use Per-Chapter Interactive Review

Using the companion website, browse through the interactive review elements, like memory tables and key term flashcards, to review the content from each chapter.

Before the year 2020, Cisco offered several CCNA certifications. Those included CCNA Routing and Switching as well as CCNA Security. In 2020, Cisco discontinued all of those, replacing them with one CCNA certification. That CCNA certification mostly resembled CCNA Routing and Switching, but with some parts of CCNA Security and CCNA Wireless included. The current CCNA certification, based on the 200-301 Exam's Version 1.1 blueprint, continues to include meaningful security and wireless LAN content.

Part III of this book discusses the largest security topics from Domain 5 of the blueprint, while leaving some security topics to other parts of the books. For instance, the wireless LAN security topics in that domain reside in Part I of this book, along with the rest of the Wireless LAN materials. This part, Part III, includes all standalone security topics.

Chapter 9 kicks off Part III with a wide description of security threats, vulnerabilities, and exploits. This introductory chapter sets the stage to help you think more like a security engineer.

Chapters 10, 11, and 12 then focus on a wide range of short security topics. Those topics include Chapter 10's discussion of how to protect router and switch logins and passwords, along with an introduction to the functions and roles of firewalls or intrusion protection systems (IPSs). Chapters 11 and 12 then get into three separate security features built into Cisco switches: port security (covered in Chapter 11), DHCP Snooping, and Dynamic ARP Inspection (DAI) (both covered in Chapter 12). All three security features use a LAN switch to examine frames as they enter the switch interface. This information enables port security, DHCP Snooping, and DAI to decide whether to allow the message to continue on its way.

Part III

Security Services

Security Architectures

This chapter covers the following exam topics:

5.0 Security Fundamentals

5.1 Define key security concepts (threats, vulnerabilities, exploits, and mitigation techniques)

5.2 Describe security program elements (user awareness, training, and physical access control)

5.4 Describe security password policies elements, such as management, complexity, and password alternatives (multifactor authentication, certificates, and biometrics)

5.8 Compare authentication, authorization, and accounting concepts

As you have learned about various networking technologies, your attention has probably been focused on using network devices to build functional networks. After all, networks should let data flow freely so that all connected users have a good experience, right? The unfortunate fact is that not all connected users can be trusted to obey the rules and be good network citizens. In this chapter, you learn about many aspects of an enterprise network that can be exploited, as well as some ways you can protect them.

"Do I Know This Already?" Quiz

Take the quiz (either here or use the PTP software) if you want to use the score to help you decide how much time to spend on this chapter. The letter answers are listed at the bottom of the page following the quiz. Appendix C, found both at the end of the book as well as on the companion website, includes both the answers and explanations. You can also find both answers and explanations in the PTP testing software.

Table 9-1 "Do I Know This Already?" Foundation Topics Section-to-Question Mapping

Foundation Topics Section	Questions
Security Terminology	1, 2
Common Security Threats	3–7
Controlling and Monitoring User Access	8
Developing a Security Program to Educate Users	9

1. Which one of the following terms means anything that can be considered to be a weakness that can compromise security?

   a. Exploit

   b. Vulnerability

    c.   Attack

    d.   Threat

2. An actual potential to exploit a vulnerability is known as which one of the following terms?

    a.   Vulnerability

    b.   Attack

    c.   Exploit

    d.   Threat

3. In a spoofing attack, which of the following parameters are commonly spoofed? (Choose two answers.)

    a.   MAC address

    b.   Source IP address

    c.   Destination IP address

    d.   ARP address

4. Suppose an attacker sends a series of packets toward a destination IP address with the TCP SYN flag set but sends no other packet types. Which of the following attacks is likely taking place?

    a.   Spoofing attack

    b.   Reflection attack

    c.   Reconnaissance attack

    d.   Denial-of-service attack

    e.   None of the other answers are correct.

5. In a reflection attack, the source IP address in the attack packets is spoofed so that it contains which one of the following entities?

    a.   The address of the attacker

    b.   The address of the reflector

    c.   The address of the victim

    d.   The address of the router

6. During a successful man-in-the-middle attack, which two of the following actions is an attacker most likely to perform?

    a.   Eavesdrop on traffic passing between hosts

    b.   Induce a buffer overflow on multiple hosts

    c.   Modify data passing between hosts

    d.   Use ping sweeps and port scans to discover the network

7. Which one of the following is the goal of a brute-force attack?

    a.   Try every possible TCP port until a service answers.

    b.   Try every possible combination of keyboard characters to guess a user's password.

    c   Initiate a denial-of-service operation on every possible host in a subnet.

    d.   Spoof every possible IP address in an organization.

8. Which one of the following is an example of a AAA server?

    a. DHCP

    b. DNS

    c. SNMP

    d. ISE

9. Physical access control is important for which one of the following reasons?

    a. It prevents unauthorized people from sitting at a corporate user's desk and using their computer.

    b. It prevents users from getting angry and damaging computer equipment.

    c. It prevents unauthorized access to network closets.

    d. It prevents fires from destroying data centers.

Foundation Topics

Security Terminology

In a perfect world, you might build a network that supports every user in an enterprise, with the assumption that every user is known, every user is approved to access everything on the network, and every user will use the available resources exactly according to some corporate guidelines. The network shown in Figure 9-1 might represent such a scenario. Even this ideal, closed system is not completely secure because a user might decide to misbehave in order to pester a coworker or to view information on the corporate server that should be restricted or confidential.

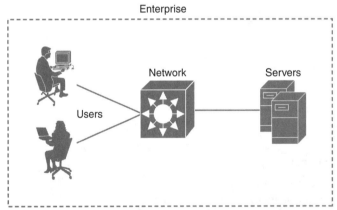

Figure 9-1 *An Example of an Enterprise Closed System*

Now consider that almost no enterprise uses such a limited, closed environment. After all, the enterprise will probably want to somehow connect itself to the public Internet and perhaps to some corporate partners. It will also probably want to allow its workers to be mobile and carry laptops, tablets, and smartphones in and out of the corporate boundaries for convenience. The enterprise might want to provide network access to guests who visit. If the enterprise offers wireless connectivity to its employees (and guests), it might also unknowingly offer its wireless access to people who are within range of the signals. And the list goes on and on. As the network and its connectivity expand, as Figure 9-2 shows, the enterprise will have more difficulty maintaining the safe, closed boundary around itself.

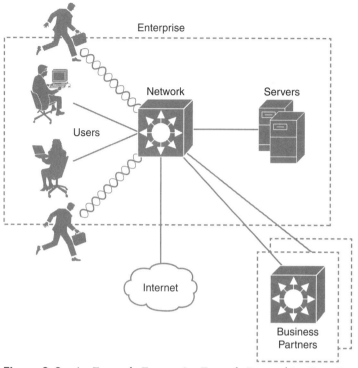

Figure 9-2   *An Example Enterprise Extends Beyond Its Own Boundary*

To begin securing a network, you first need to understand what might go wrong with it. Think of an enterprise network as a simple box-shaped facility, as shown in part A of Figure 9-3. When all of the walls, floor, and ceiling are made of a very strong material and are very thick, the contents inside the box will likely remain safe from harm or theft. The owner, however, might have a hard time getting in and out of the box.

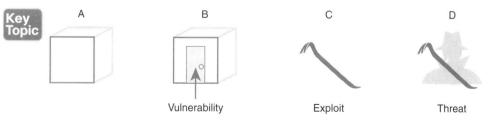

Figure 9-3   *Security Terminology Illustrated*

Suppose a door is introduced for convenience, as shown in part B of Figure 9-3. The owner can now come and go, but so might anyone else. Even if the door is locked, someone might find a way to get the door open and access the treasures inside. Because no door is impenetrable, the door becomes a **vulnerability**. In terms of security, a vulnerability is anything that can be considered to be a weakness that can compromise the security of something else, such as the integrity of data or how a system performs.

Just because a vulnerability exists, nothing is necessarily in jeopardy. In the locked door example, nobody but the trusted owner can open the door unless some sort of tool other than the key is used. Such a tool can be used to exploit a vulnerability. In fact, the tool itself is called an **exploit**, as shown by the pry bar in part C of Figure 9-3. An exploit is not very effective if it is used against anything other than the targeted weakness or vulnerability.

Technically, an exploit such as the pry bar is not very effective at all by itself. Someone must pick it up and use it against the vulnerability. In part D of Figure 9-3, a malicious user possesses the pry bar and intends to use it to open the locked door. Now there is an actual potential to break in, destroy, steal, or otherwise modify something without permission. This is known as a **threat**.

In the IT world of networks, systems, workstations, and applications, there are many, many different vulnerabilities and exploits that can be leveraged by malicious users to become threats to an organization and its data. The remainder of this chapter provides an overview of many of them, along with some techniques you can leverage to counteract or prevent the malicious activity. Such measures are known as **mitigation techniques**. You might be thinking of some ways the Figure 9-3 building owner could mitigate the threats from attack. Perhaps the owner could add stronger, more secure locks to the door, a more robust door frame to withstand prying forces, or an alarm system to detect an intrusion and alert the authorities.

Common Security Threats

Because modern enterprise networks are usually made up of many parts that all work together, securing them can become a very complex task. As with the simple box analogy, you cannot effectively try to secure it until you have identified many of the vulnerabilities, assessed the many exploits that exist, and realized where the threats might come from. Only then can the appropriate countermeasures and mitigations be put in place.

You should also consider some important attributes of enterprise resources that should be protected and preserved. As you work through the many threats that are discussed in this chapter, think about the vulnerability and exploit that make the threat possible. Notice how many different parts of the enterprise network exhibit vulnerabilities and how the threats are crafted to take advantage of the weaknesses.

Attacks That Spoof Addresses

When systems behave normally, parameters and services can be trusted and used effectively. For example, when a machine sends an IP packet, everyone expects the source IP address to be the machine's own IP address. The source MAC address in the Ethernet frame is expected to be the sender's own MAC address. Even services like DHCP and DNS should follow suit; if a machine sends a DHCP or DNS request, it expects any DHCP or DNS reply to come from a legitimate, trusted server.

Spoofing attacks focus on one vulnerability; addresses and services tend to be implicitly trusted. Attacks usually take place by replacing expected values with spoofed or fake values. Address spoofing attacks can be simple and straightforward, where one address value is substituted for another.

Answers to the "Do I Know This Already?" quiz:

1 B **2** D **3** A, B **4** D **5** C **6** A, C **7** B **8** D **9** C

For example, an attacker can send packets with a spoofed source IP address instead of its own, as shown in Figure 9-4. When the target receives the packets, it will send return traffic to the spoofed address, rather than the attacker's actual address. If the spoofed address exists, then an unsuspecting host with that address will receive the packet. If the address does not exist, the packet will be forwarded and then dropped further out in the network.

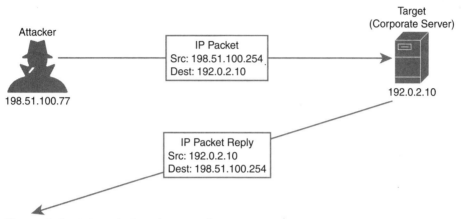

Figure 9-4 *A Sample Spoofing Attack*

An attacker can send spoofed MAC addresses too, to add false information to the forwarding tables used by Layer 2 switches or ARP tables used by other hosts and routers. DHCP requests with spoofed MAC addresses can also be sent to a legitimate DHCP server, filling its address lease table and leaving no free IP addresses for normal use.

Note that Chapter 11, "Implementing Switch Port Security," discusses a tool that can be used to help mitigate MAC address spoofing. In Chapter 12, "DHCP Snooping and ARP Inspection," you can learn more about Dynamic ARP Inspection (DAI) and how to use it to mitigate IP address spoofing using ARP.

Denial-of-Service Attacks

In the normal operation of a business application, clients open connections to corporate servers to exchange information. This operation might occur in the form of web-based sessions that are open to internal users as well as external users on the Internet. The process is simple: users open a web browser to the corporate site, which then opens a TCP connection with the corporate web server; then some transaction can take place. If all the users are well behaved and conduct legitimate transactions, the corporate servers are (hopefully) not stressed and many clients can do business normally.

Now suppose a malicious user finds a way to open an abnormal connection to the same corporate server. The TCP connection begins with the malicious user sending a SYN flag to the server, but the source IP address is replaced with a fake address. The server adds the TCP connection to its table of client connections and replies to the fake address with a SYN-ACK. Because the fake address is not involved in the TCP connection, there is no ACK reply to complete the TCP three-way handshake. The incomplete connection stays in the server's table until it eventually times out and is removed. During this time, the attacker can try to open many, many more abnormal connections at such a rate that the server's connection table fills. At that point, the server is no longer able to maintain TCP connections with legitimate users, so their business transactions all halt. Figure 9-5 illustrates this process.

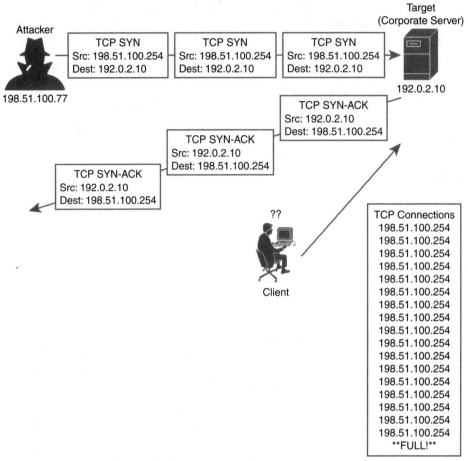

Figure 9-5 *A Sample Denial-of-Service Attack*

When an attacker is able to deplete a system resource, services and systems become unavailable or crash. This is called a **denial-of-service (DoS) attack** because it denies service to legitimate users or operations. DoS attacks can involve something as simple as ICMP echo (ping) packets, a flood of UDP packets, and TCP connections, such as the TCP SYN flood attack previously described. Such attacks can be successful provided a system has a vulnerability with the protocol or type of traffic that is exploited.

Attackers can carry the DoS idea even further by enlisting many other systems to participate. To do this, the attacker sets up a master control computer somewhere on the Internet. Next, many computers must first be infected with malicious code or malware by leveraging vulnerabilities present in those machines. Each machine then silently becomes a "bot," appearing to operate normally, while awaiting commands from the master control. When the time comes for an attack to begin, the master control sends a command to every bot and tells it to initiate a denial-of-service attack against a single target host. This is called a **distributed denial-of-service (DDoS) attack** because the attack is distributed across a large number of bots, all flooding or attacking the same target.

Reflection and Amplification Attacks

Recall that in a spoofing attack, the attacker sends packets with a spoofed source address to a target. The goal is to force the target to deal with the spoofed traffic and send return traffic toward a nonexistent source. The attacker does not care where the return traffic goes or that it cannot be delivered successfully.

In a somewhat related attack, the attacker again sends packets with a spoofed source address toward a live host. However, the host is not the intended target; the goal is to get the host to reflect the exchange toward the spoofed address that is the target. This is known as a **reflection attack**, as illustrated in Figure 9-6, and the host reflecting the traffic toward the target is called the reflector. The attacker might also send the spoofed packets to multiple reflectors, causing the target to receive multiple copies of the unexpected traffic.

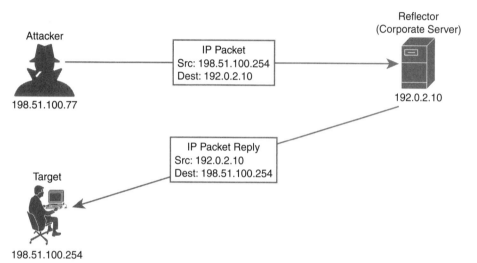

Figure 9-6   *A Sample Reflection Attack*

The impact of a reflection attack might seem limited because a single target host is the victim, and the amount of traffic being reflected to the target is in proportion to the packets sent by the attacker. If an attacker sends a small amount of traffic to a reflector and leverages a protocol or service to generate a large volume of traffic toward a target, then an **amplification attack** has occurred. In effect, such an attack amplifies the attacker's efforts to disrupt the target. Another result is that large amounts of network bandwidth can be consumed forwarding the amplified traffic toward the target, especially if many reflectors are involved. Some mechanisms of DNS and NTP have been exploited in the past to set new records for enormous bandwidth consumption during an amplification attack.

Man-in-the-Middle Attacks

Many types of attacks are meant to disrupt or directly compromise targeted systems, often with noticeable results. Sometimes an attacker might want to eavesdrop on data that passes from one machine to another, avoiding detection. A **man-in-the-middle attack** does just that, by allowing the attacker to quietly wedge itself into the communication path as an intermediary between two target systems.

One type of man-in-the-middle attack exploits the ARP table that each host maintains to communicate with other hosts on its local network segment. Normally, if one host needs to send data to another, it looks for the destination host in its ARP table. If an entry is found, the Ethernet frame can be sent directly to the destination MAC address; otherwise, the sender must broadcast an ARP request containing the destination's IP address and wait for the destination to answer with an ARP reply and its own MAC address.

Figure 9-7 illustrates a successful man-in-the-middle attack.

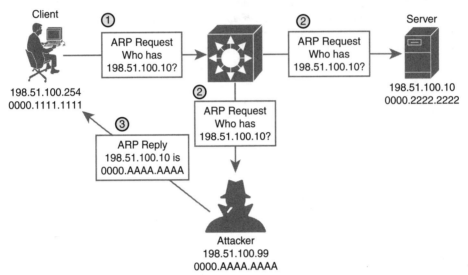

Figure 9-7 *A Man-in-the-Middle Attack Begins*

In step 1, a client broadcasts an ARP request to find out what MAC address is used by the host with IP address 198.51.100.10. In step 2, the ARP request is flooded to all hosts in the broadcast domain. This allows the attacker to overhear the ARP request and prepare to exploit the information learned. The legitimate owner of 198.51.100.10 may indeed respond with its own ARP reply and real MAC address, as expected. However, in step 3, the attacker simply waits a brief time and then sends a spoofed ARP reply containing its own MAC address, rather than that of the actual destination. The goal is for the attacker to send the last ARP reply so that any listening host will update its ARP table with the most recent information.

This process effectively poisons the ARP table entry in any system receiving the spoofed ARP reply. From that point on, a poisoned system will blindly forward traffic to the attacker's MAC address, who is now masquerading as the destination. The attacker is able to know the real destination's MAC address because the attacker received an earlier ARP reply from the destination host. Figure 9-8 depicts the end result. The attacker can repeat this process by poisoning the ARP entries on multiple hosts and then relay traffic between them without easy detection.

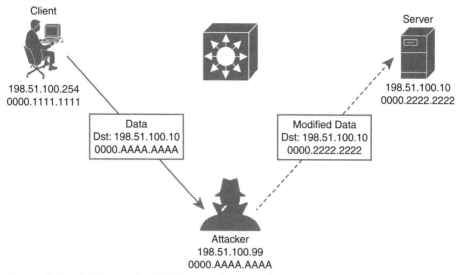

Figure 9-8   *A Man-in-the-Middle Attack Succeeds*

After attackers have inserted themselves between two hosts, they can passively eavesdrop on and inspect all traffic passing between them. The attackers might also take an active role and modify the data passing through.

Address Spoofing Attack Summary

As you work through the various types of address spoofing attacks, remember that the attackers' goal is to disguise their identity and fool other systems in a malicious way. Use Table 9-2 to review the concepts and characteristics of each attack type.

Table 9-2   Summary of Address Spoofing Attacks

Goal	DoS/DDoS	Reflection	Amplification	Man-in-the-Middle
Exhaust a system service or resource; crash the target system	Yes	Yes	Yes	No
Trick an unwitting accomplice host to send traffic to target	No	Yes	Yes	No
Eavesdrop on traffic	No	No	No	Yes
Modify traffic passing through	No	No	No	Yes

Reconnaissance Attacks

When an attacker intends to launch an attack on a target, that attacker might want to identify some vulnerabilities so the attack can be focused and more effective. A **reconnaissance attack** can be used to discover more details about the target and its systems prior to an actual attack.

During a reconnaissance attack, the attacker can use some common tools to uncover public details like who owns a domain and what IP address ranges are used there. For example, the **nslookup** command exists in many operating systems and can perform a DNS lookup to resolve an IP address from a fully qualified domain name. If an attacker knows the domain name of a business, nslookup can reveal the owner of the domain and the IP address space registered to it. The **whois** and **dig** commands are complementary tools that can query DNS information to reveal detailed information about domain owners, contact information, mail servers, authoritative name servers, and so on.

Then the attacker can progress to using ping sweeps to send pings to each IP address in the target range. Hosts that answer the ping sweep then become live targets. Port scanning tools can then sweep through a range of UDP and TCP ports to see if a target host answers on any port numbers. Any replies indicate that a corresponding service is running on the target host.

Keep in mind that a reconnaissance attack is not a true attack because nothing is exploited as a result. It is used for gathering information about target systems and services so that vulnerabilities can be discovered and exploited using other types of attacks.

Buffer Overflow Attacks

Operating systems and applications normally read and write data using buffers and temporary memory space. Buffers are also important when one system communicates with another, as IP packets and Ethernet frames come and go. As long as the memory space is maintained properly and data is placed within the correct buffer boundaries, everything should work as expected.

However, some systems and applications have vulnerabilities that can allow buffers to overflow. This means some incoming data might be stored in unexpected memory locations if a buffer is allowed to fill beyond its limit. An attacker can exploit this condition by sending data that is larger than expected, in what is called a **buffer overflow attack**. If a vulnerability exists, the target system might store that data, overflowing its buffer into another area of memory, eventually crashing a service or the entire system. The attacker might also be able to specially craft the large message by inserting malicious code in it. If the target system stores that data as a result of a buffer overflow, then it can potentially run the malicious code without realizing.

Malware

Some types of security threats can come in the form of malicious software or **malware**. For example, a **Trojan horse** is malicious software that is hidden and packaged inside other software that looks normal and legitimate. If a well-meaning user decides to install it, the Trojan horse software is silently installed too. Then the malware can run attacks of its own on the local system or against other systems. Trojan horse malware can spread from one computer to another only through user interaction such as opening email attachments, downloading software from the Internet, and inserting a USB drive into a computer.

In contrast, **viruses** are malware that can propagate between systems more readily. To spread, virus software must inject itself into another application, then rely on users to transport the infected application software to other victims.

One other type of malware is able to propagate to and infect other systems on its own. An attacker develops **worm** software and deposits it on a system. From that point on, the worm replicates itself and spreads to other systems through their vulnerabilities, then replicates and spreads again and again.

To summarize, Table 9-3 lists the key ideas behind each type of malware described in this section.

Table 9-3   Summary of Malware Types

Characteristic	Trojan Horse	Virus	Worm
Packaged inside other software	Yes	No	No
Self-injected into other software	No	Yes	No
Propagates automatically	No	No	Yes

Human Vulnerabilities

Many types of attacks must take advantage of a vulnerability in an operating system, service, or other types of application software. In other words, an attacker or the malware involved must find a weakness in the target computer system. There are still many other attacks that can succeed by exploiting weaknesses in the humans who use computer systems.

One rather straightforward attack is called **social engineering**, where human trust and social behaviors can become security vulnerabilities. For example, an attacker might pose as an IT staff member and attempt to contact actual end users through phone calls, emails, and social media. The end goal might be to convince the users to reveal their credentials or set their passwords to a "temporary" value due to some fictitious IT maintenance that will take place, allowing the attacker to gain easy access to secure systems. Attackers might also be physically present and secretly observe users as they enter their credentials.

Phishing is a technique that attackers use to lure victims into visiting malicious websites. The idea is to either disguise the invitation as something legitimate, frighten victims into following a link, or otherwise deceive users into browsing content that convinces them to enter their confidential information.

Phishing comes in many forms. For instance, **spear phishing** begins with research to discover facts about one person or people in a specific group using social media. The attacker then forms a message for that person or group that sounds much more convincing because of the facts dropped into the message. **Whaling** uses spear phishing but targets high-profile individuals in corporations, governments, and organizations. Phishing can also occur over traditional communications, such as voice calls (*vishing*) and SMS text messages (*smishing*).

Pharming also attempts to send victims to a malicious website, but it takes a more drastic approach. Rather than enticing victims to follow a disguised link, pharming involves compromising the services that direct users toward a well-known or trusted website. For instance, an attacker can compromise a DNS service or edit local hosts files to change the entry for a legitimate site. When a victim tries to visit the site using its actual link, the altered name resolution returns the address of a malicious site instead.

In a **watering hole attack**, an attacker determines which users frequently visit a site; then that site is compromised and malware is deposited there. The malware infects only the target users who visit the site, while leaving other users unscathed.

You can refer to Table 9-4 to review the key ideas behind each type of human vulnerability that is commonly exploited.

9

Table 9-4   Summary of Human Security Vulnerabilities

Attack Type	Goal
Social engineering	Exploits human trust and social behavior
Phishing	Disguises a malicious invitation as something legitimate
Spear phishing	Targets one person or a small group with targeted messaging based on prior research
Whaling	Directs spear phishing techniques toward high-profile individuals
Vishing	Uses voice calls
Smishing	Uses SMS text messages
Pharming	Uses legitimate services to send users to a compromised site
Watering hole	Targets specific victims who visit a compromised site

Password Vulnerabilities

Most systems in an enterprise network use some form of authentication to grant or deny user access. When users access a system, a username and password are usually involved. It might be fairly easy to guess someone's username based on that person's real name. If the user's password is set to some default value or to a word or text string that is easy to guess, an attacker might easily gain access to the system too.

Think like an attacker for a moment and see if you can make some guesses about passwords you might try if you wanted to log in to a random system. Perhaps you thought of passwords like *password*, *password123*, *123456*, and so on. Perhaps you could try username *admin* and password *admin*.

An attacker can launch an online attack by actually entering each **password guess** as the system prompts for user credentials. In contrast, an offline attack occurs when the attacker is able to retrieve the encrypted or hashed passwords ahead of time, then goes offline to an external computer and uses software there to repeatedly attempt to recover the actual password.

Attackers can also use software to perform **dictionary attacks** to discover a user's password. The software will automatically attempt to log in with passwords taken from a dictionary or word list. It might have to go through thousands or millions of attempts before discovering the real password. In addition, the software can perform a **brute-force attack** by trying every possible combination of letter, number, and symbol strings. Brute-force attacks require very powerful computing resources and a large amount of time.

To mitigate password attacks, an enterprise should implement password policies for all users. Such a policy might include guidelines that require a long password string made up of a combination of upper- and lowercase characters along with numbers and some special characters. The goal is to require all passwords to be complex strings that are difficult to guess or reveal by a password attack. As well, password management should require all passwords to be changed periodically so that even lengthy brute-force attacks would not be able to recover a password before it is changed again.

Password Alternatives

A simple password string is the single factor that a user must enter to be authenticated. Because a password should be remembered and not written down anywhere, you might think of your password as "something you know." Hopefully nobody else knows it too; otherwise, they could use it to impersonate you when authenticating.

An enterprise might also consider using alternative credentials that bring more complexity and more security. Multifactor credentials require users to provide values or factors that come from different sources, reducing the chance that an attacker might possess all of the factors. An old saying describes two-factor credentials as "something you have" (a dynamic changing cryptographic key or a text message containing a time-limited code) and "something you know" (a password).

A digital certificate can serve as one alternative factor because it serves as a trusted form of identification, adheres to a standardized format, and contains encrypted information. If an enterprise supports certificate use, then a user must request and be granted a unique certificate to use for specific purposes. For example, certificates used for authenticating users must be approved for authentication. To be trusted, certificates must be granted and digitally signed by a trusted certificate authority (CA). As long as the services used by the enterprise know and trust the CA, then individual certificates signed by that CA can be trusted as well.

Digital certificates are also time sensitive, as each is approved for a specific time range. After a certificate expires, any attempts to authenticate with it will be rejected. The user who possesses the certificate can request a new one prior to the expiration date or at any time afterward. Certificates can also be revoked, if the business decides to revoke privileges from a user, if the user separates from the business, and so on. Even if the user still possesses a revoked certificate, that user will be refused access when trying to authenticate with it.

Because digital certificates exist as files on a computer or device, you might think they can be freely copied and used to identify people other than the original owners. Each digital certificate must also carry proof of possession to show that it was truly granted to the user who presents it during authentication. This proof is built into the encrypted certificate content, as a result of combining public keys that the user's machine and the authentication server can publicly share, along with private keys that each party keeps private and secret. As long as the authentication server can verify that the certificate was created using the correct public and private keys, then the certificate must be possessed by the expected owner. If not, then authentication will be rejected to keep an imposter out.

Biometric credentials carry the scheme even further by providing a factor that represents "something you are." The idea is to use some physical attribute from a user's body to uniquely identify that person. Physical attributes are usually unique to each individual's body structure and cannot be easily stolen or duplicated. For example, a user's fingerprint can be scanned and used as an authentication factor. Other examples include face recognition, palm prints, voice recognition, iris recognition, and retinal scans. As you might expect, some methods can be trusted more than others. Sometimes facial recognition systems can be fooled when presented by photographs or masks of trusted individuals. Injuries and the aging process can also alter biometric patterns such as fingerprints, facial shapes, and iris patterns. To help mitigate potential weaknesses, multiple biometric credentials can be collected and used to authenticate users as well.

To summarize, Table 9-5 lists the key ideas used in each alternative to password authentication.

Table 9-5   Summary of Password Authentication and Alternatives

Characteristic	Password Only	Two-Factor	Digital Certificates	Biometric
Something you know	Yes	Yes		
Something you have		Yes	Yes	
Something you are				Yes

Controlling and Monitoring User Access

You can manage user activity to and through systems with authentication, authorization, and accounting (**AAA**, also pronounced "triple-A") mechanisms. AAA uses standardized methods to challenge users for their credentials before access is allowed or authorized. Accounting protocols also can record user activity on enterprise systems. AAA is commonly used to control and monitor access to network devices like routers, switches, firewalls, and so on.

In a nutshell, you can think of AAA in the following manner:

- **Authentication:** Who is the user?

- **Authorization:** What is the user allowed to do?

- **Accounting:** What did the user do?

AAA begins with centralized management of login credentials used for authentication. Authentication refers to confirming the user is who they claim to be. The user can supply information (username and password) or use something they have (like responding to a text from their phone).

Using a centralized authentication process has many advantages over the distributed configuration options found in network device configuration. For instance, users should update passwords from time to time. Companies that rely on per-device password configuration on thousands of networking devices seldom systematically update those passwords. A centralized AAA system would solve that problem.

The second A in AAA, authorization, defines the capabilities allowed for the user. For example, on routers and switches, you should be familiar with user mode, reached via simple login, and privileged mode, reached with the **enable** command. In effect, those modes act as two authorization levels. IOS supports additional authorization levels you can configure, defining different commands allowed at each level.

As an example, user mode does not allow the **show running-config** or **configure terminal** commands. With IOS authorization features, you could define a new level that includes all user mode commands plus the **show running-config** command, which lets the user see the configuration. However, you may not want to allow the **configure terminal** command, which would let the user change the configuration. That authorization level can be associated with the user as identified during the authentication process.

Accounting, the third A in AAA, defines the need to record information about user activity. For network device users, that often comes in the form of log messages (as discussed further in Chapter 13, "Device Management Protocols.") Devices generate information messages—log messages—when events of note occur. Some log messages track user actions, like configuring the device or reloading it.

IT departments used centralized AAA services for end users as well as for network device access. Cisco's Identity Services Engine (ISE) product implements authentication and authorization for network-focused activities. It uses the following two protocols to communicate with enterprise resources:

- **TACACS+:** A Cisco proprietary protocol that separates each of the AAA functions. Communication is secure and encrypted over TCP port 49.

- **RADIUS:** A standards-based protocol that combines authentication and authorization into a single resource. Communication uses UDP ports 1812 and 1813 (accounting) but is not completely encrypted.

Ignoring the differences for now, you can think of these protocols as the basis for exchanging user credentials between the user and the AAA server. Both TACACS+ and RADIUS are arranged as a client/server model, where an authenticating device acts as a client talking to a AAA server. Figure 9-9 shows a simplified view of the process, where a user is attempting to connect to a switch for management purposes. In the AAA client role, the switch is often called Network Access Device (NAD) or Network Access Server (NAS). When a user tries to connect to the switch, the switch challenges the user for credentials, then passes the credentials along to the AAA server. In simple terms, if the user passes authentication, the AAA server returns an "accept" message to the switch. If the AAA server requires additional credentials, as in **multifactor authentication**, it returns a "challenge" message to the switch. Otherwise, a "reject" message is returned, denying access to the user.

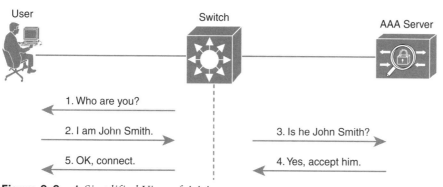

Figure 9-9   *A Simplified View of AAA*

Comparing RADIUS and TACACS+, RADIUS tends to be used more often for end-user AAA services, whereas TACACS+ (created by Cisco) is used more often to protect networking devices. TACACS+ can authorize the specific CLI commands allowed by a user, whereas RADIUS does not, making it useful for AAA with devices that have a CLI. Table 9-6 summarizes the differences between the two protocols.

Table 9-6   Comparisons Between TACACS+ and RADIUS

Features	TACACS+	RADIUS
Most often used for	Network devices	Users
Transport protocol	TCP	UDP
Authentication port number(s)	49	1645, 1812
Protocol encrypts the password	Yes	Yes
Protocol encrypts entire packet	Yes	No
Supports function to authorize each user to a subset of CLI commands	Yes	No
Defined by	Cisco	RFC 2865

Developing a Security Program to Educate Users

One effective approach an enterprise can take to improve information security is to educate its user community through a corporate security program. Most users may not have an IT background, so they might not recognize vulnerabilities or realize the consequences of their own actions. For example, if corporate users receive an email message that contains a message concerning a legal warrant for their arrest or a threat to expose some supposed illegal behavior, they might be tempted to follow a link to a malicious site. Such an action might infect a user's computer and then open a back door or introduce malware or a worm that could then impact the business operations.

An effective security program should have the following basic elements:

- **User awareness:** All users should be made aware of the need for data confidentiality to protect corporate information, as well as their own credentials and personal information. They should also be made aware of potential threats, schemes to mislead, and proper procedures to report security incidents. Users should also be instructed to follow strict guidelines regarding data loss. For example, users should not include sensitive information in emails or attachments, should not keep or transmit that information from a smartphone, or store it on cloud services or removable storage drives.

- **User training:** All users should be required to participate in periodic formal training so that they become familiar with all corporate security policies. (This also implies that the enterprise should develop and publish formal security policies for its employees, users, and business partners to follow.)

- **Physical access control:** Infrastructure locations, such as network closets and data centers, should remain securely locked. Badge access to sensitive locations is a scalable solution, offering an audit trail of identities and timestamps when access is granted. Administrators can control access on a granular basis and quickly remove access when an employee is dismissed.

Chapter Review

One key to doing well on the exams is to perform repetitive spaced review sessions. Review this chapter's material using either the tools in the book or interactive tools for the same material found on the book's companion website. Refer to the "Your Study Plan" element for more details. Table 9-7 outlines the key review elements and where you can find them. To better track your study progress, record when you completed these activities in the second column.

Table 9-7 Chapter Review Tracking

Review Element	Review Date(s)	Resource Used
Review key topics		Book, website
Review key terms		Book, website
Answer DIKTA questions		Book, PTP
Review memory tables		Website

Review All the Key Topics

Table 9-8 Key Topics for Chapter 9

Key Topic Element	Description	Page Number
Figure 9-3	Security terminology	187
Table 9-3	Types of malware	195
Table 9-4	Human security vulnerabilities	196
Paragraph	Password vulnerabilities	196
List	AAA functions	198
Table 9-6	TACACS+ and RADIUS compared	200
List	User education	200

Key Terms You Should Know

AAA, amplification attack, brute-force attack, buffer overflow attack, denial-of-service (DoS) attack, dictionary attack, distributed denial-of-service (DDoS) attack, exploit, malware, man-in-the-middle attack, mitigation technique, multifactor authentication, password guessing, pharming, phishing, reconnaissance attack, reflection attack, social engineering, spear phishing, spoofing attack, threat, Trojan horse, virus, vulnerability, watering hole attack, whaling, worm

9

CHAPTER 10

Securing Network Devices

This chapter covers the following exam topics:

1.0 Network Fundamentals

  1.1 Explain the role and function of network components

    1.1.c Next-generation firewalls and IPS

4.0 IP Services

  4.8 Configure network devices for remote access using SSH

5.0 Security Fundamentals

  5.3 Configure and verify device access control using local passwords

All devices in the network—endpoints, servers, and infrastructure devices like routers and switches—include some methods for the devices to legitimately communicate using the network. To protect those devices, the security plan will include a wide variety of tools and mitigation techniques, with the chapters in Part III of this book discussing a large variety of those tools and techniques.

This chapter focuses on two particular security needs in an enterprise network. First, access to the CLI of the network devices needs to be protected. The network engineering team needs to be able to access the devices remotely, so the devices need to allow remote SSH (and possibly Telnet) access. The first half of this chapter discusses how to configure passwords to keep them safe and how to filter login attempts at the devices themselves.

The second half of the chapter turns to two different security functions most often implemented with purpose-built appliances: firewalls and IPSs. These devices together monitor traffic in transit to determine if the traffic is legitimate or if it might be part of some exploit. If considered to be part of an exploit, or if contrary to the rules defined by the devices, they can discard the messages, stopping any attack before it gets started.

"Do I Know This Already?" Quiz

Take the quiz (either here or use the PTP software) if you want to use the score to help you decide how much time to spend on this chapter. The letter answers are listed at the bottom of the page following the quiz. Appendix C, found both at the end of the book as well as on the companion website, includes both the answers and explanations. You can also find both answers and explanations in the PTP testing software.

Table 10-1 "Do I Know This Already?" Foundation Topics Section-to-Question Mapping

Foundation Topics Section	Questions
Securing IOS Passwords	1–4
Firewalls and Intrusion Prevention Systems	5, 6

1. Imagine that you have configured the **enable secret** command, followed by the **enable password** command, from the console. You log out of the switch and log back in at the console. Which command defines the password that you had to enter to access privileged mode?

   a. **enable password**

   b. **enable secret**

   c. Neither

   d. The **password** command, if it's configured

2. Some IOS commands store passwords as clear text, but you can then encrypt the passwords with the **service password-encryption** global command. By comparison, other commands store a computed hash of the password instead of storing the password. Comparing the two options, which one answer is the *most accurate* about why one method is better than the other?

   a. Using hashes is preferred because encrypted IOS passwords can be easily decrypted.

   b. Using hashes is preferred because of the large CPU effort required for encryption.

   c. Using encryption is preferred because it provides stronger password protection.

   d. Using encryption is preferred because of the large CPU effort required for hashes.

3. A network engineer issues a **show running-config** command and sees only one line of output that mentions the **enable secret** command, as follows:

   ```
   enable secret 5 $1$ZGMA$e8cmvkz4UjiJhVp7.maLE1
   ```

   Which of the following is true about users of this router?

   a. A user must type **1ZGMA$e8cmvkz4UjiJhVp7.maLE1** to reach enable mode.

   b. The router will hash the clear-text password that the user types to compare to the hashed password.

   c. A **no service password-encryption** configuration command would decrypt this password.

   d. The router will decrypt the password in the configuration to compare to the clear-text password typed by the user.

4. The **show running-config** command output on a router includes the following line: **username test05 secret 8 8rTJqzmkwdI20WU$.mktApC8shjjwgABbQp7Uj-OmttmJaiIDfvBBJOpcns6**. Which answer best describes the command the network engineer used to configure this **username** command with its clear-text password?

   a. **username test05 algorithm-type scrypt secret cisco**

   b. **username test05 algorithm-type sha256 secret cisco**

    c. username test05 algorithm-type md5 secret cisco

    d. username test05 secret cisco

5. A next-generation firewall sits at the edge of a company's connection to the Internet. It has been configured to prevent Telnet clients residing in the Internet from accessing Telnet servers inside the company. Which of the following might a next-generation firewall use that a traditional firewall would not?

    a. Match message destination well-known port 23

    b. Match message application data

    c. Match message IP protocol 23

    d. Match message source TCP ports greater than 49152

6. Which actions show a behavior typically supported by a Cisco next-generation IPS (NGIPS) beyond the capabilities of a traditional IPS? (Choose two answers.)

    a. Gather and use host-based information for context

    b. Comparisons between messages and a database of exploit signatures

    c. Logging events for later review by the security team

    d. Filter URIs using reputation scores

Foundation Topics

Securing IOS Passwords

The ultimate way to protect passwords in Cisco IOS devices is to not store passwords in IOS devices. That is, for any functions that can use an external authentication, authorization, and accounting (AAA) server, use it. However, it is common to store some passwords in a router or switch configuration, and this first section of the chapter discusses some of the ways to protect those passwords.

As a brief review, Figure 10-1 summarizes some typical login security configuration on a router or switch. On the lower left, you see Telnet support configured, with the use of a password only (no username required). On the right, the configuration adds support for login with both username and password, supporting both Telnet and SSH users. The upper left shows the one command required to define an enable password in a secure manner.

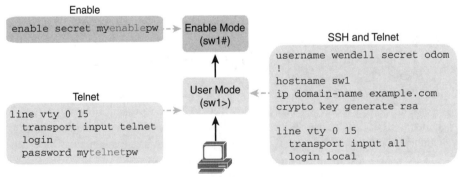

Figure 10-1 *Sample Login Security Configuration*

> **NOTE**   The configuration on the far right of the figure supports both SSH and Telnet, but consider allowing SSH only by instead using the **transport input ssh** command. The Telnet protocol sends all data unencrypted, so any attacker who copies the message with a Telnet login will have a copy of the password.

The rest of this first section discusses how to make these passwords secure. In particular, this section looks at ways to avoid keeping clear-text passwords in the configuration and storing the passwords in ways that make it difficult for attackers to learn the password.

Encrypting Older IOS Passwords with service password-encryption

Some older-style IOS passwords create a security exposure because the passwords exist in the configuration file as clear text. These clear-text passwords might be seen in printed versions of the configuration files, in a backup copy of the configuration file stored on a server, or as displayed on a network engineer's display.

Cisco attempted to solve this clear-text problem by adding a command to encrypt those passwords: the **service password-encryption** global configuration command. This command encrypts passwords that are normally held as clear text, specifically the passwords for these commands:

password *password* (console or vty mode)

username *name* **password** *password* (global)

enable password *password* (global)

To see how it works, Example 10-1 shows how the **service password-encryption** command encrypts the clear-text console password. The example uses the **show running-config | section line con 0** command both before and after the encryption; this command lists only the section of the configuration about the console.

Example 10-1   *Encryption and the* **service password-encryption** *Command*

```
Switch3# show running-config | section line con 0
line con 0
 password cisco
 login


Switch3# configure terminal
Enter configuration commands, one per line.    End with CNTL/Z.
Switch3(config)# service password-encryption
Switch3(config)# ^Z


Switch3# show running-config | section line con 0
line con 0
 password 7 070C285F4D06
 login
```

A close examination of the before and after **show running-config** command output reveals both the obvious effect and a new concept. The encryption process now hides the original

10

clear-text password. Also, IOS needs a way to signal that the value in the **password** command lists an encrypted password rather than the clear text. IOS adds the encryption or encoding type of "7" to the command, which specifically refers to passwords encrypted with the **service password-encryption** command. (IOS considers the clear-text passwords to be type 0; some commands list the 0, and some do not.)

While the **service password-encryption** global command encrypts passwords, the **no service password-encryption** global command does not immediately decrypt the passwords back to their clear-text state. Instead, the process works as shown in Figure 10-2. Basically, after you enter the **no service password-encryption** command, the passwords remain encrypted until you change a password.

Figure 10-2   *Encryption Is Immediate; Decryption Awaits Next Password Change*

Unfortunately, the **service password-encryption** command does not protect the passwords very well. Armed with the encrypted value, you can search the Internet and find sites with tools to decrypt these passwords. In fact, you can take the encrypted password from this example, plug it into one of these sites, and it decrypts to "cisco." So, the **service password-encryption** command will slow down the curious, but it will not stop a knowledgeable attacker.

Encoding the Enable Passwords with Hashes

In the earliest days of IOS, Cisco used the **enable password** *password* global command to define the password that users had to use to reach enable mode (after using the **enable** EXEC command). However, as just noted, the **enable password** *password* command stored the password as clear text, and the **service password-encryption** command encrypted the password in a way that was easily decrypted.

Cisco solved the problem of only weak ways to store the password of the **enable password** *password* global command by making a more secure replacement: the **enable secret** *password* global command. However, both of these commands exist in IOS even today. The next few pages look at these two commands from a couple of angles, including interactions between these two commands, why the **enable secret** command is more secure, along with a note about some advancements in how IOS secures the **enable secret** password.

Interactions Between Enable Password and Enable Secret

First, for real life: use the **enable secret** *password* global command, and ignore the **enable password** *password* global command. That has been true for around 20 years.

However, to be complete, Cisco has never removed the much weaker **enable password** command from IOS. So, on a single switch (or router), you can configure one or the other, both,

---

or neither. What, then, does the switch expect you to type as the password to reach enable mode? It boils down to these rules:

Both commands configured: Users must use the password in the **enable secret** *password* command (and ignore the **enable password** *password* command).

Only one command configured: Use the password in that one command.

Neither command configured (default): Console users move directly to enable mode without a password prompt; Telnet and SSH users are rejected with no option to supply an enable password.

Making the Enable Secret Truly Secret with a Hash

The Cisco **enable secret** command protects the password value by never even storing the clear-text password in the configuration. However, that one sentence may cause you a bit of confusion: If the router or switch does not remember the clear-text password, how can the switch know that the user typed the right password after using the **enable** command? This section works through a few basics to show you how and appreciate why the password's value is secret.

First, by default, IOS uses a hash function called Message Digest 5 (MD5) to store an alternative value in the configuration, rather than the clear-text password. Think of MD5 as a rather complex mathematical one-way formula. This formula is chosen so that even if you know the exact result of the formula—that is, the result after feeding the clear-text password through the formula as input—it is computationally difficult to compute the original clear-text password. Figure 10-3 shows the main ideas:

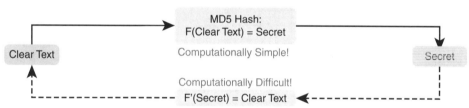

Figure 10-3 *One-Way Nature of MD5 Hash to Create Secret*

NOTE "Computationally difficult" is almost a code phrase, meaning that the designers of the function hope that no one is willing to take the time to compute the original clear text.

So, if the original clear-text password cannot be re-created, how can a switch or router use it to compare to the clear-text password typed by the user? The answer depends on another fact about these security hashes like MD5: each clear-text input results in a unique result from the math formula.

The **enable secret fred** command generates an **MD5 hash**. If a user types **fred** when trying to enter enable mode, IOS will run MD5 against that value and get the same MD5 hash as is listed in the **enable secret** command, so IOS allows the user to access enable mode. If the user typed any other value besides **fred**, IOS would compute a different MD5 hash than the value stored with the **enable secret** command, and IOS would reject that user's attempt to reach enable mode.

10

Knowing that fact, the switch can make a comparison when a user types a password after using the **enable** EXEC command as follows:

Step 1.   IOS computes the MD5 hash of the password in the **enable secret** command and stores the hash of the password in the configuration.

Step 2.   When the user types the **enable** command to reach enable mode, a password that needs to be checked against that configuration command, IOS hashes the clear-text password as typed by the user.

Step 3.   IOS compares the two hashed values: if they are the same, the user-typed password must be the same as the configured password.

As a result, IOS can store the hash of the password but never store the clear-text password; however, it can still determine whether the user typed the same password.

Switches and routers already use the logic described here, but you can see the evidence by looking at the switch configuration. Example 10-2 shows the creation of the **enable secret** command, with a few related details. This example shows the stored (hashed) value as revealed in the **show running-configuration** command output. That output also shows that IOS changed the **enable secret fred** command to list the encryption type 5 (which means the listed password is actually an MD5 hash of the clear-text password). The gobbledygook long text string is the hash, preventing others from reading the password.

Example 10-2   *Cisco IOS Encoding Password "fred" as Type 5 (MD5)*

```
Switch3(config)# enable secret fred
Switch3(config)# ^Z
Switch3# show running-config | include enable secret

enable secret 5 $1$ZGMA$e8cmvkz4UjiJhVp7.maLE1

Switch3# configure terminal
Enter configuration commands, one per line.    End with CNTL/Z.
Switch3(config)# no enable secret
Switch3(config)# ^Z
```

The end of the example also shows an important side point about deleting the **enable secret** password: after you are in enable mode, you can delete the **enable secret** password using the **no enable secret** command, without even having to enter the password value. You can also overwrite the old password by just repeating the **enable secret** command. But you cannot view the original clear-text password.

NOTE   Example 10-2 shows another shortcut illustrating how to work through long **show** command output, this time using the pipe to the **include** command. The **| include enable secret** part of the command processes the output from **show running-config** to include only the lines with the case-sensitive text "enable secret."

Improved Hashes for Cisco's Enable Secret

The use of any hash function to encode passwords relies on several key features of the particular hash function. In particular, every possible input value must result in a single hashed value, so that when users type a password, only one password value matches each hashed value. Also, the hash algorithm must result in computationally difficult math (in other words, a pain in the neck) to compute the clear-text password based on the hashed value to discourage attackers.

The MD5 hash algorithm has been around 30 years. Over those years, computers have gotten much faster, and researchers have found creative ways to attack the MD5 algorithm, making MD5 less challenging to crack. That is, someone who saw your running configuration would have an easier time re-creating your clear-text secret passwords than in the early years of MD5.

These facts are not meant to say that MD5 is bad, but like many cryptographic functions before MD5, progress has been made, and new functions were needed. To provide more recent options that would create a much greater challenge to attackers, Cisco added two additional hashes in the 2010s, as noted in Figure 10-4.

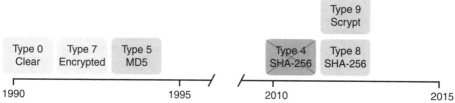

Figure 10-4 *Timeline of Encryptions/Hashes of Cisco IOS Passwords*

Of the newer types shown in the figure, Cisco continues to use types 8 and 9. Cisco found a security exposure with their type 4 password implementation, so they deprecated it, later replacing it with type 8. Both types 4 and 8 use the same underlying algorithm (PBKDF2) that combines with the SHA-256 algorithm. (You might see both terms mentioned in documentation about type 8 passwords.) Type 9 uses a different hash algorithm called Scrypt (pronounced "es crypt.")

IOS now supports two alternative algorithm types in the more recent router and switch IOS images. Table 10-2 shows the configuration of all three algorithm types on the **enable secret** command.

Table 10-2 Commands and Encoding Types for the **enable secret** Command

Command	Type	Algorithm
enable algorithm-type md5 secret *password*	5	MD5
enable algorithm-type sha256 secret *password*	8	SHA-256
enable algorithm-type scrypt secret *password*	9	Scrypt

10

Example 10-3 shows the **enable secret** command being changed from MD5 to the Scrypt algorithm. Of note, the example shows that only one **enable secret** command should exist between those three commands in Table 10-2. Basically, if you configure another **enable** secret command with a different algorithm type, that command replaces any existing **enable secret** command.

Example 10-3   *Cisco IOS Encoding Password "mypass1" as Type 9 (SHA-256)*

```
R1# show running-config | include enable
enable secret 5 $1$ZSYj$725dBZmLUJOnx8gFPTtTv0
R1# configure terminal
Enter configuration commands, one per line. End with CNTL/Z.
R1(config)# enable algorithm-type scrypt secret mypass1
R1(config)# ^Z
R1#
R1# show running-config | include enable
enable secret 9 $9$II/EeKiRW91uxE$fwYuOE5EHoii16AWv2wSywkLJ/KNeGj8uK/24BOTVU6
R1#
```

Following the process shown in the example, the first command confirms that the current **enable secret** command uses encoding type 5, meaning it uses MD5. Second, the user configures the password using algorithm type scrypt. The last command confirms that only one **enable secret** command exists in the configuration, now with encoding type 9.

Also, think through how IOS takes the command with the clear-text password and then stores the command in a different syntax. In the example, the user issues the **enable algorithm-type scrypt secret mypass** command, referencing the algorithm type by name. However, the **show running-config** output shows how IOS removed the **algorithm-type scrypt** parameters, but it also left the number 9 behind the **secret** parameter. As a result, the command stored by IOS identifies the algorithm type by number. Because of that, take time to memorize both the names and numbers of the algorithm types per Table 10-2.

Finally, note that IOS and IOS XE differ slightly with the **enable secret** command. When configuring without using the **algorithm-type** keyword, IOS defaults to MD5, whereas IOS XE defaults to Scrypt.

Encoding the Passwords for Local Usernames

The **username password** and **username secret** commands have a similar history to the **enable password** and **enable secret** commands. Originally, IOS supported the **username** *user* **password** *password* command—a command that had those same issues of being a clear-text password or a poorly encrypted value (with the **service password-encryption** feature). Many years later, Cisco added the **username** *user* **secret** *password* global command, which encoded the password as an MD5 hash, with Cisco adding support for the newer hashes later. Note that Cisco uses the term **local username** to refer to these usernames configured on individual routers and switches, in contrast to those configured centrally on a AAA server.

Today, the **username secret** command is preferred over the **username password** command; however, keep these rules in mind for **username** commands:

- IOS allows only one **username** command for a given username—either a **username** *name* **password** *password* command or a **username** *name* **secret** *password* command.

- IOS allows a mix of commands (**username password** and **username secret**) in the same router or switch (for different usernames).

As mentioned, IOS on both switches and routers uses the additional encoding options beyond MD5, just as supported with the **enable secret** command. Table 10-3 shows the syntax of those three options in the **username** command.

Table 10-3 Commands and Encoding Types for the **username secret** Command

Command	Type	Algorithm
username *name* **algorithm-type md5 secret** *password*	5	MD5
username *name* **algorithm-type sha256 secret** *password*	8	SHA-256
username *name* **algorithm-type scrypt secret** *password*	9	SHA-256

IOS and IOS XE also differ with the **username secret** command, with the same defaults as for the **enable secret** command: MD5 for IOS and Scrypt for IOS XE. Also, for the **username secret** command, IOS XE does not support the MD5 option at all. (As always, treat any comments about IOS and IOS XE differences for general awareness because the CCNA exam topics do not mention the need to know such distinctions.)

Firewalls and Intrusion Prevention Systems

The next topic examines the roles of a couple of different kinds of networking devices: firewalls and intrusion prevention systems (IPSs). Both devices work to secure networks but with slightly different goals and approaches.

This second major section of the chapter takes a look at each. This section first discusses the core traditional features of both firewalls and IPSs. The section closes with a description of the newer features in the current generation of these products, called next-generation products, which improve the functions of each.

Traditional Firewalls

Traditionally, a **firewall** sits in the forwarding path of all packets so that the firewall can then choose which packets to discard and which to allow through. By doing so, the firewall protects the network from different kinds of issues by allowing only the intended types of traffic to flow in and out of the network. In fact, in its most basic form, firewalls do the same kinds of work that routers do with ACLs, but firewalls can perform that packet-filtering function with many more options, as well as perform other security tasks.

Figure 10-5 shows a typical network design for a site that uses a physical firewall. The figure shows a firewall, like the Cisco Adaptive Security Appliance (ASA) firewall, connected to a Cisco router, which in turn connects to the Internet. All enterprise traffic going to or from the Internet would be sent through the firewall. The firewall would consider its rules and make a choice for each packet, whether the packet should be allowed through.

10

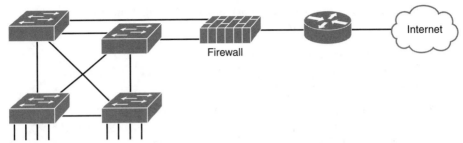

Figure 10-5 *Firewall as Positioned in the Packet Forwarding Path*

Although firewalls have some router-like features (such as packet forwarding and packet filtering), they provide much more advanced security features than a traditional router. For example, most firewalls can use the following kinds of logic to make the choice of whether to discard or allow a packet:

■ Like router IP ACLs, match the source and destination IP addresses

■ Like router IP ACLs, identify applications by matching their static well-known TCP and UDP ports

■ Watch application-layer flows to know what additional TCP and UDP ports are used by a particular flow, and filter based on those ports

■ Match the text in the URI of an HTTP request—that is, look at and compare the contents of what is often called the web address—and match patterns to decide whether to allow or deny the download of the web page identified by that URI

■ Keep state information by storing information about each packet, and make decisions about filtering future packets based on the historical state information (called *stateful inspection*, or being a stateful firewall)

The stateful firewall feature provides the means to prevent a variety of attacks and is one of the more obvious differences between the ACL processing of a router versus security filtering by a firewall. Routers must spend as little time as possible processing each packet so that the packets experience little delay passing through the router. The router cannot take the time to gather information about a packet, and then for future packets, consider some saved state information about earlier packets when making a filtering decision. Because they focus on network security, firewalls do save some information about packets and can consider that information for future filtering decisions.

As an example of the benefits of using a stateful firewall, consider a simple denial-of-service (DoS) attack. An attacker can make this type of attack against a web server by using tools that create (or start to create) a large volume of TCP connections to the server. The firewall might allow TCP connections to that server normally, but imagine that the server might typically receive 10 new TCP connections per second under normal conditions and 100 per second at the busiest times. A DoS attack might attempt thousands or more TCP connections per second, driving up CPU and RAM use on the server and eventually overloading the server to the point that it cannot serve legitimate users.

A stateful firewall could be tracking the number of TCP connections per second—that is, recording state information based on earlier packets—including the number of TCP connection requests from each client IP address to each server address. The stateful firewall could notice a large number of TCP connections, check its state information, and then notice that the number of requests is very large from a small number of clients to that particular server, which is typical of some kinds of DoS attacks. The stateful firewall could then start filtering those packets, helping the web server survive the attack, whereas a stateless firewall or a router ACL would not have had the historical state information to realize that a DoS attack was occurring.

Security Zones

Firewalls not only filter packets but also pay close attention to which host initiates communications. That concept is most obvious with TCP as the transport layer protocol, where the client initiates the TCP connection by sending a TCP segment that sets the SYN bit only (as seen in Figure 5-5 in Chapter 5, "Introduction to TCP/IP Transport and Applications").

Firewalls use logic that considers which host initiated a TCP connection by watching these initial TCP segments. To see the importance of who initiates the connections, think about a typical enterprise network with a connection to the Internet, as shown in Figure 10-6. The company has users inside the company who open web browsers, initiating connections to web servers across the Internet. However, by having a working Internet connection, that same company opens up the possibility that an attacker might try to create a TCP connection to the company's internal web servers used for payroll processing. Of course, the company does not want random Internet users or attackers to be able to connect to their payroll server.

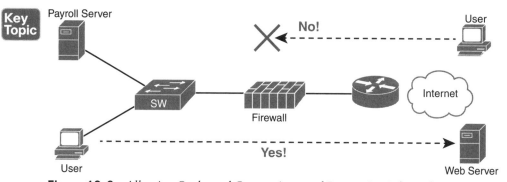

Figure 10-6   *Allowing Outbound Connections and Preventing Inbound Connections*

Firewalls use the concept of *security zones* (also called a *zone* for short) when defining which hosts can initiate new connections. The firewall has rules, and those rules define which host can initiate connections from one zone to another zone. Also, by using zones, a firewall can place multiple interfaces into the same zone, in cases for which multiple interfaces should have the same security rules applied. Figure 10-7 depicts the idea with the inside part of the enterprise considered to be in a separate zone compared to the interfaces connected toward the Internet.

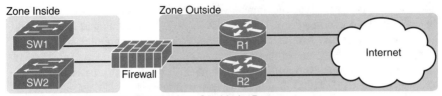

Figure 10-7 *Using Security Zones with Firewalls*

The most basic firewall rule when using two zones like Figure 10-7 reduces to this logic:

Allow hosts from zone inside to initiate connections to hosts in zone outside, for a predefined set of safe well-known ports (like HTTP port 80, for instance).

Note that with this one simple rule, the correct traffic is allowed while filtering the unwanted traffic by default. Firewalls typically disallow all traffic unless a rule specifically allows the packet. So, with this simple rule to allow inside users to initiate connections to the outside zone, and that alone, the firewall also prevents outside users from initiating connections to inside hosts.

Most companies have an inside and outside zone, as well as a special zone called the *demilitarized zone (DMZ)*. Although the DMZ name comes from the real world, it has been used in IT for decades to refer to a firewall security zone used to place servers that need to be available for use by users in the public Internet. For example, Figure 10-8 shows a typical Internet edge design, with the addition of a couple of web servers in its DMZ connected through the firewall. The firewall then needs another rule that enables users in the zone outside—that is, users in the Internet—to initiate connections to those web servers in the DMZ. By separating those web servers into the DMZ, away from the rest of the enterprise, the enterprise can prevent Internet users from attempting to connect to the internal devices in the inside zone, preventing many types of attacks.

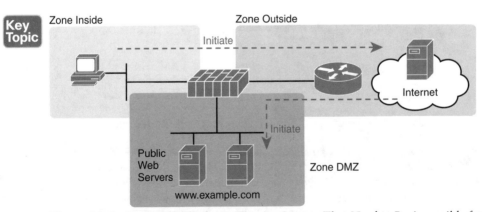

Figure 10-8 *Using a DMZ for Enterprise Servers That Need to Be Accessible from the Internet*

Intrusion Prevention Systems (IPS)

Traditionally, a firewall works with a set of user-configured rules about where packets should be allowed to flow in a network. The firewall needs to sit in the path of the packets so it can filter the packets, redirect them for collection and later analysis, or let them continue toward their destination.

A traditional intrusion prevention system (**IPS**) can sit in the path packets take through the network, and it can filter packets, but it makes its decisions with different logic. The IPS first downloads a database of exploit signatures. Each signature defines different header field values found in sequences of packets used by different exploits. Then the IPS can examine packets, compare them to the known exploit signatures, and notice when packets may be part of a known exploit. Once identified, the IPS can log the event, discard packets, or even redirect the packets to another security application for further examination.

A traditional IPS differs from firewalls in that instead of an engineer at the company defining rules for that company based on applications (by port number) and zones, the IPS applies the logic based on signatures supplied mostly by the IPS vendor. Those signatures look for these kinds of attacks:

- DoS

- DDoS

- Worms

- Viruses

To accomplish its mission, the IPS needs to download and keep updating its signature database. Security experts work to create the signatures. The IPS must then download the exploit signature database and keep downloading updates over time, as shown in Figure 10-9.

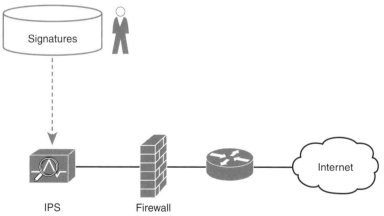

Figure 10-9   *IPS and Signature Database*

For example, think about what happens when an entirely new computer virus has been created. Host-based security products, like antivirus software, should be installed on the computers inside the company. These tools use a similar model as the IPS, keeping an updated database of virus signatures. The signatures might look for patterns in how a computer virus could be stored inside files on the computer, or in files sent to the computer via email or web browsers. But there will be some time lag between the day when the virus is discovered (called zero-day attacks) and when researchers develop a virus signature, change their database, and allow time for all the hosts to update their antivirus software. The hosts are at risk during this time lag.

The IPS provides a complimentary service to prevent viruses. Researchers will look for ways an IPS could recognize the same virus while in flight through the network with new IPS signatures—for instance, looking for packets with a particular port and a particular hex string in the application payload. Once developed, the IPS devices in the network need to be updated with the new signature database, protecting against that virus. Both the host-based and IPS-based protections play an important role, but the fact that one IPS protects sections of a network means that the IPS can sometimes more quickly react to new threats to protect hosts.

Cisco Next-Generation Firewalls

The CCNA 200-301 exam topics mention the terms *firewall* and *IPS* but prefaced with the term *next-generation*. Around the mid-2010s, Cisco and some of their competitors started using the term *next generation* when discussing their security products to emphasize some of the newer features. In short, a **next-generation firewall (NGFW)** and a **next-generation IPS (NGIPS)** are the now-current firewall and IPS products from Cisco.

However, the use of the term *next generation* goes far beyond just a marketing label: the term emphasizes some major shifts and improvements over the years. The security industry sees endless cycles of new attacks followed by new solutions. Some solutions might require entirely new product features or even new products. Some of the changes that have required new security features include the proliferation of mobile devices—devices that leave the enterprise, connect to the Internet, and return to the enterprise—creating a whole new level of risk. Also, no single security function or appliance (firewall, IPS, anti-malware) can hope to stop some threats, so the next-generation tools must be able to work better together to provide solutions. In short, the next-generation products have real useful features not found in their predecessor products.

As for Cisco products, for many years Cisco branded its firewalls as the Cisco Adaptive Security Appliance (ASA). Around 2013, Cisco acquired Sourcefire, a security product company. Many of the next-generation firewall (and IPS) features come from software acquired through that acquisition. For a while, Cisco sold security appliances that ran multiple security features, such as NGFW, with branding similar to the old Sourcefire name: Cisco Firepower firewalls. As of the publication of this book, Cisco had moved on to branding with the name Cisco Secure Firewall (see www.cisco.com/go/firewalls).

An NGFW still does the traditional functions of a firewall, of course, like stateful filtering by comparing fields in the IP, TCP, and UDP headers, and using security zones when defining firewall rules. To provide some insight into some of the newer next-generation features, consider the challenge of matching packets with ports:

1. Each IP-based application should use a well-known port.

2. Attackers know that firewalls will filter most well-known ports from sessions initiated from the outside zone to the inside zone (see Figure 10-8).

3. Attackers use port scanning to find any port that a company's firewall will allow through right now.

4. Attackers attempt to use a protocol of their choosing (for example, HTTP) but with the nonstandard port found through port scanning as a way to attempt to connect to hosts inside the enterprise.

The sequence lists a summary of some of the steps attackers need to take but does not list every single task. However, even to this depth, you can see how attackers can find a way to send packets past the corporate firewall.

The solution? A next-generation firewall that looks at the application layer data to identify the application instead of relying on the TCP and UDP port numbers used. Cisco performs their deep packet inspection using a feature called **Application Visibility and Control (AVC)**. Cisco AVC can identify many applications based on the data sent (application layer headers plus application data structures far past the TCP and UDP headers). When used with a Cisco NGFW, instead of matching port numbers, the firewall matches the application, defeating attacks like the one just described.

The following list mentions a few of the features of an NGFW. Note that while *NGFW* is a useful term, the line between a traditional firewall and a next-generation firewall can be a bit blurry because the terms describe products that have gone through repeated changes over long periods of time. This list does summarize a few of the key points, however:

- **Traditional firewall:** An NGFW performs traditional firewall features, like stateful firewall filtering, NAT/PAT, and VPN termination.

- **Application Visibility and Control (AVC):** This feature looks deep into the application layer data to identify the application. For instance, it can identify the application based on the data, rather than port number, to defend against attacks that use random port numbers.

- **Advanced Malware Protection:** NGFW platforms run multiple security services, not just as a platform to run a separate service, but for better integration of functions. A network-based antimalware function can run on the firewall itself, blocking file transfers that would install malware, and saving copies of files for later analysis.

- **URL Filtering:** This feature examines the URLs in each web request, categorizes the URLs, and either filters or rate-limits the traffic based on rules. The Cisco Talos security group monitors and creates reputation scores for each domain known in the Internet, with URL filtering being able to use those scores in its decision to categorize, filter, or rate limit.

- **NGIPS:** Cisco's NGFW products can also run their NGIPS feature along with the firewall.

Note that for any of the services that benefit from being in the same path that packets traverse, like a firewall, it makes sense that over time those functions could migrate to run on the same product. So, when the design needs both a firewall and IPS at the same location in the network, these NGFW products can run the NGIPS feature as shown in the combined device in Figure 10-10.

10

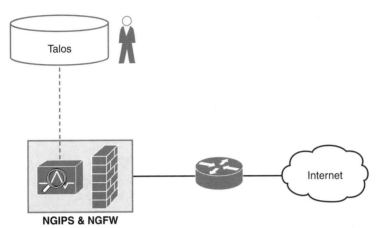

Figure 10-10 *Next-Generation Firewall with Next-Generation IPS Module*

Cisco Next-Generation IPS

The Cisco next-generation IPS (NGIPS) products have followed a similar path as the Cisco NGFW products. Cisco first added NGIPS features primarily through its Sourcefire acquisition. Current Cisco IPS products now run as applications in appliances that use the Cisco Secure Firewall name. In fact, as for products, think more like the previous figure, with an appliance that runs both the NGFW and NGIPS.

As with the NGFW, the NGIPS adds features to a traditional IPS. One of the biggest issues with a traditional IPS comes with the volume of security events logged by the IPS. For instance:

1. An IPS compares the signature database, which lists all known exploits, to all messages.
2. It generates events, often far more than the security staff can read.
3. The staff must mentally filter events to find the proverbial needle in the haystack, possible only through hard work, vast experience, and a willingness to dig.

An NGIPS helps with this issue in a couple of ways. First, an NGIPS examines the context by gathering data from all the hosts and the users of those hosts. The NGIPS will know the OS, software revision levels, what apps are running, open ports, the transport protocols and port numbers in use, and so on. Armed with that data, the NGIPS can make much more intelligent choices about what events to log.

For instance, consider an NGIPS placed into a network to protect a campus LAN where end users connect, but no data center exists in that part of the network. Also, all PCs happen to be running Windows, and possibly the same version, by corporate policy. The signature database includes signatures for exploits of Linux hosts, Macs, Windows versions nonexistent in that part of the network, and exploits that apply to server applications that are not running on those hosts. After gathering those facts, an NGIPS can suggest de-emphasizing checks for exploits that do not apply to those endpoints, spending more time and focus on events that could occur, greatly reducing the number of events logged.

The following are a few of the Cisco NGIPS features:

- **Traditional IPS:** An NGIPS performs traditional IPS features, like using exploit signatures to compare packet flows, creating a log of events, and possibly discarding and/or redirecting packets.

- **Application Visibility and Control (AVC):** As with NGFWs, an NGIPS has the ability to look deep into the application layer data to identify the application.

- **Contextual Awareness:** NGFW platforms gather data from hosts—OS, software version/level, patches applied, applications running, open ports, applications currently sending data, and so on. Those facts inform the NGIPS as to the often more limited vulnerabilities in a portion of the network so that the NGIPS can focus on actual vulnerabilities while greatly reducing the number of logged events.

- **Reputation-Based Filtering:** The Cisco Talos security intelligence group researches security threats daily, building the data used by the Cisco security portfolio. Part of that data identifies known bad actors, based on IP address, domain, name, or even specific URL, with a reputation score for each. A Cisco NGIPS can perform reputation-based filtering, taking the scores into account.

- **Event Impact Level:** Security personnel need to assess the logged events, so an NGIPS provides an assessment based on impact levels, with characterizations as to the impact if an event is indeed some kind of attack.

If you want to learn a little more about these topics for your own interest, let me refer you to a couple of resources. First, check out articles and blog posts from the Cisco Talos Intelligence Group (www.talosintelligence.com). The Cisco Talos organization researches security issues around the globe across the entire spectrum of security products. Additionally, one Cisco Press book has some great information about both next-generation firewalls and IPSs, written at a level appropriate as a next step. If you want to read more, check out this book with the long name: *Integrated Security Technologies and Solutions, Volume I: Cisco Security Solutions for Advanced Threat Protection with Next Generation Firewall, Intrusion Prevention, AMP, and Content Security* (or just use its ISBN, 9781587147067), with one chapter each on NGFW and NGIPS.

Chapter Review

One key to doing well on the exams is to perform repetitive spaced review sessions. Review this chapter's material using either the tools in the book or interactive tools for the same material found on the book's companion website. Refer to the "Your Study Plan" element for more details. Table 10-4 outlines the key review elements and where you can find them. To better track your study progress, record when you completed these activities in the second column.

10

Table 10-4   Chapter Review Tracking

Review Element	Review Date(s)	Resource Used
Review key topics		Book, website
Review key terms		Book, website
Repeat DIKTA questions		Book, PTP
Do labs		Blog
Review command tables		Book

Review All the Key Topics

Table 10-5   Key Topics for Chapter 10

Key Topic Element	Description	Page Number
List	Commands whose passwords are encrypted by **service password-encryption**	205
List	Rules for when IOS uses the password set with the **enable password** versus **enable secret** commands	207
List	Logic by which IOS can use the **enable secret** hash when a user types a clear-text password to reach enable mode	208
List	Rule for combinations of the **username** command	210
Figure 10-6	Typical client filtering by firewall at Internet edge	213
Figure 10-8	Firewall security zones with DMZ	214
List	Features of next-generation firewalls	217
List	Features of next-generation IPSs	219

Key Terms You Should Know

Application Visibility and Control, enable secret, firewall, IPS, local username, MD5 hash, next-generation firewall (NGFW), next-generation IPS (NGIPS), username secret

Do Labs

The Sim Lite software is a version of Pearson's full simulator learning product with a subset of the labs, included free with this book. The Sim Lite with this book includes a couple of labs about various password-related topics. Also, check the author's blog site pages for configuration exercises (Config Labs) at https://www.certskills.com/config-labs.

Command References

Tables 10-6 and 10-7 list configuration and verification commands used in this chapter. As an easy review exercise, cover the left column in a table, read the right column, and try to recall the command without looking. Then repeat the exercise, covering the right column, and try to recall what the command does.

Table 10-6   Chapter 10 Configuration Commands

Command	Mode/Purpose/Description
line console 0	Command that changes the context to console configuration mode.
line vty *1st-vty last-vty*	Command that changes the context to vty configuration mode for the range of vty lines listed in the command.
login	Console and vty configuration mode. Tells IOS to prompt for a password.
password *pass-value*	Console and vty configuration mode. Lists the password required if the **login** command is configured.
login local	Console and vty configuration mode. Tells IOS to prompt for a username and password, to be checked against locally configured **username** global configuration commands.
username *name* [algorithm-type md5 | sha256 | scrypt] secret *pass-value*	Global command. Defines one of possibly multiple usernames and associated passwords, stored as a hashed value (default MD5), with other hash options as well.
username *name* password *pass-value*	Global command. Defines a username and password, stored in clear text in the configuration by default.
crypto key generate rsa [modulus 512 | 768 | 1024]	Global command. Creates and stores (in a hidden location in flash memory) the keys required by SSH.
transport input {telnet | ssh | all | none}	vty line configuration mode. Defines whether Telnet and/or SSH access is allowed into this switch.
[no] service password-encryption	Global command that encrypts all clear-text passwords in the running-config. The **no** version of the command disables the encryption of passwords when the password is set.
enable password *pass-value*	Global command to create the enable password, stored as a clear text instead of a hashed value.
enable [algorithm-type md5 | sha256 | scrypt] secret *pass-value*	Global command to create the enable password, stored as a hashed value instead of clear text, with the hash defined by the algorithm type.
no enable secret no enable password	Global command to delete the **enable secret** or **enable password** commands, respectively.

Table 10-7   Chapter 10 EXEC Command Reference

Command	Purpose
show running-config | section vty	Lists the vty lines and subcommands from the configuration.
show running-config | section con	Lists the console and subcommands from the configuration.
show running-config | include enable	Lists all lines in the configuration with the word *enable*.

10

CHAPTER 11

Implementing Switch Port Security

This chapter covers the following exam topics:

5.0 Security Fundamentals

    5.7 Configure and verify Layer 2 security features (DHCP snooping, dynamic ARP inspection, and port security)

In modern networks, security must be implemented in depth. The security architecture should use firewalls and intrusion prevention systems (IPS) at strategic locations, and hosts should use antivirus and antimalware tools. Routers, which already need to exist throughout the enterprise at the edge between local-area networks and wide-area networks, can be configured with IP access control lists to filter packets related to different IP address ranges in that enterprise.

LAN switches have a unique opportunity as a security enforcement point, particularly LAN switches connected to endpoint devices. Attackers often launch attacks from the endpoints connected to an enterprise LAN switch. The attacker might gain physical access to the endpoint or first infect the device to then launch an attack. Additionally, a mobile device can become infected while outside the company network and then later connect to the company network, with the attack launching at that point.

Engineers should assume that attacks might be launched from end-user devices connected directly to access ports on the enterprise's LAN switches, so Cisco switches include a number of useful tools to help prevent several types of attacks. This chapter discusses one such tool: port security. Chapter 12, "DHCP Snooping and ARP Inspection," discusses two other switch security tools that take advantage of the switch's access layer role.

This short chapter takes a straightforward approach to the port security feature. The first section discusses the concepts, configuration, and verification, using the primary port security operational mode: shutdown mode. The second section then discusses some of the intricacies of the three operational modes: shutdown, protect, and restrict.

"Do I Know This Already?" Quiz

Take the quiz (either here or use the PTP software) if you want to use the score to help you decide how much time to spend on this chapter. The letter answers are listed at the bottom of the page following the quiz. Appendix C, found both at the end of the book as well as on the companion website, includes both the answers and explanations. You can also find both answers and explanations in the PTP testing software.

Table 11-1 "Do I Know This Already?" Foundation Topics Section-to-Question Mapping

Foundation Topics Section	Questions
Port Security Concepts and Configuration	1–3
Port Security Violation Modes	4, 5

1. Which of the following is required when configuring port security with sticky learning?

    a. Setting the maximum number of allowed MAC addresses on the interface with the **switchport port-security maximum** interface subcommand.

    b. Enabling port security with the **switchport port-security** interface subcommand.

    c. Defining the specific allowed MAC addresses using the **switchport port-security mac-address** interface subcommand.

    d. All the other answers list required commands.

2. A Cisco Catalyst switch connects to what should be individual user PCs. Each port has the same port security configuration, configured as follows:

    ```
    interface range gigabitethernet 0/1 - 24
    switchport mode access
    switchport port-security
    switchport port-security mac-address sticky
    ```

    Which of the following answers describe the result of the port security configuration created with these commands? (Choose two answers.)

    a. Prevents unknown devices with unknown MAC addresses from sending data through the switch ports.

    b. If a user connects a switch to the cable, prevents multiple devices from sending data through the port.

    c. Will allow any one device to connect to each port and *will* save that device's MAC address into the startup-config.

    d. Will allow any one device to connect to each port but *will not* save that device's MAC address into the startup-config.

3. Which of the following commands list the MAC address table entries for MAC addresses configured by port security? (Choose two answers.)

    a. show mac address-table dynamic

    b. show mac address-table

    c. show mac address-table static

    d. show mac address-table port-security

4. The **show port-security interface f0/1** command lists a port status of secure-shutdown. Which one of the following answers must be true about this interface at this time?

    a. The **show interface status** command lists the interface status as connected.

    b. The **show interface status** command lists the interface status as err-disabled.

   c. The **show port-security interface** command could list a mode of shutdown or restrict, but not protect.

   d. The **show port-security interface** command violation counter can increase while in the secure-shutdown port state.

5. A switch's port Gi0/1 has been correctly enabled with port security. The configuration sets the violation mode to restrict. A frame that violates the port security policy enters the interface, followed by a frame that does not. Which of the following answers correctly describe what happens in this scenario? (Choose two answers.)

   a. The switch puts the interface into an err-disabled state when the first frame arrives.

   b. The switch generates syslog messages about the violating traffic for the first frame.

   c. The switch increments the violation counter for Gi0/1 by 1.

   d. The switch discards both the first and second frames.

Foundation Topics

Port Security Concepts and Configuration

If the network engineer knows what devices should be cabled and connected to particular interfaces on a switch, the engineer can use **port security** to restrict that interface so that only the expected devices can use it. This approach reduces exposure to attacks in which the attacker connects a laptop to some unused switch port. When that inappropriate device attempts to send frames to the switch interface, the switch can take different actions, ranging from simply issuing informational messages to effectively shutting down the interface.

Port security identifies devices based on the source MAC address of Ethernet frames that the devices send. For example, in Figure 11-1, PC1 sends a frame, with PC1's MAC address as the source address. SW1's F0/1 interface can be configured with port security, and if so, SW1 would examine PC1's MAC address and decide whether PC1 was allowed to send frames into port F0/1.

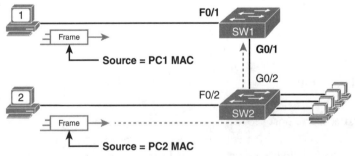

Figure 11-1 *Source MAC Addresses in Frames as They Enter a Switch*

Port security also has no restrictions on whether the frame came from a local device or was forwarded through other switches. For example, switch SW1 could use port security on its G0/1 interface, checking the source MAC address of the frame from PC2, when forwarded up to SW1 from SW2.

Port security has several flexible options, but all operate with the same core concepts. First, switches enable port security per port, with different settings available per port. Each port has a maximum number of allowed MAC addresses, meaning that for all frames entering that port, only that number of *different* source MAC addresses can be used before port security thinks a violation has occurred. When a frame with a new source MAC address arrives, pushing the number of MAC addresses past the allowed maximum, a port security violation occurs. At that point, the switch takes action—by default, discarding all future incoming traffic on that port.

The following list summarizes these ideas common to all variations of port security:

- It examines frames received on the interface to determine if a violation has occurred.

- It defines a maximum number of unique source MAC addresses allowed for all frames coming in the interface.

- It keeps a list and counter of all unique source MAC addresses on the interface.

- It monitors newly learned MAC addresses, considering those MAC addresses to cause a violation if the newly learned MAC address would push the total number of MAC table entries for the interface past the configured maximum allowed MAC addresses for that port.

- It takes action to discard frames from the violating MAC addresses, plus other actions depending on the configured violation mode.

Those rules define the basics, but port security allows other options as well, including options like these:

- Define a maximum of three MAC addresses, defining all three specific MAC addresses.

- Define a maximum of three MAC addresses but allow those addresses to be dynamically learned, allowing the first three MAC addresses learned.

- Define a maximum of three MAC addresses, predefining one specific MAC address, and allowing two more to be dynamically learned.

You might like the idea of predefining the MAC addresses for port security, but finding the MAC address of each device can be a bother. Port security provides a useful compromise using a feature called *sticky secure MAC addresses*. With this feature, port security learns the MAC addresses off each port so that you do not have to preconfigure the values. It also adds the learned MAC addresses to the port security configuration (in the running-config file). This feature helps reduce the big effort of finding out the MAC address of each device.

As you can see, port security has a lot of detailed options. The next few sections walk you through these options to pull the ideas together.

Configuring Port Security

Port security configuration involves several steps. First, port security works on both access ports and trunk ports, but it requires you to statically configure the port as a trunk or an access port, rather than let the switch dynamically decide whether to use trunking. The following configuration checklist details how to enable port security, set the maximum allowed MAC addresses per port, and configure the actual MAC addresses:

Step 1. Use the **switchport mode access** or the **switchport mode trunk** interface subcommands, respectively, to make the switch interface either a static access or trunk interface.

Step 2. Use the **switchport port-security** interface subcommand to enable port security on the interface.

Step 3. (Optional) Use the **switchport port-security maximum** *number* interface subcommand to override the default maximum number of allowed MAC addresses associated with the interface (1).

Step 4. (Optional) Use the **switchport port-security violation {protect | restrict | shutdown}** interface subcommand to override the default action to take upon a security violation (shutdown).

Step 5. (Optional) Use the **switchport port-security mac-address** *mac-address* interface subcommand to predefine any allowed source MAC addresses for this interface. Use the command multiple times to define more than one MAC address.

Step 6. (Optional) Use the **switchport port-security mac-address sticky** interface subcommand to tell the switch to "sticky learn" dynamically learned MAC addresses.

To demonstrate how to configure this variety of the settings, Figure 11-2 and Example 11-1 show four examples of port security. Three ports operate as access ports, while port F0/4, connected to another switch, operates as a trunk.

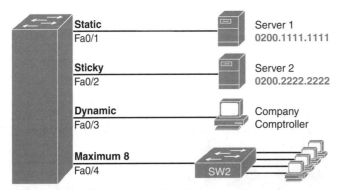

Figure 11-2 *Port Security Configuration Example*

Answers to the "Do I Know This Already?" quiz:

1 B **2** B, D **3** B, C **4** B **5** B, C

Example 11-1 *Variations on Port Security Configuration*

```
SW1# show running-config
(Lines omitted for brevity)

interface FastEthernet0/1
 switchport mode access
 switchport port-security
 switchport port-security mac-address 0200.1111.1111
 !
interface FastEthernet0/2
 switchport mode access
 switchport port-security
 switchport port-security mac-address sticky
 !
interface FastEthernet0/3
 switchport mode access
 switchport port-security
 !
interface FastEthernet0/4
 switchport mode trunk
 switchport port-security
 switchport port-security maximum 8
```

First, scan the configuration for all four interfaces in Example 11-1, focusing on the first two interface subcommands in each case. Note that the first three interfaces in the example use the same first two interface subcommands, matching the first two configuration steps noted before Figure 11-2. The **switchport port-security** command enables port security, with all defaults, with the **switchport mode access** command meeting the requirement to configure the port as either an access or trunk port. The final port, F0/4, has a similar configuration, except that it has been configured as a trunk rather than as an access port.

Next, scan all four interfaces again, and note that the configuration differs on each interface after those first two interface subcommands. Each interface simply shows a different example for perspective.

The first interface, FastEthernet 0/1, adds one optional port security subcommand: **switchport port-security mac-address 0200.1111.1111**, which defines a specific source MAC address. With the default maximum source address setting of 1, only frames with source MAC 0200.1111.1111 will be allowed in this port. When a frame with a source other than 0200.1111.1111 enters F0/1, the switch would normally perform MAC address learning and want to add the new source MAC address to the MAC address table. Port security will see that action as learning one too many MAC addresses on the port, taking the default violation action to disable the interface.

As a second example, FastEthernet 0/2 uses the same logic as FastEthernet 0/1, except that it uses the sticky learning feature. For port F0/2, the configuration of the **switchport port-security mac-address sticky** command tells the switch to dynamically learn source

11

MAC addresses and add **port-security** commands to the running-config. Example 11-2 shows the running-config file that lists the sticky-learned MAC address in this case.

Example 11-2 *Configuration Added by the Port Security Sticky Feature*

```
SW1# show running-config interface f0/2
Building configuration...
Current configuration : 188 bytes
!
interface FastEthernet0/2
  switchport mode access
  switchport port-security
  switchport port-security mac-address sticky
  switchport port-security mac-address sticky 0200.2222.2222
```

Port security does not save the configuration of the sticky addresses, so use the **copy running-config startup-config** command if desired.

The other two interfaces in Example 11-1 do not predefine MAC addresses, nor do they sticky-learn the MAC addresses. The only difference between these two interfaces' port security configuration is that FastEthernet 0/4 supports eight MAC addresses because it connects to another switch and should receive frames with multiple source MAC addresses. Interface F0/3 uses the default maximum of one MAC address.

NOTE   Switches can also use port security on voice ports and EtherChannels. For voice ports, make sure to configure the maximum MAC address to at least two (one for the phone, or for a PC connected to the phone). On EtherChannels, the port security configuration should be placed on the port-channel interface, rather than the individual physical interfaces in the channel.

Verifying Port Security

The **show port-security interface** command provides the most insight into how port security operates, as shown in Example 11-3. This command lists the configuration settings for port security on an interface; plus it lists several important facts about the current operation of port security, including information about any security violations. The two commands in the example show interfaces F0/1 and F0/2, based on Example 11-1's configuration.

Example 11-3 *Using Port Security to Define Correct MAC Addresses of Particular Interfaces*

```
SW1# show port-security interface fastEthernet 0/1
Port Security              : Enabled
Port Status                : Secure-shutdown
Violation Mode             : Shutdown
Aging Time                 : 0 mins
Aging Type                 : Absolute
```

```
SecureStatic Address Aging : Disabled
Maximum MAC Addresses       : 1
Total MAC Addresses         : 1
Configured MAC Addresses    : 1
Sticky MAC Addresses        : 0
Last Source Address:Vlan    : 0013.197b.5004:1
Security Violation Count    : 1


SW1# show port-security interface fastEthernet 0/2
Port Security               : Enabled
Port Status                 : Secure-up
Violation Mode              : Shutdown
Aging Time                  : 0 mins
Aging Type                  : Absolute
SecureStatic Address Aging  : Disabled
Maximum MAC Addresses       : 1
Total MAC Addresses         : 1
Configured MAC Addresses    : 1
Sticky MAC Addresses        : 1
Last Source Address:Vlan    : 0200.2222.2222:1
Security Violation Count    : 0
```

The two commands in Example 11-3 confirm that a security violation has occurred on FastEthernet 0/1, but no violations have occurred on FastEthernet 0/2. The **show port-security interface fastethernet 0/1** command shows that the interface is in a *secure-shutdown* state, which means that the interface has been disabled because of port security. In this case, another device connected to port F0/1, sending a frame with a source MAC address other than 0200.1111.1111, is causing a violation. However, port Fa0/2, which used sticky learning, simply learned the MAC address used by Server 2.

Port Security MAC Addresses

To complete this chapter, take a moment to think about Layer 2 switching, along with all those examples of output from the **show mac address-table dynamic** EXEC command.

Once a switch port has been configured with port security, the switch no longer considers MAC addresses associated with that port as being dynamic entries as listed with the **show mac address-table dynamic** EXEC command. Even if the MAC addresses are dynamically learned, once port security has been enabled, you need to use one of these options to see the MAC table entries associated with ports using port security:

- **show mac address-table secure:** Lists MAC addresses associated with ports that use port security

- **show mac address-table static:** Lists MAC addresses associated with ports that use port security, as well as any other statically defined MAC addresses

11

Example 11-4 proves the point. It shows two commands about interface F0/2 from the port security example shown in Figure 11-2 and Example 11-1. In that example, port security was configured on F0/2 with sticky learning, so from a literal sense, the switch learned a MAC address off that port (0200.2222.2222). However, the **show mac address-table dynamic** command does not list the address and port because IOS considers that MAC table entry to be a static entry. The **show mac address-table secure** command does list the address and port.

Example 11-4 *Using the* secure *Keyword to See MAC Table Entries When Using Port Security*

```
SW1# show mac address-table secure interface F0/2
          Mac Address Table
-------------------------------------------


Vlan    Mac Address      Type         Ports
----    -----------      --------     -----
 1      0200.2222.2222   STATIC       Fa0/2
Total Mac Addresses for this criterion: 1

SW1# show mac address-table dynamic interface f0/2
          Mac Address Table
-------------------------------------------


Vlan    Mac Address      Type         Ports
----    -----------      --------     -----
SW1#
```

Port Security Violation Modes

The first half of the chapter discussed many details of port security, but it mostly ignored one major feature: the port security violation mode. The **violation mode** defines how port security should react when a violation occurs.

First, to review, what is a port security violation? Any received frame that breaks the port security rules on an interface. For example:

- For an interface that allows any two MAC addresses, a violation occurs when the total of preconfigured and learned MAC addresses on the interface exceeds the configured maximum of two.

- For an interface that predefines all the specific MAC addresses allowed on the interface, a violation occurs when the switch receives a frame whose source MAC is not one of those configured addresses.

With port security, each switch port can be configured to use one of three violation modes that defines the actions to take when a violation occurs. All three options cause the switch to discard the offending frame (a frame whose source MAC address would push the number of learned MAC addresses over the limit). However, the modes vary in how many other steps they take. For instance, some modes include the action of the switch generating syslog messages and SNMP Trap messages, while some define the action to disable the interface. Table 11-2 lists the three modes, their actions, along with the keywords that enable each mode on the **switchport port-security violation** {**protect** | **restrict** | **shutdown**} interface subcommand:

Table 11-2   Actions When Port Security Violation Occurs

Option on the switchport port-security violation Command	Protect	Restrict	Shutdown
Discards offending traffic	Yes	Yes	Yes
Sends log and SNMP messages	No	Yes	Yes
Disables the interface by putting it in an err-disabled state, discarding all traffic	No	No	Yes

Because IOS reacts so differently with shutdown mode as compared to restrict and protect modes, the next few pages explain the differences—first for shutdown mode, then for the other two modes.

Port Security Shutdown Mode

When the (default) shutdown violation mode is used and a port security violation occurs on a port, port security stops all frame forwarding on the interface, both in and out of the port. In effect, it acts as if port security has shut down the port; however, it does not literally configure the port with the **shutdown** interface subcommand. Instead, port security uses the **err-disabled** feature. Cisco switches use the err-disabled state for a wide range of purposes, but when using port security shutdown mode and a violation occurs, the following happens:

- The switch interface state (per **show interfaces** and **show interfaces status**) changes to an err-disabled state.

- The switch interface port security state (per **show port-security**) changes to a secure-shutdown state.

- The switch stops sending and receiving frames on the interface.

Once port security has placed a port in err-disabled state, by default, the port remains in an err-disabled state until someone takes action. To recover from an err-disabled state, the interface must be shut down with the **shutdown** command and then enabled with the **no shutdown** command. Alternately, the switch can be configured to automatically recover from the err-disabled state, when caused by port security, with these commands:

- **errdisable recovery cause psecure-violation:** A global command to enable automatic recovery for interfaces in an err-disabled state caused by port security

- **errdisable recovery interval** *seconds*: A global command to set the time to wait before recovering the interface

To take a closer look at shutdown mode, start by checking the configuration state of the switch. You can check the port security configuration on any interface with the **show port-security interface** *type number* command, as seen previously in Example 11-2, but the

11

show port-security command (as listed in Example 11-5) shows briefer output, with one line per enabled interface.

Example 11-5 *Confirming the Port Security Violation Mode*

```
SW1# show port-security
Secure Port  MaxSecureAddr  CurrentAddr  SecurityViolation  Security Action
             (Count)        (Count)      (Count)
-------------------------------------------------------------------------
    Fa0/13             1            1                  1         Shutdown
-------------------------------------------------------------------------
Total Addresses in System (excluding one mac per port) : 0
Max Addresses limit in System (excluding one mac per port) : 8192
```

Note that for these next examples, a switch has configured port security on port Fa0/13 only. In this case, the switch appears to be configured to support one MAC address, has already reached that total, and has a security violation action of "shutdown."

Next, Example 11-6 shows the results after a port security violation has already occurred on port F0/13. The first command confirms the err-disabled state (per the **show interfaces status** command) and the secure-shutdown state (per the **show port-security** command).

Example 11-6 *Port Security Status in Shutdown Mode After a Violation*

```
! The next lines show the log message generated when the violation occurred.
Jul 31 18:00:22.810: %PORT_SECURITY-2-PSECURE_VIOLATION: Security violation
occurred, caused by MAC address 0200.3333.3333 on port FastEthernet0/13

! The next command shows the err-disabled state, implying a security violation.
SW1# show interfaces Fa0/13 status

Port     Name            Status         Vlan   Duplex  Speed  Type
Fa0/13                   err-disabled   1      auto    auto   10/100BaseTX
!
! The next command's output has shading for several of the most important facts.
SW1# show port-security interface Fa0/13
Port Security              : Enabled
Port Status                : Secure-shutdown
Violation Mode             : Shutdown
Aging Time                 : 0 mins
Aging Type                 : Absolute
SecureStatic Address Aging : Disabled
Maximum MAC Addresses      : 1
Total MAC Addresses        : 1
Configured MAC Addresses   : 1
Sticky MAC Addresses       : 0
Last Source Address:Vlan   : 0200.3333.3333:2
Security Violation Count   : 1
```

The output of the **show port-security interface** command lists the current port-security status (secure-shutdown) as well as the configured mode (shutdown). The last line of output lists the number of violations that caused the interface to fail to an err-disabled state, while the second-to-last line identifies the MAC address and VLAN of the device that caused the violation.

Figure 11-3 summarizes these behaviors, assuming the same scenario shown in the example.

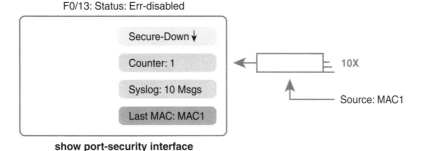

Figure 11-3 *Summary of Actions: Port Security Violation Mode Shutdown*

The violations counter notes the number of times the interface has been moved to the err-disabled (secure-shutdown) state. For instance, the first time it fails, the counter increments to 1; while err-disabled, many frames can arrive, but the counter remains at 1. IOS will reset the counter to 0 when you recover the interface using a shutdown/no shutdown command combination, so that the next violation will cause the counter to increment to 1.

Port Security Protect and Restrict Modes

The restrict and protect violation modes take a much different approach to securing ports. These modes still discard offending traffic, but the interface remains in a connected (up/up) state and in a port security state of secure-up. As a result, the port continues to forward good traffic but discards offending traffic.

Having a port in a seemingly good state that also discards traffic can be a challenge when troubleshooting. Basically, you have to know about the feature and then know how to tell when port security is discarding some traffic on a port even though the interface status looks good.

With protect mode, the only action the switch takes for a frame that violates the port security rules is to discard the frame. The switch does not change the port to an err-disabled state, does not generate messages, and does not even increment the violations counter.

Example 11-7 shows a sample with protect mode after several violations have occurred. Note that the **show** command confirms the mode (protect) as configured in the top part of the example, with a port security state of secure-up—a state that will not change in protect mode. Also, note that the counter at the bottom shows 0, even though several violations have occurred, because protect mode does not count the violating frames.

11

Example 11-7   *Port Security Using Protect Mode*

```
SW1# show running-config
! Lines omitted for brevity
interface FastEthernet0/13
  switchport mode access
  switchport port-security
  switchport port-security mac-address 0200.1111.1111
  switchport port-security violation protect
! Lines omitted for brevity


SW1# show port-security interface Fa0/13
Port Security                : Enabled
Port Status                  : Secure-up
Violation Mode               : Protect
Aging Time                   : 0 mins
Aging Type                   : Absolute
SecureStatic Address Aging   : Disabled
Maximum MAC Addresses        : 1
Total MAC Addresses          : 1
Configured MAC Addresses     : 1
Sticky MAC Addresses         : 0
Last Source Address:Vlan     : 0000.0000.0000:0
Security Violation Count     : 0
```

NOTE   The small particulars of the violation counters and last source address might be slightly different with some older switch models and IOS versions. Note that this edition's testing is based on 2960XR switches running IOS 15.2.(6)E2.

While shutdown mode disables the interface, and protect mode does nothing more than discard the offending traffic, restrict mode provides a compromise between the other two modes. If Example 11-7 had used the restrict violation mode instead of protect, the port status would have also remained in a secure-up state; however, IOS would show some indication of port security activity, such as an accurate incrementing violation counter, as well as syslog messages. Example 11-8 shows an example of the violation counter and ends with a sample port security syslog message. In this case, 97 incoming frames so far violated the rules, with the most recent frame having a source MAC address of 0200.3333.3333 in VLAN 1.

Example 11-8   *Port Security Using Violation Mode Restrict*

```
SW1# show port-security interface fa0/13
Port Security                : Enabled
Port Status                  : Secure-up
Violation Mode               : Restrict
```

```
Aging Time                    : 0 mins
Aging Type                    : Absolute
SecureStatic Address Aging    : Disabled
Maximum MAC Addresses         : 1
Total MAC Addresses           : 1
Configured MAC Addresses      : 1
Sticky MAC Addresses          : 0
Last Source Address:Vlan      : 0200.3333.3333:1
Security Violation Count      : 97
!
! The following log message also points to a port security issue.
!
01:46:58: %PORT_SECURITY-2-PSECURE_VIOLATION: Security violation occurred, caused by
MAC address 0200.3333.3333 on port FastEthernet0/13.
```

Figure 11-4 summarizes the key points about the restrict mode for port security. In this case, the figure matches the same scenario as the example again, with 97 total violating frames arriving so far, with the most recent being from source MAC address MAC3.

F0/13: Status: Connected

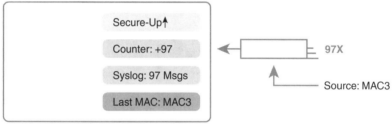

show port-security interface

Figure 11-4 *Summary of Actions: Port Security Violation Mode Restrict*

Chapter Review

One key to doing well on the exams is to perform repetitive spaced review sessions. Review this chapter's material using either the tools in the book or interactive tools for the same material found on the book's companion website. Refer to the "Your Study Plan" element for more details. Table 11-3 outlines the key review elements and where you can find them. To better track your study progress, record when you completed these activities in the second column.

Table 11-3 Chapter Review Tracking

Review Element	Review Date(s)	Resource Used
Review key topics		Book, website
Review key terms		Book, website

11

Review Element	Review Date(s)	Resource Used
Answer DIKTA questions		Book, PTP
Review command tables		Book
Review memory tables		Book, website
Review config checklists		Book, website
Do labs		Sim Lite, blog
Watch video		Website

Review All the Key Topics

Table 11-4   Key Topics for Chapter 11

Key Topic Element	Description	Page Number
List	Summary of port security concepts	225
List	Port security configuration checklist	226
Example 11-1	Port security configuration samples	227
Table 11-2	Port security actions and the results of each action	231
List	Switch actions with a port in err-disabled state	231

Key Terms You Should Know

error disabled (err-disable), port security, violation mode

Do Labs

The Sim Lite software is a version of Pearson's full simulator learning product with a subset of the labs, included free with this book. The Sim Lite with this book includes a couple of labs about port security. Also, check the author's blog site pages for configuration exercises (Config Labs) at https://www.certskills.com/config-labs.

Command References

Tables 11-5 and 11-6 list configuration and verification commands used in this chapter. As an easy review exercise, cover the left column in a table, read the right column, and try to recall the command without looking. Then repeat the exercise, covering the right column, and try to recall what the command does.

Table 11-5   Chapter 11 Configuration Command Reference

Command	Mode/Purpose/Description
**switchport mode {access	trunk}**	Interface configuration mode command that tells the switch to always be an access port, or always be a trunk port
switchport port-security mac-address *mac-address*	Interface configuration mode command that statically adds a specific MAC address as an allowed MAC address on the interface

Command	Mode/Purpose/Description
switchport port-security mac-address sticky	Interface subcommand that tells the switch to learn MAC addresses on the interface and add them to the configuration for the interface as secure MAC addresses
switchport port-security maximum *value*	Interface subcommand that sets the maximum number of static secure MAC addresses that can be assigned to a single interface
switchport port-security violation {protect | restrict | shutdown}	Interface subcommand that tells the switch what to do if an inappropriate MAC address tries to access the network through a secure switch port
errdisable recovery cause psecure-violation	Global command that enables the automatic recovery from err-disabled state for ports that reach that state due to port security violations
errdisable recovery interval *seconds*	Global command that sets the delay, in seconds, before a switch attempts to recover an interface in err-disabled mode, regardless of the reason for that interface being in that state
shutdown no shutdown	Interface subcommands that administratively disable and enable an interface, respectively

Table 11-6   Chapter 11 EXEC Command Reference

Command	Purpose
show running-config	Lists the currently used configuration
show running-config | interface *type number*	Displays the running-configuration excerpt of the listed interface and its subcommands only
show mac address-table dynamic [interface *type number*]	Lists the dynamically learned entries in the switch's address (forwarding) table
show mac address-table secure [interface *type number*]	Lists MAC addresses defined or learned on ports configured with port security
show mac address-table static [interface *type number*]	Lists static MAC addresses and MAC addresses learned or defined with port security
show interfaces [interface *type number*] status	Lists one output line per interface (or for only the listed interface if included), noting the description, operating state, and settings for duplex and speed on each interface
show port-security interface *type number*	Lists an interface's port security configuration settings and security operational status
show port-security	Lists one line per interface that summarizes the port security settings for any interface on which it is enabled

11

CHAPTER 12

DHCP Snooping and ARP Inspection

This chapter covers the following exam topics:

5.0 Security Fundamentals

> **5.7 Configure and verify Layer 2 security features (DHCP snooping, dynamic ARP inspection, and port security)**

To understand the kinds of risks that exist in modern networks, you have to first understand the rules. Then you have to think about how an attacker might take advantage of those rules in different ways. Some attacks might cause harm as part of a denial-of-service (DoS) attack, while a reconnaissance attack may gather more data to prepare for some other attack. For every protocol and function you learn in networking, there are possible methods to take advantage of those features to give an attacker an advantage.

This chapter discusses two switch features that help prevent some types of attacks that can result in the attacker getting copies of packets sent to/from a legitimate host. One of these features, DHCP Snooping, notices DHCP messages that fall outside the normal use of DHCP—messages that may be part of an attack—and discards those messages. It also watches the DHCP messages that flow through a LAN switch, building a table that lists the details of legitimate DHCP flows, so that other switch features can know what legitimate DHCP leases exist for devices connected to the switch.

The second such feature, Dynamic ARP Inspection (DAI), also helps prevent packets being redirected to an attacking host. Some ARP attacks try to convince hosts to send packets to the attacker's device instead of the true destination. The switch watches ARP messages as they flow through the switch. The switch checks incoming ARP messages, checking those against normal ARP operation as well as checking the details against other data sources, including the DHCP Snooping binding table. When the ARP message does not match the known information about the legitimate addresses in the network, the switch filters the ARP message.

This chapter examines DHCP Snooping concepts and configuration in the first major section and DAI in the second.

"Do I Know This Already?" Quiz

Take the quiz (either here or use the PTP software) if you want to use the score to help you decide how much time to spend on this chapter. The letter answers are listed at the bottom of the page following the quiz. Appendix C, found both at the end of the book as well as on the companion website, includes both the answers and explanations. You can also find both answers and explanations in the PTP testing software.

Table 12-1 "Do I Know This Already?" Foundation Topics Section-to-Question Mapping

Foundation Topics Section	Questions
DHCP Snooping	1–4
Dynamic ARP Inspection	5–7

1. An engineer hears about DHCP Snooping and decides to implement it. Which of the following are the devices on which DHCP Snooping could be implemented? (Choose two answers.)

   a. Layer 2 switches

   b. Routers

   c. Multilayer switches

   d. End-user hosts

2. Layer 2 switch SW2 connects a Layer 2 switch (SW1), a router (R1), a DHCP server (S1), and three PCs (PC1, PC2, and PC3). All PCs are DHCP clients. Which of the following are the most likely DHCP Snooping trust state configurations on SW2 for the ports connected to the listed devices? (Choose two answers.)

   a. The port connected to the router is untrusted.

   b. The port connected to switch SW1 is trusted.

   c. The port connected to PC1 is untrusted.

   d. The port connected to PC3 is trusted.

3. Switch SW1 needs to be configured to use DHCP Snooping in VLAN 5 and only VLAN 5. Which commands must be included, assuming at least one switch port in VLAN 5 must be an untrusted port? (Choose two answers.)

   a. no ip dhcp snooping trust

   b. ip dhcp snooping untrust

   c. ip dhcp snooping

   d. ip dhcp snooping vlan 5

4. On a multilayer switch, a switch needs to be configured to perform DHCP Snooping on some Layer 2 ports in VLAN 3. Which command may or may not be needed depending on whether the switch also acts as a DHCP relay agent?

   a. no ip dhcp snooping information option

   b. ip dhcp snooping limit rate 5

   c. errdisable recovery cause dhcp-rate-limit

   d. ip dhcp snooping vlan 3

5. Switch SW1 has been configured to use Dynamic ARP Inspection with DHCP Snooping in VLAN 5. An ARP request arrives on port G0/1. Which answer describes two items DAI always compares regardless of the configuration?

   a. The message's ARP sender hardware address and the message's Ethernet header source MAC address

   b. The message's ARP sender hardware address and the DHCP Snooping binding table

   c. The message's ARP target IP address and the DHCP Snooping binding table

   d. The message's ARP target IP address and the switch's ARP table

6. Switch SW1 needs to be configured to use Dynamic ARP Inspection along with DHCP Snooping in VLAN 6 and only VLAN 6. Which commands must be included, assuming at least one switch port in VLAN 6 must be a trusted port? (Choose two answers.)

   a. no ip arp inspection untrust

   b. ip arp inspection trust

   c. ip arp inspection

   d. ip arp inspection vlan 6

7. A Layer 2 switch needs to be configured to use Dynamic ARP Inspection along with DHCP Snooping. Which command would make DAI monitor ARP message rates on an interface at an average rate of 4 received ARP messages per second? (Choose two answers.)

   a. ip arp inspection limit rate 4 burst interval 2

   b. ip arp inspection limit rate 10 burst interval 2

   c. ip arp inspection limit rate 16 burst interval 4

   d. ip arp inspection limit rate 4

Foundation Topics

DHCP Snooping

DHCP servers play a vital role in most every network today, with almost every user endpoint using DHCP to learn its IP address, mask, default gateway, and DNS server IP addresses. Chapter 19, "IP Addressing on Hosts," in the *CCNA 200-301 Official Certification Guide, Volume 1*, Second Edition, shows how DHCP should work under normal circumstances. This section now examines how attackers might use DHCP for their own ends and how two specific tools—DHCP Snooping and Dynamic ARP Inspection (DAI)—help defeat those attacks.

This section begins with an examination of the need for DHCP Snooping concepts, including the types of attacks it can try to prevent, followed by details of how to configure DHCP Snooping.

DHCP Snooping Concepts

DHCP Snooping on a switch acts like a firewall or an ACL in many ways. It analyzes incoming messages on the specified subset of ports in a VLAN. DHCP Snooping never filters non-DHCP messages, but it may choose to filter DHCP messages, applying logic to make a choice—to allow the incoming DHCP message or discard the message.

While DHCP itself provides a Layer 3 service, DHCP Snooping operates on LAN switches and is commonly used on Layer 2 LAN switches and enabled on Layer 2 ports. The reason to put DHCP Snooping on the switch is that the function needs to be performed between a typical end-user device—the type of device that acts as a DHCP client—and DHCP servers or DHCP relay agents.

Figure 12-1 shows a sample network that provides a good backdrop to discuss DHCP Snooping. First, all devices connect to Layer 2 switch SW2, with all ports as Layer 2 switch ports, all in the same VLAN. The typical DHCP clients sit on the right of the figure. The left shows other devices that could be the path through which to reach a DHCP server.

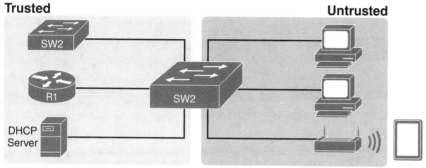

Figure 12-1 *DHCP Snooping Basics: Client Ports Are Untrusted*

DHCP Snooping works first on all ports in a VLAN, but with each port being trusted or untrusted by DHCP Snooping. To understand why, consider this summary of the general rules used by DHCP Snooping. Note that the rules differentiate between messages normally sent by servers (like DHCPOFFER and DHCPACK) versus those normally sent by DHCP clients (DHCPDISCOVER and DHCPREQUEST):

■ DHCP messages received on an **untrusted port**, for messages normally sent by a server, will always be discarded.

■ DHCP messages received on an untrusted port, as normally sent by a DHCP client, may be filtered if they appear to be part of an attack.

■ DHCP messages received on a **trusted port** will be forwarded; trusted ports do not filter (discard) any DHCP messages.

A Sample Attack: A Spurious DHCP Server

To give you some perspective, Figure 12-2 shows a legitimate user's PC on the far right and the legitimate DHCP server on the far left. However, an attacker has connected a laptop to the LAN and started a DHCP attack by acting like a DHCP server. Following the steps in the figure, assume PC1 is attempting to lease an IP address while the attacker is making this attack:

1. PC1 sends a LAN broadcast with PC1's first DHCP message (DHCPDISCOVER).

2. The attacker's PC—acting as a spurious DHCP server—replies to the DHCPDISCOVER with a DHCPOFFER.

In this example, the DHCP server created and used by the attacker actually leases a useful IP address to PC1, in the correct subnet, with the correct mask. Why? The attacker wants PC1 to function, but with one twist. Notice the default gateway assigned to PC1: 10.1.1.2, which is the attacker's PC address, rather than 10.1.1.1, which is router R1's address. Now PC1 thinks it has all it needs to connect to the network, and it does—but now all the packets sent by PC1 to what it thinks is its default router flow first through the attacker's PC, creating a man-in-the-middle attack, as shown in Figure 12-3.

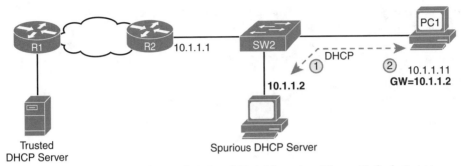

Figure 12-2 *DHCP Attack Supplies Good IP Address but Wrong Default Gateway*

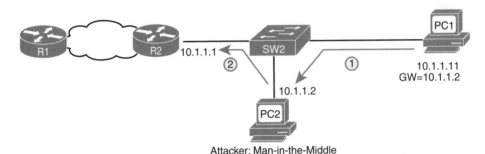

Figure 12-3 *Unfortunate Result: DHCP Attack Leads to Man-in-the-Middle*

Note that the legitimate DHCP also returns a DHCPOFFER message to host PC1, but most hosts use the first received DHCPOFFER, and the attacker will likely be first in this scenario.

The two steps in the figure show data flow once DHCP has completed. For any traffic destined to leave the subnet, PC1 sends its packets to its default gateway, 10.1.1.2, which happens to be the attacker. The attacker forwards the packets to R1. The PC1 user can connect to any and all applications just like normal, but now the attacker can keep a copy of anything sent by PC1.

DHCP Snooping Logic

The preceding example shows just one attack in which the attacker acts like a DHCP server (spurious DHCP server). DHCP Snooping defeats such attacks by making most ports untrusted, which by definition would filter the DHCP server messages that arrive on the untrusted ports. For instance, in Figures 12-2 and 12-3, making the port connected to the attacker, a DHCP Snooping untrusted port defeats the attack.

To appreciate the broader set of DHCP Snooping rules and logic, it helps to have a handy reference of some of the more common DHCP messages and processes. For a quick review, the normal message flow includes this sequence: DISCOVER, OFFER, REQUEST, ACK (DORA). In particular:

- Clients send DISCOVER and REQUEST.

- Servers send OFFER and ACK.

Answers to the "Do I Know This Already?" quiz:

1 A, C **2** B, C **3** C, D **4** A **5** B **6** B, D **7** C, D

Additionally, DHCP clients also use the DHCP RELEASE and DHCP DECLINE messages. When a client has a working lease for an address but no longer wants to use the address, the DHCP client can tell the DHCP server it no longer needs the address, releasing it back to the DHCP server, with the DHCP RELEASE message. Similarly, a client can send a DHCP DECLINE message to turn down the use of an IP address during the normal DORA flow on messages.

Now to the logic for DHCP Snooping untrusted ports. Figure 12-4 summarizes the ideas, with two switch ports. On the left, the switch port connects to a DHCP server, so it should be trusted; otherwise, DHCP would not work because the switch would filter all DHCP messages sent by the DHCP server. On the right, PC1 connects to an untrusted port with a DHCP client.

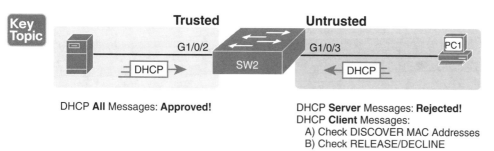

DHCP **All** Messages: **Approved!**

DHCP **Server** Messages: **Rejected!**
DHCP **Client** Messages:
   A) Check DISCOVER MAC Addresses
   B) Check RELEASE/DECLINE

Figure 12-4 *Summary of Rules for DHCP Snooping*

The DHCP Snooping rules are as follows:

1. Examine all incoming DHCP messages.
2. If normally sent by servers, discard the message.
3. If normally sent by clients, filter as follows:

    a. For DISCOVER and REQUEST messages, check for MAC address consistency between the Ethernet frame and the DHCP message.

    b. For RELEASE or DECLINE messages, check the incoming interface plus IP address versus the DHCP Snooping binding table.

4. For messages allowed by DHCP Snooping, observe the details in the messages, and if they result in a DHCP lease, build a new entry to the DHCP Snooping binding table.

The next few pages complete the discussion of concepts by explaining a little more about steps 3 and 4 in the list.

Filtering DISCOVER Messages Based on MAC Address

DHCP Snooping does one straightforward check for the most common client-sent messages: DISCOVER and REQUEST. First, note that DHCP messages define the chaddr (client hardware address) field to identify the client. Hosts on LANs include the device's MAC address as part of chaddr. As usual, Ethernet hosts encapsulate the DHCP messages inside Ethernet frames, and those frames of course include a source MAC address—an address that should be the same MAC address used in the DHCP chaddr field. DHCP Snooping does a simple check to make sure those values match.

Figure 12-5 shows how an attacker could attempt to overload the DHCP server and lease all the addresses in the subnet. The attacker's PC uses pseudo MAC address A, so all three DISCOVER messages in the figure show a source Ethernet address of "A." However, each message (in the DHCP data) identifies a different MAC address in the chaddr value (shown as MAC1, MAC2, and MAC3 in the figure for brevity), so from a DHCP perspective, each message appears to be a different DHCP request. The attacker can attempt to lease every IP address in the subnet so that no other hosts could obtain a lease.

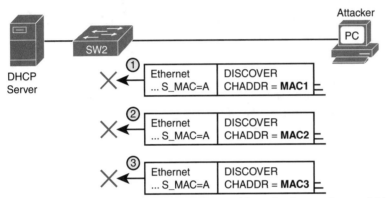

Figure 12-5 *DHCP Snooping Checks chaddr and Ethernet Source MAC*

The core feature of DHCP Snooping defeats this type of attack on untrusted ports. It checks the Ethernet header source MAC address and compares that address to the MAC address in the DHCP header, and if the values do not match, DHCP Snooping discards the message.

Filtering Messages That Release IP Addresses

Before looking at the next bit of logic, you need to first understand the DHCP Snooping binding table.

DHCP Snooping builds the **DHCP Snooping binding table** for all the DHCP flows it sees that it allows to complete. That is, for any working legitimate DHCP flows, it keeps a list of some of the important facts. Then DHCP Snooping, and other features like Dynamic ARP Inspection, can use the table to make decisions.

As an example, consider Figure 12-6, which repeats the same topology as Figure 12-4, now with one entry in its DHCP Snooping binding table.

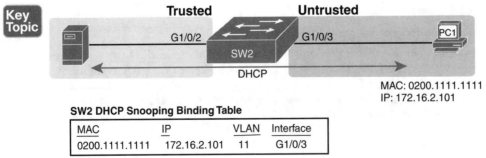

Figure 12-6 *Legitimate DHCP Client with DHCP Binding Entry Built by DHCP Snooping*

In this simple network, the DHCP client on the right leases IP address 172.16.2.101 from the DHCP server on the left. The switch's DHCP Snooping feature combines the information from the DHCP messages, with information about the port (interface G1/0/3, assigned to VLAN 11 by the switch), and puts that in the DHCP Snooping binding table.

DHCP Snooping then applies additional filtering logic that uses the DHCP Snooping binding table: it checks client-sent messages like RELEASE and DECLINE that would cause the DHCP server to be allowed to release an address. For instance, a legitimate user might lease address 172.16.2.101, and at some point release the address back to the server; however, before the client has finished with its lease, an attacker could send a DHCP RELEASE message to release that address back into the pool. The attacker could then immediately try to lease that address, hoping the DHCP server assigns that same 172.16.2.101 address to the attacker.

Figure 12-7 shows an example. PC1 already has a DHCP address (172.16.2.101), with SW2 listing an entry in the DHCP Snooping binding table. The figure shows the action by which the attacker off port G1/0/5 attempts to release PC1's address. DHCP Snooping compares the incoming message, incoming interface, and matching table entry:

1. The attacker, PC A, sends a DHCP RELEASE message, received by switch SW2 in port G1/0/5. The message attempts to DHCP RELEASE address 172.16.2.101.

2. Switch SW2 compares the DHCP Snooping binding table to find the entry matching the listed address: 172.16.2.101.

3. Switch SW2 notes that the binding table lists the legitimate entry with port G1/0/3, but the new DHCP RELEASE arrived in port G1/0/5. As a result, DHCP Snooping discards the DHCP RELEASE message.

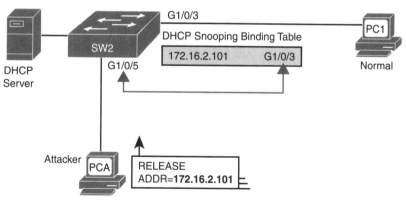

Figure 12-7 *DHCP Snooping Defeats a DHCP RELEASE from Another Port*

DHCP Snooping Configuration

DHCP Snooping requires several configuration steps to make it work. First, you need to use a pair of associated global commands: one to enable DHCP Snooping and another to list the VLANs on which to use DHCP Snooping. Both must be included for DHCP Snooping to operate.

Second, while not literally required, you will often need to configure a few ports as trusted ports. Most switches that use DHCP Snooping for a VLAN have some trusted ports and some untrusted ports, and with a default of untrusted, you need to configure the trusted ports.

This section begins with an example that shows how to configure a typical Layer 2 switch to use DHCP Snooping, with required commands as just described, and with other optional commands.

Configuring DHCP Snooping on a Layer 2 Switch

The upcoming examples all rely on the topology illustrated in Figure 12-8, with Layer 2 switch SW2 as the switch on which to enable DHCP Snooping. The DHCP server sits on the other side of the WAN, on the left of the figure. As a result, SW2's port connected to router R2 (a DHCP relay agent) needs to be trusted. On the right, two sample PCs can use the default untrusted setting.

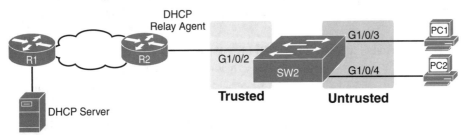

Figure 12-8 *Sample Network Used in DHCP Snooping Configuration Examples*

Switch SW2 places all the ports in the figure in VLAN 11. To enable DHCP Snooping in VLAN 11, SW2 requires two commands, as shown near the top of Example 12-1: **ip dhcp snooping** and **ip dhcp snooping vlan 11**. Then, to change the logic on port G1/0/2 (connected to the router) to be trusted, the configuration includes the **ip dhcp snooping trust** interface subcommand.

Example 12-1 *DHCP Snooping Configuration to Match Figure 12-8*

```
ip dhcp snooping
ip dhcp snooping vlan 11
no ip dhcp snooping information option
!
interface GigabitEthernet1/0/2
 ip dhcp snooping trust
```

Note that the **no ip dhcp snooping information option** command in Example 12-1 will be explained in a better context just after Example 12-2 but is listed in Example 12-1 to make the example complete.

With this configuration, the switch follows the logic steps detailed in the earlier section titled "DHCP Snooping Logic." To see some support for that claim, look at Example 12-2, which shows the output from the **show ip dhcp snooping** command on switch SW2.

Example 12-2 *SW2 DHCP Snooping Status*

```
SW2# show ip dhcp snooping
Switch DHCP snooping is enabled
Switch DHCP gleaning is disabled
DHCP snooping is configured on following VLANs:
11
DHCP snooping is operational on following VLANs:
11
Smartlog is configured on following VLANs:
none
Smartlog is operational on following VLANs:
none
DHCP snooping is configured on the following L3 Interfaces:


Insertion of option 82 is disabled
   circuit-id default format: vlan-mod-port
   remote-id: bcc4.938b.a180 (MAC)
Option 82 on untrusted port is not allowed
Verification of hwaddr field is enabled
Verification of giaddr field is enabled
DHCP snooping trust/rate is configured on the following Interfaces:

Interface               Trusted     Allow option    Rate limit (pps)
----------------------  -------     ------------    ----------------
GigabitEthernet1/0/2    yes         yes             unlimited
  Custom circuit-ids:
```

The highlighted lines in the example point out a few of the key configuration settings. Starting at the top, the first two confirm the configuration of the **ip dhcp snooping** and **ip dhcp snooping vlan 11** commands, respectively. Also, the highlighted lines at the bottom of the output show a section that lists trusted ports—in this case, only port G1/0/2.

Also, you might have noticed that highlighted line in the middle that states **Insertion of option 82 is disabled**. That line confirms the addition of the **no ip dhcp information option** command to the configuration back in Example 12-1. To understand why the example includes this command, consider these facts about DHCP relay agents:

- DHCP relay agents add new fields to DHCP requests—defined as option 82 DHCP header fields (in RFC 3046).

- DHCP Snooping uses default settings that work well if the switch acts as a Layer 3 switch and as a DHCP relay agent, meaning that the switch should insert the DHCP option 82 fields into DHCP messages. In effect, the switch defaults to use **ip dhcp snooping information option.**

- When the switch does not also act as a DHCP relay agent, the default setting stops DHCP from working for end users. The switch sets fields in the DHCP messages as if it were a DHCP relay agent, but the changes to those messages cause most DHCP servers (and most DHCP relay agents) to ignore the received DHCP messages.

■ The conclusion: To make DHCP Snooping work on a switch that is not also a DHCP relay agent, and to avoid the problem of preventing legitimate DHCP leases, disable the option 82 feature using the **no ip dhcp snooping information option** global command.

That concludes the DHCP Snooping configuration that is both required and that you will most often need to make the feature work. The rest of this section discusses a few optional DHCP Snooping features.

Limiting DHCP Message Rates

Knowing that DHCP Snooping prevents their attacks, what might attackers do in response? Devise new attacks, including attacking DHCP Snooping itself.

One way to attack DHCP Snooping takes advantage of the fact that it uses the general-purpose CPU in a switch. Knowing that, attackers can devise attacks to generate large volumes of DHCP messages in an attempt to overload the DHCP Snooping feature and the switch CPU itself. The goal can be as a simple denial-of-service attack or a combination of attacks that might cause DHCP Snooping to fail to examine every message, allowing other DHCP attacks to then work.

To help prevent this kind of attack, DHCP Snooping includes an optional feature that tracks the number of incoming DHCP messages. If the number of incoming DHCP messages exceeds that limit over a one-second period, DHCP Snooping treats the event as an attack and moves the port to an err-disabled state. Also, the feature can be enabled both on trusted and untrusted interfaces.

Although rate limiting DHCP messages can help, placing the port in an err-disabled state can itself create issues. As a reminder, once in the err-disabled state, the switch will not send or receive frames for the interface. However, the err-disabled state might be too severe an action because the default recovery action for an err-disabled state requires the configuration of a **shutdown** and then a **no shutdown** subcommand on the interface.

To help strike a better balance, you can enable DHCP Snooping rate limiting and then also configure the switch to automatically recover from the port's err-disabled state, without the need for a **shutdown** and then **no shutdown** command.

Example 12-3 shows how to enable DHCP Snooping rate limits and err-disabled recovery. First, look at the lower half of the configuration, to the interfaces, to see the straightforward setting of the per-interface limits using the **ip dhcp snooping rate limit** *number* interface subcommands. The top of the configuration uses two global commands to tell IOS to recover from an err-disabled state if it is caused by DHCP Snooping, and to use a nondefault number of seconds to wait before recovering the interface. Note that the configuration in Example 12-3 would rely on the core configuration for DHCP Snooping as shown in Example 12-1.

Example 12-3   *Configuring DHCP Snooping Message Rate Limits*

```
errdisable recovery cause dhcp-rate-limit
errdisable recovery interval 30
!
interface GigabitEthernet1/0/2
 ip dhcp snooping limit rate 10
!
interface GigabitEthernet1/0/3
 ip dhcp snooping limit rate 2
```

A repeat of the **show ip dhcp snooping** command now shows the rate limits near the end of the output, as noted in Example 12-4.

Example 12-4   *Confirming DHCP Snooping Rate Limits*

```
SW2# show ip dhcp snooping
! Lines omitted for brevity

Interface                 Trusted   Allow option   Rate limit (pps)
----------------------    -------   ------------   ----------------
GigabitEthernet1/0/2      yes       yes            10
  Custom circuit-ids:
GigabitEthernet1/0/3      no        no             2
  Custom circuit-ids:
```

DHCP Snooping Configuration Summary

The following configuration checklist summarizes the commands included in this section about how to configure DHCP Snooping.

Step 1.   Configure this pair of commands (both required):

    A. Use the **ip dhcp snooping** global command to enable DHCP Snooping on the switch.

    B. Use the **ip dhcp snooping vlan** *vlan-list* global command to identify the VLANs on which to use DHCP Snooping.

Step 2.   (Optional): Use the **no ip dhcp snooping information option** global command on Layer 2 switches to disable the insertion of DHCP Option 82 data into DHCP messages, specifically on switches that do not act as a DHCP relay agent.

Step 3.   Configure the **ip dhcp snooping trust** interface subcommand to override the default setting of not trusted.

Step 4.   (Optional): Configure DHCP Snooping rate limits and err-disabled recovery:

    Step A. (Optional): Configure the **ip dhcp snooping limit rate** *number* interface subcommand to set a limit of DHCP messages per second.

    Step B. (Optional): Configure the **no ip dhcp snooping limit rate** *number* interface subcommand to remove an existing limit and reset the interface to use the default of no rate limit.

Step C. (Optional): Configure the **errdisable recovery cause dhcp-rate-limit** global command to enable the feature of automatic recovery from err-disabled mode, assuming the switch placed the port in err-disabled state because of exceeding DHCP Snooping rate limits.

Step D. (Optional): Configure the **errdisable recovery interval** *seconds* global commands to set the time to wait before recovering from an interface err-disabled state (regardless of the cause of the err-disabled state).

Dynamic ARP Inspection

The **Dynamic ARP Inspection (DAI)** feature on a switch examines incoming ARP messages on untrusted ports to filter those it believes to be part of an attack. DAI's core feature compares incoming ARP messages with two sources of data: the DHCP Snooping binding table and any configured ARP ACLs. If the incoming ARP message does not match the tables in the switch, the switch discards the ARP message.

This section follows the same sequence as with the DHCP Snooping section, first examining the concepts behind DAI and ARP attacks, and then showing how to configure DAI with both required and optional features.

DAI Concepts

To understand the attacks DAI can prevent, you need to be ready to compare normal ARP operations with the abnormal use of ARP used in some types of attacks. This section uses that same flow, first reviewing a few important ARP details, and then showing how an attacker can just send an **ARP reply**—called a **gratuitous ARP**—triggering hosts to add incorrect ARP entries to their ARP tables.

Review of Normal IP ARP

If all you care about is how ARP works normally, with no concern about attacks, you can think of ARP to the depth shown in Figure 12-9. The figure shows a typical sequence. Host PC1 needs to send an IP packet to its default router (R2), so PC1 first sends an ARP request message in an attempt to learn the MAC address associated with R2's 172.16.2.2 address. Router R2 sends back an ARP reply, listing R2's MAC address (note the figure shows pseudo MAC addresses to save space).

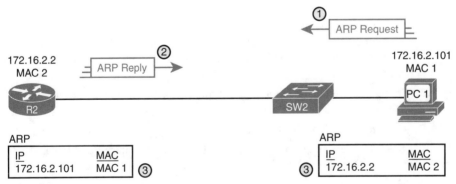

Figure 12-9 *Legitimate ARP Tables After PC1 DHCP and ARP with Router R2*

12

The ARP tables at the bottom of the figure imply an important fact: both hosts learn the other host's MAC address with this two-message flow. Not only does PC1 learn R2's MAC address based on the ARP reply (message 2), but router R2 learns PC1's IP and MAC address because of the ARP request (message 1). To see why, take a look at the more detailed view of those messages as shown in Figure 12-10.

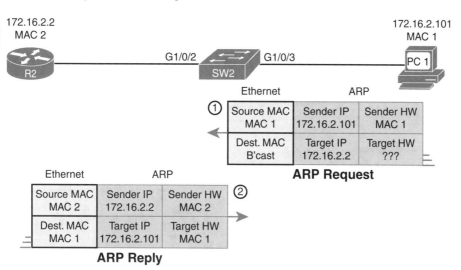

Figure 12-10 *A Detailed Look at ARP Request and Reply*

The ARP messages define four related fields: the **sender hardware address**, **sender protocol address**, target hardware address, and target protocol address. Those terms use general wording, but the word hardware refers to MAC addresses and the word protocol refers to IP. So, you should expect to see many descriptions about ARP that use similar terms like sender MAC address and **sender IP address**.

The sender fields of every ARP message list the sending device's IP address and MAC, no matter whether the message is an ARP reply or ARP request. For instance, message 1 in the figure, sent by PC1, lists PC1's IP and MAC addresses in the sender fields, which is why router R2 could learn that information. PC1 likewise learns of R2's MAC address per the sender address fields in the ARP reply.

Gratuitous ARP as an Attack Vector

Normally, a host uses ARP when it knows the IP address of another host and wants to learn that host's MAC address. However, for legitimate reasons, a host might also want to inform all the hosts in the subnet about its MAC address. That might be useful when a host changes its MAC address, for instance. So, ARP supports the idea of a gratuitous ARP message with these features:

- It is an ARP reply.

- It is sent without having first received an ARP request.

- It is sent to an Ethernet destination broadcast address so that all hosts in the subnet receive the message.

For instance, if a host's MAC address is MAC A, and it changes to MAC B, to cause all the other hosts to update their ARP tables, the host could send a gratuitous ARP that lists a sender MAC of MAC B.

Attackers can take advantage of gratuitous ARPs because they let the sending host make other hosts change their ARP tables. Figure 12-11 shows just such an example initiated by PC A (an attacker) with a gratuitous ARP. However, this ARP lists PC1's IP address but a different device's MAC address (PC A) at step 1, causing the router to update its ARP table (step 2).

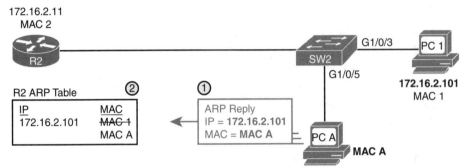

Figure 12-11 *Nefarious Use of ARP Reply Causes Incorrect ARP Data on R2*

At this point, when R2 forwards IP packets to PC1's IP address (172.16.2.101), R2 will encapsulate them in an Ethernet frame with PC A as the destination rather than with PC1's MAC address. At first, this might seem to stop PC1 from working, but instead it could be part of a man-in-the-middle attack so that PC A can copy every message. Figure 12-12 shows the idea of what happens at this point:

1. PC1 sends messages to some server on the left side of router R2.

2. The server replies to PC1's IP address, but R2 forwards that packet to PC A's MAC address, rather than to PC1.

3. PC A copies the packet for later processing.

4. PC A forwards the packet inside a new frame to PC1 so that PC1 still works.

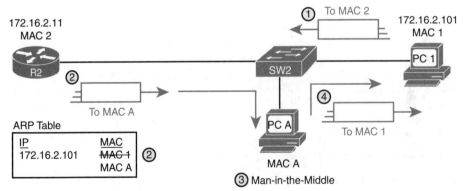

Figure 12-12 *Man-in-the-Middle Attack Resulting from Gratuitous ARP*

12

Dynamic ARP Inspection Logic

DAI has a variety of features that can prevent these kinds of ARP attacks. To understand how, consider the sequence of a typical client host with regards to both DHCP and ARP. When a host does not have an IP address yet—that is, before the DHCP process completes—it does not need to use ARP. Once the host leases an IP address and learns its subnet mask, it needs to use ARP to learn the MAC addresses of other hosts or the default router in the subnet, so it sends some ARP messages. In short, DHCP happens first, then ARP.

DAI takes an approach for untrusted interfaces that confirms an ARP's correctness based on DHCP Snooping's data about the earlier DHCP messages. The correct normal DHCP messages list the IP address leased to a host as well as that host's MAC address. The DHCP Snooping feature also records those facts into the switch's DHCP Snooping binding table.

For any DAI untrusted ports, DAI compares the ARP message's sender IP and sender MAC address fields to the DHCP Snooping binding table. If found in the table, DAI allows the ARP through, but if not, DAI discards the ARP. For instance, Figure 12-13 shows step 1 in which the attacker at PC A attempts the gratuitous ARP shown earlier in Figure 12-11. At step 2, DAI makes a comparison to the DHCP Snooping binding table, not finding a match with MAC A along with IP address 172.16.2.101, so DAI would discard the message.

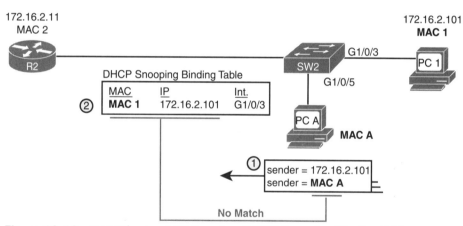

Figure 12-13 *DAI Filtering ARP Based on DHCP Snooping Binding Table*

DAI also works with a concept of trusted and untrusted ports, with the logic generally matching the logic used with DHCP Snooping. Ports connected to local DHCP clients can remain in the default DAI untrusted state. Configure all other switch ports as trusted for DAI.

Note that although DAI can use the DHCP Snooping table as shown here, it can also use similar statically configured data that lists correct pairs of IP and MAC addresses via a tool called *ARP ACLs*. Using ARP ACLs with DAI becomes useful for ports connected to devices that use static IP addresses rather than DHCP. Note that DAI looks for both the DHCP Snooping binding data and ARP ACLs.

Beyond that core feature, note that DAI can optionally perform other checks as well. For instance, the Ethernet header that encapsulates the ARP should have addresses that match the ARP sender and target MAC addresses. Figure 12-14 shows an example of the comparison of the Ethernet source MAC address and the ARP message sender hardware field.

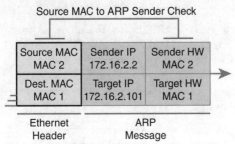

Source MAC to ARP Sender Check

Figure 12-14 *DAI Filtering Checks for Source MAC Addresses*

DAI can be enabled to make the comparisons shown in the figure, discarding these messages:

- Messages with an Ethernet header source MAC address that is not equal to the ARP sender hardware (MAC) address

- ARP reply messages with an Ethernet header destination MAC address that is not equal to the ARP target hardware (MAC) address

- Messages with unexpected IP addresses in the two ARP IP address fields

Finally, like DHCP Snooping, DAI does its work in the switch CPU rather than in the switch ASIC, meaning that DAI itself can be more susceptible to DoS attacks. The attacker could generate large numbers of ARP messages, driving up CPU usage in the switch. DAI can avoid these problems through rate limiting the number of ARP messages on a port over time.

Dynamic ARP Inspection Configuration

Configuring DAI requires just a few commands, with the usual larger variety of optional configuration settings. This section examines DAI configuration, first with mostly default settings and with reliance on DHCP Snooping. It then shows a few of the optional features, like rate limits, automatic recovery from err-disabled state, and how to enable additional checks of incoming ARP messages.

Configuring ARP Inspection on a Layer 2 Switch

Before configuring DAI, you need to think about the feature and make a few decisions based on your goals, topology, and device roles. The decisions include the following:

- Choose whether to rely on DHCP Snooping, ARP ACLs, or both.

- If using DHCP Snooping, configure it and make the correct ports trusted for DHCP Snooping.

- Choose the VLAN(s) on which to enable DAI.

- Make DAI trusted (rather than the default setting of untrusted) on select ports in those VLANs, typically for the same ports you trusted for DHCP Snooping.

All the configuration examples in this section use the same sample network used in the DHCP Snooping configuration topics, repeated here as Figure 12-15. Just as with DHCP Snooping, switch SW2 on the right should be configured to trust the port connected to the router (G1/0/2), but not trust the two ports connected to the PCs.

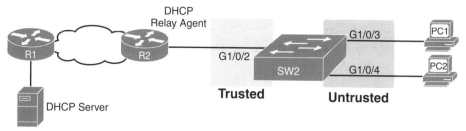

Figure 12-15 *Sample Network Used in ARP Inspection Configuration Examples*

Example 12-5 shows the required configuration to enable DAI on switch SW2 in Figure 12-15—a configuration that follows a similar progression compared to DHCP Snooping. All ports in the figure connect to VLAN 11, so to enable DAI in VLAN 11, just add the **ip arp inspection vlan 11** global command. Then, to change the logic on port G1/0/2 (connected to the router) to be trusted by DAI, add the **ip arp inspection trust** interface subcommand.

Example 12-5 *IP ARP Inspection Configuration to Match Figure 12-15*

```
ip arp inspection vlan 11
!
interface GigabitEthernet1/0/2
 ip arp inspection trust
```

Example 12-5 configures DAI, but it omits both DHCP Snooping and ARP ACLs. (If you were to configure a switch only with commands shown in Example 12-5, the switch would filter all ARPs entering all untrusted ports in VLAN 11.) Example 12-6 shows a complete and working DAI configuration that adds the DHCP Snooping configuration to match the DAI configuration in Example 12-5. Note that Example 12-6 combines Example 12-1's earlier DHCP Snooping configuration for this same topology to the DAI configuration just shown in Example 12-5, with highlights for the DAI-specific configuration lines.

Example 12-6 *IP DHCP Snooping Configuration Added to Support DAI*

```
ip arp inspection vlan 11
ip dhcp snooping
ip dhcp snooping vlan 11
no ip dhcp snooping information option
!
interface GigabitEthernet1/0/2
 ip dhcp snooping trust
 ip arp inspection trust
```

Remember, DHCP occurs first with DHCP clients, and then they send ARP messages. With the configuration in Example 12-6, the switch builds its DHCP Snooping binding table by analyzing incoming DHCP messages. Next, any incoming ARP messages on DAI untrusted ports must have matching information in that binding table.

Example 12-7 confirms the key facts about correct DAI operation in this sample network based on the configuration in Example 12-6. The **show ip arp inspection** command gives both configuration settings along with status variables and counters. For instance, the highlighted lines show the total ARP messages received on untrusted ports in that VLAN and the number of dropped ARP messages (currently 0).

Example 12-7 *SW2 IP ARP Inspection Status*

```
SW2# show ip arp inspection

Source Mac Validation      : Disabled
Destination Mac Validation : Disabled
IP Address Validation      : Disabled


Vlan     Configuration   Operation   ACL Match            Static ACL
----     -------------   ---------   ---------            ----------
  11     Enabled         Active


Vlan     ACL Logging     DHCP Logging      Probe Logging
----     -----------     ------------      -------------
  11     Deny            Deny              Off


Vlan     Forwarded       Dropped     DHCP Drops     ACL Drops
----     ---------       -------     ----------     ---------
  11            59             0              0             0


Vlan   DHCP Permits    ACL Permits   Probe Permits    Source MAC Failures
----   ------------    -----------   -------------    -------------------
  11              7             0              49                        0


Vlan   Dest MAC Failures   IP Validation Failures   Invalid Protocol Data
----   -----------------   ----------------------   ---------------------


Vlan   Dest MAC Failures   IP Validation Failures   Invalid Protocol Data
----   -----------------   ----------------------   ---------------------
  11                   0                        0                       0
SW2# show ip dhcp snooping binding
MacAddress         IpAddress      Lease(sec) Type          VLAN  Interface
-----------------  -------------  ---------- -------------  ----  -----------------
--
02:00:11:11:11:11  172.16.2.101   86110      dhcp-snooping   11  GigabitEthernet1/0/3
02:00:22:22:22:22  172.16.2.102   86399      dhcp-snooping   11  GigabitEthernet1/0/4
Total number of bindings: 2
```

The end of Example 12-7 shows an example of the **show ip dhcp snooping binding** command on switch SW2. Note that the first two columns list a MAC and IP address as learned from the DHCP messages. Then, imagine an ARP message arrives from PC1, a message that should list PC1's 0200.1111.1111 MAC address and 172.16.2.101 as the sender MAC and IP address, respectively. Per this output, the switch would find that matching data and allow the ARP message.

Example 12-8 shows some detail of what happens when switch SW2 receives an invalid ARP message on port G1/0/4 in Figure 12-15. In this case, to create the invalid ARP message, PC2 in the figure was configured with a static IP address of 172.16.2.101 (which is PC1's DHCP-leased IP address). The highlights in the log message at the top of the example show PC2's claimed sender MAC and sender IP addresses in the ARP message. If you refer back to the bottom of Example 12-7, you can see that this sender MAC/IP pair does not exist in the DHCP Snooping binding table, so DAI rejects the ARP message.

Example 12-8 *Sample Results from an ARP Attack*

```
Jul 25 14:28:20.763: %SW_DAI-4-DHCP_SNOOPING_DENY: 1 Invalid ARPs (Req) on Gi1/0/4,
vlan 11.([0200.2222.2222/172.16.2.101/0000.0000.0000/172.16.2.1/09:28:20 EST Thu Jul
25 2019])


SW2# show ip arp inspection statistics


 Vlan       Forwarded        Dropped      DHCP Drops      ACL Drops
 ----       ---------        -------      ----------      ---------
  11              59              17              17               0


 Vlan    DHCP Permits    ACL Permits   Probe Permits   Source MAC Failures
 ----    ------------    -----------   -------------   -------------------
  11               7              0              49                     0


 Vlan   Dest MAC Failures    IP Validation Failures   Invalid Protocol Data
 ----   -----------------    ----------------------   ---------------------
  11                   0                         0                       0
```

The statistics from the **show ip arp inspection** command also confirm that the switch has dropped some ARP messages. The highlighted lines in the middle of the table show 17 total dropped ARP messages in VLAN 11. That same highlighted line confirms that it dropped all 17 because of the DHCP Snooping binding table ("DHCP Drops"), with zero dropped due to an ARP ACL ("ACL Drops").

Limiting DAI Message Rates

Like DHCP Snooping, DAI can also be the focus of a DoS attack with the attacker generating a large number of ARP messages. Like DHCP Snooping, DAI supports the configuration of rate limits to help prevent those attacks, with a reaction to place the port in an err-disabled state, and with the ability to configure automatic recovery from that err-disabled state.

The DHCP Snooping and DAI rate limits do have some small differences in operation, defaults, and in configuration, as follows:

- DAI defaults to use rate limits for all interfaces (trusted and untrusted), with DHCP Snooping defaulting to not use rate limits.

- DAI allows the configuration of a burst interval (a number of seconds), so that the rate limit can have logic like "*x* ARP messages over *y* seconds" (DHCP Snooping does not define a burst setting).

It helps to look at DAI and DHCP Snooping rate limit configuration together to make comparisons, so Example 12-9 shows both. The example repeats the exact same DHCP Snooping commands in earlier Example 12-3 but adds the DAI configuration (highlighted). The configuration in Example 12-7 could be added to the configuration shown in Example 12-6 for a complete DHCP Snooping and DAI configuration.

Example 12-9 *Configuring ARP Inspection Message Rate Limits*

```
errdisable recovery cause dhcp-rate-limit
errdisable recovery cause arp-inspection
errdisable recovery interval 30
!
interface GigabitEthernet1/0/2
 ip dhcp snooping limit rate 10
 ip arp inspection limit rate 8
!
interface GigabitEthernet1/0/3
 ip dhcp snooping limit rate 2
 ip arp inspection limit rate 8 burst interval 4
```

Example 12-10 lists output that confirms the configuration settings. For instance, Example 12-9 configures port G1/0/2 with a rate of 8 messages for each (default) burst of 1 second; the output in Example 12-10 for interface G1/0/2 also lists a rate of 8 and burst interval of 1. Similarly, Example 12-9 configures port G1/0/3 with a rate of 8 over a burst of 4 seconds, with Example 12-10 confirming those same values for port G1/0/3. Note that the other two interfaces in Example 12-10 show the default settings of a rate of 15 messages over a one-second burst.

Example 12-10 *Confirming ARP Inspection Rate Limits*

```
SW2# show ip arp inspection interfaces
  Interface         Trust State     Rate (pps)     Burst Interval
  ---------------   -----------     ----------     --------------
  Gi1/0/1           Untrusted            15                     1
  Gi1/0/2           Trusted               8                     1
  Gi1/0/3           Untrusted             8                     4
  Gi1/0/4           Untrusted            15                     1
! Lines omitted for brevity
```

Configuring Optional DAI Message Checks

As mentioned in the section titled "Dynamic ARP Inspection Logic," DAI always checks the ARP message's sender MAC and sender IP address fields versus some table in the switch, but it can also perform other checks. Those checks require more CPU, but they also help prevent other types of attacks.

Example 12-11 shows how to configure those three additional checks. Note that you can configure one, two, or all three of the options: just configure the **ip arp inspection validate** command again with all the options you want in one command, and it replaces the previous global configuration command. The example shows the three options, with the **src-mac** (source mac) option configured.

Example 12-11 *Confirming ARP Inspection Rate Limits*

```
SW2# configure terminal
Enter configuration commands, one per line.  End with CNTL/Z.

SW2(config)# ip arp inspection validate ?
  dst-mac  Validate destination MAC address
  ip       Validate IP addresses
  src-mac  Validate source MAC address

SW2(config)# ip arp inspection validate src-mac
SW2(config)# ^z
SW2#
SW2# show ip arp inspection

Source Mac Validation      : Enabled
Destination Mac Validation : Disabled
IP Address Validation      : Disabled
```

IP ARP Inspection Configuration Summary

The following configuration checklist summarizes the commands included in this section about how to configure Dynamic IP ARP Inspection:

Step 1. Use the **ip arp inspection vlan** *vlan-list* global command to enable Dynamic ARP Inspection (DAI) on the switch for the specified VLANs.

Step 2. Separate from the DAI configuration, also configure DHCP Snooping and/or ARP ACLs for use by DAI.

Step 3. Configure the **ip arp inspection trust** interface subcommand to override the default setting of not trusted.

Step 4. (Optional): Configure DAI rate limits and err-disabled recovery:

    Step A. (Optional): Configure the **ip arp inspection limit rate** *number* [**burst interval** *seconds*] interface subcommand to set a limit of ARP messages per second, or ARP messages for each configured interval.

    Step B. (Optional): Configure the **ip arp inspection limit rate none** interface subcommand to disable rate limits.

    Step C. (Optional): Configure the **errdisable recovery cause arp-inspection** global command to enable the feature of automatic recovery from err-disabled mode, assuming the switch placed the port in err-disabled state because of exceeding DAI rate limits.

    Step D. (Optional): Configure the **errdisable recovery interval** *seconds* global commands to set the time to wait before recovering from an interface err-disabled state (regardless of the cause of the err-disabled state).

Step 5. (Optional): Configure the **ip arp inspection validate** {[**dst-mac**] [**src-mac**] [**ip**]} global command to enable optional items to validate with DAI on untrusted ports.

Chapter Review

One key to doing well on the exams is to perform repetitive spaced review sessions. Review this chapter's material using either the tools in the book or interactive tools for the same material found on the book's companion website. Refer to the "Your Study Plan" element for more details. Table 12-2 outlines the key review elements and where you can find them. To better track your study progress, record when you completed these activities in the second column.

Table 12-2 Chapter Review Tracking

Review Element	Review Date(s)	Resource Used
Review key topics		Book, website
Review key terms		Book, website
Answer DIKTA questions		Book, PTP
Review config checklists		Book, website

Review All the Key Topics

Table 12-3 Key Topics for Chapter 12

Key Topic Element	Description	Page Number
Figure 12-4	DHCP filtering actions on trusted and untrusted ports	243
List	DHCP Snooping logic	243
Figure 12-6	DHCP Snooping Binding Table Concept	244
Example 12-1	DHCP Snooping configuration	246
List	DHCP Snooping configuration checklist	249
Figure 12-10	Detail inside ARP messages with sender and target	251
List	Gratuitous ARP details	251
Figure 12-13	Core Dynamic ARP Inspection logic	253
Example 12-6	Dynamic ARP Inspection configuration with associated DHCP Snooping configuration	255
List	Dynamic ARP Inspection checklist	259

Key Terms You Should Know

ARP reply, DHCP Snooping, DHCP Snooping binding table, Dynamic ARP Inspection, gratuitous ARP, (ARP) sender hardware address, (ARP) sender IP address, (ARP) sender protocol address, trusted port, untrusted port

Command References

Tables 12-4 and 12-5 list the configuration and verification commands used in this chapter. As an easy review exercise, cover the left column in a table, read the right column, and try to recall the command without looking. Then repeat the exercise, covering the right column, and try to recall what the command does.

Table 12-4   Chapter 12 Configuration Command Reference

Command	Mode/Purpose/Description
ip dhcp snooping	Global command that enables DHCP Snooping if combined with enabling it on one or more VLANs
ip dhcp snooping vlan *vlan-list*	Global command that lists VLANs on which to enable DHCP Snooping, assuming the **ip dhcp snooping** command is also configured
[no] ip dhcp snooping information option	Command that enables (or disables with **no** option) the feature of inserting DHCP option 82 parameters by the switch when also using DHCP Snooping
[no] ip dhcp snooping trust	Interface subcommand that sets the DHCP Snooping trust state for an interface (default **no**, or untrusted)
ip dhcp snooping limit rate *number*	Interface subcommand that sets a limit to the number of incoming DHCP messages processed on an interface, per second, before DHCP Snooping discards all other incoming DHCP messages in that same second
err-disable recovery cause dhcp-rate-limit	Global command that enables the switch to automatically recover an err-disabled interface if set to that state because of exceeding a DHCP rate limit setting
err-disable recovery interval *seconds*	Global command that sets the number of seconds IOS waits before recovering any err-disabled interfaces which, per various configuration settings, should be recovered automatically
err-disable recovery cause arp-inspection	Global command that enables the switch to automatically recover an err-disabled interface if set to that state because of an ARP Inspection violation
ip arp inspection vlan *vlan-list*	Global command to enable Dynamic ARP Inspection (DAI) on the switch for the specified VLANs
ip arp inspection trust	Interface subcommand to override the default setting of not trusted
ip arp inspection limit rate *number* [burst interval *seconds*]	Interface subcommand to set a limit of ARP messages per second, or ARP messages for each configured interval
ip arp inspection limit rate none	Interface subcommand to disable rate limits
ip arp inspection validate {[dst-mac] [src-mac] [ip]}	Global command to enable optional items to validate with DAI on untrusted ports

Table 12-5   Chapter 12 EXEC Command Reference

Command	Purpose
show ip dhcp snooping	Lists a large variety of DHCP Snooping configuration settings
show ip dhcp snooping statistics	Lists counters regarding DHCP Snooping behavior on the switch
show ip dhcp snooping binding	Displays the contents of the dynamically created DHCP Snooping binding table

Command	Purpose
show ip arp inspection	Lists both configuration settings for Dynamic ARP Inspection (DAI) as well as counters for ARP messages processed and filtered
show ip arp inspection statistics	Lists the subset of the show ip arp inspection command output that includes counters
show ip arp inspection interfaces	Lists one line per DAI-enabled interface, listing trust state and rate limit settings

Part III Review

Keep track of your part review progress with the checklist shown in Table P3-1. Details on each task follow the table.

Table P3-1   Part 3 Review Checklist

Activity	1st Date Completed	2nd Date Completed
Repeat All DIKTA Questions		
Answer Part Review Questions		
Review Key Topics		
Do Labs		
Review Videos		

Repeat All DIKTA Questions

For this task, use the PTP software to answer the "Do I Know This Already?" questions again for the chapters in this part of the book.

Answer Part Review Questions

For this task, use PTP to answer the Part Review questions for this part of the book.

Review Key Topics

Review all key topics in all chapters in this part, either by browsing the chapters or by using the Key Topics application on the companion website.

Do Labs

Depending on your chosen lab tool, here are some suggestions for what to do in lab:

Pearson Network Simulator: If you use the full Pearson CCNA simulator, focus more on the configuration scenario and troubleshooting scenario labs associated with the topics in this part of the book. These types of labs include a larger set of topics and work well as Part Review activities. (See the Introduction for some details about how to find which labs are about topics in this part of the book.)

Blog Config Labs: The author's blog (https://www.certskills.com) includes a series of configuration-focused labs that you can do on paper, each in 10–15 minutes. Review and performs labs for this part of the book by using the menus to navigate to the per-chapter content and then finding all config labs related to that chapter. (You can see more detailed instructions at https://www.certskills.com/config-labs.)

Other: If using other lab tools, here are a few suggestions: make sure to experiment with the variety of configuration topics in this part, including router and switch passwords, switch port security, Dynamic ARP Inspection, and DHCP Snooping.

Watch Videos

Two chapters in this part mention videos included as extra material related to those chapters. Check out the reference in Chapter 9 to a video about using RADIUS protocol, as well as Chapter 10's reference to a video about troubleshooting switch port security.

Use Per-Chapter Interactive Review

Using the companion website, browse through the interactive review elements, like memory tables and key term flashcards, to review the content from each chapter.

Part IV shifts to a variety of topics that can be found in most every network. None are required for a network to work, but many happen to be useful services. Most happen to use IP or support the IP network in some way, so Part IV groups the topics together as IP services.

Part IV begins and ends with chapters that examine a series of smaller topics. First, Chapter 13 examines several IP services for which the CCNA 200-301 version 1.1 exam blueprint requires you to develop configuration and verification skills. Those services include logging and syslog, the Network Time Protocol (NTP), as well as two related services: CDP and LLDP.

The next two chapters in Part IV also focus on IP-based services, beginning with Chapter 14's examination of Network Address Translation (NAT). Almost every network uses NAT with IPv4, although in many cases, the firewall implements NAT. This chapter shows how to configure and verify NAT in a Cisco router.

Chapter 15 at first may give the appearance of a large chapter about one topic— Quality of Service—and it does focus on QoS. However, QoS by nature includes a wide variety of individual QoS tools. This chapter walks you through the basic concepts of the primary QoS features.

Chapters 16 and 17, at the end of Part IV, close with another series of smaller topics that require only conceptual knowledge rather than configuration skills. Chapter 16 covers First Hop Redundancy Protocols (FHRPs), while Chapter 17 covers Simple Network Management Protocol (SNMP), and two related protocols: TFTP and FTP.

Part IV

IP Services

CHAPTER 13

Device Management Protocols

This chapter covers the following exam topics:

2.0 Network Access

    2.3 Configure and verify Layer 2 discovery protocols (Cisco Discovery Protocol and LLDP)

4.0 IP Services

    4.2 Configure and verify NTP operating in a client and server mode

    4.5 Describe the use of syslog features including facilities and severity levels

This chapter begins Part IV with a discussion of the concepts, configuration, and verification of three functions found on Cisco routers and switches. These functions focus more on managing the network devices themselves than on managing the network that devices create.

The first major section of this chapter focuses on log messages and syslog. Most computing devices have a need to notify the administrator of any significant issue; generally, across the world of computing, messages of this type are called log messages. Cisco devices generate log messages as well. The first section shows how a Cisco device handles those messages and how you can configure routers and switches to ignore the messages or save them in different ways.

Next, different router and switch functions benefit from synchronizing their time-of-day clocks. Like most every computing device, routers and switches have an internal clock function to keep time. Network Time Protocol (NTP) provides a means for devices to synchronize their time, as discussed in the second section.

The final major section focuses on two protocols that do the same kinds of work: Cisco Discovery Protocol (CDP) and Link Layer Discovery Protocol (LLDP). Both provide a means for network devices to learn about neighboring devices, without requiring that IPv4 or IPv6 be working at the time.

"Do I Know This Already?" Quiz

Take the quiz (either here or use the PTP software) if you want to use the score to help you decide how much time to spend on this chapter. The letter answers are listed at the bottom of the page following the quiz. Appendix C, found both at the end of the book as well as on the companion website, includes both the answers and explanations. You can also find both answers and explanations in the PTP testing software.

Table 13-1 "Do I Know This Already?" Foundation Topics Section-to-Question Mapping

Foundation Topics Section	Questions
System Message Logging (Syslog)	1, 2
Network Time Protocol (NTP)	3, 4
Analyzing Topology Using CDP and LLDP	5, 6

1. What level of logging to the console is the default for a Cisco device?

    a. Informational

    b. Errors

    c. Warnings

    d. Debugging

2. What command limits the messages sent to a syslog server to levels 4 through 0?

    a. logging trap 0-4

    b. logging trap 0,1,2,3,4

    c. logging trap 4

    d. logging trap through 4

3. Which of the following is accurate about the NTP client function on a Cisco router?

    a. The client synchronizes its time-of-day clock based on the NTP server.

    b. It counts CPU cycles of the local router CPU to keep time more accurately.

    c. The client synchronizes all Ethernet interfaces to use the same speed.

    d. The client must be connected to the same subnet as an NTP server.

4. The only NTP configuration on router R1 is the **ntp server 10.1.1.1** command. Which answer describes how NTP works on the router?

    a. As an NTP server only

    b. As an NTP client only

    c. As an NTP server only after the NTP client synchronizes with NTP server 10.1.1.1

    d. As an NTP server regardless of whether the NTP client synchronizes with NTP server 10.1.1.1

5. Imagine that a switch connects through an Ethernet cable to a router, and the router's host name is Hannah. Which of the following commands could tell you information about the IOS version on Hannah without establishing a Telnet connection to Hannah? (Choose two answers.)

    a. show neighbors Hannah

    b. show cdp

    c. show cdp neighbors

    d. show cdp neighbors Hannah

    e. show cdp entry Hannah

    f. show cdp neighbors detail

6. A switch is cabled to a router whose host name is Hannah. Which of the following LLDP commands could identify Hannah's enabled capabilities? (Choose two answers.)

   a. show neighbors

   b. show neighbors Hannah

   c. show lldp

   d. show lldp interface

   e. show lldp neighbors

   f. show lldp entry Hannah

Foundation Topics

System Message Logging (Syslog)

It is amazing just how helpful Cisco devices try to be to their administrators. When major (and even not-so-major) events take place, these Cisco devices attempt to notify administrators with detailed system messages. As you learn in this section, these messages vary from the mundane to those that are incredibly important. Thankfully, administrators have a large variety of options for storing these messages and being alerted to those that could have the largest impact on the network infrastructure.

When an event happens that the device's OS thinks is interesting, how does the OS notify us humans? Cisco IOS can send the messages to anyone currently logged in to the device. It can also store the message so that a user can later look at the messages. The next few pages examine both topics.

NOTE Included in the CCNA 200-301 exam topics is one about logging and syslog: "Describe the use of syslog features including facilities and severity levels." This exam topic does not require you to understand the related configuration. However, the configuration reveals many of the core concepts, so this section includes the configuration details as a means to help you understand how logging and syslog work.

Sending Messages in Real Time to Current Users

Cisco IOS running on a device at least tries to allow current users to see **log messages** when they happen. Not every router or switch may have users connected, but if some user is logged in, the router or switch benefits by making the network engineer aware of any issues.

By default, IOS shows log messages to console users for all severity levels of messages. That default happens because of the default **logging console** global configuration command. In fact, if you have been using a console port throughout your time reading this book, you likely have already noticed many syslog messages, like messages about interfaces coming up or going down.

For other users (that is, Telnet and SSH users), the device requires a two-step process before the user sees the messages. First, IOS has another global configuration setting—**logging monitor**—that tells IOS to enable the sending of log messages to all connected users. However, that default configuration is not enough to allow the user to see the log messages. The user must also issue the **terminal monitor** EXEC command during the login session, which tells IOS that this terminal session would like to receive log messages.

Figure 13-1 summarizes these key points about how IOS on a Cisco router or switch processes log messages for currently connected users. In the figure, user A sits at the console and always receives log messages. On the right, the fact that user B sees messages (because user B issued the **terminal monitor** EXEC command after login) and user C does not shows that users can individually control whether or not they receive log messages.

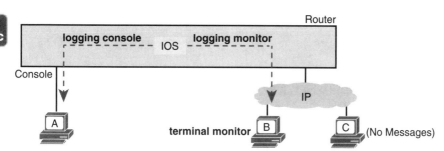

Figure 13-1 *IOS Processing for Log Messages to Current Users*

Storing Log Messages for Later Review

With logging to the console and to terminals, when an event happens, IOS sends the messages to the console and terminal sessions, and then IOS can discard the message. However, clearly, it would be useful to keep a copy of the log messages for later review, so IOS provides two primary means to keep a copy.

IOS can store copies of the log messages in RAM by virtue of the **logging buffered** global configuration command. Then any user can come back later and see the old log messages by using the **show logging** EXEC command.

As a second option—an option used frequently in production networks—all devices store their log messages centrally to a **syslog server**. RFC 5424 defines the Syslog protocol, which provides the means by which a device like a switch or router can use a UDP protocol to send messages to a syslog server for storage. All devices can send their log messages to the server. Later, a user can connect to the server (typically with a graphical user interface) and browse the log messages from various devices. To configure a router or switch to send log messages to a syslog server, add the **logging host** {*address* | *hostname*} global command, referencing the IP address or host name of the syslog server.

Figure 13-2 shows the ideas behind the buffered logging and syslog logging.

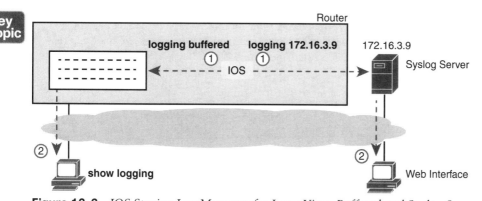

Figure 13-2 *IOS Storing Log Messages for Later View: Buffered and Syslog Server*

Log Message Format

IOS defines the format of log messages. The message begins with some data fields about the message, followed by some text more easily read by humans. For example, take a close look at this sample message:

```
*Dec 18 17:10:15.079: %LINEPROTO-5-UPDOWN: Line protocol on Interface
FastEthernet0/0, changed state to down
```

Notice that by default on this particular device, we see the following:

A timestamp: *Dec 18 17:10:15.079

The facility on the router that generated the message: %LINEPROTO

The severity level: 5

A mnemonic for the message: UPDOWN

The description of the message: Line protocol on Interface FastEthernet0/0, changed state to down

IOS dictates most of the contents of the messages, but you can at least toggle on and off the use of the timestamp (which is included by default) and a log message sequence number (which is not enabled by default). Example 13-1 reverses those defaults by turning off timestamps and turning on sequence numbers.

Example 13-1 *Disabling Timestamps and Enabling Sequence Numbers in Log Messages*

```
R1(config)# no service timestamps
R1(config)# service sequence-numbers
R1(config)# end
R1#
000011: %SYS-5-CONFIG_I: Configured from console by console
```

To see the change in format, look at the log message at the end of the example. As usual, when you exit configuration mode, the device issues yet another log message. Comparing this message to the previous example, you can see it now no longer lists the time of day but does list a sequence number.

Log Message Severity Levels

Log messages may just tell you about some mundane event, or they may tell you of some critical event. To help you make sense of the importance of each message, IOS assigns each message a severity level (as noted in the same messages in the preceding page or so). Figure 13-3 shows the severity levels: the lower the number, the more severe the event that caused the message. (Note that IOS commands use both the keywords and numbers from the figure.)

Answers to the "Do I Know This Already?" quiz:

1 D **2** C **3** A **4** C **5** E, F **6** E, F

Keyword	Numeral	Description	
Emergency	0	System unusable	Severe
Alert	1	Immediate action required	
Critical	2	Critical Event (Highest of 3)	Impactful
Error	3	Error Event (Middle of 3)	
Warning	4	Warning Event (Lowest of 3)	
Notification	5	Normal, More Important	Normal
Informational	6	Normal, Less Important	
Debug	7	Requested by User Debug	Debug

Figure 13-3 *Syslog Message Severity Levels by Keyword and Numeral*

Figure 13-3 breaks the eight severity levels into four sections just to make a little more sense of the meaning. The two top levels in the figure are the most severe. Messages from this level mean a serious and immediate issue exists. The next three levels, called Critical, Error, and Warning, also tell about events that impact the device, but they are not as immediate and severe. For instance, one common log message about an interface failing to a physically down state shows as a severity level 3 message.

Continuing down the figure, IOS uses the next two levels (5 and 6) for messages that are more about notifying the user rather than identifying errors. Finally, the last level in the figure is used for messages requested by the **debug** command, as shown in an example later in this chapter.

Table 13-2 summarizes the configuration commands used to enable logging and to set the severity level for each type. When the severity level is set, IOS will send messages of that severity level and more severe (lower severity numbers) to the service identified in the command. For example, the command **logging console 4** causes IOS to send severity level 0–4 messages to the console. Also, note that the command to disable each service is the **no** version of the command, with *no* in front of the command (**no logging console, no logging monitor**, and so on).

Table 13-2   How to Configure Logging Message Levels for Each Log Service

Service	To Enable Logging	To Set Message Levels
Console	**logging console**	**logging console** *level-name* | *level-number*
Monitor	**logging monitor**	**logging monitor** *level-name* | *level-number*
Buffered	**logging buffered**	**logging buffered** *level-name* | *level-number*
Syslog	**logging host** *address* | *hostname*	**logging trap** *level-name* | *level-number*

Configuring and Verifying System Logging

With the information in Table 13-2, configuring syslog in a Cisco IOS router or switch should be relatively straightforward. Example 13-2 shows a sample, based on Figure 13-4. The figure shows a syslog server at IP address 172.16.3.9. Both switches and both routers will use the same configuration shown in Example 13-2, although the example shows the configuration process on a single device, router R1.

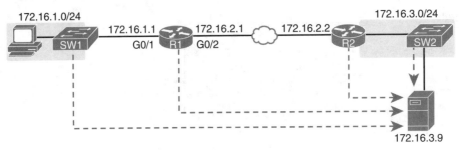

Figure 13-4 *Sample Network Used in Logging Examples*

Example 13-2 *Syslog Configuration on R1*

```
logging console 7
logging monitor debug
logging buffered 4
logging host 172.16.3.9
logging trap warning
```

First, note that the example configures the same message level at the console and for terminal monitoring (level 7, or debug), and the same level for both buffered and logging to the syslog server (level 4, or warning). The levels may be set using the numeric severity level or the name as shown earlier in Figure 13-3.

The **show logging** command confirms those same configuration settings and also lists the log messages per the logging buffered configuration. Example 13-3 shows a sample, with the configuration settings to match Example 13-2 highlighted in gray.

Example 13-3 *Viewing the Configured Log Settings per the Earlier Example*

```
R1# show logging
Syslog logging: enabled (0 messages dropped, 3 messages rate-limited, 0 flushes, 0
overruns, xml disabled, filtering disabled)


No Active Message Discriminator.


No Inactive Message Discriminator.

    Console logging: level debugging, 45 messages logged, xml disabled,
                   filtering disabled
    Monitor logging: level debugging, 0 messages logged, xml disabled,
                   filtering disabled
    Buffer logging: level warnings, 0 messages logged, xml disabled,
                   filtering disabled
    Exception Logging: size (8192 bytes)
    Count and timestamp logging messages: disabled
    Persistent logging: disabled
No active filter modules.
```

```
      Trap logging: level warnings, 0 message lines logged
         Logging to 172.16.3.9 (udp port 514, audit disabled,
              link up),
              0 message lines logged,
              0 message lines rate-limited,
              0 message lines dropped-by-MD,
              xml disabled, sequence number disabled
              filtering disabled
         Logging Source-Interface:     VRF Name:
      TLS Profiles:

Log Buffer (8192 bytes):
```

You might notice by now that knowing the names of all eight log message levels can be handy if you want to understand the output of the commands. Most of the **show** commands list the log message levels by name, not by number. As you can see in the gray highlights in this example, two levels list "debug," and two list "warning," even though some of the configuration commands referred to those levels by number.

Also, you cannot know this from the output, but in Example 13-3, router R1 has no buffered log messages. (Note the counter value of 0 for buffered logging messages.) If any log messages had been buffered, the actual log messages would be listed at the end of the command. In this case, I had just booted the router, and no messages had been buffered yet. (You could also clear out the old messages from the log with the **clear logging** EXEC command.)

The next example shows the difference between the current severity levels. This example shows the user disabling interface G0/1 on R1 with the **shutdown** command and then re-enabling it with the **no shutdown** command. If you look closely at the highlighted messages, you will see several severity 5 messages and one severity 3 message. The **logging buffered 4** global configuration command on R1 (see Example 13-2) means that R1 will not buffer the severity level 5 log messages, but it will buffer the severity level 3 message. Example 13-4 ends by showing that log message at the end of the output of the **show logging** command.

Example 13-4 *Seeing Severity 3 and 5 Messages at the Console, and Severity 3 Only in the Buffer*

```
R1# configure terminal
Enter configuration commands, one per line. End with CNTL/Z.
R1(config)# interface g0/1
R1(config-if)# shutdown
R1(config-if)#
*Oct 21 20:07:07.244: %LINK-5-CHANGED: Interface GigabitEthernet0/1, changed state
  to administratively down
*Oct 21 20:07:08.244: %LINEPROTO-5-UPDOWN: Line protocol on Interface
  GigabitEthernet0/1, changed state to down
R1(config-if)# no shutdown
R1(config-if)#
*Oct 21 20:07:24.312: %LINK-3-UPDOWN: Interface GigabitEthernet0/1, changed state to up
*Oct 21 20:07:25.312: %LINEPROTO-5-UPDOWN: Line protocol on Interface
  GigabitEthernet0/1, changed state to up
```

```
R1(config-if)# ^Z
R1#
*Oct 21 20:07:36.546: %SYS-5-CONFIG_I: Configured from console by console
R1# show logging
! Skipping about 20 lines, the same lines in Example 13-3, until the last few lines


Log Buffer (8192 bytes):

*Oct 21 20:07:24.312: %LINK-3-UPDOWN: Interface GigabitEthernet0/1, changed state to up
```

The debug Command and Log Messages

Of the eight log message severity levels, one level, debug level (7), has a special purpose: for messages generated as a result of a user logged in to the router or switch who issues a **debug** command.

The **debug** EXEC command gives the network engineer a way to ask IOS to monitor for certain internal events, with that monitoring process continuing over time, so that IOS can issue log messages when those events occur. The engineer can log in, issue the **debug** command, and move on to other work. The user can even log out of the device, and the debug remains enabled. IOS continues to monitor the request in that **debug** command and generate log messages about any related events. The debug remains active until some user issues the **no debug** command with the same parameters, disabling the debug.

> **NOTE** While the **debug** command is just one command, it has a huge number of options, much like the **show** command may be one command, but it also has many, many options.

The best way to see how the **debug** command works, and how it uses log messages, is to see an example. Example 13-5 shows a sample debug of OSPF Hello messages for router R1 in Figure 13-4. The router (R1) enables OSPF on two interfaces and has established one OSPF neighbor relationship with router R2 (RID 2.2.2.2). The debug output shows one log message for the Hello messages sent on ports G0/1 and G0/2, plus one message for a received Hello arriving in port G0/2.

Example 13-5 *Using* debug ip ospf hello *from R1's Console*

```
R1# debug ip ospf hello
OSPF hello debugging is on
R1#
*Aug 10 13:38:19.863: OSPF-1 HELLO Gi0/1: Send hello to 224.0.0.5 area 0 from
   172.16.1.1
*Aug 10 13:38:21.199: OSPF-1 HELLO Gi0/2: Rcv hello from 2.2.2.2 area 0 172.16.2.2
*Aug 10 13:38:22.843: OSPF-1 HELLO Gi0/2: Send hello to 224.0.0.5 area 0 from
   172.16.2.1
R1#
```

The console user sees the log messages created on behalf of that **debug** command after the **debug** command completes. Per the earlier configuration in Example 13-2, R1's **logging** console 7 command tells us that the console user will receive severity levels 0–7, which includes level 7 debug messages. Also, if you examine the log messages generated by the **debug** command, you will not find the severity level listed. So, the absence of a severity level number in a log message points to the message coming from the **debug** command.

Many companies may not want to keep copies of debug messages with the longer-term options to store log messages. For instance, with the current settings per Example 13-2, these debug messages would not be in the local log message buffer (because of the level in the **logging buffered warning** command). The router would also not send debug messages to the syslog server (because of the level in the **logging trap 4** command).

Note that the console user automatically sees the log messages as shown in Example 13-4. However, as noted in the text describing Figure 13-1, a user who connects to R1 using SSH or Telnet would need to also issue the **terminal monitor** command, even with the **logging monitor debug** command configured on router R1.

Note that all enabled debug options use router CPU, which can cause problems for the router. You can monitor CPU use with the **show process cpu** command, but you should use caution when using **debug** commands on production devices. Also, note the more CLI users who receive debug messages, the more CPU is consumed. So, some installations choose not to include debug-level log messages for console and terminal logging, requiring users to look at the logging buffer or syslog for those messages, just to reduce router CPU load.

Network Time Protocol (NTP)

Each networking device has some concept of a date and a time-of-day clock. For instance, the log messages discussed in the first major section of this chapter had a timestamp with the date and time of day listed. Now imagine looking at all the log messages from all routers and switches stored at a syslog server. All those messages have a date and timestamp, but how do you make sure the timestamps are consistent? How do you make sure that all devices synchronize their time-of-day clocks so that you can make sense of all the log messages at the syslog server? How could you make sense of the messages for an event that impacted devices in three different time zones?

For example, consider the messages on two routers, R1 and R2, as shown in Example 13-6. Routers R1 and R2 do not synchronize their NTP clocks. A problem keeps happening on the Ethernet WAN link between the two routers. A network engineer looks at all the log messages as stored on the syslog server. However, when seeing some messages from R1, at 13:38:39 (around 1:40 p.m.), the engineer does not think to look for messages from R2 that have a timestamp of around 9:45 a.m.

Example 13-6 *Log Messages from Two Routers, Compared*

```
*Oct 19 13:38:37.568: %OSPF-5-ADJCHG: Process 1, Nbr 2.2.2.2 on GigabitEthernet0/2
from FULL to DOWN, Neighbor Down: Interface down or detached
*Oct 19 13:38:40.568: %LINEPROTO-5-UPDOWN: Line protocol on Interface
GigabitEthernet0/2, changed state to down
```

```
! These messages happened on router R2
Oct 19 09:44:09.027: %LINK-3-UPDOWN: Interface GigabitEthernet0/1, changed state to down
Oct 19 09:44:09.027: %OSPF-5-ADJCHG: Process 1, Nbr 1.1.1.1 on GigabitEthernet0/1
from FULL to DOWN, Neighbor Down: Interface down or detached
```

In reality, the messages in both parts of Example 13-6 happened within 0.5 second of each other because I issued a **shutdown** command on router R1 (not shown). However, the two routers' time-of-day clocks were not synchronized, which makes the messages on the two routers look unrelated. With synchronized clocks, the two routers would have listed practically identical timestamps of almost the exact same time when these messages occurred, making it much easier to read and correlate messages.

Routers, switches, other networking devices, and pretty much every device known in the IT world has a time-of-day clock. For a variety of reasons, it makes sense to synchronize those clocks so that all devices have the same time of day, other than differences in time zone. The **Network Time Protocol (NTP)** provides the means to do just that.

NTP gives any device a way to synchronize its time-of-day clocks. NTP provides protocol messages that devices use to learn the timestamp of other devices. Devices send timestamps to each other with NTP messages, continually exchanging messages, with one device changing its clock to match the other, eventually synchronizing the clocks. As a result, actions that benefit from synchronized timing, like the timestamps on log messages, work much better.

This section works through a progression of topics that lead to the more common types of NTP configurations seen in real networks. The section begins with basic settings, like the time zone and initially configured time on a router or switch, followed by basic NTP configuration. The text then examines some NTP internals regarding how NTP defines the sources of time data (reference clocks) and how good each time source is (stratum). The section closes with more configuration that explains typical enterprise configurations, with multiple **ntp** commands for redundancy and the use of loopback interfaces for high availability.

Setting the Time and Time Zone

NTP's job is to synchronize clocks, but NTP works best if you set the device clock to a reasonably close time before enabling the **NTP client** function with the **ntp server** command. For instance, my wristwatch says 8:52 p.m. right now. Before starting NTP on a new router or switch so that it synchronizes with another device, I should set the time to 8:52 p.m., set the correct date and time zone, and even tell the device to adjust for daylight savings time—and then enable NTP. Setting the time correctly gives NTP a good start toward synchronizing.

Example 13-7 shows how to set the date, time, time zone, and daylight savings time. Oddly, it uses two configuration commands (for the time zone and daylight savings time) and one EXEC command to set the date and time on the router.

Example 13-7 *Setting the Date/Time with* **clock set***, Plus Time Zone/DST*

```
R1# configure terminal
Enter configuration commands, one per line. End with CNTL/Z.
R1(config)# clock timezone EST -5
R1(config)# clock summer-time EDT recurring
R1(config)# ^Z
R1#
R1# clock set 12:32:00 19 January 2023
*Jan 19 17:32:00.005: %SYS-6-CLOCKUPDATE: System clock has been updated from
12:32:16 EST Thu Jan 19 2023 to 12:32:00 EST Thu Jan 19 2023, configured from
console by console.
R1# show clock
12:32:06.146 EST Thu Jan 19 2023
```

Focus on the two configuration commands first. You should set the first two commands before setting the time of day with the **clock set** EXEC command because the two configuration commands impact the time that is set. In the first command, the **clock timezone** part defines the command and a keyword. The next parameter, "EST" in this case, is any value you choose, but choose the name of the time zone of the device. This value shows up in **show** commands, so although you make up the value, the value needs to be meaningful to all. I chose EST, the acronym for US Eastern Standard Time. The "-5" parameter means that this device is 5 hours behind Universal Time Coordinated (UTC).

The **clock summer-time** part of the second command defines what to do, again with the "EDT" being a field in which you could have used any value. However, you should use a meaningful value. This is the value shown with the time in **show** commands when daylight savings time is in effect, so I chose EDT because it is the acronym for daylight savings time in that same EST time zone. Finally, the **recurring** keyword tells the router to spring forward an hour and fall back an hour automatically over the years.

The **clock set** EXEC command then sets the time, day of the month, month, and year. However, note that IOS interprets the time as typed in the command in the context of the time zone and daylight savings time. In the example, the **clock set** command lists a time of 20:52:49 (the command uses a time syntax with a 24-hour format, not with a 12-hour format plus a.m./p.m.). As a result of that time plus the two earlier configuration commands, the **show clock** command (issued seconds later) lists that time but also notes the time as EDT rather than UTC time.

Basic NTP Configuration

With NTP, servers supply information about the time of day to clients, and clients react by adjusting their clocks to match. The process requires repeated small adjustments over time to maintain that synchronization. The configuration itself can be simple, or it can be extensive once you add security configuration and redundancy.

Cisco supplies two **ntp** configuration commands that dictate how NTP works on a router or switch, as follows:

- **ntp master** {*stratum-level*}: NTP server mode—the device acts only as an **NTP server**, and not as an NTP client. The device gets its time information from the internal clock on the device.

- **ntp server** {*address | hostname*}: NTP client/server mode—the device acts as both client and server. First, it acts as an NTP client, to adjust its time to synchronize time with another server. Once synchronized, the device can then act as an NTP server, to supply time to other NTP clients.

For an example showing the basic configuration syntax and **show** commands, consider Figure 13-5. With this simple configuration:

- R3 acts as an NTP server only.

- R2 acts in client/server mode—first as an NTP client to synchronize time with NTP server R3, then as a server to supply time to NTP client R1.

■ R1 acts in client/server mode—first as an NTP client to synchronize time with NTP server R2. (R1 will be willing to act as a server, but no devices happen to reference R1 as an NTP server in this example.)

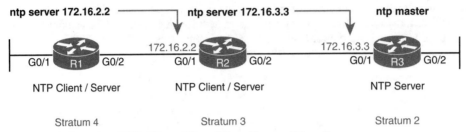

Figure 13-5 *R1 as NTP Client, R2 as Client/Server, R3 as Server*

As you can see, NTP requires little configuration to make it work with a single configuration command on each device. Example 13-8 collects the configuration from the devices shown in the figure for easy reference.

Example 13-8 *NTP Client/Server Configuration*

```
! Configuration on R1:
ntp server 172.16.2.2
```
```
! Configuration on R2:
ntp server 172.16.3.3
```
```
! Configuration on R3:
ntp master 2
```

Example 13-9 lists the output from the **show ntp status** command on R1, with the first line of output including a few important status items. First, it lists a status of synchronized, which confirms the NTP client has completed the process of changing its time to match the server's time. Any router acting as an NTP client will list "unsynchronized" in that first line until the **NTP synchronization** process completes with at least one server. It also confirms the IP address of the server—this device's *reference clock*—with the IP address configured in Example 13-8 (172.16.2.2).

Example 13-9 *Verifying NTP Client Status on R1 and R2*

```
R1# show ntp status
Clock is synchronized, stratum 4, reference is 172.16.2.2
nominal freq is 250.0000 Hz, actual freq is 250.0000 Hz, precision is 2**21
ntp uptime is 1553800 (1/100 of seconds), resolution is 4000
reference time is DA5E7147.56CADEA7 (15:24:38.694 EST Thu Jan 19 2023)
clock offset is 0.0986 msec, root delay is 2.46 msec
root dispersion is 22.19 msec, peer dispersion is 5.33 msec
loopfilter state is 'CTRL' (Normal Controlled Loop), drift is 0.000000009 s/s
system poll interval is 64, last update was 530 sec ago.
```

Next, look at the **show ntp associations** command output from both R1 and R2, as shown in Example 13-10. This command lists all the NTP servers that the local device can attempt to use, with status information about the association between the local device (client) and the various NTP servers. Beginning with R1, note that it has one association (that is, relationship with an NTP server), based on the one **ntp server 172.16.2.2.2** configuration command on R1. The * means that R1 has successfully contacted the server. You will see similar data from the same command output taken from router R2.

13

Example 13-10   *Verifying NTP Client Status on R1 and R2*

```
R1# show ntp associations
! This output is taken from router R1, acting in client/server mode
   address    ref clock st when poll reach  delay  offset disp
*~172.16.2.2 10.1.3.3   3  50  64    377  1.223  0.090  4.469
 * sys.peer, # selected, + candidate, - outlyer, x falseticker, ~ configured

R2# show ntp associations
! This output is taken from router R2, acting in client/server mode
   address      ref clock    st  when poll  reach  delay offset  disp
*~172.16.3.3  127.127.1.1  2   49   64    377    1.220  -7.758  3.695
 * sys.peer, # selected, + candidate, - outlyer, x falseticker, ~ configured
```

NTP Reference Clock and Stratum

NTP servers must learn the time from some device. For devices acting in **NTP client/server mode**, the device uses the NTP client function to learn the time. However, devices that act solely as an NTP server get their time from either internal device hardware or from some external clock using mechanisms other than NTP.

For instance, when configured with the **ntp master** command, a Cisco router/switch uses its internal device hardware to determine the time. All computers, networking devices included, need some means to keep time for a myriad of reasons, so they include both hardware components and software processes to keep time even over periods in which the device loses power.

Additionally, NTP servers and clients use a number to show the perceived accuracy of their reference clock data based on stratum level. The lower the stratum level, the more accurate the reference clock is considered to be. An NTP server that uses its internal hardware or external reference clock sets its own stratum level. Then, an NTP client adds 1 to the stratum level it learns from its NTP server, so that the stratum level increases the more hops away from the original clock source.

For instance, back in Figure 13-5, you can see the NTP primary server (R3) with a stratum of 2. R2, which references R3, adds 1 so it has a stratum of 3. R1 uses R2 as its NTP server, so R1 adds 1 to have a stratum of 4. These increasing stratum levels allow devices to refer to several NTP servers and then use time information from the best NTP server, *best* being the server with the lowest stratum level.

Routers and switches use the default stratum level of 8 for their internal reference clock based on the default setting of 8 for the stratum level in the **ntp master** [*stratum-level*] command. The command allows you to set a value from 1 through 15; in Example 13-8, the **ntp master 2** command set router R3's stratum level to 2.

NOTE NTP considers 15 to be the highest useful stratum level, so any devices that calculate its stratum as 16 consider the time data unusable and do not trust the time. So, avoid setting higher stratum values on the **ntp master** command.

To see the evidence, refer back to Example 13-10, which shows two commands based on the same configuration in Example 13-8 and Figure 13-5. The output highlights details about reference clocks and stratum levels, as follows:

R1: Per the configured **ntp server 172.16.2.2** command, the **show** command lists the same address (which is router R2's address). The ref clock (reference clock) and st (stratum) fields represent R2's reference clock as 172.16.3.3—in other words, the NTP server R2 uses, which is R3 in this case. The st field value of 3 shows R2's stratum.

R2: Per the configured **ntp server 172.16.3.3** command, the **show** command lists 172.16.3.3, which is an address on router R3. The output notes R3's ref clock as 127.127.1.1—an indication that the server (R3) gets its clock internally. It lists R3's st (stratum) value of 2—consistent with the configured **ntp master 2** command on R3 (per Example 13-8).

On the NTP primary server itself (R3 in this case), the output has more markers indicating the use of the internal clock. Example 13-11 shows output from R3, with a reference clock of the 127.127.1.1 loopback address, used to refer to the fact that this router gets its clock data internally. Also, in the **show ntp associations** command output at the bottom, note that same address, along with a reference clock value of ".LOCL." In effect, R3, per the **ntp master** configuration command, has an association with its internal clock.

Example 13-11 *Examining NTP Server, Reference Clock, and Stratum Data*

```
R3# show ntp status
Clock is synchronized, stratum 2, reference is 127.127.1.1
nominal freq is 250.0000 Hz, actual freq is 250.0000 Hz, precision is 2**20
ntp uptime is 595300 (1/100 of seconds), resolution is 4000
reference time is E0F9174C.87277EBB (15:27:54.252 EST Thu Jan 19 2023)
clock offset is 0.0000 msec, root delay is 0.00 msec
root dispersion is 0.33 msec, peer dispersion is 0.23 msec
loopfilter state is 'CTRL' (Normal Controlled Loop), drift is 0.000000000 s/s
system poll interval is 16, last update was 8 sec ago.

R3# show ntp associations
  address         ref clock       st   when   poll reach  delay  offset    disp
*~127.127.1.1     .LOCL.           1     15     16   377  0.000   0.000   0.232
 * sys.peer, # selected, + candidate, - outlyer, x falseticker, ~ configured
```

NOTE Appendix D, "Topics from Previous Editions," includes a few pages about adding redundancy to NTP. For those moving on to CCNP, you might want to read that topic when convenient. You can find Appendix D on this book's companion website.

Analyzing Topology Using CDP and LLDP

The first two major sections of this chapter showed two features—syslog and NTP—that work the same way on both routers and switches. This final section shows yet another feature common to both routers and switches, with two similar protocols: the Cisco Discovery Protocol (**CDP**) and the Link Layer Discovery Protocol (**LLDP**). This section focuses on CDP, followed by LLDP.

Examining Information Learned by CDP

CDP discovers basic information about neighboring routers and switches without needing to know the passwords for the neighboring devices. To discover information, routers and switches send CDP messages out each of their interfaces. The messages essentially announce information about the device that sent the CDP message. Devices that support CDP learn information about others by listening for the advertisements sent by other devices.

CDP discovers several useful details from the neighboring Cisco devices:

- **Device identifier:** Typically the hostname

- **Address list:** Network and data-link addresses

- **Port identifier:** The interface on the remote router or switch on the other end of the link that sent the CDP advertisement

- **Capabilities list:** Information on what type of device it is (for example, a router or a switch)

- **Platform:** The model and OS level running on the device

CDP plays two general roles: to provide information to the devices to support some function and to provide information to the network engineers who manage the devices. For example, Cisco IP Phones use CDP to learn the data and voice VLAN IDs as configured on the access switch. For that second role, CDP has **show** commands that list information about neighboring devices, as well as information about how CDP is working. Table 13-3 describes the three **show** commands that list the most important CDP information.

Table 13-3   show cdp Commands That List Information About Neighbors

Command	Description
show cdp neighbors [*type number*]	Lists one summary line of information about each neighbor or just the neighbor found on a specific interface if an interface was listed
show cdp neighbors detail	Lists one large set (approximately 15 lines) of information, one set for every neighbor
show cdp entry *name*	Lists the same information as the **show cdp neighbors detail** command, but only for the named neighbor (case sensitive)

NOTE   Cisco routers and switches support the same CDP commands, with the same parameters and same types of output.

The next example shows the power of the information in CDP commands. The example uses the network shown in Figure 13-6, with Example 13-12 listing the output of several **show cdp** commands.

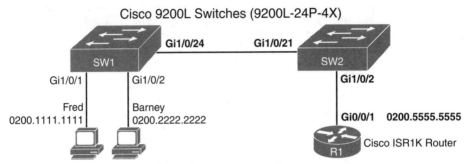

Figure 13-6 *Small Network Used in CDP Examples*

Example 13-12 show cdp neighbors *Command Examples: SW2*

```
SW2# show cdp neighbors
Capability Codes: R - Router, T - Trans Bridge, B - Source Route Bridge
                  S - Switch, H - Host, I - IGMP, r - Repeater, P - Phone,
                  D - Remote, C - CVTA, M - Two-port Mac Relay


Device ID        Local Intrfce    Holdtme    Capability  Platform  Port ID
SW1              Gig 1/0/21       155              S I   WS-C2960X Gig 1/0/24
R1               Gig 1/0/2        131            R S I   C1111-8P  Gig 0/0/1


Total cdp entries displayed : 2
```

The **show cdp neighbors** command lists one line per neighbor. (Look for the Device ID column and the list that includes SW1 and R1.) Each of those two lines lists the most important topology information about each neighbor: the neighbor's hostname (Device ID), the local device's interface, and the neighboring device's interface (under the Port heading).

Pay close attention to the local device's interface and the neighboring device's interface, comparing the example to the figure. For example, SW2's **show cdp neighbors** command lists an entry for SW1, with SW2's local interface of Gi1/0/21 (listed under the heading "Local Intrfce") and SW1's interface of Gi1/0/24 (listed under the heading "Port ID").

This command also lists the platform, identifying the specific model of the neighboring router or switch. So, even using this basic information, you could either construct a figure like Figure 13-6 or confirm that the details in the figure are correct.

Figure 13-6 and Example 13-12 provide a good backdrop as to why devices learn about direct neighbors with CDP, but not other neighbors. First, CDP defines encapsulation that uses the data-link header, but no IP header. To ensure all devices receive a CDP message, the Ethernet header uses a multicast destination MAC address (0100.0CCC.CCCC). However, when any device that supports CDP receives a CDP message, the device processes the message and then discards it, rather than forwarding it. So, for instance, when router R1 sends a

CDP message to Ethernet multicast address 0100.0CCC.CCCC, switch SW2 receives it, processes it, but does not forward it to switch SW1—so SW1 will not list router R1 as a CDP neighbor. Likewise, R1 will not list SW1 as a neighbor.

Next, consider the **show cdp neighbors detail** command as shown in Example 13-13, again taken from switch SW2. This command lists more detail, as you might have guessed. The detail lists the full name of the switch model (C9200L-24P-4X) and the IP address configured on the neighboring device. You have to look closely, but the example has one long group of messages for each of the two neighbors, separated by a line of dashes.

Example 13-13 show cdp neighbors detail *Command on SW2*

```
SW2# show cdp neighbors detail
-------------------------
Device ID: SW1
Entry address(es):
  IP address: 1.1.1.1
Platform: cisco C9200L-24P-4X,  Capabilities: Switch IGMP
Interface: GigabitEthernet1/0/21,  Port ID (outgoing port): GigabitEthernet1/0/24
Holdtime : 144 sec

Version :
Cisco IOS Software [Bengaluru], Catalyst L3 Switch Software (CAT9K_LITE_IOSXE),
Version 17.6.3, RELEASE SOFTWARE (fc4)
Technical Support: http://www.cisco.com/techsupport
Copyright (c) 1986-2022 by Cisco Systems, Inc.
Compiled Wed 30-Mar-22 21:23 by mcpre

advertisement version: 2
VTP Management Domain: 'fred'
Native VLAN: 1
Duplex: full
Management address(es):
  IP address: 1.1.1.1


-------------------------
Device ID: R1
Entry address(es):
  IP address: 10.12.25.5
Platform: cisco C1111-8P,  Capabilities: Router Switch IGMP
Interface: GigabitEthernet1/0/2,  Port ID (outgoing port): GigabitEthernet0/0/1
Holdtime : 151 sec

Version :
Cisco IOS Software [Fuji], ISR Software (ARMV8EB_LINUX_IOSD-UNIVERSALK9_IAS-M),
Version 16.8.1, RELEASE SOFTWARE (fc3)
Technical Support: http://www.cisco.com/techsupport
```

```
Copyright (c) 1986-2018 by Cisco Systems, Inc.
Compiled Tue 27-Mar-18 10:56 by mcpre

advertisement version: 2
VTP Management Domain: ''
Duplex: full
Management address(es):
  IP address: 10.12.25.5



Total cdp entries displayed : 2
```

NOTE The **show cdp entry** *name* command lists the exact same details shown in the output of the **show cdp neighbors detail** command, but for only the one neighbor listed in the command. The *name* parameter must be a neighbor's case-sensitive name.

Configuring and Verifying CDP

Most of the work you do with CDP relates to what CDP can tell you with **show** commands. However, it is an IOS feature, so you can configure CDP and use some **show** commands to examine the status of CDP itself.

IOS typically enables CDP globally and on each interface by default. You can then disable CDP per interface with the **no cdp enable** interface subcommand and later re-enable it with the **cdp enable** interface subcommand. To disable and re-enable CDP globally on the device, use the **no cdp run** and **cdp run** global commands, respectively.

To examine the status of CDP itself, use the commands in Table 13-4.

Table 13-4 Commands Used to Verify CDP Operations

Command	Description
show cdp	States whether CDP is enabled globally and lists the default update and holdtime timers
show cdp interface [*type number*]	States whether CDP is enabled on each interface, or a single interface if the interface is listed, and states update and holdtime timers on those interfaces
show cdp traffic	Lists global statistics for the number of CDP advertisements sent and received

Example 13-14 lists sample output from each of the commands in Table 13-4, based on switch SW2 in Figure 13-6.

Example 13-14 show cdp *Commands That Show CDP Status*

```
SW2# show cdp
Global CDP information:
        Sending CDP packets every 60 seconds
        Sending a holdtime value of 180 seconds
        Sending CDPv2 advertisements is enabled

SW2# show cdp interface GigabitEthernet1/0/2
GigabitEthernet1/0/2 is up, line protocol is up
  Encapsulation ARPA
  Sending CDP packets every 60 seconds
  Holdtime is 180 seconds

SW2# show cdp traffic
CDP counters :
        Total packets output: 304, Input: 305
        Hdr syntax: 0, Chksum error: 0, Encaps failed: 0
        No memory: 0, Invalid packet: 0,
        CDP version 1 advertisements output: 0, Input: 0
        CDP version 2 advertisements output: 304, Input: 305
```

The first two commands in the example list two related settings about how CDP works: the send time and the hold time. CDP sends messages every 60 seconds by default, with a hold time of 180 seconds. The hold time tells the device how long to wait after no longer hearing from a device before removing those details from the CDP tables. You can override the defaults with the **cdp timer** *seconds* and **cdp holdtime** *seconds* global commands, respectively. Table 13-5 summarizes the configuration commands for CDP and LLDP timers for easier review and study.

Table 13-5 CDP and LLDP Timer Configuration

CDP Command	LLDP Command	Description
cdp timer *seconds*	lldp timer *seconds*	Defines how often CDP or LLDP sends messages on each interface
cdp holdtime *seconds*	lldp holdtime *seconds*	Defines how long to wait after the most recent incoming message from a neighbor before deleting that neighbor's information
N/A	lldp reinit *seconds*	(LLDP only) Defines a wait time before the first message sent after an interface comes up

Examining Information Learned by LLDP

Cisco created the Cisco-proprietary CDP before any standard existed for a similar protocol. CDP has many benefits. As a Layer 2 protocol, sitting on top of Ethernet, it does not rely on a working Layer 3 protocol. It provides device information that can be useful in a variety of ways. Cisco had a need but did not see a standard that met the need, so Cisco made up a protocol, as has been the case many times over history with many companies and protocols.

Link Layer Discovery Protocol (LLDP), defined in IEEE standard 802.1AB, provides a standardized protocol that provides the same general features as CDP. LLDP has similar configuration and practically identical **show** commands as compared with CDP.

The LLDP examples all use the same topology used in the CDP examples per Figure 13-6 (the same figure used in the CDP examples). Example 13-15 lists switch SW2's LLDP neighbors as learned after LLDP was enabled on all devices and ports in that figure. The example highlights the items that match the similar output from the **show cdp neighbors** command listed at the end of the example, also from switch SW2.

Example 13-15 show lldp neighbors *on SW2 with Similarities to CDP Highlighted*

```
SW2# show lldp neighbors
Capability codes:
    (R) Router, (B) Bridge, (T) Telephone, (C) DOCSIS Cable Device
    (W) WLAN Access Point, (P) Repeater, (S) Station, (O) Other

Device ID          Local Intf     Hold-time  Capability    Port ID
R1                 Gi1/0/2        120        R             Gi0/0/1
SW1                Gi1/0/21       120        B             Gi1/0/24

Total entries displayed: 2


SW2# show cdp neighbors
Capability Codes: R - Router, T - Trans Bridge, B - Source Route Bridge
                  S - Switch, H - Host, I - IGMP, r - Repeater, P - Phone,
                  D - Remote, C - CVTA, M - Two-port Mac Relay

Device ID        Local Intrfce    Holdtme    Capability  Platform  Port ID
SW1              Gig 1/0/21       155            S I     WS-C2960X Gig 1/0/24
R1               Gig 1/0/2        131          R S I     C1111-8P  Gig 0/0/1
Total entries displayed: 2
```

The most important take-away from the output is the consistency between CDP and LLDP in how they refer to the interfaces. Both the **show cdp neighbors** and **show lldp neighbors** commands have "local intf" (interface) and "port ID" columns. These columns refer to the local device's interface and the neighboring device's interface, respectively.

However, the LLDP output in the example does differ from CDP in a few important ways:

- LLDP uses **B** as the capability code for switching, referring to **bridge**, a term for the device type that existed before switches that performed the same basic functions.

- LLDP does not identify IGMP as a capability, while CDP does (I).

- CDP lists the neighbor's **platform**, a code that defines the device type, while LLDP does not.

- LLDP lists capabilities with different conventions (see upcoming Example 13-19).

The last item in the list requires a closer look with more detail. Interestingly, CDP lists all capabilities supported by the neighbor in the **show cdp neighbors** command output, whether enabled or not. LLDP instead lists only the enabled (configured) capabilities, rather than all supported capabilities, in the output from the **show lldp neighbors** command.

The **show lldp neighbors detail** and **show lldp entry** *hostname* commands provide identical detailed output, with the first command providing detail for all neighbors, and the second providing detail for the single listed neighbor. Example 13-16 shows the detail for neighbor R1. Note that the parameter "R1" is case sensitive, and should match the name listed by the **show lldp neighbors** command.

Example 13-16   show lldp entry r2 *Command on SW2*

```
SW2# show lldp entry R1

Capability codes:
    (R) Router, (B) Bridge, (T) Telephone, (C) DOCSIS Cable Device
    (W) WLAN Access Point, (P) Repeater, (S) Station, (O) Other
-------------------------------------------------
Local Intf: Gi1/0/2
Chassis id: 70ea.1a9a.d300
Port id: Gi0/0/1
Port Description: GigabitEthernet0/0/1
System Name: R1

System Description:
Cisco IOS Software [Fuji], ISR Software (ARMV8EB_LINUX_IOSD-UNIVERSALK9_IAS-M),
Version 16.8.1, RELEASE SOFTWARE (fc3)
Technical Support: http://www.cisco.com/techsupport
Copyright (c) 1986-2022 by Cisco Systems, Inc.
Compiled Fri 08-Apr-22 12:42 by mcp

Time remaining: 100 seconds
System Capabilities: B,R
Enabled Capabilities: R
Management Addresses:
    IP: 10.12.25.5
Auto Negotiation - not supported
Physical media capabilities - not advertised
Media Attachment Unit type - not advertised
Vlan ID: - not advertised


Total entries displayed: 1
```

First, regarding the device capabilities, note that the LLDP command output lists two lines about the neighbor's capabilities:

System Capabilities: What the device can do

Enabled Capabilities: What the device does now with its current configuration

For instance, in Example 13-16, the neighboring R1 claims the ability to perform routing and switching (codes **R** and **B**) but also claims to currently be using only its routing capability, as noted in the "enabled capabilities" line.

Also, take a moment to look at the output for the similarities to CDP. For instance, this output lists detail for neighbor R1, which uses its local port G0/0/1, with a hostname of R1. The output also notes the IOS name and version, from which an experienced person can infer the model number, but there is no explicit mention of the model.

> **NOTE** LLDP uses the same messaging concepts as CDP, encapsulating messages directly in data-link headers. Devices do not forward LLDP messages, so LLDP learns only of directly connected neighbors. LLDP sends messages to multicast MAC address 0180.C200.000E, while CDP uses 0100.0CCC.CCCC.

Configuring and Verifying LLDP

LLDP uses a similar configuration model as CDP, but with a few key differences. First, Cisco devices default to disable LLDP. Additionally, LLDP separates the sending and receiving of LLDP messages as separate functions. For instance, LLDP support processing receives LLDP messages on an interface so that the switch or router learns about the neighboring device while not transmitting LLDP messages to the neighboring device. To support that model, the commands include options to toggle on/off the transmission of LLDP messages separately from the processing of received messages.

The three LLDP configuration commands are as follows:

- **[no] lldp run:** A global configuration command that sets the default mode of LLDP operation for any interface that does not have more specific LLDP subcommands (**lldp transmit, lldp receive**). The **lldp run** global command enables LLDP in both directions on those interfaces, while **no lldp run** disables LLDP.

- **[no] lldp transmit:** An interface subcommand that defines the operation of LLDP on the interface regardless of the global **[no] lldp run** command. The **lldp transmit** interface subcommand causes the device to transmit LLDP messages, while **no lldp transmit** causes it to not transmit LLDP messages.

- **[no] lldp receive:** An interface subcommand that defines the operation of LLDP on the interface regardless of the global **[no] lldp run** command. The **lldp receive** interface subcommand causes the device to process received LLDP messages, while **no lldp receive** causes it to not process received LLDP messages.

For example, consider a switch that has no LLDP configuration commands at all. Example 13-17 adds configuration that first enables LLDP for all interfaces (in both directions) with the **lldp run** global command. It then shows how to disable LLDP in both directions on Gi1/0/17 and how to disable LLDP in one direction on Gi1/0/18.

Example 13-17   *Enabling LLDP on All Ports, Disabling on a Few Ports*

```
lldp run
!
interface gigabitEthernet1/0/17
 no lldp transmit
 no lldp receive
!
interface gigabitEthernet1/0/18
 no lldp receive
```

Example 13-18 adds another example that again begins with a switch with all default settings. In this case, the configuration does not enable LLDP for all interfaces with the **lldp run** command, meaning that all interfaces default to not transmit and not receive LLDP messages. The example does show how to then enable LLDP for both directions on one interface and in one direction for a second interface.

Example 13-18   *Enabling LLDP on Limited Ports, Leaving Disabled on Most*

```
interface gigabitEthernet1/0/19
 lldp transmit
 lldp receive
!
interface gigabitEthernet1/0/20
 lldp receive
```

Finally, checking LLDP status uses the exact same commands as CDP as listed in Table 13-4, other than the fact that you use the **lldp** keyword instead of **cdp**. For instance, **show lldp interface** lists the interfaces on which LLDP is enabled. Example 13-19 shows some examples from switch SW2 based on earlier Figure 13-6 (the same figure used in the CDP examples), with LLDP enabled in both directions on all interfaces with the **cdp run** global command.

Example 13-19   show lldp *Commands That Show LLDP Status*

```
SW2# show lldp
Global LLDP Information:
    Status: ACTIVE
    LLDP advertisements are sent every 30 seconds
    LLDP hold time advertised is 120 seconds
    LLDP interface reinitialisation delay is 2 seconds

SW2# show lldp interface g1/0/2

GigabitEthernet1/0/2:
    Tx: enabled
    Rx: enabled
    Tx state: IDLE
    Rx state: WAIT FOR FRAME
```

```
SW2# show lldp traffic

LLDP traffic statistics:
    Total frames out: 259
    Total entries aged: 0
    Total frames in: 257
    Total frames received in error: 0
    Total frames discarded: 0
    Total TLVs discarded: 0
    Total TLVs unrecognized: 0
```

Also, note that like CDP, LLDP uses a send timer and hold timer for the same purposes as CDP. The example shows the default settings of 30 seconds for the send timer and 120 seconds for the hold timer. You can override the defaults with the **lldp timer** *seconds* and **lldp holdtime** *seconds* global commands, respectively.

LLDP-MED and TLVs

The LLDP 802.1AB standard defines a method to expand LLDP for new functions using a *type-length-value (TLV)* concept. The term refers to three fields in a data structure. The first defines the type of data held there, the length lists the length of the TLV, and the value lists the data. Any device processing received messages with TLVs can quickly identify one TLV after another based on the specified length.

Figure 13-7 shows a sample LLDP message. Devices encapsulate LLDP messages directly in the data-link protocol. The LLDP message consists of a series of TLVs.

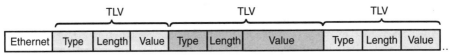

Figure 13-7 *Type-Length-Value Concept in LLDP Messages*

Over time, new endpoint-focused LLDP TLVs emerged. The LLDP Media Endpoint Discovery (**LLDP-MED**) protocol uses a variety of endpoint-focused LLDP TLVs useful for operations between a switch and an endpoint device. (While IEEE standard 802.1AB defines LLDP, the Telecommunications Industry Association [TIA] defines LLDP-MED as an industry-standard in their TIA-1057 document.) For instance, Chapter 17, "SNMP, FTP, and TFTP," discusses Power over Ethernet (PoE), with devices using LLDP-MED to exchange data about the power needed by the endpoint device.

IP Phones connected to LAN switches can also use LLDP-MED or CDP to learn information like the voice and data VLAN IDs used by the switch. Figure 13-8 shows an example for context, with three phones, each with a connected PC. The design uses VLAN 20 as the voice VLAN and VLAN 21 as the data VLAN. (Refer to the *CCNA 200-301 Official Cert Guide, Volume 1*, Second Edition, Chapter 8, Figure 8-13, and surrounding text to review voice and data VLAN configuration.)

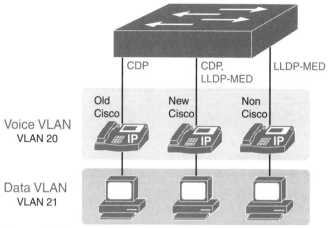

Figure 13-8 *Sample Access Switch with IP Phones*

The phones need to learn the voice VLAN to use because the phone adds an 802.1Q trunking header to any Ethernet frames generated by the phone. You do not preconfigure the phone with the voice VLAN ID; instead, the phone learns it using LLDP-MED or CDP. Originally, Cisco IP phones supported only CDP to learn the voice VLAN ID. Cisco IP phones have supported both LLDP-MED and CDP for over a decade. Non-Cisco IP phones, which do not support Cisco-proprietary CDP, use only LLDP-MED.

On a final note about LLDP-MED, you configure LLDP-MED with the same commands as LLDP. The devices on the link dynamically discover that they need to include the TLVs defined by LLDP-MED; no additional configuration is required.

Chapter Review

One key to doing well on the exams is to perform repetitive spaced review sessions. Review this chapter's material using either the tools in the book or interactive tools for the same material found on the book's companion website. Refer to the "Your Study Plan" element for more details. Table 13-6 outlines the key review elements and where you can find them. To better track your study progress, record when you completed these activities in the second column.

Table 13-6 Chapter Review Tracking

Review Element	Review Date(s)	Resource Used
Review key topics		Book, website
Review key terms		Book, website
Answer DIKTA questions		Book, PTP
Review memory tables		Book, app
Do labs		Blog
Review command references		Book
Watch video		Website

Review All the Key Topics

Table 13-7   Key Topics for Chapter 13

Key Topic Element	Description	Page Number
Figure 13-1	Logging to console and terminal	271
Figure 13-2	Logging to syslog and buffer	271
Figure 13-3	Log message levels	273
Table 13-2	Logging configuration commands	273
List	The **ntp master** and **ntp server** commands	279
List	Facts that CDP can learn about neighbors	283
Table 13-3	Three CDP **show** commands that list information about neighbors	283
List	How LLDP output in the example differs from CDP	288
List	LLDP configuration commands	290
Figure 13-7	Type-length-value concept	292

Key Terms You Should Know

CDP, LLDP, LLDP-MED, log message, Network Time Protocol (NTP), NTP client, NTP client/server mode, NTP server, NTP synchronization, syslog server

Command References

Tables 13-8 and 13-9 list configuration and verification commands used in this chapter. As an easy review exercise, cover the left column in a table, read the right column, and try to recall the command without looking. Then repeat the exercise, covering the right column, and try to recall what the command does.

Table 13-8   Configuration Command Reference

Command	Description
[no] logging console	Global command that enables (or disables with the **no** option) logging to the console device.
[no] logging monitor	Global command that enables (or disables with the **no** option) logging to users connected to the device with SSH or Telnet.
[no] logging buffered	Global command that enables (or disables with the **no** option) logging to an internal buffer.
logging [host] *ip-address* | *hostname*	Global command that enables logging to a syslog server.
logging console *level-name* | *level-number*	Global command that sets the log message level for console log messages.
logging monitor *level-name* | *level-number*	Global command that sets the log message level for log messages sent to SSH and Telnet users.

Command	Description
logging buffered *level-name* | *level-number*	Global command that sets the log message level for buffered log messages displayed later by the **show logging** command.
logging trap *level-name* | *level-number*	Global command that sets the log message level for messages sent to syslog servers.
[no] service sequence-numbers	Global command to enable or disable (with the **no** option) the use of sequence numbers in log messages.
clock timezone *name +/– hours-offset [minutes-offset]*	Global command that names a time zone and defines the +/– offset versus UTC.
clock summertime *name* recurring	Global command that names a daylight savings time for a time zone and tells IOS to adjust the clock automatically.
ntp server *address | hostname*	Global command that configures the device as an NTP client by referring to the address or name of an NTP server.
ntp master *stratum-level*	Global command that configures the device as an NTP server and assigns its local clock stratum level.
ntp source *name/number*	Global command that tells NTP to use the listed interface (by name/number) for the source IP address for NTP messages.
interface loopback *number*	Global command that, at first use, creates a loopback interface. At all uses, it also moves the user into interface configuration mode for that interface.
[no] cdp run	Global command that enables and disables (with the **no** option) CDP for the entire switch or router.
[no] cdp enable	Interface subcommand to enable and disable (with the **no** option) CDP for a particular interface.
cdp timer *seconds*	Global command that changes the CDP send timer (the frequency at which CDP sends messages).
cdp holdtime *seconds*	Global command that changes how long CDP waits since the last received message from a neighbor before believing the neighbor has failed, removing the neighbor's information from the CDP table.
[no] lldp run	Global command to enable and disable (with the **no** option) LLDP for the entire switch or router.
[no] lldp transmit	Interface subcommand to enable and disable (with the **no** option) the transmission of LLDP messages on the interface.
[no] lldp receive	Interface subcommand to enable and disable (with the **no** option) the processing of received LLDP messages on the interface.
lldp timer *seconds*	Global command that changes the LLDP send timer (the frequency at which LLDP sends messages).
lldp holdtime *seconds*	Global command that changes how long LLDP waits since the last received message from a neighbor before believing the neighbor has failed, removing the neighbor's information from the LLDP table.

13

Table 13-9 Chapter 13 EXEC Command Reference

Command	Description
show logging	Lists the current logging configuration and lists buffered log messages at the end
terminal monitor terminal no monitor	For a user (SSH or Telnet) session, toggles on (**terminal monitor**) or off (**terminal no monitor**) the receipt of log messages, for that one session, if **logging monitor** is also configured
[no] debug {*various*}	EXEC command to enable or disable (with the **no** option) one of a multitude of debug options
show clock	Lists the time of day and the date per the local device
show ntp associations	Shows all NTP clients and servers with which the local device is attempting to synchronize with NTP
show ntp status	Shows current NTP client status in detail
show interfaces loopback *number*	Shows the current status of the listed loopback interface
show cdp | lldp neighbors [*type number*]	Lists one summary line of information about each neighbor; optionally, lists neighbors off the listed interface
show cdp | lldp neighbors detail	Lists one large set of information (approximately 15 lines) for every neighbor
show cdp | lldp entry *name*	Displays the same information as **show cdp|lldp neighbors detail** but only for the named neighbor
show cdp | lldp	States whether CDP or LLDP is enabled globally and lists the default update and holdtime timers
show cdp | lldp interface [*type number*]	States whether CDP or LDP is enabled on each interface or a single interface if the interface is listed
show cdp | lldp traffic	Displays global statistics for the number of CDP or LDP advertisements sent and received

CHAPTER 14

Network Address Translation

This chapter covers the following exam topics:

1.0 Network Fundamentals

　　1.7 Describe private IPv4 addressing

4.0 IP Services

　　4.1 Configure and verify inside source NAT using static and pools

Most enterprises and small office/home office (SOHO) networks use Network Address Translation (NAT). NAT helped solve a big problem with IPv4: the IPv4 address space would have been completely assigned by the mid-1990s without it. If that had happened, Internet growth would have slowed significantly. NAT helped delay the exhaustion of the IPv4 public address space by several decades, giving time for the long-term solution—IPv6—to mature.

This chapter breaks the topics into two major sections. The first explains the basic concept behind NAT, how several variations of NAT work, and how the Port Address Translation (PAT) variation conserves the IPv4 address space. The final section shows how to configure NAT from the Cisco IOS Software command-line interface (CLI) and how to troubleshoot NAT.

"Do I Know This Already?" Quiz

Take the quiz (either here or use the PTP software) if you want to use the score to help you decide how much time to spend on this chapter. The letter answers are listed at the bottom of the page following the quiz. Appendix C, found both at the end of the book as well as on the companion website, includes both the answers and explanations. You can also find both answers and explanations in the PTP testing software.

Table 14-1 "Do I Know This Already?" Foundation Topics Section-to-Question Mapping

Foundation Topics Section	Questions
Network Address Translation Concepts	1–3
NAT Configuration and Troubleshooting	4–6

　1. Which of the following are not private addresses according to RFC 1918? (Choose two answers.)

　　a. 172.31.1.1

　　b. 172.33.1.1

　　c. 10.255.1.1

    d. 10.1.255.1

    e. 191.168.1.1

2. What causes the NAT router to create NAT table entries when using static NAT for inside addresses only?

    a. The first packet from the inside network to the outside network

    b. The first packet from the outside network to the inside network

    c. Configuration using the **ip nat inside source** command

    d. Configuration using the **ip nat outside source** command

3. What causes the NAT router to create NAT table entries when using dynamic NAT for inside addresses only?

    a. The first packet from the inside network to the outside network

    b. The first packet from the outside network to the inside network

    c. Configuration using the **ip nat inside source** command

    d. Configuration using the **ip nat outside source** command

4. An enterprise uses inside source NAT for packets that flow into the Internet, with a working NAT configuration that includes the command **ip nat inside source list alice pool barney**. Which statements must be true for the router to apply NAT to a packet entering an inside interface?

    a. ACL alice must match the packet with a permit action.

    b. ACL alice must match the packet with a deny action.

    c. Pool barney must include the packet's source IP address.

    d. Pool barney must include the packet's destination IP address.

5. An engineer created the incomplete configuration shown here. The configuration should achieve a typical router source NAT function at a router that connects an enterprise to the Internet and uses a single public IP address. Which answers list commands or parameters that would help complete the configuration? (Choose two answers.)

```
interface GigabitEthernet0/0/0
 description LAN interface (private)
 ip address 10.1.1.1 255.255.255.0
 ip nat inside
interface GigabitEthernet0/0/1
 description WAN interface (public)
 ip address 200.1.1.249 255.255.255.252
ip nat inside source list 1 interface GigabitEthernet0/0/1
access-list 1 permit 10.1.1.0 0.0.0.255
```

    a. The **ip nat outside** command

    b. The **ip nat pat** command

    c. The **overload** keyword

    d. The **ip nat pool** command

    e. The **inside** keyword

6. Examine the following **show** command output on a router configured for dynamic NAT:

```
-- Inside Source
access-list 1 pool fred refcount 2288
 pool fred: netmask 255.255.255.240
 start 200.1.1.1 end 200.1.1.7
 type generic, total addresses 7, allocated 7 (100%), misses 965
```

Users are complaining about not being able to reach the Internet. Which of the following is the most likely cause?

a. The problem is not related to NAT, based on the information in the command output.

b. The NAT pool does not have enough entries to satisfy all requests.

c. Standard ACL 1 cannot be used; an extended ACL must be used.

d. The command output does not supply enough information to identify the problem.

Foundation Topics

Network Address Translation Concepts

The original design for the Internet required every organization to ask for and receive one or more registered public classful IPv4 network numbers. However, the world would have run out of unique public IPv4 addresses decades ago following that plan. Network Address Translation (NAT) served as part of the short-term solution, delaying the day when the world ran out of public IPv4 addresses.

IPv4 Address Conservation with NAT

Figure 14-1 shows some examples of using private and public addresses in enterprises today and how they reduce the use of public IPv4 addresses. Each company uses NAT on a router connected to the Internet. With the original plan, both companies would have needed a public Class B IPv4 network containing 65,536 public IPv4 addresses each. Instead, one company uses a small Classless InterDomain Routing (**CIDR**) block of 16 public addresses, while the other uses only 8. For the addresses used internally by the computers, per their settings, both companies use any **private IP networks** they choose, making the most common choice: to use Class A private network 10.0.0.0.

The design uses NAT but relies on private networks and public CIDR blocks. To review from Part IV of the Volume 1 book, RFC 1918 reserves a set of networks never to be used as registered public IP networks. Companies and households can use these networks internally, as shown in Figure 14-1. (Much of the rest of the chapter explains how and why.) Table 14-2 shows the private address space.

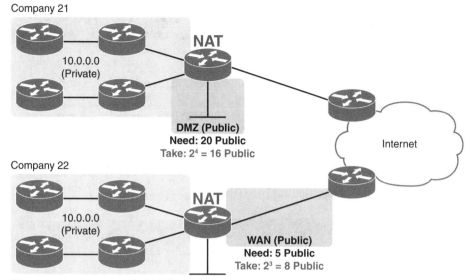

Figure 14-1   *NAT with Small CIDR Blocks Saving IPv4 Addresses*

Table 14-2   RFC 1918 Private Address Space

Range of IP Addresses	Network(s)	Class of Networks	Number of Networks
10.0.0.0 to 10.255.255.255	10.0.0.0	A	1
172.16.0.0 to 172.31.255.255	172.16.0.0 – 172.31.0.0	B	16
192.168.0.0 to 192.168.255.255	192.168.0.0 – 192.168.255.0	C	256

Any organization can use these network numbers. However, no organization can advertise these networks using a routing protocol on the Internet, and routers in the Internet will not attempt to forward packets sent to private addresses.

The short-term public address conservation plan combines NAT with CIDR blocks of public addresses, as shown in Figure 14-1. These *CIDR blocks* act like a public IP network, giving each company a consecutive set of public IPv4 addresses but allowing sizes of any power of 2. Internet routers will advertise routes for these public addresses so that the routers will forward those packets to the NAT router.

Comparing private and public addresses used with NAT, a company needs enough private IP addresses so all devices within the company have a unique address. However, companies require only a small set of public addresses when using NAT because the hosts inside the enterprise will share the public IP addresses. Table 14-3 summarizes these critical features that have helped extend the life of IPv4 by decades.

Table 14-3 Three Important Functions That Extended the Life of IPv4

Feature	RFC(s)	Main Benefits
CIDR*	4632	Assign more-specific public IPv4 address blocks to companies than Class A, B, and C networks. Aggregate routes to public IPv4 addresses based on a worldwide address allocation plan.
NAT*	3022	Enable approximately 65,000 TCP/UDP sessions to be supported by a single public IPv4 address.
Private Networks	1918	Enable the use of NAT for enterprise Internet connections, with private addresses used inside the enterprise.

*CIDR and NAT may be better known for their original RFCs (1518, 1519 for CIDR; 1631 for NAT).

> **NOTE** This chapter shows NAT implemented on routers, but firewalls also support NAT.

Inside Source NAT

The NAT feature of routers and firewalls includes several variations. However, the one CCNA exam topic about NAT uses the phrase **inside source NAT**, which refers to NAT as typically used at the edge of an enterprise, as shown in Figure 14-1. This next topic introduces the core concepts of inside source NAT, but be aware that all discussions in this chapter refer to only inside source NAT.

NAT, defined in RFC 3022, allows a host using a private IP address to communicate with other hosts through the Internet. NAT achieves its goal by using a valid registered public IP address to represent the private address to the rest of the Internet. The NAT function changes the private IP addresses to publicly registered IP addresses inside each IP packet, as shown in Figure 14-2.

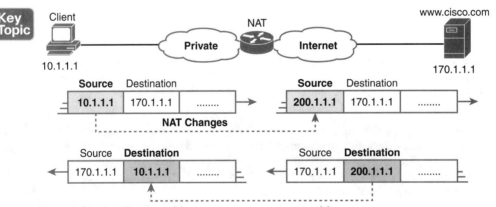

Figure 14-2 *NAT IP Address Swapping: Private Addressing*

Answers to the "Do I Know This Already?" quiz:

1 B, E **2** C **3** A **4** A **5** A, C **6** B

Notice that the router, performing NAT, changes the packet's source IP address when the packet leaves the private organization. The router performing NAT also changes the destination address in each packet returned to the private network. (Network 200.1.1.0 is a registered network in Figure 14-2.) The NAT feature, configured in the router labeled NAT, performs the translation.

The next few pages discuss three variants of inside source NAT: static NAT, dynamic NAT, and **Port Address Translation (PAT)**, also called **NAT overload**. All translate the addresses as shown in Figure 14-2; however, most IPv4 networks use PAT because it is the only variant that conserves public IP addresses.

Static NAT

Static NAT works as shown in Figure 14-2 but with a static one-to-one mapping of private and public addresses. To help you understand the implications of static NAT and to explain several key terms, Figure 14-3 shows a similar example with more information.

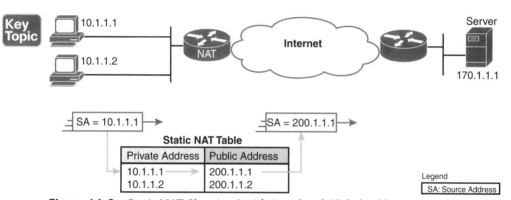

Figure 14-3 *Static NAT Showing Inside Local and Global Addresses*

First, the concepts: The company's ISP has assigned it a registered public Class C network 200.1.1.0. The settings on all the computers inside the enterprise use addresses in private Class A network 10.0.0.0. Therefore, the NAT router must make the private IP addresses in packets appear as part of network 200.1.1.0. So, the NAT router changes the source IP addresses in the packets going from left to right in the figure.

Static NAT requires the direct configuration of the NAT table entries that tell NAT the addresses to change. In Figure 14-3, inside source NAT (as mentioned in the exam topics) relies on global command **ip nat inside source static 10.1.1.1 200.1.1.1** to add the first table entry. You could then add other static NAT table entries up to the number of available public addresses.

With a one-to-one mapping between private and public addresses, static NAT does not reduce the use of public IP addresses. In Figure 14-3, because the enterprise has a single registered Class C network, it can support at most 254 private IP addresses with NAT, with the usual two reserved numbers (the network number and network broadcast address).

Inside Local and Inside Global Addresses

The NAT table depicted in Figure 14-3 uses the terms *private address* and *public address* for clarity. However, Cisco commands use the terms **inside local** for the private addresses and **inside global** for the public addresses.

To better understand NAT terminology, first think of any network diagram that includes NAT. Separate it into two parts, on either side of the router performing NAT. One side contains the enterprise's network (or your home network with a SOHO router). The other side contains the Internet. In Cisco NAT terminology, *inside* refers to the enterprise side, and *outside* refers to the Internet side.

Two other terms refer to the address pair in a NAT table entry. For instance, Figures 14-2 and 14-3 show a host with private address 10.1.1.1. Those figures also show NAT translating that address to public address 200.1.1.1. So NAT on Cisco routers refers to these associated addresses as follows:

Inside local address: The address which represents the inside host in packets that travel through the enterprise (local) network. You find this address in the host's settings. It is typically a private IP address when using inside source NAT. For example, address 10.1.1.1 in Figure 14-4.

Inside global address: The address represents the inside host in packets traveling over the global Internet. You do not find this address in a host's settings but rather in the NAT table. It is typically a public IP address, so Internet routers can forward the packet. For example, 200.1.1.1 in Figure 14-4.

Figure 14-4 repeats the same example as Figure 14-3, with some of the terminology shown.

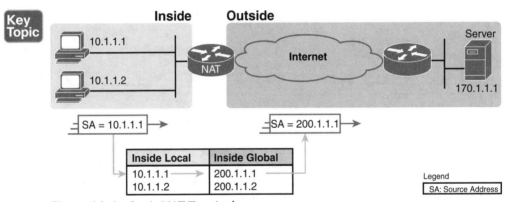

Figure 14-4 *Static NAT Terminology*

Dynamic NAT

Dynamic NAT is similar to static NAT but with one crucial difference. Like static NAT, the NAT router creates a one-to-one mapping between an inside local and inside global address and changes the IP addresses in packets as they exit and enter the inside network. Because of the one-to-one mappings, it also does not conserve public IPv4 addresses. But the name *dynamic NAT* gives away the big difference: it dynamically creates NAT table entries. That dynamic behavior also adds some protection against attackers in the Internet.

Dynamic NAT sets up a pool of possible inside global addresses and defines matching criteria to determine which inside local IP addresses should be translated with NAT. For example, in Figure 14-5, the NAT router has a pool of five inside global IP addresses: 200.1.1.1 through 200.1.1.5. Dynamic NAT also needs matching logic to initiate the translation of any inside local addresses that start with 10.1.1.

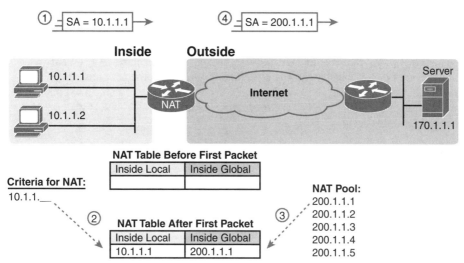

Figure 14-5 *Dynamic NAT*

The numbers 1, 2, 3, and 4 in the figure refer to the following sequence of events:

1. Host 10.1.1.1 sends its first packet to the server at 170.1.1.1.

2. As the packet enters the NAT router, the router matches packets with source addresses (inside local addresses) that begin with 10.1.1. Matched packets trigger a new NAT table entry as needed. In this case, a packet sourced from 10.1.1.1 causes a new NAT table entry.

3. To create the new NAT table entry, the NAT router must allocate an IP address from the valid inside global address pool. It picks the first one available (200.1.1.1, in this case) and adds it to the NAT table to complete the entry.

4. The NAT router translates the source IP address and forwards the packet.

The dynamic entry stays in the table as long as continuing packets match the NAT table entry. If no packets need a NAT table entry for a configured timeout value, the router will remove the dynamic entry. You can also manually clear the dynamic entries from the table using the **clear ip nat translation *** command.

On an important security note, dynamic NAT allows new NAT table entries if initiated by inside hosts only. Dynamic NAT triggers new NAT table entries only for packets entering inside interfaces. For example, a PC user in the inside network can connect to a website in the Internet. The first packet it sends to the web server in the Internet enters the NAT router's inside interface, triggering a new entry. However, a PC user in the Internet cannot connect to a web server in the inside network. The first packet it sends would enter the outside interface and not trigger a new NAT table entry. That simple difference with dynamic NAT provides a primary security feature of only allowing new connections initiated by inside users.

Note that with predefined NAT table entries, static NAT has no restrictions for triggering new NAT table entries: a static NAT table entry would allow connections initiated by Internet users. So, engineers often use static NAT when that is the goal—to allow new connections from hosts in the Internet to a server inside the company.

By design, the NAT pool typically contains fewer addresses than the total number of hosts inside the enterprise. The router allocates addresses from the pool until none remain. If a new packet arrives, triggering the need for a new NAT table entry, but the pool has no unused addresses, the router simply discards the packet. The user must try again until a NAT entry times out, at which point the NAT function works for the next host that sends a packet. Essentially, the inside global address pool needs to be as large as the maximum number of concurrent hosts that need to use the Internet simultaneously—unless you use PAT, as explained in the next section.

Overloading NAT with Port Address Translation

Static NAT and dynamic NAT use one-to-one mappings between inside local and inside global addresses, so they do not reduce the number of public IPv4 addresses an enterprise needs. The NAT Overload feature, also called Port Address Translation (PAT), solves this problem. Overloading uses a one-to-many mapping, allowing NAT to scale to support many inside hosts with only a few public IP addresses.

PAT uses the transport layer protocols as a means to share public addresses. To see how, first consider the idea of three separate TCP connections to a web server, from three different hosts, as shown in Figure 14-6.

Figure 14-6 *Three TCP Connections from Three PCs*

Next, compare those three TCP connections in Figure 14-6 to three similar ones, now with all three TCP connections from one client, as shown in Figure 14-7. The server does realize a difference because the server sees the IP address and TCP port number used by the clients in both figures. However, the server does not care whether the TCP connections come from different hosts or the same host; the server just sends and receives data over each connection.

Figure 14-7 *Three TCP Connections from One PC*

NAT takes advantage of the fact that, from a transport layer perspective, the server doesn't care whether it has one connection each to three different hosts or three connections to a single host IP address. PAT translates the IP address and the port number when necessary, making what looks like many TCP or UDP flows from different hosts (as in Figure 14-6) look like the same number of flows from one host (as in Figure 14-7). Figure 14-8 outlines the logic, with three TCP connections from three different hosts, with the NAT router making them appear as three TCP connections from a single host.

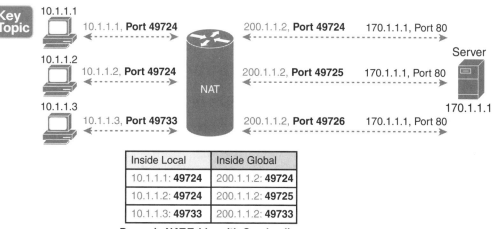

Figure 14-8   *NAT Overload (PAT)*

Work through the specifics of the NAT table in Figure 14-8. The inside global column lists a single inside global (public) IP address. Look at the specific port numbers on the inside local side of the table: the TCP connections from 10.1.1.1 and 10.1.1.2 both use TCP ports 49,724. On those same table entries on the inside global side, NAT had to change one of the port numbers to make each address/port combination unique. For the third TCP connection, the port number used by the host (49,733) is not used with NAT inside global address 200.1.1.1, so the NAT router did not need to change the port number.

More generally, PAT works like dynamic NAT, but it uses both address and port numbers in the translation. When PAT creates the dynamic mapping, it notes the incoming packet's source IP address and source transport port for the inside local entry in the table. For a new dynamic table entry, it selects an inside global IP address from the pool and then a port number not already in use with the inside global address.

The NAT router keeps a NAT table entry for every unique combination of inside local IP address and port associated with an inside global address and a unique port. In addition, because the port number field has 16 bits, NAT overload can use 216 port numbers with each inside global (public) address. PAT scales well without needing many registered IP addresses—in many cases, requiring only one inside global IP address.

Real networks use PAT far more than the others of the three inside source NAT types discussed here. Static NAT and Dynamic NAT have their uses, but the fact that they do not reduce public IP address consumption makes them a poor option for the primary NAT feature between an enterprise and the Internet.

NAT Configuration and Troubleshooting

The sections that follow describe how to configure the three most common variations of NAT: static NAT, dynamic NAT, and PAT, along with the **show** and **debug** commands used to troubleshoot NAT.

Static NAT Configuration

Static NAT configuration requires only a few configuration steps. The configuration must include each static mapping between an inside local (private) address and an inside global (public) address. Additionally, NAT must be enabled on the necessary interfaces, identifying the interface as inside or outside. The specific steps are as follows:

Step 1. Use the **ip nat inside** command in interface configuration mode to configure interfaces in the inside part of the NAT design.

Step 2. Use the **ip nat outside** command in interface configuration mode to configure interfaces in the outside part of the NAT design.

Step 3. Use the **ip address** *address mask* command in interface configuration mode to configure a subnet that includes the inside global (public) addresses intended for the design.

Step 4. Use the **ip nat inside source static** *inside-local inside-global* command in global configuration mode to configure the static mappings.

The upcoming examples use the familiar network design and addresses in Figure 14-9. You can see that Certskills has obtained Class C network 200.1.1.0 as a registered network number. That entire network, with mask 255.255.255.0, is configured on the Internet access link between Certskills and the Internet. The two routers on the link use two of the addresses, leaving 252 addresses for use by NAT. The NAT table shows two of those available addresses in static entries.

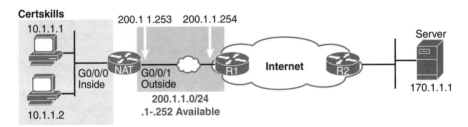

Figure 14-9 *Sample Network for NAT Examples, with Public Class C 200.1.1.0/24*

Example 14-1 lists the NAT configuration, using 200.1.1.1 and 200.1.1.2 for the two static NAT mappings.

Example 14-1 *Static NAT Configuration*

```
NAT# show running-config
!
! Lines omitted for brevity
!
interface GigabitEthernet0/0/0
```

```
 ip address 10.1.1.3 255.255.255.0
 ip nat inside
!
interface GigabitEthernet0/0/1
 ip address 200.1.1.253 255.255.255.0
 ip nat outside
!
ip nat inside source static 10.1.1.2 200.1.1.2
ip nat inside source static 10.1.1.1 200.1.1.1
```

To further explore the configuration, these steps analyze the configuration using the same numbered steps as the configuration checklist just before the example:

1. Interface G0/0/0, connected to the enterprise network, shows an **ip nat inside** command, enabling NAT and identifying it as an inside interface.

2. Interface G0/0/1, connected to the enterprise network, shows an **ip nat outside** command, enabling NAT and identifying it as an outside interface.

3. Interface G0/0/1 uses command **ip address 200.1.1.251 255.255.255.0**, defining connecting subnet 200.1.1.0/24. Unused addresses in this subnet will be available for static mappings.

4. The **ip nat inside source static** global configuration command creates the static mappings, referring to the addresses of the two inside hosts and two addresses in subnet 200.1.1.0/24.

Example 14-2 provides a couple of **show** commands listing essential NAT information. The **show ip nat translations** command lists the two static NAT entries created in the configuration. It shows the headings as Cisco terms inside local (with private addresses listed) and inside global (with public addresses listed). The **show ip nat statistics** command mentions the number of currently active translation table entries (with static NAT) that value matches the number of configured NAT table entries. The statistics also include the number of hits, which increments for every packet NAT must translate addresses.

Example 14-2 *Static NAT Verification*

```
NAT# show ip nat translations
Pro Inside global     Inside local      Outside local      Outside global
--- 200.1.1.1         10.1.1.1          ---                ---
--- 200.1.1.2         10.1.1.2          ---                ---

NAT# show ip nat statistics
Total active translations: 2 (2 static, 0 dynamic; 0 extended)
Outside interfaces:
  GigabitEthernet0/0/1
Inside interfaces:
  GigabitEthernet0/0/0
Hits: 100 Misses: 0
Expired translations: 0
Dynamic mappings:
```

Before leaving static NAT, again consider the public addresses used by NAT. A typical NAT design relies on a subnet connected to the NAT router, with that connected subnet including all the inside global (public) addresses needed by NAT.

The example in this section shows a classic case of using the entire public address block, in this case, 200.1.1.0/24, on the Internet access link between the enterprise and the ISP. The routers on the link use addresses 200.1.1.253 and 200.1.1.254. The **ip address 200.1.1.253 255.255.255.0** command on router R1 in the enterprise results in a connected route for subnet 200.1.1.0/24. That subnet includes the two reserved values (200.1.1.0 and 200.1.1.255) and the two interface addresses (200.1.1.253 and 200.1.1.254). That leaves addresses 200.1.1.1–200.1.1.252 available for use by NAT on the router.

So, the configuration requires a familiar **ip address** interface subcommand, but the address planning requires some thought, with configuration to create a connected route that includes all the public addresses needed for NAT. Any interface on the NAT router will work for this purpose, with the link to the ISP being the most common. The NAT router can also use a loopback interface.

Dynamic NAT Configuration

Dynamic NAT configuration has a few similarities with static NAT configuration. You configure the inside and outside interfaces in the same way. You also need to configure a router interface with an IP address and mask so the connected subnet contains all the inside global addresses planned for the design. Unsurprisingly, the difference is that dynamic NAT requires no preconfigured static NAT table entries.

Instead, dynamic NAT monitors packets entering inside interfaces, matching the packets' source addresses with an access control list (ACL). Incoming packets matching an ACL with a permit action trigger the NAT process. Once triggered, the NAT router will create a new NAT table entry if needed. Additionally, the dynamic NAT configuration includes some inside global (public) addresses in the form of a NAT pool. The specific steps are as follows:

Step 1. Use the **ip nat inside** command in interface configuration mode to configure interfaces in the inside part of the NAT design (just like with static NAT).

Step 2. Use the **ip nat outside** command in interface configuration mode to configure interfaces in the outside part of the NAT design (just like with static NAT).

Step 3. Use the **ip address** *address mask* command in interface configuration mode to configure a subnet that includes the inside global (public) addresses intended for the design.

Step 4. Configure an ACL that matches, with a permit action, the packets entering inside interfaces for which the router should apply NAT.

Step 5. Use the **ip nat pool** *name first-address last-address* {**netmask** *subnet-mask* | **prefix-length** *length*} command in global configuration mode to configure the pool of public registered IP addresses.

Step 6. Use the **ip nat inside source list** *acl-number* **pool** *pool-name* command in global configuration mode to enable dynamic NAT. Note the command references the ACL and pool per the previous steps.

The following example shows a sample dynamic NAT configuration using the same network topology as the previous example (see Figure 14-9). The two inside local addresses—10.1.1.1 and 10.1.1.2—need translation. Unlike the previous static NAT example, however, the configuration in Example 14-3 places the public IP addresses (200.1.1.1 and 200.1.1.2) into a pool of dynamically assignable inside global addresses.

Example 14-3 *Dynamic NAT Configuration*

```
NAT# show running-config
!
! Lines omitted for brevity
!
interface GigabitEthernet0/0/0
 ip address 10.1.1.3 255.255.255.0
 ip nat inside
!
interface GigabitEthernet0/0/1
 ip address 200.1.1.253 255.255.255.0
 ip nat outside
!
ip nat pool fred 200.1.1.1 200.1.1.2 netmask 255.255.255.252
ip nat inside source list 1 pool fred
!
access-list 1 permit 10.1.1.2
access-list 1 permit 10.1.1.1
```

Dynamic NAT configures the public (global) addresses pool with the **ip nat pool** command listing the first and last numbers in an inclusive range of inside global addresses. For example, if the pool needed 10 addresses, the command might have listed 200.1.1.1 and 200.1.1.10, which means that NAT can use 200.1.1.1 through 200.1.1.10.

Dynamic NAT also performs a verification check on the **ip nat pool** command with the required **netmask** parameter. The addresses in the pool should be in the same subnet, assuming you applied the **netmask** (or **prefix-length**) parameter as a subnet mask. If the addresses reside in different subnets per that math, IOS rejects the **ip nat pool** command. For example, as configured in Example 14-3, IOS approves the values per this logic:

- 200.1.1.1 with mask 255.255.255.252 implies subnet 200.1.1.0, broadcast address 200.1.1.3.

- 200.1.1.2 with mask 255.255.255.252 implies subnet 200.1.1.0, broadcast address 200.1.1.3.

If the example had used addresses 200.1.1.1 and 200.1.1.6, with mask 255.255.255.252, IOS would reject that command per this logic:

- 200.1.1.1 with mask 255.255.255.252 implies subnet 200.1.1.0, broadcast address 200.1.1.3.

- 200.1.1.6 with mask 255.255.255.252 implies subnet 200.1.1.4, broadcast address 200.1.1.7.

14

Dynamic NAT also needs one **ip nat inside source** global command. The command refers to the name of the NAT pool it wants to use for inside global addresses—in this case, fred. It also refers to an IP ACL, which defines the matching logic for inside local IP addresses. So, the logic for the **ip nat inside source list 1 pool fred** command in this example is as follows:

Create NAT table entries that map between hosts matched by ACL 1, for packets entering any inside interface, allocating an inside global address from the pool called fred.

Dynamic NAT Verification

Example 14-4 shows the NAT status on the NAT router before creating any dynamic NAT table entries, with Example 14-5 showing the same commands after user traffic triggered dynamic NAT table entries. In Example 14-4, the **show ip nat translations** command output shows a blank line, meaning no NAT table entries exist. The **show ip nat statistics** command shows a counter of the number of dynamic NAT table entries, showing zero active translations.

Example 14-4 *Dynamic NAT Verifications Before Generating Traffic*

```
! The next command lists one empty line because NAT has not yet added table entries.
NAT# show ip nat translations

NAT# show ip nat statistics
Total active translations: 0 (0 static, 0 dynamic; 0 extended)
Peak translations: 8, occurred 00:02:44 ago
Outside interfaces:
  GigabitEthernet0/0/1
Inside interfaces:
  GigabitEthernet0/0/0
Hits: 0 Misses: 0
CEF Translated packets: 0, CEF Punted packets: 0
Expired translations: 0
Dynamic mappings:
-- Inside Source
[id 1] access-list 1 pool fred refcount 0
 pool fred: netmask 255.255.255.252
    start 200.1.1.1 end 200.1.1.2
    type generic, total addresses 2, allocated 0 (0%), misses 0

Total doors: 0
Appl doors: 0
Normal doors: 0
Queued Packets: 0
```

Before leaving Example 14-4, look closely at the **show ip nat statistics** command at the end of the example. It lists some fascinating troubleshooting information with two different counters labeled "Misses," as highlighted in the example. The first occurrence of this counter, around the midpoint of the command's output, counts the number of times a new packet comes along, needing a NAT entry, but no matching entry exists. At that point, dynamic NAT reacts and builds an entry.

At the end of the command output, the second Misses counter relates to the pool. This counter increments only when dynamic NAT tries to allocate a new NAT table entry, looks for an unused address from the pool, but finds no available addresses. In that case, NAT cannot add the table entry, so the packet cannot be translated—probably resulting in an end user not getting to the application.

Next, Example 14-5 updates the output of both commands from Example 14-4, this time after the user of the host at 10.1.1.1 telnets to host 170.1.1.1.

Example 14-5 *Dynamic NAT Verifications After Generating Traffic*

```
NAT# show ip nat translations
Pro Inside global      Inside local      Outside local      Outside global
--- 200.1.1.1          10.1.1.1          ---                ---


NAT# show ip nat statistics
Total active translations: 1 (0 static, 1 dynamic; 0 extended)
Peak translations: 11, occurred 00:04:32 ago
Outside interfaces:
  GigabitEthernet0/0/1
Inside interfaces:
  GigabitEthernet0/0/0
Hits: 69 Misses: 1
Expired translations: 0
Dynamic mappings:
-- Inside Source
access-list 1 pool fred refcount 1
[eml fred: netmask 255.255.255.252
    start 200.1.1.1 end 200.1.1.2
    type generic, total addresses 2, allocated 1 (50%), misses 0
```

The example begins with host 10.1.1.1 telnetting to 170.1.1.1 (not shown), with the NAT router creating a NAT entry. The NAT table shows a single entry, mapping 10.1.1.1 to 200.1.1.1. And the first line in the output of the **show ip nat statistics** command lists a counter for 1 active translation, as shown in the NAT table at the top of the example.

Take an extra moment to consider the highlighted line, where the **show ip nat statistics** command lists 1 miss and 69 hits. The first miss counter, now at 1, means that one packet arrived that needed NAT, but there was no NAT table entry. NAT reacted and added a NAT table entry, so the hit counter of 69 means that the following 69 packets used the newly added NAT table entry.

At the bottom of the example, the second misses counter remains at 0. The counter did not increment because the NAT pool had enough inside global IP addresses to allocate the new NAT table entry. Also, note that the last line lists statistics on the number of pool members allocated (1) and the percentage of the pool currently in use (50%).

The dynamic NAT table entries time out after a period of inactivity, releasing the inside global addresses for future use. Example 14-6 shows a sequence in which two different hosts use inside global address 200.1.1.1. Host 10.1.1.1 uses inside global address 200.1.1.1 at the beginning of the example. Then, instead of just waiting on the NAT entry to time out, the example clears the NAT table entry with the **clear ip nat translation** * command. At that point, the user at 10.1.1.2 telnets to 170.1.1.1, and the new NAT table entry appears, using the same 200.1.1.1 inside global address.

Example 14-6 *Example of Reuse of a Dynamic Inside Global IP Address*

```
! Host 10.1.1.1 currently uses inside global 200.1.1.1
NAT# show ip nat translations
Pro Inside global      Inside local      Outside local      Outside global
--- 200.1.1.1          10.1.1.1          ---                ---
NAT# clear ip nat translation *

!
! telnet from 10.1.1.2 to 170.1.1.1 happened next; not shown
!
! Now host 10.1.1.2 uses inside global 200.1.1.1

NAT# show ip nat translations
Pro Inside global      Inside local      Outside local      Outside global
--- 200.1.1.1          10.1.1.2          ---                ---
!
! Telnet from 10.1.1.1 to 170.1.1.1 happened next; not shown
!
NAT# debug ip nat
IP NAT debugging is on

Oct 20 19:23:03.263: NAT*: s=10.1.1.1->200.1.1.2, d=170.1.1.1 [348]
Oct 20 19:23:03.267: NAT*: s=170.1.1.1, d=200.1.1.2->10.1.1.1 [348]
Oct 20 19:23:03.464: NAT*: s=10.1.1.1->200.1.1.2, d=170.1.1.1 [349]
Oct 20 19:23:03.568: NAT*: s=170.1.1.1, d=200.1.1.2->10.1.1.1 [349]
```

Finally, at the end of Example 14-6, you see that host 10.1.1.1 has telnetted to another host in the Internet, plus the **debug ip nat** command output. This **debug** command causes the router to issue a message every time a packet has its address translated for NAT. You generate the output results by entering a few lines from the Telnet connection from 10.1.1.1 to 170.1.1.1. The debug output tells you that host 10.1.1.1 uses inside global address 200.1.1.2 for this new connection.

NAT Overload (PAT) Configuration

The static and dynamic NAT configurations matter, but this section's NAT overload (PAT) configuration matters more. PAT allows NAT to support many inside local IP addresses with only one or a few inside global IP addresses. By translating the inside local address and port number to a single inside global address but with a unique port number, NAT can support many (over 65,000) concurrent TCP and UDP flows with only one public global address.

PAT configuration includes two variations:

- One with a pool of several addresses

- One with a single inside global address from an existing interface

PAT configuration that uses a pool of addresses looks exactly like dynamic NAT, except the **ip nat inside source list** global command has an **overload** keyword added to the end. Summarizing the configuration differences between PAT, when using a pool of addresses, and dynamic NAT:

Use the same steps for configuring dynamic NAT, as outlined in the previous section, but include the **overload** keyword at the end of the **ip nat inside source list** global command.

Alternatively, PAT can use a single inside global address effectively. Your router at home likely does that. It leases a single public IP address from your ISP and performs NAT using it as the inside global (public) address. An enterprise router can do the same and use a public IP address on an interface, typically the interface connecting the router to the Internet. With that single address, NAT can support over 65,000 concurrent flows. If each computer averaged 10 concurrent flows, one public IP address would support around 6500 inside hosts.

The following checklist details the configuration when using an interface IP address as the sole inside global IP address:

Step 1. As with dynamic and static NAT, configure the **ip nat inside** interface subcommand to identify inside interfaces.

Step 2. As with dynamic and static NAT, configure the **ip nat outside** interface subcommand to identify outside interfaces.

Step 3. As with dynamic and static NAT, use the **ip address** *address mask* command in interface configuration mode to configure a subnet that includes the inside global (public) addresses intended for the design.

Step 4. As with dynamic NAT, configure an ACL that matches the packets entering inside interfaces.

Step 5. Configure the **ip nat inside source list** *acl-number* **interface** *type/number* **overload** global configuration command, referring to the ACL from the previous step and to the interface whose connected subnet includes the NAT inside global addresses used for translations.

The vital difference between dynamic NAT versus PAT configuration comes from the use of the **overload** keyword. Step 5 notes the PAT version of the **ip nat inside source** command, which ends with **overload**. Dynamic NAT (without PAT) omits the **overload** keyword.

The following example demonstrates PAT configuration using a single interface IP address. Figure 14-10 shows the same familiar network with a few changes: CIDR block 200.1.1.248/30 instead of Class C network 200.1.1.0. The CIDR block has two usable addresses: 200.1.1.249 and 200.1.1.250. The NAT feature on the Certskills router translates all NAT addresses to its interface address: 200.1.1.249.

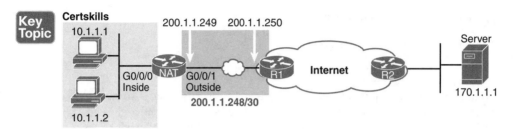

NAT Table (Overload)

Inside Local	Inside Global
10.1.1.1: 49712	200.1.1.249: 49712
10.1.1.2: 49713	200.1.1.249: 49713
10.1.2.2: 49913	200.1.1.249: 49913

Figure 14-10 *PAT Example Using an Interface Inside Global Address*

In Example 14-7, which shows the NAT overload configuration, NAT translates using inside global address 200.1.1.249 only, so the NAT pool is not required.

Example 14-7 *NAT Overload Configuration*

```
NAT# show running-config
!
! Lines Omitted for Brevity
!
interface GigabitEthernet0/0/0
 ip address 10.1.1.3 255.255.255.0
 ip nat inside
!
interface GigabitEthernet0/0/1
 ip address 200.1.1.249 255.255.255.252
 ip nat outside
!
ip nat inside source list 1 interface GigabitEthernet0/0/1 overload
!
access-list 1 permit 10.1.1.2
access-list 1 permit 10.1.1.1
```

The **ip nat inside source list 1 interface gigabitethernet0/0/1 overload** command has several parameters, but if you understand the dynamic NAT configuration, the new parameters shouldn't be too hard to grasp. The **list 1** parameter means the same thing as for dynamic NAT: inside local IP addresses matching ACL 1 have their addresses translated. The **interface gigabitethernet 0/0/1** parameter indicates that the only inside global IP address available is the IP address of the NAT router's interface gigabitethernet 0/0/1. Finally, the **overload** parameter enables NAT overload (PAT). Without this parameter, the router does not perform overload, just dynamic NAT.

Example 14-8 shows the NAT translation table after the two hosts created a total of three TCP connections. Take some time with the output of the **show ip nat translations** command.

It shows the three dynamic entries in the table. Now the inside global and inside local columns list both an IP address and port number (with the numbers matching Figure 14-10).

Example 14-8   *NAT Overload Verification*

```
NAT# show ip nat translations
Pro  Inside global      Inside local      Outside local      Outside global
tcp  200.1.1.249:49712  10.1.1.1:49712    170.1.1.1:23       170.1.1.1:23
tcp  200.1.1.249:49713  10.1.1.2:49713    170.1.1.1:23       170.1.1.1:23
tcp  200.1.1.249:49913  10.1.1.2:49913    170.1.1.1:23       170.1.1.1:23


NAT# show ip nat statistics
Total active translations: 3 (0 static, 3 dynamic; 3 extended)
Peak translations: 12, occurred 00:01:11 ago
Outside interfaces:
  GigabitEthernet0/0/1
Inside interfaces:
  GigabitEthernet0/0/0
Hits: 103 Misses: 3
Expired translations: 0
Dynamic mappings:
-- Inside Source
access-list 1 interface GigabitEthernet0/0/1 refcount 3
```

Finally, in the output of the **show ip nat statistics** command, the hits and misses counters work as with dynamic NAT. The three misses count the first packet in each TCP connection, which triggered the creation of the NAT table entries. Later packets that arrive with a pre-existing NAT table entry cause an increment in the hits counter.

NAT Troubleshooting

The majority of NAT troubleshooting issues relate to getting the configuration correct. Inside source NAT has several configuration options—static, dynamic, and PAT—with several configuration commands for each. You should work hard at building skills with the configuration to quickly recognize configuration mistakes. The following troubleshooting checklist summarizes the most common source NAT issues, most of which relate to incorrect configuration.

- **Reversed inside and outside:** Ensure that the configuration includes the **ip nat inside** and **ip nat outside** interface subcommands and that the commands are not reversed (the **ip nat inside** command on outside interfaces, and vice versa). With source NAT, only the packets entering inside interfaces trigger new translations, so designating the correct inside interfaces is particularly important.

- **Static NAT:** Check the **ip nat inside source static** command to ensure it lists the inside local address first and the inside global IP address second.

- **Dynamic NAT (ACL):** Ensure that the ACL configured to match packets sent by the inside hosts match that host's packets before any NAT translation has occurred. For example, if an inside local address of 10.1.1.1 should be translated to 200.1.1.1, ensure that the ACL matches source address 10.1.1.1, not 200.1.1.1.

14

- **Dynamic NAT (pool):** For dynamic NAT without PAT, ensure the pool has enough IP addresses. When not using PAT, each inside host consumes one IP address from the pool. A large or growing value in the second misses counter in the **show ip nat statistics** command output can indicate this problem. Also, compare the configured pool to the list of addresses in the NAT translation table (**show ip nat translations**). Finally, if the pool is small, the problem may be that the configuration intended to use PAT and is missing the **overload** keyword (see the next item).

- **PAT:** It is easy to forget to add the **overload** option on the end of **ip nat inside source list** command. PAT configuration with a pool is identical to a valid dynamic NAT configuration, except that PAT requires the **overload** keyword. Without it, dynamic NAT works, but often with too few inside global addresses in the pool. The NAT router will not translate or forward traffic for hosts if there is no available pool IP address for their traffic, so some hosts experience an outage.

- **ACL:** As mentioned in Chapter 8, "Applied IP ACLs," you can always add a check for ACLs that cause a problem. Perhaps NAT has been configured correctly, but an ACL exists on one of the interfaces, discarding the packets. Note that the order of operations inside the router matters in this case. For packets entering an interface, IOS processes ACLs before inside source NAT. For packets exiting an interface, IOS processes any outbound ACL after translating the addresses due to inside source NAT.

- **User traffic required:** Dynamic NAT and PAT react to user traffic. If you configure NAT in a lab, NAT does not act to create translations (**show ip nat translations**) until some user traffic enters the NAT router on an inside interface, triggering NAT to do a translation. The NAT configuration can be perfect, but if no inbound traffic occurs that matches the NAT configuration, NAT does nothing.

- **IPv4 routing:** IPv4 routing could prevent packets from arriving on either side of the NAT router. Note that the routing must work for the destination IP addresses used in the packets. For instance, routers in the Internet must have routes that match the public addresses used by NAT so that packets destined to those addresses arrive at the NAT router.

Chapter Review

One key to doing well on the exams is to perform repetitive spaced review sessions. Review this chapter's material using either the tools in the book or interactive tools for the same material found on the book's companion website. Refer to the "Your Study Plan" element for more details. Table 14-4 outlines the key review elements and where you can find them. To better track your study progress, record when you completed these activities in the second column.

Table 14-4 Chapter Review Tracking

Review Element	Review Date(s)	Resource Used
Review key topics		Book, website
Review key terms		Book, website
Answer DIKTA questions		Book, PTP

Review Element	Review Date(s)	Resource Used
Review memory tables		Book, website
Review command tables		Book
Do labs		Blog
Watch video		Website

Review All the Key Topics

Table 14-5   Key Topics for Chapter 14

Key Topic Element	Description	Page Number
Table 14-2	List of private IP network numbers	301
Figure 14-2	Main concept of NAT translating private IP addresses into publicly unique global addresses	302
Figure 14-3	Static NAT showing inside local and global addresses	303
List	Terms: Inside local and inside global	304
Figure 14-4	Typical NAT network diagram with key NAT terms listed	304
Figure 14-8	Concepts behind address conservation achieved by NAT overload (PAT)	307
Paragraph	Summary of differences between dynamic NAT configuration and PAT using a pool	315
Figure 14-10	Dynamic NAT with PAT (NAT Overload) example	316

Key Terms You Should Know

CIDR, inside global, inside local, inside source NAT, NAT overload, Port Address Translation (PAT), private IP network

Command References

Tables 14-6 and 14-7 list configuration and verification commands used in this chapter. As an easy review exercise, cover the left column in a table, read the right column, and try to recall the command without looking. Then repeat the exercise, covering the right column, and try to recall what the command does.

Table 14-6   Chapter 14 Configuration Command Reference

Command	Description
ip nat {**inside** | **outside**}	Interface subcommand to enable NAT and identify whether the interface is in the inside or outside of the network
ip nat inside source {**list** {*access-list-number* | *access-list-name*}} {**interface** *type number* | **pool** *pool-name*} [**overload**]	Global command that enables NAT globally, referencing the ACL that defines which source addresses to NAT, and the interface or pool from which to find global addresses

Command	Description
ip nat pool *name start-ip end-ip* {netmask *netmask* | **prefix-length** *prefix-length*}	Global command to define a pool of NAT addresses
ip nat inside source *inside-local inside-global*	Global command that lists the inside and outside address (or an outside interface whose IP address should be used) to be paired and added to the NAT translation table

Table 14-7 Chapter 14 EXEC Command Reference

Command	Description
show ip nat statistics	Lists counters for packets and NAT table entries, as well as basic configuration information
show ip nat translations [verbose]	Displays the NAT table
clear ip nat translation {* | [inside *global-ip local-ip*] [outside *local-ip global-ip*]}	Clears all or some of the dynamic entries in the NAT table, depending on which parameters are used
clear ip nat translation *protocol* inside *global-ip global-port local-ip local-port* [outside *local-ip global-ip*]	Clears some of the dynamic entries in the NAT table, depending on which parameters are used
debug ip nat	Issues a log message describing each packet whose IP address is translated with NAT

CHAPTER 15

Quality of Service (QoS)

This chapter covers the following exam topics:

4.0 IP Services

> **4.7 Explain the forwarding per-hop behavior (PHB) for QoS such as classification, marking, queuing, congestion, policing, and shaping**

Quality of Service (QoS) refers to tools that network devices can use to manage several related characteristics of what happens to a packet while it flows through a network. Specifically, these tools manage the bandwidth made available to that type of packet, the delay the packet experiences, the jitter (variation in delay) between successive packets in the same flow, and the percentage of packet loss for packets of each class. These tools balance the tradeoffs of which types of traffic receive network resources and when, giving more preference to some traffic and less preference to others.

QoS tools define actions a device can apply to a message between the time it enters the device until it exits the device. QoS defines these actions as **per-hop behaviors (PHBs)**, which is a formal term to refer to actions other than storing and forwarding a message. These actions can delay the message, discard it, or even change header fields. The device can choose different PHBs for different kinds of messages, improving the QoS behavior for some messages, while worsening the QoS behavior for others.

This chapter works through the QoS tools listed in the single QoS exam topic: "Explain the forwarding per-hop behavior (PHB) for QoS such as classification, marking, queuing, congestion, policing, and shaping." Each topic emphasizes the problems each tool solves and how each tool manages bandwidth, delay, jitter, and loss.

"Do I Know This Already?" Quiz

Take the quiz (either here or use the PTP software) if you want to use the score to help you decide how much time to spend on this chapter. The letter answers are listed at the bottom of the page following the quiz. Appendix C, found both at the end of the book as well as on the companion website, includes both the answers and explanations. You can also find both answers and explanations in the PTP testing software.

Table 15-1 "Do I Know This Already?" Foundation Topics Section-to-Question Mapping

Foundation Topics Section	Questions
Introduction to QoS	1
Classification and Marking	2, 3
Queuing	4
Shaping and Policing	5
Congestion Avoidance	6

1. Which of the following attributes do QoS tools manage? (Choose three answers.)
   a. Bandwidth
   b. Delay
   c. Load
   d. MTU
   e. Loss

2. Which of the following QoS marking fields could remain with a packet while being sent through four different routers, over different LAN and WAN links? (Choose two answers.)
   a. CoS
   b. IPP
   c. DSCP
   d. MPLS EXP

3. Which of the following are available methods of classifying packets in DiffServ on Cisco routers? (Choose three answers.)
   a. Matching the IP DSCP field
   b. Matching the 802.1p CoS field
   c. Matching fields with an extended IP ACL
   d. Matching the SNMP Location variable

4. Which of the following behaviors are applied to a low latency queue in a Cisco router or switch? (Choose two answers.)
   a. Shaping
   b. Policing
   c. Priority scheduling
   d. Round-robin scheduling

5. Enterprise router R1 sends data over a WAN link to ISP router ISP1. R1 shapes outgoing traffic to 200 Mbps, while ISP1 polices incoming traffic at a 250-Mbps rate. For an extended period (long enough to exhaust any bursting abilities of the shaper and policer), R1 receives 300 Mbps of traffic that it routes out the link connected to ISP1. Which answers describe the most likely shaping and policing actions in this scenario? (Choose two answers.)
   a. The policer measures an incoming rate that exceeds the policing rate.
   b. The policer measures an incoming rate that does not exceed the policing rate.
   c. The shaper is not queuing packets to slow down the sending rate.
   d. The shaper is queuing packets to slow down the sending rate.

6. A queuing system has three queues serviced with round-robin scheduling and one low latency queue that holds all voice traffic. Round-robin queue 1 holds predominantly UDP traffic, while round-robin queues 2 and 3 hold predominantly TCP traffic. The packets in each queue have a variety of DSCP markings per the QoS design. In which queues would it make sense to use a congestion avoidance (drop management) tool? (Choose two answers.)

    a. The LLQ

    b. Queue 1

    c. Queue 2

    d. Queue 3

Foundation Topics

Introduction to QoS

Routers typically sit at the WAN edge, with both WAN interfaces and LAN interfaces. Those LAN interfaces typically run at much faster speeds, while the WAN interfaces run at slower speeds. While that slower WAN interface is busy sending the packets waiting in the router, hundreds or even thousands more IP packets could arrive in the LAN interfaces, all needing to be forwarded out that same WAN interface. What should the router do? Send them all, in the same order in which they arrived? Prioritize the packets, to send some earlier than others, preferring one type of traffic over another? Discard some of the packets when the number of packets waiting to exit the router gets too large?

The preceding paragraph describes some of the many classic **Quality of Service (QoS)** questions in networking. QoS refers to the tools that networking devices use to apply some different treatment to packets in the network as they pass through the device. For instance, the WAN edge router would queue packets waiting for the WAN interface to be available. The router could also use a queue scheduling algorithm to determine which packets should be sent next, using some other order than the arrival order—giving some packets better service and some worse service.

QoS: Managing Bandwidth, Delay, Jitter, and Loss

Cisco offers a wide range of QoS tools on both routers and switches. All these tools give you the means to manage four characteristics of network traffic:

- Bandwidth

- Delay

- Jitter

- Loss

Bandwidth refers to the speed of a link, in bits per second (bps). But while we think of bandwidth as speed, it helps to also think of bandwidth as the capacity of the link, in terms of how many bits can be sent over the link per second. The networking device's QoS tools determine what packet is sent over the link next, so the networking device is in control of which messages get access to the bandwidth next and how much of that bandwidth (capacity) each type of traffic gets over time.

For example, consider a typical WAN edge router that has hundreds of packets waiting to exit the WAN link. An engineer might configure a queuing tool to reserve 10 percent of the bandwidth for voice traffic, 50 percent for mission-critical data applications, and leave the rest of the bandwidth for all other types of traffic. The queuing tool could then use those settings to make the choice about which packets to send next.

Delay can be described as one-way delay or round-trip delay. *One-way delay* refers to the time between sending one packet and that same packet arriving at the destination host. *Round-trip delay* counts the one-way delay plus the time for the receiver of the first packet to send back a packet—in other words, the time it takes to send one packet between two hosts and receive one back. Many different individual actions impact delay; this chapter discusses a few of those, including queuing and shaping delay.

Jitter refers to the variation in one-way delay between consecutive packets sent by the same application. For example, imagine an application sends a few hundred packets to one particular host. The first packet's one-way delay is 300 milliseconds (300 ms, or .3 seconds). The next packet's one-way delay is 300 ms; so is the third's; and so on. In that case, there is no jitter. However, if instead the first packet has a one-way delay of 300 ms, the next has a one-way delay of 310 ms, and the next has 325 ms, then there is some variation in the delay, 10 ms between packets 1 and 2, and another 15 ms between packets 2 and 3. That difference is called jitter.

Finally, **loss** refers to the number of lost messages, usually as a percentage of packets sent. The comparison is simple: if the sender for some application sends 100 packets, and only 98 arrive at the destination, that particular application flow experienced 2 percent loss. Loss can be caused by many factors, but often, people think of loss as something caused by faulty cabling or poor WAN services. That is one cause. However, more loss happens because of the normal operation of the networking devices, in which the devices' queues get too full, so the device has nowhere to put new packets, and it discards the packet. Several QoS tools manage queuing systems to help control and avoid loss.

Types of Traffic

With QoS, a network engineer sets about to prefer one type of traffic over another in regard to bandwidth, delay, jitter, and loss. Sometimes, that choice relates to the specific business. For example, if all the mission-critical applications sit on servers in three known subnets, then the QoS plan could be set up to match packets going to/from that subnet and give that traffic better treatment compared to other traffic. However, in other cases, the choice of how to apply QoS tools relates to the nature of different kinds of applications. Some applications have different QoS needs than others. This next topic compares the basic differences in QoS needs based on the type of traffic.

Data Applications

First, consider a basic web application, with a user at a PC or tablet. The user types in a URI to request a web page. That request may require a single packet going to the web server, but it may result in hundreds or thousands of packets coming back to the web client, as shown in Figure 15-1.

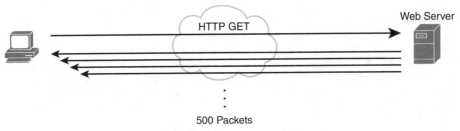

Figure 15-1   *Interactive Data Application*

NOTE   If you wonder how one web page might require thousands of packets, consider this math: with a 1500-byte IP maximum transmission unit (MTU), the data part of a TCP segment could be at most 1460 bytes (1500 bytes minus 20 bytes each for the IP and TCP header). In this example, 1000 such packets total to 1,460,000 bytes, or about 1.5 MB. It is easy to imagine a web page with just a few graphics that totals more than 1.5 MB in size.

So, what is the impact of bandwidth, delay, jitter, and loss on an interactive web-based application? First, the packets require a certain amount of bandwidth capacity. As for delay, each of those packets from the server to the client takes some amount of one-way delay, with some jitter as well. Of the 500 packets shown in Figure 15-1, if some are lost (transmission errors, discarded by devices, or other reasons), then the server's TCP logic will retransmit, but parts of the web page may not show up right away.

While QoS tools focus on managing bandwidth, delay, jitter, and loss, the user mainly cares about the quality of the overall experience. For instance, with a web application, how long after clicking do you see something useful in your web browser? So, as a user, you care about the *quality of experience (QoE)*, which is a term referring to users' perception of their use of the application on the network. QoS tools directly impact bandwidth, delay, jitter, and loss, which then should have some overall good effect to influence the users' QoE. And you can use QoS tools to create a better QoE for more important traffic; for instance, you might give certain business-critical applications better QoS treatment, which improves QoE for users of those apps.

In contrast, a noninteractive data application (historically called *batch* traffic)—for instance, data backup or file transfers—has different QoS requirements than interactive data applications. Batch applications typically send more data than interactive applications, but because no one is sitting there waiting to see something pop on the screen, the delay and jitter do not matter much. Much more important for these applications is meeting the need to complete the larger task (transferring files) within a larger time window. QoS tools can be used to provide enough bandwidth to meet the capacity needs of these applications and manage loss to reduce the number of retransmissions.

Answers to the "Do I Know This Already?" quiz:

1 A, B, E **2** B, C **3** A, B, C **4** B, C **5** A, D **6** C, D

Voice and Video Applications

Voice and video applications each have a similar breakdown of interactive and noninteractive flows. To make the main points about both voice and video, this section looks more deeply at voice traffic.

Before looking at voice, though, first think about the use of the term *flow* in networking. A flow is all the data moving from one application to another over the network, with one flow for each direction. For example, if you open a website and connect to a web server, the web page content that moves from the server to the client is one flow. Listen to some music with a music app on your phone, and that creates a flow from your app to the music app's server and a flow from the server back to your phone. From a voice perspective, a phone call between two IP phones would create a flow for each direction. For video, it could be the traffic from one video surveillance camera collected by security software.

Now on to voice, specifically voice over IP (VoIP). VoIP defines the means to take the sound made at one telephone and send it inside IP packets over an IP network, playing the sound back on the other telephone. Figure 15-2 shows the general idea. The figure includes these steps:

Step 1. The phone user makes a phone call and begins speaking.

Step 2. A chip called a *codec* processes (digitizes) the sound to create a binary code (160 bytes with the G.711 codec, for example) for a certain time period (usually 20 ms).

Step 3. The phone places the data into an IP packet.

Step 4. The phone sends the packet to the destination IP phone.

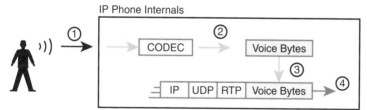

Figure 15-2 *Creating VoIP Packets with an IP Phone and a G.711 Codec*

If you work through the math a bit, this single call, with the G.711 codec, requires about 80 Kbps of bandwidth (ignoring the data-link header and trailer overhead). Counting the headers and VoIP payload as shown in the figure, each of the IP packets has 200 bytes. Each holds 20 ms of digitized voice, so the phone sends 50 packets per second. These 50 packets at 200 bytes each equal 10,000 bytes per second, or 80,000 bits per second, which is 80 Kbps. Other voice codecs require even less bandwidth, with the commonly used G.729 taking about 24 Kbps (again ignoring data-link overhead).

At first, it might look as though VoIP calls require little in regard to QoS. For bandwidth, a single voice call or flow requires only a little bandwidth in comparison to many data applications. However, interactive voice does require a much better level of quality for delay, jitter, and loss.

For instance, think about making a phone call with high one-way delay. You finish speaking and pause for the other person to respond. And that person does not, so you speak again—and hear the other person's voice overlaid on your own. The problem: too much delay. Or consider calls for which the sound breaks up. The problem? It could have been packet loss, or it could have been jitter.

You can achieve good-quality voice traffic over an IP network, but you must implement QoS to do so. QoS tools set about to give different types of traffic the QoS behavior they need. Cisco's *Enterprise QoS Solution Reference Network Design Guide*, which itself quotes other sources in addition to relying on Cisco's long experience in implementing QoS, suggests the following guidelines for interactive voice:

- **Delay (one-way):** 150 ms or less
- **Jitter:** 30 ms or less
- **Loss:** 1% or less

In comparison, interactive voice requires more attention than interactive data applications for QoS features. Data applications generally tolerate more delay, jitter, and loss than voice (and video). A single voice call does generally take less bandwidth than a typical data application, but that bandwidth requirement is consistent. Data applications tend to be bursty, with data bursts in reaction to the user doing something with the application.

Video has a much more varied set of QoS requirements. Generally, think of video like voice, but with a much higher bandwidth requirement than voice (per flow) and similar requirements for low delay, jitter, and loss. As for bandwidth, video can use a variety of codecs that impact the amount of data sent, but many other technical features impact the amount of bandwidth required for a single video flow. (For instance, a sporting event with lots of movement on screen takes more bandwidth than a news anchor reading the news in front of a solid background with little movement.) This time quoting from *End-to-End QoS Network Design*, Second Edition (Cisco Press, 2013), some requirements for video include

- **Bandwidth:** 384 Kbps to 20+ Mbps
- **Delay (one-way):** 200–400 ms
- **Jitter:** 30–50 ms
- **Loss:** 0.1%–1%

QoS as Mentioned in This Book

QoS tools change the QoS characteristics of certain flows in the network. The rest of the chapter focuses on the specific tools mentioned in the lone CCNA 200-301 version 1.1 exam topic about QoS, presented in the following major sections:

- "Classification and Marking" is about the marking of packets and the definition of trust boundaries.
- "Queuing" describes the scheduling of packets to give one type of packet priority over another.

- "Shaping and Policing" explains these two tools together because they are often used on opposite ends of a link.

- "Congestion Avoidance" addresses how to manage the packet loss that occurs when network devices get too busy.

QoS on Switches and Routers

Before moving on to several sections of the chapter about specific QoS tools, let me make a point about the terms *packet* and *frame* as used in this chapter.

The QoS tools discussed in this chapter can be used on both switches and routers. There are some differences in the features and differences in implementation, due to the differences of internal architecture between routers and switches. However, to the depth discussed here, the descriptions apply equally to both LAN switches and IP routers.

This chapter uses the word *packet* in a general way, to refer to any message being processed by a networking device, just for convenience. Normally, the term *packet* refers to the IP header and encapsulated headers and data, but without the data-link header and trailer. The term *frame* refers to the data-link header/trailer with its encapsulated headers and data. For this chapter, those differences do not matter to the discussion, but at the same time, the discussion often shows a message that sometimes is literally a packet (without the data-link header/trailer) and sometimes a frame.

Throughout the chapter, the text uses *packet* for all messages, because the fact of whether or not the message happens to have a data-link header/trailer at that point is immaterial to the basic discussion of features.

Additionally, note that all the examples in the chapter refer to routers, just to be consistent.

Classification and Marking

The first QoS tool discussed in this chapter, classification and marking, or simply marking, refers to a type of QoS tool that classifies packets based on their header contents, and then marks the message by changing some bits in specific header fields. This section looks first at the role of classification across all QoS tools, and then it examines the marking feature.

Classification Basics

QoS tools sit in the path that packets take when being forwarded through a router or switch, much like the positioning of ACLs. Like ACLs, QoS tools are enabled on an interface. Also like ACLs, QoS tools are enabled for a direction: packets entering the interface (before the forwarding decision) or for messages exiting the interface (after the forwarding decision).

The term **classification** refers to the process of matching the fields in a message to make a choice to take some QoS action. So, again comparing QoS tools to ACLs, ACLs perform classification and filtering; that is, ACLs match (classify) packet headers. ACLs can have the purpose (action) of choosing which packets to discard. QoS tools perform classification (matching of header fields) to decide which packets to take certain QoS actions against. Those actions include the other types of QoS tools discussed in this chapter, such as queuing, shaping, policing, and so on.

For example, consider the internal processing done by a router as shown in Figure 15-3. In this case, an output queuing tool has been enabled on an interface. Routers use queuing tools to place some packets in one output queue, other packets in another, and so on, when the outgoing interface happens to be busy. Then, when the outgoing interface becomes available to send another message, the queuing tool's scheduler algorithm can pick the next message from any one of the queues, prioritizing traffic based on the rules configured by the network engineer.

Router Internals

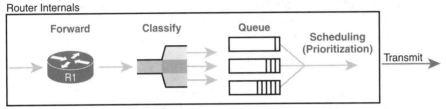

Figure 15-3 *Big Idea: Classification for Queuing in a Router*

The figure shows the internals of a router and what happens to the packet during part of that internal processing, moving left to right inside the router, as follows:

Step 1.   The router makes a forwarding (routing) decision.

Step 2.   The output queuing tool uses classification logic to determine which packets go into which output queue.

Step 3.   The router holds the packets in the output queue waiting for the outgoing interface to be available to send the next message.

Step 4.   The queuing tool's scheduling logic chooses the next packet, effectively prioritizing one packet over another.

While the example shows a queuing tool, note that the queuing tool requires the ability to classify messages by comparing the messages to the configuration, much like ACLs.

Matching (Classification) Basics

Now think about classification from an enterprise-wide perspective, which helps us appreciate the need for marking. Every QoS tool can examine various headers to make comparisons to classify packets. However, you might apply QoS tools on most every device in the network, sometimes at both ingress and egress on most of the interfaces. Using complex matching of many header fields in every device and on most interfaces requires lots of configuration. The work to match packets can even degrade device performance of some devices. So, while you could have every device use complex packet matching, doing so is a poor strategy.

A better strategy, one recommended both by Cisco and by RFCs, suggests doing complex matching early in the life of a packet and then marking the packet. **Marking** means that the QoS tool changes one or more header fields, setting a value in the header. Several header fields have been designed for the purpose of marking the packets for QoS processing. Then, devices that process the packet later in its life can use much simpler classification logic.

Figure 15-4 shows an example, with a PC on the left sending an IP packet to some host off the right side of the figure (not shown). Switch SW1, the first networking device to forward the packet, does some complex comparisons and marks the packet's **Differentiated**

Services Code Point (DSCP) field, a 6-bit field in the IP header meant for QoS marking. The next three devices that process this message—SW2, R1, and R2—then use simpler matching to classify the packet by comparing the packet's DSCP value, placing packets with one DSCP value in class 1, and packets with another DSCP value in class 2.

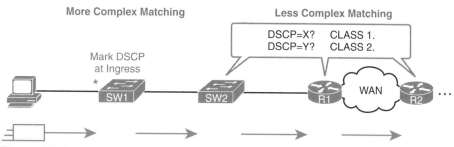

Figure 15-4 *Systematic Classification and Marking for the Enterprise*

Classification on Routers with ACLs and NBAR

Now that you know the basics of what classification and marking do together, this section takes the discussion a little deeper with a closer look at classification on routers, which is followed by a closer look at the marking function.

First, QoS classification sounds a lot like what ACLs do, and it should. In fact, many QoS tools support the ability to simply refer to an IP ACL, with this kind of logic:

> For any packet matched by the ACL with a permit action, consider that packet a match for QoS, so do a particular QoS action.

As a reminder, Figure 15-5 shows the IP and TCP header. All these fields are matchable for QoS classification.

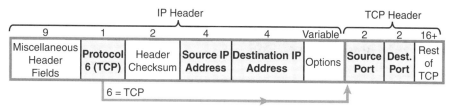

Figure 15-5 *Classification with Five Fields Used by Extended ACLs*

Now think about the enterprise's QoS plan for a moment. That plan should list details such as which types of traffic should be classified as being in the same class for queuing purposes, for shaping, and for any other QoS tool. That plan should detail the fields in the header that can be matched. For instance, if all the IP phones sit in subnets within the range of addresses 10.3.0.0/16, then the QoS plan should state that. Then the network engineer could config-ure an extended ACL to match all packets to/from IP addresses inside 10.3.0.0/16 and apply appropriate QoS actions to that voice traffic.

However, not every classification can be easily made by matching with an ACL. In more challenging cases, Cisco Network Based Application Recognition (NBAR) can be used. NBAR is basically in its second major version, called NBAR2, or next-generation NBAR.

In short, NBAR2 matches packets for classification in a large variety of ways that are very useful for QoS.

NBAR2 looks far beyond what an ACL can examine in a message. Many applications cannot be identified based on well-known port alone. NBAR solves those problems.

Cisco also organizes what NBAR can match in ways that make it easy to separate the traffic into different classes. For instance, the Cisco WebEx application provides audio and video conferencing on the web. In a QoS plan, you might want to classify WebEx differently than other video traffic and classify it differently than voice calls between IP phones. That is, you might classify WebEx traffic and give it a unique DSCP marking. NBAR provides easy built-in matching ability for WebEx, plus well over 1000 different subcategories of applications.

Just to drive the point home with NBAR, Example 15-1 lists several lines of help output for one of many NBAR configuration commands. I chose a variety of items that might be more memorable. With the use of the keywords in the help lines in the correct configuration command, you could match traffic related to various Amazon public cloud offerings. NBAR refers to this idea of defining the characteristics of different applications as *application signatures*.

Example 15-1   *Example of the Many NBAR2 Matchable Applications*

```
R1#(config)# class-map matchingexample
R1(config-cmap)# match protocol ?

! output heavily edited for length
   amazon-ec2              Secure and resizable compute capacity in the cloud.
   amazon-instant-video    VOD service by Amazon
   amazon-s3               Amazon S3 (Simple Storage Service) is a cloud
                           computing web service.
   amazon-web-services     Amazon collection of remote computing services
! Output snipped.
```

Marking IP DSCP and Ethernet CoS

The QoS plan for an enterprise centers on creating classes of traffic that should receive certain types of QoS treatment. That plan would note how to classify packets into each classification and the values that should be marked on the packets, basically labeling each packet with a number to associate it with that class. For example, that plan might state the following:

- Classify all voice payload traffic that is used for business purposes as IP DSCP EF and CoS 5.

- Classify all video conferencing and other interactive video for business purposes as IP DSCP AF41 and CoS 4.

- Classify all business-critical data application traffic as IP DSCP AF21 and CoS 2.

This next topic takes a closer look at the specific fields that can be marked, defining the DSCP and CoS marking fields.

Marking the IP Header

Marking a QoS field in the IP header works well with QoS because the IP header exists for the entire trip from the source host to the destination host. When a host sends data, the host sends a data-link frame that encapsulates an IP packet. Each router that forwards the IP packet discards the old data-link header and adds a new header. Because IP routing retains the IP header, the marking in the IP header stays with the data from the first place at which the IP header is marked until it reaches the destination host.

IPv4 defines a type of service (ToS) byte in the IPv4 header, as shown in Figure 15-6. The original RFC defined a 3-bit **IP Precedence (IPP)** field for QoS marking. That field gave us eight separate values—binary 000, 001, 010, and so on, through 111—which when converted to decimal are decimals 0 through 7.

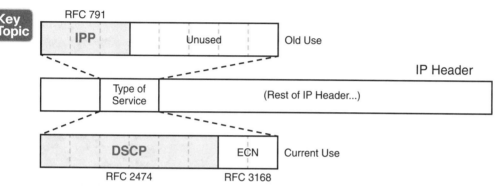

Key Topic

15

Figure 15-6 *IP Precedence and Differentiated Services Code Point Fields*

NOTE Those last 5 bits of the ToS byte per RFC 791 were mostly defined for some purpose but were not used in practice to any significant extent.

While a great idea, IPP gave us only eight different values to mark, so later RFCs redefined the ToS byte with the DSCP field. DSCP increased the number of marking bits to 6 bits, allowing for 64 unique values that can be marked. The **Differentiated Services (DiffServ)** RFCs, which became RFCs back in the late 1990s, have become accepted as the most common method to use when doing QoS, and using the DSCP field for marking has become quite common.

IPv6 has a similar field to mark as well. The 6-bit field also goes by the name DSCP, with the byte in the IPv6 header being called the IPv6 *Traffic Class* byte. Otherwise, think of IPv4 and IPv6 being equivalent in terms of marking.

IPP and DSCP fields can be referenced by their decimal values as well as some convenient text names. The later section titled "DiffServ Suggested Marking Values" details some of the names.

Marking the Ethernet 802.1Q Header

Another useful marking field exists in the 802.1Q header, in a field originally defined by the IEEE 802.1p standard. This field sits in the third byte of the 4-byte 802.1Q header, as a 3-bit field, supplying eight possible values to mark (see Figure 15-7). It goes by two different names: **class of service (CoS)** and *priority code point (PCP)*.

Ethernet Frame

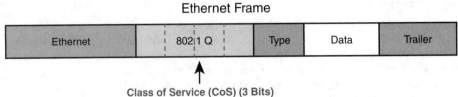

Figure 15-7 *Class of Service Field in 802.1Q/p Header*

The figure uses two slightly different shades of gray (in print) for the Ethernet header and trailer fields versus the 802.1Q header, as a reminder: the 802.1Q header is not included in all Ethernet frames. The 802.1Q header exists only when 802.1Q trunking is used on a link. As a result, QoS tools can make use of the CoS field only for QoS features enabled on interfaces that use trunking, as shown in Figure 15-8.

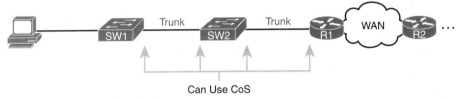

Figure 15-8 *Useful Life of CoS Marking*

For instance, if the PC on the left were to send data to a server somewhere off the figure to the right, the DSCP field would exist for that entire trip. However, the CoS field would exist over the two trunks only and would be useful mainly on the four interfaces noted with the arrow lines.

Other Marking Fields

Other marking fields also exist in other headers. Table 15-2 lists those fields for reference.

Table 15-2 Marking Fields

Field Name	Header(s)	Length (bits)	Where Used
DSCP	IPv4, IPv6	6	End-to-end packet
IPP	IPv4, IPv6	3	End-to-end packet
CoS	802.1Q	3	Over VLAN trunk
TID	802.11	3	Over Wi-Fi
EXP	MPLS Label	3	Over MPLS WAN

Defining Trust Boundaries

The end-user device can mark the DSCP field—and even the CoS field if trunking is used on the link. Would you, as the network engineer, trust those settings and let your networking devices trust and react to those markings for their various QoS actions?

Most of us would not, because anything the end user controls might be used inappropriately at times. For instance, a PC user could know enough about DiffServ and DSCPs to know that most voice traffic is marked with a DSCP called Expedited Forwarding (EF), which has a decimal value of 46. Voice traffic gets great QoS treatment, so PC users could mark all their traffic as DSCP 46, hoping to get great QoS treatment.

The people creating a QoS plan for an enterprise have to choose where to place the trust boundary for the network. The *trust boundary* refers to the point in the path of a packet flowing through the network at which the networking devices can trust the current QoS markings. That boundary typically sits in a device under the control of the IT staff.

For instance, a typical trust boundary could be set in the middle of the first ingress switch in the network, as shown in Figure 15-9. The markings on the message as sent by the PC cannot be trusted. However, because SW1 performed classification and marking as the packets entered the switch, the markings can be trusted at that point.

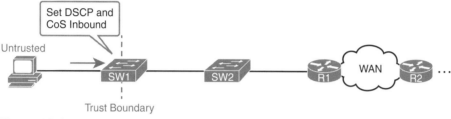

Figure 15-9 *Trusting Devices—PC*

Interestingly, when the access layer includes an IP Phone, the phone is typically the trust boundary, instead of the access layer switch. IP Phones can set the CoS and DSCP fields of the messages created by the phone, as well as those forwarded from the PC through the phone. Figure 15-10 shows the typical trust boundary in this case, with notation of what the phone's marking logic usually is: mark all of the PC's traffic with a particular DSCP and/or CoS, and the phone's traffic with different values.

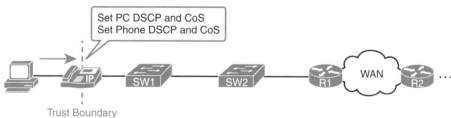

Figure 15-10 *Trusting Devices—IP Phone*

DiffServ Suggested Marking Values

Everything in this chapter follows the DiffServ architecture as defined originally by RFC 2475, plus many other DiffServ RFCs. In particular, DiffServ goes beyond theory in several areas, including making suggestions about the specific DSCP values to use when marking IP packets. By suggesting specific markings for specific types of traffic, DiffServ hoped to create a consistent use of DSCP values in all networks. By doing so, product vendors could provide good default settings for their QoS features, QoS could work better between an enterprise and service provider, and many other benefits could be realized.

The next two topics outline three sets of DSCP values as used in DiffServ.

Expedited Forwarding (EF)

DiffServ defines the *Expedited Forwarding (EF)* DSCP value—a single value—as suggested for use for packets that need low latency (delay), low jitter, and low loss. The Expedited Forwarding RFC (RFC 3246) defines the specific DSCP value (decimal 46) and an equivalent text name (Expedited Forwarding). QoS configuration commands allow the use of the decimal value or text name, but one purpose of having a text acronym to use is to make the value more memorable, so many QoS configurations refer to the text names.

Most often QoS plans use EF to mark voice payload packets. With voice calls, some packets carry voice payload, and other packets carry call signaling messages. Call signaling messages set up (create) the voice call between two devices, and they do not require low delay, jitter, and loss. Voice payload packets carry the digitized voice, as shown back in Figure 15-2, and these packets do need better QoS. By default, Cisco IP Phones mark voice payload with EF, and mark voice signaling packets sent by the phone with another value called CS3.

Assured Forwarding (AF)

The *Assured Forwarding (AF)* DiffServ RFC (2597) defines a set of 12 DSCP values meant to be used in concert with each other. First, it defines the concept of four separate queues in a queuing system. Additionally, it defines three levels of drop priority within each queue for use with congestion avoidance tools. With four queues, and three drop priority classes per queue, you need 12 different DSCP markings, one for each combination of queue and drop priority. (Queuing and congestion avoidance mechanisms are discussed later in this chapter.)

Assured Forwarding defines the specific AF DSCP text names and equivalent decimal values as listed in Figure 15-11. The text names follow a format of AFXY, with X referring to the queue (1 through 4) and Y referring to the drop priority (1 through 3).

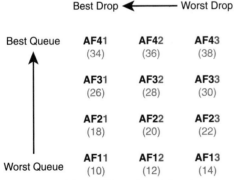

Figure 15-11 *Differentiated Services Assured Forwarding Values and Meaning*

For example, if you marked packets with all 12 values, those with AF11, AF12, and AF13 would all go into one queue; those with AF21, AF22, and AF23 would go into another queue; and so on. Inside the queue with all the AF2Y traffic, you would treat the AF21, AF22, and AF23 each differently in regard to drop actions (congestion avoidance), with AF21 getting the preferred treatment and AF23 the worst treatment.

Class Selector (CS)

Originally, the ToS byte was defined with a 3-bit IP Precedence (IPP) field. When DiffServ redefined the ToS byte, it made sense to create eight DSCP values for backward compatibility with IPP values. The *Class Selector (CS)* DSCP values are those settings.

Figure 15-12 shows the main idea along with the eight CS values, both in name and in decimal value. Basically, the DSCP values have the same first 3 bits as the IPP field, and with binary 0s for the last 3 bits, as shown on the left side of the figure. CSx represents the text names, where x is the matching IPP value (0 through 7).

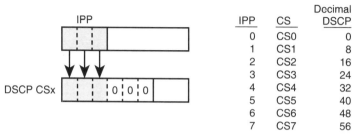

IPP	CS	Decimal DSCP
0	CS0	0
1	CS1	8
2	CS2	16
3	CS3	24
4	CS4	32
5	CS5	40
6	CS6	48
7	CS7	56

Figure 15-12 *Class Selector*

15

This section on classification and marking has provided a solid foundation for understanding the tools explored in the next three major sections of this chapter: queuing, shaping and policing, and congestion avoidance.

Guidelines for DSCP Marking Values

Even with this introduction to the various DSCP marking values, you could imagine that an enterprise needs to follow a convention for how to use the markings. With so many different values, having different uses of different DSCP values by different devices in the same enterprise would make deploying QoS quite difficult at best.

Among its many efforts to standardize QoS, Cisco helped to develop RFC 4954, an RFC that defines several conventions for how to use the DSCP field. The RFC provides alternative plans with different levels of detail. Each plan defines a type of traffic and the DSCP value to use when marking data. Without getting into the depth of any one plan, the plans all specify some variation for how all devices should mark data as follows:

- DSCP EF: Voice payload

- AF4x: Interactive video (for example, videoconferencing)

- AF3x: Streaming video

- AF2x: High priority (low latency) data

- CS0: Standard data

Cisco not only worked to develop the RFC standards but also uses those standards. Cisco uses default marking conventions based on the marking data in RFC 4594, with some small exceptions. If you want to read more about these QoS marking plans, refer to a couple of sources. First, look for the Cisco QoS Design Guides at Cisco.com. Also refer to RFC 4594.

Queuing

All networking devices use queues. Network devices receive messages, make a forwarding decision, and then send the message…but sometimes the outgoing interface is busy. So, the device keeps the outgoing message in a queue, waiting for the outgoing interface to be available—simple enough.

The term **queuing** refers to the QoS toolset for managing the queues that hold packets while they wait their turn to exit an interface (and in other cases in which a router holds packets waiting for some resource). But queuing refers to more than one idea, so you have to look inside devices to think about how they work. For instance, consider Figure 15-13, which shows the internals of a router. The router, of course, makes a forwarding decision, and it needs to be ready to queue packets for transmission once the outgoing interface is available. At the same time, the router may take a variety of other actions as well—ingress ACL, ingress NAT (on the inside interface), egress ACLs after the forwarding decision is made, and so on.

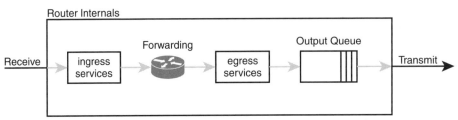

Figure 15-13 *Output Queuing in a Router: Last Output Action Before Transmission*

The figure shows *output queuing* in which the device holds messages until the output interface is available. The queuing system may use a single output queue, with a first-in, first-out (FIFO) scheduler. (In other words, it's like ordering lunch at the sandwich shop that has a single ordering line.)

Next, think a little more deeply about the queuing system. Most networking devices can have a queuing system with multiple queues. To use multiple queues, the queuing system needs a classifier function to choose which packets are placed into which queue. (The classifier can react to previously marked values or do a more extensive match.) The queuing system needs a scheduler as well, to decide which message to take next when the interface becomes available, as shown in Figure 15-14.

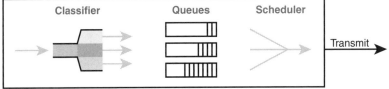

Figure 15-14 *Queuing Components*

Of all these components of the queuing system, the scheduler can be the most interesting part because it can perform prioritization. *Prioritization* refers to the concept of giving priority to one queue over another in some way.

Round-Robin Scheduling (Prioritization)

One scheduling algorithm used by Cisco routers and switches uses round-robin logic. In its most basic form, **round robin** cycles through the queues in order, taking turns with each queue. In each cycle, the scheduler either takes one message or takes a number of bytes from each queue by taking enough messages to total that number of bytes. Take some messages from queue 1, move on and take some from queue 2, then take some from queue 3, and so on, starting back at queue 1 after finishing a complete pass through the queues.

Round-robin scheduling also includes the concept of *weighting* (generally called *weighted round robin*). Basically, the scheduler takes a different number of packets (or bytes) from each queue, giving more preference to one queue over another.

For example, routers use a popular tool called *Class-Based Weighted Fair Queuing (CBWFQ)* to guarantee a minimum amount of bandwidth to each class. That is, each class receives at least the amount of bandwidth configured during times of congestion, but maybe more. Internally, CBWFQ uses a weighted round-robin scheduling algorithm, while letting the network engineer define the weightings as a percentage of link bandwidth. Figure 15-15 shows an example in which the three queues in the system have been given 20, 30, and 50 percent of the bandwidth each, respectively.

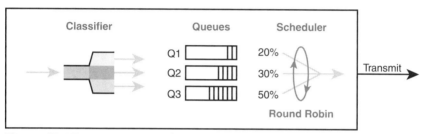

Figure 15-15 *CBWFQ Round-Robin Scheduling*

With the queuing system shown in the figure, if the outgoing link is congested, the scheduler guarantees the percentage bandwidth shown in the figure to each queue. That is, queue 1 gets 20 percent of the link even during busy times.

Low Latency Queuing

Earlier in the chapter, the section titled "Voice and Video Applications" discussed the reasons why voice and video, particularly interactive voice and video like phone calls and videoconferencing, need low latency (low delay), low jitter, and low loss. Unfortunately, a round-robin scheduler does not provide low enough delay, jitter, or loss. The solution: add Low Latency Queuing (LLQ) to the scheduler.

First, for a quick review, Table 15-3 lists the QoS requirements for a voice call. The numbers come from the *Enterprise QoS Solution Reference Network Design Guide*, referenced earlier in the chapter. The amount of bandwidth required per call varies based on the codec used by the call. However, the delay, jitter, and loss requirements remain the same for all voice calls. (Interactive video has similar requirements for delay, jitter, and loss.)

Table 15-3 QoS Requirements for a VoIP Call per Cisco Voice Design Guide

Bandwidth/call	One-way Delay (max)	Jitter (max)	Loss (max)
30–320 Kbps	150 ms	30 ms	<1%

A round-robin queuing system adds too much delay for these voice and video packets. To see why, imagine a voice packet arrives and is routed to be sent out some interface with the queuing system shown in Figure 15-16. However, that next voice packet arrives just as the round-robin scheduler moves on to service the queue labeled "data 1." Even though the voice queue has been given 50 percent of the link bandwidth, the scheduler does not send that voice message until it sends some messages from the other three queues—adding delay and jitter.

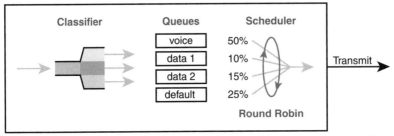

Figure 15-16   *Round Robin Not Good for Voice Delay (Latency) and Jitter*

The solution, LLQ, tells the scheduler to treat one or more queues as special **priority queues**. The LLQ scheduler always takes the next message from one of these special priority queues. Problem solved: very little delay for packets in that queue, resulting in very little jitter as well. Plus, the queue never has time to fill up, so there are no drops due to the queue filling up. Figure 15-17 shows the addition of the LLQ logic for the voice queue.

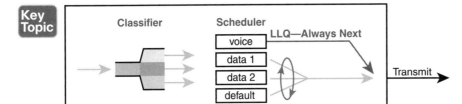

Figure 15-17   *LLQ Always Schedules Voice Packet Next*

Using LLQ, or a priority queue, provides the needed low delay, jitter, and loss for the traffic in that queue. However, think about those other queues. Do you see the problem? What happens if the speed of the interface is X bits per second, but more than X bits per second come into the voice queue? The scheduler never services the other queues (called *queue starvation*).

As you might guess, there is a solution: limit the amount of traffic placed into the priority queue, using a feature called *policing*. The next section talks about policers in more detail, but for now, think of it as a cap on the bandwidth used by the priority queue. For instance, you could reserve 20 percent of the link's bandwidth for the voice queue and make it a priority queue. However, in this case, instead of 20 percent being the minimum bandwidth, it is the maximum for that queue. If more than 20 percent of the link's worth of bits shows up in that queue, the router will discard the excess.

Limiting the amount of bandwidth in the priority queue protects the other queues, but it causes yet another problem. Voice and video need low loss, and with LLQ, we put the voice and video into a priority queue that will discard the excess messages beyond the bandwidth limit. The solution? Find a way to limit the amount of voice and video that the network routes out this link, so that the policer never discards any of the traffic. There are QoS tools to help you do just that, called call admission control (CAC) tools. However, CAC tools did not get a mention in the exam topics, so this chapter leaves those tools at a brief mention.

A Prioritization Strategy for Data, Voice, and Video

This section about queuing introduces several connected ideas, so before leaving the discussion of queuing, think about this strategy for how most enterprises approach queuing in their QoS plans:

1. Use a round-robin queuing method like CBWFQ for data classes and for noninteractive voice and video.

2. If faced with too little bandwidth compared to the typical amount of traffic, give data classes that support business-critical applications much more guaranteed bandwidth than is given to less important data classes.

3. Use a priority queue with LLQ scheduling for interactive voice and video, to achieve low delay, jitter, and loss.

4. Put voice in a separate queue from video so that the policing function applies separately to each.

5. Define enough bandwidth for each priority queue so that the built-in policer should not discard any messages from the priority queues.

6. Use call admission control (CAC) tools to avoid adding too much voice or video to the network, which would trigger the policer function.

Shaping and Policing

This section introduces two related QoS tools—**shaping** and **policing**. These tools have a more specialized use and are not found in as many locations in a typical enterprise. These tools are most often used at the WAN edge in an enterprise network design.

Both policing and shaping monitor the bit rate of the combined messages that flow through a device. Once enabled, the policer or shaper notes each packet that passes and measures the number of bits per second over time. Both attempt to keep the bit rate at or below the configured speed, but by using two different actions: policers discard packets, and shapers hold packets in queues to delay the packets.

Shapers and policers monitor the traffic rate (the bits per second that move through the shaper or policer) versus a configured **shaping rate** or **policing rate**, respectively. The basic question that both ask is listed below, with the actions based on the answers:

1. Does this next packet push the measured rate past the configured shaping rate or policing rate?

2. If no:

   a. Let the packet keep moving through the normal path and do nothing extra to the packet.

3. If yes:

   a. If shaping, delay the message by queuing it.

   b. If policing, either discard the message or mark it differently.

This section first explains policing, which discards or re-marks messages that exceed the policing rate, followed by shaping, which slows down messages that exceed the shaping rate.

Policing

Focus on the traffic rate versus the configured policing rate for a moment, and the policing action of discarding messages. Those concepts sit at the core of what the policing function does.

Traffic arrives at networking devices at a varying rate, with valleys and spikes. That is, if you graph the bit rate of the collective bits that enter or exit any interface, the graph would look something like the one on the left side of Figure 15-18. The policer would measure that rate and make a similar measurement. Still on the left side of the figure, the horizontal dashed line represents the policing rate, which is the rate configured for the policer. So, the policer has some awareness of the measured bit rate over time, which can be compared to the configured rate.

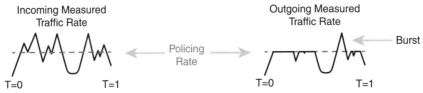

Figure 15-18 *Effect of a Policer and Shaper on an Offered Traffic Load*

The right side of the figure shows a graph of what happens to the traffic when a policer discards any messages that would have otherwise pushed the rate over the configured policing rate. In effect, the policer chops off the top of the graph at the policing rate.

The graph on the right also shows one example of a policer allowing a burst of traffic. Policers allow for a burst beyond the policing rate for a short time, after a period of low activity. So, that one peak that exceeds the policing rate on the graph on the right side allows for the nature of bursty data applications.

Where to Use Policing

Now that you understand the basics of policing, take a moment to ponder. Policers monitor messages, measure a rate, and discard some messages. How does that help a network in regard to QoS? At first glance, it seems to hurt the network, discarding messages, many of which the transport or application layer will have to resend. How does that improve bandwidth, delay, jitter, or loss?

Policing makes sense only in certain cases, and as a general tool, it can be best used at the edge between two networks. For instance, consider a typical point-to-point metro Ethernet WAN connection between two enterprise routers, R1 and R2. Usually, the enterprise network engineers just view the WAN as a cloud, with Ethernet interfaces on the routers, as shown at the top of Figure 15-19.

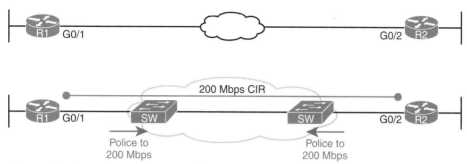

Figure 15-19 *Ethernet WAN: Link Speed Versus CIR*

Now think about the contract for this MetroE connection, as shown at the bottom of Figure 15-19. In this case, this connection uses Gigabit Ethernet for the access links, and a 200-Mbps *committed information rate (CIR)*. That is, the SP providing the WAN service agrees to allow the enterprise to send 200 Mbps of traffic in each direction. However, remember that the enterprise routers transmit the data at the speed of the access link, or 1 Gbps in this case.

Think like the SP for a moment, and think about supporting tens of thousands of Gigabit Ethernet links into your WAN service, all with 200-Mbps CIRs. What would happen if you just let all those customers send data that, over time, averaged close to 1000 Mbps (1 Gbps)? That is, if all customers kept sending data far beyond their contracted CIR, that much traffic could cause congestion in the WAN service. Also, those customers might choose to pay for a lower CIR, knowing that the SP would send the data anyway. And customers who were well behaved and did not send more data than their CIR might suffer from the congestion just as much as the customers who send far too much data.

Figure 15-19 also notes the solution to the problem: The SP can police incoming packets, setting the policing rate to match the CIR that the customer chooses for that link. By doing so, the SP protects all customers from the negative effects of the customers who send too much traffic. Customers receive what they paid for. And the SP can provide reports of actual traffic rates, so the enterprise knows when to buy a faster CIR for each link.

Policers can discard excess traffic, but they can also re-mark packets. Think again about what an SP does with an ingress policer, as shown in Figure 15-19: they are discarding their customers' messages. So, the SP might want to make a compromise that works better for its customers, while still protecting the SP's network. The SP could mark the messages with a new marking value, with this strategy:

1. Re-mark packets that exceed the policing rate, but let them into the SP's network.

2. If other SP network devices are experiencing congestion when they process the packet, the different marking means that device can discard the packet. However…

3. …if no other SP network devices are experiencing congestion when forwarding that re-marked packet, it gets through the SP network anyway.

With this strategy, the SP can treat their customers a little better by discarding less traffic, while still protecting the SP's network during times of stress.

Summarizing the key features of policing:

- Policing measures the traffic rate over time for comparison to the configured policing rate.

- Policing allows for a burst of data after a period of inactivity.

- Policing is enabled on an interface, in either direction, but typically at ingress.

- Policing can discard excess messages but can also re-mark the message so that it is a candidate for more aggressive discard later in its journey.

Shaping

You have a 1-Gbps link from a router into a SP, but a 200-Mbps CIR for traffic to another site, as seen in Figure 15-19. The SP has told you that it always discards incoming traffic that exceeds the CIR. The solution? Use a shaper to slow down the traffic—in this case to a 200-Mbps shaping rate.

That scenario—shaping before sending data to an SP that is policing—is one of the typical uses of a shaper. Shapers can be useful in other cases as well, but generally speaking, shapers make sense when a device can send at a certain speed, but there is a benefit to slowing down the rate.

The shaper slows down messages by queuing the messages. The shaper then services the shaping queues, but not based on when the physical interface is available. Instead, the shaper schedules messages from the shaping queues based on the shaping rate, as shown in Figure 15-20. Following the left-to-right flow in the figure, for a router, the packet is routed out an interface; the shaper queues packets so that the sending rate through the shaper does not exceed the shaping rate; and then output queuing works as normal, if needed.

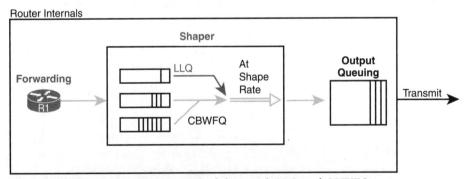

Figure 15-20 *Shaping Queues: Scheduling with LLQ and CBWFQ*

Note that in some cases, the output queuing function has little to do. For instance, in the earlier example shown in Figure 15-19, the SP is policing incoming messages at 200 Mbps. If the router (R1, for instance) were to shape all traffic exiting toward the SP to 200 Mbps as well, with that 1-Gbps interface, the output queue would seldom if ever be congested.

Because shapers create queues where messages wait, you should apply a queuing tool to those queues. It is perfectly normal to apply the round-robin and priority queuing features of CBWFQ and LLQ, respectively, to the shaping queues, as noted in the figure.

Setting a Good Shaping Time Interval for Voice and Video

Once again, a QoS tool has attempted to solve one QoS problem but introduces another. The unfortunate side effect of a shaper is that it slows down packets, which then creates more delay and probably more jitter. The delay occurs in part because of the message simply waiting in a queue, but partly because of the mechanisms used by a shaper. Thankfully, you can (and should) configure a shaper's setting that changes the internal operation of the shaper, which then reduces the delay and jitter caused to voice and video traffic.

A shaper's *time interval* refers to its internal logic and how a shaper averages, over time, sending at a particular rate. A shaper basically sends as fast as it can and then waits; sends and waits; sends and waits. For instance, the policing and shaping example in this section suggests shaping at 200 Mbps on a router that has a 1000-Mbps (1-Gbps) outgoing interface. In that case, the shaper would result in the interface sending data 20 percent of the time and being silent 80 percent of the time.

Figure 15-21 shows a graph of the shaping time interval concept, assuming a time interval of 1 second. To average 200 million bits per second, the shaper would allow 200 million bits to exit its shaping queues and exit the interface each second. Because the interface transmits bits at 1 Gbps, it takes just .2 seconds, or 200 ms, to send all 200 million bits. Then the shaper must wait for the rest of the time interval, another 800 ms, before beginning the next time interval.

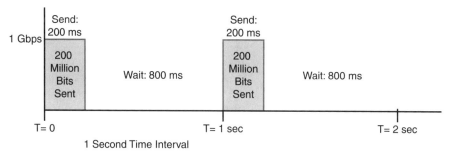

Figure 15-21   *One Second (1000 ms) Shaping Time Interval, Shaping at 20% of Line Rate*

Now think about a voice or video packet that needs very low delay and jitter—and unfortunately, it arrives just as the shaper finishes sending data for a time interval. Even if that voice or video packet is in a priority shaping queue, the packet will wait 800 ms before the shaper schedules the next packet—far too long compared to the 150-ms one-way delay goal for voice.

The solution to this problem: configure a short time interval. For example, consider the following time intervals (abbreviated Tc), and their effects, for this same example (1-Gbps link, shaping to 200 Mbps), but with shorter and shorter time intervals:

Tc = **1 second (1000 ms):** Send at 1 Gbps for 200 ms, rest for 800 ms

Tc = **.1 second (100 ms):** Send at 1 Gbps for 20 ms, rest for 80 ms

Tc = **.01 second (10 ms):** Send at 1 Gbps for 2 ms, rest for 8 ms

When shaping, use a short time interval. By recommendation, use a 10-ms time interval to support voice and video. With that setting, a voice or video packet should wait no more than

10 ms while waiting for the next shaping time interval, at which point the priority queue scheduling should take all the voice and video messages next.

Summarizing the key features of shapers:

- Shapers measure the traffic rate over time for comparison to the configured shaping rate.

- Shapers allow for bursting after a period of inactivity.

- Shapers are enabled on an interface for egress (outgoing packets).

- Shapers slow down packets by queuing them and over time releasing them from the queue at the shaping rate.

- Shapers use queuing tools to create and schedule the shaping queues, which is very important for the same reasons discussed for output queuing.

Congestion Avoidance

The QoS feature called *congestion avoidance* attempts to reduce overall packet loss by pre-emptively discarding some packets used in TCP connections. To see how it works, you first need to look at how TCP works in regard to windowing and then look at how congestion avoidance features work.

TCP Windowing Basics

TCP uses a flow control mechanism called *windowing*. Each TCP receiver grants a window to the sender. The window, which is a number, defines the number of bytes the sender can send over the TCP connection before receiving a TCP acknowledgment for at least some of those bytes. More exactly, the window size is the number of unacknowledged bytes that the sender can send before the sender must simply stop and wait.

The TCP window mechanism gives the receiver control of the sender's rate of sending data. Each new segment sent by the receiver back to the sender grants a new window, which can be smaller or larger than the previous window. By raising and lowering the window, the receiver can make the sender wait more or wait less.

> **NOTE**   Each TCP connection has two senders and two receivers; that is, each host sends and receives data. For this discussion, focus on one direction, with one host as the sender and the other as the receiver. If calling one host the "sender" and one the "receiver," note that the receiver then acknowledges data in TCP segments sent back to the sender by the receiver.

By choice, when all is well, the receiver keeps increasing the granted window, doubling it every time the receiver acknowledges data. Eventually, the window grows to the point that the sender never has to stop sending: the sender keeps receiving TCP acknowledgments before sending all the data in the previous window. Each new acknowledgment (as listed in a TCP segment and TCP header) grants a new window to the sender.

Also by choice, when a TCP receiver senses the loss of a TCP segment, the receiver shrinks the window with the next window size listed in the next TCP segment the receiver sends back to the sender. For each TCP segment lost, the window can shrink by one-half, with multiple segment losses causing the window to shrink by half multiple times, slowing down the sender's rate significantly.

Now think about router queues for a moment. Without a congestion avoidance tool, an event called a *tail drop* causes the most drops in a network. Figure 15-22 illustrates the idea, showing the same queuing system, but in three separate conditions—little congestion, medium congestion, and much congestion. On the left, with little congestion, the output queues on an interface have not yet filled. In the middle, the queues have started to fill, with one queue being totally full. Any new packets that arrive for that queue right now will be dropped because there is no room at the tail of the queue (tail drop).

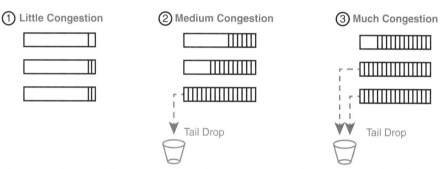

Figure 15-22   *Stable TCP Window: Acknowledgment Received Before Window Expires*

The worse the congestion in the queues, the more likely tail drop will occur, as shown with the most congested case on the right side of the figure. The more congestion, the bigger the negative impact on traffic—both in terms of loss and in terms of increasing delay in TCP connections.

Congestion Avoidance Tools

Congestion avoidance tools attempt to avoid the congestion, primarily through using TCP's own windowing mechanisms. These tools discard some TCP segments before the queues fill, hoping that enough TCP connections will slow down, reducing congestion, and avoiding a much worse problem: the effects of many more packets being dropped due to tail drop. The strategy is simple: discard some now in hopes that the device discards far fewer in the long term.

Congestion avoidance tools monitor the average queue depth over time, triggering more severe actions the deeper the queue, as shown in Figure 15-23. The height of the box represents the queue depth, or the number of packets in the queue. When the queue depth is low, below the minimum threshold values, the congestion avoidance tool does nothing. When the queue depth is between the minimum and maximum thresholds, the congestion avoidance tool discards a percentage of the packets—usually a small percentage, like 5, 10, or 20 percent. If the queue depth passes the maximum threshold, the tool drops all packets, in an action called a *full drop*.

Of course, like all the QoS tools mentioned in this chapter, congestion avoidance tools can classify messages to treat some packets better than others. In the same queue, packets with one marking might be dropped more aggressively, and those with better DSCP markings dropped less aggressively.

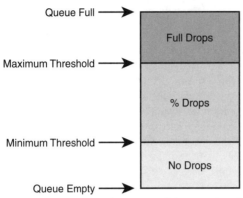

Figure 15-23 *Mechanisms of Congestion Avoidance*

Chapter Review

One key to doing well on the exams is to perform repetitive spaced review sessions. Review this chapter's material using either the tools in the book or interactive tools for the same material found on the book's companion website. Refer to the "Your Study Plan" element for more details. Table 15-4 outlines the key review elements and where you can find them. To better track your study progress, record when you completed these activities in the second column.

Table 15-4   Chapter Review Tracking

Review Element	Review Date(s)	Resource Used
Review key topics		Book, website
Review key terms		Book, website
Answer DIKTA questions		Book, PTP
Review memory tables		Book, website
Watch video		Website

Review All the Key Topics

Table 15-5   Key Topics for Chapter 15

Key Topic Element	Description	Page Number
List	Four QoS characteristics	324
List	Voice call QoS requirements	328
List	Video QoS requirements	328
Figure 15-6	IP Precedence and IP DSCP marking fields	333
Figure 15-7	802.1Q CoS marking field	334
Figure 15-10	Trust boundary with IP Phones	335
Figure 15-14	Queuing components	338
Figure 15-17	LLQ scheduling logic with a priority queue	340

Key Topic Element	Description	Page Number
List	A strategy for using queuing (congestion management) to prioritize traffic	341
List	Logic steps for shapers and policers	341
List	Key features of policers	344
List	Key features of shapers	346

Key Terms You Should Know

bandwidth, Class of Service (CoS), classification, delay, Differentiated Services (DiffServ), Differentiated Services Code Point (DSCP), IP Precedence (IPP), jitter, loss, marking, per-hop behavior (PHB), policing, policing rate, priority queue, Quality of Service (QoS), queuing, round robin, shaping, shaping rate

15

CHAPTER 16

First Hop Redundancy Protocols

This chapter covers the following exam topics:

3.0 IP Connectivity

3.5 Describe the purpose, functions, and concepts of First Hop Redundancy Protocols

Any host's default router serves as the first router, or first hop, in the routing path from sender to receiver. However, IPv4 did not include high-availability and redundancy features related to the default router. IP hosts use a single setting with a single default router IP address. Also, IP did not define a backup or load-sharing mechanism for multiple routers connected to the same subnet.

First Hop Redundancy Protocols (FHRPs) add the function of redundancy and load sharing for the default router function in any subnet.

This chapter begins with the concepts central to all FHRPs. All FHRPs define how multiple routers work together to appear as a single default router, sharing responsibility. All the FHRPs hide their existence from the hosts, so there is no change to host routing logic. The second section examines the most popular FHRP: Hot Standby Router Protocol (HSRP). The final section compares HSRP with the other two FHRPs: Virtual Router Redundancy Protocol (VRRP) and Global Load Balancing Protocol (GLBP).

"Do I Know This Already?" Quiz

Take the quiz (either here or use the PTP software) if you want to use the score to help you decide how much time to spend on this chapter. The letter answers are listed at the bottom of the page following the quiz. Appendix C, found both at the end of the book as well as on the companion website, includes both the answers and explanations. You can also find both answers and explanations in the PTP testing software.

Table 16-1 "Do I Know This Already?" Foundation Topics Section-to-Question Mapping

Foundation Topics Section	Questions
First Hop Redundancy Protocols	1, 2
Hot Standby Router Protocol	3, 4
VRRP and GLBP Concepts	5, 6

1. R1 and R2 attach to the same Ethernet VLAN, with subnet 10.1.19.0/25, with addresses 10.1.19.1 and 10.1.19.2, respectively, configured with the **ip address** interface subcommand. Host A refers to 10.1.19.1 as its default router, and host B refers to 10.1.19.2 as its default router. The routers do not use an FHRP. Which of the following is a problem for this LAN?

   a. The design breaks IPv4 addressing rules because two routers cannot connect to the same LAN subnet.

   b. If one router fails, neither host can send packets off-subnet.

   c. If one router fails, both hosts will use the one remaining router as a default router.

   d. If one router fails, the host that uses that router as a default router cannot send packets off-subnet.

2. R1 and R2 attach to the same Ethernet VLAN, with subnet 10.1.19.0/25, with addresses 10.1.19.1 and 10.1.19.2, respectively, configured with the **ip address** interface subcommand. The routers use an FHRP. Host A and host B attach to the same LAN and have correct default router settings per the FHRP configuration. Which of the following statements is true for this LAN?

   a. The design breaks IPv4 addressing rules because two routers cannot connect to the same LAN subnet.

   b. If one router fails, neither host can send packets off-subnet.

   c. If one router fails, both hosts will use the one remaining router as a default router.

   d. If one router fails, only one of the two hosts will still be able to send packets off-subnet.

3. R1 and R2 attach to the same Ethernet VLAN, with subnet 10.1.19.0/25, with addresses 10.1.19.1 and 10.1.19.2, respectively, configured with the **ip address** interface subcommand. The routers use HSRP. The network engineer prefers to have R1 be the default router when both R1 and R2 are up. Which of the following is the likely default router setting for hosts in this subnet?

   a. 10.1.19.1

   b. 10.1.19.2

   c. Another IP address in subnet 10.1.19.0/25 other than 10.1.19.1 and 10.1.19.2

   d. A host name that the FHRP mini-DNS will initially point to 10.1.19.1

4. Routers R1, R2, and R3, with addresses 10.1.1.1, 10.1.1.2, and 10.1.1.3, respectively, are in HSRPv2 group 16, and use VIP 10.1.1.8. R2 is the current HSRP active router. Which statement is true about HSRP operation in the subnet?

   a. Traffic from hosts in the subnet balances across all routers (R1, R2, and R3).

   b. Traffic from hosts in the subnet flows into only router R2.

   c. Router R1 only replies to ARP requests for address 10.1.1.8.

   d. The HSRP group uses virtual MAC 0000.0C9F.F016.

5. Routers R1, R2, and R3, with addresses 10.1.1.1, 10.1.1.2, and 10.1.1.3, respectively, are in VRRPv3 group 32. R3 is the current VRRP active router. Which statements are true about VRRP operation in the subnet? (Choose two answers.)

    a. The current VIP may be 10.1.1.3.

    b. The current VIP must be 10.1.1.3.

    c. VRRP sends its group messages to multicast address 224.0.0.18.

    d. VRRP sends its group messages to multicast address 224.0.0.2.

6. Which answer best describes a mechanism that enables GLBP to achieve active/active load balancing, with all routers in the group forwarding packets as a default router?

    a. By configuring a VIP that matches one of the router's interface IP addresses

    b. By using a different VIP per router in the same group

    c. By using a separate GLBP group for each router

    d. By using a different virtual MAC address per router in the same group

Foundation Topics

First Hop Redundancy Protocols

When networks use a design that includes redundant routers, switches, LAN links, and WAN links, in some cases, other protocols are required to take advantage of that redundancy and prevent problems caused by it.

For instance, imagine a WAN with many remote branch offices. If each remote branch has two WAN links connecting it to the rest of the network, those routers can use an IP routing protocol to pick the best routes. The routing protocol learns routes over both WAN links, adding the best route into the routing table. When the better WAN link fails, the routing protocol adds the alternate route to the IP routing table, taking advantage of the redundant link.

As another example, consider a LAN with redundant links and switches. Those LANs have problems unless the switches use Spanning Tree Protocol (STP) or Rapid STP (RSTP). STP/RSTP prevents the problems created by frames that loop through those extra redundant paths in the LAN.

This section examines yet another protocol that helps when a network uses some redundancy, this time with redundant default routers. When two or more routers connect to the same LAN subnet, the hosts in that subnet could use any of the routers as their default router. However, another protocol is needed to use the redundant default routers best. The term **First Hop Redundancy Protocol (FHRP)** refers to the category of protocols that enable hosts to take advantage of redundant routers in a subnet.

This first major section of the chapter discusses the major concepts behind how different FHRPs work. This section begins by discussing a network's need for redundancy in general and the need for redundant default routers.

The Need for Redundancy in Networks

Networks need redundant links to improve the availability of those networks. Eventually, something in a network will fail. A router power supply might fail, or a link might break, or a switch might lose power. And those WAN links, shown as simple lines in most drawings in this book, represent the most complicated physical parts of the network, with many individual components that can fail as well.

Depending on the design of the network, the failure of a single component might mean an outage that affects at least some part of the user population. Network engineers refer to any one component that, if it fails, brings down that part of the network as a *single point of failure*. For instance, in Figure 16-1, the LANs appear to have some redundancy, whereas the WAN does not. If most of the traffic flows between sites, many single points of failure exist, as shown in the figure.

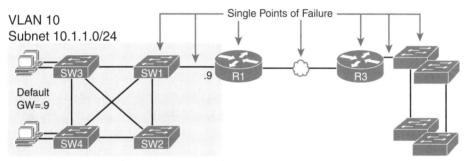

Figure 16-1 *R1 and the One WAN Link as Single Points of Failure*

The figure notes several components as a single point of failure. If any of the network's noted parts fail, packets cannot flow from the left side of the network to the right.

To improve availability, the network engineer first looks at a design and finds the single points of failure. Then the engineer chooses where to add to the network so that one (or more) single point of failure now has redundant options, increasing availability. In particular, the engineer

- Adds redundant devices and links

- Implements any necessary functions that take advantage of the redundant device or link

For instance, of all the single points of failure in Figure 16-1, the most expensive over the long term would likely be the WAN link because of the ongoing monthly charge. However, statistically, the WAN links are the most likely component to fail. So, a good upgrade from the network in Figure 16-1 would be to add a WAN link and possibly even connect to another router on the right side of the network, as shown in Figure 16-2.

Many real enterprise networks follow designs like Figure 16-2, with one router at each remote site, two WAN links connecting back to the main site, and redundant routers at the main site (on the right side of the figure). Compared to Figure 16-1, the design in Figure 16-2 has fewer single points of failure. Of the remaining single points of failure, a risk remains, but it is a calculated risk. For many outages, a reload of the router solves the problem, and the outage is short. But the risk still exists that the switch or router hardware will fail and require time to deliver a replacement device on-site before that site can work again.

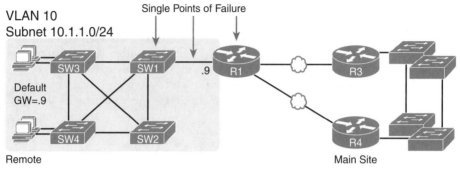

Figure 16-2 *Higher Availability but with R1 Still as a Single Point of Failure*

For enterprises that can justify more expense, the next step in higher availability for that remote site is to protect against those catastrophic router and switch failures. In this particular design, adding one router on the left side of the network in Figure 16-2 removes all the single points of failure noted earlier. Figure 16-3 shows the design with a second router, which connects to a different LAN switch so that SW1 is no longer a single point of failure.

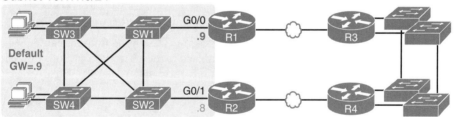

Figure 16-3 *Removing All Single Points of Failure from the Network Design*

> **NOTE** Medium to large enterprise networks work hard to balance high-availability features versus the available budget dollars. Cisco.com has many design documents that discuss tradeoffs in high-availability design. If interested in learning more, search Cisco.com for the Cisco Design Zone section of the site.

The Need for a First Hop Redundancy Protocol

Of the designs shown so far in this chapter, only Figure 16-3's design has two routers to support the LAN on the left side of the figure, specifically the same VLAN and subnet.

Answers to the "Do I Know This Already?" quiz:

1 D **2** C **3** C **4** B **5** A, C **6** D

While having the redundant routers on the same subnet helps, the network must use an FHRP when these redundant routers exist.

To see the need and benefit of using an FHRP, first think about how these redundant routers could be used as default routers by the hosts in VLAN 10/subnet 10.1.1.0/24, as shown in Figure 16-4. The host logic will remain unchanged, so each host has a single default router setting. So, some design options for default router settings include the following:

- All hosts in the subnet use R1 (10.1.1.9) as their default router, and they statically reconfigure their default router setting to R2's 10.1.1.8 if R1 fails.

- All hosts in the subnet use R2 (10.1.1.8) as their default router, and they statically reconfigure their default router setting to R1's 10.1.1.9 if R2 fails.

- Half the hosts use R1 and half use R2 as their default router, and if either router fails, half of the users statically reconfigure their default router setting.

VLAN 10, Subnet 10.1.1.0/24

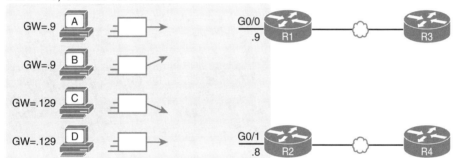

Figure 16-4 *Balancing Traffic by Assigning Different Default Routers to Different Clients*

To ensure the concept is clear, Figure 16-4 shows this third option, with half the hosts using R1 and the other half using R2. The figure removes all the LAN switches just to unclutter the figure. Hosts A and B use R1 as their default router, and hosts C and D use R2 as their default router.

All these options have a problem: the users must act. They have to know an outage occurred. They have to know how to reconfigure their default router setting. And they have to know when to change it back to the original setting.

FHRPs use the redundant default routers without the end users being aware of any changes. The two routers appear to be a single default router. The users never have to do anything: their default router setting remains the same, and their ARP tables remain the same.

To allow the hosts to remain unchanged, the routers must do more work, as defined by one of the FHRP protocols. Generically, each FHRP makes the following happen:

1. All hosts act like they always have, with one default router setting that never has to change.

2. The default routers share a virtual IP address in the subnet, defined by the FHRP.

3. Hosts use the FHRP virtual IP address as their default router address.

4. The routers exchange FHRP protocol messages so that both agree as to which router does what work at any point in time.

5. When a router fails or has some other problem, the routers use the FHRP to choose which router takes over responsibilities from the failed router.

The Three Solutions for First-Hop Redundancy

The term *First Hop Redundancy Protocol* does not name any one protocol. Instead, it names a family of protocols that fill the same role. For a given network, like the left side of Figure 16-4, the engineer would pick one of the protocols from the FHRP family.

> **NOTE** *First Hop* refers to the default router being the first router, or first router hop, through which a packet must pass.

Table 16-2 lists the three FHRP protocols in chronological order as first used in the market. Cisco first introduced the proprietary **Hot Standby Router Protocol (HSRP)**, which worked well for many customers. Later, the IETF developed an RFC for a similar protocol, **Virtual Router Redundancy Protocol (VRRP)**. Finally, Cisco developed a more robust option, **Gateway Load Balancing Protocol (GLBP)**.

Table 16-2 Three FHRP Options

Acronym	Full Name	Origin	Redundancy Approach	Load Balancing Per...
HSRP	Hot Standby Router Protocol	Cisco	active/standby	subnet
VRRP	Virtual Router Redundancy Protocol	RFC 5798	active/standby	subnet
GLBP	Gateway Load Balancing Protocol	Cisco	active/active	host

The CCNA 200-301 version 1.1 blueprint requires you to know the purpose, functions, and concepts of an FHRP. To do that, the next section takes a deep look at HSRP concepts, while the final section of the chapter compares VRRP and GLBP to HSRP. (This chapter does not discuss FHRP configuration, but if you want to learn beyond the plain wording of the exam topics, note that Appendix D, "Topics from Previous Editions," contains a short section about HSRP and GLBP configuration, copied from an earlier edition of the book.)

Hot Standby Router Protocol

HSRP operates with an active/standby model (more generally called *active/passive*). HSRP allows two (or more) routers to cooperate, all willing to act as the default router. However, at any one time, only one router actively supports the end-user traffic. The packets sent by hosts to their default router flow to that one active router. Then the other routers sit there patiently waiting to take over should the active HSRP router have a problem.

This next section of the chapter discusses how HSRP achieves its goal of providing default router redundancy. It progresses briefly through the mechanisms of virtual IP and MAC addresses, failover, load balancing, object tracking, and HSRP versions.

HSRP Virtual IP and MAC Addresses

The **HSRP active** router implements a **virtual IP address (VIP)** and matching **virtual MAC address**. This virtual IP address is part of the HSRP configuration, an additional configuration item compared to the usual **ip address** interface subcommand. This virtual IP address is in the same subnet as the interface IP address, but it is a different IP address. The router then automatically creates the virtual MAC address. All the cooperating HSRP routers know these virtual addresses, but only the HSRP active router uses these addresses at any one point in time.

Using HSRP protocol messages between the routers, the routers negotiate and settle in either the HSRP active or **HSRP standby** state. The router with the highest **HSRP priority** wins and becomes active, with the other router becoming the standby router. If the priorities tie, the router with the highest IP address wins and becomes active. (Also, note that while FHRPs often have only two routers in a group, if using three or more, HSRP uses only one standby router, with the other routers in a listen state, waiting to become the new standby router one day.)

The active router implements the virtual IP and MAC addresses on its interface in addition to its configured interface IP address. Hosts refer to the virtual IP address as their default router address instead of any router's interface IP address. For instance, in Figure 16-5, R1 and R2 use HSRP. The HSRP virtual IP address is 10.1.1.1, with the virtual MAC address referenced as VMAC1 for simplicity's sake.

16

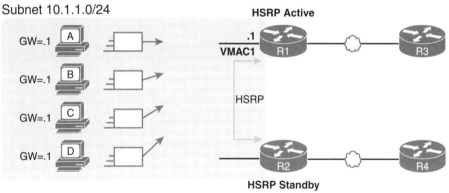

Figure 16-5 *All Traffic Goes to .1 (R1, Which Is Active); R2 Is Standby*

HSRP Failover

Under normal conditions, with all devices and interfaces working, one HSRP router is the default router, with another standing by. That might happen for months before the standby router needs to take over. However, so that the standby router knows when to act, the two routers continue to send HSRP messages to each other.

HSRP uses HSRP Hello messages to let the other HSRP routers in the same HSRP group know that the active router continues to work. HSRP defines a Hello timer, which dictates how often (in seconds) between successive Hello messages sent by the active router. HSRP also defines a Hold timer, typically more than three times the Hello timer. When the standby router fails to receive a Hello from the active router within the time defined by the hold time, the standby router believes the active router has failed, and begins taking over as the active router.

For example, Figure 16-6 shows the result when R1, the HSRP active router in Figure 16-5, loses power. R2 fails to receive additional HSRP Hellos from router R1 for hold time. At that point, R2, the new active router, starts using the virtual IP and MAC addresses.

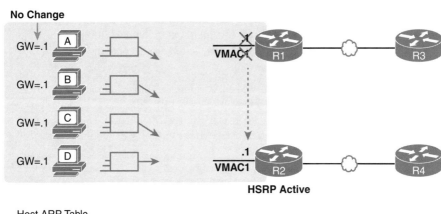

Figure 16-6 *Packets Sent Through R2 (New Active) After It Takes Over for Failed R1*

The figure shows packets flowing from the hosts toward router R2, with no changes on the hosts. The host keeps the same default router setting, referencing the virtual IP address (10.1.1.1). The host's ARP table does not have to change either, with the ARP entry for the default router listing the virtual MAC.

To direct the Ethernet frames that formerly flowed to router R1 to instead flow to router R2, changes occur on both the routers and the LAN switches. The new active router (R2) must be ready to receive packets (encapsulated inside frames) using the virtual IP and MAC addresses. The LAN switches, hidden in the last few figures, must also change their MAC address tables. Formerly, their MAC tables directed frames destined for VMAC1 to router R1, but now the switches must know to send the frames to the new active router, R2.

To make the switches change their MAC address table entries for VMAC1, R2 sends an Ethernet frame with VMAC1 as the source MAC address. The switches, as normal, learn the source MAC address (VMAC1) but with new ports that point toward R2. The frame is also a LAN broadcast, so all the switches learn a MAC table entry for VMAC1 that leads toward R2. (By the way, this Ethernet frame holds an ARP Reply message, called a gratuitous ARP, because the router sends it without first receiving an ARP Request.)

HSRP Load Balancing

The active/standby model of HSRP means that all hosts send their off-subnet packets through only one router. In other words, the routers do not share the workload; instead, one router forwards all the packets. For instance, back in Figure 16-5, R1 was the active router. All hosts in the subnet sent their packets through R1, and none of them sent their packets through R2.

HSRP does support load balancing by preferring different routers to be the active router in different subnets. Most sites that require a second router for redundancy also use several VLANs and subnets at the site. The two routers will likely connect to all the VLANs, acting as the default router in each subnet. The HSRP configuration settings can result in one router being active in one subnet and another router being active in another subnet, balancing the traffic. Or you can configure multiple instances of HSRP in the same subnet (called multiple HSRP groups), preferring one router to be active in one group and the other router to be selected as active in another.

For instance, Figure 16-7 shows a redesigned LAN with two hosts in VLAN 1 and two in VLAN 2. R1 and R2 connect to the LAN using a VLAN trunking and router-on-a-stick (ROAS) configuration. The two routers define two HSRP groups, one to support each of the two subnets. In this case, R1 wins and becomes active in Subnet 1, while router R2 becomes active in Subnet 2.

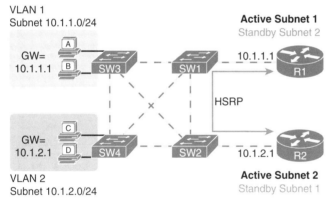

Figure 16-7 *Load Balancing with HSRP by Using Different Active Routers per Subnet*

Note that the design uses both routers and WAN links by having each router act as the HSRP active router in some subnets.

The example surrounding Figure 16-7 raises the question of where to consider using HSRP. You should consider an FHRP on any router or Layer 3 switch interface with an IP address that connects to hosts that rely on a default router setting. If only one router connects to the subnet, you do not need an FHRP, but if two or more connect to the subnet, you benefit from using an FHRP.

HSRP Interface Tracking

Another feature supported by all the FHRPs tracks the operational state of other router features. IOS allows for tracking of interface state, tracking routes in the IP routing table, and other types of objects. When the tracked interface or object fails, HSRP reduces that router's

HSRP priority. With well-chosen priority and tracking settings, you can arrange the HSRP configuration so that when everything works perfectly, one router is active. Later, when something fails related to that router, another router preempts and takes over as the active router.

Figure 16-8 shows one classic failure case that can occur without tracking. In this example, router R1 uses priority 110, with router R2 using 100 (the default), so R1 wins and becomes HSRP active. However, the one WAN link connected to R1 fails. R1 remains the HSRP active router. In this failure case, hosts forward packets to router R1, which has to forward them to router R2, which has the only working WAN link.

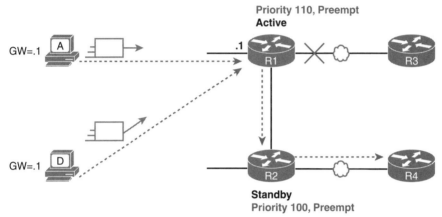

Figure 16-8   *Problem: Extra Routing Hop When the R1 WAN Link Fails*

A better plan links the HSRP role to the WAN link state. For instance, with interface tracking and preemption, you can configure HSRP as follows:

If R1's WAN link is up, make R1 HSRP active.

If R1's WAN link is down, make R2 HSRP active.

To do so, HSRP object tracking on R1 monitors the state of the R1 WAN interface. If the interface fails, HSRP lowers R1's HSRP priority, allowing R2 to preempt R1. For example:

1.   R1 notices its WAN interface fails.

2.   R1 lowers its HSRP priority by 20 points.

3.   HSRP messages allow both R1 and R2 to realize that R2 has a better (higher) priority and has the right to preempt.

4.   R2, using preemption, becomes the HSRP active router.

As a result, while router R1's WAN link is down, packets from the hosts on the left flow first to R2 and then out a WAN link. Later, when R1's WAN link recovers, it preempts router R2 and becomes active again.

HSRP Recovery and Preemption

The **HSRP preemption** also dictates what happens when a formerly active router recovers, independent of any HSRP tracking. HSRP disables preemption by default but supports it on any router.

First, consider the following scenario:

1. R1 has priority 110, and R2 has priority 100, so R1 wins and becomes active, while R2 becomes standby.

2. Later, R1 fails, so R2 becomes active.

3. When R1 recovers, what happens?

With the default setting of no preemption, R2 remains the active router. With only two routers in the HSRP group, when R1 recovers, it moves to a standby state, ready to take over from R2 when R2 next fails. In that case, the operations staff can choose when to make the failover happen, for instance, off-shift, when a minor outage has no impact.

If you prefer, you can enable preemption. With preemption, in this case, or any case in which a new router appears in the group that has a better (higher) priority than the active router, it takes over as the active router. The switch to a new active router is methodical but quick, without waiting for timers like the Hello and Hold timers to expire, but it might cause a disruption in packet flow for a second or two. (Note that preemption does not apply to cases where the priorities tie, but only when the new router has a higher priority.)

HSRP Versions

Cisco routers and Layer 3 switches support two versions of HSRP: versions 1 and 2. The versions have enough differences, like multicast IP addresses used and message formats, so routers in the same HSRP group must use the same version. Suppose two routers configured in the same HSRP group mistakenly use different versions. In that case, they will not understand each other and will ignore each other for the purposes of HSRP.

There are good reasons to use the more recent HSRP version 2 (HSRPv2). HSRPv2 added IPv6 support. It also supports faster convergence when changes happen using shorter Hello and Hold timers, while HSRPv1 typically had a minimum of a 1-second Hello timer. Table 16-3 lists the differences between HSRPv1 and HSRPv2.

Table 16-3   HSRPv1 Versus HSRPv2

Feature	Version 1	Version 2
IPv6 support	No	Yes
Smallest unit for Hello timer	Second	Millisecond
Range of group numbers	0..255	0..4095
Virtual MAC address used (*xx* or *xxx* is the hex group number)	0000.0C07.AC*xx*	0000.0C9F.F*xxx*
IPv4 multicast address used	224.0.0.2	224.0.0.102

Ensure you understand how a router chooses the virtual MAC shown in the table. HSRPv1 supports 256 groups per interface, while HSRPv2 supports 4096. You can represent decimal values 0..255 with two-digit hexadecimal equivalents of 00..FF, while decimal values 0..4095 require three hex digits from 000..FFF. The HSRP virtual MAC addresses use the hex equivalents of the configured decimal HSRP group number as the last two or three digits of the virtual MAC address as follows:

HSRPv1: 0000.0C07.AC*xx*, where *xx* is the hex group number

HSRPv2: 0000.0C9F.F*xxx*, where *xxx* is the hex group number

For example, an HSRPv1 group 1 would use virtual MAC address 0000.0C07.AC**01**, while an HSRPv2 group would use 0000.0C9F.F**001**. For group decimal 100 (hex 64), they would use 0000.0C07.AC**64** and 0000.0C9F.F**064**, respectively.

VRRP and GLBP Concepts

Now that you have a thorough understanding of the purpose, functions, and concepts of HSRP, this third major section of the chapter examines the two other FHRPs: VRRP and GLBP. Both provide the same primary functions as HSRP. VRRP has more similarities with HSRP, while GLBP goes beyond HSRP with better load-balancing features.

Virtual Router Redundancy Protocol (VRRP)

HSRP and VRRP emerged in the 1990s when TCP/IP and routers first became common in corporate networks. As is often the case, Cisco saw a need, but with no standards-based solution, so they defined HSRP as a proprietary solution for first hop router redundancy. Later, the IETF created VRRP, providing similar features. However, unlike many stories of Cisco-proprietary pre-standard features, HSRP has not faded into history; you will still find both HSRP and VRRP support in many Cisco product families.

> **NOTE**   While VRRP includes versions 1, 2, and 3, all references in this chapter refer to VRRPv3 (RFC 5798.)

For similarities, note that VRRP supports all the same functions as HSRP, as described earlier in this chapter. The purpose remains to provide a standby backup for the default router function, preemption if desired, and load balancing the default router role by using multiple VRRP groups.

The differences come with default settings, protocol details, and addresses used. Table 16-4 lists some comparison points between HSRP, VRRP, and GLBP (ignore GLBP for now.)

Table 16-4   Comparing Features of the Three FHRP Options

Acronym	HSRPv2	VRRPv3	GLBP
Cisco Proprietary	Yes	No	Yes
VIP must differ from the routers' interface IP addresses	Yes	No	Yes
Preemption off by default	Yes	No	Yes
Allows preemption (or not)	Yes	Yes	Yes
Default priority value (decimal)	100	100	100
Supports tracking to change the priority	Yes	Yes	Yes
Supports IPv4 and IPv6	Yes	Yes	Yes
Active/active load balancing with multiple active routers in one group	No	No	Yes
IPv4 multicast address used	224.0.0.102	224.0.0.18	224.0.0.102
Group numbers supported in IOS	0–4095	1–255	0–1023
Virtual MAC address pattern	0000.0c9f.fxxx	0000.5e00.01xx	0007.b40x.xxrr

You can configure VRRP so that it appears to work like HSRP. Two or more VRRP routers form a group within one subnet. VRRP routers define one VIP, use multicast messages to communicate with each other, use an active/standby approach, select the active router with the same logic as HSRP, allow tracking, and fail over when the master (active) router fails. (Note that VRRP uses the terms *master* and *backup* rather than *active* and *standby*.)

One difference comes in the choice of VIP. You can use the same IP address as one of the VRRP routers' interface addresses or, like HSRP, use another IP address in the subnet. For example, the HSRP discussion around Figures 16-5 and 16-6 used VIP 10.1.1.1, with router addresses 10.1.1.9 and 10.1.1.8. You could do the same with VRRP or use 10.1.1.9 (the same IP address as router R1's interface IP address).

VRRP has protocol differences as well. It uses a multicast IPv4 address (224.0.0.18) for its messages. While it uses a single virtual MAC per group, the MAC address follows a different pattern. VRRP configuration uses decimal group numbers from 1 to 255 decimal. The virtual MAC uses the equivalent two-digit hex group number at the end of the virtual MAC, with VRRP routers choosing their virtual MAC based on this pattern:

VRRPv3: 0000.5e00.01xx, where xx is the hex group number

GLBP Concepts

16

Cisco-proprietary GLBP, defined after HSRP and VRRP, provides the same benefits as HSRP and VRRP but with different implementation details. But it also includes different internals that allow much more effective load balancing. So, while used for redundancy (the *R* in FHRP), GLBP also adds robust load balancing, per its name.

This GLBP section begins with comparisons to the other FHRPs and then discusses its improved approach to load balancing.

Similarities of GLBP, HSRP, and VRRP

GLBP provides redundancy for the default router function while hiding that redundancy from the hosts using that default router address. But most of the core features follow a familiar theme:

■ It uses a virtual IP address (VIP), which is the address used by endpoints as their default router.

■ It identifies the best router in the group based on the highest priority.

■ It allows for the preemption of the best router when a new router with a better (higher) priority joins the group.

■ It supports tracking, which dynamically lowers one router's priority, allowing another router to preempt the first based on conditions like an interface failure.

■ It sends messages using multicasts but uses a different address: 224.0.0.102.

GLBP uses virtual MAC addresses differently than the other FHRPs as part of the underlying support for load balancing. Like HSRP and VRRP, a GLBP group has one VIP. Unlike HSRP and VRRP, the routers in a group do not use one virtual MAC address whose function resides with the one active router. Instead, GLBP uses a unique virtual MAC address per GLBP router.

The MAC address value includes three hex digits to represent the decimal GLBP group number, with the unique last two digits (01, 02, 03, or 04) representing the four allowed GLBP routers in a group. The MAC address pattern is 0007.b40x.xxrr. For instance, for two routers in the same GLBP group:

Router R1: 0007:b400:**1401** (Decimal group 20, which is hex group 014, assigned router number 01)

Router R2: 0007:b400:**1402** (Decimal group 20, which is hex group 014, assigned router number 02)

GLBP Active/Active Load Balancing

With a name like Gateway Load Balancing Protocol, load balancing should be a key feature. The term *gateway* refers to the alternate term for default router (*default gateway*), so by name, GLBP claims to load balance across the default routers in a subnet—and it does.

GLBP manipulates the hosts' IP ARP tables in a subnet so that some hosts forward packets to one router and some to another. As usual, all the hosts use the same VIP as their default router address. Under normal conditions, with multiple GLBP routers working in the subnet, GLBP spreads the default router workload across all GLBP group members. When one of those routers fails, GLBP defines the methods by which the remaining router or routers take over the role of the failed router.

To achieve this active/active load balancing, one GLBP performs the role of **GLBP active virtual gateway (AVG)**. The AVG handles all ARP functions for the VIP. Knowing the virtual MAC addresses of all the routers in the group, the AVG replies to some ARP Requests with one virtual MAC and some with the other. As a result, some hosts in the subnet send frames to the Ethernet MAC address of one of the routers, with different hosts sending their frames to the MAC address of the second router.

All routers serve as a **GLBP active virtual forwarder (AVF)** to support load balancing. All the AVFs sit ready to receive Ethernet frames addressed to their unique virtual MAC address and to route the encapsulated packets as usual. Note that one router serves as both AVG and AVF.

Figures 16-9 and 16-10 show the results of two ARP Reply messages from AVG R1. First, Figure 16-9 shows how a GLBP balances traffic for host A based on the ARP Reply sent by the AVG (R1). The two AVF routers support virtual IP address 10.1.1.1, with the hosts using that address as their default router setting.

The figure shows three messages, top to bottom, with the following action:

1. Host A has no ARP table entry for its default router, 10.1.1.1, so host A sends an ARP Request to learn 10.1.1.1's MAC address.

2. The GLBP AVG, R1 in this case, sends back an ARP Reply. The AVG includes its virtual MAC address in the ARP Reply, VMAC1.

3. Host A encapsulates future IP packets in Ethernet frames destined for VMAC1, so they arrive at R1 (also an AVF).

10.1.1.0/24

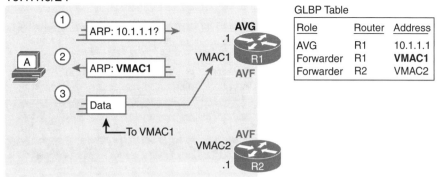

Figure 16-9 *GLBP Directs Host A by Sending Back the ARP Reply with R1's VMAC1*

To balance the load, the AVG answers each new ARP Request with the MAC addresses of alternating routers. Figure 16-10 continues the load-balancing effect with host B's ARP Request for 10.1.1.1. The router acting as AVG (R1) still sends the ARP Reply, but this time with R2's virtual MAC (VMAC2).

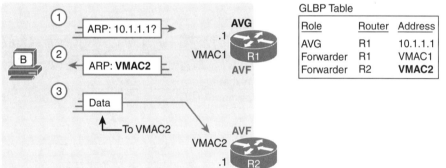

Figure 16-10 *GLBP Directs Host B by Sending Back the ARP Reply with R2's VMAC2*

Here are the steps in the figure:

1. Host B sends an ARP Request to learn 10.1.1.1's MAC address.

2. The GLBP AVG (R1) sends back an ARP Reply, listing VMAC2, R2's virtual MAC address.

3. Host B cncapsulates future IP packets in Ethernet frames destined for VMAC2, so they arrive at R2.

Finally, to capture a few related points beyond this GLBP example, note that GLBP uses priority, preemption, and tracking. However, those rules apply to the AVG only; all GLBP routers serve as AVFs. So, if the AVG fails, the remaining routers in a GLBP group elect a new AVG.

That model requires additional logic to deal with AVF failures. When a router serving as only an AVF fails, the AVG recognizes the failure and causes a still-functional AVF to begin receiving frames sent to the failed AVF's virtual MAC address.

Chapter Review

One key to doing well on the exams is to perform repetitive spaced review sessions. Review this chapter's material using either the tools in the book or interactive tools for the same material found on the book's companion website. Refer to the "Your Study Plan" element for more details. Table 16-5 outlines the key review elements and where you can find them. To better track your study progress, record when you completed these activities in the second column.

Table 16-5   Chapter Review Tracking

Review Element	Review Date(s)	Resource Used
Review key topics		Book, website
Review key terms		Book, website
Answer DIKTA questions		Book, PTP
Review memory tables		Website

Review All the Key Topics

Table 16-6   Key Topics for Chapter 16

Key Topic Element	Description	Page Number
List	Common characteristics of all FHRPs	355
Table 16-2	Comparisons of HSRP, VRRP, GLBP	356
Figure 16-5	HSRP concepts	357
Figure 16-6	HSRP failover results	358
Table 16-3	Comparing HSRPv1 and HSRPv2	361
Table 16-4	Comparing HSRP, VRRP, and GLBP	362
List	GLBP virtual MAC addresses	364
Figure 16-10	GLBP AVG ARP Reply referring to a different GLBP router	365

Key Terms You Should Know

First Hop Redundancy Protocol (FHRP), Gateway Load Balancing Protocol (GLBP), GLBP active virtual forwarder (AVF), GLBP active virtual gateway (AVG), Hot Standby Router Protocol (HSRP), HSRP active, HSRP preemption, HSRP priority, HSRP standby, virtual IP address (VIP), virtual MAC address, Virtual Router Redundancy Protocol (VRRP)

CHAPTER 17

SNMP, FTP, and TFTP

This chapter covers the following exam topics:

4.0 Infrastructure Services

> **4.4 Explain the function of SNMP in network operations**
>
> **4.9 Describe the capabilities and functions of TFTP/FTP in the network**

To close this part of the book about a variety of IP Services, this chapter focuses on two topics of managing routers and switches as an end to themselves.

Network engineers have used Simple Network Management Protocol (SNMP) as the main network management protocol for decades. As per the associated exam topic, the first major section focuses on SNMP concepts rather than configuration, including how managed devices—SNMP agents—can be interrogated by network management systems—SNMP clients—to find the current status of each device.

The second major section of the chapter examines the mechanics of transferring files with the FTP and TFTP protocols. The first topic of this section focuses on a few practical uses of TFTP and FTP when working with Cisco routers to upgrade the IOS. Armed with that practical knowledge, you then look at the protocol details of both FTP and TFTP in the rest of the section.

"Do I Know This Already?" Quiz

Take the quiz (either here or use the PTP software) if you want to use the score to help you decide how much time to spend on this chapter. The letter answers are listed at the bottom of the page following the quiz. Appendix C, found both at the end of the book as well as on the companion website, includes both the answers and explanations. You can also find both answers and explanations in the PTP testing software.

Table 17-1 "Do I Know This Already?" Foundation Topics Section-to-Question Mapping

Foundation Topics Section	Questions
Simple Network Management Protocol	1–3
FTP and TFTP	4–6

1. A Network Management Station (NMS) is using SNMP to manage some Cisco routers and switches with SNMPv2c. Which of the following answers most accurately describes how the SNMP agent on a router authenticates any SNMP Get requests received from the NMS?

    a. Using a username and hashed version of a password

    b. Using either the read-write or read-only community string

    c.   Using only the read-write community string

    d.   Using only the read-only community string

2. Which of the following SNMP messages are typically sent by an SNMP agent? (Choose two answers.)

    a.   Trap

    b.   Get Request

    c.   Inform

    d.   Set Request

3. Which SNMP verbs were added for SNMP Version 2 to improve the efficiency of retrieving lists of related MIB variables?

    a.   GetBulk

    b.   Get

    c.   GetNext

    d.   Inform

4. An FTP client connects to an FTP server using active mode and retrieves a copy of a file from the server. Which of the answers describes a TCP connection initiated by the FTP client?

    a.   The FTP control connection only

    b.   The FTP data connection only

    c.   Both the FTP data and control connections

    d.   Neither the FTP data nor control connections

5. Which of the following functions are supported by FTP but not by TFTP? (Choose two answers.)

    a.   Transferring files from client to server

    b.   Changing the current directory on the server

    c.   Transferring files from server to client

    d.   Listing directory contents of a server's directory

6. In an IOS XE router, the **pwd** command output lists directory "bootflash:". Which answers describe what you would expect to see in the output of the **show bootflash:** and **dir** commands? (Choose two answers.)

    a.   The **dir** command lists all files in file system bootflash:, including files in subdirectories.

    b.   The **show bootflash:** command lists all files in file system bootflash:, including files in subdirectories.

    c.   The **dir** command lists files in the root of bootflash:, but not files in subdirectories.

    d.   The **show bootflash:** command lists files in the root of bootflash:, but not files in subdirectories.

Foundation Topics

Simple Network Management Protocol

In 1988, RFC 1065, "Structure and Identification of Management Information for TCP/IP-based Internets," was published. SNMP uses a model of breaking down the information about devices on a TCP/IP-based network—configuration settings, status information, counters, and so on—into a database of variables. Management software could then collect those variables to monitor and manage the IP-based network. After all, the elements of any IP-based machines would have commonalities. For example, a PC, a network printer, and a router would all have commonalities such as interfaces, IP addresses, and buffers. Why not create a standardized database of these variables and a simple system for monitoring and managing them? This idea was brilliant, caught on, and became what we know today as **Simple Network Management Protocol (SNMP)**.

In this major section of the chapter, we now turn our attention to SNMP by looking at the major concepts along with the two common versions used today: **SNMPv2c** and **SNMPv3**.

SNMP defines request and response messages for communication between **SNMP managers** and **SNMP agents**. An SNMP manager is a network management application running on a PC or server, with that host typically called a **Network Management System (NMS)**. Many SNMP agents exist in the network, one per device that is managed. The SNMP agent is software running inside each device (router, switch, and so on), with knowledge of all the variables on that device that describe the device's configuration, status, and counters. The SNMP manager uses SNMP protocols to communicate with each SNMP agent.

Each agent keeps a database of variables that comprise the parameters, status, and counters for the device's operations. This database, called the **Management Information Base (MIB)**, has some core elements in common across most networking devices. It also has many variables unique to that type of device—for instance, router MIBs will include variables not needed on switch MIBs, and vice versa. (For perspective, I checked a router when writing this section and found a little over 7000 MIB variables on a router.)

Figure 17-1 connects a few of these ideas and terms. First, many companies sell SNMP management products. For example, the Cisco Catalyst Center (formerly Cisco DNA Center) controller (www.cisco.com/go/catalystcenter) uses SNMP (and other protocols) to manage networks. IOS on routers and switches include an SNMP agent with built-in MIB.

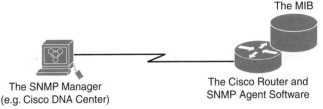

The MIB

The SNMP Manager
(e.g. Cisco DNA Center)

The Cisco Router and
SNMP Agent Software

Figure 17-1 *Elements of Simple Network Management Protocol*

Answers to the "Do I Know This Already?" quiz:

1 B **2** A, C **3** A **4** A **5** B, D **6** B, C

SNMP Variable Reading and Writing: SNMP Get and Set

The NMS typically polls the SNMP agent on each device. The NMS can notify the human user in front of the PC or send emails, texts, and so on to notify the network operations staff of any issues identified by the data found by polling the devices. You can even reconfigure the device through these SNMP variables in the MIB if you permit this level of control.

Specifically, the NMS uses the **SNMP Get** request message to ask for information from an agent. The NMS sends an **SNMP Set** request message to write variables on the SNMP agent to configure the device. These messages come in pairs, with, for instance, a Get Request asking the agent for the contents of a variable, and the Get Response supplying that information. Figure 17-2 shows an example of a typical flow, with the NMS using an SNMP Get to ask for the MIB variable that describes the status of a particular router interface.

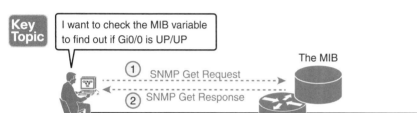

Figure 17-2 *SNMP Get Request and Get Response Message Flow*

The original SNMP Version 1 (SNMPv1) standard defined two types of Get requests: Get and GetNext. The Get request lists one or more specific variable names, with the SNMP agent sending back a Get response that lists the values of those specific variables. However, the Get response requires the listing of a specific variable, which requires some processing by the NMS.

The GetNext request takes a slightly different approach that reduces some processing at the NMS. GetNext also asks for the contents of variables; however, a GetNext request asks for the next variable in the agent's MIB after the listed variable. So, the NMS can do the work to find the specific name of one variable, and then issue a series of GetNext requests to get the next instance of that variable, and the next, and so on.

For instance, imagine a router has many interfaces, as usual. The router's MIB has variables for each interface, for instance, for interface MAC and IP addresses. First, the NMS identifies the specific variable names for the first interface and uses a Get request on those variables. However, to get those same variables for the second interface, GetNext can refer to the names of the variables for the first interface, without having to do the processing to derive the specific variable names for the second interface. It reduces the overhead to traverse and retrieve variables in a list.

SNMP Version 2 (SNMPv2) added the GetBulk request as an additional improvement over GetNext. While one GetNext requests the next variable in a list or table, GetBulk can request more than one successive variable. For instance, to retrieve data for eight router interfaces, the NMS could begin with one Get and then be more efficient with seven more GetNext requests, for each additional interface. One GetBulk request could ask for the MAC and IP address of the next eight interfaces on a router, again making the process more efficient.

17

SNMP permits much flexibility in how you monitor variables in the MIB. A network administrator gathers and stores statistics over time using the NMS. With the stored data, the NMS can analyze various statistical facts such as averages, minimums, and maximums. To be proactive, administrators can set thresholds for certain key variables, telling the NMS to send a notification (email, text, and so on) when a threshold is passed.

SNMP Notifications: Traps and Informs

In addition to asking for information with Get commands and setting variables on agents with the Set command, SNMP agents can initiate communications to the NMS. These messages, generally called *notifications*, use two specific SNMP messages: Trap and Inform. Agents send an SNMP Trap or **SNMP Inform** message to the NMS to list the value of certain MIB variables when those variables reach a certain state.

As an example of a Trap, suppose that Router 1's G0/0 interface fails, as shown at step 1 of Figure 17-3. With Traps configured, the router would send an **SNMP Trap** message to the NMS, with that Trap message noting the down state of the G0/0 interface. Then, the NMS software can send a text message to the network support staff, pop up a window on the NMS screen, change the color of the correct router icon to red on the graphical interface, and so on.

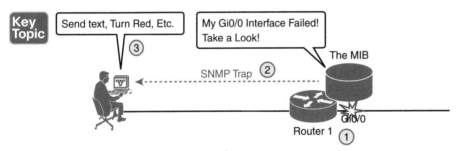

Figure 17-3 *SNMP Trap Notification Process*

SNMP Trap and Inform messages have the exact same purpose but differ in the protocol mechanisms. SNMP Traps, available since the first version of SNMP (SNMPv1), use a fire-and-forget process. The SNMP agent sends the Trap to the IP address of the NMS, with UDP as the transport protocol as with all SNMP messages, and with no application layer error recovery. If the Trap arrives, great; if it is lost in transit, it is lost.

Inform messages inform the NMS but with reliability added. Added to the protocol with SNMPv2, Informs also use UDP, but add application layer reliability. The NMS must acknowledge receipt of the Inform with an SNMP Response message, or the SNMP agent will time out and resend the Inform.

Note that Traps and Informs both have a useful role today, and Traps are still frequently used. Both inform the NMS. Traps use less overhead on the agent, while Informs improve reliability of the messages but require a little more overhead effort.

The Management Information Base

Every SNMP agent has its own Management Information Base. The MIB defines variables whose values are set and updated by the agent. The MIB variables on the devices in the network enable the management software to monitor/control the network device.

Each agent organizes its MIB in a hierarchical structure, with the individual variables called an *object ID* (OID). Each node in the tree can be described based on the tree structure sequence, either by name or by number. Figure 17-4 shows a small part of the tree structure of an MIB that happens to be part of the Cisco-proprietary part of the MIB.

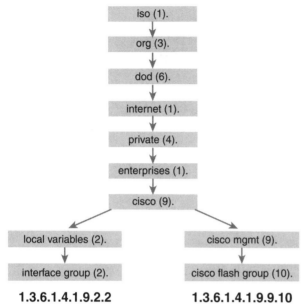

Figure 17-4   *Management Information Base (MIB)*

Working directly with an MIB, with long variable names and numbers, can be a bit of a challenge, so NMS software typically hides the complexity of the MIB variable numbering and names. However, to get a sense for the variable names, Figure 17-4 shows the tree structure for two variables, with the variable names being the long string of numbers shown at the bottom of the figure. Working with those numbers and the tree structure can be difficult at best. As a result, most people manage their networks using an NMS. For perspective, you could use an SNMP manager and type **MIB variable 1.3.6.1.4.1.9.2.1.58.0** and click a button to get that variable, to see the current CPU usage percentage from a Cisco router. However, most users of an NMS would much prefer to ignore those details and have a simple graphical interface to ask for the same information, never having to know that 1.3.6.1.4.9.2.1.58.0 represents the router CPU utilization MIB variable.

For an SNMP manager to manage each agent, the SNMP manager must have the same MIBs used by the various SNMP agents installed for proper SNMP operation. Each agent comes with a set of standard and vendor-proprietary MIBs built into the product. Expecting that, SNMP manager products also preload the most common MIBs in anticipation of managing those agents. Figure 17-5 shows the concept, with an SNMP manager on the left. It also shows a Cisco and non-Cisco switch on the right. The switches both support the standard MIB-II MIB plus a larger proprietary MIB built by each switch vendor.

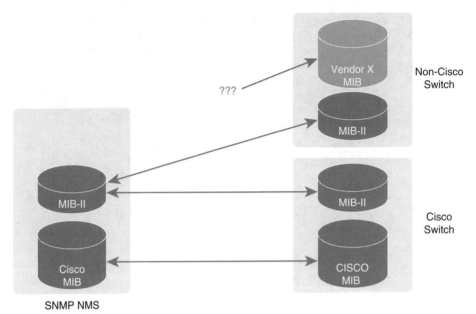

SNMP NMS

Figure 17-5 *Proprietary MIB Concepts*

The Cisco NMS comes preloaded with the MIBs for Cisco products, but not for all non-Cisco products. The arrow lines show the MIBs that match between the devices (agents) and the NMS. For those MIB variables, the NMS can issue Get requests to the Cisco switch. The NMS will also understand those variables in Trap or Inform messages. Likewise, the NMS can support Gets, Sets, Traps, and Informs using the MIB II in the non-Cisco switch. However, without the non-Cisco vendor's MIB loaded into the NMS, the NMS cannot ask for data from the non-Cisco vendor's MIB, and it will not understand Traps and Informs that use variables from that MIB. The solution? Download and install the other vendor's MIB into the NMS.

Securing SNMP

SNMP supports a few security mechanisms, depending in part on the particular version. This section works through the options.

First, one strong method to secure SNMP is to use ACLs to limit SNMP messages to those from known servers only. SNMP agents on Cisco routers and switches support SNMP messages that flow in both IPv4 and IPv6 packets. The SNMP agent can configure an IPv4 ACL to filter incoming SNMP messages that arrive in IPv4 packets and an IPv6 ACL to filter SNMP messages that arrive in IPv6 packets.

Using an IPv4 and IPv6 ACL to secure an agent makes good sense. The only hosts that should be sending SNMP messages to the SNMP agent in a router or switch are the NMS hosts. Those NMS hosts seldom move and their IP addresses should be well known to the networking staff. It makes good sense to configure an ACL that permits packets sourced from the IP addresses of all NMS hosts, but no others.

As for the SNMP protocol messages, all versions of SNMP support a basic clear-text password mechanism, although none of those versions refer to the mechanism as using a password. SNMP Version 3 (SNMPv3) adds more modern security as well.

SNMPv1 defined clear-text passwords called **SNMP communities**. Basically, both the SNMP agent and the SNMP manager need prior knowledge of the same SNMP community value (called a *community string*). The SNMP Get messages and the Set message include the appropriate community string value, in clear text. If the NMS sends a Get or Set with the correct community string, as configured on the SNMP agent, the agent processes the message.

SNMPv1 defines both a read-only community and a read-write community. The **read-only (RO) community** allows Get messages, and the **read-write (RW) community** allows both reads and writes (Gets and Sets). Figure 17-6 shows the concepts. At steps 1 and 2, the agent is configured with particular RO and RW community strings, and the NMS configures the matching values. At step 3, the SNMP Get can flow with either community, but at step 4, the Set Request must use the RW community.

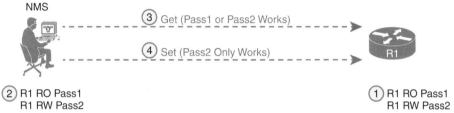

Figure 17-6 *RO and RW Communities with the Get and Set Commands*

SNMPv2 and the related Community-based SNMP Version 2 (SNMPv2c) added a wrinkle in naming but basically kept the same community security feature as SNMPv1 once the standards process completed. The original specifications for SNMPv2 did not include SNMPv1 communities; however, the marketplace still wanted communities, so an additional RFC added the SNMPv1 communities mechanism back to SNMPv2. This updated RFC, "Community-based SNMPv2," came to be known simply as SNMPv2c. Vendors (including Cisco) implemented SNMPv2c; however, security was still relatively weak.

SNMPv3 arrived with much celebration among network administrators. Finally, security had arrived with the powerful network management protocol. SNMPv3 does away with communities and replaces them with the following features:

- **Message integrity:** This mechanism, applied to all SNMPv3 messages, confirms whether or not each message has been changed during transit.

- **Authentication:** This optional feature adds authentication with both a username and password, with the password never sent as clear text. Instead, it uses a hashing method like many other modern authentication processes.

- **Encryption (privacy):** This optional feature encrypts the contents of SNMPv3 messages so that attackers who intercept the messages cannot read their contents.

NOTE The CCNA 200-301 version 1.1 exam blueprint lists SNMP in one exam topic, with that exam topic reduced to "explain SNMP." Some previous versions of the exam required configuration. Refer to Appendix D, "Topics from Previous Editions," if you're interested in learning about SNMP configuration and verification.

FTP and TFTP

This final major section of the chapter focuses on two topics: File Transfer Protocol (**FTP**) and Trivial File Transfer Protocol (**TFTP**). Both exist as TCP/IP protocols defined in RFCs. Both use a client and server model, in which the client connects to a server and then the client can copy files to the server or from the server. Both exist as a myriad of implementations of both client and server code, from command-line clients to apps with graphical interfaces, using the respective FTP or TFTP protocols behind the scenes.

This section discusses FTP and TFTP with two branches. First, we take a practical view of the most common use of TFTP and FTP by network engineers while on the job: the job of updating IOS images. The process can make use of TFTP and FTP, so this section provides the basics. Second, we move on to talk about FTP and TFTP in a much broader sense, with details about each protocol, their capabilities, and what capabilities each provides to any user.

Managing Cisco IOS Images with FTP/TFTP

IOS exists as a file—a single file—that the router then loads into RAM to use as its operating system. To better understand the process, you must understand a few more details about how IOS works. In particular, you need to understand the **IOS file system (IFS)**, which defines how IOS stores files (including the IOS file). The **IOS image** upgrade process occurs by copying new IOS files into the router and then booting the router with that new IOS.

The IOS File System

Every OS creates file systems to store files. A computer needs some type of permanent storage, but it needs more than just a place to store bytes. The OS organizes the storage into a file system, which includes directories, a structure, and filenames, with the associated rules. By using a file system, the OS can keep data organized so the user and the applications can find the data later.

Every OS defines its own file system conventions. Windows OSs, for instance, use a left-leaning slash (\) in directory structures, like \Desktop\Applications. Linux and macOS use a right-leaning slash, for example, /Desktop. Each OS refers to physical disks slightly differently as well, and IOS is no different.

As for the physical storage, Cisco routers typically use **flash memory**, with no hard disk drive. Flash memory is rewriteable, permanent storage, which is ideal for storing files that need to be retained when the router loses power. Cisco purposefully uses flash memory rather than hard disk drives in its products because there are no moving parts in flash memory, so there is a smaller chance of failure as compared with disk drives. Some routers have flash memory on the motherboard. Others have flash memory slots that allow easy removal and replacement of the flash card, but with the intent that the card remain in the device most of the time. Also, many devices have USB slots that support USB flash drives.

For each physical memory device in the router, IOS creates a simple IOS file system of type *disk*. In Example 17-1, a Cisco 1108 ISR router has an internal flash memory, with just under 3 GB of memory, which can be referenced as either bootflash:, flash:, or crashinfo:. The bottom of the output confirms that the single USB flash slot holds a flash drive with just under 32 GB, referenced by name usb0:.

Example 17-1   *Cisco IOS File Systems on a Router*

```
R2# show file systems
File Systems:


      Size(b)        Free(b)        Type  Flags  Prefixes
            -              -      opaque    rw    system:
            -              -      opaque    rw    tmpsys:
*   2968264704     1416036352        disk    rw    bootflash: flash: crashinfo:
    1634713600     1557024768        disk    ro    webui:
            -              -      opaque    rw    null:
            -              -      opaque    ro    tar:
            -              -     network    rw    tftp:
            -              -      opaque    wo    syslog:
      33554432       33534559       nvram    rw    nvram:
            -              -     network    rw    rcp:
            -              -     network    rw    http:
            -              -     network    rw    ftp:
            -              -     network    rw    scp:
            -              -     network    rw    sftp:
            -              -     network    rw    https:
            -              -      opaque    ro    cns:
    31022530560    31022514176        disk    rw    usb0:
```

Beyond the physical disks, IFS creates other types of disks for use by the operating system, as noted in this list. Example 17-1 also shows examples of each.

■ **Opaque:** To represent logical internal file systems for the convenience of internal functions and commands

■ **Network:** To represent external file systems found on different types of servers for the convenience of reference in different IOS commands

■ **Disk:** For physical disks, either internal or external flash

■ **NVRAM:** A special type for NVRAM memory, the default location of the startup-config file

Many IOS commands refer to files in an IFS, but only some commands refer directly to the files by their formal names. The formal names use the prefix as seen in the far right column of Example 17-1. For instance, the command **more flash0:/wotemp/fred** would display the contents of file *fred* in directory */wotemp* in the first flash memory slot in the router. (The **more** command itself displays the contents of a file.) However, many commands use a keyword that indirectly refers to a formal filename, to reduce typing. For example:

■ **show running-config** command: Refers to file system:running-config

■ **show startup-config** command: Refers to file nvram:startup-config

17

Upgrading IOS Images

One of the first steps to upgrade a router's IOS to a new version is to obtain the new IOS image and put it in the right location. Typically, Cisco routers have their IOS in one of the local physical file systems, most often in permanent flash. The only requirement is that the IOS be in some reachable file system—even if the file sits on an external server and the device loads the OS over the network. However, the best practice is to store each device's IOS file in flash that will remain with the device permanently.

Figure 17-7 illustrates the process to upgrade an IOS image into flash memory, using the following steps:

Step 1.   Obtain the IOS image from Cisco, usually by downloading the IOS image from Cisco.com using HTTP or FTP.

Step 2.   Place the IOS image someplace that the router can reach. Locations include TFTP or FTP servers in the network or a USB flash drive that is then inserted into the router.

Step 3.   Issue the **copy** command from the router, copying the file into the flash memory that usually remains with the router on a permanent basis.

Figure 17-7   *Copying an IOS Image as Part of the Cisco IOS Software Upgrade Process*

Copying a New IOS Image to a Local IOS File System Using TFTP

Example 17-2 provides an example of step 3 from Figure 17-7, copying the IOS image into flash memory. In this case, router R2, a Cisco ISR 1108 router, copies an IOS image from a TFTP server at IP address 2.2.2.1.

Example 17-2   copy tftp flash *Command Copies the IOS Image to Flash Memory*

```
R2# copy tftp: flash:
Address or name of remote host []? 2.2.2.1
Source filename []? c1100-universalk9.17.06.03a.SPA.bin
Destination filename [c1100-universalk9.17.06.03a.SPA.bin]?
Accessing tftp://2.2.2.1/c1100-universalk9.17.06.03a.SPA.bin...
Loading c1100-universalk9.17.06.03a.SPA.bin from 2.2.2.1 (via GigabitEthernet0/0/0):
!!!!!!!!!!!!!!!!!!!!!!!!!!!!!!!!!!!!!!!!!!!!!!!!!!!!!!!!!!!!!!!!!!!!!!!!!!!!!!!!!!!!!!!!
!!!!!!!!!!!!!!!!!!!!!!!!!!!!!!!!!!!!!!!!!!!!!!!!!!!!!!!!!!!!!!!!!!!!!!!!!!!!!!!!!!!!!!!!
!!!!!!!!!!!!!!!!!!!!!!!!!!!!!!!!!!!!!!!!!!!!!!!!!!!!!!!!!!!!!!!!!!!!!!!!!!!!!!!!!!!!!!!!
!!!!!!!!!!!!!!!!!!!!!!!!!!!!!!!!!!!!!!!!!!!!
[OK - 706422748 bytes]

706422748 bytes copied in 187.876 secs (3760047 bytes/sec)
R2#
```

The **copy** command does a simple task—copy a file—but the command also has several small items to check. It needs a few pieces of information from the user, so the command prompts the user for that information by showing the user some text and waiting for the user's input. The bold items in the example show the user's input. The router then has to check to make sure the copy will work. The command works through these kinds of questions:

1. What is the IP address or host name of the TFTP server?

2. What is the name of the file?

3. Ask the server to learn the size of the file, and then check the local router's flash to ask whether enough space is available for this file in flash memory.

4. Does the server actually have a file by that name?

5. Do you want the router to erase any old files in flash?

The router prompts you for answers to some of these questions, as necessary. For each question, you should either type an answer or press **Enter** if the default answer (shown in square brackets at the end of the question) is acceptable. Afterward, the router erases flash memory if directed, copies the file, and then verifies that the checksum for the file shows that no errors occurred in transmission.

NOTE   Most people use the IOS filenames that Cisco supplies because these names embed information about the IOS image, like the version. Also, if you want to use the same destination filename as the source, avoid the mistake of typing "y" or "yes" to confirm the selection; instead, you would be setting the destination filename to "y" or "yes." Simply press **Enter** to confirm the selection listed in brackets.

17

Listing the Files in the IOS File System

You can view the contents of the flash file system to see the IOS file that was just copied by using a couple of commands. It helps to think of each IFS as a disk on your favorite desktop operating system, with directories, subdirectories, and files, because those exist in IFS disks as well. For instance, you can use both the **show flash:** and **dir flash:** commands and see files, both showing some evidence of directories.

First, the **show flash:** command displays all files in the flash: file system in one list, regardless of what subdirectory the file resides in. The output lists each file with its directory structure; however, IOS uses both the bootflash: and flash: aliases to represent this disk, so the output lists directories that begin bootflash: rather than flash:. For instance, line 5 in the output in Example 17-3 (the first line with gray highlights) lists

A directory of /bootflash/.installer

A filename of watchlist

Example 17-3   *The* **show flash:** *Command Displays All Files and All Subdirectories*

```
R2# show flash:
-#- --length-- ---------date/time---------             path
  1        4096 Aug 01 2022 17:12:23.0000000000 +00:00 /bootflash/
  2        4096 Aug 01 2022 16:12:30.0000000000 +00:00 /bootflash/.installer
  3           5 Aug 01 2022 16:10:40.0000000000 +00:00 /bootflash/.installer/
install_global_trans_lock
  4          50 Aug 01 2022 16:10:40.0000000000 +00:00 /bootflash/.installer/
last_pkgconf_shasum
  5          11 Aug 01 2022 16:11:15.0000000000 +00:00 /bootflash/.installer/
watchlist
! Skipped many lines for brevity...
571  706422748 Jun 27 2022 17:08:17.0000000000 +00:00 /bootflash/c1100-
universalk9.17.06.03a.SPA.bin
! Many lines skipped for brevity...
1416802304 bytes available (1400680448 bytes used)
```

The columns of the **show flash:** command provide some key facts. First, IFS numbers the files with a unique number. The # (file number) column lists those numbers. Notice that the **show flash:** command lists the files in file number order. Moving to the right, the length column notes the number of bytes in each file. On the far right, the path column lists the filenames with the entire directory path (beginning with /bootflash: in this case).

Next, look for the line for file 571 near the bottom of Example 17-3, which happens to be the IOS file copied into this disk earlier in Example 17-2. It has a length of just over 700 MB. If you look back to the **copy** command in Example 17-2, you can see the output there that lists the exact size of the file copy, which matches the file size listed by **show flash:**.

The **dir** command lets you display files by directory instead of as a long list of sequential files. To do so, you navigate using the **cd** (change directory) command and discover the current directory with the **pwd** (present working directory) command. IOS begins with a default IFS disk, typically bootflash: (which holds the IOS file). To show the commands in action, Example 17-4 shows these steps:

1. The **pwd** command confirms the default pwd of "bootflash:".

2. Use the **dir** command to lists files/directories in the current directory.

3. Change to a subdirectory of bootflash: (license_evlog).

4. Repeat the **dir** command to list files in the new current directory.

5. Confirm the present working directory again.

Example 17-4   *The* **dir** *Command: Display Files in the Present Working Directory*

```
R2# pwd
bootflash:/

R2# dir
Directory of bootflash:/
```

```
88177     drwx           40960    Aug 1 2022 20:34:05 +00:00  tracelogs
64129     drwx            4096    Aug 1 2022 16:12:30 +00:00  .installer
56113     drwx            4096    Aug 1 2022 16:11:48 +00:00  license_evlog
15        -rw-              30    Aug 1 2022 16:11:39 +00:00  throughput_monitor_params
12        -rw-          134935    Aug 1 2022 16:11:23 +00:00  memleak.tcl
11        -rw-            1546    Aug 1 2022 16:11:00 +00:00  mode_event_log
40081     drwx            4096    Jun 27 2022 17:15:02 +00:00  .prst_sync
19        -rw-            1923    Jun 27 2022 17:14:30 +00:00  trustidrootx_ca_092024.ca
18        -rw-       706422748    Jun 27 2022 17:08:17 +00:00  c1100-universalk9.
17.06.03a.SPA.bin
! Lines omitted for brevity
2968264704 bytes total (1416704000 bytes free)


R2# cd license_evlog
R2# dir
Directory of bootflash:/license_evlog/


56121    -rw-           1656    Aug 1 2022 16:13:19 +00:00  SAEventRegular20220801_
161148.log
56120    -rw-           1927    Jul 29 2022 16:13:37 +00:00  SAEventRegular20220727_
161208.log
56119    -rw-           1809    Jul 1 2022 20:28:37 +00:00  SAEventRegular20220701_
184140.log
56118    -rw-           1555    Jun 27 2022 17:22:22 +00:00  SAEventRegular20220627_
171513.log


2968264704 bytes total (1416802304 bytes free)


R2# pwd
bootflash:/license_evlog/
```

Finally, take a moment to compare the usage memory usage statistics from the **show flash:** (Example 17-3) and **dir** (Example 17-4) commands. Both commands end with one line showing memory use statistics. Both list the number of free (unused) bytes; however, the **dir** command lists total bytes (used + unused), while the **show flash:** command lists total bytes used. Make sure you understand the difference. Then use these statistics to check if enough memory exists to copy in new IOS images, and if not, you should expect to remove some old files to make room.

Verifying IOS Code Integrity with MD5 or SHA512

You download the IOS from Cisco, copy it to your router, and run it. Is it really the code from Cisco? Or did some nefarious attacker somehow get you to download a fake IOS that has a virus?

Cisco provides a means to check the **code integrity** of the IOS file to prevent this type of problem by creating a hash value based on the IOS image. First, when Cisco builds a new IOS image, it calculates and publishes both an MD5 and SHA512 hash value for that specific

IOS file. To create the MD5 hash, Cisco uses as input the IOS file itself and runs the MD5 math algorithm against that file. To create the SHA512 hash, Cisco uses the same process, but with the SHA512 algorithm.

To verify that the IOS file on your router or switch has not been changed, use the **verify** command to re-create the same math that Cisco used to create the hash values. To do so, follow the process shown in Figure 17-8. As shown on the right side of the figure, first, find the hash(es) created by Cisco by finding your IOS file in the downloads area of cisco.com. Then, you run that same MD5 or SHA512 math on your router against the IOS file on the router, using the IOS **verify** command. That command will generate the same hash as listed at the Cisco site: if both hashes are equal, the file has not changed.

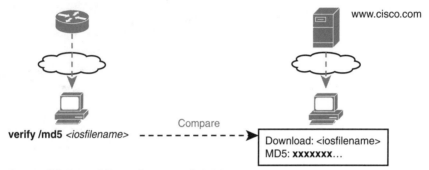

Figure 17-8   *MD5 Verification of IOS Images—Concepts*

The **verify /sha512** command generates the SHA512 hash on your router, as shown in Example 17-5. Note that you can include the hash value computed by Cisco as the last parameter or omit it. If you include it (as in the example), IOS will compare the locally computed value to the value you pasted into the command and tell you if they match. If you omit the value from the command, the **verify** command lists the locally computed SHA512 hash, but you have to do the picky character-by-character check of the values yourself.

Example 17-5   *Verifying Flash Memory Contents with the* **verify** *Command*

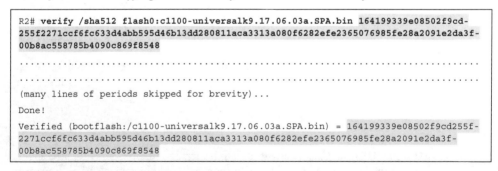

Copying Images with FTP

The networking world has many options for file transfer, several of which IOS supports for the transfer of files into and out of the IOS file systems that reside on the router. TFTP and FTP have been supported for the longest time, with more recent support added for protocols like Secure Copy Protocol (SCP), which uses the SSH File Transfer Protocol (SFTP). Table 17-2 lists some of the names of file transfer protocols that you might come across when working with routers.

Table 17-2   Common Methods to Copy Files Outside a Router

Method	Method (Full Name)	Encrypted?
TFTP	Trivial File Transfer Protocol	No
FTP	File Transfer Protocol	No
SCP	Secure Copy Protocol	Yes

To copy files with FTP, you follow the same kind of process you use with TFTP (see Example 17-6). You can follow the interactive prompts after using an EXEC command like **copy ftp flash:**. However, the **copy** command allows you to use a URI for the source and/or destination, which lets you put most or all of the information in the command line itself. Each URI refers to the formal name of a file in the IFS.

Example 17-6   *Installing a New IOS with FTP*

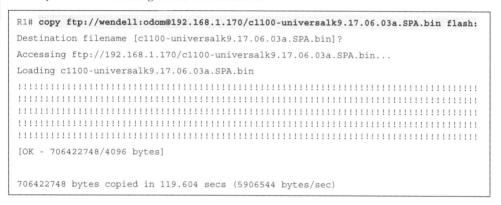

```
R1# copy ftp://wendell:odom@192.168.1.170/c1100-universalk9.17.06.03a.SPA.bin flash:
Destination filename [c1100-universalk9.17.06.03a.SPA.bin]?
Accessing ftp://192.168.1.170/c1100-universalk9.17.06.03a.SPA.bin...
Loading c1100-universalk9.17.06.03a.SPA.bin
!!!!!!!!!!!!!!!!!!!!!!!!!!!!!!!!!!!!!!!!!!!!!!!!!!!!!!!!!!!!!!!!!!!!!!!!!!!!!!!!!!!
!!!!!!!!!!!!!!!!!!!!!!!!!!!!!!!!!!!!!!!!!!!!!!!!!!!!!!!!!!!!!!!!!!!!!!!!!!!!!!!!!!!
!!!!!!!!!!!!!!!!!!!!!!!!!!!!!!!!!!!!!!!!!!!!!!!!!!!!!!!!!!!!!!!!!!!!!!!!!!!!!!!!!!!
!!!!!!!!!!!!!!!!!!!!!!!!!!!!!!!!!!!!!!!!!!!!!!!!!!!!!!!!!!!!!!!!!!!!!!!!!!!!!!!!!!!
!!!!!!!!!!!!!!!!!!!!!!!!!!!!!!!!!!!!!!!!!!!!!!!!!!!!!!!!!!!!!!!!!!!!!!!!!!!!!!!!!!!
[OK - 706422748/4096 bytes]

706422748 bytes copied in 119.604 secs (5906544 bytes/sec)
```

First, take a close look at the long URI in the command that begins with "ftp." The "ftp" part identifies the protocol, of course. After the //, the text references the username (wendell) and password (odom), as well as the FTP server's IP address. After the single / comes the filename on the server.

Although the command is long, it has only two parameters, with the long first parameter and the short keyword **flash:** as the second parameter. The **copy** command lists the source location as the first parameter and the destination as the second. The destination in this case, **flash:**, refers to the internal flash file system, but it does not mention the filename. As a result, IOS prompts the user for a specific destination filename, with a default (in brackets) to keep the source filename. In this case, the user just pressed Enter to accept the default. To avoid being prompted at all, the command could have listed **flash:c1100-universalk9.17.06.03a.SPA.bin** as that second parameter, fully defining the destination file.

Finally, with another twist, you can configure the FTP username and password on the router so that you do not have to include them in the **copy** command. For instance, the global configuration commands **ip ftp username wendell** and **ip ftp password odom** would have configured those values. Then the **copy** command would have begun with **copy**

17

ftp://192.168.1.170/..., omitting the username:password in the command, without needing to then prompt the user for the username and password.

The FTP and TFTP Protocols

The IOS **copy** command, when using the **tftp** or **ftp** keyword, makes the command act as a client. The client connects to a TFTP or FTP server and then attempts to transfer the file. In the examples from the IOS, that **copy** command copied the file from the server into the client device (a router). The rest of this section takes a closer look at both FTP and TFTP as protocols and tools.

FTP Protocol Basics

FTP has long been a core Internet protocol, serving as the primary file transfer protocol for several decades. RFC 959, which standardizes FTP, dates back to 1985. FTP uses TCP as its transport protocol, relying on TCP to provide an error-free in-order delivery of data so that the FTP application knows that each file transfer creates an exact copy of the file with no omissions. FTP uses well-known TCP port 21, and in some cases, also uses well-known port 20.

As for normal operation, FTP uses a client/server model for file transfer, as shown in the example in Figure 17-9. The figure shows the major steps but not every message. For instance, step 1 shows host A creating a TCP connection to the server (which takes the usual three TCP messages). Step 2 represents the exchange that allows the server to authenticate the client. Step 3 shows the idea that, once authenticated, the client and server can send FTP commands over the connection to tell the other device what to do.

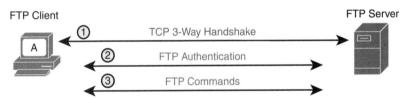

Figure 17-9 *Major Concepts with FTP Clients and Servers*

The commands that flow over this initial TCP connection—called the **FTP control connection**—define the kinds of functions supported by FTP. Those commands allow the client to navigate around the directory structures of the server, list files, and then transfer files from the server (FTP GET) or to the server (FTP PUT). A summary of some of the FTP actions is as follows:

- **Navigate directories:** List the current directory, change the current directory to a new directory, go back to the home directory, all on both the server and client side of the connection.

- **Add/remove directories:** Create new directories and remove existing directories on both the client and server.

- **List files:** List files on both the client and server.

- **File transfer:** Get (client gets a copy of the file from the server), Put (client takes a file that exists on the client and puts a copy on the FTP server).

While many OSs support command-line FTP clients, which require you to learn the various FTP commands and use those from the command line, most users instead use an FTP client app that issues the FTP commands behind the scenes. Clients typically display files on the local system as well as the server with a user interface that has a similar appearance as a file browser on a desktop OS (for instance, Windows Explorer, macOS Finder). Figure 17-10 shows a sample user interface from the FileZilla FTP client (Filezilla-project.org).

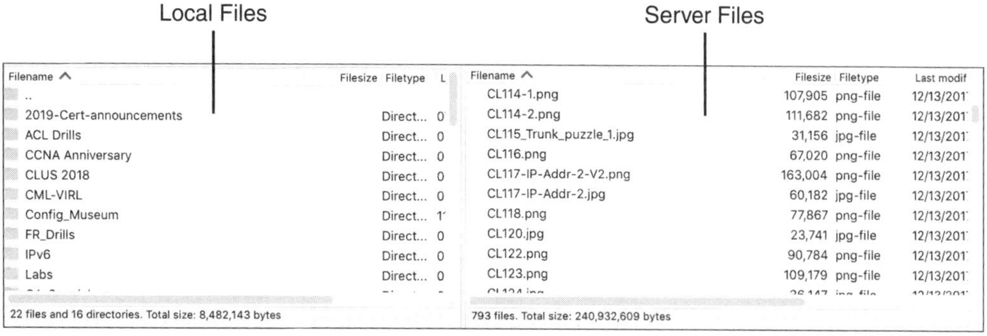

Local Files   Server Files

Filename ∧	Filesize	Filetype	L	Filename ∧	Filesize	Filetype	Last modif
..				CL114-1.png	107,905	png-file	12/13/201
2019-Cert-announcements				CL114-2.png	111,682	png-file	12/13/201
ACL Drills		Direct...	0	CL115_Trunk_puzzle_1.jpg	31,156	jpg-file	12/13/201
CCNA Anniversary		Direct...	0	CL116.png	67,020	png-file	12/13/201
CLUS 2018		Direct...	0	CL117-IP-Addr-2-V2.png	163,004	png-file	12/13/201
CML-VIRL		Direct...	0	CL117-IP-Addr-2.jpg	60,182	jpg-file	12/13/201
Config_Museum		Direct...	1	CL118.png	77,867	png-file	12/13/201
FR_Drills		Direct...	0	CL120.jpg	23,741	jpg-file	12/13/201
IPv6		Direct...	0	CL122.png	90,784	png-file	12/13/201
Labs		Direct...	0	CL123.png	109,179	png-file	12/13/201
				CL124.jpg	26,147	jpg-file	12/13/201

22 files and 16 directories. Total size: 8,482,143 bytes   793 files. Total size: 240,932,609 bytes

Figure 17-10 *FTP Client Example with FileZilla*

The client application in Figure 17-10 lists the client computer's local file system on the left and the FTP server's file system on the right. The user can click on the right to change directories, much like using any app that browses a file system, with FTP performing the commands behind the scenes. The user can also drag and drop files from the left to the right to put a file on the server, or vice versa to get a file from the server.

The FTP server can be a server application installed and managed by others, or you can install or enable an FTP server for your own use. For instance, a network engineer might install an FTP server application on a laptop for use in upgrading IOS files, while the IT staff may keep an FTP server available 24/7 for all employees of the company to use. A simple Internet search can show a variety of FTP server applications that run on the common desktop OSs. Additionally, both Windows and macOS come with an FTP or FTPS (FTP Secure) server option built into the OS; all you have to do is enable it. (The Linux distributions all have FTP servers available via simple downloads.) (The aforementioned FileZilla also has a free open-source FTP server option, which can be an easy way to get started.)

Once it is installed, the server can be configured with a variety of settings. For instance, the server needs to specify which users can access the server, so it can use the same login credentials allowed for the host where it resides or specify other credentials. It can specify the directories that each user can access, and whether the user has read-only or read-write access.

FTP Active and Passive Modes

FTP can operate in either active or passive mode. The choice of mode may impact whether the FTP client can or cannot connect to the server and perform normal functions. The user at the FTP client can choose which mode to use, so this section works through the underlying details to explain why FTP passive mode may be the more likely option to work.

17

First, note that FTP uses two types of TCP connections:

- **Control Connection:** Used to exchange FTP commands

- **Data Connection:** Used for sending and receiving data, both for file transfers and for output to display to a user

Given the two roles, when a client connects to an FTP server, the client first creates the FTP control connection as shown in Figure 17-11. The server listens for new control connections on its well-known port 21; the client allocates any new dynamic port (49222 in this case) and creates a TCP connection to the server.

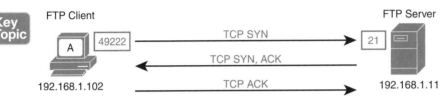

Figure 17-11   *FTP Client Creates an FTP Control Connection*

After creating the TCP connection, the user authenticates to the FTP server and takes some actions. Some of those actions require only the control connection, but eventually the user will take an action (like getting a file) that requires a data connection. When that happens, to create the **FTP data connection**, the client will either use active mode or passive mode, as shown in the next two examples.

Figure 17-12 shows an example of what happens in active mode. Following the steps in the figure:

1. The FTP client allocates a currently unused dynamic port and starts listening for new connections on that port.

2. The client identifies that port (and its IP address) to the FTP server by sending an FTP **PORT** command to the server over the control connection.

3. The server, because it also operates in active mode, expects the **PORT** command; the server reacts and initiates the FTP data connection to the client's address (192.168.1.102) and port (49333).

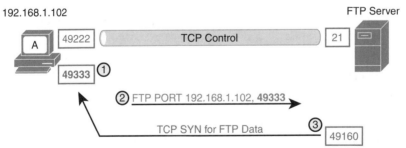

Figure 17-12   *FTP Active Mode Process to Create the Data Connection*

Note that in active mode, the server initiates the TCP connection for data. That works well with both the FTP client and server sitting inside the same enterprise network. When within the same network, typically no NAT function and no firewall sit between the two.

However, if the FTP client sits in an enterprise network, and the FTP server resides some-where in the Internet, an active mode connection typically fails. Most firewalls do not allow Internet-based hosts to initiate TCP connections to hosts inside the enterprise without a specific firewall rule allowing connections to a known port, and in this case, the FTP client allocates any available port number. For instance, in Figure 17-12, the TCP connection (step 3) would be discarded by a firewall.

> **NOTE**   When using Active mode, the server may use its well-known data port 20 or a dynamic port. (Figure 17-12 shows the use of dynamic port 49160.)

Passive mode helps solve the firewall restrictions by having the FTP client initiate the FTP data connection to the server. However, passive mode does not simply cause the FTP client to connect to a well-known port on the server; it requires more exchanges of port numbers to use between the server and client, as shown in Figure 17-13, with these steps:

1. Via messages sent over the control connection, the FTP client changes to use FTP passive mode, notifying the server using the FTP **PASV** command.

2. The server chooses a port to listen on for the upcoming new TCP connection, in this case TCP port 49444.

3. Again using the control connection, the FTP server notifies the FTP client of its IP address and chosen port with the FTP **PORT** command.

4. The FTP client opens the TCP data connection to the IP address and port learned at the previous step.

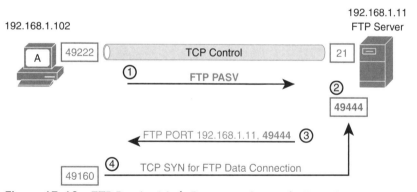

Figure 17-13   *FTP Passive Mode Process to Create the Data Connection*

TFTP Protocol Basics

FTP has a role as a general file transfer tool for any user, with a good number of FTP client application options available. TFTP plays a much smaller role as a tool for the average user, but it does play a more useful role for IT support staff.

For the basics, Trivial File Transfer Protocol uses UDP well-known port 69. Because it uses UDP, TFTP adds a feature to check each file for transmission errors by using a checksum process on each file after the transfer completes.

The word *trivial* in the name refers to its relatively small number of features, meant to be an advantage by making the tool lightweight. For instance, TFTP supports far fewer commands than FTP (fewer functions), meaning that the code requires less space to install, which can be useful for devices with limited memory. TFTP can Get and Put files, but it includes no commands to change directories, create/remove directories, or even to list files on the server. TFTP does not support even simple clear-text authentication. In effect, if a TFTP server is running, it should accept requests from any TFTP client.

Ideally, TFTP has its best use as a temporary tool for quick file transfers in a controlled environment, particularly when the data itself does not have to be secure. For instance, imagine this scenario:

1. A network engineer keeps all router and switch IOS images in a folder.

2. The engineer enables a TFTP server on a laptop as needed; otherwise, the TFTP server remains disabled.

3. The engineer connects the laptop to a LAN and enables the TFTP server long enough to transfer IOS images into or out of a few devices.

4. If the engineer forgets to disable TFTP, the only risk is that someone may copy an IOS image—an image that is already available from Cisco.com to any customer.

Chapter Review

One key to doing well on the exams is to perform repetitive spaced review sessions. Review this chapter's material using either the tools in the book or interactive tools for the same material found on the book's companion website. Refer to the "Your Study Plan" element for more details. Table 17-3 outlines the key review elements and where you can find them. To better track your study progress, record when you completed these activities in the second column.

Table 17-3 Chapter Review Tracking

Review Element	Review Date(s)	Resource Used
Review key topics		Book, website
Review key terms		Book, website
Answer DIKTA questions		Book, PTP

Review All the Key Topics

Table 17-4 Key Topics for Chapter 17

Key Topic Element	Description	Page Number
Figure 17-2	The SNMP Get Request and Get Response message flow	371
Figure 17-3	SNMP notification with SNMP Trap messages	372
Figure 17-6	The use of SNMP RO and RW communities with SNMP Get and Set	375

Key Topic Element	Description	Page Number
List	SNMP security benefits	375
Figure 17-7	Process of upgrading IOS using TFTP	378
Example 17-2	Example of using TFTP to load new IOS	378
Example 17-6	Example of using FTP to load new IOS	383
List	FTP functions	384
List	FTP data and control connections	386
Figure 17-11	FTP Control connection establishment	386
Figure 17-13	FTP data connection establishment in passive mode	387
Paragraph	Description of limited functions of TFTP	388

Key Terms You Should Know

code integrity, flash memory, FTP, FTP control connection, FTP data connection, IOS file system, IOS image, Management Information Base (MIB), Network Management System (NMS), read-only community, read-write community, Simple Network Management Protocol (SNMP), SNMP agent, SNMP community, SNMP Get, SNMP Inform, SNMP manager, SNMP Set, SNMP Trap, SNMPv2c, SNMPv3, TFTP

Command References

Tables 17-5 and 17-6 list configuration and verification commands used in this chapter. As an easy review exercise, cover the left column in a table, read the right column, and try to recall the command without looking. Then repeat the exercise, covering the right column, and try to recall what the command does.

Table 17-5 Chapter 17 Configuration Command Reference

Command	Description
boot system flash [*flash-fs*:] [*filename*]	Global command that identifies the location of an IOS image in flash memory
boot system {tftp | ftp} *filename* [*ip-address*]	Global command that identifies an external server, protocol, and filename to use to load an IOS from an external server
ip ftp username *name*	Global command to define the username used when referencing the **ftp:** IOS file system but not supplying a username
ip ftp password *pass*	Global command to define the password used when referencing the **ftp:** IOS file system but not supplying a password

17

Table 17-6   Chapter 17 EXEC Command Reference

Command	Description
copy *from-location to-location*	Enable mode EXEC command that copies files from one file location to another. Locations include the startup-config and running-config files, files on TFTP and RPC servers, and flash memory.
show flash:	Lists the names and size of the files in internal flash memory, and notes the amount of flash memory consumed and available.
dir *filesystem:/* dir *filesystem:directory*	Lists the files in the referenced file system or file system directory.
verify {/md5 | /sha512} *filesystem:name [hash-value]*	Performs an MD5 or SHA512 hash of the referenced file and displays the results. If listed, the command compares the hash in the command with the results of performing MD5 or SHA512 hash on the local file.
cd *directory-name*	If the directory exists, this command changes the present working directory (pwd) variable to refer to the listed directory.
cd ..	Changes the present working directory setting to one directory above the current directory.
pwd	Displays the present working directory, a variable used by commands like **dir** to identify a file system directory in which to check for files needed for a command.

Part IV Review

Keep track of your part review progress with the checklist shown in Table P4-1. Details on each task follow the table.

Table P4-1 Part 4 Review Checklist

Activity	1st Date Completed	2nd Date Completed
Repeat All DIKTA Questions		
Answer Part Review Questions		
Review Key Topics		
Do Labs		
Watch Video		
Use Per-Chapter Interactive Review		

Repeat All DIKTA Questions

For this task, use the PTP software to answer the "Do I Know This Already?" questions again for the chapters in this part of the book.

Answer Part Review Questions

For this task, use PTP to answer the Part Review questions for this part of the book.

Review Key Topics

Review all key topics in all chapters in this part, either by browsing the chapters or by using the Key Topics application on the companion website.

Labs

Depending on your chosen lab tool, here are some suggestions for what to do in lab:

Pearson Network Simulator: If you use the full Pearson CCNA simulator, focus more on the configuration scenario and troubleshooting scenario labs associated with the topics in this part of the book. These types of labs include a larger set of topics and work well as Part Review activities. (See the Introduction for some details about how to find which labs are about topics in this part of the book.)

Blog Config Labs: The author's blog (https://www.certskills.com) includes a series of configuration-focused labs that you can do on paper, each in 10–15 minutes. Review and performs labs for this part of the book by using the menus to navigate to the per-chapter content and then finding all config labs related to that chapter. (You can see more detailed instructions at https://www.certskills.com/config-labs).

Other: If using other lab tools, here are a few suggestions: All the exam topics in Part IV that include the word configure exist in Chapters 13 and 14, so focus on those chapters. Those chapters touch on CDP/LLDP, NTP, syslog, and NAT/PAT.

Watch Video

The companion website includes a variety of common mistake and Q&A videos organized by part and chapter. Use these videos to challenge your thinking, dig deeper, review topics, and better prepare for the exam. Make sure to bookmark a link to the companion website and use the videos for review whenever you have a few extra minutes.

Use Per-Chapter Interactive Review

Using the companion website, browse through the interactive review elements, like memory tables and key term flashcards, to review the content from each chapter.

Part V delivers content related to concept-only exam topics. As a result, it moves away from the concept-configure-verify approach of the earlier chapters of this book. Instead, this part collects exam topics better understood from an architecture and design perspective. In fact, the CCNA 200-301 V1.1 exam blueprint organizes six exam topics with this same approach, all listed under exam topic 1.2 "Describe characteristics of network topology architectures." The chapters in this part examine most of those topics.

First, Chapter 18 revisits LAN switching, discussing campus LAN design concepts and terminology, such as the *two-tier* and *three-tier* terms listed in the exam topics. This chapter also discusses how to supply power over that LAN infrastructure using Power over Ethernet (PoE), what the term *small office/home office* (SOHO) means, and the particulars of cabling choices in a campus LAN.

Chapter 19 takes the brief mentions of WAN technologies in the CCNA 200-301 V1.1 blueprint and expands that into a story of three major WAN architectures to explain the topics of MPLS VPN WANs, Ethernet WANs, and Internet VPNs.

Chapter 20 completes the architecture-focused chapters with a discussion of cloud computing and networking. This chapter begins by defining basic concepts and terms related to data centers and cloud, and closes with design discussions that show packet flows in a public cloud environment.

Part V

Network Architecture

CHAPTER 18

LAN Architecture

This chapter covers the following exam topics:

1.0 Network Fundamentals

    1.1 Explain the role and function of network components

        1.1.h PoE

    1.2 Describe characteristics of network topology architectures

        1.2.a Two-tier

        1.2.b Three-tier

        1.2.e Small office/home office (SOHO)

    1.3 Compare physical interface and cabling types

        1.3.a Single-mode fiber, multimode fiber, copper

By now you have learned a lot about Ethernet and Ethernet switches. You have learned how individual links work, with cabling, duplex settings, and framing. You know how addresses work and how switches forward frames based on those addresses. You have seen how switches deal with redundancy, using STP/RSTP and collecting links into EtherChannels. And here in Volume 2, you have learned about various security features available for switches, including Dynamic ARP Inspection, DHCP Snooping, and ARP Inspection.

What the earlier discussions of individual features do not do to any great extent is discuss architecture and design. You now know how switches work, but why would you connect switches in one topology versus another? If you could connect switches in two different topologies, why would you prefer one? This chapter examines a few such design questions, specifically the topic areas mentioned in the CCNA 200-301 V1.1 exam blueprint.

This chapter covers four specific topics that have design-related considerations. The first section looks at the topology of a campus Ethernet LAN and the design terms *two-tier* and *three-tier*, which describe how many switch layers exist between the endpoints and the devices that lead out of the campus to some other site. The second section discusses copper and multimode fiber cabling options for campus links. A third short section examines small office/home office (SOHO) LANs and how they differ from enterprise LANs. The final section introduces the concepts behind Power over Ethernet (PoE) and the reasons why LAN design activities need to consider PoE.

"Do I Know This Already?" Quiz

Take the quiz (either here or use the PTP software) if you want to use the score to help you decide how much time to spend on this chapter. The letter answers are listed at the bottom of the page following the quiz. Appendix C, found both at the end of the book as well as on the companion website, includes both the answers and explanations. You can also find both answers and explanations in the PTP testing software.

Table 18-1 "Do I Know This Already?" Foundation Topics Section-to-Question Mapping

Foundation Topics Section	Questions
Analyzing Campus LAN Topologies	1–3
Ethernet Physical Media and Standards	4
Small Office/Home Office	5
Power over Ethernet	6, 7

1. Which answers best describe the topology in a two-tier campus LAN design? (Choose two answers.)

   a. The design uses a full mesh of links between access and distribution switches.

   b. The design uses a partial mesh of links between access and distribution switches.

   c. The design uses a partial mesh of links between the distribution and core switches.

   d. The end-user and server devices connect directly to access layer switches.

2. In a three-tier campus LAN design, which answers best describe the topology? (Choose two answers.)

   a. The design uses a partial mesh of links between access and distribution switches.

   b. The design uses a full mesh of links between access and distribution switches.

   c. The design uses a partial mesh of links between the distribution and core switches.

   d. The end-user and server devices connect directly to distribution layer switches.

3. Which topology term refers to a network in which one node connects to all other nodes with no other links?

   a. Partial mesh

   b. Full mesh

   c. Hybrid topology

   d. Star topology

4. Which cable categories support 1000BASE-T at distances up to 100 meters? (Choose two answers.)

   a. CAT 5

   b. CAT 5E

   c. CAT 6

   d. OM1

   e. OM3

5.   Which answers list criteria typical of a SOHO network? (Choose two answers.)

   a.   The AP functions using standalone mode.

   b.   The AP functions using a split-MAC architecture using a WLC.

   c.   A single networking device implements the router, switch, AP, and firewall functions.

   d.   Separate networking devices implement each function (router, switch, AP, and firewall).

6.   After deciding the attached device wants to receive power over the UTP cable, how does a PoE LAN switch choose the initial power level to apply?

   a.   It applies a standard small amount of voltage.

   b.   It asks using CDP messages.

   c.   It asks using LLDP messages.

   d.   It applies voltage based on a configured value.

7.   Which of the following refers to standards that deliver power over all four pairs in a UTP cable? (Choose two answers.)

   a.   PoE

   b.   UPoE

   c.   PoE+

   d.   UPoE+

Foundation Topics

Analyzing Campus LAN Topologies

The term *campus LAN* refers to the LAN created to support the devices in a building or in multiple buildings close to one another. For example, a company might lease office space in several buildings in the same office park. The network engineers can then build a campus LAN that includes switches in each building, plus Ethernet links between the switches in the buildings, to create a larger campus LAN.

When planning and designing a campus LAN, the engineers must consider the types of Ethernet available and the cabling lengths each type supports. The engineers also need to choose the speeds required for each Ethernet segment. In addition, engineers use switches in different roles—some connect directly to end-user devices, and others connect switches. Finally, most projects require that engineers consider the type of equipment already installed and whether an increase in speed on some segments is worth the cost of buying new equipment.

This first major section of this chapter discusses the topology of a campus LAN design. Network designers do not just plug in devices to any port and arbitrarily connect switches like you might do with a few devices in a lab. Instead, most traditional campus LAN designs follow either two- or three-tier designs, as discussed in the following pages.

Two-Tier Campus Design (Collapsed Core)

Figure 18-1 shows a typical design of a large campus LAN plus some key terms. This LAN has around 1000 PCs connected to switches that support around 25 ports each. Explanations of the terminology follow the figure.

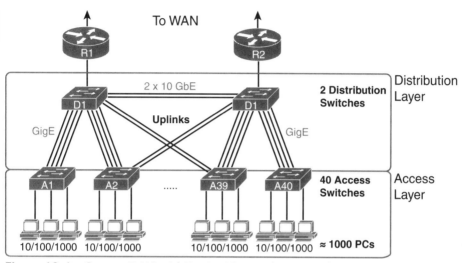

Figure 18-1 *Campus LAN with Design Terminology Listed*

Cisco uses three terms to describe the role of each switch in a campus design: *access*, *distribution*, and *core*. The roles differ based on whether the switch forwards traffic from user devices and the rest of the LAN (access) or whether the switch forwards traffic between other LAN switches (distribution and core).

Access switches connect directly to end users, providing user device access to the LAN. Access switches normally send traffic to and from the end-user devices to which they are connected and sit at the edge of the LAN. **Access links** connect the access switch to the various endpoint devices. The following list summarizes the more common features implemented by access switches:

- Physical network access links for endpoints and wireless APs

- Power over Ethernet (PoE)

- Redundant uplinks with EtherChannel and STP/RSTP

- Security (port security, DHCP Snooping, and DAI)

- A QoS trust boundary created using QoS classification and marking

Distribution switches provide a path through which the access switches can forward traffic to each other and outside the campus to the rest of the enterprise. The links between the access and distribution switches—uplinks or **distribution links**—typically connect each access switch to two distribution switches, often with multiple links in an EtherChannel.

Beyond that basic connectivity, the **distribution layer** provides many features that affect the endpoints connected to the access switches. Because designs use only a few distribution switches, and some of the services require additional processing, distribution switches will often need more powerful processors and more memory. The following list summarizes the more common features implemented by distribution switches:

- Connects access switches into the network

- Creates a core with other distribution switches, either directly (two-tier) or using core switches (three-tier)

- Provides Layer 3 features such as interVLAN routing, default router, FHRPs

- Implements dynamic IP routing protocols (e.g., OSPF)

- Load balances over redundant links and devices (EtherChannels, STP/RSTP, FHRPs)

- Provides QoS (queuing, policing, drop)

- Filters IPv4 and IPv6 packets with ACLs

Figure 18-1 shows a two-tier design, with the tiers being the access tier (or layer) and the distribution tier (or layer). A two-tier design solves two major design needs:

- Provides a place to connect end-user devices (the **access layer**, with access switches), typically within 100 meters

- Creates paths between all devices with a reasonable number of cables and switch ports by connecting all 40 access switches to two distribution switches

Three-Tier Campus Design (Core)

The two-tier design of Figure 18-1, with a **partial mesh** of distribution links, happens to be the most common campus LAN design. It also goes by two common names: a two-tier design (for obvious reasons) and a **collapsed core design** (for less obvious reasons). The term *collapsed core* refers to the two-tier design without a third tier (the core tier). A two-tier design has a core, but the distribution switches implement the core; the core is collapsed into the distribution switches. This next topic examines a three-tier design with a **core layer** for perspective while further detailing the purpose of the core.

Imagine your campus has just two or three buildings. Each building has a two-tier design inside the building, with a pair of distribution switches in each building and access switches spread around the building as needed. How would you connect the LANs in each building? Well, with just a few buildings, it makes sense to simply cable the distribution switches together in a **full mesh**, as shown in Figure 18-2.

The design in Figure 18-2 works well, and many companies use this design. Sometimes the center of the network uses a full mesh, sometimes a partial mesh, depending on the availability of cables between the buildings.

Answers to the "Do I Know This Already?" quiz:

1 B, D **2** A, C **3** D **4** B, C **5** A, C **6** A **7** B, D

Using a third tier in the center of the campus—the core tier—has several advantages in large campuses. For instance, you can use far fewer switch ports and links while connecting the building LANs. And note that with the links between buildings, the cables run outside, are often more expensive to install, and are almost always fiber cabling with more expensive switch ports, so conserving the number of cables used between buildings can help reduce costs.

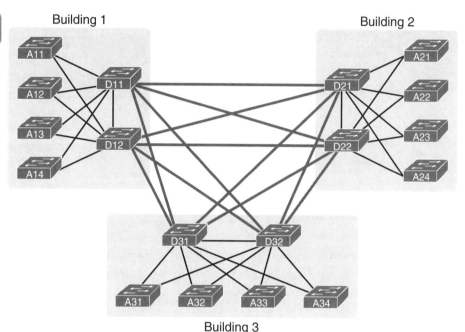

Figure 18-2   *Two-Tier Building Design, No Core, Three Buildings*

A three-tier **core design**, unsurprisingly at this point, adds a few more switches (core switches), which provide one primary function: to connect the distribution switches. Figure 18-3 shows the migration of Figure 18-2's collapsed core (a design without a core) to a three-tier core design. Note that topologically, the core switches reside in the middle of the network as shown; however, you typically install them in the wiring closet of one of the buildings, along with the distribution switches.

Using a core design, with a partial mesh of links in the core, you still provide connectivity to all parts of the LAN and to the routers that send packets over the WAN, with fewer links between buildings. But the emphasis turns to speed, low delay, and high availability—which oddly enough also means avoiding doing too much in the core. Summarizing the key roles for the core switches:

- Connectivity between distribution switches while conserving links and ports

- Fast transport

- High availability (redundant hardware and design)

- Low latency

- Avoidance of all services that might slow message delivery

18

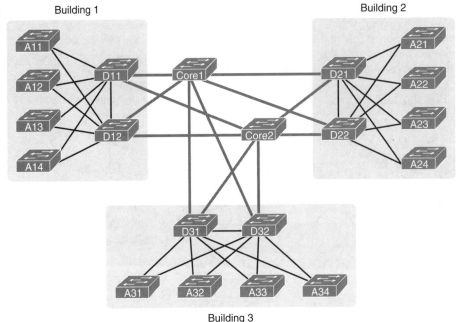

Figure 18-3 *Three-Tier Building Design (Core Design), Three Buildings*

The following list summarizes the terms that describe the roles of campus switches:

- **Access:** Provides a connection point (access) for end-user devices and connections to the distribution layer. They also implement services focused on endpoint devices, like Power over Ethernet (PoE), switch port security, and DHCP Snooping.

- **Distribution:** Provides an aggregation point for access switches, providing connectivity to the rest of the devices in the LAN, forwarding frames between switches, but not connecting directly to end-user devices. These switches implement most of the services for the campus LAN.

- **Core:** Aggregates distribution switches in large campus LANs, providing high forwarding rates for the larger traffic volume due to the network's size, while purposefully implementing few services.

Topology Design Terminology

The next topic applies some generic topology terms to a typical two-tier design to close the discussion of enterprise LAN topology.

Access switch drawings often show a series of parallel vertical cables, shown on the far left of Figure 18-4. However, an access switch and its access links are often called a **star topology**. Why? Look at the redrawn access switch in the center of the figure, with the cables radiating out from the center. It looks a little like a child's drawing of a star, hence the term *star topology*.

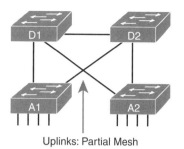

Access Switch | Access Switch: Star | Uplinks: Partial Mesh

Figure 18-4 *LAN Design Terminology*

The right side of the figure repeats a typical two-tier design, focusing on the mesh of distribution links. Any group of nodes that connect with more links than a star topology is typically called a *mesh*. In this case, the mesh is a *partial mesh* because not all nodes have a direct link between each other. A design that connects all nodes with a link would be a *full mesh*.

Why not use a full mesh between the access and distribution switches? A full mesh would connect the access switches to each other, create more links than needed, and use too many switch ports. Traffic seldom flows between endpoint devices on access switches. Instead, traffic flows between an endpoint and a server outside the campus LAN, so traffic rarely needs to flow between access switches when all links work. Most traffic flows endpoint-to-server: from the endpoint, to an access switch, to a distribution switch, and out to the WAN.

Regarding the number of links, imagine a two-tier design with 40 access switches and two distribution switches. If the design calls for two uplinks to each distribution switch from each access switch, you need 160 uplinks. (Four per access switch, with 40 switches.) Alternately, a full mesh between the distribution and access switches (42 switches), with just one link between each pair, requires 861 distribution links. (The math uses the formula $N(N - 1) / 2$, or in this case, $42 * 41 / 2 = 861$ links.)

Real networks use these topology ideas, but often a network combines the ideas. For instance, the right side of Figure 18-4 combines the access layer's star topology with the distribution layer's partial mesh. So you might hear these designs that combine concepts called a *hybrid topology*.

18

Ethernet Physical Media and Standards

In the two-tier and three-tier designs discussed in this chapter, the individual links use the Ethernet data-link protocol, supporting Ethernet frames—but often use different physical layer standards. Those standards define the maximum link segment length and transmission speeds. This next section takes a closer look at some of the considerations and decisions when choosing the cabling to use in a campus LAN, first focusing on access links, which often use UTP cabling, followed by distribution and core links, which use UTP and fiber-optic links.

Ethernet UTP Links at the Access Layer

Most, if not all, access links use unshielded twisted-pair (UTP) cabling—and that is no accident. From the early days of Ethernet, the IEEE set about to ensure Ethernet would be commercially viable, making it highly useful and affordable, with UTP cabling as the least expensive option. For instance:

- Knowing that UTP cabling costs less than the other options, the IEEE emphasized standards that supported UTP for the most common links in a typical network: access links.

- Early studies showed that a 100-meter cable could reach from the wiring closet to any point on the floor for most office buildings.

- Therefore, the IEEE used a 100-meter maximum length convention in their successive UTP-based standards over the years.

Most building construction plans include a structured cabling system. On each building floor, the cables run from a wiring panel in a central wiring closet to most locations around the floor. For instance, on a floor used for office cubicles, the structured cabling system includes UTP cables from the wiring closet to every cubicle location, often terminating with an RJ-45 connector in a wall plate.

Not all UTP cables have the same physical transmission characteristics, so the cabling industry and standards bodies have long-defined standards for the UTP cables used by Ethernet. Ethernet standards refer to UTP cable rating categories defined by the Telecommunications Industry Association and the US American National Standards Institute (TIA/ANSI). These categories define the physical transmission qualities when using the cable.

While the TIA and ANSI do not define Ethernet, and the IEEE does not define cabling standards, the Ethernet UTP-based standards refer to the minimum quality of **UTP cable category** that supports each Ethernet standard. For the TIA/ANSI categories, the higher the number and letter, the higher the quality, the more recent the standard release, and the more recent the IEEE standard that uses the cabling. The categories include CAT 3, CAT 5, CAT 5E, CAT 6, CAT 6A, and CAT 8.

Table 18-2 lists the data about the cable categories and matching Ethernet standards. Note that the higher the cable category number/letter, the better for supporting faster Ethernet standards. Also, the table does not list every combination; however, the table does list standards that support a 100-meter cable length.

Table 18-2 Ethernet and Cable Standards to Support a 100-Meter Segment

Standard (Common)	Standard (Original Document)	Year of Standard	(Minimum) ANSI/TIA Category	Max Speed
10BASE-T	802.3	1990	CAT 3	10 Mbps
100BASE-T	802.3u	1995	CAT 5	100 Mbps
1000BASE-T	802.3ab	1999	CAT 5E	1 Gbps
10GBASE-T	802.3an	2006	CAT 6A*	10 Gbps
40GBASE-T	802.3ba	2010	CAT 8	40 Gbps
2.5GBASE-T	802.3bz	2016	CAT 5E	2.5 Gbps
5GBASE-T	802.3bz	2016	CAT 5E	5 Gbps

*10GBASE-T can also use a CAT 6 cable, but with a distance limit of 55 meters.

The table lists the minimum cable category, with better cable categories also working. For instance, the original 10BASE-T worked on then-current CAT 3 cabling (or better). 100BASE-T, the next IEEE UTP Ethernet standard, required CAT 5 (or better). The following Ethernet UTP standard, 1000BASE-T, required even better cabling (CAT 5E) to reach 100 meters.

Today, the IEEE and others work hard to improve Ethernet standards for UTP cabling with that 100-meter access link as a critical design point. As shown by the dates in Table 18-2, about every five years from 1990 to 2010, the IEEE supplied a new UTP-based standard faster than UTP. Those standards deliver plenty of speed for the access layer, assuming you have the required cable types installed.

Multigig Ethernet on CAT 5E Cabling

After the introduction of 1000BASE-T, over time, the access layer in campus LANs reached a comfortable place in the market. Many buildings completed migrations to use **CAT 5E** cabling. Prices quickly became reasonable for 10/100/1000 switch ports and NICs. And a 1-Gbps speed for each access link connected to a desktop or laptop PC provided more than enough capacity for the PC.

In the 2010s, the IEEE anticipated a potential migration problem for the campus LAN access layer. To move endpoints beyond the 1-Gbps speed required 10GBASE-T, which would not run on CAT 5E cabling, at least per the IEEE standard. Per its standard, 10GBASE-T requires

- CAT 6 cabling to reach 55 meters

- **CAT 6A** cabling to reach 100 meters

The IEEE saw that to move from 1000BASE-T to 10GBASE-T at the access layer, with links up to 100 meters, would require a migration to CAT 6E cabling or better, making those migrations much more expensive. So, they set about creating an alternative Ethernet standard that ran faster than 1 Gbps but also worked on the large installed base of CAT 5E cabling.

The solution, **multigig Ethernet**, comes from the 2016 IEEE 802.3bz addendum. It defines two new UTP-based physical transmission standards: 2.5GBASE-T and 5GBASE-T. Both work on CAT 5E cabling (like 1000BASE-T) but run faster at 2.5 Gbps and 5 Gbps. Figure 18-5 shows the basic migration concept and cable categories.

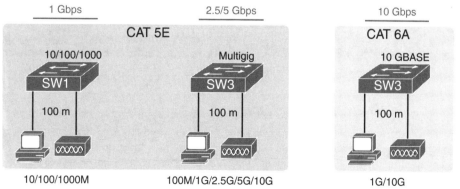

Figure 18-5   *Concept: Multigig as Faster Option Than 1 Gbps Using CAT 5E*

More than PCs, wireless access points (APs) have driven the multigig Ethernet market. IEEE 802.11ac (WI-FI 5) and 802.11ax (WI-FI 6) APs support more than 1 Gbps of wireless traffic, so they need an Ethernet interface faster than 1 Gbps. Using an AP with a multigig NIC connected to a multigig switch port, the AP can support 2.5- or 5-Gbps speeds so that the Ethernet link does not become a bottleneck.

To use multigig Ethernet, you need multigig host NICs and switch ports. Multigig NICs and switch ports use IEEE autonegotiation to choose the best speed. So, instead of a 10/100/1000 port, multigig ports typically support 100 Mbps, 1 Gbps, 2.5 Gbps, and 5 Gbps, all using CAT 5E cabling. They can also negotiate to use 10 Gbps if connected to upgraded CAT 6/6E cabling.

Fiber Uplinks

For all uplinks, you need to choose the required speed and the physical layer Ethernet standard. The installed cabling influences the choices because using installed cabling, rather than installing new cables, can significantly reduce the cost.

If possible, use UTP cables for all uplinks. For instance, Table 18-2 lists 10GBASE-T as needing CAT 6A UTP cabling to handle distances to 100 meters. If your structured cabling system had plenty of CAT 6A already installed, using 10GBASE-T uplinks makes great sense.

However, several factors will drive a decision to use fiber Ethernet options. Why fiber? The original cabling design may have needed cable segments longer than 100 meters, so they anticipated your choice to use Ethernet standards that use fiber-optic cabling. With preinstalled fiber cabling, you can then concentrate on what Ethernet standards will work on that cabling, choosing the best switch hardware (for instance, SFPs to add to the switch), and so on.

Multimode fiber cabling has quality standards akin to UTP cable categories. Those standards, called **Optical Multimode (OM)**, include OM1, OM2, OM3, and OM4, with the higher numbers representing newer, more-capable cabling standards. The cable standards define some attributes of the cabling—for instance, the diameter of the core and cladding. (In *CCNA 200-301 Official Cert Guide, Volume 1*, Second Edition, see Chapter 2's section titled "Fiber Cabling Transmission Concepts" for some figures that show a fiber cable core and cladding.) Table 18-3 lists those OM standards and some supported Ethernet standards.

Table 18-3 Optical Multimode (OM) and Related Ethernet Standards

(Minimum) ISO Cable Category	Core/Cladding Diameter	1000BASE-SX Max Distance per Standard	10GBASE-SR Max Distance per Standard
OM1	62.5/125	220 m	33 m
OM2	50/125	550 m	82 m
OM3	50/125	N/A	300 m
OM4	50/125	N/A	400 m

When attempting to use an existing installed base of multimode fiber, determine the OM category required by the Ethernet standard to meet the desired speeds. You can then analyze the data in the table, or similar data about other Ethernet standards, to determine the maximum cable lengths supported by each Ethernet standard. (Note that vendors often suggest that their optical transceivers—SFP, SFP+, and so on—can support distances longer than the standards.) As you can see in Table 18-3, the **1000BASE-SX** supports distances longer than 1000BASE-T's 100 meters, which may be helpful. The 10GBASE-SR standard supports similar distances but at 10 Gbps.

Also, use the numbers in the table for initial planning, but be aware of a couple of essential points:

- The standards typically give a conservative distance estimate, but you may be able to make links work at longer distances.

- In practice, 1000BASE-SX works on OM3 and OM4. The table lists N/A (not applicable) because the 1000BASE-SX standard pre-dates the OM3 and OM4 standards. But formally, the 1000BASE-SX part of the Ethernet standard does not mention OM3 and OM4.

After identifying the specific cables, you can plan for the Ethernet standard and switch ports. For instance, you might make a standard of buying access and distribution switches with modular ports that support 1 or 10 Gbps. You could then buy a 1000BASE-SX SFP or **10GBASE-SR** SFP+ to match the standard that meets each case's needs.

Small Office/Home Office

Now that you know more about design choices and terms for an enterprise LAN, this next section examines one type of smaller LAN: the small office/home office (**SOHO**) LAN. SOHO refers to designs and implementations with such a small volume of requirements— few switch ports, APs, routers, and WAN links—that the design differs significantly. The term itself refers to the two most common cases: a user who works from home or a small office with a small number of workers and devices. This next short topic points out a few highlights that differentiate a SOHO network from an enterprise network.

First, as a reminder, the IEEE defines Ethernet and wireless LANs (WLANs). All IEEE 802.3 Ethernet standards use cables—that is, Ethernet defines wired LANs. The IEEE 802.11 working group defines wireless LANs, also called *Wi-Fi* per a trademarked term from the Wi-Fi Alliance (www.wi-fi.org).

Most of you have used Wi-Fi and may use it daily. Some of you may have set up Wi-Fi at home, as shown in Figure 18-6. You probably used a single consumer device called a *wireless router* in a home. One side of the device connects to the Internet, while the other connects to the home's devices. In the home, the devices can connect with Wi-Fi or with a wired Ethernet cable.

SOHO

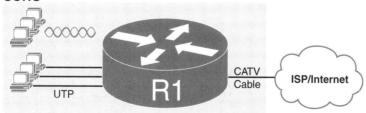

Figure 18-6 *A Typical Home Wired and Wireless LAN*

While the figure shows the hardware as a single router icon, internally, that one wireless router acts like separate devices you would find in an enterprise campus:

■ An Ethernet switch, for the wired Ethernet connections

■ A wireless access point (AP), to communicate with the wireless devices and forward the frames to/from the wired network

■ A router, to route IP packets to/from the LAN and WAN (Internet) interfaces

■ A firewall, which often defaults to allow only clients to connect to servers in the Internet, but not vice versa

Figure 18-7 repeats the previous figure, breaking out the internal components as if they were separate physical devices, just to make the point that a single consumer wireless router acts like several devices.

SOHO

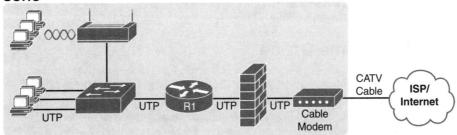

Figure 18-7   *A Representation of the Functions Inside a Consumer Wireless Routing Product*

In a SOHO wireless LAN, the wireless AP acts autonomously, rather than with a WLC, doing all the work required to create and control the WLAN. In other words, the autonomous AP communicates with various wireless devices using 802.11 protocols and radio waves. It uses Ethernet protocols on the wired side. It converts the differences in header formats between 802.11 and 802.3 frames before forwarding to/from 802.3 Ethernet and 802.11 wireless frames. But it does not encapsulate frames in CAPWAP because the AP will not send them to a WLC.

For the Internet connection, the router (combo) device connects with any available Internet access technology, including cable Internet, DSL, 4G/5G wireless, or fiber Ethernet. Note that Chapter 19, "WAN Architecture," introduces those technologies.

Power over Ethernet (PoE)

Just walk around any building and you see electrical power outlets everywhere. When finishing the interior of a building, electricians run electrical cables and install electrical outlets to any and every location that might need power. They also run power cables directly to devices like light fixtures. And when network engineers thought about electrical power, they thought about making sure the electricians had run enough power to the wiring closets and other locations to power the networking devices.

Power over Ethernet (**PoE**) changes that thinking so that the responsibility to provide electrical power to some devices can fall to the network engineering team. Some modern devices can pull power from an Ethernet cable rather than a separate power cord. To make that work, the LAN switch connected to the cable must supply that power over the cable. Using PoE, companies can gain several advantages, including reduced cost by requiring fewer cable runs and better power management capabilities than traditional electrical power cable runs and power outlets. This final section of the chapter examines PoE.

PoE Basics

The family of standards that supply power goes by the general name *Power over Ethernet* (PoE). With PoE, some device, typically a LAN switch, acts as the **power sourcing equipment (PSE)**—that is, the device that supplies DC power over the Ethernet UTP cable (as shown in Figure 18-8). A device that can be powered over the Ethernet cable rather than by some other power connector on the device is called the **powered device (PD)**.

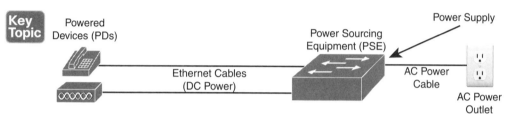

Figure 18-8 *Power over Ethernet Terminology*

PoE has an excellent advantage for devices installed in locations that often do not have a pre-installed power cable or power output. For instance, wireless networks locate APs across a wide range of places in the ceiling of most floors. Also, IP video cameras might be placed in the ceiling corners inside or at various outside locations. Instead of running both power and network cables to each device, a single Ethernet cable run can supply power to the device while allowing routine Ethernet communications over the same cable and wire pairs.

PoE also helps in some less obvious practical ways because it supplies DC power over the Ethernet cable, so the device does not need an AC/DC converter. For instance, devices like laptops and IP phones use a power cord that includes a power brick—an AC-to-DC converter—which converts the AC power from the power outlet to the DC power needed by the device. PoE supplies DC current over the Ethernet cable. So, for an IP phone, for instance, no more power cable and no more power brick cluttering the desk or taking up a power outlet.

PoE Operation

PoE must have the means to avoid harming the devices on the end of the circuit. Every electrical device can be damaged by receiving too much current into the device, which is why electricians install circuit breakers and why we use surge protectors. Applying power over an Ethernet cable could have the same effect, harming the device on the other end if the device does not support PoE.

PoE first performs **power detection** and then **power classification**. Power detection defines how the PSE can detect whether the attached device is a PD. To do so, the PSE sends a low-power signal. PDs complete the circuit, while non-PDs do not. Also, PDs add a defined resistance to the circuit, which allows the PSE not only to detect that the PD completed the circuit, but that it also added the right amount of resistance—confirming to the PSE that the attached device is a PD.

PoE power classification determines how much power the PSE should apply to the circuit. The process identifies a specific power class defined by PoE, with each power class defining electrical characteristics like voltage and current.

Layer 1 power classification uses the electrical signals on the cable, choosing among a small set of low-power classes with less chance of harming a device. But Layer 1 power classification has the great advantage of assigning a power class and supplying enough power to boot a simple OS that can participate in Layer 2 power classification.

Layer 2 power classification follows Layer 1 power classification. Layer 2 power classification uses LLDP and CDP messages, defined as Layer 2 protocols because they do not include IP headers, to determine the power class. The PD sends the message to the PSE, telling the PSE the desired class. If the PSE has enough power, it supplies it; if not, it stops supplying power. (See Chapter 13, "Device Management Protocols," for a broad discussion of LLDP and CDP.)

You can also configure PoE settings on the switch. By default, the PoE ports use automatic power detection and classification as discussed in this section. Alternatively, you can disable PoE on a port, or set a specific power class, reserving power on that port, and bypassing the need for power classification.

The standards allow for various paths through the power detection and classification processes. The following list gives a typical example (note that the list does not attempt to describe every process combination).

Step 1.   Do not supply power on a PoE-capable port unless power detection identifies that the device needs power.

Step 2.   The PSE performs Layer 1 power detection of the presence of a PD by sending low-power signals and monitoring the return signal to determine if the device is a PD.

Step 3.   If identified as a PD, determine an initial power level based on Layer 1 power classification and supply that power level, giving the PD enough power to perform some software initialization steps.

Step 4.   Perform Layer 2 power classification using LLDP or CDP, with the PD announcing a specific power class. If choosing a new power class, adjust the power level.

The processes result in the PDs signaling how many watts of power they would like to receive from the PSE. Depending on the specific PoE standard, the PSE will supply the power over two or four pairs, as noted in Table 18-4.

Table 18-4   Power over Ethernet Standards

Name	Standard	Watts at PSE	Power Class	Powered Wire Pairs
PoE	802.3af	15	0	2
PoE+	802.3at	30	4	2
UPoE	802.3bt	60	6	4
UpoE+	802.3bt	90	8	4

As an aside, the table shows PoE standards, but Cisco created an earlier pre-standard PoE feature called Cisco Inline Power (ILP). However, for the most part, Cisco's literature refers to the more familiar names in the first column of the table. Cisco long ago migrated to use the IEEE PoE standards in their product line rather than their proprietary Cisco inline power.

PoE and LAN Design

Most of the LAN switch features discussed in this book (and in *CCNA 200-301 Official Cert Guide, Volume 1*, Second Edition) exist as software features. Once you learn about a software feature, to use it, you just need to configure it. (Sometimes, you might need to research and add software licenses first.) Regardless, adding software-based features takes little or no prior planning.

PoE requires more planning and engineering effort, both when planning for the cable plant (both Ethernet and electrical) and when choosing new networking hardware. The following list includes some of the key points to consider when planning a LAN design that includes PoE:

■ **Powered devices:** Determine the types of devices, specific models, and their power requirements.

■ **Power requirements:** Plan the number of different types of PDs to connect to each wiring closet to build a power budget. Then analyze the data to determine the amount of PoE power to make available through each switch.

■ **Switch ports:** Some switches support PoE standards on all ports, some on no ports, and some on a subset of ports. Some switches support PoE+ but not **UPoE** or UPoE+. Research the various switch models so that you purchase enough PoE-capable ports with the needed standards for the switches planned for each wiring closet.

■ **Switch power supplies:** A PoE switch acts as a distributor of electrical power, so the switch power supply must deliver many more watts than needed for the switch itself. You will need to create a power budget per switch, based on the number of connected PDs and each device's power needs, and purchase power supplies to match those requirements.

■ **PoE standards versus actual:** Consider the number of PoE switch ports needed, the standards they support, the standards supported by the PDs, and how much power they consume. For instance, a PD and a switch port may both support PoE+, which supports up to 30 watts supplied by the PSE. However, that powered device may need at most 9 watts to operate, so your power budget needs to reserve less power than the maximum for those devices.

18

Chapter Review

One key to doing well on the exams is to perform repetitive spaced review sessions. Review this chapter's material using either the tools in the book or interactive tools for the same material found on the book's companion website. Refer to the "Your Study Plan" element for more details. Table 18-5 outlines the key review elements and where you can find them. To better track your study progress, record when you completed these activities in the second column.

Table 18-5 Chapter Review Tracking

Review Element	Review Date(s)	Resource Used
Review key topics		Book, app
Review key terms		Book, app
Answer DIKTA questions		Book, PTP
Review memory tables		Book, app

Review All the Key Topics

Table 18-6 Key Topics for Chapter 18

Key Topic Element	Description	Page Number
Figure 18-1	Campus LAN design terms	399
List	Access switch functions	399
List	Distribution switch functions	400
Figure 18-2	A two-tier (collapsed core) LAN topology	401
Figure 18-3	A three-tier (core) LAN topology	401
List	Core switch functions	402
List	Switch roles in campus LAN design	402
Figure 18-4	Network topology terms and campus LANs	403
Table 18-2	UTP cable categories	404
Table 18-3	Optical Multimode (OM) cable categories	406
List	Components in an integrated SOHO network device	408
Figure 18-8	PoE roles and terms	409
List	Typical steps to discover power requirements with PoE	410

Key Terms You Should Know

10BASE-T, 100BASE-T, 1000BASE-T, 10GBASE-SR, 1000BASE-SX, 2.5GBASE-T, 5GBASE-T, 10GBASE-T, 40GBASE-T, access layer, access link, CAT 5E, CAT 6A, collapsed core design, core design, core layer, distribution layer, distribution link, full mesh, multigig Ethernet, Optical Multimode, partial mesh, PoE, power classification, power detection, power sourcing equipment (PSE), powered device (PD), SOHO, star topology, UPoE, UTP cable category

CHAPTER 19

WAN Architecture

This chapter covers the following exam topics:

1.0 Network Fundamentals

    1.2 Describe the characteristics of network topology architectures

        1.2.d WAN

5.0 Security Fundamentals

    5.5 Describe IPsec remote access and site-to-site VPNs

The *CCNA 200-301 Official Cert Guide, Volume 1*, Second Edition introduces just enough detail about two types of WAN links—point-to-point serial and point-to-point Ethernet WAN links—so that you could understand IP routing, which is a major focus in CCNA. This chapter now turns our attention to WAN topics, from the perspective of the enterprise, as the customer of some WAN **service provider (SP)**. (Cisco's Service Provider certification track explores how an SP implements its network.)

This chapter begins with a discussion of Metro Ethernet, in the first major section, a technology that defines how to use Ethernet links between a customer site and the SP. The second section then examines MPLS VPNs, even though MPLS VPNs came before Metro Ethernet historically. The chapter introduces Metro Ethernet first because the many similarities between using Ethernet in the LAN and WAN make this topic easier to learn.

The chapter closes with a third section about how to use the Internet as a private WAN service by using virtual private network (VPN) technology. The Internet does not inherently provide a private service, meaning that any attacker who gets a copy of your packets as they pass through the Internet can read the contents. VPNs secure the data sent over the Internet, effectively creating a private WAN service over the public Internet.

"Do I Know This Already?" Quiz

Take the quiz (either here or use the PTP software) if you want to use the score to help you decide how much time to spend on this chapter. The letter answers are listed at the bottom of the page following the quiz. Appendix C, found both at the end of the book as well as on the companion website, includes both the answers and explanations. You can also find both answers and explanations in the PTP testing software.

Table 19-1 "Do I Know This Already?" Foundation Topics Section-to-Question Mapping

Foundation Topics Section	Questions
Metro Ethernet	1–3
Multiprotocol Label Switching (MPLS)	4, 5
Internet VPNs	6

1. Which of the following topology terms most closely describe the topology created by a Metro Ethernet Tree (E-Tree) service? (Choose two answers.)

   a. Full mesh

   b. Partial mesh

   c. Hub and spoke

   d. Point-to-point

2. Which of the following is the most likely technology used for an access link to a Metro Ethernet service?

   a. 100BASE-LX10

   b. High-speed TDM (for example, T3, E3)

   c. MPLS

   d. 100BASE-T

3. An enterprise uses a Metro Ethernet WAN with an Ethernet LAN (E-LAN) service, connecting the company headquarters to ten remote sites. The enterprise uses OSPF at all sites, with one router connected to the service from each site. Which of the following are true about the Layer 3 details most likely used with this service and design? (Choose two answers.)

   a. The WAN uses one IP subnet.

   b. The WAN uses ten or more IP subnets.

   c. A remote site router would have one OSPF neighbor.

   d. A remote site router would have ten OSPF neighbors.

4. An enterprise uses an MPLS Layer 3 VPN, connecting the company headquarters to ten remote sites. The enterprise uses OSPF at all sites, with one router connected to the service from each site. Which of the following are true about the Layer 3 details most likely used with the routers connected using MPLS? (Choose two answers.)

   a. The WAN uses one IP subnet.

   b. The WAN uses ten or more IP subnets.

   c. A remote site router would have one OSPF neighbor.

   d. A remote site router would have ten or more OSPF neighbors.

5. Which of the following answers about access link options for an MPLS network is most accurate?

   a. Uses only TDM (T1, T3, E1, E3, etc.)

   b. Uses only Ethernet

   c. Uses only DSL and cable

   d. Uses a wide variety of Layer 1 and Layer 2 networking technologies

6. A colleague mentions a remote access VPN using a VPN client on their laptop. Which protocols might the VPN concentrator choose to require of the VPN client? (Choose two answers.)

   a. TLS

   b. IPsec

   c. GRE

   d. FTPS

Foundation Topics

Metro Ethernet

Metro Ethernet (MetroE) includes various WAN services with some common features. Each MetroE service uses Ethernet physical links to connect the customer's device to the service provider's device. Second, it delivers a Layer 2 service in that the WAN provider forwards Ethernet frames from one customer device to another.

Conceptually, Metro Ethernet acts as if the WAN service were created by one Ethernet switch, as shown in Figure 19-1. The figure shows four sites in the same company, each with a router. Each router connects to the WAN service with an Ethernet link; those Ethernet links typically use one of the fiber Ethernet standards due to the distances involved. From the customer's perspective (that is, from the perspective of the enterprise that is the customer of the WAN SP), the WAN service acts like a LAN switch in that it forwards Ethernet frames.

NOTE   Throughout this chapter, the word *customer* refers to the customer of the service provider—the enterprise purchasing the WAN service.

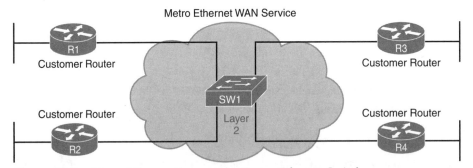

Figure 19-1   *Metro Ethernet Concept as a Large Ethernet Switch*

This first major section of the chapter examines the physical connections in a Metro Ethernet service. Also, enterprises typically connect to MetroE services with a router or Layer 3 switch, so this section also describes IP subnetting and routing protocols when using MetroE.

Metro Ethernet Physical Design and Topology

From an enterprise perspective, to use a Metro Ethernet service, each site needs to connect to the service with (at least) one Ethernet link. However, the enterprise's routers need not connect directly to each other. For instance, in Figure 19-1, each of the four enterprise routers uses one physical Ethernet link to connect to the SP's MetroE service—but not to each other.

The SP needs to build a network to create the Metro Ethernet service. To keep costs lower, the SP installs many devices, typically Ethernet switches, physically near as many customer sites as possible in an SP facility called a **point of presence (PoP)**. The goal: Locate a switch within the distance limitations of physical Ethernet fiber-optic standards. Figure 19-2 collects some of these terms and ideas together.

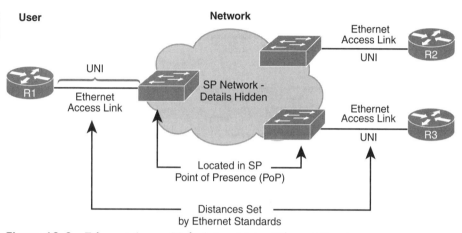

Figure 19-2 *Ethernet Access Links into a Metro Ethernet Service*

SPs generally refer to any link that connects the customer and SP as an **access link**, so when using Metro Ethernet, the link is an *Ethernet access link*. Everything on that link falls within the definition of the *user network interface*, or UNI. Breaking down the term *UNI*, the word *network* refers to the SP's network, while the SP's customer (the enterprise) is known as the *user* of the network.

The SP's network remains hidden from the customer, as depicted in the center of Figure 19-2. The SP promises to deliver Ethernet frames across the WAN. As you can imagine, the switch will look at the Ethernet header's MAC address fields and 802.1Q trunking headers for VLAN tags, but the details inside the network remain hidden.

The UNI supports any IEEE Ethernet standard. Table 19-2 lists some standards you might expect to see used as Ethernet access links, given their support of longer distances than the standards that use UTP cabling.

Table 19-2 IEEE Ethernet Standards Useful for Metro Ethernet Access

Name	Speed	Distance
100BASE-LX10	100 Mbps	10 Km
1000BASE-LX	1 Gbps	5 Km
1000BASE-LX10	1 Gbps	10 Km
1000BASE-ZX	1 Gbps	100 Km

Name	Speed	Distance
10GBASE-LR	10 Gbps	10 Km
10GBASE-ER	10 Gbps	40 Km

Ethernet WAN Services and Topologies

Beyond adding a physical Ethernet connection from each site into the SP's Metro **Ethernet WAN** service, the enterprise must choose between several possible variations of MetroE services. Those variations use different topologies that meet different customer needs.

MEF (www.mef.net) defines the standards for Metro Ethernet, including the specifications for different MetroE services. Table 19-3 lists three service types described in this chapter and their topologies.

Table 19-3   Three MEF Service Types and Their Topologies

MEF Service Name	MEF Short Name	Topology Terms	Description
Ethernet Line Service	E-Line	**Point-to-point**	Two customer premise equipment (CPE) devices can exchange Ethernet frames, similar in concept to a leased line.
Ethernet LAN Service	E-LAN	**Full mesh**	This service acts like a LAN so that all devices can send frames to all other devices.
Ethernet Tree Service	E-Tree	**Hub and spoke; partial mesh;** point-to-multipoint	A central site can communicate with a defined set of remote sites, but the remote sites cannot communicate directly.

> **NOTE**   You might see the term *Virtual Private Wire Service* (VPWS) used for what MEF defines as E-Line service and *Virtual Private LAN Service* (VPLS) used for what MEF defines as E-LAN service. You might also see the term *Ethernet over MPLS* (EoMPLS). All these terms refer to cases in which the SP uses MPLS internally to create what the customer sees as an Ethernet WAN service.

Ethernet Line Service (Point-to-Point)

The Ethernet Line Service, or **E-Line**, is the simplest of the Metro Ethernet services. The customer connects two sites with access links. Then the MetroE service allows the two customer devices to send Ethernet frames to each other. Figure 19-3 shows an example, with routers as the CPE devices.

Answers to the "Do I Know This Already?" quiz:

1 B, C **2** A **3** A, D **4** B, C **5** D **6** A, B

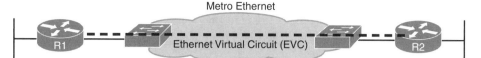

Figure 19-3 *Point-to-Point Topology in Metro Ethernet E-Line Service Between Routers*

As with all MetroE services, the promise made by the service is to deliver Ethernet frames across the service, as if the two customer routers had a rather long crossover cable connected between them. The E-Line service is the same Ethernet WAN service you have seen in many examples throughout this book and *CCNA 200-301 Official Cert Guide, Volume 1, Second Edition*. For instance, in this case:

- The routers would use physical Ethernet interfaces.

- The routers would configure IP addresses in the same subnet as each other.

- Their routing protocols would become neighbors and exchange routes.

The MetroE specifications define the concept of an *Ethernet Virtual Connection*, or EVC, which defines which user (customer) devices can communicate with which. By definition, an E-Line service creates a point-to-point EVC, meaning that the service allows two endpoints to communicate.

An enterprise might want to implement a network exactly as shown in Figure 19-3, but other variations exist. For example, think of a typical enterprise WAN topology with a central site and 100 remote sites. As shown so far, with an E-Line service, the central site router would need 100 physical Ethernet interfaces to connect to those 100 remote sites. That could be expensive. Instead, the enterprise could use a design with one high-speed Ethernet access link. Figure 19-4 shows the design concept with just three remote sites. In this case:

- The central site router uses a single 10-Gbps access link.

- The central site connects to 100 E-Lines (only three lines shown).

- All the E-Lines send and receive frames over the same access link.

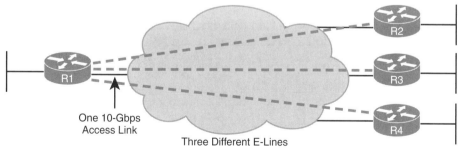

Figure 19-4 *Using Multiple E-Lines, One for Each Remote Site*

Ethernet LAN Service (Full Mesh)

Imagine an enterprise needs to connect several sites to a WAN, and the goal is to allow every site to send frames directly to every other site. You could do that with E-Lines, but you would need many. For instance, to connect six sites, you need 15 E-Lines, but with 20 sites, you need 190 E-Lines. Instead, you need an any-to-any service, more like a LAN.

A MetroE *Ethernet LAN service*, or **E-LAN**, connects all sites in a full mesh, meeting the need for direct connectivity between all WAN sites. One E-LAN service allows all devices connected to that service to send Ethernet frames directly to every other device as if the Ethernet WAN service were one big Ethernet switch. Figure 19-5 shows a representation of a single E-LAN EVC, allowing routers R1, R2, R3, and R4 to send frames directly to each other. All reside in the same Layer 3 subnet on the WAN.

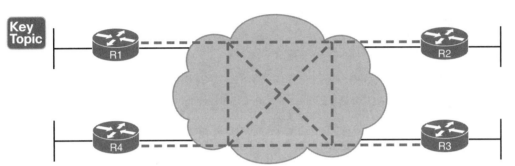

Figure 19-5   *MetroE Ethernet LAN Service—Any-to-Any Forwarding over the Service*

Layer 3 Design Using Metro Ethernet

How should the engineer plan for IP addresses and subnets when using Ethernet WAN services? What is the impact on routing protocols? This section answers those questions. Note that this section uses routers as the enterprise's WAN edge devices, but the concepts also apply to Layer 3 switches.

Layer 3 Design with E-Line Service

Every E-Line creates a point-to-point topology. For Layer 3 protocols, that results in

- One subnet per E-Line

- Routing protocol neighbor relationships occur between the two routers on the E-Line, but not between routers without an E-Line

Figure 19-6 shows a design with two E-Lines, with IP subnetting details added. Router pairs R1-R2 and R1-R3 connect with an E-Line, but R2-R3 do not. As a result,

1. The R1-R2 E-Line uses a subnet (10.1.12.0/24 in this case).
2. The R1-R3 E-Line uses a subnet (10.1.13.0/24 in this case).
3. R1 will become a routing protocol neighbor with R2 and R3.
4. R2 and R3 will not become routing protocol neighbors or learn IP routes directly from each other.

The figure also shows router R3's IP routing table. Note that the next-hop address for all OSPF-learned routes refers to router R1's 10.1.13.1 IP address: R1's address on the other end of the R1-R3 E-Line. Look at R3's route for subnet 10.1.2.0/24, the LAN subnet connected to router R2. With no E-Line or routing protocol neighbor relationship between R2 and R3,

R3 learns its route for subnet 10.1.2.0/24 from R1, with R1's 10.1.13.1 address as the next-hop address.

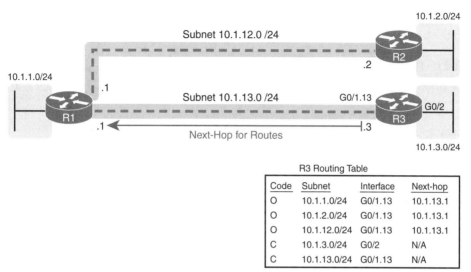

Figure 19-6 *Layer 3 Forwarding Between Remote Sites—Through Central Site*

Layer 3 Design with E-LAN Service

Typically, with four routers connected to the same LAN switch, on the same VLAN, using the same routing protocol, normally all four routers would have IP addresses in the same subnet, and all would become neighbors. The same IP addressing and routing protocol relationships occur with an E-LAN service. Figure 19-7 shows an example with four routers connected to an E-LAN service, all with addresses in subnet 10.1.99.0/24.

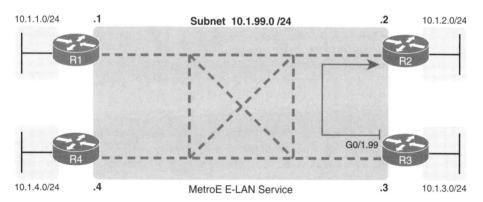

Figure 19-7 *Layer 3 Forwarding Between Sites with E-LAN Service*

To show the differences in IP routing when using an E-LAN service, focus on R3's route to R2's LAN subnet (10.1.2.0/24). In this case, R3's next-hop address is the WAN address on R2 (10.1.99.2), and R3 will send packets directly to R2. Note also that the other two routes in the routing table list the next-hop addresses of R1 (10.1.99.1) and R4 (10.1.99.4), showing an example of routers sending packets directly to each other over the WAN.

Multiprotocol Label Switching (MPLS)

From your CCNA preparation so far, you already understand much about Layer 3 routing, as represented by the packet flowing left to right in Figure 19-8. Each router makes a separate forwarding decision to forward the packet, as shown in steps 1, 2, and 3 in the figure. Each router compares the packet's destination IP address and that router's IP routing table; the matching IP routing table entry tells the router where to forward the packet next. The routers typically run some routing protocol to learn those routes.

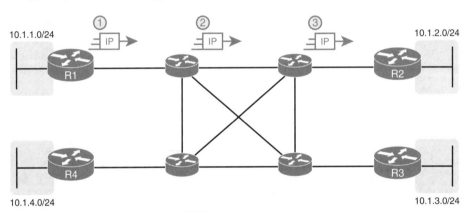

Figure 19-8 *Basic IP Routing of IP Packets*

MPLS creates a WAN service that routes IP packets between customer sites. The enterprise deploys routers and switches as usual. The SP then creates its IP network, spanning a large geographic area. The customer can then connect to the MPLS network, with an access link from each site, with the SP routing IP packets from one customer site to the other. For instance, in Figure 19-8, the middle four routers could represent the SP's MPLS network, with the numbered routers on the edges owned by one company.

However, an SP cannot just build a large IP network and connect all its customers to that same IP network using only the same IP routing rules you have learned so far. For instance, many customers will use the same private IP network (for example, network 10.0.0.0), so the SP's IP network would learn large numbers of routes to overlapping subnets. The SP's routers would be confused as to where to forward packets.

To overcome this and other issues, the SP builds its IP network to use **Multiprotocol Label Switching (MPLS)**, particularly **MPLS VPNs**. MPLS VPNs allow the SP to make one extensive MPLS network, creating a private IP-based WAN, but it keeps the IP routes separate for each customer. With MPLS VPNs, the SP can separate the routes learned from one customer from those learned for the next customer; consequently, the SP can support each customer while preventing packets from leaking from one customer to the next.

To give you a little insight into why MPLS is not just an IP network with routers, internally, the devices in an MPLS network use label switching—hence, the name MPLS. The routers on the edge of the MPLS network add and remove an MPLS header to packets as they enter and exit the MPLS network. The devices inside the MPLS network then use the label field inside that MPLS header when forwarding data across the MPLS network. The choices of the labels to use, along with other related logic, allow the MPLS VPN to create separate VPNs to keep different customers' traffic separate.

NOTE While MPLS VPNs provide a Layer 3 service to customers, MPLS itself is sometimes called a Layer 2.5 protocol because it adds the MPLS header between the data-link header (Layer 2) and the IP header (Layer 3).

As usual, the discussion of WAN services in this book ignores as much of the SP's network as possible. For instance, you do not need to know how MPLS labels work. However, because MPLS VPNs create a Layer 3 service, the customer must be more aware of what the SP does than with other WAN servers, so you need to know a few facts about how an MPLS network approaches some Layer 3 functions. In particular, the SP's MPLS VPN network

- Will build routing protocol neighbor relationships with customer routers

- Will learn customer subnets/routes with those routing protocols

- Will advertise a customer's routes with a routing protocol so that all routers connected to the MPLS VPN can learn all routes as advertised through the MPLS VPN network

- Will make decisions about MPLS VPN forwarding, including what MPLS labels to add and remove, based on the customer's IP address space and customer IP routes

As an aside, MPLS VPNs create a private network by keeping customer data separate but not by encrypting the data. Some VPN services encrypt the data, expecting that attackers might be able to receive copies of the packets. With MPLS, even though the packets for two customers may pass through the same devices and links inside the MPLS network, MPLS logic can keep the packets separate for each customer.

19

MPLS networks can offer Quality of Service (QoS) features as well. The MPLS provider controls their entire network. As a result, each device that forwards customer traffic can react to markings and apply different QoS features. Note that Metro Ethernet can also provide QoS services, but with different marking fields. However, Internet WANs cannot support QoS, because the Internet consists of many ISPs, and the ISP to which a company connects cannot guarantee the other ISPs will follow any particular QoS commitment.

This second of two major sections of the chapter works through the basics of MPLS, specifically MPLS VPNs. This section first looks at the design, topology, and terminology related to building the customer-facing parts of an MPLS network. It then looks at the MPLS network providing a Layer 3 service.

MPLS VPN Physical Design and Topology

MPLS provides a Layer 3 service, promising to forward Layer 3 packets (IPv4 and IPv6). To support that service, MPLS SPs typically use routers at the edge of the MPLS networks because routers provide the function of forwarding Layer 3 packets.

Figure 19-9 shows two important MPLS terms in context: **customer edge (CE)** and **provider edge (PE)**. Because MPLS requires so much discussion about the devices on the edge of the customer and SP networks, MPLS uses specific terms for each. The term *customer edge* refers to a router at the customer site—that is, at a site in the company buying the MPLS service. The *provider edge* devices sit at the edge of the SP's network, on the other end of the access link.

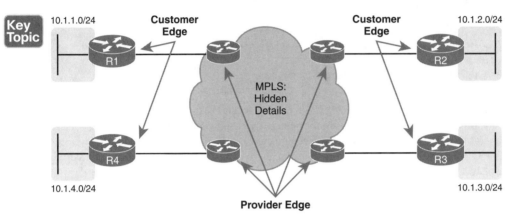

Figure 19-9 *MPLS Layer 3 Design, with PE and CE Routers*

Next, to appreciate what MPLS does, think back to router de-encapsulation and re-encapsulation. When routing a packet, routers discard an incoming data-link frame's data-link header and trailer. Once the router knows the outgoing interface, it builds a new data-link header/trailer. That action allows the incoming packet to arrive inside a frame of one data-link protocol and leave out an interface with another data-link protocol. As a result, MPLS supports any data-link protocol that could be used on MPLS access links, as shown in Figure 19-10.

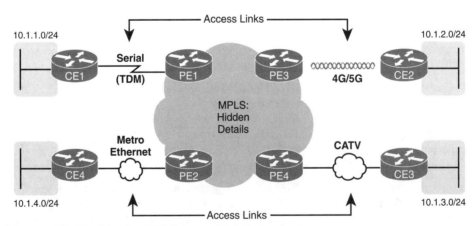

Figure 19-10 *Popular MPLS Access Link Technologies*

Layer 3 with MPLS VPN

Because MetroE provides a Layer 2 service, the SP does not need to understand anything about the customer's Layer 3 design. The SP knows nothing about the customer's IP addressing plan and does not need to participate with routing protocols.

MPLS VPNs take the completely opposite approach. As a Layer 3 service, MPLS must know the customers' IP addressing. The SP uses routing protocols and advertises those customer routes across the WAN. This section takes a closer look at what that means.

First, keep the primary goal in mind: to deliver IP packets between sites. The CE routers must learn routes for the subnets known to all the other CE routers; however, MPLS routing protocol design creates routing protocol neighbor relationships between the CE and PE routers but not between CE routers, as seen in Figure 19-11. MPLS supports all the standard routing protocols: RIPv2, EIGRP, OSPF, and even eBGP.

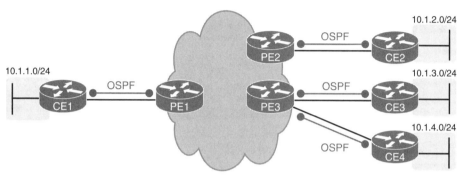

Figure 19-11 *Routing Protocol Neighbor Relationships with MPLS Customer Edge Routers*

The CE routers learn all the routes because the PE routers also exchange routes; however, the PE routers must use additional routing protocol features beyond the topics already discussed in this book. First, the MPLS SP uses a variation of BGP called **Multiprotocol BGP (MP-BGP)** between the PE routers. MP-BGP provides the means for the PE routers to keep customer routes separate using virtual routing and forwarding (VRF) instances. (Chapter 20, "Cloud Architecture," discusses VRFs in the context of data center networks.) So, the CE routers learn routes from each other.

For instance, in Figure 19-12, for CE3 to learn routes from CE1, the process begins with CE1 advertising the routes to PE1. PE1 redistributes the routes into MP-BGP and advertises them to PE3. PE3 redistributes them into OSPF and advertises them to CE3. As a result, CE3's routes that forward packets over the MPLS WAN will list PE3's IP address as the next-hop router.

19

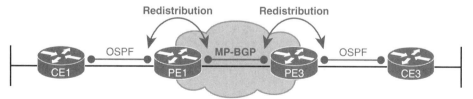

Figure 19-12 *MPLS VPN Using Redistribution with MP-BGP at the PE Router*

Internet VPNs

To build the Internet, Internet service providers (ISPs) need links to other ISPs and the ISPs' customers. The Internet core connects ISPs using various high-speed technologies. Additionally, Internet access links connect an ISP to each customer, again with different technologies.

The combination of ISP and customer networks that connect to the ISPs together creates the worldwide Internet.

While consumers typically connect to the Internet to reach destinations on the Internet, businesses can also use the Internet as a WAN service. First, the enterprise can connect each business site to the Internet. Then, using virtual private network (VPN) technology, the enterprise can create an Internet VPN. An Internet VPN can keep the enterprise's packet private through encryption and other means, even while sending the data over the Internet.

This final major section of the chapter discusses some of the basics of Internet access links. The section then details how an enterprise can communicate securely over the Internet, making the public Internet act like a private network by creating an Internet VPN.

Internet Access

Enterprises can use private WAN technology to access an ISP's network, including the Ethernet WAN and MPLS technologies discussed earlier in this chapter. Figure 19-13 shows a visual reminder of these options.

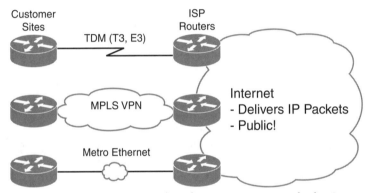

Figure 19-13   *Three Examples of Internet Access Links for Companies*

Additionally, enterprises can also use Internet access technologies more commonly used by consumers, including DSL, cable, 4G/5G, and fiber Ethernet. The chapter includes this information about Internet access technologies to provide helpful background information before getting into VPN topics.

Digital Subscriber Line

Telephone companies (telcos) have offered Internet access services since the early days of the Internet via the pre-existing phone lines connecting to most homes. Originally, that access used analog modems attached to the phone lines. Later, Integrated Services Digital Network (ISDN) created faster digital services over the same phone line. The third wave of technology to use local phone lines, digital subscriber line (DSL), added more improvements, with much faster speeds.

Figure 19-14 details how DSL works on a home phone line. The phone can do what it has always done: plug into a phone jack and send analog signals. For the data, a DSL modem connects to a spare phone outlet. The DSL modem sends and receives the data, as digital signals, at frequencies other than those used for voice, over the same local loop, even at the same time as a telephone call. (Note that the physical installation often uses frequency filters not shown in the figure or discussed here.)

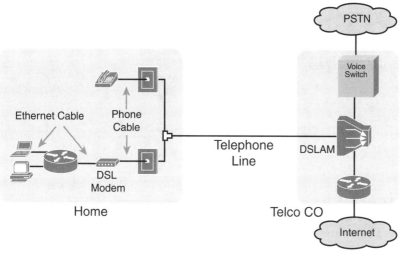

Figure 19-14 *Wiring and Devices for a Home DSL Link*

Because DSL sends analog (voice) and digital (data) signals on the same line, the telco has to somehow split those signals on the telco side of the connection. The local loop connects to a *DSL access multiplexer* (DSLAM) in the nearby telco central office (CO). The DSLAM splits the digital data over to the router on the lower right in Figure 19-14, completing the Internet connection. The DSLAM also splits out the analog voice signals over to the voice switch on the upper right.

Cable Internet

DSL uses the local link (telephone line) from the local telco. Cable Internet instead uses the cabling from what has become the primary competitor to the telco in most markets: the cable company.

Cable Internet creates an Internet access service that, when viewed generally rather than specifically, has many similarities to DSL. Like DSL, cable Internet takes full advantage of existing cabling, using the existing cable TV (CATV) cable to send data. Like DSL, cable Internet uses asymmetric speeds, sending data faster downstream than upstream, which works well for most consumer locations. And cable Internet still allows the original service (cable TV) while adding Internet access service.

Cable Internet uses CATV cabling but the same general model as telco with phone lines and DSL. The left side of Figure 19-15 shows a TV connected to the CATV cabling, just as it would normally connect. At another cable outlet, a cable modem connects to the same cable. The Internet service flows over one frequency, like another TV channel, just reserved for Internet service.

19

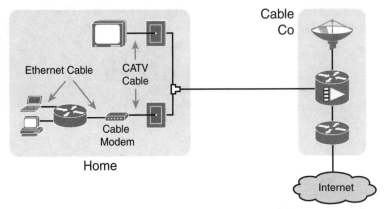

Figure 19-15 *Wiring and Devices for a Home Cable Internet Link*

Similar to DSL, on the CATV company side of the connection (on the right side of the figure), the CATV company must split out the data and video traffic. Data flows to the lower right, through a router, to the Internet. The video comes in from video dishes for distribution to the TVs in people's homes.

Wireless WAN (4G, 5G)

Many of you reading this book have a mobile phone with Internet access. You can use your phone to check your email, surf the web, download apps, and watch videos. This section touches on the big concepts behind the Internet access technology connecting those mobile phones.

Mobile phones use radio waves to communicate through a nearby mobile phone tower. The phone has a small radio antenna, and the provider has a much larger one sitting at the top of a tower within miles of you and your phone. Phones, tablet computers, laptops, and even routers (with the correct interface cards) can communicate through the Internet using this technology, as represented in Figure 19-16.

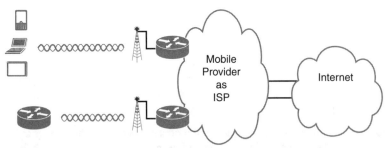

Figure 19-16 *Wireless Internet Access Using 3G/4G/5G Technology*

The mobile phone radio towers also have cabling and equipment, including routers. The mobile provider builds its IP network much like an ISP builds an IP network. The customer IP packets pass through the IP router at the tower into the mobile provider's IP network and then out to the Internet.

The market for mobile phones and wireless Internet access for other devices is large and competitive. As a result, mobile providers spend a lot of money advertising their services, with lots of names for one service or the other. Frankly, it can be difficult to tell what all the marketing jargon means, but the industry uses many of these terms:

Wireless Internet: This general term refers to Internet services from a mobile phone or any device that uses the same technology.

1G/2G/3G Wireless: Short for the first, second, and third generations of mobile phone access networks, which have come and gone from the market. (For perspective, note that the major carriers in the USA shut down their 3G services in 2022.)

4G and 4G LTE Wireless: Short for fourth generation, 4G improved both upload and download data rates versus 3G. 4G refers to the entire standard, but over time, the term *Long-Term Evolution (LTE)* came to refer to improved 4G.

5G Non-standalone (NSA) Wireless (sub-6): 5G refers to the fifth generation of wireless WAN technologies. 5G Non-standalone (NSA) refers to a subset of the 5G standard that works with the older 4G LTE network (hence non-standalone), with similar characteristics to 4G LTE, but with improvements in speed and latency. It also goes by sub-6 because it uses frequencies just beneath 6 GHz.

5G Standalone (SA) Wireless (mmWave): A higher performance part of the 5G standards, 5G standalone (SA) offers much faster data rates than 5G NSA. However, 5G SA works over shorter distances than 5G NSA, requiring more antennas to cover the same geographical footprint. 5G SA also goes by the name millimeter Wave (mmWave), because the wavelengths of the signals happen to be millimeters long.

The takeaway from all this jargon is this: when you hear about wireless Internet services with a mobile phone tower in the picture—whether the device is a phone, tablet, or PC—it is probably a 4G or 5G wireless Internet connection.

Enterprises can use this same wireless technology to connect to the Internet. For instance, a network engineer can install a 5G wireless card in a router. ISPs team with wireless operators to create contracts for wireless and Internet service.

Fiber (Ethernet) Internet Access

The consumer-focused Internet access technologies discussed in this section use a couple of different physical media. DSL uses the copper wiring installed between the telco CO and the home. Cable uses the copper CATV cabling installed from the cable company to the home. And, of course, wireless WAN technologies do not use cables for Internet access.

The cabling used by DSL and cable Internet uses copper wires, but, comparing different types of physical media, fiber-optic cabling generally supports faster speeds for longer distances. That is, just comparing physical layer technologies across the breadth of networking, fiber-optic cabling supports longer links, and those links often run at equivalent or faster speeds.

Some ISPs now offer Internet access that goes by the name *fiber Internet*, or simply *fiber*. To make that work, some local company that owns the rights to install cabling underground in a local area (often a telephone company) installs new fiber-optic cabling. Once the cable plant is in place (a process that often takes years and a large budget), the fiber ISP connects customers to the Internet using the fiber-optic cabling. Often not stated, the SP uses Ethernet protocols over the fiber. The result is high-speed Internet to the home.

19

Internet VPN Fundamentals

Private WANs have some wonderful security features. In particular, the customers who send data through the WAN have good reason to believe that no attackers saw the data in transit or even changed the data to cause some harm. The private WAN service provider promises to send one customer's data to other sites owned by that customer but not to sites owned by other customers, and vice versa.

VPNs try to provide the same secure features as a private WAN while sending data over a network open to other parties (such as the Internet). Compared to a private WAN, the Internet does not provide a secure environment that protects the privacy of an enterprise's data. Internet VPNs provide essential security features, such as

- **Confidentiality (privacy):** Preventing anyone in the middle of the Internet (man in the middle) from being able to read the data

- **Authentication:** Verifying that the sender of the VPN packet is a legitimate device and not a device used by an attacker

- **Data integrity:** Verifying that nothing changed the packet as it transited the Internet

- **Anti-replay:** Preventing a man in the middle from copying packets sent by a legitimate user, so they can later send those packets and appear to be that legitimate user

To accomplish these goals, two devices near the edge of the Internet create a VPN, sometimes called a *VPN tunnel*. These devices add headers to the original packet, with these headers including fields that allow the VPN devices to make the traffic secure. The VPN devices also encrypt the original IP packet, meaning that its contents are undecipherable to anyone who examines a copy of the packet as it traverses the Internet.

Figure 19-17 shows a VPN between branch office router R1 and a Cisco firewall (FW1). By definition, a VPN that connects two sites to support traffic from all hosts at those sites goes by the name **site-to-site VPN**.

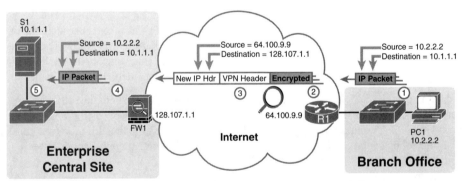

Figure 19-17 *VPN Tunnel Concepts for a Site-to-Site Intranet VPN*

The figure shows the following steps, which explain the overall flow:

  1. Host PC1 (10.2.2.2) on the right sends a packet destined for the web server (10.1.1.1), just as it would without a VPN.

2. Router R1 encrypts the packet, adds some VPN headers, adds another IP header (with public IP addresses), and forwards the packet, as shown in the upper-center of the figure.

3. Even if an attacker in the Internet copied the packet (called a man-in-the-middle attack), they could not change the packet without being noticed. The attacker also cannot read the contents of the original packet.

4. Firewall FW1 receives the packet, confirms the sender's authenticity, confirms no changes occurred in the packet, and decrypts the original packet. FW1 then forwards the original packet to the web server.

5. Server S1 receives the unencrypted packet.

Internet-based VPNs give enterprises great options for WAN servers. High-speed Internet access often costs less than private WAN access links. The Internet is seemingly everywhere, making this kind of solution available worldwide. If the enterprise uses VPN technology and protocols, the communications are secure.

> **NOTE**   The term *tunnel* refers to any protocol's packet that is sent by encapsulating the packet inside another packet. The term *VPN tunnel* may or may not imply that the tunnel also uses encryption.

Site-to-Site VPNs with IPsec

A site-to-site VPN provides VPN services for the devices at two sites with a single VPN tunnel. For instance, if each site has dozens of devices that need to communicate between sites, the various devices do not have to act to create the VPN. Instead, the network engineers configure devices such as routers and firewalls to create one VPN tunnel. The tunnel remains up and operating all the time, so it is always available when end-user devices send data. All the endpoint devices at each site can communicate using the VPN, unaware of the VPN, without needing to create a VPN for themselves.

IPsec defines one popular set of rules for creating secure VPNs. IPsec is an architecture or framework for security services for IP networks. The name derives from the title of the RFC that defines it (RFC 4301, "Security Architecture for the Internet Protocol"), more generally called IP Security, or IPsec.

IPsec defines how two devices, both of which connect to the Internet, can achieve the main goals of a VPN, as listed at the beginning of this section: confidentiality, authentication, data integrity, and anti-replay. IPsec does not define just one way to implement a VPN but allows several different protocol options for each feature. IPsec provides a solid architectural VPN framework by allowing for changes and improvements to individual security functions over time.

IPsec encryption might sound intimidating, but if you ignore the math—and thankfully, you can—IPsec encryption is not too difficult to understand. IPsec encryption uses a pair of encryption algorithms, essentially math formulas, to meet a couple of requirements. First, the two math formulas are a matched set:

- One to hide (encrypt) the data

- Another to re-create (decrypt) the original data based on the encrypted data

19

The choice of encryption and decryption formulas helps thwart attackers. For instance, if an attacker intercepted the encrypted packet but did not have the secret password (called an *encryption key*), the attacker could only decrypt the packet through great effort. Also, if an attacker happened to decrypt one packet, the formulas also give them no insights in how they might decrypt a second packet.

The process for encrypting data for an IPsec VPN works generally as shown in Figure 19-18. Note that the *encryption key* is also known as the *session key*, **shared key**, or *shared session key*.

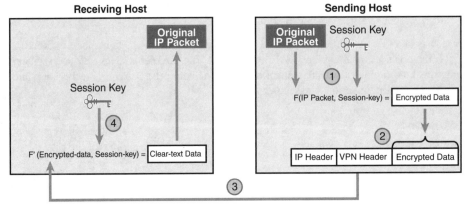

Figure 19-18 *Basic IPsec Encryption Process*

The four steps highlighted in the figure are as follows:

1. The sending VPN device (router R1 in Figure 19-17) feeds the original packet and the session key into the encryption formula, calculating the encrypted data.

2. The sending device encapsulates the encrypted data into a packet, which includes the new IP header and VPN header.

3. The sending device sends this new packet to the destination VPN device (FW1 back in Figure 19-17).

4. The receiving VPN device runs the corresponding decryption formula using the encrypted data and session key—the same key value used on the sending VPN device—to decrypt the data.

While Figure 19-18 shows the basic encryption process, Figure 19-19 shows a broader view of an Enterprise IPsec VPN. Devices use some related VPN technology like Generic Routing Encapsulation (GRE) to create the concept of a tunnel (a virtual link between the routers), with three such tunnels shown in the figure. The router configuration then adds IPsec security features to the data that flows over the tunnel. (Note that the figure shows IPsec and GRE, but IPsec teams with other VPN technologies as well.)

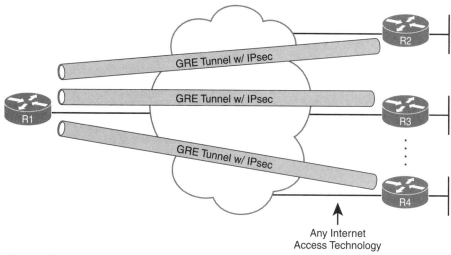

Figure 19-19 *Site-to-Site VPN Tunnels with GRE and IPsec*

Remote Access VPNs with IPsec

A site-to-site VPN exists to support multiple devices at each site, with the IT staff creating a permanent VPN connection to support all users. In contrast, user devices can dynamically initiate VPN connections in cases where a permanent site-to-site VPN does not exist. Such a VPN connection, terminated by and initiated from the end-user device, is called a **remote access VPN**.

For instance, a user can walk into a coffee shop and connect to the free Wi-Fi with a tablet or laptop, but that coffee shop does not have a site-to-site VPN to the user's enterprise network. Instead, software on the endpoint device creates a secure VPN connection back to the enterprise network, as shown in Figure 19-20.

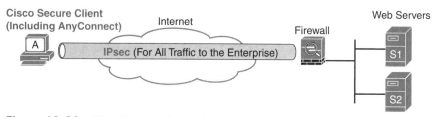

Figure 19-20 *IPsec Remote Access IPsec VPN*

Many companies use the remote access VPN model in the figure for employees doing remote work, connecting from their home, a hotel, or any off-site location. The company can choose whether to use IPsec or Transport Layer Security **(TLS)** to secure the traffic.

To support all traffic sent by the computer, the end-user device requires VPN client software. The networking staff also installs and configures a device to act as a VPN concentrator, defining whether to use TLS or IPsec. Employee devices then connect to the VPN concentrator. While routers can play that role, companies typically use firewall products.

NOTE For many years, Cisco branded its VPN client software as the Cisco AnyConnect Secure Mobility Client. Cisco has replaced that product with the **Cisco Secure Client (Including AnyConnect)**. See www.cisco.com/go/secureclient for more info.

IPsec works a little differently when used for remote access versus site-to-site VPNs. **IPsec tunnel mode** is used for site-to-site encryption, which encrypts the entire original packet. **IPsec transport mode** is used for remote access VPNs, which encrypts the data of the original IP packet—that is, everything after the IP header—but not the IP header itself. Figure 19-21 shows a visual comparison of the two modes.

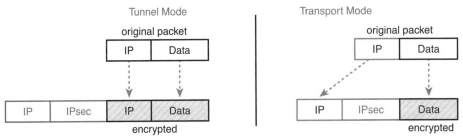

Figure 19-21 *IPsec Tunnel and Transport Mode—What Is Encrypted*

Site-to-site and remote access IPsec VPNs also have other differences, given their different roles. Table 19-4 summarizes the differences for easier study.

Table 19-4 Comparisons of Site-to-Site and Remote Access IPsec VPNs

Attribute	Site-to-Site IPsec VPN	Remote Access IPsec VPN
Does the end-user device need VPN client software?	No	Yes
Devices supported by one VPN: one or many	Many	One
Typical use: on-demand or permanent	Permanent	On-demand
Does the VPN use IPsec tunnel mode?	Yes	No
Does the VPN use IPsec transport mode?	No	Yes

Remote Access VPNs with TLS

While the exam topics specifically mention IPsec VPNs, VPN technologies include many protocols beyond IPsec. This final topic discusses one that most people use every day: Transport Layer Security, or TLS.

For most websites today, when you connect, your browser uses HTTPS (RFC 9110), which secures the HTTP protocol. HTTPS secures HTTP by using TLS (RFC 8446).

The world has migrated away from HTTP to HTTPS. Just look at most URIs you see in your web browser: they all start with HTTPS. As a result, a browser completes the secure connection using HTTPS, which uses TLS, before connecting to the site.

When opening a new web page, the browser creates a TCP connection to well-known port 443 (default) and then initializes a TLS session. TLS encrypts data sent between the browser and the server (application layer header and data—but not the IP or TCP header) while authenticating the user. Then the HTTPS messages flow over the TLS VPN connection.

> **NOTE**   In years past, Secure Sockets Layer (SSL) played the same role as TLS. SSL has been deprecated (see RFC 7568) and replaced by TLS.

In its most common use, TLS creates a host-to-host secure connection between one client's web browser and one web server. If you open a web browser tab and connect to a website, your browser creates a TLS connection to that server. Open more browser tabs, and your browser creates additional TLS host-to-host connections, all secured with TLS. TLS can also be used for remote access VPNs. For instance, the Cisco Secure Client can use TLS when connecting to a firewall, supporting all traffic sent by that host. Figure 19-22 shows both.

 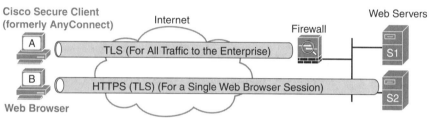

Figure 19-22   *Remote Access VPN Options (TLS)*

Chapter Review

One key to doing well on the exams is to perform repetitive spaced review sessions. Review this chapter's material using either the tools in the book or interactive tools for the same material found on the book's companion website. Refer to the "Your Study Plan" element for more details. Table 19-5 outlines the key review elements and where you can find them. To better track your study progress, record when you completed these activities in the second column.

Table 19-5   Chapter Review Tracking

Review Element	Review Date(s)	Resource Used
Review key topics		Book, website
Review key terms		Book, website
Answer DIKTA questions		Book, PTP
Review memory tables		Book, website

19

Review All the Key Topics

Table 19-6   Key Topics for Chapter 19

Key Topic Element	Description	Page Number
Figure 19-2	Metro Ethernet terminology in context	417
Table 19-3	MetroE service types per MEF	418
Figure 19-5	MetroE Ethernet LAN (E-LAN) service concept	420
List	Ideas about customer Layer 3 addressing and what an MPLS VPN provider needs to know	423
Figure 19-9	MPLS terminology in context	424
Figure 19-19	Concepts of site-to-site VPNs with IPsec and GRE	433
Figure 19-20	IPsec remote access VPN	433
Table 19-4	Comparisons of site-to-site and remote access VPNs	434
Figure 19-22	Concepts of remote access VPNs with TLS	435

Key Terms You Should Know

access link, Cisco Secure Client (including AnyConnect), customer edge (CE), E-LAN, E-Line, Ethernet WAN, full mesh, hub and spoke, IPsec, IPsec transport mode, IPsec tunnel mode, Metro Ethernet, MPLS VPN, Multiprotocol BGP (MP-BGP), Multiprotocol Label Switching (MPLS), partial mesh, point-to-point, point of presence (PoP), provider edge (PE), remote access VPN, service provider (SP), shared key, site-to-site VPN, TLS

CHAPTER 20

Cloud Architecture

This chapter covers the following exam topics:

1.0 Network Fundamentals

    1.1 Explain the role and function of network components

        1.1.g Servers

    1.2 Describe the characteristics of network topology architectures

        1.2.f On-premises and cloud

    1.12 Explain virtualization fundamentals (server virtualization, containers, and VRFs)

Cloud computing is an approach to offering IT services to customers. However, cloud computing is not a product, a set of products, a protocol, or any single thing. So, while there are accepted descriptions and definitions of cloud computing today, it takes a broad knowledge of IT beyond networking to know whether a particular IT service is or is not worthy of being called a cloud computing service.

To categorize an IT service as a cloud computing service, it should have these characteristics: It can be requested on-demand; it can dynamically scale (that is, it is elastic); it uses a pool of resources; it has a variety of network access options; and it can be measured and billed back to the user based on the amount used.

Cloud computing relies on automated data centers. For instance, to service requests, a cloud computing system will create virtual server instances—virtual machines (VMs)—and configure the settings on each VM to provide the requested service.

This chapter gives you a general idea of cloud services and network architecture. To do that, this chapter begins by discussing server virtualization basics. The following section then discusses the big ideas in cloud computing, with the final section discussing the impact of public clouds on packet flows in enterprise networks.

"Do I Know This Already?" Quiz

Take the quiz (either here or use the PTP software) if you want to use the score to help you decide how much time to spend on this chapter. The letter answers are listed at the bottom of the page following the quiz. Appendix C, found both at the end of the book as well as on the companion website, includes both the answers and explanations. You can also find both answers and explanations in the PTP testing software.

Table 20-1 "Do I Know This Already?" Foundation Topics Section-to-Question Mapping

Foundation Topics Section	Questions
Server Virtualization	1, 2
Cloud Computing Services	3, 4
WAN Traffic Paths to Reach Cloud Services	5, 6

1. Three virtual machines run on one physical server. Which server resources does a virtualization system typically virtualize so each VM can use the required amount of that resource? (Choose three correct answers.)

   a. NIC

   b. RAM

   c. Power

   d. Hypervisor

   e. CPU

2. Eight virtual machines run on one physical server; the server has two physical Ethernet NICs. Which answer describes a method that allows all eight VMs to communicate?

   a. The VMs must share two IP addresses and coordinate to avoid using duplicate TCP or UDP ports.

   b. The hypervisor acts as an IP router using the NICs as routed IP interfaces.

   c. Each VM uses a virtual NIC mapped to a physical NIC.

   d. Each VM uses a virtual NIC that logically connects to a virtual switch.

3. Which cloud service is most likely to be used for software development?

   a. IaaS

   b. PaaS

   c. SaaS

   d. SLBaaS

4. With which of the following cloud services would you purchase the service and then later install your software applications?

   a. IaaS

   b. PaaS

   c. SaaS

   d. SLBaaS

5. An enterprise plans to use a public cloud service and considers different WAN options. The answers list four options under consideration. Which option causes the most challenges when migrating from the original cloud provider to a different one?

   a. Using private WAN connections directly to the cloud provider

   b. Using an Internet connection without VPN

    c. Using an intercloud exchange

    d. Using an Internet connection with VPN

6. An enterprise plans to use a public cloud service and considers different WAN options. Which answers list a WAN option that provides good security by keeping the data private while also providing good QoS services? (Choose two answers.)

    a. Using private WAN connections directly to the cloud provider

    b. Using an Internet connection without VPN

    c. Using an intercloud exchange

    d. Using an Internet connection with VPN

Foundation Topics

Server Virtualization

When you think of a server, what comes to mind? Is it a desktop computer with a fast CPU? A desktop computer with lots of RAM? Is it hardware that would not sit upright on the floor, but something easily bolted into a rack in a data center? Do you not even think of hardware, but instead think of the server operating system (OS) running somewhere as a virtual machine (VM)?

All those answers are accurate from one perspective or another, but we ignore those details in almost every other discussion within the scope of the CCNA certification. From the perspective of most CCNA discussions, a server is a place to run applications, with users connecting to those applications over the network. This book represents the server with an icon that looks like a desktop computer (that is the standard Cisco icon for a server). This first topic breaks down different perspectives on what it means to be a server and prepares us to discuss cloud computing.

Cisco Server Hardware

Think about the form factor of servers for a moment—that is, the shape and size of the physical server. If you were to build a server of your own, what would it look like? How big, how wide, how tall, and so on? Even if you have never seen a device characterized as a server, consider these key facts:

No KVM: For most servers, no permanent user sits near the server; all the users and administrators connect to the server over the network. As a result, there is no need for a permanent keyboard, video display, or mouse (collectively referred to as KVM).

Racks of servers in a data center: In the early years of servers, a server was any computer with a relatively fast CPU, large amounts of RAM, and so on. Today, companies put many servers into one room—a data center—and one goal is not to waste space. So, making servers with a form factor that fits in a standard rack makes for more efficient use of the available space—especially when you do not expect people to be sitting in front of each server.

For example, Figure 20-1 shows a photo of server hardware from Cisco. While you might think of Cisco as a networking company, around 2010, Cisco expanded its product line into the server market with the Cisco **Unified Computing System (UCS)** product line. The photo shows a UCS B-Series (Blade series) rack-mountable chassis, which fits in a 19-inch-wide rack and is 10.5 inches (six rack units) high. It supports 16 servers: two per each of the eight removable server blades. The bottom of the chassis holds four power supplies.

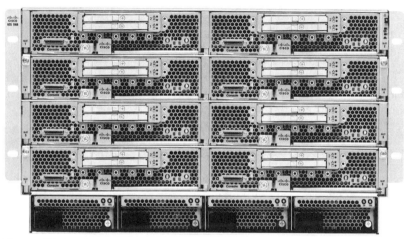

Figure 20-1   *Cisco UCS Servers: B-Series (Blade)*

No matter the form factor, server hardware today supplies some capacity of CPU chips, RAM, storage, and network interface cards (NICs). But you also have to think differently about the OS that runs on the server because of a tool called *server virtualization*.

Server Virtualization and Virtual Machine Basics

Think of a server—the hardware—as one computer. It can be one of the servers in a blade in Figure 20-1, a powerful computer you can buy at the local computer store. . . whatever. Traditionally, when you think of one server, that one server runs one OS. The hardware includes a CPU, RAM, permanent storage (like disk drives), and one or more NICs. And that one OS can use all the hardware inside the server and then run one or more applications. Figure 20-2 shows those main ideas.

20

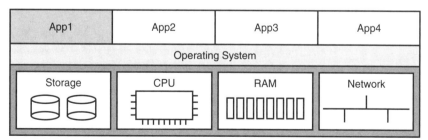

Figure 20-2   *Physical Server Model: Physical Hardware, One OS, and Applications*

With the physical server model shown in Figure 20-2, each physical server runs one OS, and that OS uses all the hardware in that one server. That was true of servers in the days before server virtualization.

Today, most companies use server hardware as part of a virtualized data center. That means the company purchases server hardware, installs it in racks, and then treats all the CPU, RAM, and so on as capacity in the data center. Then, each OS instance is decoupled from the hardware and is therefore virtual (in contrast to physical). Each piece of hardware that we would formerly have thought of as a server runs multiple instances of an OS at the same time, with each virtual OS instance called a **virtual machine**, or **VM**.

A single physical host (server) often has more processing power than you need for one OS. Thinking about processors, modern server CPUs have multiple cores (processors) in a single CPU chip. Each core may also be able to run multiple threads with a feature called *multithreading*. So, when you read about a particular Intel processor with 40 cores and multithreading (typically two threads per core), one CPU chip can execute 80 programs concurrently. The hypervisor (introduced shortly) can then treat each available thread as a **virtual CPU (vCPU)**, assigning each VM vCPUs as needed.

A VM—that is, an OS instance decoupled from the server hardware—still must execute on hardware. Each VM configures the number of vCPUs it needs, minimum RAM, and so on. The virtualization system then starts each VM on some physical server so that enough physical server hardware capacity exists to support all the VMs running on that host. So, at any one time, each VM is running on a physical server, using a subset of the CPU, RAM, storage, and NICs on that server. Figure 20-3 shows a graphic of that concept, with four separate VMs running on one physical server.

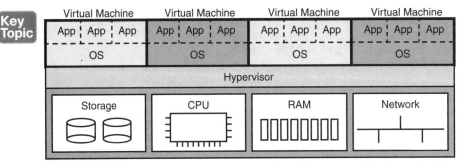

Figure 20-3 *Four VMs Running on One Host; Hypervisor Manages the Hardware*

To make server virtualization work, each physical server (called a **host** in the server virtualization world) uses a **hypervisor**. The hypervisor manages and allocates the host hardware (CPU, RAM, etc.) to each VM based on the settings for the VM. Each VM runs as if it is running on a self-contained physical server, with a specific number of virtual CPUs and NICs and a set amount of RAM and storage. For instance, if one VM defines a need for four CPUs with 8 GB of RAM, the hypervisor allocates those resources to the VM.

Answers to the "Do I Know This Already?" quiz:

1 A, B, E **2** D **3** B **4** A **5** A **6** A, C

The following are a few of the vendors and product family names associated with virtualized data centers:

- VMware vCenter

- Microsoft HyperV

- Citrix Hypervisor (formerly XenServer)

- Red Hat KVM

Beyond the hypervisor, companies sell complete virtualization systems. These systems allow virtualization engineers to dynamically create VMs, start them, move them (manually and automatically) to different servers, and stop them. For instance, before powering off server hardware to perform maintenance, the staff can move the VMs to another host (often while running).

Networking with Virtual Switches on a Virtualized Host

Server virtualization tools provide a wide variety of options for connecting VMs to networks. This book does not attempt to discuss them all, but it can help to get some of the basics down before thinking more about cloud computing.

First, what does a physical server include for networking functions? Typically, it has one or more NICs, maybe as slow as 1 Gbps, often 10 Gbps today, and maybe as fast as 40 Gbps.

Next, think about the VMs. Normally, an OS has one NIC, maybe more. Each VM has (at least) one NIC, but for a VM, it is a **virtual NIC**. (For instance, in VMware's virtualization systems, the VM's virtual NIC is called a vNIC.)

Finally, the server must combine the ideas of the physical NICs with the vNICs used by the VMs into a network. Each server uses an internal Ethernet switch concept, often called (you guessed it) a **virtual switch**, or **vSwitch**. Figure 20-4 shows an example, with four VMs, each with one vNIC. The physical server has two physical NICs. The vNICs and physical NICs connect internally to a virtual switch.

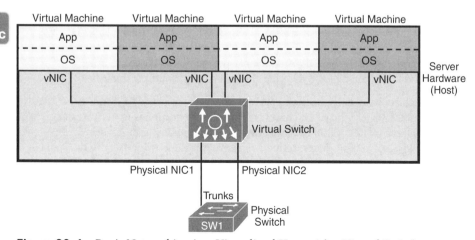

Figure 20-4 *Basic Networking in a Virtualized Host with a Virtual Switch*

In most cases today, the hypervisor vendor supplies the vSwitch, but sometimes, a different vendor (like Cisco) may supply an alternate vSwitch. For instance, Cisco offers the Cisco ACI Virtual Edge switch, supporting Cisco ACI networking.

The vSwitch shown in Figure 20-4 uses the same networking features you now know from your CCNA studies. In particular:

- **Ports connected to VMs:** The vSwitch can configure a port so that the VM will be in its own VLAN, or share the same VLAN with other VMs, or even use VLAN trunking to the VM itself.

- **Ports connected to physical NICs:** The vSwitch uses the physical NICs in the server hardware so that the switch is adjacent to the external physical LAN switch. The vSwitch can (and likely does) use VLAN trunking.

- **Automated configuration:** The configuration can be easily done within the same virtualization software that controls the VMs. That programmability allows the virtualization software to move VMs between hosts (servers) and reprogram the vSwitches so that the VM has the same networking capabilities no matter where the VM is running.

Software Containers

Software containers have the same goal as VMs but use different methods. Compared to VMs, containers take less CPU and memory while also taking less time to initialize and shut down—making them more appealing in some cases.

To appreciate the differences, consider VMs again for a moment. A single VM exists on disk, waiting to run, as one large file—typically many gigabytes because it holds an entire OS. Starting a VM takes minutes; think of VM initialization time as similar to the time it takes to boot your desktop or laptop computer. Also, VMs require some work: both the OS and application must be installed, and you need to apply software fixes over time.

Some of those perceived drawbacks of VMs led to a second wave of server virtualization, called software containers, or simply containers.

First, consider the word *container* as a generic term to understand the fundamentals. What do you imagine? Maybe you think of shipping containers that fill huge ships or ride behind tractor-trailer trucks. Perhaps you think of the plastic container you use to bring your lunch to school. Generically, containers hold other things, typically multiple things.

Software containers hold an application plus every other file it needs to work—other than the OS. For instance, the primary executable file for the application is in the container. The container has all the related files that come with the app, plus any libraries (standard code often used by applications) at the prescribed versions. It includes files used by the application, for instance, maybe a text file with application settings. The container—a file with a defined format that collects and includes all the component files—holds all the files. Because a container does not include the OS, however, it is usually smaller than a VM, often measured in megabytes rather than gigabytes.

NOTE By convention, the term **container image** refers to the file on disk that holds all the files that make up the application. The term **container** refers to a container once it has been started. For example, you might use a container image for a web server application. When you start that image five times on a server, you have five containers, that is, five instances of the web server running on the server.

So, if the container does not include the OS, how does it execute? It seems like something is missing. The answer: Architecturally, server hardware runs one instance of the OS—an OS that supports containers, like Windows or Linux. Additionally, you need a *container engine*, which is software that can install, start, stop, and monitor containers. Figure 20-5 shows the general idea.

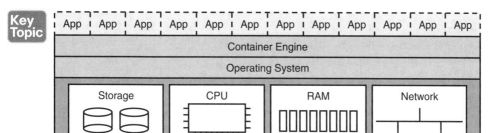

Figure 20-5 *Twelve Containers Running on One Host Managed by Container Engine*

Starting a container requires a container engine, software that understands container file formats and operations. The container engine supplies a GUI to start, stop, and monitor the containers. Most data center operational activities happen remotely, however, so the container image includes shell commands and APIs to aid remote control and automation by virtualization software. Furthermore, when you start a container, it takes the time typical of starting an application (seconds or tens of seconds) rather than the minutes required to boot an OS.

While Linux and Windows include support for containers, containers became popular in the 2010s when some companies began offering related software services. Some of the most popular and common companies and sites include

- Docker (Docker.com)
- Kubernetes (k8s.io)
- Terraform (hashicorp.com)

Docker (www.docker.com) probably had the most significant early impact in popularizing containers, with the name *Docker* becoming almost synonymous with containers. For instance, Docker created rules for packaging container images. It also offers the docker engine as a container engine.

Docker also helps speed application development through Docker Hub (hub.docker.com), a website that offers over 100,000 container images. To begin developing an application, a developer can find an existing Docker container image that includes most of what the

20

application needs. For instance, the Docker container image for the world's most popular web server software (Apache) has been downloaded over one billion times per Docker Hub.

> **NOTE**   Docker has long had free and paid accounts and software. You can download Docker on your computer at no cost, download Docker containers from Docker Hub, and start running and using containers on your desktop if you want to learn more.

The Physical Data Center Network

Next, consider the physical network in a virtualized data center. Each host—the physical host—needs a physical connection to the network. Looking again at Figure 20-4, that host, with two physical NICs, needs to connect those two physical NICs to a LAN switch in the data center.

Figure 20-6 shows the traditional cabling for a data center LAN. Each taller rectangle represents one rack inside a data center, with the tiny squares representing NIC ports and the lines representing cables.

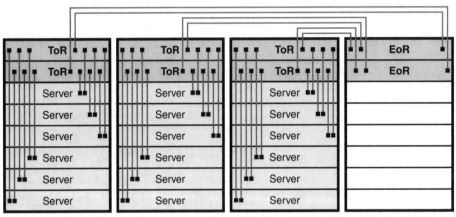

Figure 20-6   *Traditional Data Center Top-of-Rack and End-of-Row Physical Switch Topology*

Often, each host is cabled to two different switches in the top of the rack—called Top of Rack (ToR) switches—to provide redundant paths into the LAN. Each ToR switch acts as an access layer switch from a design perspective. Each ToR switch connects to an End of Row (EoR) switch, which acts as a distribution switch and also connects to the rest of the network.

The design in Figure 20-6 uses a traditional data center cabling plan. Some data center technologies call for different topologies, in particular, Cisco Application Centric Infrastructure (ACI). ACI places the server and switch hardware into racks, but cables the switches with a different topology—a topology required for proper operation of the ACI fabric. Chapter 21 introduces ACI concepts.

Workflow with a Virtualized Data Center

The first part of this chapter describes background information important to the upcoming discussions of cloud computing. Server virtualization greatly improves the operations of many data centers, but virtualization alone does not create a cloud computing environment. Consider this example of a workflow through a virtualized (not cloud-based) data center to see the differences.

Some IT staff—call them server or virtualization engineers or administrators—order and install new hosts (servers). They gather requirements, plan for the required capacity, shop for hardware, order it, and install the hardware. They play the role of long-time server administrators and engineers, but now they also work with virtualization tools.

For the virtualization parts of the effort, the virtualization engineers also install and customize the virtualization tools beyond the hypervisor. For instance, one tool might give the engineers a view of the data center as a whole, with all VMs running there, with the idea that one data center is just a lot of capacity to run VMs. The server/virtualization engineers add new physical servers to the data center, configure the virtualization systems to use the new physical servers, and ensure it all works.

So far in this scenario, the work has been in preparation for providing services to some internal customer—a development team member, the operations staff, and so on. Now, an internal customer requests a "server." In truth, the customer wants many VMs, each with requirements for vCPUs, RAM, and so on. The customer makes a request to the virtualization/server engineer to set up the VMs, as shown in Figure 20-7.

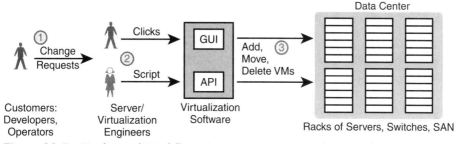

Figure 20-7   *Traditional Workflow: Customer (Human) Asks Virtualization (Human) for Service*

The figure emphasizes what happens after the customer makes a request, which flows something like this:

Step 1.   The customer of the IT group, such as a developer or a member of the operations staff, wants some service, like a set of new VMs.

Step 2.   The virtualization/server engineer reacts to the request from the customer. The server/virtualization engineer clicks away at the user interface or, if the number of VMs is significant, often runs a program called a script to create the VMs.

Step 3.   Regardless of whether the virtualization engineer clicked or used scripts, the virtualization software could then create many new VMs and start those on some hosts inside the data center.

The process shown in Figure 20-7 works great. However, that approach to providing services breaks some of the basic criteria of a cloud service. For instance, cloud computing requires self-service. Automated software processes should complete the request at step 2 rather than require a human. Want some new VMs in a cloud world? Click a user interface to ask for some new VMs, get a cup of coffee, and your VMs will be set up and started, to your specification, in minutes.

Summarizing some of the key points about a virtualized data center made so far, which enable cloud computing:

- The OS is decoupled from the hardware on which it runs, so the OS, as a VM/container, can run on any server in a data center with enough resources to run the VM/container.

- The virtualization software can automatically start and move the VM/container between servers in the data center.

- Data center networking includes virtual switches and NICs within each host (server).

- The virtualization software can program data center networking features, allowing new VMs/containers to be configured, started, moved, and stopped, with the networking details changing automatically.

Cloud Computing Services

> **NOTE** Cloud services support VMs and containers, but the rest of the chapter refers mostly to VMs just to avoid repetitive references to "VMs and containers."

Cloud computing uses virtualization products and products built specifically to enable cloud features. However, cloud computing is not just a set of products; instead, it is a way of offering IT services. So, understanding what cloud computing is—and is not—takes a little work; this next section introduces the basics.

From the just-completed discussions about virtualization, you already know one characteristic of a cloud service: it must allow self-service provisioning by the consumer. That is, the consumer or customer of the service must be able to request the service and receive that service without the delay of waiting for a human to have time to work on it, consider the request, do the work, and so on.

The US National Institute of Standards and Technology (NIST) defines cloud computing with the following list of paraphrased attributes:

On-demand self-service: The IT consumer chooses when to start and stop using the service, without any direct interaction with the provider of the service.

Broad network access: The service must be available from many types of devices and over many types of networks (including the Internet).

Resource pooling: The provider creates a pool of resources (rather than dedicating specific servers for use only by certain consumers) and dynamically allocates resources from that pool for each new request from a consumer.

Rapid elasticity: To the consumer, the resource pool appears unlimited (that is, it expands quickly, so it is called *elastic*), and the requests for new services are filled quickly.

Measured service: The provider can measure the usage and report that usage to the consumer for transparency and billing.

Keep this list of five criteria in mind while you work through the rest of the chapter. Later parts of the chapter refer back to the list.

To further develop this definition, the next few pages look at two branches of the cloud universe—private cloud and public cloud—also to further explain some of the points from the NIST definition.

Private Cloud (On-Premise)

Look back to the workflow example in Figure 20-7 with a virtualized data center. Now think about the five NIST criteria for cloud computing. If you break down the list versus the example around Figure 20-7, it seems as though the workflow may meet at least some of these five NIST cloud criteria, and it does. In particular, as described in this chapter, a virtualized data center pools resources to allow dynamic allocation. You could argue that a virtualized data center is elastic, in that the resource pool expands. However, the process may not be rapid because the workflow requires human checks, balances, and time before provisioning new services.

Private cloud creates a service, inside a company for internal customers, that meets the five criteria from the NIST list. To create a private cloud, an enterprise often expands its IT tools (like virtualization tools), changes internal workflow processes, adds additional tools, and so on.

NOTE   The world of cloud computing has long used the terms **private cloud** and **public cloud**. In more recent years, you may also find references that instead use a different pair of terms for the same ideas, with *on-premise* meaning *private cloud*, and *cloud* meaning *public cloud*. Note that the CCNA 200-301 exam topics use the newer pair of terms.

As some examples, consider what happens when an application developer at a company needs VMs to use when developing an application. With private cloud, the developer can request a service. The associated VMs automatically start and are available within minutes, with most of the time lag being the time to boot the VMs. If the developer wants many more VMs, the developer can assume that the private cloud will have enough capacity, with new requests serviced rapidly. And all parties should know that the IT group can measure the usage of the services for internal billing.

Cloud computing services enable self-service through a **cloud services catalog**. The catalog has a web page that lists all services available via the company's cloud infrastructure. With private cloud, the (internal) consumers of IT services—developers, operators, and the like—can click to choose from the cloud services catalog. And if the request is for a new set of VMs, the VMs appear and are ready for use in minutes, without human interaction for that step, as seen at step 2 of Figure 20-8.

20

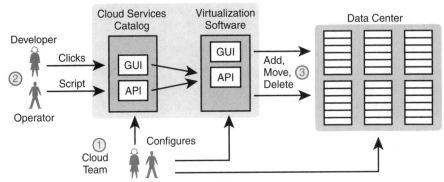

Figure 20-8 *Basic Private Cloud Workflow to Create One VM*

The cloud team adds some tools and processes to its virtualized data center to make this process work. For instance, it installs software to create the cloud services catalog, both with a user interface and code that interfaces to the APIs of the virtualization systems. That services catalog software can react to consumer requests, using APIs in the virtualization software to add, move, and create VMs, for instance. Also, the cloud team—composed of server, virtualization, network, and storage engineers—focuses on building the resource pool, testing and adding new services to the catalog, handling exceptions, and watching usage reports, so they can create the capacity to be ready to handle future requests.

Notably, with the cloud model, the cloud team no longer handles individual requests for adding 10 VMs here, and 50 there, with change requests from different groups.

Summarizing, with private cloud, the enterprise owns and manages the cloud service. The term *private cloud* emphasizes ownership by the company that uses the service. The alternate terms *on-premise* and *on-premise cloud* refer to the cloud service existing within a company-controlled site. Most importantly, to be a cloud service rather than an internal data center, a private cloud service meets the NIST criteria.

Public Cloud

With a private cloud, the cloud provider and the cloud consumer are part of the same company. With public cloud, the reverse is true: a public cloud provider offers services, selling those services to consumers in other companies. Internet service providers sell Internet services to many enterprises; public cloud providers have a similar business model, selling their services to many enterprises.

The workflow in public cloud happens somewhat like private cloud when you start from the point of a consumer asking for some service (like a new VM). As shown on the right of Figure 20-9, at step 1, the consumer asks for the new service from the service catalog web page. At step 2, the virtualization tools react to the request to create the service. Once started, the services are available but running in a data center that resides elsewhere in the world, and certainly not at the enterprise's data center (step 3).

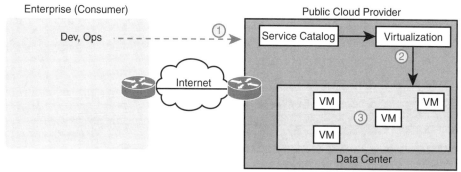

Figure 20-9 *Public Cloud Provider in the Internet*

Public cloud services exist in a data center owned by the cloud provider, so the customer needs some network connection to the public cloud provider. Cloud providers support multiple network options. They each connect to the Internet so that apps and users inside the consumer's network can communicate with the apps that the consumer runs in the cloud provider's network. However, broad network access is one of the five NIST criteria for cloud computing. Cloud providers offer different networking options, including virtual private network (VPN) and private wide-area network (WAN) connections between consumers and the cloud.

Cloud and the "As a Service" Model

So, what do you get with cloud computing? So far, this chapter has just shown a VM (or container) as a service. With cloud computing, there are a variety of services, and three stand out as the most commonly seen in the market today.

In cloud computing, categories of services use names that end in "as a Service" or aaS. Cloud computing delivers services, a more abstract concept than a physical server or a software package. So, the industry uses a variety of terms that end in "as a Service." And each "aaS" term has a different meaning.

This next topic explains the three most common cloud services: Infrastructure as a Service, Software as a Service, and Platform as a Service.

Infrastructure as a Service

Infrastructure as a Service (IaaS) may be the easiest cloud computing service for most people to understand. For perspective, think about any time you have shopped for a computer. You thought about the OS to run (the latest Microsoft OS, or Linux, or macOS if shopping for a Mac). You compared prices based on the CPU and its speed, how much RAM the computer had, the disk drive size, and so on.

IaaS offers a similar idea, but the consumer receives the use of a VM. You specify the amount of hardware performance/capacity to allocate to the VM (number of virtual CPUs, amount of RAM, and so on), as shown in Figure 20-10. You can even pick an OS to use. Once you've made your selection, the cloud provider starts the VM, which boots the chosen OS. You can even think of IaaS as a generic VM-as-a-service.

20

NOTE   In the virtualization and cloud world, starting a VM is often called *spinning up a VM* or *instantiating a VM*.

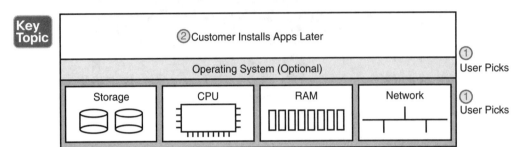

Figure 20-10   *IaaS Concept*

The provider also gives the consumer details about the VM so the consumer can connect to the OS's user interface, install more software, and customize settings. For example, imagine the customer wants to run a particular application on the server. If that customer wanted to use Microsoft Exchange as an email server, the customer would need to connect to the VM and install Exchange.

Figure 20-11 shows a web page from Amazon Web Services (AWS), a public cloud provider, where you could create a VM as part of its IaaS service. The screenshot shows that the user selected a small VM called "micro." If you look closely at the text, you can read the heading and numbers to see that this particular VM has 1 vCPU and 1 GB of RAM.

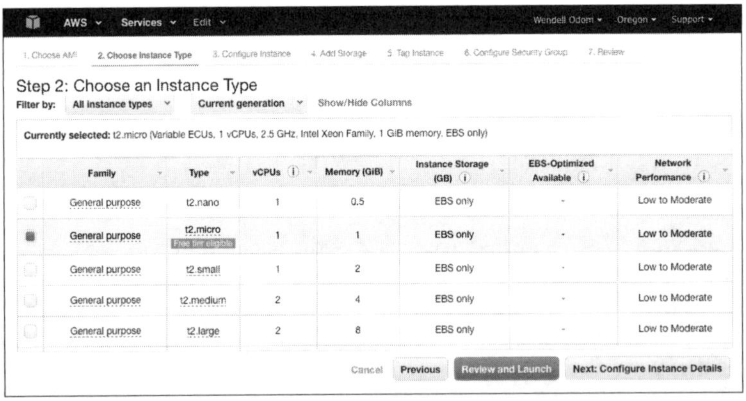

Figure 20-11   *AWS Screenshot—Set Up VM with Different CPU/RAM/OS*

Software as a Service

With **Software as a Service (SaaS)**, the consumer receives a service with working software. The cloud provider may use many VMs and containers to create the service, but those are hidden from the consumer. The cloud provider licenses, installs, and supports whatever software is required. The cloud provider then monitors performance of the application. However, the consumer chooses to use the application, signs up for the service, and starts using the application—no further installation work required. Figure 20-12 shows these main concepts.

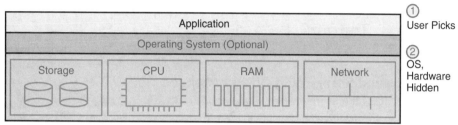

Figure 20-12   *SaaS Concept*

Many of you have probably used or at least heard of many public SaaS offerings. File storage services like Apple iCloud, Google Drive, Dropbox, and Box are all SaaS offerings. Most online email offerings can be considered SaaS services today. As another example, Microsoft offers its Exchange email server software as a service so that you can have private email services but offered as a service, along with all the other features included with Exchange— without having to license, install, and maintain the Exchange software on some VMs.

(Development) Platform as a Service

Platform as a Service (PaaS) is a development platform prebuilt as a service. A PaaS service is like IaaS in some ways. Both supply the consumer with one or more VMs, with a configurable amount of CPU, RAM, and other resources.

The key difference between PaaS and IaaS is that PaaS includes many more software tools beyond the basic OS. Those tools are useful to a software developer during the software development process. The servers running the application in production do not need the development tools, so those servers would not use the PaaS service. Instead, software developers use PaaS to create systems with tools useful when developing.

A PaaS offering includes a set of development tools, and each PaaS offering has a different combination of tools. PaaS VMs often include an integrated development environment (IDE), a set of related tools that enable the developer to write and test code easily. PaaS VMs include continuous integration tools that allow the developer to update code and have that code automatically tested and integrated into a larger software project. Examples include Google's App Engine PaaS offering (https://cloud.google.com/appengine), the Eclipse integrated development environment (see www.eclipse.org), and the Jenkins continuous integration and automation tool (see https://jenkins.io).

The primary reason to choose one PaaS service over another or a PaaS solution instead of IaaS is the mix of development tools. If you do not have experience as a developer, it can be difficult to tell whether one PaaS service might be better. You can still make some choices about sizing the PaaS VMs, similar to IaaS tools when setting up some PaaS services, as shown in Figure 20-13, but the developer tools included are the key to a PaaS service.

20

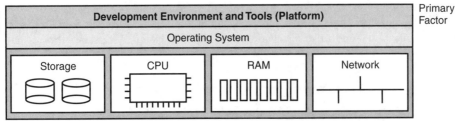

Figure 20-13 *PaaS Concept*

Virtual Routing and Forwarding (VRF) Instances

Public cloud services must support many customers concurrently. However, those different customers may, and often do, use overlapping IP subnets. Many companies use private IPv4 networks internally, and the subnets they use for their private and public cloud VMs and containers use addresses from those subnets. Unsurprisingly, those customers use overlapping subnets and addresses.

Overlapping subnets cause problems for a router (or Layer 3 switch) when using traditional conventions. Working through some of the key points:

- Typically, one router has one IP routing table.

- Typically, a router allows only one interface connected to the same subnet.

- If an engineer attempts to connect a second interface to the same subnet, the router will not bring the interface up.

- Data center virtualization software can locate and move VMs and re-program networking, so VMs from multiple customers can exist on one physical server—creating a case of overlapping subnets within that physical server.

As an example, consider customers A and B, whose VMs reside in the server shown in Figure 20-14. The customers use private class A network 10.0.0.0, and both use subnets 10.1.1.0/24 and 10.1.2.0/24. In this example, the virtual switch performs Layer 2 switching only, with no IP routing. Instead, it uses four separate VLANs, as shown. Within that limited scope, no problems exist.

Next, focus on router R1, outside the host. R1 needs to have interfaces configured in the four subnets shown in the figure so it can receive data from those VMs; however, the overlapping subnets confuse R1. For instance, the router and virtual switch define their link as a VLAN trunk. The router uses a router-on-a-stick (ROAS) configuration as shown in the figure (see Volume 1's Chapter 18, "IP Routing in the LAN," for more detail). That configuration gives router R1 an interface with an IP address in all four subnets shown inside the server.

One set of R1 interfaces would fail, however. If R1 were to configure the statements on the left first and then the ones on the right, IOS would not bring up the two interfaces on the right side of the figure due to the overlapping subnets implied by the **ip address** subcommands.

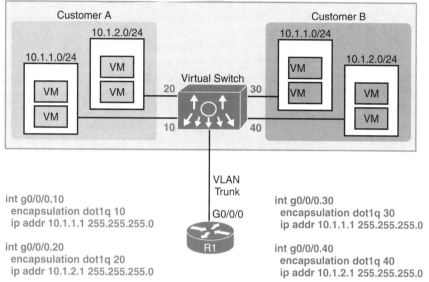

Figure 20-14 *Overlapping Subnets with Two Customers' VMs on the Same Server*

Virtual Routing and Forwarding (VRF) instances solve this problem by expanding the logic used within a router. VRFs create multiple virtual routers inside a single router or Layer 3 switch. The router configuration associates interfaces and routing protocol neighbors to VRFs, with a separate routing table per VRF. In this case, router R1 would create two VRFs, one for each customer. On the ROAS link, R1 will assign the interfaces for VLANs 10 and 20 into one VRF and the ROAS interfaces for VLANs 30 and 40 into another.

By using a separate IP routing table per VRF, the router can support overlapping subnets by placing them in different VRFs. Figure 20-15 expands Figure 20-14 to represent that concept, adding VRFs to the router. It places two VLAN interfaces in each VRF and shows the per-VRF routing tables to the left and right of the router. Note the exact same subnets in each routing table, now allowed by using VRFs.

You will find a use for VRFs throughout the world of networking. For instance, MPLS, as discussed in Chapter 19, "WAN Architecture," makes use of VRFs. One MPLS provider can support thousands of customers with the same MPLS network, even those using overlapping IP addresses, using VRFs. Summing up some of the critical points about VRFs:

- The VRF must be created via configuration in each device that performs routing (router or Layer 3 switch).

- Each router will have a separate IP routing table for each VRF, each holding routes for only that VRF.

- The configuration assigns each interface to a VRF so that the router places the associated connected route into that VRF's routing table.

- Each VRF has its own routing protocol instance and associated neighbor relationships. The routes learned from those neighbors land in the IP routing table for the VRF.

■ The router keeps its original routing table, called the global routing table. The global routing table holds routes related to interfaces and routing protocol neighbors not associated with any VRF.

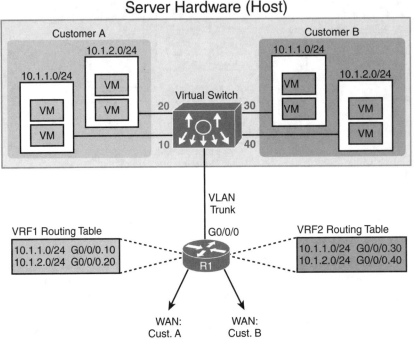

Figure 20-15   *Overlapping Subnets with Two Customers' VMs on the Same Server*

WAN Traffic Paths to Reach Cloud Services

This final major section of the chapter focuses on WAN options for public cloud, and the pros and cons of each. This section ignores private cloud for the most part, because using a private cloud—which is internal to an enterprise—has much less of an impact on an enterprise WAN compared to public cloud. With public cloud, a WAN resides between the cloud service and the consumer, so network engineers must consider how best to build a WAN when using public cloud services.

Enterprise WAN Connections to Public Cloud

Using the Internet to communicate between the enterprise and a public cloud provider is easy and convenient. However, it also has some negatives. This first section describes the basics and points out the issues, which leads to some reasons why using other WAN connections may be preferred.

Accessing Public Cloud Services Using the Internet

Consider a common workflow after moving an internal application to the public cloud as depicted in Figure 20-16, while using the Internet for connectivity. The cloud provider's services catalog can be reached by enterprise personnel, over the Internet, as shown at step 1. After the desired services—for instance, some VMs for an IaaS service—are chosen, the cloud provider (step 2) instantiates the VMs. Then, not shown as a step in the figure, the VMs are customized to run the app that was formerly running inside the enterprise's data center.

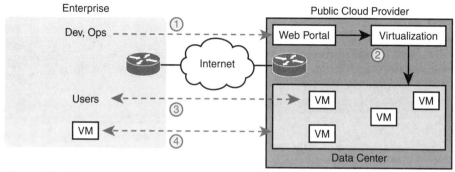

Figure 20-16   *Accessing a Public Cloud Service Using the Internet*

With the application running in the cloud, enterprise users need to access it. Step 3 shows users communicating with the application, but with the traffic flowing over the Internet. Additionally, many apps send data to other apps—some of which might still reside in the enterprise (as shown in step 4). For instance, you might use authentication services on an internal server. So, at step 4, any application communication between VMs hosted in the cloud to/from VMs hosted inside the enterprise must also occur.

Pros and Cons with Connecting to Public Cloud with Internet

Using the Internet to connect from the enterprise to the public cloud has several advantages. Every enterprise and public cloud provider already connects to the Internet. As a result, using Internet connectivity greatly speeds migration to public cloud. The following list summarizes some good reasons to use the Internet as the WAN connection to a public cloud service:

Agility: An enterprise can get started using public cloud without waiting to order a private WAN connection to the cloud provider because cloud providers support Internet connectivity.

Migration: An enterprise can switch its workload from one cloud provider to another more easily because cloud providers all connect to the Internet.

Remote work: Remote workers already use the Internet, so accessing SaaS apps available over the Internet works well.

While using the Internet for public cloud has some advantages, it has some negatives as well, including the following:

Security: The Internet is less secure than private WAN connections in that a "man in the middle" can attempt to read the contents of data that passes to/from the public cloud.

Capacity: Moving an internal application to the public cloud increases network traffic, so consider whether the enterprise's Internet links can handle the additional load.

Quality of service (QoS): The Internet does not provide QoS, whereas private WANs can. Using the Internet may result in a worse user experience than desired because of higher delay (latency), jitter, and packet loss.

No WAN SLA: ISPs typically will not provide a service-level agreement (SLA) for WAN performance and availability to all destinations of a network. Private WAN service providers are much more likely to offer performance and availability SLAs.

20

This list of concerns does not mean that an enterprise cannot use the Internet to access its public cloud services. It does mean that it should consider the pros and cons of each WAN option.

Private WAN and Internet VPN Access to Public Cloud

The NIST definition for cloud computing lists broad network access as one of the five main criteria. In the case of public cloud, that often means supporting a variety of WAN connections, including the most common enterprise WAN technologies. Basically, an enterprise can connect to a public cloud provider with WAN technologies discussed in this book. Figure 20-17 breaks it down into two broad categories.

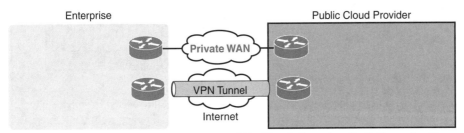

Figure 20-17   *Using Private WAN to a Public Cloud: Security, QoS, Capacity, Reporting*

To create a VPN tunnel between the enterprise and the cloud provider, use the same VPN features discussed in Chapter 19 in this volume. The cloud provider can offer a VPN service, with the cloud provider implementing one end of the tunnel and the customer implementing the other. Or the enterprise can use its own router inside the cloud provider's network—a virtual router running as a VM—and configure VPN services on that router. Cisco makes the Cloud Services Router (CSR to do exactly that: to be a router, but a router that runs as a VM in a cloud service, controlled by the cloud consumer, to do various functions that routers do, including terminating VPNs.

> **NOTE**   Cisco has introduced the Catalyst 8000v Edge Software, or simply Catalyst 8000v, as a replacement for the CSR. As of the publication date, the CSR was still available.

To make a private Multiprotocol Label Switching (MPLS) VPN or Ethernet WAN connection, the enterprise must work with the cloud and WAN providers. Because cloud providers connect to many customers with private WAN connections, they often have a published set of instructions to follow. When a customer connects using MPLS, the MPLS provider creates an MPLS VPN between the customer and the cloud provider. The same basic process happens with Ethernet WAN services, with one or more Ethernet Virtual Connections (EVCs) created between the public WAN and the enterprise.

> **NOTE**   Often, the server/virtualization engineers will dictate whether the WAN connection needs to support Layer 2 or Layer 3 connectivity, depending on other factors.

Private WAN connections also require some physical planning. Each of the larger public cloud providers has several large data centers spread around the planet and with prebuilt connection points into the major WAN services to aid the creation of private WAN connections to customers. An enterprise might then look at the cloud provider's documentation and work with that provider to choose the best place to install the private WAN connection. (Those larger public cloud companies include Amazon Web Services, Google Compute Cloud, Microsoft Azure, and Rackspace if you want to look at their websites for information about their locations.)

Pros and Cons of Connecting to Cloud with Private WANs

Private WANs overcome some of the issues of using the Internet without a VPN, so working through those issues, consider some of the different WAN options.

First, considering the issue of security, all the private options, including adding a VPN to the existing Internet connection, improve security significantly. An Internet VPN would encrypt the data to keep it private. Private WAN connections with MPLS and Ethernet have traditionally been considered secure without encryption. Still, companies sometimes encrypt data sent over private WAN connections to make the network more secure.

Regarding QoS, using an Internet VPN solution still fails to provide QoS because the Internet does not provide QoS. WAN services like MPLS VPN and Ethernet WANs can. Private WAN providers can apply QoS tools to the traffic as it passes through the service provider's network.

Finally, as for the capacity issue, the concern of planning network capacity exists for every type of WAN. Moving an app away from an internal data center to a public cloud provider requires extra thought and planning.

Several negatives exist for using a private WAN, as you might expect. Installing the new private WAN connections takes time, delaying when a company starts in cloud computing. Private WANs typically cost more than using the Internet. If a company uses a WAN connection to one cloud provider, migrating to a new cloud provider can require another round of private WAN installation, again delaying work projects. Using the Internet (with or without VPN) would make that migration much easier, but the next section shows a strong compromise solution.

Intercloud Exchanges

Public cloud computing also introduces a whole new level of competition because cloud consumers can move their workload from one cloud provider to another. Moving the workload takes some effort, for reasons beyond the scope of this book. (Suffice it to say that most cloud providers differ in how they implement services.) But enterprises can migrate their workload from one cloud provider to another, for many reasons, including looking for a less expensive cloud provider.

Now, focus on the networking connections again. Using a private WAN for the cloud adds setup time and expense. However, an intercloud exchange (or simply an intercloud) reduces the time when you migrate cloud providers.

The term *intercloud exchange* refers to any company that creates a private network as a service. First, an intercloud exchange connects to multiple cloud providers on one side. On the other side, the intercloud connects to cloud consumers. Figure 20-18 shows the idea.

20

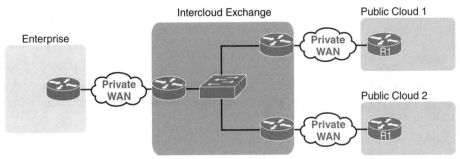

Figure 20-18 *Permanent Private WAN Connection to an Intercloud Exchange*

With access links to all cloud providers and to the cloud customer, the intercloud exchange can configure a private WAN connection to specific cloud provider sites. Later, if the consumer wants to migrate to use a different cloud provider, the consumer keeps the same private WAN links. That consumer just has to ask the intercloud exchange to reconfigure to set up new private WAN connections to the new cloud provider.

As for pros and cons, with an intercloud exchange, you get the same benefits as when connecting with a private WAN connection to a public cloud, but with the additional pro of easier migration to a new cloud provider. The main con is that using an intercloud exchange introduces another company.

Summarizing the Pros and Cons of Public Cloud WAN Options

Table 20-2 summarizes some of these key pros and cons for the public WAN options for cloud computing, for study and reference.

Table 20-2 Comparison of Public Cloud WAN Options

	Internet	Internet VPN	MPLS VPN	Ethernet WAN	Intercloud Exchange
Makes data private	No	Yes	Yes	Yes	Yes
Supports QoS	No	No	Yes	Yes	Yes
Requires capacity planning	Yes	Yes	Yes	Yes	Yes
Eases migration to a new provider	Yes	Yes	No	No	Yes
Speeds initial installation	Yes	Yes	No	No	No

Understanding Cloud Management

Cloud management is a popular method for managing your cloud-based or hosted infrastructure. There are multiple methods of cloud management. Cisco has recently added it to the CCNA blueprint, and this section covers a few of the most common methods when managing Cisco devices from a cloud perspective. The most common method is not that unfamiliar from what you have already learned, and that is to use the console capabilities of the virtual device to log in to the CLI and issue commands as you would if the device were a physical device. In this use case, a console or a serial port is mapped to the virtual device and you simply telnet or SSH to the IP of the virtual device to be put right into the CLI.

From here, you simply issue any CLI configuration commands to configure the cloud-based device.

Alternatively, there are two methods that require some experience inside the hypervisor environment such as VMware ESXi, Microsoft Hyper-V, Citrix XenServer, or KVM. Using the **Cisco Catalyst 8000V** router as an example, when the router VM first boots up, you have, by default, 5 seconds to select the console option you want to use.

NOTE   The Cisco 8000V is the latest version of the Cisco virtual router family. Previously, there was the Cisco CSR1000v, which was deployed in a similar fashion but is now End-of-Sale.

One hypervisor option is called the *virtual console*, and it enables you to click into the virtual machine within the hypervisor GUI and access the CLI that way. This is also called the hypervisor virtual VGA console. It is similar to how a virtual server that is running as a VM would be accessed. By default, this is the method the Cisco 8000V router VM boots in to.

Another hypervisor option for the Cisco 8000V is called the *serial console*. The serial console option maps to a serial port on the Cisco 8000V router VM. This enables you to use telnet to access the specific port number you specify when configuring the serial console option. The telnet syntax that follows is for a VM and UNIX xTerm terminal:

```
VM: telnet://host-ipaddress:portnumber
```

```
From a UNIX xTerm terminal: telnet host-ipaddress portnumber
```

NOTE   Telnet is used only to initially configure the Cisco 8000V router VM when using serial console. After the device is fully configured, it is highly recommended to enable SSH to ensure enhanced security and privacy because telnet utilizes clear text data in its communications.

Additionally, it is important to understand the benefits of cloud management compared to the traditional method of managing devices on a one-by-one basis. The following list highlights some of the key advantages of using cloud management and their associated definitions:

- **Centralized management:** Provides centralized control and visibility over network devices and services. This makes it easier to manage distributed networks with multiple devices across different locations.

- **Accessibility:** Devices can be accessed from anywhere in the world via an Internet connection. This enables the remote management capability of the network infrastructure. This is especially relevant for remote network operations staff.

- **Scale:** Environments can grow and shrink their scale from a small deployment to be very large and can do this very rapidly without having a constraint on resources such as storage, compute, and bandwidth. This is what "cloud elasticity" refers to.

20

■ **Automation:** Cloud management platforms often include automation capabilities that streamline repetitive tasks such as configuration management, provisioning, and troubleshooting. This reduces the manual interaction for network management, increases operational efficiency, and lowers the risk of human error.

■ **Security:** Cloud management platforms typically include built-in security mechanisms to protect network data and infrastructure from cyber threats. Role-based access control, encryption, and security monitoring are among the most common features.

■ **Lower cost of ownership:** Cloud-based infrastructure can eliminate the need for some on-premises hardware and software, which could potentially reduce capital expenditures, support, and operational costs associated with managing on-premise network infrastructure.

Cisco also offers a cloud managed solution called *Meraki*. Meraki leverages completely cloud-based management for onsite devices. All of the key advantages and benefits of cloud management mentioned previously also apply to Meraki. The centralized cloud-based web portal to manage Meraki devices is called the **Meraki Dashboard**. The Meraki Dashboard provides an informative and intuitive view of your entire Meraki network, along with the current and historical status of all managed devices. The following are some advantages of Meraki Dashboard:

■ **Zero touch provisioning (ZTP):** You can create predefined locations and install devices in a remote location and they will check in with the Meraki Dashboard and instantiate themselves by downloading their appropriate software images and configuration without needing an on-site expert to configure the devices. This saves significant costs due to lowered travel expenses and lowers the risk of misconfigured devices.

■ **Topology:** This is a live topological view of the network and how devices are connected to each other. This is an excellent way to see what is connected in your environment and how it is performing. The Topology view can be carved out in layers to see certain aspects of the network, with more focus on the devices you are interested in inspecting.

■ **Path visualization:** Allows for visual network traffic monitoring. This includes device path and directional traffic flows and can be seen in the dashboard.

■ **Single-click into devices:** Enables you to see performance and management options.

■ **Color-coded states of operation:** Simplifies monitoring and can give a quick view into the state of the network.

Figure 20-19 showcases the default client page view when logging into the Meraki Dashboard. It can be seen that there is a tremendous amount of information that is available without clicking or drilling down into any other page or link. Looking at the top of the page, we can see that there are some tiles that show the status of the Uplinks, WAN Appliances, Switches, and Access Points. All are green and show online. From there you can look further down and see the client usage graph and pie chart that highlights the bandwidth usage and details about the applications operating within the network.

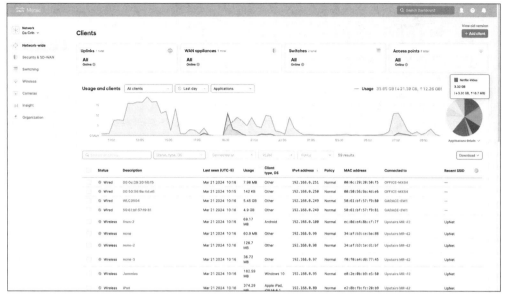

Figure 20-19 *Default View of Meraki Dashboard*

What is useful about this view is that you can hover your mouse over the graph or pie chart to display more information without navigating away from this default view. For example, you can see that there are 3.32 GB of Netflix-Video traffic running over the network on the last day, along with the corresponding upload and download statistics.

Moving to the bottom section of the screen, you can see some very helpful pieces of information, such as the device status, description, when the device was last seen on the network, the client usage, client operation system, IP address, policy, MAC address, uplink information, and most recent SSID. The sheer amount of information that is accessible from just logging into the dashboard is pretty remarkable. Furthermore, you can select many other values to view on this screen by clicking the gear and selecting additional data points. In many traditional networks, you would have to log into a standalone **network management system (NMS)** or multiple devices in the network to gain the amount of data that you can access within the Meraki Dashboard. This is one of the major benefits of centralized cloud management.

From a troubleshooting perspective, Topology and Path Visualization are some of the handiest tools within Meraki. Looking at this sample network you can see some interesting information by simply clicking the Topology view within the dashboard. You can also see that when you hover over devices or links with your mouse, you can get more detailed information about each component. In the case illustrated in Figure 20-20, you can see that there is an issue with the GARAGE-SW1 device and that there is a high amount of CRC errors on Port 3. This example shows the Layer 2 Link layer, although you can see that Layer 3 networking information is available as well.

There are many advantages to using cloud-management versus traditional methods, covered throughout this section of the chapter. Table 20-3 summarizes and compares some of the most common differences between the two.

20

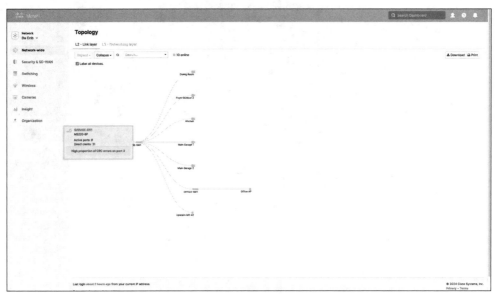

Figure 20-20 *Topology View of Meraki Dashboard*

Table 20-3 Comparing Cloud Management and Traditional Management

Use Case	Cloud Management	Traditional Management
Centralized device management	Typically, a single point of management for all devices	Unless using a third-party NMS or tool, devices are typically managed individually
Scale and speed of deployment	Zero touch provisioning (ZTP)	Manual or automated provisioning through scripting or third-party tools
Security policy and enforcement	Security polices can be applied to multiple devices within a single central dashboard	Unless using third-party tools or automation, typically security policies have to be applied on a device-by-device basis
Troubleshooting	Centralized management makes troubleshooting much more effective due to the ability to see the whole network in a single dashboard	Typically is more difficult and time-consuming from having to troubleshoot on a device-by-device basis
Monitoring and reporting	Cloud management enables you to monitor your network centrally to see and report on issues across all devices	Traditional networks monitor or report on devices using a third-party tool, which may require you to correlate the data

Chapter Review

One key to doing well on the exams is to perform repetitive spaced review sessions. Review this chapter's material using either the tools in the book or interactive tools for the same material found on the book's companion website. Refer to the "Your Study Plan" element for more details. Table 20-4 outlines the key review elements and where you can find them. To better track your study progress, record when you completed these activities in the second column.

Table 20-4 Chapter Review Tracking

Review Element	Review Date(s)	Resource Used
Review key topics		Book, website
Review key terms		Book, website
Answer DIKTA questions		Book, PTP
Review memory tables		Book, website

Review All the Key Topics

Table 20-5 Key Topics for Chapter 20

Key Topic Element	Description	Page Number
Figure 20-3	Organization of applications, on a VM, on an OS, with a hypervisor allocating and managing the host hardware	442
Figure 20-4	Virtual switch concept	443
Figure 20-5	Software container architecture	445
List	Definition of cloud computing (paraphrased) based on the NIST standard	448
Figure 20-10	Organization and concepts for an IaaS service	452
Figure 20-12	Organization and concepts for an SaaS service	453
Figure 20-13	Organization and concepts for a PaaS service	454
List	VRF features	455
List	Cons for using the Internet to access public WAN services	457
Table 20-2	Summary of pros and cons with different public cloud WAN access options	460
Table 20-3	Comparing cloud management versus traditional management	464

20

Key Terms You Should Know

Cisco Catalyst 8000V, cloud management, cloud services catalog, container, container image, host (context: DC), hypervisor, Infrastructure as a Service (IaaS), Meraki Dashboard, network management system (NMS), on-demand self-service, Platform as a Service (PaaS), private cloud, public cloud, rapid elasticity, resource pooling, Software as a Service (SaaS), Unified Computing System (UCS), virtual CPU (vCPU), virtual machine (VM), virtual NIC (vNIC), Virtual Routing and Forwarding (VRF), virtual switch (vSwitch), zero touch provisioning (ZTP)

Part V Review

Keep track of your part review progress with the checklist shown in Table P5-1. Details on each task follow the table.

Table P5-1   Part V Part Review Checklist

Activity	1st Date Completed	2nd Date Completed
Repeat All DIKTA Questions		
Answer Part Review Questions		
Review Key Topics		

Repeat All DIKTA Questions

For this task, use the PTP software to answer the "Do I Know This Already?" questions again for the chapters in this part of the book.

Answer Part Review Questions

For this task, use PTP to answer the Part Review questions for this part of the book.

Review Key Topics

Review all key topics in all chapters in this part, either by browsing the chapters or by using the Key Topics application on the companion website.

Use Per-Chapter Interactive Review

Using the companion website, browse through the interactive review elements, like memory tables and key term flashcards, to review the content from each chapter.

Part VI of this book includes most of the network automation topics from the CCNA blueprint; however, this part includes as much discussion of how Cisco and others have changed the way networks work to enable better automation as it discusses tools and processes to automate networks.

Chapters 21 and 22 examine a wide range of products and architectures that also enable better operations and automation. Chapter 21 discusses how controllers can separate out part of the work formerly done by networking devices. The chapter shows the advantages of these new controller-based models and details a few examples. Chapter 22 then goes on to give more detail about Cisco Software-Defined Access (Cisco SD-Access), a controller-based networking approach to building enterprise campus networks.

Chapters 23 and 24 discuss a few more specific details about network automation. Controllers typically include REST APIs and often return data to automation programs in the form of formatted data like JSON. Chapter 23 introduces these concepts. Chapter 24 then moves on to discuss IT automation tools, specifically Ansible and Terraform.

Part VI

Network Automation

CHAPTER 21

Introduction to Controller-Based Networking

This chapter covers the following exam topics:

The CCNA certification focuses on the traditional model for operating and controlling networks, a model that has existed for decades. You understand protocols that the devices use, along with the commands that can customize how those protocols operate. Then you plan and implement distributed configuration to the devices, device by device, to implement the network.

A new network operational model was introduced in the 2010s: Software-Defined Networking (SDN). SDN makes use of a controller that centralizes some network functions. The controller also creates many new capabilities to operate networks differently; in particular, controllers enable programs to automatically configure and operate networks through the power of application programming interfaces (APIs).

With traditional networking, the network engineer configured the various devices and changes requiring a long timeframe to plan and implement changes. With controller-based networking and SDN, network engineers and operators can implement changes more quickly, with better consistency, and often with better operational practices.

This chapter introduces the concepts of network programmability and SDN. Note that the topic area is large, with this chapter providing enough detail for you to understand the basics and to be ready for the other three chapters in this part.

The first major section of this chapter introduces the basic concepts of data and control planes, along with controllers and the related architecture. The second section then shows separate product examples of network programmability using controllers, all of which use different methods to implement networking features. The last section takes a little more exam-specific approach to these topics, comparing the benefits of traditional networking with the benefits of controller-based networking.

"Do I Know This Already?" Quiz

Take the quiz (either here or use the PTP software) if you want to use the score to help you decide how much time to spend on this chapter. The letter answers are listed at the bottom of the page following the quiz. Appendix C, found both at the end of the book as well as on the companion website, includes both the answers and explanations. You can also find both answers and explanations in the PTP testing software.

Table 21-1 "Do I Know This Already?" Foundation Topics Section-to-Question Mapping

Foundation Topics Section	Questions
SDN and Controller-Based Networks	1–3
Examples of Network Programmability and SDN	4, 5
Comparing Traditional Versus Controller-Based Networks	6

1. A Layer 2 switch examines a frame's destination MAC address and chooses to forward that frame out port G0/1 only. That action occurs as part of which plane of the switch?

   a. Data plane

   b. Management plane

   c. Control plane

   d. Table plane

2. A router uses OSPF to learn routes and adds those to the IPv4 routing table. That action occurs as part of which plane of the router?

   a. Data plane

   b. Management plane

   c. Control plane

   d. Table plane

3. A network uses an SDN architecture with switches and a centralized controller. Which of the following terms describes a function or functions expected to be found on the switches but not on the controller?

   a. A northbound interface

   b. A southbound interface

   c. Data plane functions

   d. Control plane functions

4. Which of the following controllers (if any) uses a mostly centralized control plane model?

    a. OpenDaylight Controller

    b. Cisco Application Policy Infrastructure Controller (APIC)

    c. Cisco Catalyst 9800 Series Controller

    d. None of these controllers use a mostly centralized control plane.

5. To which types of nodes should an ACI leaf switch connect in a typical single-site design? (Choose two answers.)

    a. All of the other leaf switches

    b. A subset of the spine switches

    c. All of the spine switches

    d. Some of the endpoints

    e. None of the endpoints

6. Which answers list an advantage of controller-based networks versus traditional networks? (Choose two answers.)

    a. The ability to configure the features for the network rather than per device

    b. The ability to have forwarding tables at each device

    c. Programmatic APIs available per device

    d. More consistent device configuration

Foundation Topics

SDN and Controller-Based Networks

Networking devices forward data in the form of messages, typically data-link frames like Ethernet frames. You have learned about how switches and routers do that forwarding for the entire length of preparing for the CCNA exam.

Network programmability and **Software-Defined Networking (SDN)** take those ideas, analyze the pieces, find ways to improve them for today's needs, and reassemble those ideas into a new way of making networks work. At the end of that rearrangement, the devices in the network still forward messages, but the how and why have changed.

This first major section explains the most central concepts of SDN and network programmability. It starts by breaking down some of the components of what exists in traditional networking devices. Then this section explains how some centralized controller software, called a controller, creates an architecture for easier programmatic control of a network.

The Data, Control, and Management Planes

Stop and think about what networking devices do. What does a router do? What does a switch do?

Many ideas should come to mind. For instance, routers and switches physically connect to each other with cables, and with wireless, to create networks. They forward messages: switches forward Ethernet frames, and routers forward packets. They use many different protocols to learn useful information such as routing protocols for learning network layer routes.

Everything that networking devices do can be categorized as being in a particular plane. This section takes those familiar facts about how networking devices work and describes the three planes most often used to describe how network programmability works: the data plane, the control plane, and the management plane.

The Data Plane

The term **data plane** refers to the tasks that a networking device does to forward a message. In other words, anything to do with receiving data, processing it, and forwarding that same data—whether you call the data a frame, a packet, or, more generically, a message—is part of the data plane.

For example, think about how routers forward IP packets, as shown in Figure 21-1. If you focus on the Layer 3 logic for a moment, the host sends the packet (Step 1) to its default router, R1. R1 does some processing on the received packet, makes a forwarding (routing) decision, and forwards the packet (Step 2). Routers R3 and R4 also receive, process, and forward the packet (Steps 3 and 4).

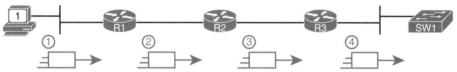

Figure 21-1 *Data Plane Processing on Routers: Basics*

Now broaden your thinking for a moment and try to think of everything a router or switch might do when receiving, processing, and forwarding a message. Of course, the forwarding decision is part of the logic; in fact, the data plane is often called the *forwarding plane*. But think beyond matching the destination address to a table. For perspective, the following list details some of the more common actions that a networking device does that fit into the data plane:

- De-encapsulating and re-encapsulating a packet in a data-link frame (routers, Layer 3 switches)

- Adding or removing an 802.1Q trunking header (routers and switches)

- Matching an Ethernet frame's destination Media Access Control (MAC) address to the MAC address table (Layer 2 switches)

- Matching an IP packet's destination IP address to the IP routing table (routers, Layer 3 switches)

- Encrypting the data and adding a new IP header (for virtual private network [VPN] processing)

- Changing the source or destination IP address (for Network Address Translation [NAT] processing)

- Discarding a message due to a filter (access control lists [ACLs], port security)

All the items in the list make up the data plane, because the data plane includes all actions done per message.

21

The Control Plane

Next, take a moment to ponder the kinds of information that the data plane needs to know beforehand so that it can work properly. For instance, routers need IP routes in a routing table before the data plane can forward packets. Layer 2 switches need entries in a MAC address table before they can forward Ethernet frames out the one best port to reach the destination. Switches must use Spanning Tree Protocol (STP) to limit which interfaces can be used for forwarding so that the data plane works well and does not loop frames forever.

From one perspective, the information supplied to the data plane controls what the data plane does. For instance, a router needs a route that matches a packet's destination address for the router to know how to route (forward) the packet. When a router's data plane tries to match the routing table and finds no matching route, the router discards the packet. And what controls the contents of the routing table? Various control plane processes.

The term **control plane** refers to any action that controls the data plane. Most of these actions have to do with creating the tables used by the data plane, tables like the IP routing table, an IP Address Resolution Protocol (ARP) table, a switch MAC address table, and so on. By adding to, removing, and changing entries to the tables used by the data plane, the control plane processes control what the data plane does. You already know about many control plane protocols—for instance, all the IP routing protocols.

Traditional networks use both a distributed data plane and a distributed control plane. In other words, each device has a data plane and a control plane, and the network distributes those functions into each individual device, as shown in the example in Figure 21-2.

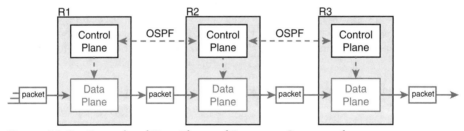

Figure 21-2 *Control and Data Planes of Routers—Conceptual*

In the figure, Open Shortest Path First (OSPF), the control plane protocol, runs on each router (that is, it is distributed among all the routers). OSPF on each router then adds to, removes from, and changes the IP routing table on each router. Once populated with useful routes, the data plane's IP routing table on each router can forward incoming packets, as shown from left to right across the bottom of the figure. The following list includes many of the more common control plane protocols:

- Routing protocols (OSPF, Enhanced Interior Gateway Routing Protocol [EIGRP], Routing Information Protocol [RIP], Border Gateway Protocol [BGP])

- IPv4 ARP

Answers to the "Do I Know This Already?" quiz:

1 A **2** C **3** C **4** A **5** C, D **6** A, D

- IPv6 Neighbor Discovery Protocol (NDP)

- Switch MAC learning

- STP

Without the protocols and activities of the control plane, the data plane of traditional networking devices would not function well. Routers would be mostly useless without routes learned by a routing protocol. Without learning MAC table entries, a switch could still forward unicasts by flooding them, but doing that for all frames would create much more load on the local-area network (LAN) compared to normal switch operations. So the data plane must rely on the control plane to provide useful information.

The Management Plane

The control plane performs overhead tasks that directly impact the behavior of the data plane. The **management plane** performs overhead work as well, but that work does not directly impact the data plane. Instead, the management plane includes protocols that allow network engineers to manage the devices.

Telnet and Secure Shell (SSH) are two of the most obvious management plane protocols. To emphasize the difference with control plane protocols, think about two routers: one configured to allow Telnet and SSH into the router and one that does not. Both could still be running a routing protocol and routing packets, whether or not they support Telnet and SSH.

Figure 21-3 extends the example shown in Figure 21-2 by now showing the management plane, with several management plane protocols.

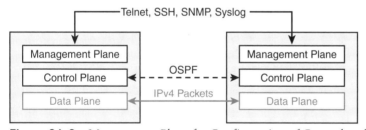

Figure 21-3 *Management Plane for Configuration of Control and Data Planes*

Cisco Switch Data Plane Internals

To better understand SDN and network programmability, it helps to think about the internals of switches. This next topic does just that.

From the very first days of devices called LAN switches, switches had to use specialized hardware to forward frames, because of the large number of frames per second (fps) required. To get a sense for the volume of frames a switch must be able to forward, consider the minimum frame size of an Ethernet frame, the number of ports on a switch, and the speeds of the ports; even low-end switches need to be able to forward millions of frames per second. For example, if a switch manufacturer wanted to figure out how fast its data plane needed to be in a new access layer switch with 24 ports, it might work through this bit of math:

- The switch has 24 ports.

- Each port runs at 1 Gbps.

21

- For this analysis, assume frames 125 bytes in length (to make the math easier, because each frame is 1000 bits long).

- With a 1000-bit-long frame and a speed of 1,000,000,000 bits/second, a port can send 1,000,000 frames per second (fps).

- Use full duplex on all ports, so the switch can expect to receive on all 24 ports at the same time.

- Result: Each port would be receiving 1,000,000 fps, for 24 million fps total, so the switch data plane would need to be ready to process 24 million fps.

Although 24 million fps may seem like a lot, the goal here is not to put an absolute number on how fast the data plane of a switch needs to be for any given era of switching technology. Instead, from their first introduction into the marketplace in the mid-1990s, LAN switches needed a faster data plane than a generalized CPU could process in software. As a result, hardware switches have always had specialized hardware to perform data plane processing.

First, the switching logic occurs not in the CPU with software, but in an **application-specific integrated circuit (ASIC)**. An ASIC is a chip built for specific purposes, such as for message processing in a networking device.

Second, the ASIC needs to perform table lookup in the MAC address table, so for fast table lookup, the switch uses a specialized type of memory to store the equivalent of the MAC address table: **ternary content-addressable memory (TCAM)**. TCAM memory does not require the ASIC to execute loops through an algorithm to search the table. Instead, the ASIC can feed the fields to be matched, like a MAC address value, into the TCAM, and the TCAM returns the matching table entry, without a need to run a search algorithm.

Note that a switch still has a general-purpose CPU and RAM as well, as shown in Figure 21-4. IOS runs in the CPU and uses RAM. Most of the control and management plane functions run in IOS. The data plane function (and the control plane function of MAC learning) happens in the ASIC.

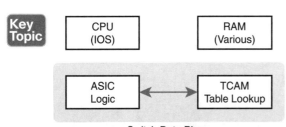

Figure 21-4 *Key Internal Processing Points in a Typical Switch*

Note that some routers also use hardware for data plane functions, for the same kinds of reasons that switches use hardware. (For instance, check out the Cisco Quantum Flow Processor (QFP) for interesting reading about hardware data plane forwarding in Cisco routers.) The ideas of a hardware data plane in routers are similar to those in switches: use a purpose-built ASIC for the forwarding logic, and TCAM to store the required tables for fast table lookup.

Controllers and Software Defined Architecture

New approaches to networking emerged in the 2010s, approaches that change where some of the control plane functions occur. Many of those approaches move parts of the control plane work into software that runs as a centralized application called a *controller*. This next topic looks at controller concepts, and the interfaces to the devices that sit below the controller and to any programs that use the controller.

> **NOTE**   The term *Software Defined Networking (SDN)* became common in the 2010s to refer to the types of controller-based networks described in the next few pages. More often today you might see terms like *software defined architecture* or **controller-based networking**.

Controllers and Centralized Control

Most traditional control plane processes use a distributed architecture. For example, each router runs its own OSPF routing protocol process. To do their work, those distributed control plane processes use messages to communicate with each other, like OSPF protocol messages between routers. As a result, traditional networks are said to use a **distributed control plane**.

The people who created today's control plane concepts, like STP, OSPF, EIGRP, and so on, could have chosen to use a **centralized control plane**. That is, they could have put the logic in one place, running on one device, or on a server. Then the centralized software could have used protocol messages to learn information from the devices, but with all the processing of the information at a centralized location. But they instead chose a distributed architecture.

There are pros and cons to using distributed and centralized architectures to do any function in a network. Many control plane functions have a long history of working well with a distributed architecture. However, a centralized application can be easier to write than a distributed application, because the centralized application has all the data gathered into one place. And this emerging world of software defined architectures often uses a centralized architecture, with a centralized control plane, with its foundations in a service called a controller.

A *controller*, or *SDN controller*, centralizes the control of the networking devices. The degree of control—and the type of control—varies widely. For instance, the controller can perform all control plane functions, replacing the devices' distributed control plane. Alternately, the controller can simply be aware of the ongoing work of the distributed data, control, and management planes on the devices, without changing how those operate. And the list goes on, with many variations.

To better understand the idea of a controller, consider one specific case as shown in Figure 21-5, in which one SDN controller centralizes all important control plane functions. First, the controller sits anywhere in the network that has IP reachability to the devices in the network. Each of the network devices still has a data plane; however, note that not one of the devices has a control plane. In the variation of SDN as shown in Figure 21-5, the controller directly programs the data plane entries into each device's tables. The networking devices do not populate their forwarding tables with traditional distributed control plane processes.

21

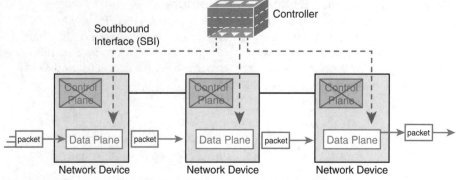

Figure 21-5 *Centralized Control Plane and a Distributed Data Plane*

> **NOTE**   Figure 21-5 shows the model used by one of the original SDN implementations that uses an industry standard called **OpenFlow**.

Figure 21-5 shows one model for network programmability and SDN, but not all. The figure does give us a great backdrop to discuss a few more important basic concepts, in particular, the idea of a southbound interface (SBI) and northbound interface (NBI).

The Southbound Interface

In a controller-based network architecture, the controller needs to communicate to the networking devices. In most network drawings and architecture drawings, those network devices typically sit below the controller, as shown in Figure 21-5. There is an interface between the controller and those devices, and given its location at the bottom part of drawings, the interface came to be known as the **southbound interface (SBI)**, as labeled in Figure 21-5.

> **NOTE**   In the context of this chapter's discussion of SDN, the word *interface* (including in the names of SBI, NBI, and API) refers to software interfaces unless otherwise noted.

Several different options exist for the SBI. The overall goal is network programmability, so the interface moves away from being only a protocol. An SBI often includes a protocol, so that the controller and devices can communicate, but it often includes an **application programming interface (API)**. An API is a method for one application (program) to exchange data with another application. Rearranging the words to describe the idea, an API is an interface to an application program. Programs process data, so an API lets two programs exchange data. While a protocol exists as a document, often from a standards body, an API often exists as usable code—functions, variables, and data structures—that can be used by one program to communicate and copy structured data between the programs across a network.

So, back to the term *SBI*: it is an interface between a program (the controller) and a program (on the networking device) that lets the two programs communicate, with one goal being to allow the controller to program the data plane forwarding tables of the networking device.

Unsurprisingly, in a network architecture meant to enable network programmability, the capabilities of the SBIs and their APIs tell us a lot about what that particular architecture can and cannot do. For instance, some controllers might support one or a few SBIs, for a specific purpose, while others might support many more SBIs, allowing a choice of SBIs to use. The comparisons of SBIs go far beyond this chapter, but it does help to think about a few; the second major section gives three sample architectures that happen to show three separate SBIs, specifically:

- OpenFlow (from the ONF; www.opennetworking.org)

- OpFlex (from Cisco; used with ACI)

- CLI (Telnet/SSH) and SNMP, and NETCONF (used with Cisco Software-Defined Access)

The Northbound Interface

Think about the programming required at the controller related to the example in Figure 21-5. The figure focuses on the fact that the controller can add entries to the networking device's forwarding tables; however, how does the controller know what to add? How does it choose? What kind of information would your program need to gather before it could attempt to add something like MAC table entries or IP routes to a network? You might think of these:

- A list of all the devices in the network

- The capabilities of each device

- The interfaces/ports on each device

- The current state of each port

- The topology—which devices connect to which, over which interfaces

- Device configuration—IP addresses, VLANs, and so on as configured on the devices

A controller does much of the work needed for the control plane in a centralized control model. It gathers all sorts of useful information about the network, like the items in the preceding list. The controller itself can create a centralized repository of all this useful information about the network.

A controller's **northbound interface (NBI)** opens the controller so its data and functions can be used by other programs, enabling network programmability, with much quicker development. Programs can pull information from the controller, using the controller's APIs. The NBIs also enable programs to use the controller's capabilities to program flows into the devices using the controller's SBIs.

To see where the NBI resides, first think about the controller itself. The controller is software, running on some server, which can be a VM or a physical server. An application can run on the same server as the controller and use an NBI, which is an API, so that two programs can communicate.

21

Figure 21-6 shows just such an example. The big box in the figure represents the system where the controller software resides. This particular controller happens to be written in Java and has a Java-based native API. Anyone—the same vendor as the controller vendor, another company, or even you—can write an app that runs on this same operating system that uses the controller's Java API. By using that API to exchange data with the controller, the application can learn information about the network. The application can also program flows in the network—that is, ask the controller to add the specific match/action logic (flows) into the forwarding tables of the networking devices.

Inside the Controller

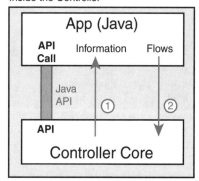

Figure 21-6 *Java API: Java Applications Communicates with Controller*

NOTE   The northbound interface (NBI) gets its name from its normal location as shown above the controller—that is, in what would be north on a map.

Before we leave the topic of NBIs, let's close with a brief explanation of a REST API as used for a controller. REST (*REpresentational State Transfer*) describes a type of API that allows applications to sit on different hosts, using HTTP messages to transfer data over the API. When you see SDN figures like Figure 21-6, with the application running on the same system as the controller, the API does not need to send messages over a network because both programs run on the same system. But when the application runs on a different system somewhere else in the network other than running on the controller, the API needs a way to send the data back and forth over an IP network, and RESTful APIs meet that need.

Figure 21-7 shows the big ideas with a REST API. The application runs on a host at the top of the figure. In this case, at Step 1, it sends an HTTP GET request to a particular URI. The HTTP GET is like any other HTTP GET, even like those used to retrieve web pages. However, the URI is not for a web page, but rather identifies an object on the controller, typically a data structure that the application needs to learn and then process. For example, the URI might identify an object that is the list of physical interfaces on a specific device along with the status of each.

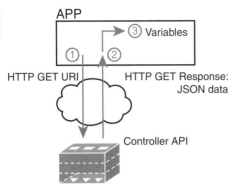

Figure 21-7 *Process Example of a GET Using a REST API*

At Step 2, the controller sends back an HTTP GET response message with the object. Most REST APIs will ask for and receive structured data. That is, instead of receiving data that is a web page, like a web browser would receive, the response holds variable names and their values, in a format that can be easily used by a program. The common formats for data used for network programmability are JavaScript Object Notation (JSON) and eXtensible Markup Language (XML), shown as Step 3.

Software Defined Architecture Summary

SDN and network programmability introduce a new way to build networks. The networking devices still exist and still forward data, but the control plane functions and locations can change dramatically. The centralized controller acts as the focal point, so that at least some of the control plane functions move from a distributed model to a centralized model.

However, the world of network programmability and SDN includes a wide array of options and solutions. Some options pull most control plane functions into the controller, whereas others pull only some of those functions into the controller. The next section takes a look at two different options, each of which takes a different approach to network programmability and the degree of centralized control.

Examples of Network Programmability and SDN

This second of three major sections of the chapter introduces two different SDN and network programmability solutions available from Cisco. Others exist as well. These two were chosen because they give a wide range of comparison points:

- OpenDaylight Controller
- Cisco Application Centric Infrastructure (ACI)

OpenDaylight and OpenFlow

One common form of SDN comes from the Open Networking Foundation (ONF) and is billed as Open SDN. The ONF (www.opennetworking.org) acts as a consortium of users (operators) and vendors to help establish SDN in the marketplace. Part of that work defines protocols, SBIs, NBIs, and anything that helps people implement their vision of SDN.

The ONF model of SDN features OpenFlow. OpenFlow defines the concept of a controller along with an IP-based SBI between the controller and the network devices. Just as

21

important, OpenFlow defines a standard idea of what a switch's capabilities are, based on the ASICs and TCAMs commonly used in switches today. (That standardized idea of what a switch does is called a *switch abstraction*.) An OpenFlow switch can act as a Layer 2 switch, a Layer 3 switch, or in different ways and with great flexibility beyond the traditional model of a Layer 2/3 switch.

The Open SDN model centralizes most control plane functions, with control of the network done by the controller plus any applications that use the controller's NBIs. In fact, Figure 21-5 (shown previously) showed the network devices without a control plane, which represents this mostly centralized OpenFlow model of SDN.

In the OpenFlow model, applications may use any APIs (NBIs) supported on the controller platform to dictate what kinds of forwarding table entries are placed into the devices; however, it calls for OpenFlow as the SBI protocol. Additionally, the networking devices need to be switches that support OpenFlow.

Because the ONF's Open SDN model has this common thread of a controller with an Open-Flow SBI, the controller plays a big role in the network. The next few pages provide a brief background about two such controllers.

The OpenDaylight Controller

First, if you were to look back at the history of OpenFlow, you could find information on dozens of different SDN controllers that support the OpenFlow SDN model. Some were more research oriented, during the years in which SDN was being developed and was more of an experimental idea. As time passed, more and more vendors began building their own controllers. And those controllers often had many similar features because they were trying to accomplish many of the same goals. As you might expect, some consolidation eventually needed to happen.

The OpenDaylight open-source SDN controller is one of the more successful SDN controller platforms to emerge from the consolidation process over the 2010s. OpenDaylight took many of the same open-source principles used with Linux, with the idea that if enough vendors worked together on a common open-source controller, then all would benefit. All those vendors could then use the open-source controller as the basis for their own products, with each vendor focusing on the product differentiation part of the effort, rather than the fundamental features. The result was that back in the mid-2010s, the *OpenDaylight SDN controller* (www.opendaylight.org) was born. OpenDaylight (ODL) began as a separate project but now exists as a project managed by the Linux Foundation.

Figure 21-8 shows a generalized version of the ODL architecture. In particular, note the variety of SBIs listed in the lower part of the controller box: OpenFlow, NetConf, PCEP, BGP-LS, and OVSDB; many more exist. The ODL project has enough participants so that it includes a large variety of options, including multiple SBIs, not just OpenFlow.

ODL has many features, with many SBIs, and many core features. A vendor can then take ODL, use the parts that make sense for that vendor, add to it, and create a commercial ODL controller.

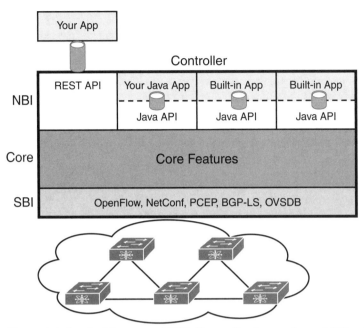

Figure 21-8 *Architecture of NBI, Controller Internals, and SBI to Network Devices*

The Cisco Open SDN Controller (OSC)

At one point back in the 2010s, Cisco offered a commercial version of the OpenDaylight controller called the Cisco *Open SDN Controller* (OSC). That controller followed the intended model for the ODL project: Cisco and others contributed labor and money to the ODL open-source project; once a new release was completed, Cisco took that release and built new versions of their product.

Cisco no longer produces and sells the Cisco OSC, but I decided to keep a short section about OSC here in this chapter for a couple of reasons. First, if you do any of your own research, you will find mention of Cisco OSC; however, well before this chapter was written, Cisco had made a strong strategic move toward different approaches to SDN using **intent-based networking (IBN)**. That move took Cisco away from OpenFlow-based SDN. But because you might see references to Cisco OSC online, or in the previous edition of this book, I wanted to point out this transition in Cisco's direction.

This book describes two Cisco offerings that use an IBN approach to SDN. The next topic in this chapter examines one of those: Application Centric Infrastructure (ACI), Cisco's data center SDN product. Chapter 22, "Cisco Software-Defined Access (Cisco SD-Access)," discusses yet another Cisco SDN option that uses intent-based networking: Software-Defined Access (Cisco SD-Access).

NOTE Examples of specific products are used only to help readers internalize the concepts of SDN and controller-based networks. Examples of these products would include Cisco Application Centric Infrastructure (ACI) and Cisco Software-Defined Access with Cisco Catalyst Center (Cisco SD-Access).

Cisco Application Centric Infrastructure (ACI)

Interestingly, many SDN offerings began with research that discarded many of the old networking paradigms in an attempt to create something new and better. For instance, OpenFlow came to be from the Stanford University Clean Slate research project that had researchers reimagining (among other things) device architectures. Cisco took a similar research path, but Cisco's work happened to arise from different groups, each focused on different parts of the network: data center, campus, and WAN. That research resulted in Cisco's current SDN offerings of ACI in the data center: Software-Defined Access (Cisco SD-Access) in the enterprise campus and Software-Defined WAN (Cisco SD-WAN) in the enterprise WAN.

When reimagining networking for the data center, the designers of ACI focused on the applications that run in a data center and what they need. As a result, they built networking concepts around application architectures. Cisco made the network infrastructure become application centric, hence the name of the Cisco data center SDN solution: **Application Centric Infrastructure (ACI)**.

For example, Cisco looked at the data center world beyond networking and saw lots of automation and control. As discussed in Chapter 20, "Cloud Architecture," virtualization software routinely starts, moves, and stops VMs. Additionally, cloud software enables self-service for customers so they can enable and disable highly elastic services as implemented with VMs and containers in a data center. From a networking perspective, some of those VMs need to communicate, but some do not. And those VMs can move based on the needs of the virtualization and cloud systems.

ACI set about to create data center networking with the flexibility and automation built into the operational model. Old data center networking models with a lot of per-physical-interface configuration on switches and routers were just poor models for the rapid pace of change and automated nature of modern data centers. This section looks at some of the detail of ACI to give you a sense of how ACI creates a powerful and flexible network to support a modern data center in which VMs and containers are created, run, move, and are stopped dynamically as a matter of routine.

ACI Physical Design: Spine and Leaf

The Cisco ACI uses a specific physical switch topology called **spine** and **leaf**. While the other parts of a network might need to allow for many different physical topologies, the data center could be made standard and consistent. But what particular standard and consistent topology? Cisco decided on the spine and leaf design, also called a Clos network after one of its creators.

With ACI, the physical network has a number of spine switches and a number of leaf switches, as shown in Figure 21-9. The figure shows the links between switches, which can be single links or multiple parallel links. Of note in this design (assuming a single-site design):

- Each leaf switch must connect to every spine switch.

- Each spine switch must connect to every leaf switch.

- Leaf switches cannot connect to each other.

- Spine switches cannot connect to each other.

- Endpoints connect only to the leaf switches.

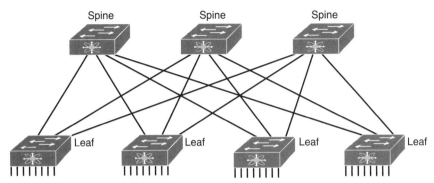

Figure 21-9 *Spine-Leaf Network Design*

Endpoints connect only to leaf switches and never to spine switches. To emphasize the point, Figure 21-10 shows a more detailed version of Figure 21-9, this time with endpoints connected to the leaf switches. None of the endpoints connect to the spine switches; they connect only to the leaf switches. The endpoints can be connections to devices outside the data center, like the router on the left. By volume, most of the endpoints will be either physical servers running a native OS or servers running virtualization software with numbers of VMs and containers as shown in the center of the figure.

Key Topic

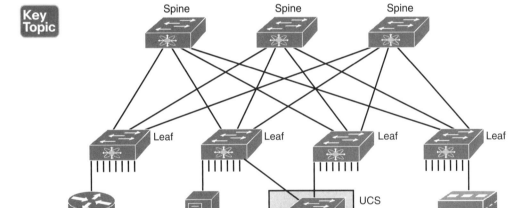

Figure 21-10 *Endpoints Found on the Leaf Switches Only*

Also, note that the figure shows a typical design with multiple leaf switches connecting to a single hardware endpoint like a Cisco Unified Computing System (UCS) server. Depending on the design requirements, each UCS might connect to at least two leaf switches, both for redundancy and for greater capacity to support the VMs and containers running on the UCS hardware. (In fact, in a small design with UCS or similar server hardware, every UCS might connect to every leaf switch.)

21

ACI Operating Model with Intent-Based Networking

The model that Cisco defines for ACI uses a concept of endpoints and policies. The *endpoints* are the VMs, containers, or even traditional servers with the OS running directly on the hardware. ACI then uses several constructs as implemented via the **Application Policy Infrastructure Controller (APIC)**, the software that serves as the centralized controller for ACI.

This section hopes to give you some insight into ACI, rather than touch on every feature. To do that, consider the application architecture of a typical enterprise web app for a moment. Most casual observers think of a web application as one entity, but one web app often exists as three separate servers:

- **Web server:** Users from outside the data center connect to a web server, which sends web page content to the user.

- **App (Application) server:** Because most web pages contain dynamic content, the app server does the processing to build the next web page for that particular user based on the user's profile and latest actions and input.

- **DB (Database) server:** Many of the app server's actions require data; the DB server retrieves and stores the data as requested by the app server.

To accommodate those ideas, ACI uses an intent-based networking (IBN) model. With that model, the engineer, or some automation program, defines the policies and intent for which endpoints should be allowed to communicate and which should not. Then the controller determines what that means for this network at this moment in time, depending on where the endpoints are right now.

For instance, when starting the VMs for this app, the virtualization software would create (via the APIC) several endpoint groups (EPGs) as shown in Figure 21-11. The controller must also be told the access polices, which define which EPGs should be able to communicate (and which should not), as implied in the figure with arrowed lines. For example, the routers that connect to the network external to the data center should be able to send packets to all web servers, but not to the app servers or DB servers.

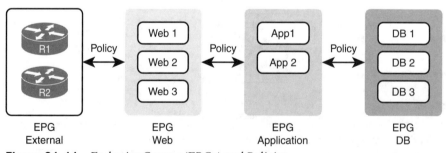

Figure 21-11 *Endpoint Groups (EPGs) and Policies*

Note that at no point did the previous paragraph talk about which physical switch interfaces should be assigned to which VLAN or which ports are in an EtherChannel; the discussion moves to an application-centric view of what happens in the network. Once all the endpoints, policies, and related details are defined, the controller can then direct the network as to what needs to be in the forwarding tables to make it all happen—and to more easily react when the VMs start, stop, or move.

To make it all work, ACI uses a centralized controller called the Application Policy Infrastructure Controller (APIC), as shown in Figure 21-12. The name defines the function in this case: it is the controller that creates application policies for the data center infrastructure. The APIC takes the intent (EPGs, policies, and so on), which completely changes the operational model away from configuring VLANs, trunks, EtherChannels, ACLs, and so on.

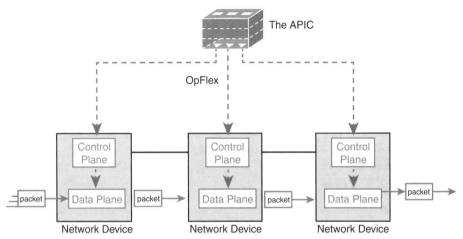

Figure 21-12 *Architectural View of ACI with APIC Pushing Intent to Switch the Control Plane*

The APIC, of course, has a convenient GUI, but the power comes in software control—that is, network programmability. The same virtualization software, or cloud or automation software, even scripts written by the network engineer, can define the endpoint groups, policies, and so on to the APIC. But all these players access the ACI system by interfacing to the APIC as depicted in Figure 21-13; the network engineer no longer needs to connect to each individual switch and configure CLI commands.

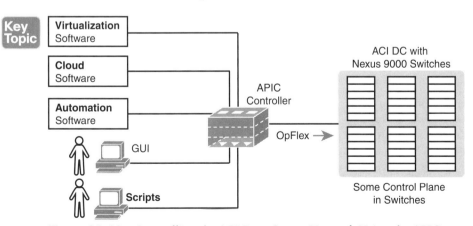

Figure 21-13 *Controlling the ACI Data Center Network Using the APIC*

For more information on Cisco ACI, go to www.cisco.com/go/aci.

Summary of the SDN Examples

The sample SDN architectures in this section of the book were chosen to provide a wide variety for the sake of learning. However, they differ to some degree in how much of the control plane work is centralized. Table 21-2 lists those and other comparison points taken from this section, for easy review and study.

Table 21-2   Points of Comparison: OpenFlow and ACI

Criteria	OpenFlow	ACI
Changes how the device control plane works versus traditional networking	Yes	Yes
Creates a centralized point from which humans and automation control the network	Yes	Yes
Degree to which the architecture centralizes the control plane	Mostly	Partially
SBIs used	OpenFlow	OpFlex
Controllers mentioned in this chapter	OpenDaylight	APIC
Organization that is the primary definer/owner	ONF	Cisco

If you want to learn more about the Cisco solutions, consider using both Cisco DevNet (the Cisco Developer Network) and dCloud (Demo cloud). Cisco provides its DevNet site (https://developer.cisco.com) for anyone interested in network programming, and the Demo Cloud site (https://dcloud.cisco.com) for anyone to experience or demo Cisco products. At the time this book went to press, DevNet had many REST API labs, while both sites had a variety of ACI-based labs.

Comparing Traditional Versus Controller-Based Networks

Before finishing the chapter, this final topic turns directly toward the CCNA 200-301 V1.1 exam. Two of the CCNA 200-301 exam topics in domain 6.0, "Automation and Programmability," ask us to compare some aspect of traditional networks versus new networking using controllers and automation. Those exam topics include

6.1: Explain how automation impacts network management

6.2: Compare traditional networks with controller-based networking

First, the wording in both exam topics can be reduced to "compare and contrast." One uses the word *compare*. The other uses a longer phrase "explain how automation impacts...," which asks us to compare what was before to what happens now that automation has been added to the network.

Network management can be broken down into two distinct categories: configuration management and operational management.

Configuration management refers to any feature that changes device configuration, with automated configuration management doing so with software (program) control. For instance, Cisco's ACI uses the APIC controller. You do not configure the devices directly, but the APIC pushes configuration down to the ACI switches that it builds based on its inter-pretation of the policies configured by the engineer. With ACI, the configuration manage-ment occurs as a part of the overall system. Other configuration management tools can be more focused on automating traditional configuration processes, with tools like NETCONF/RESTCONF, Ansible, and Terraform, as discussed in Chapter 23, "Understanding REST and JSON," and Chapter 24, "Understanding Ansible and Terraform."

Operational network management includes monitoring, gathering operational data, report-ing, and alerting humans to possible issues. For instance, **Cisco Catalyst Center** has a capability that checks the IOS images on Cisco devices to make sure only approved versions are used and that no changes have occurred to the images in comparison to the images cre-ated by Cisco.

NOTE   Cisco DNA Center was rebranded to Cisco Catalyst Center; however, all features and functionality remain the same. Please visit www.cisco.com/go/catalystcenter for more information. Catalyst Center is used because it is an example of a commonly used campus controller.

The other exam topic (6.2) described in this section focuses on controller-based networking instead of network management. That exam topic includes any SDN network as character-ized by the use of a controller. Today people might use that term or these other synonyms to describe some of the newer networking options that happen to use controllers:

■ Software Defined Networking

■ Software Defined Architecture

■ Programmable Networks

■ Controller-Based Networks

Table 21-3 summarizes the chapters that have content related to these two exam topics.

Table 21-3   Exam Topics and Most Relevant Chapters

Exam Topic	Exam Topic Text	Most Relevant Chapter(s)
6.1	Explain how automation impacts network management	21–24
6.2	Compare traditional networks with controller-based networking	21, 22

How Automation Impacts Network Management

This chapter introduces many of the features that enable automation in SDNs, but so far it has not made any overt statements about how automation impacts network management. This next topic works through a couple of examples that show the power of automation as enabled through controller-based networks.

First, centralized controllers formalize and define data models for the configuration and operational data about networks. We humans might be comfortable with visually scanning the output of **show** commands to find the tidbit of information we need. Programs need to be able to identify the specific fact. To build a controller-based network with APIs, all the

21

data about the network needs to be defined in a data model so programs can use that data via API calls. Before using controllers, automation scripts often had to begin by processing the text output of a **show** command, but with controllers and the data models behind the APIs, the data can be readily available to any automation script or vendor application through a **northbound API**.

For instance, Example 21-1 shows some output from a command on a switch. With a northbound API on a controller, and the data model it supplies, an automation program could issue this command and begin by parsing this text. The goal: find the configuration setting on the **switchport mode** command and the current trunking state.

Example 21-1   *Small Output from a Switch Command*

```
SW1# show interfaces gigabit 0/1 switchport
Name: Gi0/1
Switchport: Enabled
Administrative Mode: dynamic auto
Operational Mode: static access
Administrative Trunking Encapsulation: dot1q
Operational Trunking Encapsulation: native
Negotiation of Trunking: On
```

Example 21-2 shows a simple example of the starting point for a program using a controller's northbound API. Instead of asking for the text from a **show** command, the API call will result in the program having a series of variables set. In this case, there are variables for that same interface that list the trunk configuration setting and the trunk operational state.

Example 21-2   *Python Dictionary with Variables Set to Needed Values*

```
>>> interface1
{'trunk-config': 'dynamic auto', 'trunk-status': 'static access'}
>>>
```

Using a controller-based model not only supplies APIs that give us the exact same data a human could see in **show** commands, but often they also supply much more useful information. A controller collects data from the entire network; consequently, the controller can be written so that it analyzes and presents more useful data via the API. As a result, software that uses the APIs—whether automation written by local engineers or applications written by vendors—can be written more quickly and can often create features that would have been much more difficult without a controller.

For instance, Cisco Catalyst Center provides a path trace feature. The application shows the path of a packet from source to destination, with the forwarding logic used at each node.

Now imagine writing that application with either of these two approaches.

- One API call that returns a list of all devices and their running configuration, with other API calls to collect each device's MAC address tables and/or their IP routing tables. Then you have to process that data to find the end-to-end path.

- One API call to which you pass the source and destination IP addresses and TCP/UDP ports, and the API returns variables that describe the end-to-end path, including device hostnames and interfaces. The variables spell out the path the packet takes through the network.

The second option does most of the work, while the first option leaves most of the work to you and your program. But that second option becomes possible because of the centralized controller. The controller has the data if it at least collects configuration and forwarding table information. Going beyond that, Cisco controllers analyze the data to provide much more useful data. The power of these kinds of APIs is amazing, and this is just one example.

The following list summarizes a few of the comparison points for this particular exam topic:

- Northbound APIs and their underlying data models make it much easier to automate functions versus traditional networks.

- The robust data created by controllers makes it possible to automate functions that were not easily automated without controllers.

- The new reimagined software defined networks that use new operational models simplify operations, with automation resulting in more consistent configuration and fewer errors.

- Centralized collection of operational data at controllers allows the application of modern data analytics to networking operational data, providing actionable insights that were likely not noticeable with the former model.

- Time required to complete projects is reduced.

- New operational models use external inputs, like considering time of day, day of week, and network load.

Comparing Traditional Networks with Controller-Based Networks

As for exam topic 6.2, this entire chapter begins to show the advantages created by using controller-based networks. However, this chapter only begins to describe the possibilities. By centralizing some of the functions in the network and providing robust APIs, controllers enable a large number of new operational models. Those models include the three most likely to be seen from Cisco in an enterprise: Cisco Software-Defined Access (Cisco SD-Access), Cisco Software-Defined WAN (Cisco SD-WAN), and Cisco Application Centric Infrastructure (Cisco ACI). (Chapter 22 introduces Cisco SD-Access.)

This changes the operating paradigm in many cases, with the controller determining many device-specific details:

21

- The network engineer does not need to think about every command on every device.

- The controller configures the devices with consistent and streamlined settings.

- The result: faster and more consistent changes with fewer issues.

As another example, just consider the ACI example from earlier in the chapter. Instead of configuring each port with an access VLAN, or making it a trunk, adding routing protocol configuration, and possibly updating IP ACLs, all you had to do was create some endpoint groups (EPGs) and policies. In that case, the orchestration software that started the VMs could automatically create the EPGs and policies. The new paradigm of intent-based networking was enabled through the controller-based architecture. Then the automation features enabled by the controller's northbound APIs allowed third-party applications to automatically configure the network to support the necessary changes.

Some of the advantages include the following:

- Uses new and improved operational models that allow the configuration of the network as a system rather than per-device configuration

- Enables automation through northbound APIs that provide robust methods and model-driven data

- Configures the network devices through **southbound APIs**, resulting in more consistent device configuration, fewer errors, and less time spent troubleshooting the network

- Enables a DevOps approach to networks

Chapter 22 goes into some depth comparing traditional networking with controller-based networks with descriptions of Cisco Software-Defined Access (Cisco SD-Access). Look throughout that chapter for some of the reasons and motivations for Cisco SD-Access and the features enabled by using the Cisco Catalyst Center controller.

Chapter Review

One key to doing well on the exams is to perform repetitive spaced review sessions. Review this chapter's material using either the tools in the book or interactive tools for the same material found on the book's companion website. Refer to the "Your Study Plan" element for more details. Table 21-4 outlines the key review elements and where you can find them. To better track your study progress, record when you completed these activities in the second column.

Table 21-4   Chapter Review Tracking

Review Element	Review Date(s)	Resource Used
Review key topics		Book, website
Review key terms		Book, website
Answer DIKTA questions		Book, PTP
Review memory tables		Book, app
Watch video		Website

Review All the Key Topics

Table 21-5   Key Topics for Chapter 21

Key Topic Element	Description	Page Number
List	Sample actions of the networking device data plane	473
List	Sample actions of the networking device control plane	474
Figure 21-4	Switch internals with ASIC and TCAM	476
Figure 21-5	Basic SDN architecture, with the centralized controller programming device data planes directly	478
Paragraph	Description of the role and purpose of the NBI	479
Figure 21-7	REST API basic concepts	481
List	Spine-leaf topology requirements	484
Figure 21-10	Spine-leaf design	485
Figure 21-13	Controlling the ACI data center network using APIC	487
Table 21-2	Comparisons of Open SDN and Cisco ACI options	488
List	Comparisons of how automation improves network management	491
List	Comparisons of how controller-based networking works versus traditional networking	492

Key Terms You Should Know

Application Centric Infrastructure (ACI), Application Policy Infrastructure Controller (APIC), application programming interface (API), application-specific integrated circuit (ASIC), centralized control plane, Cisco Catalyst Center, control plane, controller-based networking, data plane, distributed control plane, intent-based networking (IBN), leaf, management plane, northbound API, northbound interface (NBI), OpenFlow, Software Defined Networking (SDN), southbound API, southbound interface (SBI), spine, ternary content-addressable memory (TCAM)

21

Cisco Software-Defined Access (Cisco SD-Access)

This chapter covers the following exam topics:

Cisco Software-Defined Access (SD-Access) is a software-defined approach to build converged wired and wireless campus networks or LANs. The word *access* in the name refers to the three-tier network architecture design that consists of the core, distribution, and access layers of a network. The access layer is where the endpoint devices connect to the network, while *software-defined* refers to many of the software-defined architectural features discussed in Chapter 21, "Introduction to Controller-Based Networking." These features include a centralized controller—called Cisco Catalyst Center—and use both southbound and northbound protocols and APIs. It also includes a completely different operational model within Cisco SD-Access when compared to that of a traditional network. Cisco SD-Access creates a network fabric composed of an underlay network and an overlay network.

> **NOTE** Cisco DNA Center was rebranded to Cisco Catalyst Center; however, all features and functionality remain the same. Please visit www.cisco.com/go/catalystcenter for more information.

Cisco SD-Access is Cisco's main campus offering and fits within Cisco Digital Network Architecture (DNA). Cisco DNA defines the entire architecture for the new world of software-defined networks, digitization, and how Cisco networks should be operated in the future. This chapter introduces Cisco SD-Access, which exists as one implementation of Cisco DNA.

The discussion of Cisco SD-Access and Cisco DNA provides a great backdrop to discuss a few other topics from the CCNA blueprint: Cisco Catalyst Center controller and network management. Cisco SD-Access uses the Cisco Catalyst Center controller to configure and operate Cisco SD-Access. However, Cisco Catalyst Center also acts as a complete network management platform. To understand Cisco Catalyst Center, you also need to understand traditional network management as well as the new management models using controllers.

"Do I Know This Already?" Quiz

Take the quiz (either here or use the PTP software) if you want to use the score to help you decide how much time to spend on this chapter. The letter answers are listed at the bottom of the page following the quiz. Appendix C, found both at the end of the book as well as on the companion website, includes both the answers and explanations. You can also find both answers and explanations in the PTP testing software.

Table 22-1 "Do I Know This Already?" Foundation Topics Section-to-Question Mapping

Foundation Topics Section	Questions
Cisco SD-Access Fabric, Underlay, and Overlay	1–3
Cisco Catalyst Center and Cisco SD-Access Operation	4, 5
Cisco Catalyst Center as a Network Management Platform	6
Artificial Intelligence (AI), Machine Learning (ML), and Operational Management	7

1. In Cisco Software-Defined Access (Cisco SD-Access), which term refers to the devices and cabling, along with configuration that allows the network device nodes enough IP connectivity to send IP packets to each other?

   a. Fabric

   b. Overlay

   c. Underlay

   d. VXLAN

2. In Cisco Software-Defined Access (Cisco SD-Access), which term refers to the functions that deliver endpoint packets across the network using tunnels between the ingress and egress fabric nodes?

   a. Fabric

   b. Overlay

   c. Underlay

   d. VXLAN

3. In Software-Defined Access (Cisco SD-Access), which of the answers are part of the overlay data plane?

   a. LISP

   b. GRE

   c. OSPF

   d. VXLAN

4. Which answers best describe options of how to implement security with scalable groups using Cisco Catalyst Center and Cisco SD-Access? (Choose two answers.)

   a. A human user from the Cisco Catalyst Center GUI

   b. An automation application using NETCONF

   c. A human user using the CLI of a Cisco SD-Access fabric edge node

   d. An automation application using REST

5. Which of the following protocols or tools could be used as part of the Cisco Catalyst Center southbound interface? (Choose three answers.)

   a. Ansible

   b. SSH

   c. NETCONF

   d. SNMP

   e. Puppet

6. Which of the following are network management features performed by both traditional network management software as well as by Cisco Catalyst Center? (Choose two answers.)

   a. Network device discovery

   b. Software-Defined Access configuration

   c. End-to-end path discovery with ACL analysis

   d. Device installation (day 0), configuration (day 1), and monitoring (day n) operations

7. What distinguishes Narrow AI from Generative AI?

   a. Narrow AI lacks broad cognitive capabilities, while Generative AI thrives in a limited scope.

   b. Narrow AI is designed for specific tasks, while Generative AI is capable of learning and decision-making.

   c. Narrow AI includes applications like speech recognition, while Generative AI focuses on conversational platforms like ChatGPT.

   d. Narrow AI relies on explicit programming, while Generative AI learns patterns and relationships from data sources.

Foundation Topics

Cisco SD-Access Fabric, Underlay, and Overlay

Cisco **Software-Defined Access (Cisco SD-Access)** creates an entirely new way to build campus LANs as compared to the traditional methods of networking discussed in most chapters of this book. In the mid-2010s, Cisco set about to reimagine campus networking, with Cisco SD-Access as the result.

Cisco SD-Access uses the software-defined architectural model introduced in Chapter 21, with a controller and various APIs. Cisco SD-Access networks are still built using a collection of physical networking equipment such as routers and switches as well as cables, and other various endpoint devices. At the top of the network is the Cisco Catalyst Center controller, as shown in Figure 22-1. Cisco Catalyst Center is where users utilize a graphical user interface (GUI) for design, configuration, and implementation settings, and the controller provides automation by leveraging APIs. In short, Cisco Catalyst Center is the controller for Cisco SD-Access networks.

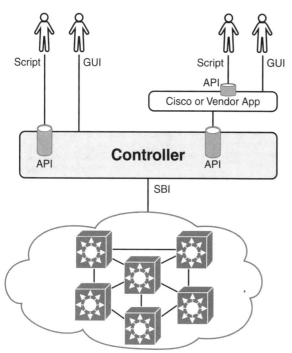

Figure 22-1 *Cisco SD-Access Architectural Model with Cisco Catalyst Center*

In terms of architecture, the southbound side of the controller contains components such as the fabric, the underlay, and the overlay. By design in SDN implementations, most of the interesting new capabilities occur on the northbound side, which are examined in the second half of this chapter. This first half of the chapter examines the details south of the controller—namely, the underlay network, overlay network, and fabric.

Underlay: The physical devices and connections, which include wired and wireless devices that provide IP connectivity to all nodes within the campus LAN. The main goal of an underlay network is to provide reachability to all Cisco SD-Access devices in order to support the dynamic creation of Virtual eXtensible Local-Area Network (**VXLAN**) overlay tunnels.

Overlay: The collection of devices that use VXLAN tunnels that are created between other Cisco SD-Access devices such as switches and fabric-enabled access points. Overlays are used to transport traffic from one endpoint to another over the fabric.

Fabric: The combination of overlay and underlay technologies, which together provide all features to deliver data across the network with the desired features and attributes. This could be all devices or a subset of devices that make up the fabric. This also means that multiple fabrics can exist within a Cisco SD-Access network.

VXLAN is defined in RFC 7348 as a technology used to create virtual networks that can span different physical locations or devices. It allows for more flexible and scalable communication between devices. VXLAN encapsulates data and extends Layer 2 networks over Layer 3 networks and is often seen in data center and cloud environments. This technology can help improve network efficiency and support the growing needs of modern applications.

In Cisco SD-Access, one main use case is something called *host mobility*. As wireless becomes a more pervasive method of connectivity, it is more common for users to move from location to location during a typical workday. These locations can be from the user's desk to the break room or from the data center to the call center. In many cases, users no longer sit and work in the same location within the corporate campus environment. This includes being wired. Users can move and plug into network jacks at other desks or also in conference rooms.

Thinking through this scenario, in the simplest terms, means that a user can hop from one wireless network with one IP address and set of security rules to another VLAN or subnet with a different IP address and set of security rules or access lists. Typically, this capability was handled by means of DHCP and the hope that the network administrator had the appropriate security policies in place to make sure that, when users went from one area of the network to another, the same rules applied. This is very often a manual process in many networks. Something had to be done to change the way users were treated technically and also from a user-experience perspective. For example, if a user moves from one area of the building to another and then suddenly couldn't access a mission-critical application because of a missing access list entry, that causes a problem for the user who is trying to get a job done.

In less formal terms, the underlay exists as multilayer switches and their links, with IP connectivity—but for a special purpose. Traffic sent by the endpoint devices flows through VXLAN tunnels in the overlay using a completely different process than traditional LAN switching and IP routing.

For instance, think about the idea of sending packets from hosts on the left of a network, over Cisco SD-Access, to hosts on the right. For instance, imagine a packet enters on the left side of the physical network at the bottom of Figure 22-2 and eventually exits the campus out switch SW2 on the far right. This underlay network looks like a more traditional network drawing, with several devices and links.

The overlay drawing at the top of the figure shows only two switches—called fabric edge nodes, because they happen to be at the edges of the Cisco SD-Access fabric—with a tunnel labeled VXLAN connecting the two. Both concepts (underlay and overlay) together create the Cisco SD-Access fabric.

The next few pages explain both the underlay and overlay in a little more depth.

Answers to the "Do I Know This Already?" quiz:

1 C **2** B **3** D **4** A, D **5** B, C, D **6** A, D **7** B

Overlay

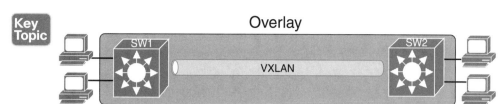

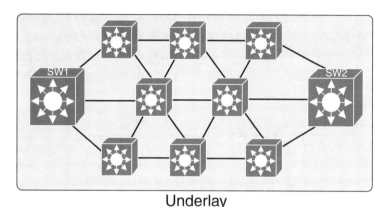

Underlay

Figure 22-2 *Fabric, Underlay, and Overlay Concepts*

The Cisco SD-Access Underlay

With Cisco SD-Access, the underlay exists to provide connectivity between the fabric edge nodes in the campus environment for the purpose of supporting VXLAN tunnels in the overlay network. To do that, the underlay includes the switches, routers, cables, and wireless links used to create the physical network. It also includes the configuration and operation of the underlay so it can support the work of the overlay network.

Using Existing Gear for the Cisco SD-Access Underlay

To build a Cisco SD-Access underlay network, companies have two basic choices. They can use supported models of their existing campus network and add new configuration to create an underlay network, while still supporting their existing production traffic with traditional routing and switching. Alternately, the company can purchase some new Catalyst switches and build the Cisco SD-Access network without concern for harming existing traffic, and migrate endpoints to the new network fabric over time.

To build Cisco SD-Access into an existing network, it helps to think for a moment about some typical campus network designs. The larger campus site may use either a two-tier or three-tier design as discussed in Chapter 18, "LAN Architecture." It has a cluster of wireless LAN controllers (WLCs) to support a number of lightweight APs (LWAPs). Engineers have configured VLANs, VLAN trunks, IP routing, IP routing protocols, ACLs, and so on. And the LAN connects to WAN routers.

22

Cisco SD-Access can be added into an existing campus LAN, but doing so has some risks and restrictions. First and foremost, you have to be careful not to disrupt the current network while adding the new features to the network. The issues include

- Because of the possibility of harming the existing production configuration, **Cisco Catalyst Center** should not be used to configure the underlay if the devices are currently used in production. (Cisco Catalyst Center will be used to configure the underlay with deployments that use all new hardware.)

- The existing hardware must be from the Cisco SD-Access compatibility list, with different models supported depending on their different roles (see a link at www.cisco.com/go/sd-access).

- The device software levels must meet the requirements, based on their roles, as detailed in that same compatibility list.

For instance, imagine an enterprise happened to have an existing campus network that uses Cisco SD-Access-compatible hardware. That company might need to update the IOS versions in a few cases. Additionally, the engineers would need to configure the underlay part of the Cisco SD-Access devices manually rather than with Cisco Catalyst Center because Cisco assumes that the existing network already supports production traffic, so they want the customer directly involved in making those changes.

The Cisco SD-Access underlay configuration requires you to think about and choose the different roles filled by each device before you can decide which devices to use and which minimum software levels each requires. If you look for the hardware compatibility list linked from www.cisco.com/go/sd-access, you will see different lists of supported hardware and software depending on the roles. These roles include

Fabric edge node: A switch that connects to endpoint devices (similar to traditional access or leaf switches)

Fabric border node: A switch that connects to devices outside the control of Cisco SD-Access—for example, switches that connect to the WAN routers or to an ACI data center

Fabric control-plane node: A switch that performs special control plane functions for the underlay (LISP), requiring more CPU and memory

For example, Cisco's compatibility list includes many Catalyst 9200, 9300, 9400, 9500, and 9600 series switches, but also some older Catalyst 3850 and 3650 switches, as fabric edge nodes. However, some products did not make the list as fabric edge nodes. For fabric control nodes, the list included higher-end Catalyst switch models (which typically have more CPU and RAM), plus several router models (routers typically have much more RAM for control plane protocol storage—for instance, for routing protocols).

The beginning of a Cisco SD-Access project will require you to look at the existing hardware and software to begin to decide whether the existing campus might be a good candidate to build the fabric with existing gear or to upgrade hardware when building the new campus fabric LAN.

Using New Gear for the Cisco SD-Access Underlay

When buying new hardware for the Cisco SD-Access fabric—that is, a greenfield design—you remove many of the challenges that exist versus deploying Cisco SD-Access on existing gear. You can simply order compatible hardware and software. Once it arrives, you can leverage Cisco Catalyst Center to then configure all the underlay features automatically.

At the same time, the usual campus LAN design decisions will still need to be made. Enterprises use Cisco SD-Access as a better way to build and operate a campus network, but it is still a campus network. It needs to provide access and connectivity to all types of users and devices. When planning a greenfield Cisco SD-Access design, plan to use appropriate compatible hardware, but also think about these traditional LAN design points:

- The number of ports needed in switches in each wiring closet

- The port speeds required

- The benefit of a switch stack in each wiring closet

- The cable length and types of cabling already installed

- The need for power (PoE/PoE+)

- The power available in each new switch versus the PoE power requirements

- Link capacity (speed and number of links) for links between switches

As far as the topology, traditional campus design does tell us how to connect devices, but Cisco SD-Access does not have to follow those traditional rules. To review, traditional campus LAN Layer 2 design (as discussed back in Chapter 18) tells us to connect each access switch to two different distribution layer switches, but not to other access layer switches, as shown in Figure 22-3. The access layer switch acts as a Layer 2 switch, with a VLAN limited to those three switches.

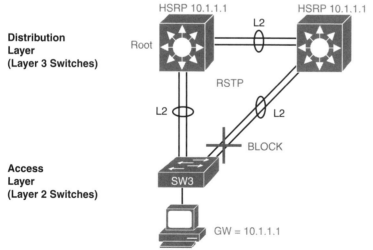

Figure 22-3 *Traditional Access Layer Design: Three Switches in STP Triangle*

22

Think through some of the traditional features shown in the figure. The distribution layer switches—Layer 3 switches—act as the default gateway used by hosts and commonly implement HSRP for better availability. The design uses more than one uplink from the access to distribution layer switches, with Layer 2 EtherChannels to allow balancing in addition to redundancy. STP/RSTP manages the small amount of Layer 2 redundancy in the campus, preventing loops by blocking traffic on some ports.

In comparison, a greenfield Cisco SD-Access fabric uses a *routed access layer* design. Routed access layer designs were around long before Cisco SD-Access, but Cisco SD-Access makes good use of the design, and it works very well for the underlay with its goal to support VXLAN tunnels in the overlay network. A routed access layer design simply means that all the LAN switches are Layer 3 switches, with routing enabled, so all the links between switches operate as Layer 3 links. This also means that there are no links in a blocking state and not being used due to STP. This increases available bandwidth and capacity due to all links being used to route traffic versus some sitting idle.

When specifying a greenfield Cisco SD-Access deployment, you can identify what gear you want Cisco Catalyst Center to configure, and it will handle the configuration of the underlay on those devices. This includes using a *routed access layer*. Because this is a greenfield deployment, Cisco Catalyst Center knows that it can configure the switches and wireless devices without any concern of causing harm to a production network. Cisco Catalyst Center will choose the best underlay configuration to support the Cisco SD-Access fabric design.

The typical underlay configuration provided by Cisco Catalyst Center includes the following features but can be modified based on specific design requirements:

- All switches act as Layer 3 switches.

- The switches use the IS-IS routing protocol.

- All links between switches (single links, EtherChannels) are routed Layer 3 links (not Layer 2 links).

- As a result, STP/RSTP is not needed, with the routing protocol instead choosing which links to use based on the IP routing tables.

- The equivalent of a traditional access layer switch—a fabric edge node—acts as the default gateway for the endpoint devices, rather than distribution switches.

- As a result, HSRP (or any FHRP) is no longer needed.

Figure 22-4 repeats the same physical design as in Figure 22-3 but shows the different features with the routed access design as configured using Cisco Catalyst Center.

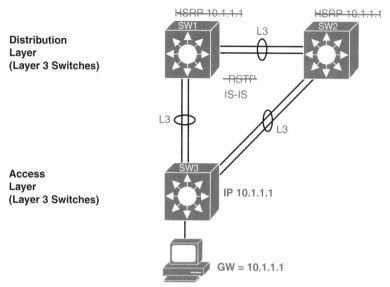

Distribution Layer (Layer 3 Switches)

Access Layer (Layer 3 Switches)

Figure 22-4 *Cisco SD-Access Fabric Layer 3 Access Benefits*

NOTE   Cisco Catalyst Center configures the underlay with consistent settings for each instance of Cisco SD-Access across an enterprise. This convention simplifies operation as an enterprise completes a migration to Cisco SD-Access.

The Cisco SD-Access Overlay

When you first think of the Cisco SD-Access overlay, think of this kind of sequence. First, an endpoint sends a frame that will be delivered across the Cisco SD-Access network. The first fabric edge node to receive the frame encapsulates the frame in a new message—using the tunneling specification VXLAN—and forwards the frame into the fabric. Once the ingress fabric edge node has encapsulated the original frame in VXLAN, the other fabric nodes forward the frame based on the VXLAN tunnel details. The last fabric edge node in the path removes the VXLAN details, leaving the original frame, and forwards the original frame on toward the destination endpoint.

While the summary steps of some of Cisco SD-Access's overlay in the previous paragraph may sound like a lot of work, all that work happens in each switch's ASIC. So, while it is more complex to understand, there is no performance penalty for the switches to perform the extra work as it is done in hardware.

Cisco's choice of using VXLAN tunnels opened up many possibilities for a number of new networking features that did not exist without VXLAN. This next topic begins with a closer look at the VXLAN tunnels in the overlay, followed by a discussion of how Cisco SD-Access uses Locator/ID Separation Protocol (**LISP**) for endpoint discovery and location information needed to create the VXLAN tunnels.

22

VXLAN Tunnels in the Overlay (Data Plane)

Cisco SD-Access has many additional needs beyond the simple message delivery—needs that let it provide improved functions. To that end, the fabric does not only route IP packets or switch Ethernet frames; it encapsulates incoming data link frames in a tunneling technology for delivery across the fabric network. VXLAN must adhere to the following functions in a Cisco SD-Access fabric:

- The VXLAN tunneling (the encapsulation and de-encapsulation) must be performed by the ASIC on each switch so that there is no performance penalty. (That is one reason for the Cisco SD-Access hardware compatibility list: the switches must have ASICs that can perform the work. These are called the Unified Access Data Plane [UADP] ASICs.)

- The VXLAN encapsulation must supply header fields that Cisco SD-Access needs for its features, so the tunneling protocol should be flexible and extensible, while still being supported by the switch ASICs.

- The tunneling encapsulation needs to encapsulate the entire data link frame instead of encapsulating the IP packet. That allows Cisco SD-Access to support Layer 2 forwarding features as well as Layer 3 forwarding features.

To achieve those goals, when creating Cisco SD-Access, Cisco chose the VXLAN protocol to create the tunnels used by Cisco SD-Access. When an endpoint (for example, an end-user computer) sends a data link frame into a fabric edge node, the ingress fabric edge node encapsulates the frame and sends it across a VXLAN tunnel to the egress fabric edge node, as shown in Figure 22-5.

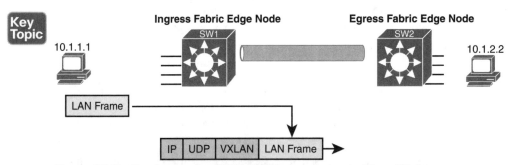

Figure 22-5 *Fundamentals of VXLAN Encapsulation in Cisco SD-Access*

To support the VXLAN encapsulation, the underlay uses a separate IP address space as compared with the rest of the enterprise, including the endpoint devices that send data over the Cisco SD-Access network. The overlay tunnels use addresses from the enterprise address space. For instance, imagine an enterprise used these address spaces:

- 10.0.0.0/8: Entire enterprise

- 172.16.0.0/16: Cisco SD-Access underlay

To make that work, first the underlay would be built using the 172.16.0.0/16 IPv4 address space, with all links using addresses from that address space. As an example, Figure 22-6 shows a small Cisco SD-Access design, with four switches, each with one underlay IP address shown (from the 172.16.0.0/16 address space).

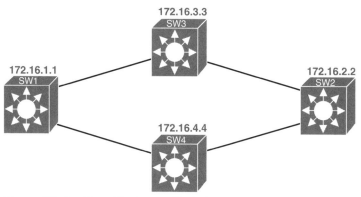

Figure 22-6   *Cisco SD-Access Underlay Using 172.16.0.0*

The overlay tunnel creates a path between two fabric edge nodes in the overlay IP address space, which is in the same address space used by all the endpoints in the enterprise. Figure 22-7 emphasizes that point by showing the endpoints (PCs) on the left and right, with IP addresses in network 10.0.0.0/8, with the VXLAN overlay tunnel shown with addresses also from 10.0.0.0/8.

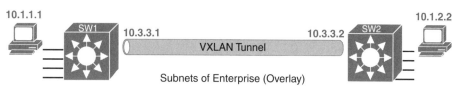

Figure 22-7   *VXLAN Tunnel and Endpoints with IPv4 Addresses in the Same IPv4 Space*

LISP for Overlay Discovery and Location (Control Plane)

Ignore Cisco SD-Access for a moment, and think about traditional Layer 2 switching and Layer 3 routing. How do their control planes work? In other words, how do these devices discover the possible destinations in the network, store those destinations, so that the data plane has all the data it needs when making a forwarding decision? To summarize:

- Traditional Layer 2 switches learn possible destinations by examining the source MAC addresses of incoming frames, storing those MAC addresses as possible future destinations in the switch's MAC address table. When new frames arrive, the Layer 2 switch data plane then attempts to match the Ethernet frame's destination MAC address to an entry in its MAC address table.

- Traditional Layer 3 routers learn destination IP subnets using routing protocols, storing routes to reach each subnet in their routing tables. When new packets arrive, the Layer 3 data plane attempts to match the IP packet's destination IP address to some entry in the IP routing table.

22

Nodes in the Cisco SD-Access network do *not* do these same control plane actions to support endpoint traffic. Just to provide a glimpse into the process for the purposes of CCNA, consider this sequence, which describes one scenario:

■ Fabric edge nodes—Cisco SD-Access nodes that connect to the edge of the fabric— learn the location of possible endpoints using traditional means, based on their MAC address, individual IP address, and by subnet, identifying each endpoint with an endpoint identifier (EID).

■ The fabric edge nodes register the fact that the node can reach a given endpoint (EID) into a database called the LISP map server.

■ The LISP map server keeps the list of endpoint identifiers (EIDs) and matching routing locators (RLOCs) (which identify the fabric edge node that can reach the EID).

■ In the future, when the fabric data plane needs to forward a message, it will look for and find the destination in the LISP map server's database.

For instance, switches SW3 and SW4 in Figure 22-8 each just learned about different subnets external to the Cisco SD-Access fabric. As noted at Step 1 in the figure, switch SW3 sent a message to the LISP map server, registering the information about subnet 10.1.3.0/24 (an EID), with its RLOC setting to identify itself as the node that can reach that subnet. Step 2 shows an equivalent registration process, this time for SW4, with EID 10.1.4.0/24, and with R4's RLOC of 172.16.4.4. Note that the table at the bottom of the figure represents that data held by the LISP map server.

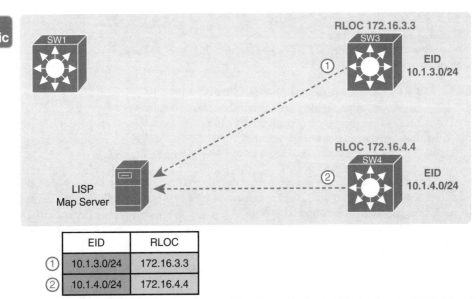

Figure 22-8 *Edge Nodes Register IPv4 Prefixes (Endpoint IDs) with the LISP Map Server*

When new incoming frames arrive, the ingress tunnel router (ITR)—the Cisco SD-Access fabric edge node that receives the new frame from outside the fabric—needs some help from the control plane. To where should the ITR forward this frame? Because Cisco SD-Access always forwards frames in the fabric over some VXLAN tunnel, what tunnel should the ITR use when forwarding the frame? For the first frame sent to a destination, the ITR must follow a process like the following steps. These steps begin at Step 3, as a continuation of Figure 22-8, with the action referenced in Figure 22-9:

3. An Ethernet frame to a new destination arrives at ingress fabric edge node SW1 (upper left), and the switch does not know where to forward the frame.

4. The ingress node sends a message to the LISP map server asking if the LISP server knows how to reach IP address 10.1.3.1.

5. The LISP map server looks in its database and finds the entry it built back at step 1 in the previous figure, listing SW3's RLOC of 172.16.3.3.

6. The LISP map server contacts SW3—the node listed as the RLOC—to confirm that the entry is correct.

7. SW3 completes the process of informing the ingress fabric edge node (SW1) that 10.1.3.1 can be reached through SW3.

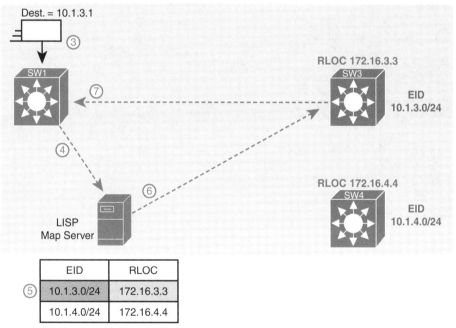

Figure 22-9 *Ingress Tunnel Router SW1 Discovers Egress Tunnel Router SW3 Using LISP*

To complete the story, now that ingress node SW1 knows that it can forward packets sent to endpoint 10.1.3.1 to the fabric edge node with RLOC 172.16.3.3 (that is, SW3), SW1 encapsulates the original Ethernet frame as shown in Figure 22-9, with the original destination IP address of 10.1.3.1. It adds the IP, UDP, and VXLAN headers shown so it can deliver the message over the Cisco SD-Access network, with that outer IP header listing a destination IP

22

address of the RLOC IP address, so that the message will arrive through the Cisco SD-Access fabric at SW3, as shown in Figure 22-10.

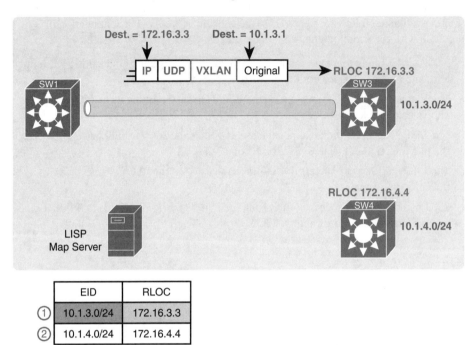

	EID	RLOC
①	10.1.3.0/24	172.16.3.3
②	10.1.4.0/24	172.16.4.4

Figure 22-10 *Ingress Tunnel Router (ITR) SW1 Forwards Based on LISP Mapping to SW3*

Now that you have a general overview of how a fabric works, how VXLAN encapsulation is used to allow for line rate switching in hardware between fabric edge nodes, and how LISP maps endpoints as they move between fabric edge nodes, let's go back to the host mobility use case of Cisco SD-Access.

Consider the following story:

When a host moves from one area of the network to another, the control-plane node (LISP mapping server) keeps track of that user's EID or identity and updates the other fabric edge nodes as they move from location to location. Think about this like a post office for mail distribution. If you move from your home to another home and do not inform the post office that you moved and provide them with your new address, your mail will be incorrectly delivered to your old home and be rendered useless. However, if you inform the post office of your new address by using a change of address form, your mail will be delivered to your new home without interruption. This is how host mobility works within a Cisco SD-Access campus fabric.

Because the identity of the user or host is known to the fabric, the reliance on IP addresses as a means to identify the user or host is no longer as important as it once was. This greatly simplifies matters when it comes to things such as security policies. For example, because the network can know when you move from location or fabric edge to fabric edge, it can enforce security policies based on your identity versus your IP address. This means that regardless of what subnet you are in, what VLAN, what IP address you have, whether it is static or DHCP, your security policy follows the user. This simplifies many things such as access control lists that have to be constantly reviewed to ensure they are covering every subnet range you might move into or out of as well as all the protocols or applications you want to permit or deny access to. Because the network knows the identity of the user, the policy can follow them, providing greater security and reduced risk of human error of an access list missing an entry because a user moved into a different subnet.

At this point, you should have a basic understanding of how the Cisco SD-Access fabric works. The underlay includes all the switches and links, along with IP connectivity, as a basis for forwarding data across the fabric. The overlay adds a different level of logic, with end-point traffic flowing through VXLAN tunnels. This chapter has not mentioned any reasons that Cisco SD-Access might want to use these tunnels, but you will see one example by the end of the chapter. Suffice it to say that with the flexible VXLAN tunnels, Cisco SD-Access can encode header fields that let Cisco SD-Access create new networking features, all without suffering a performance penalty, as all the VXLAN processing happens in the UADP ASIC.

The next section of this chapter focuses on Cisco Catalyst Center and its role in managing and controlling Cisco SD-Access fabrics.

Cisco Catalyst Center and Cisco SD-Access Operation

Cisco Catalyst Center (www.cisco.com/go/catalystcenter) has two notable roles:

- As the controller in a network that uses Cisco SD-Access

- As a network management platform for traditional (non-Cisco SD-Access) network devices

The first role as the Cisco SD-Access network controller gets most of the attention and is the topic of discussion in this second of the three major sections of this chapter. Cisco SD-Access and Cisco Catalyst Center go together, work closely together, and any serious use of Cisco SD-Access requires the use of Cisco Catalyst Center. At the same time, however, Cisco Catalyst Center can manage traditional network devices; the final major section of the chapter works through some comparisons.

Cisco Catalyst Center

Cisco Catalyst Center exists as a software application that Cisco delivers pre-installed on a Cisco Catalyst Center appliance or as a virtual appliance that can be run in a hypervisor environment. The software follows the same general controller architecture concepts as described in Chapter 21. Figure 22-11 shows the general ideas.

22

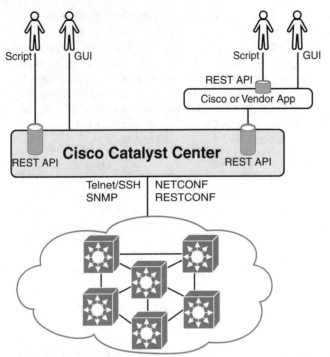

Figure 22-11 *Cisco Catalyst Center with Northbound and Southbound Interfaces*

Cisco Catalyst Center includes a robust northbound REST API along with a series of south-bound APIs. For most of us, the northbound API matters most, because as the user of Cisco SD-Access networks, you interact with Cisco SD-Access using Cisco Catalyst Center's northbound REST API or the GUI interface. (Chapter 23, "Understanding REST and JSON," discusses the concepts behind REST APIs in more detail.)

Cisco Catalyst Center supports several southbound APIs so that the controller can communicate with the devices it manages. You can think of these as two categories:

■ Protocols to support traditional networking devices/software versions: Telnet, SSH, SNMP

■ Protocols to support more recent networking devices/software versions: NETCONF, RESTCONF

Cisco Catalyst Center needs the older protocols to be able to support the vast array of older Cisco devices and OS versions. Over time, Cisco has been adding support for NETCONF and RESTCONF to their more current hardware and software.

Cisco Catalyst Center and Scalable Groups

Cisco SD-Access creates many interesting new and powerful features beyond how traditional campus networks work. Cisco Catalyst Center not only enables an easier way to configure and operate those features, but it also completely changes the operational model. While the scope of CCNA does not allow us enough space to explore all of the features of Cisco

SD-Access and Cisco Catalyst Center, this next topic looks at one feature as an example: scalable groups.

Issues with Traditional IP-Based Security

Imagine the life of one traditional IP ACL in an enterprise. Some requirements occurred, and an engineer built the first version of an ACL with three access control entries (ACEs)—that is, **access-list** commands—with a **permit any** at the end of the list. Months later, the engineer added two more lines to the ACL, so the ACL has the number of ACEs shown in Figure 22-12. The figure notes the lines added for requests one and two with the circled numbers in the figure.

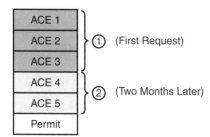

Figure 22-12 *Lines (ACEs) in an ACL After Two Changes*

Now think about that same ACL after four more requirements caused changes to the ACL, as noted in Figure 22-13. Some of the movement includes

- The ACEs for requirement two are now at the bottom of the ACL.

- Some ACEs, like ACE 5, apply to more than one of the implemented requirements.

- Some requirements, like requirement number five, required ACEs that overlap with multiple other requirements.

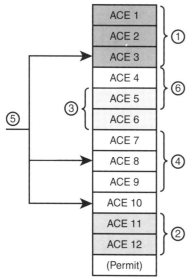

Figure 22-13 *Lines (ACEs) in an ACL After Six Changes*

Now imagine your next job is to add more ACEs for the next requirement (7). However, your boss also told you to reduce the length of the ACL, removing the ACEs from that one change made last August—you remember it, right? Such tasks are problematic at best.

With the scenario in Figure 22-13, no engineer could tell from looking at the ACL whether any lines in the ACL could be safely removed. You never know if an ACE was useful for one requirement or for many. If a requirement was removed, and you were even told which old project caused the original requirement so that you could look at your notes, you would not know if removing the ACEs would harm other requirements. Most of the time, ACL management suffers with these kinds of issues:

- ACEs cannot be removed from ACLs because of the risk of causing failures to the logic for some other past requirement.

- New changes become more and more challenging due to the length of the ACLs.

- Troubleshooting ACLs as a system—determining whether a packet would be delivered from end to end—becomes an even greater challenge.

Cisco SD-Access Security Is Based on User Groups

Imagine you could instead enforce security without even thinking about IP address ranges and ACLs. Cisco SD-Access does just that, with simple configuration, and the capability to add and remove the security policies at will.

First, for the big ideas. Imagine that over time, using Cisco SD-Access, six different security requirements occurred. For each project, the engineer would define the policy with Cisco Catalyst Center, either with the GUI or with the API. Then, as needed, Cisco Catalyst Center would configure the devices in the fabric to enforce the security, as shown in Figure 22-14.

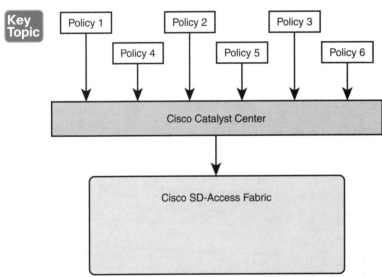

Figure 22-14 *Cisco Catalyst Center IP Security Policies (Northbound) to Simplify Operations*

NOTE The model in Figure 22-14 helps demonstrate the concept of intent-based networking (IBN). The engineer configures the intent or outcome desired from the network—in this case, a set of security policies. The controller communicates with the devices in the network, with the devices determining exactly what configuration and behavior are necessary to achieve those intended policies.

The Cisco SD-Access policy model solves the configuration and operational challenges with traditional ACLs. In fact, all those real issues with managing IP ACLs on each device are no longer issues with Cisco SD-Access's group-based security model. For instance:

- The engineer can consider each new security requirement separately, without analysis of an existing (possibly lengthy) ACL.

- Each new requirement can be considered without searching for all the ACLs in the likely paths between endpoints and analyzing each and every ACL.

- Cisco Catalyst Center (and related software) keeps the policies separate, with space to keep notes about the reason for the policy.

- Each policy can be removed without fear of impacting the logic of the other policies.

Cisco SD-Access and Cisco Catalyst Center achieve this particular feature by tying security to groups of users, called scalable groups, with each group assigned a **scalable group tag (SGT)**. Then the engineer configures a grid that identifies which SGTs can send packets to which other SGTs. For instance, the grid might include SGTs for an employee group, the Internet (for the enterprise's WAN routers that lead to the Internet), partner employees, and guests, with a grid like the one shown in Table 22-2.

Table 22-2 Access Table for Cisco SD-Access Scalable Group Access

Source\Dest.	Employee	Internet	Partner	Guest
Employee	N/A	Permit	Permit	Deny
Internet	Permit	N/A	Permit	Permit
Partner	Permit	Permit	N/A	Deny
Guest	Deny	Permit	Deny	N/A

To link this security feature back to packet forwarding, consider when a new endpoint tries to send its first packet to a new destination. The ingress Cisco SD-Access fabric edge node starts a process by sending messages to Cisco Catalyst Center. Cisco Catalyst Center then works with security tools in the network, like Cisco's Identity Services Engine (ISE), to identify the users and then match them to their respective SGTs. Cisco Catalyst Center then checks the logic similar to Table 22-2. If Cisco Catalyst Center sees a permit action between the source/destination pair of SGTs, Cisco Catalyst Center directs the edge nodes to create the VXLAN tunnel, as shown in Figure 22-15. If the security policies state that the two SGTs should not be allowed to communicate, then Cisco Catalyst Center does not direct the fabric to create the tunnel, and the packets do not flow.

22

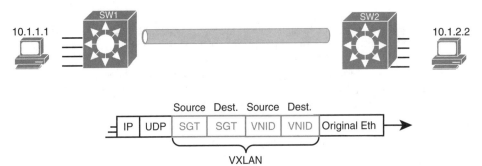

Figure 22-15 *VXLAN Header with Source and Destination SGTs and VNIDs Revealed*

NOTE The figure gives a brief insight into why Cisco SD-Access goes to the trouble of using VXLAN encapsulation for its data plane, rather than performing traditional Layer 2 switching or Layer 3 routing. The VXLAN header has great flexibility—in this case, used to define both a source and destination SGT, matching Cisco SD-Access's desired logic of allowing a subset of source/destination SGTs in the Cisco SD-Access fabric.

The operational model with scalable groups greatly simplifies security configuration and ongoing maintenance of the security policy, while focusing on the real goal: controlling access based on user, as mentioned previously in the section "LISP for Overlay Discovery and Location (Control Plane)." From a controller perspective, the fact that Cisco Catalyst Center acts as much more than a management platform, and instead as a controller of the activities in the network, makes for a much more powerful set of features and capabilities.

Cisco Catalyst Center as a Network Management Platform

Typically, a network management system (NMS) for the enterprise will include many useful features to help simplify the daily operation of your network. Although specific features will vary on a per-platform or vendor basis, many, if not most, of the following features can be found in a typical NMS:

- **Single-pane-of-glass:** Provides one GUI from which to launch all functions and features

- **Discovery, inventory, and topology:** Discovers network devices, builds an inventory, and arranges them in a topology map

- **Entire enterprise:** Provides support for traditional enterprise LAN, WAN, and data center management functions

- **Methods and protocols:** Uses SNMP, SSH, and Telnet, as well as CDP and LLDP, to discover and learn information about the devices in the network

- **Lifecycle management:** Supports different tasks to install a new device (day 0), configure it to be working in production (day 1), and perform ongoing monitoring and make changes (day *n*)

- **Application visibility:** Simplifies QoS configuration deployment to each device

- **Converged wired and wireless:** Enables you to manage both the wired and wireless LAN from the same management platform

- **Software Image Management (SWIM):** Manages software images on network devices and automates updates

- **Plug-and-Play:** Performs initial installation tasks for new network devices after you physically install the new device, connect a network cable, and power on

Cisco tends to shy away from specific product details in most of its career certifications, so it helps to think in general about network management products. It also helps to think about specific products—but temper that by focusing on the more prominent features and major functions.

Cisco Catalyst Center Similarities to Traditional Management

If you read the user's guide for Cisco Catalyst Center and look through all the features, you will find some of them are similar in nature to the traditional management features listed at the beginning of this section. For example, Cisco Catalyst Center can not only discover network devices like other network management systems but can also create a live topology map view of your network. Human operators (rather than automated processes) often start with the topology map, expecting at-a-glance notices (flashing lights, red colors) to denote issues in the network. In addition, most network management systems provide event and threshold alerting via email or SMS. As an example, Figure 22-16 shows a topology map from Cisco Catalyst Center.

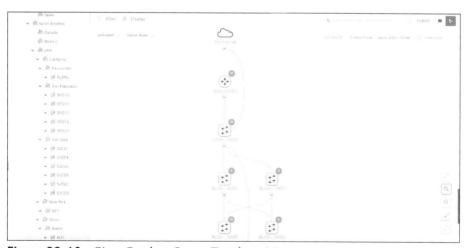

Figure 22-16   *Cisco Catalyst Center Topology Map*

The GUI mechanisms are relatively intuitive, with the ability to click into additional or less detail. Figure 22-17 shows a little more detail after hovering over and clicking on one of the nodes in the topology from Figure 22-16, typical actions and results in many management products.

22

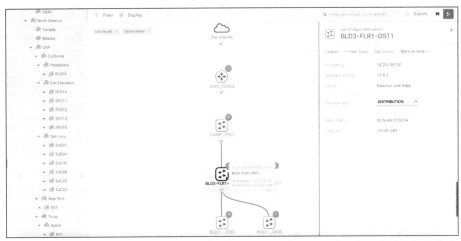

Figure 22-17 *Hover and Click Details About a Single Cisco Catalyst 9300 Switch from Cisco Catalyst Center*

I encourage you to take some time to use and watch some videos about Cisco Catalyst Center. The "Chapter Review" section for this chapter on the companion website lists some links for good videos. Also, start at https://developer.cisco.com and look for Cisco Catalyst Center sandbox labs to find a place to experiment with Cisco Catalyst Center.

Cisco Catalyst Center and Differences with Traditional Management

In a broad sense, there are several fundamental differences between Cisco Catalyst Center and traditional network management platforms. The largest difference: Cisco Catalyst Center supports Cisco SD-Access, whereas other management apps do not. So, think of network management systems as analogous to traditional device management. Cisco Catalyst Center has many similar features, but it also has more advanced features that focus on newer technology solutions like Cisco SD-Access support.

In terms of intent and strategy, Cisco focuses their development of Cisco Catalyst Center features toward simplifying the work done by enterprises, with resulting reduced costs and much faster deployment of changes. Cisco Catalyst Center features help make initial installation easier, simplify the work to implement features that traditionally have challenging configuration, and use tools to help you notice issues more quickly. Some of the features unique to Cisco Catalyst Center include

- **Application policy:** Deploys QoS, one of the most complicated features to configure manually, with just a few simple choices from Cisco Catalyst Center

- **Encrypted Traffic Analytics (ETA):** Enables Cisco DNA to use algorithms to recognize security threats even in encrypted traffic

- **Device 360 and Client 360:** Gives a comprehensive (360-degree) view of the health of the device

- **Network time travel:** Shows past client performance in a timeline for comparison to current behavior

- **Path trace:** Discovers the actual path packets would take from source to destination based on current forwarding tables

Just to expound on one feature as an example, Cisco Catalyst Center's Path Trace feature goes far beyond a traditional management application. A typical network management app might show a map of the network and let you click through to find the configuration on each device, including ACLs. The path trace feature goes much further. The Cisco Catalyst Center user (from the GUI or the API) specifies a source and destination host and optionally, the transport protocol and ports. Then the path trace feature shows a map of the path through the network and shows which ACLs are in the path, and whether they would permit or deny the packet.

All of Cisco's Digital Network Architecture sets about to help customers reach some big goals: reduced costs, reduced risks, better security and compliance, faster deployment of services through automation and simplified processes, and the list goes on. Cisco Catalyst Center plays a pivotal role, with all the functions available through its robust northbound API, and with its intent-based networking approach for Cisco SD-Access. Cisco Catalyst Center represents the future of network management for Cisco enterprises.

Artificial Intelligence (AI), Machine Learning (ML), and Operational Management

Cisco includes one exam topic in the CCNA 200-301 Version 1.1 blueprint that mentions Artificial Intelligence (AI):

6.4 Explain AI (generative and predictive) and machine learning in network operations

Tremendous amounts of industry buzz have emerged in the area of artificial intelligence and machine learning. Some of the early adopters sought benefits to alleviate some of the strain of their day-to-day operations while running the network. Before we can understand some of the benefits from AI and ML, we must first understand their definitions.

Artificial Intelligence is defined as a computer or system that can do tasks that typically require human thinking, such as learning, problem-solving, and understanding various languages. There are two major types of AI:

- **Narrow AI** is a type of AI that is designed to perform a specific task or a set of closely related tasks. Narrow AI thrives in a well-defined and limited scope. However, Narrow AI lacks the broad cognitive capabilities of human intelligence. Some common examples of Narrow AI include speech recognition systems or applications, image recognition software, and virtual personal assistants such as Amazon Alexa, Apple Siri, and Google Assistant. These assistants are often used for typical tasks like playing music, showing your calendar, or recalling a recipe when cooking.

- **Generative AI**, which could learn, be taught, and could potentially make decisions that consider facts and experiences similar to humans, is another form of AI.

22

AI also includes technologies like Machine Learning (ML). ML is used in numerous fields from healthcare to network operations and security. ML is a branch of AI that primarily focuses on the development of algorithms and complex data models. These models enable computers to learn from various data sources and not only make predictions but also make their own decisions without being explicitly programmed to. The goal of machine learning is to create systems that can continuously and automatically improve as they are fed more data or information sets.

In traditional computer programming, humans write explicit instructions to perform a task. However, in machine learning, there is a dichotomy. The computer can learn specific patterns and relationships from different data sources, which allows the computer or "AI" to make predictions on new data sets that it hasn't even seen yet. This is what the definition of **Predictive AI** is—being able to surmise what you are trying to accomplish with the least amount of prompts or input from the user.

Let's contemplate some of the benefits and use cases for the different forms of AI. Starting with a common example of Narrow AI, we can easily see the value of having virtual personal assistants. One less obvious use case is the ability to run home automation workflows and bind them to various schedules. This creates the "Smart Building" concept. Connecting and controlling various "things" such as lighting, thermostats, garage doors, and electronics typically introduces some form of intrinsic value for the user, especially when leveraging automation.

One very common advantage is creating a routine or automation that will turn off indoor lights, close the garage door, and set the temperature to a lower setting automatically when you leave your home for the day. The cost savings across all these domains can be significant. Especially if you extrapolate that out across the year. It is very frequent that lights and heat or garage doors get left on or open. Now there is a method to ensure that doesn't happen. In addition, to take this example one step further, you can automate turning on your home security system or alarm as part of this routine. It is pretty easy to see the value of how using a Narrow AI virtual personal assistant tied to automation techniques can provide real-world use cases.

Generative AI is where most of the attention seems to be these days, and for great reason. Generative AI has exploded as the next big thing and also the thing that has most of the industry cautious about the technology. Let's use the example of Microsoft's ChatGPT.

ChatGPT is a conversational artificial intelligence platform. Hence the term *chat*. Users can use text-based chat to ask ChatGPT endless amounts of questions or what the industry has termed *prompts*. This form of generative AI can be fed information to learn and can be taught and evolve. There's a lot of debate on the pros and cons of using generative AI. One example is using generative AI to create music and songs. Some think this takes the artistry out of the music creation process. But for some artists who want to quickly get some music built and distributed, this can be a mechanism to quickly and broadly create digital art. Especially if they don't have songwriting skills but have lyrics and a rhythm. Let's take a look at what ChatGPT does when having it create a song. Figure 22-18 demonstrates how to prompt ChatGPT from the initial chat window to create lyrics to a song about CCNA study habits.

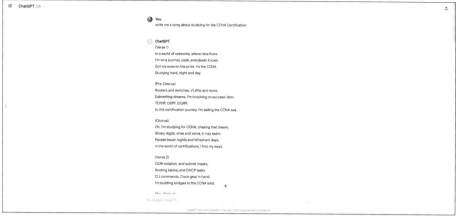

Figure 22-18 *ChatGPT 3.5 CCNA Song Prompt*

Here are the complete lyrics to the song ChatGPT created from the following prompt:

"write me a song about studying for the CCNA Certification"

(Verse 1)

In a world of networks, where data flows,

I'm on a journey, yeah, everybody knows.

Got my eyes on the prize, it's the CCNA,

Studying hard, night and day.

(Pre-Chorus)

Routers and switches, VLANs and more,

Subnetting dreams, I'm knocking on success' door.

TCP/IP, OSPF, EIGRP,

In this certification journey, I'm sailing the CCNA sea.

(Chorus)

Oh, I'm studying for CCNA, chasing that dream,

Binary digits, ones and zeros, it may seem.

Packet tracer nights and Wireshark days,

In the world of certifications, I find my ways.

(Verse 2)

CIDR notation, and subnet masks,

Routing tables, and DHCP tasks.

CLI commands, Cisco gear in hand,

I'm building bridges to the CCNA land.

22

(Pre-Chorus)
Spanning Tree Protocol, like branches on a tree,
Switches blinking, like stars, guiding me.
NAT, ACLs, and security,
I'm locking down knowledge, setting my own decree.

(Chorus)
Oh, I'm studying for CCNA, chasing that dream,
Binary digits, ones and zeros, it may seem.
Packet tracer nights and Wireshark days,
In the world of certifications, I find my ways.

(Bridge)
Late-night labs, under the moon's soft glow,
Simulations, configurations, letting my knowledge grow.
IP addressing, subnetting schemes,
I'm writing my fate in these CCNA dreams.

(Verse 3)
BGP, MPLS, and QoS,
In this networking journey, I face no loss.
Concepts intertwine like cables in a rack,
I'll conquer the CCNA, ain't no turning back.

(Pre-Chorus)
VTP and HSRP,
In this realm of routers, I'm sailing free.
Through the OSI layers, like climbing a stair,
I'll reach the summit, breathe the CCNA air.

(Chorus)
Oh, I'm studying for CCNA, chasing that dream,
Binary digits, ones and zeros, it may seem.
Packet tracer nights and Wireshark days,
In the world of certifications, I find my ways.

(Outro)
In the exam room, I'll stand tall,

Answers flowing like a waterfall.

CCNA, I'm ready to show,

In the world of networks, I'll let my knowledge glow.

ChatGPT is a very creative tool that can build out songs or configurations or anything you can think to ask it. The turnaround time is within seconds for it to create whatever you prompt it to create. There are free versions of ChatGPT like the one used in this chapter. There is also a paid version that gives you more features and access to the latest database of information and API access. These styles of data stores are called **Large Language Models (LLMs)**. The industry is seeing the need for privatized LLMs and customers are starting to build their own to house private data or knowledge bases. LLMs use a significant amount of memory, CPU, and GPU resources to look up and parse these data sources. However, for the right value to the organization, it can easily be seen as an investment to the business.

Let's now pick out a use case for ChatGPT on learning and educating yourself on various CCNA topics. It's always best to validate the source of the data, because you can find quite a lot of information on a specific subject that you may be trying to learn, but it isn't always accurate. For example, let's use ChatGPT to create a summary access list for the following subnets:

192.168.10.0/24

192.168.16.0/24

192.168.53.0/24

192.168.64.0/24

NOTE   Remember to validate anything you get from a generative AI platform especially if you plan to use any of the data for production purposes. Many issues have been created by using code or configuration from generative AI platforms and not first checking the validity of the code or configuration before deployment.

Figure 22-19 showcases using ChatGPT to summarize the previously mentioned subnets in order to use an access list that will match all four subnets.

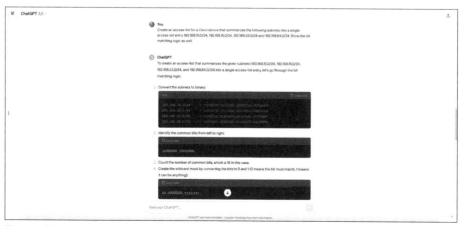

Figure 22-19   *ChatGPT 3.5 Access List Summary Prompt*

22

We can see from the initial prompt and response the four subnets we used as an example. We also can see that ChatGPT provided the bit-matching logic behind its decision on the summary to use based on the additional prompt *Show the bit matching logic as well* that we fed it. The four subnets and their bit boundaries are listed here:

192.168.10.0/24 = 11000000.10101000.00001010.00000000

192.168.16.0/24 = 11000000.10101000.00010000.00000000

192.168.53.0/24 = 11000000.10101000.00110101.00000000

192.168.64.0/24 = 11000000.10101000.01000000.00000000

Based on this output, we can see that the first 17 bits match identically. However, ChatGPT selected using a /16-bit mask vs. a /17-bit mask. Looking at Figure 22-20, we can see the rest of the chat response and confirm that it has selected 192.168.0.0/16 as the summary address to use along with the appropriate commands to configure the access list on a Cisco device.

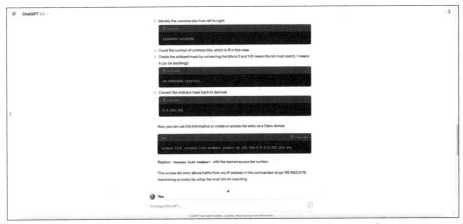

Figure 22-20   *ChatGPT 3.5 Access List Summary Prompt, Continued*

Although this is a perfectly acceptable solution to the summary access list prompt that we fed ChatGPT, one could argue that it is not the most efficient access list entry that could have been provided. A more accurate access list would be to use the following as shown in Figure 22-21:

```
access-list access-list-number permit ip 192.168.0.0 0.0.127.255 any
```

Notice that in the initial prompt, ChatGPT said that the first 16 bits were common, even though if you count them, the first 17 bits are common. This is one of the reasons we mention to validate everything you get as a response from any generative AI tool. It can be an incredible time saver. But as a wise person once mentioned: "You can automate failure just as fast as you can automate success."

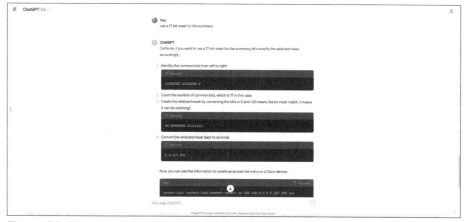

Figure 22-21   *ChatGPT 3.5 Access List Summary Prompt with 17-bit Mask*

NOTE   The version of ChatGPT used during the writing of this book may differ from the version you use or the most current version available. Features and response quality might have changed since this book was published.

There are many ways to operationalize the use of AI for networking. One of the most common methods is something called Artificial Intelligence for IT Operations (**AI Ops**). AI Ops leverages AI and ML to optimize and automate various aspects of IT operations. The primary goal of AI Ops is to improve the efficiency, reliability, and performance of IT-related systems while reducing manual interaction. This in turn should reduce human error as AI Ops takes advantage of proven and pre-tested workflows or configurations that the user specifies as beneficial to the operational process. The following list are some of the most common use cases for AI Ops:

- **Automation:** Taking routine tasks and reducing human intervention using automated processes

- **Monitoring and Data Analytics:** Providing constant analysis of data by using advanced tools to identify patterns and anomalies

- **Predictive Analysis:** Leveraging machine learning to proactively predict issues by analyzing historical data and patterns

- **Collaboration and Communication:** Promoting information sharing and troubleshooting techniques across IT operations as a whole

- **Root Cause Analysis:** Determining the underlying causes of problems by having deep visibility into the various areas of an IT environment

Automation is typically the low hanging fruit when it comes to AI Ops. Many organizations would benefit from having more automated workflows and procedures. Most businesses typically have some charter to move to a more automated operational process. Automation is one of the most common ways to get started with AI Ops.

22

However, to understand what is happening in an IT environment, the first step is to be able to "see" the environment as a whole. Monitoring the network and associated applications is the best way to determine what the network's baseline is. *Baseline* is another way of describing how the network is functioning normally with average traffic flows, average amount of users, and average data transactions. By understanding what the network is doing with a baseline, it's then easier to determine when something behaves out of the ordinary. Consider this example: the network is performing at a baseline and all of a sudden hundreds of gigs worth of data are being out pulsed to another country. This could be indicative of a data leak or malicious behavior that needs to be investigated. Without having a baseline to compare this behavior to, it could be difficult to identify the issue or its legitimacy.

Having the ability to do predictive analytics is critical in this day and age. Once upon a time, there was a bandwidth issue and the internet link was pegged at 100% utilization. By having the appropriate monitoring and analysis tools the issue was identified. The root cause was that it was the FIFA World Cup Tournament and many users were streaming the games on their internal workstations. This impacted legitimate business transactions from functioning properly because the link was so saturated. This insight gave the IT operations staff the ability to forecast out what could happen during big events like this and how to prevent it from happening again by way of policy.

When there is an issue that is impacting the network, many organizations jump into an "all hands on deck mode" or meet in a "war room" to bring together all areas of the IT teams. This is to enhance communication with each other and to minimize the impact of the issue to the business. Often, AI Ops can be used to help with this collaborative approach. For example, it is very common to see collaboration tools being used to communicate in customer environments. This is where the term **"Chat Ops"** comes from. Being able to leverage a Chat function of a tool to communicate with various teams and have video chats to discuss the current state of the network or issues that were identified can significantly streamline the path to resolution. These techniques typically lead to faster remediation and open communications between the different areas of the business.

Finally, AI Ops can help lead the IT operations staff to the Root Cause Analysis (RCA) or Root Cause of Failure (RCF) by determining what went wrong in the first place. By having tools like this in place, the process of getting to the resolution becomes a documented and repeatable procedure to follow in the event of a future outage or failure scenario.

Chapter Review

One key to doing well on the exams is to perform repetitive spaced review sessions. Review this chapter's material using either the tools in the book or interactive tools for the same material found on the book's companion website. Refer to the "Your Study Plan" element for more details. Table 22-3 outlines the key review elements and where you can find them. To better track your study progress, record when you completed these activities in the second column.

Table 22-3 Chapter Review Tracking

Review Element	Review Date(s)	Resource Used
Review key topics		Book, website
Review key terms		Book, website
Answer DIKTA questions		Book, PTP

Review All the Key Topics

Table 22-4 Key Topics for Chapter 22

Key Topic Element	Description	Page Number
List	Definitions for underlay, overlay, and fabric	497
Figure 22-2	Cisco SD-Access overlay and underlay	499
List	Cisco SD-Access fabric edge, fabric border, and fabric control-plane node roles	500
List	Attributes of the Cisco SD-Access underlay	502
List	Cisco SD-Access VXLAN tunneling benefits	504
Figure 22-5	VXLAN encapsulation process with Cisco SD-Access	504
Figure 22-8	Registering Cisco SD-Access endpoint IDs (EIDs) with the map server	506
Figure 22-14	Cisco Catalyst Center shown controlling the fabric to implement group-based security	512
List	Features unique to Cisco Catalyst Center	516
List	Artificial intelligence, large language models	517

Key Terms You Should Know

AI Ops, Artificial Intelligence, Chat Ops, Cisco Catalyst Center, Cisco SD-Access, fabric, fabric edge node, Generative AI, Large Language Models (LLM), LISP, Narrow AI, overlay, Predictive AI, scalable group tag (SGT), Software-Defined Access, underlay, VXLAN

22

CHAPTER 23

Understanding REST and JSON

This chapter covers the following exam topics:

6.0 Automation and Programmability

    6.5 Describe characteristics of REST-based APIs (CRUD, HTTP verbs, and data encoding)

    6.7 Recognize components of JSON encoded data

To automate and program networks, some automation software does several tasks. The software analyzes data in the form of variables, makes decisions based on that analysis, and then may take action to change the configuration of network devices or report facts about the state of the network.

The different automation functions reside on different devices: the network engineer's device, a server, a controller, and the various network devices themselves. For these related automation processes to work well, all these software components need useful well-defined conventions to allow easy communication between software components.

This chapter focuses on two conventions that allow automation software to communicate. The first major section discusses application programming interfaces (APIs), specifically APIs that follow a style called REpresentational State Transfer (REST). APIs of any kind create a way for software applications to communicate, while RESTful APIs (APIs that use REST conventions) follow a particular set of software rules. Many APIs used in network automation today use REST-based APIs.

The second half of the chapter focuses on the conventions and standards for the data variables exchanged over APIs, with a focus on one: JavaScript Object Notation (JSON). If REST provides one standard method of how two automation programs should communicate over a network, JSON then defines how to communicate the variables used by a program: the variable names, their values, and the data structures of those variables.

"Do I Know This Already?" Quiz

Take the quiz (either here or use the PTP software) if you want to use the score to help you decide how much time to spend on this chapter. The letter answers are listed at the bottom of the page following the quiz. Appendix C, found both at the end of the book as well as on the companion website, includes both the answers and explanations. You can also find both answers and explanations in the PTP testing software.

Table 23-1 "Do I Know This Already?" Foundation Topics Section-to-Question Mapping

Foundation Topics Section	Questions
REST-based APIs	1–3
Data Serialization and JSON	4–6

1. Which of the following are required attributes of a REST-based API? (Choose two answers.)

   a. Uses HTTP

   b. Objects noted as to whether they can be cached

   c. Stateful operation

   d. Client/server architecture

2. Which answers list a matching software development CRUD action to an HTTP verb that performs that action? (Choose two answers.)

   a. CRUD create and HTTP PATCH

   b. CRUD update and HTTP PATCH

   c. CRUD delete and HTTP PUT

   d. CRUD read and HTTP GET

3. Examine the following URI that works with a Cisco DNA Controller:

   ```
   https://dnac.example.com/dna/intent/api/v1/
   network-device?managementIPAddress=10.10.22.74
   ```

   Which part of the URI, per the API documentation, is considered to identify the resource but not any parameters?

   a. https://

   b. dna.example.com

   c. dna/intent/api/v1/network-device

   d. managementIPAddress=10.10.22.74

4. Which of the following data serialization and data modeling languages would most likely be used in a response from a REST-based server API used for networking applications? (Choose two answers.)

   a. JSON

   b. YAML

   c. JavaScript

   d. XML

5. Which answers correctly describe the format of the JSON text below? (Choose two answers.)

   ```
   { "myvariable":[1,2,3] }
   ```

   a. One JSON object that has one key:value pair

   b. One JSON object that has three key:value pairs

   c. A JSON object whose value is a second JSON object

   d. A JSON object whose value is a JSON array

6. Which answers refer to JSON values rather than JSON keys as found in the sample JSON data? (Choose two answers.)

```
{
    "response": {
            "type": "Cisco Catalyst 9300 Switch",
            "family": "Switches and Hubs",
            "role": "ACCESS",
            "managementIpAddress": "10.10.22.66"
        }
}
```

- **a.** "response"
- **b.** "type"
- **c.** "ACCESS"
- **d.** "10.10.22.66"

Foundation Topics

REST-Based APIs

Applications use *application programming interfaces (APIs)* to communicate. To do so, one program can learn the variables and data structures used by another program, making logic choices based on those values, changing the values of those variables, creating new variables, and deleting variables. APIs allow programs running on different computers to work cooperatively, exchanging data to achieve some goal.

In an API software world, some applications create an API, with many other applications using (consuming) the API. Software developers add APIs to their software so other application software can make use of the first application's features.

When writing an application, the developer will write some code, but often the developer may do a lot of work by looking for APIs that can provide the data and functions, reducing the amount of new code that must be written. As a result, much of modern software development centers on understanding and learning new APIs, along with the available libraries (prebuilt software that can be used to accomplish tasks rather than writing the equivalent from scratch).

Several types of APIs exist, each with a different set of conventions to meet different needs. The CCNA blueprint mentions one type of API—**REpresentational State Transfer (REST)**—because of its popularity as a type of API in networking automation applications. This first major section of the chapter takes a closer look at REST-based APIs.

REST-Based (RESTful) APIs

REST APIs follow a set of foundational rules about what makes a REST API and what does not. First, from a literal perspective, REST APIs include the six attributes defined a few decades back by its creator, Roy Fielding. (You can find a good summary at https:// restfulapi.net). Those six attributes are

- Client/server architecture

- Stateless operation

- Clear statement of cacheable/uncacheable

- Uniform interface

- Layered

- Code-on-demand

The first three of these attributes get at the heart of how a REST API works. You can more easily see these first three features at work with networking REST APIs, so the next few paragraphs further explain those first three points.

Client/Server Architecture

Like many applications, REST applications use a client/server architectural model. First, an application developer creates a REST API, and that application, when executing, acts as a REST server. Any other application can make a REST API call (the REST client) by executing some code that causes a request to flow from the client to the server. For instance, in Figure 23-1:

1. The REST client on the left executes a REST API call, which generates a message sent to the REST server.

2. The REST server on the right has API code that considers the request and decides how to reply.

3. The REST server sends back the response message with the appropriate data variables.

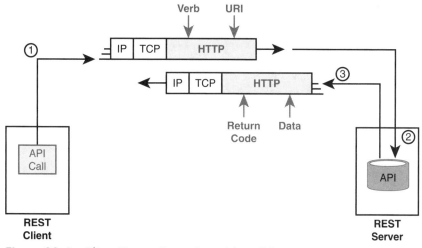

Figure 23-1 *Client/Server Operation with REST*

NOTE   Figure 23-1 shows the use of HTTP. While many REST APIs use HTTP, the use of HTTP is not a requirement for an API to be considered RESTful.

Stateless Operation

The REST **stateless** operation feature dictates that the REST server does not keep data (state information) about any prior REST requests or the REST clients. With REST, the server does not keep information from one response (state information) for use in later requests and responses. Instead, the REST client maintains all state data from prior requests to choose what future REST requests it needs to make to accomplish the app's goals.

As an example, imagine a REST server that maintains a product database. If supported by the API, a REST client could use a single request for a list of products weighing less than five pounds. The REST server would not remember the first REST request, which client made the request, or the data returned in that earlier request. As a result, when the client makes subsequent API calls, it cannot ask the server to base those future responses on the data from prior requests. Instead, the client must supply any data in each subsequent request so that each REST request is self-contained and does not require state information at the server.

Cacheable (or Not)

To appreciate what **cacheable** means, consider what happens when browsing a website. When your browser loads a new web page, the page itself contains a variety of objects (text, images, videos, audio). Some objects seldom change, so it would be better to download the object once and not download it again; in that case, the server marks that object as cacheable. For instance, a logo or other image shown on many pages of a website would almost never change and would likely be cacheable. However, the product list returned in your most recent search of the website would not be cacheable because the server would want to update and supply a new list each time you request the page.

REST APIs require that any resource requested via an API call have a clear method by which to mark the resource as cacheable or not. The goals remain the same: improve performance by retrieving resources less often (cacheable). Note that cacheable resources are marked with a timeframe so that the client knows when to ask for a new copy of the resource again.

Background: Data and Variables

To appreciate a few of the upcoming topics, it helps to have a basic idea about how programming languages use variables. Anyone who has done even a small amount of programming should have enough background, but for those who have not written programs before, this next topic gives you enough background about data and variables inside programs to understand the next topic.

If you have some programming experience and already know about simple variables, **list variables**, and **dictionary variables**, then feel free to skip ahead to the section "REST APIs and HTTP."

Simple Variables

Applications all process data with the same general actions, starting with some kind of input. The program needs data to process, so the input process reads files, sends database queries to a database server, or makes API calls to retrieve data from another application's API. The goal: gather the data that the program needs to process to do its work.

Answers to the "Do I Know This Already?" quiz:

1 B, D **2** B, D **3** C **4** A, D **5** A, D **6** C, D

Programs then process data by making comparisons, making decisions, creating new variables, and performing mathematical formulas to analyze the data. All that logic uses variables. For instance, a program might process data with the following logic:

If the router's G0/0 interface has a configuration setting of

switchport mode dynamic auto

Then gather more data to ensure that interface currently operates as a trunk rather than as an access port.

In programming, a variable is a name or label that has an assigned value. To get a general sense for programming variables, you can think of variables much like variables from algebra equations back in school. Example 23-1 shows some samples of variables of different types in a Python program (the Python language is the most popular language today for writing network automation applications). This program begins with a comment (the top three lines with triple single quotes) and then creates four variables, assigning them to different values, and prints a line of output: "The product is –12."

Example 23-1 *Simple Python Program That Shows a Product*

```
'''
Sample program to multiply two numbers and display the result
'''
x = 3
y = -4
z = 1.247
heading = "The product is "
print(heading,x*y)
```

The variables in Example 23-1 can be called *simple variables* because each variable name has a single value associated with it. Simple variables have one variable name and one associated value, so they have a simple structure.

The values of simple variables can have a variety of formats, as shown in Example 23-1. The example includes variables that contain

- Unsigned integers (x)

- Signed integers (y)

- Floating-point numbers (z)

- Text (heading)

List and Dictionary Variables

While simple variables have many great uses, programs need variables with more complex *data structures*. In programming, a data structure defines a related set of variables and values. For instance, Python uses list variables so that one variable name is assigned a value that is a list of values rather than a single value. You could imagine that a network automation program might want to have lists, such as a list of devices being managed, a list of interfaces on a device, or a list of configuration settings on an interface.

First, consider the variable named list1 in Example 23-2; note that the lines that begin with a # are comment lines.

Example 23-2 *Sample List and Dictionary Variables in Python*

```
# Variable list1 is a list in Python (called an array in Java)
list1 = ["g0/0", "g0/1", "g0/2"]


# Variable dict1 is a dictionary (called an associative array in Java)
dict1 = {"config_speed":'auto', "config_duplex":"auto", "config_ip":"10.1.1.1"}
```

Even if you have never seen Python code before, you can guess at some of the meaning of the list1 variable. The code assigns variable list1 to a value that itself is a list of three text strings. Note that the list could include text, unsigned integers, signed integers, and so on.

Figure 23-2 shows the data structure behind variable list1 in Example 23-2. The variable is assigned to the list, with the list having three list elements.

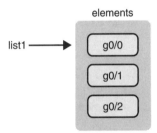

Figure 23-2 *The List Data Structure in Python*

Python supports a similar data structure called a *dictionary*. If you think of the contents of a dictionary for the English language, that dictionary lists a series of paired items: a term and a matching definition. With programming languages like Python, the dictionary data structure lists paired items as well: *keys* (like terms) and *values* (like definitions). Figure 23-3 shows the structure of that dictionary value matching the dict1 variable at the bottom of Example 23-2. Note that each key and its value is called a **key:value pair**.

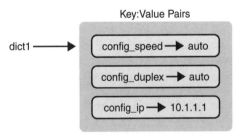

Figure 23-3 *Dictionary Data Structures in Python*

Data structures can get more complex. Additionally, the data structures can be nested. For instance, a single variable's value could be a list, with each list element being a dictionary, with the values in some key:value pairs being other lists, and so on. For now, be aware of the fact that programs use simple variables but also use list and dictionary variables to make it easier to perform different kinds of logic.

REST APIs and HTTP

APIs exist to allow two programs to exchange data. Some APIs may be designed as an interface between programs running on the same computer, so the communication between programs happens within a single operating system. Many APIs need to be available to programs that run on other computers, so an API must define the type of networking protocols supported by the API—and many REST-based APIs use the HTTP protocol.

The creators of REST-based APIs often choose HTTP because HTTP's logic matches some of the concepts defined more generally for REST APIs. HTTP uses the same principles as REST: it operates with a client/server model; it uses a stateless operational model; and it includes headers that clearly mark objects as cacheable or not cacheable. It also includes verbs—words that dictate the desired action for a pair of HTTP request and response messages—which matches how applications like to work.

This section breaks down the fundamentals of some programming terminology, how that matches HTTP verbs, and how REST APIs make use of Uniform Resource Identifiers (URIs) to specify the data desired from a RESTful API call.

Software CRUD Actions and HTTP Verbs

The software industry uses a memorable acronym—**CRUD**—for the four primary actions performed by an application. Those actions are

Create: Allows the client to create some new instances of variables and data structures at the server and initialize their values as kept at the server

Read: Allows the client to retrieve (read) the current value of variables that exist at the server, storing a copy of the variables, structures, and values at the client

Update: Allows the client to change (update) the value of variables that exist at the server

Delete: Allows the client to delete from the server different instances of data variables

For instance, if using the northbound REST API of a Cisco DNA Center or Catalyst Center controller, as discussed in Chapter 22, "Cisco Software-Defined Access (Cisco SD-Access)," you might want to create something new, like a new security policy. From a programming perspective, the security policy exists as a related set of configuration settings on the controller, internally represented by variables. To accomplish this, a user would leverage a compatible REST API client application such as Postman. Once the user has the client application set up with the appropriate HTTP methods necessary to communicate with Catalyst Center controller, a RESTful API call is made to "create" a new variable on the controller that represents the security policy mentioned previously. The variable or security policy that was built on the controller was performed using the Create function of the CRUD acronym.

NOTE Cisco used the Cisco DNA Center controller product name for many years. In 2023, Cisco rebranded the product as the Cisco Catalyst Center controller. However, given the significant number of documents that refer to the old name and acronyms DNA and DNAC, this chapter continues to refer to the controller as the DNA Center controller.

Other examples of CRUD actions include a check of the status of that new configuration (a read action), an update to change some specific setting in the new configuration (an update action), or an action to remove the security policy definition completely (a delete action).

HTTP uses verbs that mirror CRUD actions. HTTP defines the concept of an HTTP request and response, with the client sending a request and with the server answering back with a response. Each request/response lists an action verb in the HTTP request header, which defines the HTTP action. The HTTP messages also include a URI, which identifies the resource being manipulated for this request. As always, the HTTP message is carried in IP and TCP, with headers and data, as represented in Figure 23-4.

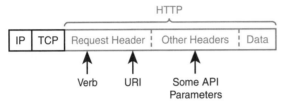

Figure 23-4 *HTTP Verb and URI in an HTTP Request Header*

To get some perspective about HTTP, ignore REST for a moment. Whenever you open a web browser and click a link, your browser generates an HTTP GET request message similar to Figure 23-4 in structure. The message includes an HTTP header with the GET verb and the URI. The resources returned in the response are the components of a web page, like text files, image files, and video files.

HTTP works well with REST in part because HTTP has verbs that match the common program actions in the CRUD paradigm. Table 23-2 lists the HTTP verbs and CRUD terms for easy reference and study.

Table 23-2   Comparing CRUD Actions to REST Verbs

Action	CRUD Term	REST (HTTP) Verb
Create new data structures and variables	Create	POST
Read (retrieve) variable names, structures, and values	Read	GET
Update or replace values of some variable	Update	PATCH, PUT
Delete some variables and data structures	Delete	DELETE

NOTE   While Table 23-2 lists HTTP POST as a create action and HTTP PATCH and PUT as CRUD update actions, all three of these HTTP verbs might be used both for create and for update actions in some cases.

Using URIs with HTTP to Specify the Resource

In addition to using HTTP verbs to perform the CRUD functions for an application, REST uses URIs to identify what resource the HTTP request acts on. For REST APIs, the resource can be any one of the many resources defined by the API. Each resource contains a set of related variables, defined by the API and identified by a URI.

For instance, imagine a user creates a REST-based API. When doing so, the user creates a set of resources to make available via the API, and also assigns a unique URI to each resource. In other words, the API creator creates a URI and a matching set of variables, and defines the actions that can be performed against those variables (read, update, and so on).

The API creator also creates API documentation that lists the resources and the URI that identifies each resource, among other details. The programmer for a REST client application can read the API documentation, build a REST API request, and ask for the specific resource, as shown in the example in Figure 23-5.

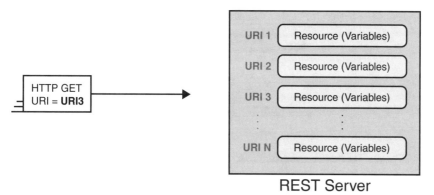

Figure 23-5   *One URI for Each API Resource—Conceptual View*

Figure 23-5 shows generic URI values; however, today's network engineers need to be able to read API documentation, see URIs in that documentation, and understand the meaning of each part of the URI. Figure 23-6 shows a URI specific to the Cisco DNA Center northbound REST API as an example of some of the components of the URI.

Scheme	Authority	Path	Query

HTTPS://dnac.example.com/dna/intent/api/v1/network-device?parm1=10.1.1.1...

Protocol	Hostname:Port	Resource	Parameters

Figure 23-6   *URI Structure for REST GET Request*

The URI has a defined format as detailed in RFC 3986. The top of Figure 23-6 lists the formal terms from the RFC. It also lists the more common terms used for those fields in some REST API documentation and tools.

- **Scheme (Protocol):** The HTTPS letters before the :// identify the scheme or protocol used—in this case, HTTP Secure (which uses HTTP with SSL encryption).

- **Authority (Host:Port):** This value sits between the // and first /, identifying the authority, which most people call the host. The authority field can list the hostname or IP address and, optionally, a transport port number. (If using a hostname, the REST client must perform name resolution to learn the IP address of the REST server.)

- **Path (Resource):** This value sits after the first / and finishes either at the end of the URI or before any additional fields (like a query field). The field uniquely identifies the resource as defined by the API. For REST, you can think of this field as data, passed from the client to the server, to identify the data referenced in the request.

- **Query (Parameter):** This value sits after the first ? at the end of the path. Following the ?, the query field allows the assignment of values to the variable names so that the URI passes data.

A tour of the API documentation for any REST-based API reveals much about the purpose and meaning of the path and query fields. For instance, Figure 23-7 shows a copy of one doc page from the Cisco Catalyst Center API documentation. (To see for yourself, go to https://developer.cisco.com and search for "Cisco Catalyst Center API documentation.")

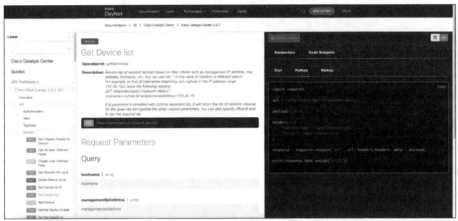

Figure 23-7   *Cisco Catalyst Center API Doc Page for the Network Device (List) Resource*

The API documentation identifies the path (resource) to use in a URI to ask for specific information. For instance, an API GET request, using the path listed at the top of Figure 23-7, asks the Cisco Catalyst Center for a list of all known devices, with Cisco Catalyst Center returning a dictionary of values for each device.

That same API documentation also lists the query parameters to refine the REST request further. For instance, instead of a list of all network devices, you might want a dictionary of values for only one device. The lower left part of Figure 23-7 lists some of the available query parameters with this API call, which allows for just that by tacking on the following to the end of the URI:

```
?managementIPAddress=10.10.22.66&macAddress=f8:7b:20:67:62:80
```

Example of REST API Call to Cisco Catalyst Center

To pull some of the REST API concepts together, the next few pages work through a few sample API calls using a software application called an API development environment tool.

For a bit of development perspective, when working to automate some part of your network operation tasks, you would eventually use a program that made API calls. However, early in the process of developing an application, you might first focus on the data available from the API and ignore all the programming details at first. API development environments let you focus on the API calls. Later, that same tool can typically generate correct code that you can copy into your program to make the API calls.

The examples in this section use an app named Postman. Postman can be downloaded for free (www.postman.co) and used as shown in this section. Note that Cisco DevNet makes extensive use of Postman in its many labs and examples.

When leveraging APIs to communicate with any software platform, application, or controller, it is important to think through what you are trying to accomplish—for example, if you wanted to use an API call to Cisco Catalyst Center to pull down an inventory of devices within the controller.

Think of making any API call to the destination application or controller like connecting to any other device in your network environment. There is an important step that must be followed to gain access to the software application or controller, and that is to authenticate. Programmatically interacting with these platforms is no different than you logging into a router from the CLI and typing in your credentials. This means that you first must authenticate to the device you're trying to connect to via API. However, there are exceptions to this rule; if the software is not secured it might not require authentication before manipulation. This is very rare and typically not seen on anything that can make changes to your network environment.

There are many different authentication methods for APIs, such as API keys, JSON Web Token (JWT), TLS/SSL client certificates, basic authentication, Java session IDs or cookies, and so on. Using Cisco Catalyst Center as an example, let's take a look at the documentation for the authentication or token API and what method is used to authenticate.

NOTE   This section focuses only on basic authentication because it is the current method of authentication used on Cisco Catalyst Center.

Figure 23-8 showcases the Cisco Catalyst Center API reference on developer.cisco.com. Notice that the first API call available in the list on the left side of the screen is the Authentication API. The way this works is that once you successfully authenticate to Cisco Catalyst Center using an HTTP POST request method to send the login credentials, you then will receive a token, which is a Base64-encoded string of the username and password. Notice the text that says

"Description: API to obtain an access token, which remains valid for 1 hour. The token obtained using this API is required to be set as value to the X-Auth-Token HTTP Header for all API calls to Cisco DNA Center."

This is stating that this API is used to authenticate to the controller, and something called an X-Auth-Token needs to be passed to the controller for all subsequent API calls after you have authenticated and received the token.

This means that once you authenticate and receive the token from Cisco Catalyst Center, you will then have to send that token back to Cisco Catalyst Center as an X-Auth-Token for all subsequent API calls you do after you initially authenticate. An example of this is done using an HTTP GET request to pull down the data or inventory from Cisco Catalyst Center.

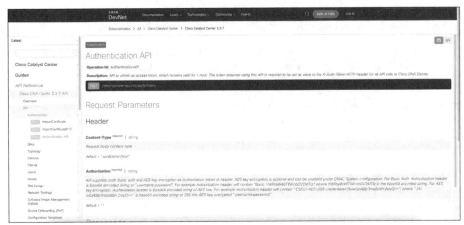

Figure 23-8   *Cisco Catalyst Center API Reference on developer.cisco.com*

Now that you understand where to find the API documentation, let's review the steps that you must authenticate to Cisco Catalyst Center and retrieve the token.

First, you must use the Authentication API to log in to the Cisco Catalyst Center and receive a token before you can make any subsequent API calls, such as pulling a device inventory from the controller. Let's look at how to authenticate using Postman. Figure 23-9 illustrates the proper setup for Postman to authenticate to Cisco Catalyst Center. The following information is used to set up Postman:

- URI for Authentication API: https://sandboxdnac2.cisco.com/dna/system/api/v1/auth/token

- HTTP POST request method

- Basic authorization

- Username and password: devnetuser / Cisco123!

Figure 23-9   *Postman Setup for Cisco Catalyst Center Authentication API*

Now Postman is set up to authenticate, click the Send button to issue the API call to Cisco Catalyst Center. Figure 23-10 displays the response from Cisco Catalyst Center, along with the token and an HTTP status code of 200 OK, indicating the authentication was successful.

Figure 23-10   *Execution of Cisco Catalyst Center Authentication API in Postman*

You use the token that was received to pass on to Cisco Catalyst Center to pull down the device inventory via an API. Looking back to the API documentation, you can see an API called Network-Device. This is the API to pull a device inventory from the Cisco Catalyst Center controller. Figure 23-11 highlights the specifics of how to use the Network-Device API from the documentation on the DevNet website. Notice, however, that the URI is different for subsequent API calls versus what was used for the Authentication API. Compare the two following URIs:

- **Authentication URI:** https://sandboxdnac2.cisco.com/dna/system/api/v1/auth/token

- **Network-Device URI:** https://sandboxdnac2.cisco.com/dna/intent/api/v1/network-device

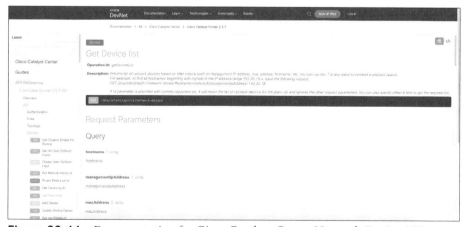

Figure 23-11   *Documentation for Cisco Catalyst Center Network-Device API*

Now that you know how to use the API by reviewing the documentation, let's demonstrate how this is done in Postman. Figure 23-12 displays the appropriate steps for using the existing token that was received via the authentication API completed earlier. In addition, the figure shows how to simply type the word X-Auth-Token into the key field under the Headers tab, then paste the token information into the Value field and ensure the appropriate URI for the Network-Device API call is being used. Once this is all confirmed, you can then issue the GET API call to Cisco Catalyst Center and pull down the device inventory.

Figure 23-12 *Postman Setup for Cisco Catalyst Center Network-Device API*

Following the same procedure done with the authentication API, click the Send button and issue the API call to Cisco Catalyst Center. In Figure 23-13, you can see the inventory was successfully pulled down via API. You can also see the list of network devices in the response section of Postman. Also note that the HTTP status code of 200 OK is present again. The resource part of the URI shows the same resource listed earlier in Figure 23-6, asking for a list of devices.

Figure 23-13 *Execution of Cisco DNA Center Network-Device API in Postman*

Take a moment to look through the data at the bottom of the Postman window in Figure 23-13. The text follows a data modeling format called JavaScript Object Notation (JSON), which is one of the main topics for the remainder of the chapter. However, armed with just a knowledge of routers, you can find a few facts that look familiar. To help you see the text, Example 23-3 shows an edited (shortened to reduce the length) view of some of the JSON output in that window, just so you can see the format and some of the data returned in this single API call.

Example 23-3 *JSON Output from a REST API Call*

```
{
    "response": {
        "family": "Switches and Hubs",
        "type": "Cisco Catalyst 9000 UADP 8 Port Virtual Switch",
        "macAddress": "52:54:00:01:c2:c0",
        "softwareType": "IOS-XE",
        "softwareVersion": "17.9.20220318:182713",
        "serialNumber": "9SB9FYAFA2O",
        "upTime": "30 days, 10:05:18.00",
        "series": "Cisco Catalyst 9000 Series Virtual Switches",
        "hostname": "sw1.ciscotest.com",
        "managementIpAddress": "10.10.20.175",
        "platformId": "C9KV-UADP-8P",
        "role": "CORE"
    }
}
```

API development tools like Postman help you work out the particulars of each API call, save the details, and share with other engineers and developers. Eventually, you will be ready to make the API call from a program. With a simple click from the Postman UI, Postman supplies the code to copy/paste into your program so that it returns all the output shown in the center/bottom of the window back as a variable to your program.

By now, you have a good foundational knowledge of the mechanics of REST APIs. By learning some skills, and using the API documentation for any REST API, you could now experiment with and try to make REST API calls. For many of those, the data will return to you as text, often in JSON format, so the second half of the chapter examines the meaning of that text.

Data Serialization and JSON

In your journey to become a modern network engineer with network automation skills, you will learn to understand several **data serialization languages**. Each data serialization language provides methods of using text to describe variables, with a goal of being able to send that text over a network or to store that text in a file. Data serialization languages give us a way to represent variables with text rather than in the internal representation used by any particular programming language.

Each data serialization language enables API servers to return data so that the API client can replicate the same variable names as well as data structures as found on the API server. To describe the data structures, the data serialization languages include special characters and conventions that communicate ideas about list variables, dictionary variables, and other more complex data structures.

This second major section of the chapter examines the concept of a data serialization language, with a focus on the one data modeling language as mentioned in the current CCNA blueprint: **JavaScript Object Notation (JSON)**.

The Need for a Data Model with APIs

This section shows some ideas of how to move variables in a program on a server to a client program. First, Figure 23-14 and surrounding text show a nonworking example as a way to identify some of the challenges with copying variable values from one device to another. Later, Figure 23-15 and its related text show how to use a data serialization language to solve the problems shown around Figure 23-14.

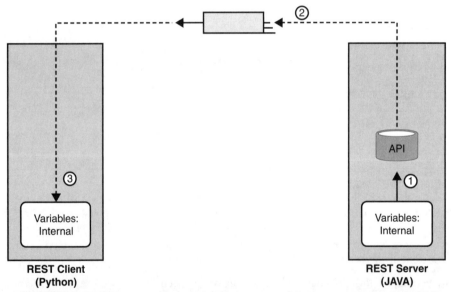

Figure 23-14 *Broken Concept: Exchanging Internal Representations of Variables*

First, for the nonworking example, consider the flow and numbered steps in Figure 23-14. A REST client sits on the left. The REST client asks for a resource, and the server needs to reply. In REST, a resource is a set of variables as defined by the API, so the REST server needs to return a set of variables to the REST client on the left. The steps in the figure run as follows:

1. The REST server (a JAVA application) takes a copy of the stored variables in RAM (step 1) in response to the REST request.

2. The REST API code creates the REST response and sends it over the network, placing an exact replica of what the REST server had in RAM to represent the variables in that resource.

3. The REST client (a Python application) receives the REST response message, storing the exact same bits and bytes into its RAM, in an attempt to have a copy of the variables, data, and data structures on the server.

The process shown in Figure 23-14 does not work (and is not attempted) because the REST client programs may not store variables in the same ways. First, programs written in different languages use different conventions to store their variables internally because there is no standard for internal variable storage across languages. In fact, programs written in the same language but with different versions of that language may not store all their variables with the same internal conventions.

To overcome these issues, applications need a standard method to represent variables for transmission and storage of those variables outside the program. *Data serialization languages* provide that function.

Figure 23-15 shows the correct process flow in comparison to Figure 23-14 with the data serialization process included:

1. The server collects the internally represented data and gives it to the API code.

2. The API converts the internal representation to a data model representing those variables (with JSON shown in the figure).

3. The server sends the data model in JSON format via messages across the network.

4. The REST client takes the received data and converts the JSON-formatted data into variables in the native format of the client application.

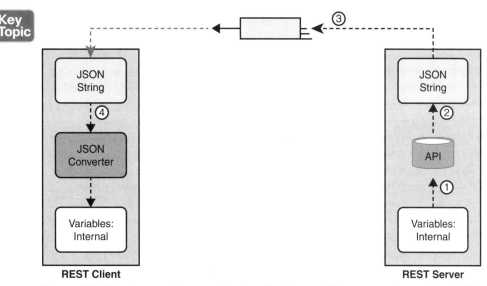

Figure 23-15   *Correct Concept: Exchanging Internal Representations of Variables*

At the end of the process, the REST client application now has equivalent variables to the ones it requested from the server in the API call. Note that the final step—to convert from the data serialization language to the native format—can be as little as a single line of code!

Finally, note that while data serialization languages like JSON enable applications to exchange variables over a network, applications can also store data in JSON format.

Data Serialization Languages

You will hear about and eventually use several data serialization and data modeling languages the more you learn about network automation. While the current CCNA blueprint mentions only JSON, learning a few facts about some of the alternatives can be helpful to add a little context to your new knowledge of JSON. These different data serialization languages exist to meet different needs that have arisen over the years. This next short section highlights four such languages.

> **NOTE**   The terms *data serialization language* and *data modeling language* should be considered equivalent for the purposes of this section.

JSON

JavaScript Object Notation attempts to strike a balance between human and machine readability. Armed with a few JSON rules, most humans can read JSON data, move past simply guessing at what it means, and confidently interpret the data structures defined by the JSON data. At the same time, JSON data makes it easy for programs to convert JSON text into variables, making it very useful for data exchange between applications using APIs.

You can find the details of JSON in IETF RFC 8259 and in a number of sites found with Internet searches, including www.json.org.

XML

Back in the 1990s, when web browsers and the World Wide Web (WWW) were first created, web pages primarily used Hypertext Markup Language (HTML) to define web pages. As a markup language, HTML defined how to add the text or a web page to a file and then add "markup"—additional text to denote formatting details for the text that should be displayed. For instance, the markup included codes for headings, font types, sizes, colors, hyperlinks, and so on.

The **eXtensible Markup Language (XML)** came later to make some improvements for earlier markup languages. In particular, over time web pages became more and more dynamic, and to make the pages dynamic, the files needed to store variables whose values could be changed and replaced over time by the web server. To define variables to be substituted into a web page, the world needed a markup language that could define data variables. XML defines a markup language that has many features to define variables, values, and data structures.

Over time, XML has grown beyond its original use as a markup language. XML's features also make it a useful general data serialization language, and it is used as such today.

While keeping human readability in mind, the creators of XML opted for less emphasis on human readability (as compared to JSON) to gain better features for computer processing. For instance, like HTML, XML uses beginning and ending tags for each variable, as seen in Example 23-4. In the highlighted line in the example, the <macAddress> and </macAddress> tags denote a variable name, with the value sitting between the tags.

Example 23-4   *XML Output from a REST API Call*

```
<?xml version="1.0" encoding="UTF-8"?>
<root>
   <response>
      <family>Switches and Hubs</family>
      <hostname>cat_9k_1</hostname>
      <interfaceCount>41</interfaceCount>
      <lineCardCount>2</lineCardCount>
      <macAddress>f8:7b:20:67:62:80</macAddress>
      <managementIpAddress>10.10.22.66</managementIpAddress>
      <role>ACCESS</role>
      <serialNumber>FCW2136L0AK</serialNumber>
      <series>Cisco Catalyst 9300 Series Switches</series>
      <softwareType>IOS-XE</softwareType>
      <softwareVersion>16.6.1</softwareVersion>
      <type>Cisco Catalyst 9300 Switch</type>
      <upTime>17 days, 22:51:04.26</upTime>
   </response>
</root>
```

YAML

YAML Ain't Markup Language (YAML) has a clever recursive name, but the name does tell us something. YAML does not attempt to define markup details (while XML does). Instead, YAML focuses on the data model (structure) details. YAML also strives to be clean and simple: of the data serialization/modeling languages listed here, YAML is easily the easiest to read for anyone new to data models.

Ansible, one of the topics in Chapter 24, "Understanding Ansible and Terraform," makes extensive use of YAML files. Example 23-5 shows a brief sample. And to make the point about readability, even if you have no idea what Ansible does, you can guess at some of the functions just reading the file. (Note that YAML denotes variables in double curly brackets: {{ }}.)

Example 23-5   *YAML File Used by Ansible*

```
---
# This comment line is a place to document this Playbook
- name: Get IOS Facts
  hosts: mylab
  vars:
```

```
   cli:
     host: "{{ ansible_host }}"
     username: "{{ username }}"
     password: "{{ password }}"

   tasks:
   - ios_facts:
       gather_subset: all
       provider: "{{ cli }}"
```

Summary of Data Serialization

As an easy reference, Table 23-3 summarizes the data serialization languages mentioned in this section, along with some key facts.

Table 23-3   Comparing Data Modeling Languages

Acronym	Name	Origin/Definition	Central Purpose	Common Use
JSON	JavaScript Object Notation	JavaScript (JS) language; RFC 8259	General data modeling and serialization	REST APIs
XML	eXtensible Markup Language	World Wide Web Consortium (W3C.org)	Data-focused text markup that allows data modeling	REST APIs, Web pages
YAML	YAML Ain't Markup Language	YAML.org	General data modeling	Ansible

Recognizing the Components of JSON

Cisco includes one exam topic in the CCNA 200-301 Version 1.1 blueprint that mentions JSON:

6.7 Recognize the components of JSON encoded data

You can think of that skill and task with two major branches. First, even ignoring the syntax and special characters, anyone who knows the topic can probably make intelligent guesses about the meaning of many of the key:value pairs. For example, without knowing anything about JSON syntax, you could probably determine from your prior knowledge of Cisco routers and switches that the JSON in Example 23-6 lists two devices (maybe their host-names) and a list of interfaces on each device.

Example 23-6   *Simple JSON That Lists a Router's Interfaces*

```
{
    "R1": ["GigabitEthernet0/0", "GigabitEthernet0/1", "GigabitEthernet0/2/0"],
    "R2": ["GigabitEthernet1/0", "GigabitEthernet1/1", "GigabitEthernet0/3/0"]
}
```

Honestly, you probably already know everything needed to do this kind of intelligent guessing. However, to perform the second type of task, where you analyze the JSON data to find the data structures, including objects, lists, and key:value pairs, you need to know a bit more about JSON syntax. This final topic in the chapter gives you the basic rules, with some advice on how to break down JSON data.

Interpreting JSON Key:Value Pairs

First, consider these rules about key:value pairs in JSON, which you can think of as individual variable names and their values:

- **Key:Value Pair:** Each and every colon identifies one key:value pair, with the key before the colon and the value after the colon.

- **Key:** Text, inside double quotes, before the colon, used as the name that references a value.

- **Value:** The item after the colon that represents the value of the key, which can be

  - **Text:** Listed in double quotes.

  - **Numeric:** Listed without quotes.

  - **Array:** A special value (more details later).

  - **Object:** A special value (more details later).

- **Multiple Pairs:** When listing multiple key:value pairs, separate the pairs with a comma at the end of each pair (except the last pair).

To work through some of these rules, consider Example 23-7's JSON data, focusing on the three key:value pairs. The text after the example provides analysis.

Example 23-7   *One JSON Object (Dictionary) with Three Key:Value Pairs*

```
{
    "1stbest": "Messi",
    "2ndbest": "Ronaldo",
    "3rdbest": "Maradona"
}
```

As an approach, just find each colon, and look for the quoted string just before each colon. Those are the keys ("1stbest", "2ndbest", and "3rdbest".) Then look to the right of each colon to find their matching values. You can know all three values are text values because JSON lists the values within double quotes.

As for other special characters, note the commas and the curly brackets. The first two key:value pairs end with a comma, meaning that another key:value pair should follow. The curly brackets that begin and end the JSON data denote a single JSON object (one pair of curly brackets, so one object). JSON files and JSON data exchanged over an API exist first as a JSON object, with an opening (left) and closing (right) curly bracket as shown.

Interpreting JSON Objects and Arrays

To communicate data structures beyond a key:value pair with a simple value, JSON uses **JSON objects** and **JSON arrays**. Objects can be somewhat flexible, but in most uses, they act like a dictionary. Arrays list a series of values.

NOTE Python, the most common language to use for network automation, converts JSON objects to Python dictionaries, and JSON arrays to Python lists. For general conversation, many people refer to the JSON structures as dictionaries and lists rather than as objects and arrays.

To begin, consider this set of rules about how to interpret the syntax for JSON objects and arrays:

- **{ }—Object:** A series of key:value pairs enclosed in a matched pair of curly brackets, with an opening left curly bracket and its matching right curly bracket.

- **[ ]—Array:** A series of values (not key:value pairs) enclosed in a matched pair of square brackets, with an opening left square bracket and its matching right square bracket.

- **Key:value pairs inside objects:** All key:value pairs inside an object conform to the earlier rules for key:value pairs.

- **Values inside arrays:** All values conform to the earlier rules for formatting values (for example, double quotes around text, no quotes around numbers).

Example 23-8 shows a single array in JSON format. Notice the JSON data begins with a [and then lists three text values (the values could have been a mix of values). It then ends with a].

Example 23-8 *A JSON Snippet Showing a Single JSON Array (List)*

```
[
    "Messi",
    "De Bruyne",
    "Pedri"
]
```

While Example 23-8 shows only the array itself, JSON arrays can be used as a value in any key:value pair. Figure 23-16 does just that, shown in a graphic to allow easier highlighting of the arrays and object. The JSON text in the figure includes two arrays (lists) as values (each found just after a colon, indicating they are values).

Now think about the entire structure of the JSON data in Figure 23-16. It has a matched pair of curly brackets to begin and end the text, encapsulating one object. That object contains two colons, so there are two key:value pairs inside the object. When you think about the broader structure, as depicted in Figure 23-17, this JSON file has one JSON object, itself with two key:value pairs. (Note that Figure 23-17 does NOT show correct JSON syntax for the lists; it instead is intended to make sure you see the structure of the one object and its two key:value pairs.)

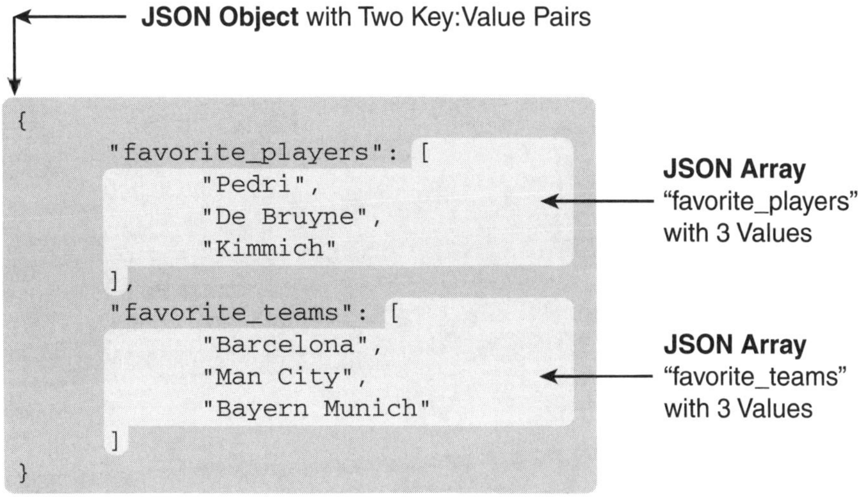

JSON Object with Two Key:Value Pairs

```
{
        "favorite_players": [
                "Pedri",
                "De Bruyne",
                "Kimmich"
        ],
        "favorite_teams": [
                "Barcelona",
                "Man City",
                "Bayern Munich"
        ]
}
```

JSON Array
"favorite_players"
with 3 Values

JSON Array
"favorite_teams"
with 3 Values

Figure 23-16 *Accurate/Complete JSON Data with One Object, Two Keys, Two JSON List Values*

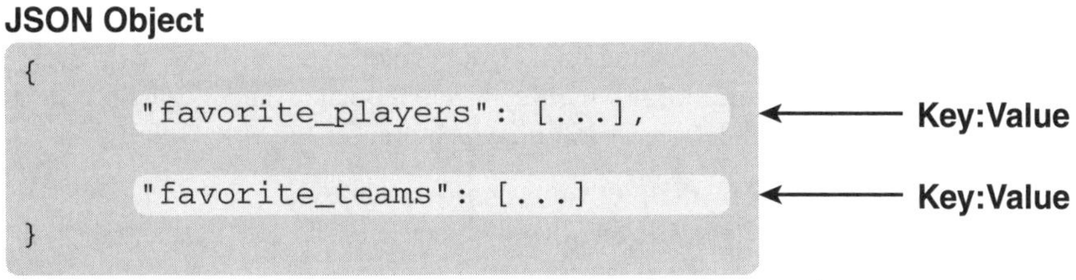

JSON Object

```
{
        "favorite_players": [...],

        "favorite_teams": [...]
}
```

Key:Value

Key:Value

Figure 23-17 *Structural Representation of Figure 23-16's Primary Object and Two Key:Value Pairs*

To drive home the idea of how to find JSON objects, consider the example shown in Figure 23-18. This figure shows correct JSON syntax. It has the following:

■ There is one object for the entire set because it begins and ends with curly brackets.

■ The outer object has two keys (Wendells_favorites and interface_config).

■ The value of each key:value pair is another object (each with curly brackets and three key:value pairs).

The JSON example in Figure 23-18 shows how JSON can nest objects and arrays; that is, JSON puts one object or array inside another. Much of the JSON output you will see as you learn more and more about network automation will include JSON data with nested arrays and objects.

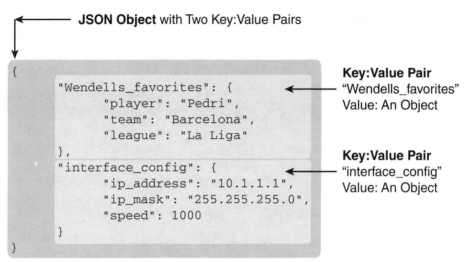

Figure 23-18 *A JSON Object, with Two Key:Value Pairs, Each Value Another Object*

Minified and Beautified JSON

So far, all the JSON examples show lots of empty space. JSON allows for whitespace, or not, depending on your needs. For humans, reading JSON can be a lot easier with the text organized with space and aligned. For instance, having the matched opening and closing brackets sit at the same left-offset makes it much easier to find which brackets go with which.

When stored in a file or sent in a network, JSON does not use whitespace. For instance, earlier in this section, Example 23-7 showed one JSON object with three key:value pairs, with whitespace, taking five lines. However, stored in a file, or sent over a network, the JSON would look like the following:

```
{"1stbest": "Messi", "2ndbest": "Ronaldo", "3rdbest": "Maradona"}
```

Most of the tools you might use when working with JSON will let you toggle from a pretty format (good for humans) to a raw format (good for computers). You might see the pretty version literally called *pretty* or *beautified* or *spaced*, while the version with no extra whitespace might be called *minified* or *raw*.

Chapter Review

One key to doing well on the exams is to perform repetitive spaced review sessions. Review this chapter's material using either the tools in the book or interactive tools for the same material found on the book's companion website. Refer to the "Your Study Plan" element for more details. Table 23-4 outlines the key review elements and where you can find them. To better track your study progress, record when you completed these activities in the second column.

Table 23-4 Chapter Review Tracking

Review Element	Review Date(s)	Resource Used
Review key topics		Book, website
Review key terms		Book, website
Answer DIKTA questions		Book, PTP
Review memory tables		Website
Watch videos		Website

Review All the Key Topics

Table 23-5 Key Topics for Chapter 23

Key Topic Element	Description	Page Number
List	Attributes of REST APIs	529
List	The meaning of the CRUD acronym	533
Table 23-2	A comparison of CRUD actions and HTTP verbs	534
Figure 23-6	Components of a URI	535
Figure 23-15	The process of sending JSON data over a REST API	543
Table 23-3	A comparison of JSON, XML, and YAML	546
List	JSON rules related to key:value pairs	547
List	JSON rules for arrays and objects	548

Key Terms You Should Know

cacheable, CRUD, data serialization language, dictionary variable, JSON (JavaScript Object Notation), JSON array, JSON object, key:value pair, list variable, REpresentational State Transfer (REST), REST API, stateless, URI path (resource), URI query (parameters), XML (eXtensible Markup Language), YAML (YAML Ain't Markup Language)

CHAPTER 24

Understanding Ansible and Terraform

This chapter covers the following exam topics:

6.0 Automation and Programmability

> **6.6 Recognize the capabilities of configuration mechanisms Ansible and Terraform**

By now, you have seen how to use the IOS CLI to configure routers and switches. To configure using the CLI, you get into configuration mode, issue configuration commands (which change the running-config file), and eventually leave configuration mode. If you decide to keep those changes, you save the configuration to the startup-config file using the **copy running-config startup-config** command. Next time the router or switch boots, the device loads the startup-config file into RAM as the running-config. Simple enough.

This chapter discusses tools for configuration management that replace that per-device configuration process. To even imagine what these tools do first requires you to make a leap of imagination to the everyday world of a network engineer at a medium to large enterprise. In a real working network, managing the configuration of the many networking devices creates challenges. Those challenges can be addressed using that same old "use configuration mode on each device" process, plus with hard work, attention to detail, and good operational practices. However, that manual per-device process becomes more and more difficult for a variety of reasons, so at some point, enterprises turn to automated configuration management tools to provide better results.

The first section of this chapter takes a generalized look at the issues of configuration management at scale along with some of the solutions to those problems. The second major section then details two configuration management tools—Ansible and Terraform—to define some of the features and terms used with each. By the end of the chapter, you should be able to see some of the reasons why these automated configuration management tools have a role in modern networks and enough context to understand as you pick one to investigate for further reading.

"Do I Know This Already?" Quiz

Take the quiz (either here or use the PTP software) if you want to use the score to help you decide how much time to spend on this chapter. The letter answers are listed at the bottom of the page following the quiz. Appendix C, found both at the end of the book as well as on the companion website, includes both the answers and explanations. You can also find both answers and explanations in the PTP testing software.

Table 24-1 "Do I Know This Already?" Foundation Topics Section-to-Question Mapping

Foundation Topics Section	Questions
Device Configuration Challenges and Solutions	1–3
Ansible and Terraform Basics	4, 5

1. Which answer best describes the meaning of the term *configuration drift*?

    a. Changes to a single device's configuration over time versus that single device's original configuration

    b. Larger and larger sections of unnecessary configuration in a device

    c. Changes to a single device's configuration over time versus other devices that have the same role

    d. Differences in device configuration versus a centralized backup copy

2. An enterprise moves away from manual configuration methods, making changes by editing centralized configuration files. Which answers list an issue solved by using a version control system with those centralized files? (Choose two answers.)

    a. The ability to find which engineer changed the central configuration file on a date/time

    b. The ability to find the details of what changed in the configuration file over time

    c. The ability to use a template with per-device variables to create configurations

    d. The ability to recognize configuration drift in a device and notify the staff

3. Configuration monitoring (also called configuration enforcement) by a configuration management tool generally solves which problem?

    a. Tracking the identity of individuals who changed files, along with which files they changed

    b. Listing differences between a former and current configuration

    c. Testing a configuration change to determine whether it will be rejected or not when implemented

    d. Finding instances of configuration drift

4. Which of the following configuration management tools by default use a push model to configure network devices? (Choose two answers.)

    a. Ansible

    b. Both use a pull model

    c. Terraform

    d. Neither uses a push model

5. Which of the following answers list a correct combination of configuration management tool and the term used for one of its primary configuration files? (Choose two answers.)

    a. Ansible Configuration

    b. Terraform Configuration

    c. Ansible Playbook

    d. Terraform Playbook

Foundation Topics

Device Configuration Challenges and Solutions

Think about any production network. What defines the exact intended configuration of each device in a production network? Is it the running-config as it exists right now or the startup-config before any recent changes were made or the startup-config from last month? Could one engineer change the device configuration so that it drifts away from that ideal, with the rest of the staff not knowing? What process, if any, might discover the configuration drift? And even with changes agreed upon by all, how do you know who changed the configuration, when, and specifically what changed?

Traditionally, CCNA teaches us how to configure one device using the **configure** terminal command to reach configuration mode, which changes the running-config file, and how to save that running-config file to the startup-config file. That manual process provides no means to answer any of the legitimate questions posed in the first paragraph; however, for many enterprises, those questions (and others) need answers, both consistent and accurate.

Not every company reaches the size to want to do something more with configuration management. Companies with one network engineer might do well enough managing device configurations, especially if the network device configurations do not change often. However, as a company moves to multiple network engineers and grows the numbers of devices and types of devices, with higher rates of configuration change, manual configuration management has problems.

This section begins by discussing a few of these kinds of configuration management issues so that you begin to understand why enterprises need more than good people and good practices to deal with device configuration. The rest of the section then details some of the features you can find in automated **configuration management tools**.

Configuration Drift

Consider the story of an enterprise of a size to need two network engineers, Alice and Bob. They both have experience and work well together. But the network configurations have grown beyond what any one person can know from memory, and with two network engineers, they may remember different details or even disagree on occasion.

One night at 1 a.m., Bob gets a call about an issue. He gets into the network from his laptop and resolves the problem with a small configuration change to branch office router BR22. Alice, the senior engineer, gets a different 4 a.m. call about another issue and makes a change to branch office router BR33.

The next day gets busy, and neither Alice nor Bob mentions the changes they made. They both follow procedures and document the changes in their change management system, which lists the details of every change. Because they both get busy, the topic never comes up, and neither mentions the changes to each for months.

The story shows how **configuration drift** can occur—an effect in which the configuration drifts away from the intended configuration over time. Alice and Bob probably agree to what a standard branch office router configuration ought to look like, but they both made an exception to that configuration to fix a problem, causing configuration drift.

Figure 24-1 shows the basic idea, with those two branch routers now with slightly different configurations than the other branch routers.

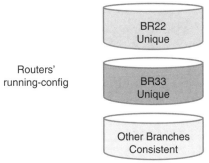

Routers'
running-config

Figure 24-1 *Configuration Drift in Branch Routers BR22 and BR33*

Configuration drift becomes a much bigger problem if using only traditional manual configuration tools. For instance:

- The on-device manual configuration process does not track change history: which lines changed, what changed on each line, what old configuration was removed, who changed the configuration, when each change was made.

- External systems used by good systems management processes, like trouble ticketing and change management software, may record details. However, those sit outside the configuration and require analysis to figure out what changed. They also rely on humans to follow the operational processes consistently and correctly; otherwise, an engineer cannot find the entire history of changes to a configuration.

- Referring to historical data in change management systems works poorly if a device has gone through multiple configuration changes over a period of time.

Centralized Configuration Files and Version Control

The manual per-device configuration model makes great sense for one person managing one device. With that model, the one network engineer can use the on-device startup-config as the intended ideal configuration. If a change is needed, the engineer gets into configuration mode and updates the running-config until happy with the change. Then the engineer saves a copy to the startup-config as the now-current ideal config for the device.

The per-device manual configuration model does not work as well for larger networks, with hundreds or even thousands of network devices, with multiple network engineers. For instance, if the team thinks of the startup-config of each device as the ideal configuration, if one team member changes the configuration (like Alice and Bob each did in the earlier story), no records exist about the change. The config file does not show what changed, when it changed, or who changed it, and the process does not notify the entire team about the change.

As a first step toward better configuration management, many medium to large enterprises store configurations in a central location. At first, storing files centrally may be a simple effort to keep backup copies of each device's configuration. They would, of course, place the files in a shared folder accessible to the entire network team, as shown in Figure 24-2.

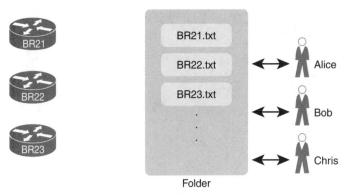

Figure 24-2   *Copying Device Configurations to a Central Location*

Which configuration file is the single source of truth in this model? The configuration files still exist on each device, but now they also exist on a centralized server, and engineers could change the on-device configuration as well as the text files on the server. For instance, if the copy of BR21's configuration on the device differs from the file on the centralized server, which should be considered as correct, ideal, the truth about what the team intends for this device?

In practice, companies take both approaches. In some cases, companies continue to use the on-device configuration files as the source of truth, with the centralized configuration files treated as backup copies in case the device fails and must be replaced. However, other enterprises make the transition to treat the files on the server as the single source of truth about each device's configuration. When using the centralized file as the source of truth, the engineers can take advantage of many configuration management tools and actually manage the configurations more easily and with more accuracy.

For example, configuration management tools use version control software to track the changes to centralized configuration files, noting who changes a file, what lines and specific characters changed, when the change occurred, and so on. The tools also allow you to compare the differences between versions of the files over time, as shown in Figure 24-3.

The figure shows a sample of a comparison between two versions of a configuration file. The upper two highlighted lines, with the minus sign, show the lines that were changed, while the two lower highlighted lines, with the plus signs, show the new versions of each line.

Version control software solves many of the problems with the lack of change tracking within the devices themselves. Figure 24-3 shows output from a popular Software-as-a-Service site called GitHub (www.github.com). GitHub offers free and paid accounts, and it uses open-source software (**Git**) to perform the version control functions.

Answers to the "Do I Know This Already?" quiz:

1 C **2** A, B **3** D **4** A, C **5** B, C

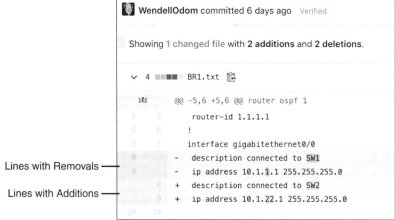

Figure 24-3 *Showing File Differences in GitHub*

Configuration Monitoring and Enforcement

With a version control system and a convention of storing the configuration files in a central location, a network team can do a much better job of tracking changes and answering the who, what, and when of knowing what changed in every device's configuration. However, using that model then introduces other challenges—challenges that can be best solved by also using an automated configuration management tool.

With this new model, engineers should make changes by editing the associated configuration files in the centralized repository. The configuration management tool can then be directed to copy or apply the configuration to the device, as shown in Figure 24-4. After that process completes, the central config file and the device's running-config (and startup-config) should be identical.

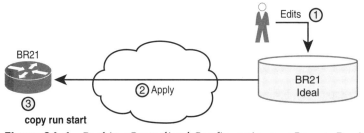

Figure 24-4 *Pushing Centralized Configuration to a Remote Device*

Using the model shown in Figure 24-4 still has dangers. For instance, the network engineers should make changes by using the configuration management tools, but they still have the ability to log in to each device and make manual changes on each device. So, while the idea of using a configuration management tool with a centralized repository of config files sounds appealing, eventually someone will change the devices directly. Former correct configuration changes might be overwritten, and made incorrect, by future changes. In other words, eventually, some configuration drift can occur.

Configuration management tools can monitor device configurations to discover when the device configuration differs from the intended ideal configuration, and then either reconfigure the device or notify the network engineering staff to make the change. This feature might be called **configuration monitoring** or *configuration enforcement*, particularly if the tool automatically changes the device configuration.

Figure 24-5 shows the general idea behind configuration monitoring. The automated configuration management software asks for a copy of the device's running-config file, as shown in steps 1 and 2. At step 3, the config management software compares the ideal config file with the just-arrived running-config file to check whether they have any differences (configuration drift). Per the configuration of the tool, it either fixes the configuration or notifies the staff about the configuration drift.

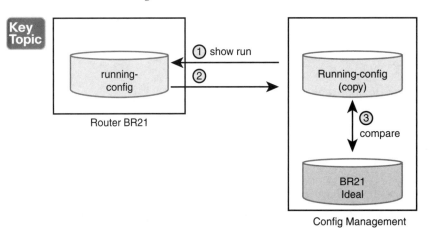

Figure 24-5   *Configuration Monitoring*

Configuration Provisioning

Configuration provisioning refers to how to provision or deploy changes to the configuration once made by changing files in the configuration management system. Included among the primary functions of a configuration management tool, you would likely see features like these:

- The core function to implement configuration changes in one device after someone has edited the device's centralized configuration file

- The capability to choose which subset of devices to configure: all devices, types with a given attribute (such as those of a particular role), or just one device, based on attributes and logic

- The capability to determine whether each change was accepted or rejected, and to use logic to react differently in each case depending on the result

- For each change, the capability to revert to the original configuration if even one configuration command is rejected on a device

- The capability to validate the change now (without actually making the change) to determine whether the change will work or not when attempted

- The capability to check the configuration after the process completes to confirm that the configuration management tool's intended configuration does match the device's configuration

- The capability to use logic to choose whether to save the running-config to startup-config or not

- The capability to represent configuration files as templates and variables so that devices with similar roles can use the same template but with different values

- The capability to store the logic steps in a file, scheduled to execute, so that the changes can be implemented by the automation tool without the engineer being present

The list could go further, but it outlines some of the major features included in all of the configuration management tools discussed in this chapter. Most of the items in the list revolve around editing the central configuration file for a device. However, the tools have many more features, so you have more work to do to plan and implement how they work. The next few pages focus on giving a few more details about the last two items in the list.

Configuration Templates and Variables

Think about the roles filled by networking devices in an enterprise. Focusing on routers for a moment, routers often connect to both the WAN and one or more LANs. You might have a small number of larger routers connected to the WAN at large sites, with enough power to handle larger packet rates. Smaller sites, like branch offices, might have small routers, maybe with a single WAN interface and a single LAN interface; however, you might have a large number of those small branch routers in the network.

For any set of devices in the same role, the configurations are likely similar. For instance, a set of branch office routers might all have the exact same configuration for some IP services, like NTP or SNMP. If using OSPF interface configuration, routers in the same OSPF area and with identical interface IDs could have identical OSPF configuration.

For instance, Example 24-1 shows a configuration excerpt from a branch router, with the unique parts of the configuration highlighted. All the unhighlighted portions could be the same on all the other branch office routers of the same model (with the same interface numbers). An enterprise might have dozens or hundreds of branch routers with nearly identical configuration.

Example 24-1 *Router BR1 Configuration, with Unique Values Highlighted*

```
hostname BR1
!
interface GigabitEthernet0/0
 ip address 10.1.1.1 255.255.255.0
 ip ospf 1 area 11
!
interface GigabitEthernet0/1
!
interface GigabitEthernet0/1/0
 ip address 10 1.12.1 255.255.255.0
 ip ospf 1 area 11
!
router ospf 1
 router-id 1.1.1.1
```

Configuration management tools can separate the components of a configuration into the parts in common to all devices in that role (the template) versus the parts unique to any one device (the variables). Engineers can then edit the standard template file for a device role as a separate file rather than each device's variable file. The configuration management tool can then process the template and variables to create the ideal configuration file for each device, as shown in Figure 24-6, which shows the configuration files being built for branch routers BR21, BR22, and BR23.

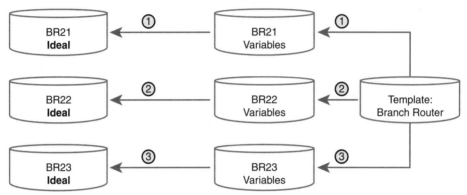

Figure 24-6   *Concept: Configuration Templates and Variables*

To give a little more insight, Example 24-2 shows a template file that could be used by Ansible for the configuration shown in Example 24-1. Each tool specifies what language to use for each type of file, with Ansible using the Jinja2 language for templates. The template mimics the configuration in Example 24-1, except for placing variable names inside sets of double curly brackets.

Example 24-2   *Jinja2 Template with Variables Based on Example 24-1*

```
hostname {{hostname}}
!
interface GigabitEthernet0/0
 ip address {{address1}} {{mask1}}
 ip ospf {{OSPF_PID}} area {{area}}
!
interface GigabitEthernet0/1
!
interface GigabitEthernet0/1/0
 ip address {{address2}} {{mask2}}
 ip ospf {{OSPF_PID}} area {{area}}
!
router ospf {{OSPF_PID}}
 router-id {{RID}}
```

To supply the values for a device, Ansible calls for defining variable files using YAML, as shown in Example 24-3. The file shows the syntax for defining the variables shown in the complete configuration in Example 24-1, but now defined as variables.

Example 24-3   *YAML Variables File Based on Example 24-2*

```
-- -
hostname: BR1
address1: 10.1.1.1
mask1: 255.255.255.0
address2: 10.1.12.1
mask2: 255.255.255.0
RID: 1.1.1.1
area: '11'
OSPF_PID: '1'
```

24

The configuration management system processes a template plus all related variables to produce the intended configuration for a device. For instance, the engineer would create and edit one template file that looks like Example 24-2 and then create and edit one variable file like Example 24-3 for each branch office router. Ansible would process the files to create complete configuration files like the text shown in Example 24-1.

It might seem like extra work to separate configurations into a template and variables, but using templates has some big advantages. In particular:

- Templates increase the focus on having a standard configuration for each device role, helping to avoid snowflakes (uniquely configured devices).

- New devices with an existing role can be deployed easily by simply copying an existing per-device variable file and changing the values.

- Templates allow for easier troubleshooting because troubleshooting issues with one standard template should find and fix issues with all devices that use the same template.

- Tracking the file versions for the template versus the variables files allows for easier troubleshooting as well. Issues with a device can be investigated to find changes in the device's settings separately from the standard **configuration template**.

Files That Control Configuration Automation

Configuration management tools also provide different methods to define logic and processes that tell the tools what changes to make, to which devices, and when. For instance, an engineer could direct a tool to make changes during a weekend change window. That same logic could specify a subset of the devices. It could also detail steps to verify the change before and after the change is attempted, and how to notify the engineers if an issue occurs.

Interestingly, you can do a lot of the logic without knowing how to program. Each tool uses a language of some kind that engineers use to define the action steps, often a language defined by that company (a domain-specific language). But they make the languages straightforward, and they are generally much easier to learn than programming languages. Configuration management tools also enable you to extend the action steps beyond what can be done in the toolset by using a general programming language. Figure 24-7 summarizes the files you could see in any of the configuration management tools.

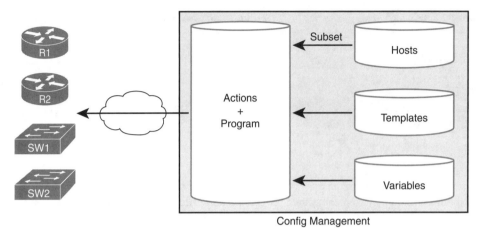

Config Management

Figure 24-7 *Important Files Used by Configuration Management Tools*

Ansible and Terraform Basics

This chapter focuses on one exam topic that asks about the capabilities of two configuration management tools: Ansible and Terraform. The first major section of the chapter describes the capabilities of both (and other) configuration management tools. This second major section examines a few of the features of each tool, focusing on terminology and major capabilities.

Ansible and Terraform are software packages. You can purchase each tool, with variations on each package. However, they also have different free options that allow you to download and learn about the tools, although you might need to run a Linux guest because some of the tools do not run in a Windows OS.

As for the names, most people use the words *Ansible* and *Terraform* to refer to the companies as well as their primary configuration management products. Both emerged as part of the transition from hardware-based servers to virtualized servers, which greatly increased the number of servers and created the need for software automation to create, configure, and remove VMs. Both also produce one or more configuration management software products that have become synonymous with their companies in many ways. (This chapter follows that convention, for the most part ignoring exact product names, and referring to products and software simply as Ansible and Terraform.) The sections that follow discuss the basics of each.

Ansible

To use **Ansible** (www.ansible.com), you need to install Ansible on some computer: Mac, Linux, or a Linux VM on a Windows host. You can use the free open-source version or use the paid Ansible Tower server version.

Once it is installed, you create several text files, many of which use YAML (Yet Another Markup Language), including

- **Playbooks:** These files provide actions and logic about what Ansible should do.

- **Inventory:** These files provide device hostnames and information about each device, like device roles, so Ansible can perform functions for subsets of the inventory.

- **Templates:** Using Jinja2 language, the templates represent a device's configuration but with variables (see Example 24-2).

- **Variables:** Using YAML, a file can list variables that Ansible will substitute into templates (see Example 24-3).

24

Ansible uses an **agentless architecture**. That means Ansible does not rely on any code (agent) running on the network device. Instead, Ansible relies on features typical in network devices, specifically SSH and NETCONF, to make changes and extract information. When using SSH, the Ansible control node changes the device like any other SSH user, logging in and using configuration mode; however, the Ansible code does the work rather than a human user.

By default, Ansible uses a **push model** (per Figure 24-8). However, it is also capable of using a **pull model** with a program called Ansible-pull if you want that capability. After installing Ansible, an engineer must create and edit various Ansible files, including an **Ansible playbook**. The playbook details the actions the engineer wants to take, acting as a program with steps taken under different conditions. Then the engineer runs the playbook, and Ansible performs the steps. Those steps can include configuring one or more devices per the various files (step 3), with the control node seen as pushing the configuration to the device.

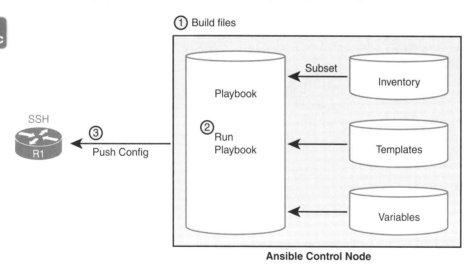

Figure 24-8 *Ansible Push Model*

Ansible can do configuration provisioning (configuring devices based on the changes made in the files) and configuration monitoring (checking to find out whether the device config matches the ideal configuration on the control node). However, Ansible's architecture more naturally fits with configuration provisioning, as seen in the figure. To do configuration monitoring, Ansible uses logic modules that detect and list configuration differences, after which the playbook defines what action to take (reconfigure or notify).

Terraform

Terraform by HashiCorp (www.terraform.io) is an infrastructure as code (IaC) tool that enables you to create both cloud and on-premises resources by leveraging easy-to-read configuration files. These files use configuration version control, can be reused, and can be shared with other developers or code contributors. Terraform provides a straightforward workflow to provision and manage your infrastructure throughout its lifecycle, making day-to-day operations much simpler to manage. Terraform can also handle components such as compute, storage, and networking as well as components such as DNS and features from Software as a Service (SaaS) applications. The following list highlights some of the main components of Terraform and their associated roles in managing your infrastructure:

- **Configuration files:** Files that describe the desired state of the infrastructure and specify resources along with their configurations.

- **Providers:** Plugins that enable interaction with different infrastructure platforms (AWS, Azure, Google Cloud).

- **Resources:** Components you want to create and manage, such as virtual machines, networks, or databases.

- **Data sources:** Reference details about existing infrastructure within your configuration.

- **Variables:** A method to reuse code and make configurations more flexible.

- **State files:** Record the infrastructure's current state and track configuration changes that are made.

- **Modules:** Organize and reuse Terraform code. Modules encapsulate a set of resources and configurations that can be treated as a single unit. Modules promote code reusability and modularity.

Terraform works with cloud providers and other services by utilizing their associated APIs. This is enabled by the use of the providers mentioned previously. This enables Terraform to connect with almost any service or platform, which is why it has become widely used as a common approach to IaC.

Terraform has its own language called HashiCorp Configuration Language (HCL). The language is human readable and fairly easy to understand like Ansible; however, Ansible is best suited for device configurations whereas Terraform is more often used for infrastructure provisioning.

There are three stages to Terraform's core workflow:

1. **Write:** This is where you define the resources that will be used across multiple cloud providers or services.

2. **Plan:** An execution plan is created that describes the infrastructure that will be created, updated, or destroyed based on the current configuration and infrastructure.

3. **Apply:** Once the plan is approved, the proposed operations will be completed in the appropriate order.

The saying "A picture is worth a thousand words" fits nicely for this technology. Figure 24-9 depicts the high-level architecture of Terraform, its core workflow, and how it interacts with various cloud providers and other infrastructure.

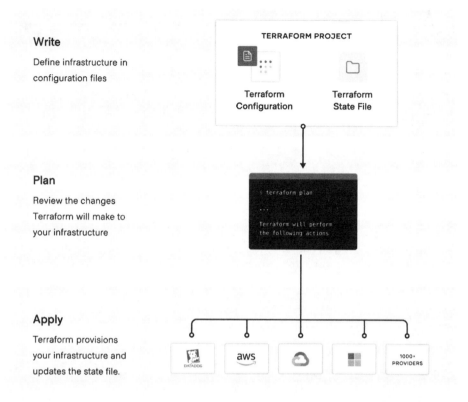

Figure 24-9 *High-level Terraform Architecture*

Summary of Configuration Management Tools

The configuration management tools discussed in this chapter have different strengths. When considering one of these tools it is best to first understand what you are trying to accomplish from a design perspective. For example, if you or your team is very fluent in CLI and want to automate device configurations across many devices, Ansible might be your first choice due to the similarity of the playbooks and the actual CLI.

However, if you are looking to lead with IaC, do more advanced capabilities of automation, need a means to keep track of configurations, and do provisioning for both on-premise or cloud infrastructure, you may consider Terraform. Sometimes, you might have both. That is the beauty of programmability and automation—there are many ways to solve business needs by leveraging different methods. Skill set, preference, and cost usually determine which tool(s) your organization will implement.

Table 24-2 summarizes a few of the most common ideas about each of the automated configuration management tools.

Table 24-2 Comparing Ansible and Terraform

Attribute	Ansible	Terraform
File type for actions or config	Playbook	Configuration
Protocol to network device	SSH, NETCONF	APIs
Execution Mode	Agentless	Client/server model
Push or pull model	Push (by default) Pull w/Ansible-pull program	Push
Modeling language	YAML	HashiCorp Configuration Language (HCL)

Chapter Review

One key to doing well on the exams is to perform repetitive spaced review sessions. Review this chapter's material using either the tools in the book or interactive tools for the same material found on the book's companion website. Refer to the "Your Study Plan" element for more details. Table 24-3 outlines the key review elements and where you can find them. To better track your study progress, record when you completed these activities in the second column.

Table 24-3 Chapter Review Tracking

Review Element	Review Date(s)	Resource Used
Review key topics		Book, website
Review key terms		Book, website
Answer DIKTA questions		Book, PTP
Review memory table		Book, website
Do DevNet Labs		DevNet

Review All the Key Topics

Table 24-4 Key Topics for Chapter 24

Key Topic Element	Description	Page Number
List	Issues that arise from configuration drift	555
Figure 24-3	Sample of showing router configuration file differences with GitHub	557
Figure 24-5	Basic configuration monitoring concepts	558
List	Primary functions of a configuration management tool	558
Example 24-2	Sample Jinja2 Ansible template	560
List	Advantages of using configuration templates	561

Key Topic Element	Description	Page Number
Figure 24-8	Ansible's push model and other features	563
Figure 24-9	Terraform's high-level architecture	565
Table 24-2	Summary of configuration management features and terms	566

24

Key Terms You Should Know

agentless architecture, Ansible, Ansible Playbook, configuration drift, configuration management tool, configuration monitoring, configuration provisioning, configuration template, Git, pull model, push model, Terraform

Do DevNet Labs

The Cisco DevNet site (https://developer.cisco.com)—a free site—includes lab environments and exercises. You can learn a lot about configuration management, and Ansible in particular, with a few of the lab tracks on the DevNet site (at the time this book was published). Navigate to https://developer.cisco.com and search for learning labs about Ansible and Terraform.

Part VI Review

Keep track of your part review progress with the checklist shown in Table P6-1. Details on each task follow the table.

Table P6-1 Part VI Review Checklist

Activity	1st Date Completed	2nd Date Completed
Repeat All DIKTA Questions		
Answer Part Review Questions		
Review Key Topics		
Watch video		
Use Per-Chapter Interactive Review		

Repeat All DIKTA Questions

For this task, answer the "Do I Know This Already?" questions again for the chapters in this part of the book, using the PTP software.

Answer Part Review Questions

For this task, answer the Part Review questions for this part of the book, using the PTP software.

Review Key Topics

Review all key topics in all chapters in this part, either by browsing the chapters or by using the Key Topics application on the companion website.

Watch video

The companion website includes a variety of common mistake and Q&A videos organized by part and chapter. Use these videos to challenge your thinking, dig deeper, review topics, and better prepare for the exam. Make sure to bookmark a link to the companion website and use the videos for review whenever you have a few extra minutes.

Use Per-Chapter Interactive Review

Using the companion website, browse through the interactive review elements, like memory tables and key term flashcards, to review the content from each chapter.

Part VII

Exam Updates and Final Review

CHAPTER 25

CCNA 200-301 Official Cert Guide, Volume 2, Second Edition, Exam Updates

The Purpose of This Chapter

For all the other chapters, the content should remain unchanged throughout this edition of the book. Instead, this chapter will change over time, with an updated online PDF posted so you can see the latest version of the chapter even after you purchase this book.

Why do we need a chapter that updates over time? For two reasons:

1. To add more technical content to the book before it is time to replace the current book edition with the next edition. This chapter will include additional technology content and possibly additional PDFs containing more content.

2. To communicate detail about the next version of the CCNA exam, to tell you about our publishing plans for that edition, and what that means to you.

To find the latest version of this chapter, follow the process below. Bookmark the link so that any time you refer to this chapter, begin by downloading a new copy. Use these steps:

If you have not yet accessed the companion website, follow these steps:

Step 1. Browse to www.ciscopress.com/register.

Step 2. Enter the print book ISBN (even if you are using an eBook): **9780138214951**.

Step 3. After registering the book, go to your account page and select the **Registered Products** tab.

Step 4. Click the **Access Bonus Content** link to access the companion website. Select the link or scroll down to that section to check for updates.

Table 25-1 summarizes the information that this version of the chapter includes. Use the table as a quick reference for the detail to expect in the rest of the chapter.

Table 25-1 Status for Available New Technical Content for This Edition

Chapter Version	1
Most recent CCNA 200-301 blueprint version when this chapter was most recently released	1.1
Is there technology content in the latter part of this chapter?	No
Is there technology content in other downloadable files?	No
Links to other file downloads	N/A
Is there information about the specifics of the new exam?	No

Any additional file downloads, or further instructions for file downloads, will be posted at this book's companion website. See the heading "How to Access the Companion Website" in the Introduction to this book for details on finding this book's companion website.

The following two sections give more detail about the primary purposes of the chapter. Any technical content or exam update detail follows later in the chapter.

Additional Technical Content

On rare occasions, the book author might want to add book content mid-edition. This chapter provides the means to do that, as we will publish updated versions of this chapter in PDF form at the publisher's website.

Several reasons exist for new content. It could just be the author looks at a chapter and feels like it needs more. It could be that the technology changes enough to warrant an update before the new edition. Cisco also can (and has) changed exam topic wording without a formal announcement or change to the blueprint version; any related new content would appear in this chapter.

You do not need to check frequently for a new PDF. You may want to check more regularly about exam updates, as discussed in the next section. But to check for new technical content, I suggest downloading the PDF at the beginning of the book and the end of the book. If you download it to begin, you can read content related to the chapters when you first read those chapters. Downloading at the end ensures you have seen the latest available version of this chapter.

> **NOTE** An equivalent chapter exists in the *CCNA 200-301 Official Cert Guide, Volume 1,* Second Edition. When doing your final study, check for a new version of that element.

Of course, if this chapter adds new technical content, treat it like any of the other chapters in the book, and study the content!

Official Blueprint Changes

Cisco introduced CCNA and CCNP in 1998. For the first 25 years of those certification tracks, Cisco updated the exams on average every 3–4 years. However, Cisco did not pre-announce the exam changes, so exam changes felt very sudden. Usually, a new exam would be announced, with new exam topics, giving you 3–6 months before your only option was to take the new exam. As a result, you could be studying with no idea about Cisco's plans, and the next day, you had a 3–6-month timeline to either pass the old exam or pivot to prepare for the new exam.

Thankfully, Cisco changed their exam release approach in 2023. Called the Cisco Certification Roadmap (https://cisco.com/go/certroadmap), the new plan includes these features:

1. Cisco considers changes to all exam tracks (CCNA, CCNP Enterprise, CCNP Security, and so on) annually.

2. Cisco uses a predefined annual schedule for each track, so you know the timing of possible changes to the exam you are studying for, even before any announcements.

3. The schedule moves in a quarterly sequence:

    a. Privately review the exam to consider what to change.

    b. Publicly announce if an exam is changing, and if so, announce details like exam topics and release date.

    c. Release the new exam.

4. Exam changes might not occur each year. If changes occur, Cisco characterizes them as minor (less than 20 percent change) or major (more than 20 percent change).

The specific dates for a given certification track can be confusing because Cisco organizes the work by fiscal year quarters. As an Example, Figure 25-1 shows the 2024 fiscal year. Their fiscal year begins in August, so, for example, the first quarter (Q1) of fiscal year (FY) 2024 began in August 2023.

Figure 25-1 *Cisco Fiscal Year and Months Example (FY2024)*

Focus more on the sequence of the quarters to understand the plan. Figure 25-2 shows an example sequence in which Cisco updates the CCNA 200-301 exam, assuming a minor release (less than 20 percent change).

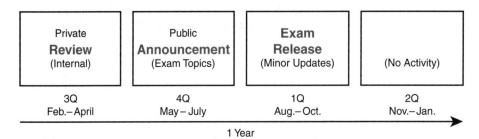

Figure 25-2 *Cisco CCNA Annual Roadmap with a Minor Release*

Over time, Cisco might make no changes in some years and minor changes in others. For example, Cisco announced CCNA 200-301 version 1.1 in the FY24-FY25 cycle (February 2024–January 2025). Figure 25-3 shows what could happen in the next four years. It first shows a year with no changes, then a year with minor changes, another year with no changes, and a year with major changes.

Figure 25-3 shows an example and does not reveal any secret knowledge about Cisco's plans; however, it shows a volume of change that matches the rate of change to the exam over its long history.

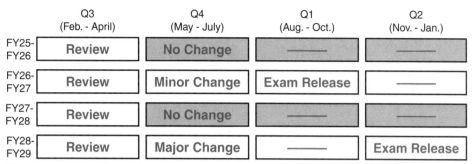

Figure 25-3   *An Example of What Could Happen with CCNA over Four Years*

Impact on You and Your Study Plan

Cisco's new policy helps you plan, but it also means that the CCNA exam might change before you pass the current exam. That impacts you, affecting how we deliver this book to you. This chapter gives us a way to communicate in detail about those changes as they occur. But you should watch other spaces as well.

Your study plan ongoing should follow this general process:

Step 1.   Continue to use the *CCNA 200-301 Official Cert Guides, Volumes 1 and 2*, Second Edition, as is.

Step 2.   Monitor for updates to this Exam Updates chapter, plus the equivalent chapter in Volume 1, to find additional content for topics Cisco may add to the exam.

Step 3.   To be aware of changes to the CCNA exam, monitor the information sources listed below.

For those other information sources to watch, bookmark and check these sites for news. In particular:

Cisco: Check their Certification Roadmap page: https://cisco.com/go/certroadmap. Make sure to sign up for automatic notifications from Cisco on that page.

Publisher: Check this page about new certification products, offers, discounts, and free downloads related to the more frequent exam updates: www.ciscopress.com/newcert.

Cisco Learning Network: Subscribe to the CCNA Community at learningnetwork.cisco.com, where I expect ongoing discussions about exam changes over time. If you have questions, search for "roadmap" in the CCNA community, and if you do not find an answer, ask a new one!

Author: Look for blog posts labeled as News at www.certskills.com. For every new edition, I post about the new exam, new topics, and how to manage the transition. I will continue to do so now with more detail about the new annual cycle. Watch that space and consider subscribing.

As changes arise, I will update this chapter with more detail about exam and book content. Given Cisco's certification roadmap, that means somewhere in each year's fiscal fourth quarter (May–July). At that point, I will publish an updated version of this chapter, listing our content plans. That detail will likely include the following:

- Content removed, so if you plan to take the new exam version, you can ignore those when studying

- New content planned per new exam topics, so you know what's coming

While I do not think Cisco will change CCNA every year—in my opinion, I predict Cisco will change it less than half the years—everyone needs to be aware of the possibility and timing of exam changes and new exam releases. I will use this chapter to communicate the exam and book content details. Look to the other sites from the previous list for brief news about plans, but look here for the detail.

The remainder of the chapter shows the new content that may change over time.

News About the Next CCNA Exam Release

This statement was last updated in March 2024, before the publication of the *CCNA 200-301 Official Cert Guide, Volume 1*, Second Edition.

This version of this chapter has no news to share about the next CCNA exam release.

At the most recent version of this chapter, the CCNA 200-301 exam version number was Version 1.1.

Updated Technical Content

The current version of this chapter has no additional technical content.

CHAPTER 26

Final Review

Congratulations! You made it through the books, and now it's time to finish getting ready for the exam. This chapter helps you get ready to take and pass the exam in two ways.

The first half of this chapter focuses on the exam event. Now you need to think about what happens during the exam and what you need to do in these last few weeks before taking the exam. At this point, everything you do should be focused on getting you ready to pass so that you can finish up this hefty task.

The second section of this chapter focuses on final content review. You should not just complete the chapters in the combined CCNA Volume 1 and 2 books. Instead, you need to review, refine, deepen, and assess your skills. This second section of this chapter gives advice and suggestions on how approach your final weeks of study before you take the CCNA 200-301 exam.

Advice About the Exam Event

Now that you have finished the bulk of this book, you could just register for your Cisco CCNA exam; show up; and take the exam. However, if you spend a little time thinking about the exam event itself, learning more about the user interface of the real Cisco exams, and the environment at the Pearson VUE testing centers, you will be better prepared, particularly if this is your first Cisco exam.

This first of two major sections in this chapter gives some advice about the Cisco exams and the exam event itself, specifically about

- Question Types

- Your Time Budget

- An Example Time-Check Method

- The Final Week Before Your Exam

- 24 Hours Before Your Exam

- The Final 30 Minutes Before Your Exam

- The Hour After Your Exam

Learn About Question Types

In the weeks leading up to your exam, you should think more about the different types of exam questions and have a plan for how to approach those questions. To get started, watch the Cisco Certification Exam Tutorial Video. You can find it these ways:

- **Direct link:** https://learningnetwork.cisco.com/s/certification-exam-tutorials

- **Internet search:** Search for "Cisco Certification Exam Tutorial Video" and you will likely find it.

- **Blog post:** Use https://www.certskills.com/final-review, which links to a blog page with a link to the video page (as well as other links useful for final review).

Cisco does not give a definitive list of all question types used on any Cisco exam; however, the videos and this section describe all the question types used at the time this book was published.

While you're watching any of the videos about the exam tutorial, the exam user interface has these conventions:

- Shows circles beside the answers in single-answer questions.

- Shows squares beside the answers in multiple-answer questions.

- Prevents you from choosing too many or too few answers.

- Supplies a popup window to tell you if you have selected too few answers if you try to move to the next question, so you can stop and go back and answer with the correct number of answers.

- Applies no penalty for guessing—so you should always supply the number of answers that the question asks for.

To emphasize: Cisco has no penalty for guessing, and the user interface helps ensure you choose the correct number of answers. Always answer, and answer with the stated number of correct answers.

Drag-and-drop questions require you to move items in the user interface with mouse actions. The draggable items begin in one location, and you will drag-and-drop them to answer. The draggables may be words, but they can also be graphics.

Within one drag-and-drop question, you can change your mind until satisfied. To do so, after dragging an item, just drag it back to its original position. The user interface does not consider you to have answered the question until you click the next button.

Lab questions directly assess your CLI skills. They present you with a lab scenario with a lab pod of virtual routers and switches running in the background, giving you console access to a few devices. Your job: find the missing or broken configuration and reconfigure the devices so that the lab scenario works. Some of the key points to consider with lab questions include

1. Learn the lab question user interface as much as possible beforehand by watching the "Cisco Certification Exam Tutorial Video."

2. Expect to navigate often between the tabs on the left of the user interface, particularly the topology (drawing) and tasks tabs. The topology shows a figure of the network, with the tasks tab listing what you need to do to gain the points for the question. (The guidelines tab typically lists generic instructions that apply to every lab question.)

3. The right side of the user interface has tabs for the console of each device—just click the tab to get to the CLI of the device.

4. Lab questions run virtualized Cisco operating systems. They do not use simulations. So, the CLI should work like real devices, with all commands supported, all options, with navigation tools like ?, tab, and up arrow.

5. You answer by changing the configuration, so make sure to issue the **copy running-config startup-config** command (or **copy run start**) to save your configuration.

6. Cisco gives partial credit on lab questions, so do as much as you can, even if you do not know how to solve the entire lab.

Figure 26-1 shows a screen capture from the video, noting the UI tabs.

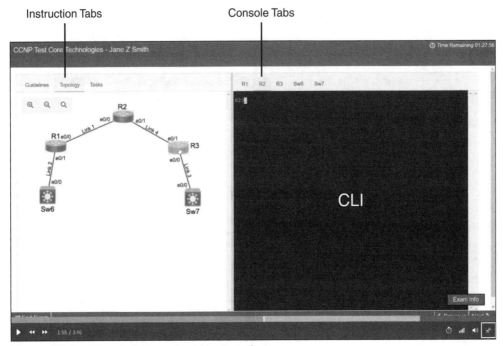

Figure 26-1 *Cisco Lab Question User Interface*

> **NOTE** Those of you with some prior experience with CCNA will notice that lab questions seem a lot like the old Sim question type. The old Sim questions required the same actions from us as test takers: read the scenario and fix the configuration. However, Sim questions used simulated Cisco devices with limited command support, which frustrated some test takers. Lab questions use virtualized Cisco operating systems, creating a much more realistic experience.

On a final note about question types, Cisco can and may change the question types, but in recent years, the CCNA exam has used the types listed here.

Think About Your Time Budget

Several factors about a Cisco exam experience make time management a challenge, including

1. The test has a time limit. The user interface shows the time count down to 0:00.

2. The test has a defined number of questions that you learn when you begin the test. The user interface shows the current question, counting up from 1 to the number of questions you will see.

3. You cannot skip a question or go back to an earlier question. Once you move on to the next question, you cannot navigate back to it.

4. You do not know how many time-consuming questions like lab questions exist on your exam, even after you start your exam. Instead, they just appear like any other question.

Because of Cisco's exam rules, you need to take extra care to manage your time and keep an eye on your speed. Going too slowly hurts you because you might not have time to answer all the questions. Going too fast hurts if you are rushing due to worry about running out of time. So, you need to be able to somehow know whether you are moving quickly enough to answer all the questions while not rushing.

You need a plan for how you will check your time, a plan that does not distract you from the exam. You can ponder the facts listed here and come up with your own plan. If you want a little more guidance, the next topic shows one way to check your time that uses some simple math so it does not take much time away from the test.

An Example Time-Check Method

As a suggestion, you can use the following math to do your time check in a way that weights the time based on those time-consuming questions. You do not have to use this method. But this math uses only addition of whole numbers, to keep it simple. It gives you a pretty close time estimate, in my opinion.

The concept is simple. Just do a simple calculation that estimates the time you should have used so far. Here's the math:

Number of questions answered so far + 7 per time-consuming question answered so far

Then you check the timer to figure out how much time you have spent:

- You have used exactly that much time, or a little more time: your timing is perfect.

- You have used less time: you are ahead of schedule.

- You have used noticeably more time: you are behind schedule.

For example, first you need to make a habit of keeping count of how many time-consuming questions you see. For instance, write "labs" on your note sheet and add a mark each time you see a lab question. For the math, for instance, if you have already finished 17 questions, 1 of which was a lab question, your time estimate is 17 + 7 = 24 minutes. If your actual time is also 24 minutes, or maybe 25 or 26 minutes, you are right on schedule. If you have spent less than 24 minutes, you are ahead of schedule.

So, the math is pretty easy: Questions answered, plus 7 per time-consuming question, is the guesstimate of how long you should have taken so far if you are right on time.

> **NOTE**   This math is an estimate; I make no guarantees that the math will be an accurate predictor on every exam.

One Week Before Your Exam

I have listed a variety of tips and advice in the next few pages, broken down by timing versus the big exam event. First, this section discusses some items to consider when your exam is about a week away:

- **Get some earplugs:** Testing centers often have some, but if you do not want to chance it, come prepared with your own. (They will not let you bring your own noise-canceling headphones into the room if they follow the rules disallowing any user electronic devices in the room, so think low-tech disposable earplugs, or even bring a cotton ball.) The testing center is typically one room within a building of a company that does something else as well, often a training center, and almost certainly you will share the room with other test takers coming and going. So, there are people talking in nearby rooms and other office noises. Earplugs can help.

- **Create a note-taking plan:** Some people like to spend the first minute of the exam writing down some notes for reference, before actually starting the exam. For example, maybe you want to write down the table of magic numbers for finding IPv4 subnet IDs. If you plan to do that, practice making those notes between now and exam day. Before each practice exam, transcribe those lists, just like you expect to do at the real exam.

- **Plan your travel to the testing center:** Leave enough time in your schedule so that you will not be rushing to make it just in time.

- **Practice your favorite relaxation techniques for a few minutes before each practice exam:** That way you can enter the exam event and be more relaxed and have more success.

24 Hours Before Your Exam

You wake up on the big day—what should you be doing and thinking? Certainly, the better prepared you are, the better chances you have on the exam. But these small tips can help you do your best on exam day:

- Rest the night before the exam rather than staying up late to study. Clarity of thought is more important than one extra fact, especially because the exam requires so much analysis and thinking rather than just remembering facts.

- Bring as few extra items with you as possible when leaving for the exam center. You may bring personal effects into the building and testing company's space, but not into the actual room in which you take the exam. So, save a little stress and bring as little extra stuff with you as possible. If you have a safe place to leave briefcases, purses, electronics, and so on, leave them there. However, the testing center should have a place to store your things as well. Simply put, the less you bring, the less you have to worry about storing. (For example, I have been asked to remove even my analog wristwatch on more than one occasion.)

- Plan time in your schedule for the day to not rush to get there and not rush when leaving, either.

- Do not drink a 64-ounce caffeinated drink on the trip to the testing center! After the exam starts, the exam timer will not stop while you go to the restroom.

- Use any relaxation techniques that you have practiced to help get your mind focused while you wait for the exam.

30 Minutes Before Your Exam

It's almost time! Here are a few tips for those last moments.

- Ask the testing center personnel for earplugs if you did not bring any—even if you cannot imagine using them. You never know whether using them might help.

- Ask for extra pens and laminated note sheets. The exam center will give you a laminated sheet and dry erase markers with which to take notes. (Test center personnel typically do not let you bring paper and pen into the room, even if supplied by the testing center.) I always ask for a second pen as well.

- Test your pens and sheets before going into the room to take the exam. Better to get a replacement pen before the clock starts.

- Grab a few tissues from the box in the room, for two reasons. One, to avoid having to get up in the middle of the exam if you need to sneeze. Two, if you need to erase your laminated sheet, doing that with a tissue paper rather than your hand helps prevent the oil from your hand making the pen stop working well.

- Find a restroom to use before going into the testing center, or just ask where one is, to avoid needing to go during the approximately two-hour exam event. Note that the exam timer does not stop if you need to go to the restroom during the exam, and you first have to go find the exam center contact before just heading to the restroom, so it can cost you a few minutes.

The Hour After Your Exam

Some people pass these exams on the first attempt, and some do not. The exams are not easy. If you fail to pass the exam that day, you will likely be disappointed. And that is understandable. But it is not a reason to give up. In fact, I added this short topic to give you a big advantage in case you do fail.

The most important study hour for your next exam attempt is the hour just after your failed attempt.

Before you take the exam, prepare for how you will react if you do not pass. That is, prepare your schedule to give yourself an hour, or at least a half an hour, immediately after the exam attempt, in case you fail. Follow these suggestions to be ready for taking notes:

- Bring pen and paper, preferably a notebook you can write in if you have to write standing up or sitting somewhere inconvenient.

- Make sure you know where pen and paper are so that you can take notes immediately after the exam. Keep these items in your backpack if using the train or bus, or on the car seat in the car.

- Install an audio recording app on your phone, and be prepared to start talking into your app when you leave the testing center.

- Before the exam, scout the testing center, and plan the place where you will sit and take your notes, preferably somewhere quiet.

Then, once you complete the exam, if you do not pass on this attempt, use the following process when taking notes:

- Write down anything in particular that you can recall from any question.

- Write down details of questions you know you got right as well, because doing so may help trigger a memory of another question.

- Draw the figures that you can remember.

- Most importantly, write down any tidbit that might have confused you: terms, configuration commands, **show** commands, scenarios, topology drawings, anything.

- Take at least three passes at remembering. That is, you will hit a wall where you do not remember more. So, start on your way back to the next place, and then find a place to pause and take more notes. And do it again.

- When you have sucked your memory dry, take one more pass while thinking of the major topics in the book, to see if that triggers any other memory of a question.

Once collected, *you cannot share the information with anyone,* because doing so would break the Cisco nondisclosure agreement (NDA). Cisco considers cheating a serious offense and strongly forbids sharing this kind of information publicly. But you can and should use everything you can recall from your first attempt to prepare for your second attempt. See the section "Adjustments for Your Second Attempt" in this chapter for the rest of the story.

Exam Review

At this point, you should have read the other chapters in the *CCNA 200-301 Official Cert Guide, Volumes 1 and 2*, and you have done the Chapter Review and Part Review tasks. Now you need to do the final study and review activities before taking the exam, as detailed in this section.

This section suggests some new activities and repeats some activities that have been previously mentioned. However, whether the activities are new or old to you, they all focus on filling in your knowledge gaps, finishing off your skills, and completing the study process.

You need to be ready to take an exam, so the Exam Review asks you to spend a lot of time answering exam questions. The next several pages discuss the best ways to make use of the practice questions that come with this book for your final preparation. The rest of the chapter then offers other suggestions for final exam preparation.

Using Practice Questions

Both this book and the associated Volume 1 book come with a set of practice questions. The Pearson Test Prep (PTP) user interface, both web and desktop app, groups questions into exams. Figure 26-2 lists the exams supplied with the Volume 1 and Volume 2 books. (You might recall some of this information from the "Your Study Plan" section of the *CCNA 200-301 Official Cert Guide, Volume 1*, Second Edition, found just before Chapter 1 of that book.)

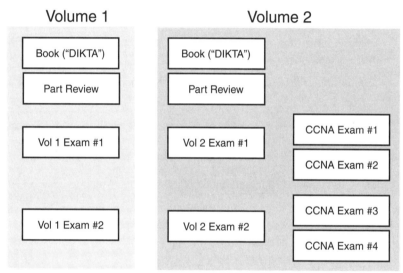

Figure 26-2 *Exams Included in the Combined CCNA 200-301 Official Cert Guide, Volumes 1 and 2*

Volume 1 comes with a set of four exams. The "book" exam holds copies of the chapter-beginning "Do I Know This Already?" quiz questions. The part review exam includes the questions meant for use during part review. Exams 1 and 2 supply additional practice questions about Volume 1 content that you could use anytime, even now during your final review.

Volume 2 includes an equivalent set of four exams, but with questions about the technologies discussed in Volume 2.

Additionally, the publisher delivers CCNA exams to you in the Volume 2 book. Those exams include questions about the technologies in both books, making them excellent candidates to be used for timed practice exams.

The next few pages suggest how to use the practice questions for review at this late stage in your CCNA journey.

Hold Practice Exam Events

One day soon, you need to pass a real Cisco exam at a Pearson VUE testing center. So, it's time to practice the real event as much as possible.

A practice exam using the PTP exam software lets you experience many of the same challenges as when taking a real Cisco exam. When you select *practice exam* mode, PTP software (both desktop and web) gives you a number of questions, with an upward question counter and a countdown timer shown in the window. When in practice exam mode, you cannot move backward to a previous question (yes, that's true on Cisco exams). And like the real exam, if you run out of time, the questions you did not answer count as incorrect.

The process of taking the timed practice exams helps you prepare in three key ways:

- To practice the exam event itself, including time pressure, the need to read carefully, and the need to concentrate for long periods

- To build your analysis and critical thinking skills when examining the network scenario built in to many questions

- To discover the gaps in your networking knowledge so that you can study those topics before the real exam

As much as possible, treat the practice exam events as if you were taking the real Cisco exam at a VUE testing center. The following list gives some advice on how to make your practice exam more meaningful, rather than just one more thing to do before exam day rolls around:

- Set aside 2.5 hours for taking a 120-minute timed practice exam.

- Make a list of what you expect to do for the 10 minutes before the real exam event. Then visualize yourself doing those things. Before taking each practice exam, practice those final 10 minutes before your exam timer starts. (The earlier section "30 Minutes Before Your Exam" lists some suggestions about what to do.)

- You cannot bring anything with you into the VUE exam room, so remove all notes and help materials from your work area before taking a practice exam. You can use blank paper, a pen, and your brain only. Do not use calculators, notes, web browsers, or any other app on your computer.

- Real life can get in the way, but if at all possible, ask anyone around you to leave you alone for the time you will practice. If you must do your practice exam in a distracting environment, wear headphones or earplugs to reduce distractions.

- To your benefit, do not guess on the practice exam event, hoping to improve your score. Answer only when you have confidence in the answer. Then, if you get the question wrong, you can go back and think more about the question in a later study session.

Hold your practice exam events using the CCNA exams listed in the PTP user interface. Just select those exams, and de-select the others. Or, select CCNA exam 1 for one event and CCNA exam 2 for the other. Also, select a 100-question limit. Then you simply need to choose the **Practice Exam** option in the upper right and start the exam.

You should plan to take between one and three practice exams with the supplied CCNA exam databases. Even people who are already well prepared should do at least one practice exam, just to experience the time pressure and the need for prolonged concentration.

Table 26-1 gives you a checklist to record your different practice exam events. Note that recording both the date and the score is helpful for some other work you will do, so note both. Also, in the Time Notes section, if you finish on time, note how much extra time you had; if you run out of time, note how many questions you did not have time to answer. Finally, note that you completed gap review (discussed later in this chapter).

Table 26-1 CCNA Practice Exam Checklist

Exam Bank(s) Used	Date Taken	Score	Time Notes	Completed Gap Review?

Exam Scoring on the Real Exam

When you take a practice exam with PTP, PTP gives you a score, on a scale from 300 to 1000. Why? Cisco gives a score of between 300 and 1000 as well. But the similarities end there.

With PTP, the score is a basic percentage but expressed as a number from 0 to 1000. For example, answer 80 percent correct, and the score is 800; get 90 percent correct, and the score is 900. If you start a practice exam and click through it without answering a single question, you get a 0.

However, Cisco does not score exams in the same way. The following is what we do know about Cisco exam scoring:

- Cisco uses a scoring scale from 300 to 1000.

- Cisco tells us that it gives partial credit but provides no further details.

So, what does an 800 or a 900 mean on the actual Cisco exams? Cisco doesn't reveal the details of scoring to us. They don't reveal the details of partial credit. It also seems like a lab question would be worth more points than a multiple-choice question. Also, some drag-and-drop questions require that you know many facts—but we do not know if Cisco weights those with more points.

Self-Assessment Suggestions

Are you ready to take and pass the real exam? We all want to be able to self-assess whether we are ready to pass. The next few pages give a few suggestions.

First, practice exam scores give you only a general indicator of exam readiness. In fact, some students use their practice exam scores as the main self-assessment tool. However, the scores give only a broad indication of your readiness given many variables that affect the scores.

As an example of a good use of the practice exam scores, imagine you hold one practice exam event and get a 650, and three weeks later (after more studying) hold another and make a 900. You probably improved your chances of passing. However, do not look at your practice exam score of 900 and think that means you're ready to get more than the 800–825 typically required on the real exam. There are too many other variables impacting the scoring to make that claim.

Why is the raw practice exam score a poor measure?

- One 100-question practice exam cannot come close to asking about the breadth and depth of CCNA topics. So the randomness of chosen questions versus your knowledge impacts your practice exam score.

- If you choose to guess like you would on the real exam, your practice test score becomes skewed by your success or failure rate at guessing, giving false confidence if you guess well and false doubts if you guess poorly.

- Question familiarity. If you have seen some of the questions before, you might get a falsely higher score.

So, use your practice exam scores as a general guide. Do not get upset with lower scores, or too excited about high scores.

In addition to practice exam scores, try some other study and review efforts that can give you a better sense of your readiness. For instance, the book identifies key topics and key terms. Those are the most important topics and terms in the books. You ought to be able to explain a few sentences about most of those topics and terms—so do just that. The following list gives some review activities that also help you assess your exam readiness:

1. **Explain each key topic:** Look at the key topic table at the end of each chapter as a reminder of each key topic. Without looking at the chapter's content, explain out loud to an imaginary colleague about the concept and technology. Note the percentage of key topics you could explain well as a measure of exam readiness (you can find the key topics in the companion website as well).

2. **Confirm mastery of subnetting math:** Review and practice all types of subnetting activities one more time. As for exam readiness, you should be able to do subnetting math confidently with 100 percent accuracy at this point.

3. **Practice config checklists:** The chapters include config checklists for the longer configuration tasks. Use the interactive versions of these checklists on the companion website. You should be able to remember most of the configuration commands for each process from memory. Practice them and note your scores, repeating until you remember all.

4. **Practice config labs:** You should be able to do all the Config Labs from my blog site, or labs of similar challenge level. Perform some of those labs to help internalize the commands and details study in the configuration checklists. While performing all labs may be too time consuming, focus on practicing weak areas.

5. **Improve recall of show commands:** For chapters with **show** commands, scan the examples and look at the fields highlighted in gray. Without looking at the notes in the book, recall and remind yourself about which values list configuration settings and

which show status information. As for exam readiness, do not expect to recall every command and output fact, but work to improve gaps.

6. **Explain key terms:** Use the key terms listed at the end of each chapter for a review exercise. Look at the list, and speaking out loud, describe each term with no other prompts. Try pretending to teach the topic to a fellow CCNA student. For any terms that make you pause too long, review the term. Note the percentage of key terms you can explain as a measure of exam readiness. (You can find the key terms in the companion website's key terms flashcards app, which can be very useful for this activity.)

Gap Analysis Using Q&A

Gap analysis refers to any activity that helps you identify differences between what you should know and what you actually know. Gap analysis helps increase your chances of passing more so than most last-stage tools, and you can use the PTP app to do effective gap analysis.

When you use exam mode in the PTP app, you cannot see the correct answers, and the app disables the answer button (which reveals a detailed explanation to the question). However, if you click Save to save your practice exam, the PTP software tracks each practice exam you take, remembering your answer for every question, and whether you got it wrong. You can view the results and move back and forth between seeing the question and seeing the results page.

Figure 26-3 shows a sample Question Review page. To know which ones you answered correctly, examine the "Your Score" column, with a 0 meaning you answered incorrectly.

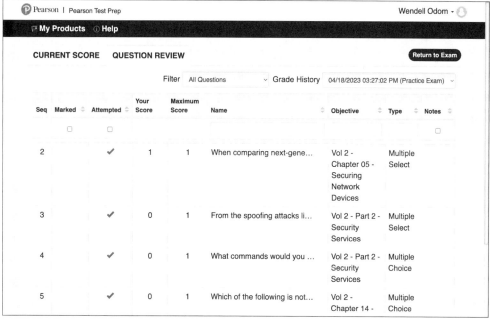

Figure 26-3 *PTP Grading Results Page*

To perform the process of reviewing questions and marking them as complete, you can move between this Question Review page and the individual questions. Just double-click a question to move back to that question, as shown in Figure 26-4.

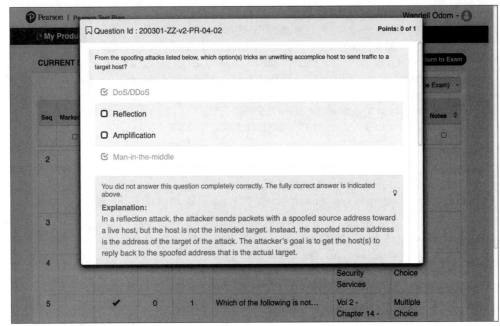

Figure 26-4   *Reviewing a Question, with the Mark Feature in the Upper Left*

From the question, you can click the Close button to move back to the grading results and to the Question Review page shown in Figure 26-3.

If you want to come back later to look through the questions you missed from an earlier exam, start at the PTP home screen. From there, instead of clicking the Start button to start a new exam, click the **Load Saved Exam** button to see your earlier exam attempts and work through any missed questions.

Find a place to track your cap analysis progress with a table like Table 26-2. PTP lists your saved practice exams by date and time, so it helps to note those values in the table for comparison to the PTP menu.

Table 26-2   Tracking Checklist for Gap Review of Practice Exams

Original Practice Exam Date/Time	Date Gap Review Was Completed

Advice on How to Answer Exam Questions

Our everyday habits have changed how we all read and think in front of a screen. Unfortunately, those same habits often hurt our scores when taking computer-based exams.

For example, open a web browser. Yes, take a break and open a web browser on any device. Do a quick search on a fun topic. Then, before you click a link, get ready to think about what you just did. Where did your eyes go for the first 5–10 seconds after you opened that web page. Now, click a link and look at the page. Where did your eyes go?

Interestingly, web browsers and the content in web pages have trained us all to scan. Web page designers actually design content expecting certain scan patterns from viewers. Regardless of the pattern, when reading a web page, almost no one reads sequentially, and no one reads entire sentences. People scan for the interesting graphics and the big words, and then scan the space around those noticeable items.

Other parts of our electronic culture have also changed how the average person reads. For example, many of you grew up using texting and social media, sifting through hundreds or thousands of messages—but each message barely fills an entire sentence. Also, we find ourselves responding to texts, tweets, and emails and later realizing we did not really understand what the other person meant.

If you use those same habits when taking the exam, you will probably make some mistakes because you missed a key fact in the question, answer, or exhibits. It helps to start at the beginning and read all the words—a process that is amazingly unnatural for many people today.

> **NOTE**   I have talked to many college professors, in multiple disciplines, and Cisco Networking Academy instructors, and they consistently tell me that the number-one test-taking issue today is that people do not read the question well enough to understand the details.

When you are taking the practice exams and answering individual questions, consider these two strategies. First, before the practice exam, think about your personal strategy for how you will read a question. Make your approach to multiple-choice questions in particular be a conscious decision on your part. Second, if you want some suggestions on how to read an exam question, use the following strategy:

Step 1.   Read the question itself, thoroughly, from start to finish.

Step 2.   Scan any exhibit or figure.

Step 3.   Scan the answers to look for the types of information. (Numeric? Terms? Single words? Phrases?)

Step 4.   Reread the question thoroughly, from start to finish, to make sure that you understand it.

Step 5.   Read each answer thoroughly, while referring to the figure/exhibit as needed. After reading each answer, before reading the next answer:

   a.   If correct, select as correct.

   b.   If for sure incorrect, mentally rule it out.

   c.   If unsure, mentally note it as a possible correct answer.

NOTE Cisco exams will tell you the number of correct answers. The exam software also helps you finish the question with the right number of answers noted. For example, for standalone multichoice questions, the software prevents you from selecting too many or too few answers. And you should guess the answer when unsure on the actual exam—there is no penalty for guessing.

Use the practice exams as a place to practice your approach to reading. Every time you click to the next question, try to read the question following your approach. If you are feeling time pressure, that is the perfect time to keep practicing your approach, to reduce and eliminate questions you miss because of scanning the question instead of reading thoroughly.

Additional Exams with the Premium Edition

Many people add practice exams and questions other than those that come with this book. Frankly, using other practice exams in addition to the questions that come with this book can be a good idea, for many reasons. The other exam questions can use different terms in different ways, emphasize different topics, and show different scenarios that make you rethink some topics.

All Cisco Press CCNA Premium Edition products include:

■ Kindle, Nook, and PDF versions of the book

■ More PTP exams

■ Links from each question to the related content in the book

Cisco Press publishes a Volume 1, Volume 2, and CCNA Library Premium Edition product. For practice questions, the CCNA Library Premium Edition is simply better. The Volume 1 and 2 products contain exams that cover only the respective book volume, whereas the CCNA Library Premium Edition has CCNA full exams, which contain exams from the full breadth of CCNA topics. (Plus, the CCNA Library Premium Edition is less expensive than buying both the Volume 1 and 2 Premium Edition products.)

NOTE In addition to the extra questions, the Premium Editions have links to every test question, including those in the print book, to the specific section of the book for further reference. This is a great learning tool if you need more detail than what you find in the question explanations.

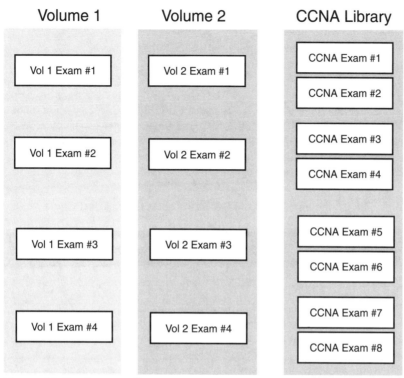

Figure 26-5   *CCNA Full Exams in the CCNA Library Premium Edition*

Practicing CLI Skills

To do well on lab questions, you need to be comfortable with many Cisco router and switch commands and how to use them from a Cisco CLI. As described in the Introduction to this book, lab questions require you to decide what configuration command(s) need to be configured to fix a problem or to complete a working configuration.

To be ready for the exam, you need to know the following kinds of information:

CLI navigation: Basic CLI mechanics of moving into and out of user, enable, and configuration modes

Individual configuration: The meaning of the parameters of each configuration command

Feature configuration: The set of configuration commands, both required and optional, for each feature

Verification of configuration: The **show** commands that directly identify the configuration settings

Verification of status: The **show** commands that list current status values, and the ability to decide incorrect configuration or other problem causes of less-than-optimal status values

To help remember and review all this knowledge and skill, you can do the tasks listed in the next several pages.

Wondering about all the topics in CCNA 200-301 that specifically include configuration or verification skills? You can just scan the CCNA 200-301 exam blueprint Version 1.1. However, Table 26-3 and Table 26-4 summarize the topics for which you could consider practicing your CLI skills. The tables organize the topics into the same order used in the *CCNA 200-301 Official Cert Guides, Volumes 1 and 2*, with chapter references.

Table 26-3 Topics with Configuration Skills in CCNA 200-301 Official Cert Guide, Volume 1

Topic	Volume 1 Chapter	Date You Finished Lab Review
Verifying LAN switching	5	
Switch IPv4	6	
Switch passwords	6	
Switch interfaces	7	
VLANs	8	
VLAN trunking	8	
STP and RSTP	10	
Layer 2 EtherChannel	10	
BPDU guard, BPDU filter, root guard, loop guard	10	
Router interfaces	16	
Router IPv4 addresses and static routes	17	
Router on a stick	18	
Layer 3 switching with SVIs	18	
Layer 3 switching with routed interfaces and L3 EtherChannels	18	
Switch interfaces on routers	18	
DHCP Client and DHCP Relay	19	
OSPF fundamentals	22	
OSPF network types and other optional features	23	
OSPF neighbor issues	24	
IPv6 addressing on routers	27	
IPv6 host addressing	28	
IPv6 static routes	29	

Table 26-4 Topics with Configuration Skills in CCNA 200-301 Official Cert Guide, Volume 2

Topic	Volume 2 Chapter	Date You Finished Lab Review
Wireless LANs	4	
Standard ACLs	6	
Extended ACLs	7	
Filtering network protocols	8	
Port security	11	
DHCP Snooping	12	
Dynamic ARP Inspection	12	
Syslog, NTP, CDP, and LLDP	13	
NAT, PAT	14	

26

You should research and choose your favorite methods and tools to get hands-on practice for CCNA. Those options include several that focus on giving you a specific activity to do. The options include the Pearson Network Simulator, Config Labs (on my blog), and Packet Tracer labs (on my blog). Look back to the Introduction to this book for more detail on the tools, and use these links for more information:

The Pearson Network Simulator (the Sim): https://www.pearsonitcertification.com/networksimulator

Config Labs at my blog: www.certskills.com/config-labs

Adjustments for Your Second Attempt

None of us wants to take and fail any exam, but some of you will. And even if you pass the CCNA exam on your first try, if you keep going with Cisco certifications, you will probably fail some exams along the way. I mention failing an exam not to focus on the negative, but to help prepare you for how to pass the next attempt after failing an earlier attempt. This section collects some of the advice I have given to readers over the years who have contacted me after a failed attempt, asking for help about what to do next.

The single most important bit of advice is to change your mindset about Cisco exams. Cisco exams are not like high school or college exams where your failing grade matters. Instead, a Cisco exam is more like an event on the road to completing an impressive major accomplishment, one that most people have to try a few times to achieve.

For instance, achieving a Cisco certification is more like training to run a marathon in under 4 hours. The first time running a marathon, you may not even finish, or you may finish at 4:15 rather than under 4:00. But finishing a marathon in 4:15 means that you have prepared and are getting pretty close to your goal.

So change your mindset. You're a marathon runner looking to improve your time. And you are getting better skills every time you study, which helps you compete in the market.

With that attitude and analogy in mind, the rest of this section lists specific study steps that can help.

First, study the notes you took about your failed attempt. (See the earlier section "The Hour After Your Exam.") Do not share that information with others, but use it to study. Before you take the exam again, you should be able to answer every actual exam question you can remember from the last attempt. Even if you never see the exact same question again, you will still get a good return for your effort.

Second, spend more time on activities that uncover your weaknesses. Do more gap analysis. When doing that, you have to slow down and be more self-aware. For instance, answer practice questions in study mode, and *do not guess*. Do not click on to the next question, but pause and ask yourself if you are really sure about both the wrong and correct answers. If unsure, fantastic! You just discovered a topic for which to go back and dig in to learn it more deeply. Or when you do a lab, hide all notes and do not use tools like Internet searches—that might be a reminder that you have not mastered those commands yet.

Third, think about your time spent on the exam. Did you run out of time? Go too fast? Too slow? If too slow, were you slow on subnetting, or lab questions, or something else? Then make a written plan as to how you will approach time on the next attempt and how you will track time use. And if you ran out of time, practice for the things that slowed you down.

Other Study Tasks

If you got to this point and still feel the need to prepare some more, this last topic gives you three suggestions.

First, the Chapter Review and Part Review sections give you some useful study tasks.

Second, use more exam questions from other sources. You can always get more questions in the Cisco Press Premium Edition eBook and Practice Test products, which include an eBook copy of this book plus additional questions in additional PTP exam banks. However, you can search the Internet for questions from many sources and review those questions as well.

NOTE   Some vendors claim to sell practice exams that contain the literal exam questions from the official exam. These exams, called "brain dumps," are against the Cisco testing policies. Cisco strongly discourages using any such tools for study.

Finally, join in the discussions on the Cisco Learning Network. Try to answer questions asked by other learners; the process of answering makes you think much harder about the topic. When someone posts an answer with which you disagree, think about why and talk about it online. This is a great way to both learn more and build confidence.

Final Thoughts

You have studied quite a bit, worked hard, and sacrificed time and money to be ready for the exam. I hope your exam goes well, that you pass, and that you pass because you really know your stuff and will do well in your IT and networking career.

I encourage you to celebrate when you pass and ask advice when you do not. The Cisco Learning Network is a great place to make posts to celebrate and to ask advice for the next time around. I personally would love to hear about your progress through LinkedIn (https://www.linkedin.com/in/WendellOdom). I wish you well, and congratulations for working through the entire book!

Part VIII

Print Appendixes

Appendix A: Numeric Reference Tables

Appendix B: Exam Topics Cross-Reference

Appendix C: Answers to the "Do I Know This Already?" Quizzes

Glossary

Numeric Reference Tables

This appendix provides several useful reference tables that list numbers used throughout this book. Specifically:

Table A-1: A decimal-binary cross reference, useful when converting from decimal to binary and vice versa.

Table A-1   Decimal-Binary Cross Reference, Decimal Values 0–255

Decimal Value	Binary Value	Decimal Value	Binary Value	Decimal Value	Binary Value	Decimal Value	Binary Value
0	00000000	32	00100000	64	01000000	96	01100000
1	00000001	33	00100001	65	01000001	97	01100001
2	00000010	34	00100010	66	01000010	98	01100010
3	00000011	35	00100011	67	01000011	99	01100011
4	00000100	36	00100100	68	01000100	100	01100100
5	00000101	37	00100101	69	01000101	101	01100101
6	00000110	38	00100110	70	01000110	102	01100110
7	00000111	39	00100111	71	01000111	103	01100111
8	00001000	40	00101000	72	01001000	104	01101000
9	00001001	41	00101001	73	01001001	105	01101001
10	00001010	42	00101010	74	01001010	106	01101010
11	00001011	43	00101011	75	01001011	107	01101011
12	00001100	44	00101100	76	01001100	108	01101100
13	00001101	45	00101101	77	01001101	109	01101101
14	00001110	46	00101110	78	01001110	110	01101110
15	00001111	47	00101111	79	01001111	111	01101111
16	00010000	48	00110000	80	01010000	112	01110000
17	00010001	49	00110001	81	01010001	113	01110001
18	00010010	50	00110010	82	01010010	114	01110010
19	00010011	51	00110011	83	01010011	115	01110011
20	00010100	52	00110100	84	01010100	116	01110100
21	00010101	53	00110101	85	01010101	117	01110101
22	00010110	54	00110110	86	01010110	118	01110110
23	00010111	55	00110111	87	01010111	119	01110111
24	00011000	56	00111000	88	01011000	120	01111000
25	00011001	57	00111001	89	01011001	121	01111001
26	00011010	58	00111010	90	01011010	122	01111010
27	00011011	59	00111011	91	01011011	123	01111011
28	00011100	60	00111100	92	01011100	124	01111100
29	00011101	61	00111101	93	01011101	125	01111101
30	00011110	62	00111110	94	01011110	126	01111110
31	00011111	63	00111111	95	01011111	127	01111111

Decimal Value	Binary Value	Decimal Value	Binary Value	Decimal Value	Binary Value	Decimal Value	Binary Value
128	10000000	160	10100000	192	11000000	224	11100000
129	10000001	161	10100001	193	11000001	225	11100001
130	10000010	162	10100010	194	11000010	226	11100010
131	10000011	163	10100011	195	11000011	227	11100011
132	10000100	164	10100100	196	11000100	228	11100100
133	10000101	165	10100101	197	11000101	229	11100101
134	10000110	166	10100110	198	11000110	230	11100110
135	10000111	167	10100111	199	11000111	231	11100111
136	10001000	168	10101000	200	11001000	232	11101000
137	10001001	169	10101001	201	11001001	233	11101001
138	10001010	170	10101010	202	11001010	234	11101010
139	10001011	171	10101011	203	11001011	235	11101011
140	10001100	172	10101100	204	11001100	236	11101100
141	10001101	173	10101101	205	11001101	237	11101101
142	10001110	174	10101110	206	11001110	238	11101110
143	10001111	175	10101111	207	11001111	239	11101111
144	10010000	176	10110000	208	11010000	240	11110000
145	10010001	177	10110001	209	11010001	241	11110001
146	10010010	178	10110010	210	11010010	242	11110010
147	10010011	179	10110011	211	11010011	243	11110011
148	10010100	180	10110100	212	11010100	244	11110100
149	10010101	181	10110101	213	11010101	245	11110101
150	10010110	182	10110110	214	11010110	246	11110110
151	10010111	183	10110111	215	11010111	247	11110111
152	10011000	184	10111000	216	11011000	248	11111000
153	10011001	185	10111001	217	11011001	249	11111001
154	10011010	186	10111010	218	11011010	250	11111010
155	10011011	187	10111011	219	11011011	251	11111011
156	10011100	188	10111100	220	11011100	252	11111100
157	10011101	189	10111101	221	11011101	253	11111101
158	10011110	190	10111110	222	11011110	254	11111110
159	10011111	191	10111111	223	11011111	255	11111111

A

Table A-2: A hexadecimal-binary cross reference, useful when converting from hex to binary and vice versa.

Table A-2   Hex-Binary Cross Reference

Hex	4-Bit Binary
0	0000
1	0001
2	0010
3	0011
4	0100
5	0101
6	0110
7	0111
8	1000
9	1001
A	1010
B	1011
C	1100
D	1101
E	1110
F	1111

Table A-3: Powers of 2, from 2^1 through 2^{32}.

Table A-3   Powers of 2

X	2^X	X	2^X
1	2	17	131,072
2	4	18	262,144
3	8	19	524,288
4	16	20	1,048,576
5	32	21	2,097,152
6	64	22	4,194,304
7	128	23	8,388,608
8	256	24	16,777,216
9	512	25	33,554,432
10	1024	26	67,108,864
11	2048	27	134,217,728
12	4096	28	268,435,456
13	8192	29	536,870,912
14	16,384	30	1,073,741,824
15	32,768	31	2,147,483,648
16	65,536	32	4,294,967,296

Table A-4: Table of all 33 possible subnet masks, in all three formats.

Table A-4   All Subnet Masks

Decimal	Prefix	Binary
0.0.0.0	/0	00000000 00000000 00000000 00000000
128.0.0.0	/1	10000000 00000000 00000000 00000000
192.0.0.0	/2	11000000 00000000 00000000 00000000
224.0.0.0	/3	11100000 00000000 00000000 00000000
240.0.0.0	/4	11110000 00000000 00000000 00000000
248.0.0.0	/5	11111000 00000000 00000000 00000000
252.0.0.0	/6	11111100 00000000 00000000 00000000
254.0.0.0	/7	11111110 00000000 00000000 00000000
255.0.0.0	/8	11111111 00000000 00000000 00000000
255.128.0.0	/9	11111111 10000000 00000000 00000000
255.192.0.0	/10	11111111 11000000 00000000 00000000
255.224.0.0	/11	11111111 11100000 00000000 00000000
255.240.0.0	/12	11111111 11110000 00000000 00000000
255.248.0.0	/13	11111111 11111000 00000000 00000000
255.252.0.0	/14	11111111 11111100 00000000 00000000
255.254.0.0	/15	11111111 11111110 00000000 00000000
255.255.0.0	/16	11111111 11111111 00000000 00000000
255.255.128.0	/17	11111111 11111111 10000000 00000000
255.255.192.0	/18	11111111 11111111 11000000 00000000
255.255.224.0	/19	11111111 11111111 11100000 00000000
255.255.240.0	/20	11111111 11111111 11110000 00000000
255.255.248.0	/21	11111111 11111111 11111000 00000000
255.255.252.0	/22	11111111 11111111 11111100 00000000
255.255.254.0	/23	11111111 11111111 11111110 00000000
255.255.255.0	/24	11111111 11111111 11111111 00000000
255.255.255.128	/25	11111111 11111111 11111111 10000000
255.255.255.192	/26	11111111 11111111 11111111 11000000
255.255.255.224	/27	11111111 11111111 11111111 11100000
255.255.255.240	/28	11111111 11111111 11111111 11110000
255.255.255.248	/29	11111111 11111111 11111111 11111000
255.255.255.252	/30	11111111 11111111 11111111 11111100
255.255.255.254	/31	11111111 11111111 11111111 11111110
255.255.255.255	/32	11111111 11111111 11111111 11111111

Exam Topics Cross-Reference

This appendix lists the exam topics defined in the CCNA 200-301 exam blueprint version 1.1. Cisco lists the exam topics on its website. Even though changes to the exam topics are rare, you should always review those exam topics for any updates; check www.cisco.com/go/certifications and navigate to the correct exam.

Cisco organizes each list of exam topics by domains, which are major topic areas. Cisco states the percentage of the exam that should come from each exam, so you get some idea of the areas of importance. Traditionally, the score report you receive after taking the exam shows your percentage score in each domain.

This appendix includes two separate types of indices to exam topics:

- **CCNA 200-301 Version 1.1 Blueprint Order:** This section uses the same order as the CCNA 200-301 V1.1 exam blueprint document. This first list shows a cross-reference from each exam topic to the chapters that include at least some material about each topic.

- **Book Chapter Order:** This section lists the chapters in this book, along with the exam topics that the chapter includes. This section basically relists the kind of information found on the first page of each chapter, just in condensed form in one place.

CCNA 200-301 Exam Topic Order

The CCNA 200-301 exam includes six major topic areas (domains), each with a percentage listed. Table B-1 lists the domains and their percentages.

Table B-1   CCNA 200-301 Version 1.1 Exam Topic Domains

Domain	Percentage
Domain 1: Network Fundamentals	20%
Domain 2: Network Access	20%
Domain 3: IP Connectivity	25%
Domain 4: IP Services	10%
Domain 5: Security Fundamentals	15%
Domain 6: Automation and Programmability	10%

Tables B-2 through B-7 list the exam topics within each of the six domains. Note that the *CCNA 200-301 Official Cert Guide, Volume 1*, Second Edition, covers some of the exam topics, while this book covers the rest. These tables show the chapters in this book; look to the equivalent appendix in Volume 1 for details of exam topic coverage in that book.

Table B-2   CCNA 200-301 Version 1.1 Domain 1 (Network Fundamentals)

Exam Topic	Vol 1 Chapter(s)	Vol 2 Chapter(s)
1.1 Explain the role and function of network components	2, 3, 5, 7	1, 10, 18, 21, 22
1.1.a Routers	3, 16	
1.1.b Layer 2 and Layer 3 Switches	2, 5, 7, 18	
1.1.c Next-generation firewalls and IPS		10
1.1.d Access points		1
1.1.e Controllers		4, 22
1.1.f Endpoints		21
1.1.g Servers		21
1.1.h PoE		18
1.2 Describe characteristics of network topology architectures	2, 3	18–21
1.2.a Two-tier		18
1.2.b Three-tier		18
1.2.c Spine-leaf		21
1.2.d WAN	3	19
1.2.e Small office/home office (SOHO)	2, 16	18
1.2.f On-premises and cloud		20
1.3 Compare physical interface and cabling types	1, 2, 7	18
1.3.a Single-mode fiber, multimode fiber, copper	1, 2	18
1.3.b Connections (Ethernet shared media and point-to-point)	1, 2, 7	18
1.4 Identify interface and cable issues (collisions, errors, mismatch duplex, and/or speed)	7	
1.5 Compare TCP to UDP		5
1.6 Configure and verify IPv4 addressing and subnetting	6, 11–16, 18	
1.7 Describe private IPv4 addressing	11, 12, 17	14
1.8 Configure and verify IPv6 addressing and prefix	25–28	
1.9 Describe IPv6 address types	25–28	
1.9.a Unicast (global, unique local, and link local)	26–28	
1.9.b Anycast	26, 27	
1.9.c Multicast	27	
1.9.d Modified EUI 64	27, 28	
1.10 Verify IP parameters for Client OS (Windows, Mac OS, Linux)	19	

Exam Topic	Vol 1 Chapter(s)	Vol 2 Chapter(s)
1.11 Describe wireless principles		1, 3
1.11.a Nonoverlapping Wi-Fi channels		1
1.11.b SSID		1
111.c RF		1
1.11.d Encryption		3
1.12 Explain virtualization fundamentals (server virtualization, containers, and VRFs)		20
1.13 Describe switching concepts	5, 8	
1.13.a MAC learning and aging	5, 8	
1.13.b Frame switching	5, 8	
1.13.c Frame flooding	5, 8	
1.13.d MAC address table	5, 8	

Table B-3 CCNA 200-301 Version 1.1 Domain 2 (Network Access)

Exam Topic	Vol 1 Chapter(s)	Vol 2 Chapter(s)
2.1 Configure and verify VLANs (normal range) spanning multiple switches	8, 18	
2.1.a Access ports (data and voice)	8	
2.1.b Default VLAN	8	
2.1.c InterVLAN connectivity	8, 18	
2.2 Configure and verify interswitch connectivity	8	
2.2.a Trunk ports	8	
2.2.b 802.1Q	8	
2.2.c Native VLAN	8	
2.3 Configure and verify Layer 2 discovery protocols (Cisco Discovery Protocol and LLDP)		13
2.4 Configure and verify (Layer 2/Layer 3) EtherChannel (LACP)	8–10, 17	
2.5 Interpret basic operations of Spanning Tree Protocols	5, 9, 10	
2.5.a Root port, root bridge (primary/secondary), and other port names	9, 10	
2.5.b Port states and port roles	9, 10	
2.5.c PortFast	9, 10	
2.5.d Root Guard, loop guard, BPDU filter, BPDU guard	9, 10	
2.6 Describe Cisco Wireless Architectures and AP modes		2
2.7 Describe physical infrastructure connections of WLAN components (AP, WLC, access/trunk ports, and LAG)		4

Exam Topic	Vol 1 Chapter(s)	Vol 2 Chapter(s)
2.8 Describe network device management access (Telnet, SSH, HTTP, HTTPS, console, and TACACS+/RADIUS, and cloud managed)	4, 6, 20	4
2.9 Interpret the wireless LAN GUI configuration for client connectivity, such as WLAN creation, security settings, QoS profiles, and advanced settings		4

Table B-4 CCNA 200-301 Version 1.1 Domain 3 (IP Connectivity)

Exam Topic	Vol 1 Chapter(s)	Vol 2 Chapter(s)
3.1 Interpret the components of routing table	17, 29	
3.1.a Routing protocol code	17, 29	
3.1.b Prefix	17, 29	
3.1.c Network mask	17, 29	
3.1.d Next hop	17, 29	
3.1.e Administrative distance	17, 24, 29	
3.1.f Metric	17	
3.1.g Gateway of last resort	17	
3.2 Determine how a router makes a forwarding decision by default	17, 21–24	
3.2.a Longest prefix match	17, 24	
3.2.b Administrative distance	17, 21–24	
3.2.c Routing protocol metric	21–24	
3.3 Configure and verify IPv4 and IPv6 static routing	17, 20, 29	
3.3.a Default route	17, 20, 29	
3.3.b Network route	17, 20, 29	
3.3.c Host route	17, 20, 29	
3.3.d Floating static	17, 20, 29	
3.4 Configure and verify single area OSPFv2	21–24	
3.4.a Neighbor adjacencies	21–24	
3.4.b Point-to-point	21–24	
3.4.c Broadcast (DR/BDR selection)	21–24	
3.4.d Router ID	21–24	
3.5 Describe the purpose, functions, and concepts of first hop redundancy protocols		16

Table B-5 CCNA 200-301 Version 1.1 Domain 4 (IP Services)

Exam Topics	Vol 1 Chapter(s)	Vol 2 Chapter(s)
4.1 Configure and verify inside source NAT using static and pools		14
4.2 Configure and verify NTP operating in a client and server mode		13
4.3 Explain the role of DHCP and DNS within the network	19	5
4.4 Explain the function of SNMP in network operations		17
4.5 Describe the use of syslog features including facilities and severity levels		13
4.6 Configure and verify DHCP client and relay	6, 19	
4.7 Explain the forwarding per-hop behavior (PHB) for QoS such as classification, marking, queuing, congestion, policing, and shaping		15
4.8 Configure network devices for remote access using SSH	6	10
4.9 Describe the capabilities and functions of TFTP/FTP in the network		17

Table B-6 CCNA 200-301 Domain 5 Exam Topics (Security Fundamentals)

Exam Topics	Vol 1 Chapter(s)	Vol 2 Chapter(s)
5.1 Define key security concepts (threats, vulnerabilities, exploits, and mitigation techniques)		9
5.2 Describe security program elements (user awareness, training, and physical access control)		9
5.3 Configure and verify device access control using local passwords	6	10
5.4 Describe security password policies elements, such as management, complexity, and password alternatives (multifactor authentication, certificates, and biometrics)		9
5.5 Describe IPsec remote access and site-to-site VPNs		19
5.6 Configure and verify access control lists		6, 7, 8
5.7 Configure and verify Layer 2 security features (DHCP snooping, dynamic ARP inspection, and port security)		11, 12
5.8 Compare authentication, authorization, and accounting concepts		9
5.9 Describe wireless security protocols (WPA, WPA2, and WPA3)		3
5.10 Configure and verify WLAN within the GUI using WPA2 PSK		4

Table B-7   CCNA 200-301 Version 1.1 Domain 6 (Programmability and Automation)

Exam Topics	Vol 1 Chapter(s)	Vol 2 Chapter(s)
6.1 Explain how automation impacts network management		21, 22
6.2 Compare traditional networks with controller-based networking		21, 22
6.3 Describe controller-based, software-defined architecture (overlay, underlay, and fabric)		21, 22
6.3.a Separation of control plane and data plane		21, 22
6.3.b Northbound and Southbound APIs		21, 22
6.4 Explain AI (generative and predictive) and machine learning in network operations		22
6.5 Describe characteristics of REST-based APIs (authentication types, CRUD, HTTP verbs, and data encoding)		23
6.6 Recognize the capabilities of configuration management mechanisms such as Ansible and Terraform		24
6.7 Recognize components of JSON-encoded data		23

Book Chapters, with Exam Topics Covered in Each

Cisco organizes its exam topics based on the outcome of your learning experience, which is typically not a reasonable order for building the content of a book or course. This section lists this book's chapters in sequence, with the exam topics covered in each chapter.

Table B-8   CCNA 200-301 Volume 2 V1.1: Chapter-to-Exam Topic Mapping

Book Chapter	Exam Topics Covered
Part I: Wireless LANs	
Chapter 1: Fundamentals of Wireless Networks	**1.0 Network Fundamentals** 1.1 Explain the role and function of network components *1.1.d Access points* 1.11 Describe wireless principles *1.11.a Non-overlapping Wi-Fi channels* *1.11.b SSID* *1.11.c RF*
Chapter 2: Analyzing Cisco Wireless Architectures	**2.0 Network Access** 2.6 Describe Cisco Wireless Architectures and AP modes

Book Chapter	Exam Topics Covered
Chapter 3: Securing Wireless Networks	**1.0 Network Fundamentals** 1.11 Describe wireless principles *1.11.d Encryption* **5.0 Security Fundamentals** 5.9 Describe wireless security protocols (WPA, WPA2, and WPA3)
Chapter 4: Building a Wireless LAN	**1.0 Network Fundamentals** 1.1 Explain the role and function of network components *1.1.e Controllers (Cisco DNA Center and WLC)* **2.0 Network Access** 2.7 Describe physical infrastructure connections of WLAN components (AP, WLC, access/trunk ports, and LAG) 2.8 Describe network device management access (Telnet, SSH, HTTP, HTTPS, console, and TACACS+/RADIUS, and cloud managed) 2.9 Interpret the wireless LAN GUI configuration for client connectivity, such as WLAN creation, security settings, QoS profiles, and advanced WLAN settings **5.0 Security Fundamentals** 5.10 Configure and verify WLAN within the GUI using WPA2 PSK
Part II: IP Access Control Lists	
Chapter 5: Introduction to TCP/IP Transport and Applications	**1.0 Network Fundamentals** 1.5 Compare TCP to UDP **4.0 IP Services** 4.3 Explain the role of DHCP and DNS in the network
Chapter 6: Basic IPv4 Access Control Lists	**5.0 Security Fundamentals** 5.6 Configure and verify access control lists
Chapter 7: Named and Extended IP ACLs	**5.0 Security Fundamentals** 5.6 Configure and verify access control lists
Chapter 8: Applied IP ACLs	**5.0 Security Fundamentals** 5.6 Configure and verify access control lists

B

Book Chapter	Exam Topics Covered
Part III: Security Services	
Chapter 9: Security Architectures	**5.0 Security Fundamentals**
	5.1 Define key security concepts (threats, vulnerabilities, exploits, and mitigation techniques)
	5.2 Describe security program elements (user awareness, training, and physical access control)
	5.4 Describe security password policies elements, such as management, complexity, and password alternatives (multifactor authentication, certificates, and biometrics)
	5.8 Compare authentication, authorization, and accounting concepts
Chapter 10: Securing Network Devices	**1.0 Network Fundamentals**
	1.1 Explain the role and function of network components
	1.1.c Next-generation firewalls and IPS
	4.0 IP Services
	4.8 Configure network devices for remote access using SSH
	5.0 Security Fundamentals
	5.3 Configure and verify device access control using local passwords
Chapter 11: Implementing Switch Port Security	**5.0 Security Fundamentals**
	5.7 Configure and verify Layer 2 security features (DHCP snooping, dynamic ARP inspection, and port security)
Chapter 12: DHCP Snooping and ARP Inspection	**5.0 Security Fundamentals**
	5.7 Configure and verify Layer 2 security features (DHCP snooping, dynamic ARP inspection, and port security)
Part IV: IP Services	
Chapter 13: Device Management Protocols	**2.0 Network Access**
	2.3 Configure and verify Layer 2 discovery protocols (Cisco Discovery Protocol and LLDP)
	4.0 IP Services
	4.2 Configure and verify NTP operating in a client and server mode
	4.5 Describe the use of syslog features including facilities and severity levels

Book Chapter	Exam Topics Covered
Chapter 14: Network Address Translation	**1.0 Network Fundamentals** 1.7 Describe the need for private IPv4 addressing **4.0 IP Services** 4.1 Configure and verify inside source NAT using static and pools
Chapter 15: Quality of Service (QoS)	**4.0 IP Services** 4.7 Explain the forwarding per-hop behavior (PHB) for QoS such as classification, marking, queuing, congestion, policing, shaping
Chapter 16: First Hop Redundancy Protocols	**3.0 IP Connectivity** 3.5 Describe the purpose, functions, and concepts of first hop redundancy protocols
Chapter 17: SNMP, FTP, and TFTP	**4.0 Infrastructure Services** 4.4 Explain the function of SNMP in network operations 4.9 Describe the capabilities and functions of TFTP/FTP in the network
Part V: Network Architecture	
Chapter 18: LAN Architecture	**1.0 Network Fundamentals** 1.1 Explain the role and function of network components *1.1.b PoE* 1.2 Describe characteristics of network topology architectures *1.2.a Two-tier* *1.2.b Three-tier* *1.2.e Small office/home office (SOHO)* 1.3 Compare physical interface and cabling types *1.3.a Single-mode fiber, multimode fiber, copper*
Chapter 19: WAN Architecture	**1.0 Network Fundamentals** 1.2 Describe the characteristics of network topology architectures *1.2.d WAN* **5.0 Security Fundamentals** 5.5 Describe IPsec remote access and site-to-site VPNs

B

Book Chapter	Exam Topics Covered
Chapter 20: Cloud Architecture	**1.0 Network Fundamentals**
	1.1 Explain the role and function of network components
	1.1.g Servers
	1.2 Describe the characteristics of network topology architectures
	1.2.f On-premises and cloud
	1.12 Explain virtualization fundamentals (server virtualization, containers, and VRFs)
Part VI: Network Automation	
Chapter 21: Introduction to Controller-Based Networking	**1.0 Network Fundamentals**
	1.1 Explain the role and function of network components
	1.1.f Endpoints
	1.1.g Servers
	1.2 Describe characteristics of network topology architectures
	1.2.c Spine-leaf
	6.0 Automation and Programmability
	6.1 Explain how automation impacts network management
	6.2 Compare traditional networks with controller-based networking
	6.3 Describe controller-based, software-defined architecture (overlay, underlay, and fabric)
	6.3.a Separation of control plane and data plane
	6.3.b Northbound and Southbound APIs
Chapter 22: Cisco Software-Defined Access (Cisco SD-Access)	**1.0 Network Fundamentals**
	1.1 Explain the role and function of network components
	1.1.e Controllers
	6.0 Automation and Programmability
	6.1 Explain how automation impacts network management
	6.2 Compare traditional networks with controller-based networking
	6.3 Describe controller-based, software-defined architecture (overlay, underlay, and fabric)
	6.4 Explain AI (generative and predictive) and machine learning in network operations

Book Chapter	Exam Topics Covered
Chapter 23: Understanding REST and JSON	**6.0 Automation and Programmability** 6.5 Describe characteristics of REST-based APIs (authentication types, CRUD, HTTP verbs, and data encoding) 6.7 Recognize components of JSON-encoded data
Chapter 24: Understanding Ansible and Terraform	**6.0 Automation and Programmability** 6.6 Recognize the capabilities of configuration mechanisms such as Ansible and Terraform

B

Answers to the "Do I Know This Already?" Quizzes

Chapter 1

1. C. The IEEE 802.3 standard defines Ethernet, while 802.11 defines Wi-Fi.

2. B. WLANs require half-duplex operation because all stations must contend for use of a channel to transmit frames.

3. C. An AP offers a basic service set (BSS). BSA is incorrect because it is a basic service area, or the cell footprint of a BSS. BSD is incorrect because it does not pertain to wireless at all. IBSS is incorrect because it is an independent BSS, or an ad hoc network, where an AP or BSS is not needed at all.

4. B. The AP at the heart of a BSS or cell identifies itself (and the BSS) with a Basic Service Set Identifier (BSSID). It also uses an SSID to identify the wireless network, but that is not unique to the AP or BSS. Finally, the radio MAC address is used as the basis for the BSSID value, but the value can be altered to form the BSSID for each SSID that the AP supports. The Ethernet MAC address is usually unique, but it is associated with the wired portion of the AP and does not identify the AP and its BSS.

5. B. A workgroup bridge acts as a wireless client but bridges traffic to and from a wired device connected to it.

6. B. In a mesh network, each mesh AP builds a standalone BSS. The APs relay client traffic to each other over wireless backhaul links, rather than wired Ethernet. Therefore, Ethernet cabling to each AP is not required.

7. D and E. Wi-Fi commonly uses the 2.5- and 5-GHz bands.

8. C and D. In the 2.4-GHz band, consecutively numbered channels are too wide to not overlap. Only channels 1, 6, and 11 are spaced far enough apart to avoid overlapping each other. In the 5-GHz band, all channels are considered to be nonoverlapping. (Note that 5-GHz channels are numbered as multiples of four, which gives sufficient spacing to avoid overlap.)

Chapter 2

1. A. An autonomous AP can operate independently without the need for a centralized wireless LAN controller.

2. B. The Cisco Meraki APs are autonomous APs that are managed through a centralized platform in the Meraki cloud.

3. C. On a lightweight AP, the MAC function is divided between the AP hardware and the WLC. Therefore, the architecture is known as split-MAC.

4. B. An AP builds a CAPWAP tunnel with a WLC.

5. A. A trunk link carrying three VLANs is not needed at all. A Cisco AP in local mode needs only an access link with a single VLAN; everything else is carried over the CAP-WAP tunnel to a WLC. The WLC will need to be connected to three VLANs so that it can work with the AP to bind them to the three SSIDs.

6. C. A centralized WLC deployment model is based around locating the WLC in a central location, to support a very large number of APs.

7. A. The local mode is the default mode, where the AP provides at least one functional BSS that wireless clients can join to connect to the network. Normal and client modes are not valid modes. Monitor mode is used to turn the AP into a dedicated wireless sensor.

8. D. The SE-Connect mode is used for spectrum analysis. "SE" denotes the Cisco Spectrum Expert software. Otherwise, an AP can operate in only one mode at a time. The local mode is the default mode.

Chapter 3

1. D. For effective security, you should leverage authentication, MIC, and encryption.

2. C. A message integrity check (MIC) is an effective way to protect against data tampering. WIPS is not correct because it provides intrusion protection functions. WEP is not correct because it does not provide data integrity along with its weak encryption. EAP is not correct because it defines the framework for authentication.

3. D. WEP is known to have a number of weaknesses and has been compromised. Therefore, it has been officially deprecated and should not be used in a wireless network. AES is not a correct answer because it is the current recommended encryption method. WPA is not correct because it defines a suite of security methods. EAP is not correct because it defines a framework for authentication.

4. C. EAP works with 802.1x to authenticate a client and enable access for it. Open authentication and WEP cannot be correct because both define a specific authentication method. WPA is not correct because it defines a suite of security methods in addition to authentication.

5. A. The TKIP method was deprecated when the 802.11 standard was updated in 2012. CCMP and GCMP are still valid methods. EAP is an authentication framework and is not related to data encryption and integrity.

6. C. WPA2 uses CCMP only. WEP has been deprecated and is not used in any of the WPA versions. TKIP has been deprecated but can be used in WPA only. WPA is not a correct answer because it is an earlier version of WPA2.

7. B. The Wi-Fi Alliance offers the WPA, WPA2, and WPA3 certifications for wireless security. WEP, AES, and 802.11 are not certifications designed and awarded by the Wi-Fi Alliance.

8. A and C. The personal mode for WPA, WPA2, and WPA3 is used to require a pre-shared key authentication. Enterprise mode uses 802.1x instead.

Chapter 4

1. A. A Cisco AP requires connectivity to only a single VLAN so that it can build CAPWAP tunnels to a controller, so access mode is used.

2. B. An autonomous AP must connect to each of the VLANs it will extend to wireless LANs. Therefore, its link should be configured as a trunk.

3. D. You can use HTTP and HTTPS to access the GUI of a wireless LAN controller, as well as SSH to access its CLI. While HTTP is a valid management protocol on a WLC, it is usually disabled to make the WLC more secure.

4. C. Controllers use a link aggregation group (LAG) to bundle multiple ports together.

5. D. A dynamic interface makes a logical connection between a WLAN and a VLAN, all internal to the AireOS controller.

6. A and D. A WLAN binds a wireless SSID to a wired VLAN through an internal controller interface.

7. C. You can configure a maximum of 512 WLANs on a controller. However, a maximum of only 16 of them can be configured on an AP.

8. A and C. A WLAN profile and a Policy profile are the only items from the list that are necessary. A channel number is not because it is supplied automatically or by more advanced AP configuration. A BSSID is not because it is the address that identifies the BSS supplied by an AP. An IP subnet is used on the VLAN and WLAN that are bound, but not for WLAN configuration.

Chapter 5

1. D and E. Many headers include a field that identifies the next header that follows inside a message. Ethernet uses the Ethernet Type field, and the IP header uses the Protocol field. The TCP and UDP headers identify the application that should receive the data that follows the TCP or UDP header by using the port number field in the TCP and UDP headers, respectively.

2. A, B, C, and F. IP, not TCP, defines routing. Many other protocols define encryption, but TCP does not. The correct answers simply list various TCP features.

3. C. TCP, not UDP, performs windowing, error recovery, and ordered data transfer. Neither performs routing or encryption.

4. C and F. The terms *segment* and *L4PDU* refer to the header and data encapsulated by the transport layer protocol. The terms *packet* and *L3PDU* refer to the header plus data encapsulated by Layer 3. *Frame* and *L2PDU* refer to the header (and trailer), plus the data encapsulated by Layer 2.

5. B. Note that the hostname is all the text between the // and the /. The text before the // identifies the application layer protocol, and the text after the / represents the name of the web page.

6. C and D. Web traffic uses TCP as the transport protocol, with HTTP as the application protocol. As a result, the web server typically uses well-known TCP port 80, which is the well-known port for HTTP traffic. Messages flowing to the web server would have a destination TCP port of 80, and messages flowing from the server would have a source TCP port of 80.

Chapter 6

1. A and C. Standard ACLs check the source IP address. An ACL can match the address range 10.1.1.1–10.1.1.4, but it requires multiple **access-list** commands. Matching all hosts in Barney's subnet can be accomplished with the **access-list 1 permit 10.1.1.0 0.0.0.255** command.

2. A and D. The range of valid ACL numbers for standard numbered IP ACLs is 1–99 and 1300–1999, inclusive.

3. D. The 0.0.0.255 wildcard mask matches all packets that have the same first three octets as the address in the ACL command. This mask is useful when you want to match a subnet in which the subnet part comprises the first three octets, as would be the case with a 255.255.255.0 subnet mask.

4. E. The 0.0.15.255 wildcard mask matches all packets with the same first 20 bits. This mask is useful when you want to match a subnet in which the subnet part comprises the first 20 bits, as in a subnet that uses the 255.255.240.0 subnet mask.

5. A. The router always searches the ACL statements in order and stops after making a match. In other words, it uses first-match logic. A packet with source IP address 1.1.1.1 would match any of the three explicitly configured commands described in the question; however, the first statement will be used.

6. B. The correct answer matches the range of addresses 172.16.4.0–172.16.5.255, which is the range of addresses in the listed subnets. Using the **access-list** command, you can add the address and wildcard mask to get 172.16.5.255 (the ending number in the range).

    One wrong answer, with wildcard mask 0.0.255.0, matches all packets that begin with 172.16, with a 5 in the last octet. Another wrong answer matches only specific IP address 172.16.5.0. A third wrong answer uses a wildcard mask of 0.0.0.127, which matches addresses 172.16.5.0 through 172.16.5.127.

Chapter 7

1. C. Named standard ACLs begin with the **ip access-list standard** *name* global command. It moves the user into ACL configuration mode, which supports the configuration of **permit** and **deny** commands. Those commands match using the same options as numbered ACLs with the **access-list** global command. And while you enable the named ACL with an interface subcommand, the matching logic is configured in ACL configuration mode.

2. C. Two incorrect answers use incorrect syntax that begins with **permit** followed by a line number. The two answers that begin with a line number followed by **permit** use correct syntax.

    The question states that the named ACL was just created, with no line numbers used in that configuration. As a result, IOS assigns the three ACEs line numbers 10, 20, and 30, respectively. To insert another **permit** or **deny** command between the second and third ACEs, the new command must use a line number from 21 to 29 inclusive. Of the two syntactically correct answers, the correct answer uses a line number in the correct range.

3. E and F. Extended ACLs can look at the Layer 3 (IP) and Layer 4 (TCP, UDP) headers and a few others, but not any application layer information. Named extended ACLs can look for the same fields as numbered extended ACLs.

4. A and E. The correct range of ACL numbers for extended IP access lists is 100 to 199 and 2000 to 2699. The answers that list the **eq www** parameter after 10.1.1.1 match the source port number, and the packets go toward the web server, not away from it.

5. E. Because the packet is going toward any web client, you need to check for the web server's port number as a source port. The question does not specify client IP address ranges, but it does specify server address ranges; the source address beginning with 172.16.5 is the correct answer.

6. C. The question states that the output comes from a command in a router so that you can rely on the access control entries (ACEs) having correct syntax. You can also expect that for the address and wildcard pairs, the address represents the lowest number in a range, with the highest number found by adding the address and wildcard mask. For instance, 10.22.33.0 + 0.0.0.63, added octet by octet, gives you 10.22.33.63. That makes the question stem's 10.22.33.99 address not match the source address field in line 10, but it is within the source address range for lines 20 and 30 (10.22.33.0–10.22.33.127) and line 40 (10.22.33.0–10.22.33.255).

    Analyzing the destination address fields, all four ACL lines include destination address 10.33.22.22. The ranges include 10.33.22.0–10.33.22.127, 10.33.22.0–10.33.22.63, and 10.33.22.31.

    So far, that analysis rules out only line 10.

    Line 20 matches the source port, not the destination port, so its logic cannot match packets destined to an SSH server. SSH uses port 22, not 24, so the lines that use port number 24 (lines 20 and 40) cannot match SSH. Those facts rule out lines 20 and 40.

    Line 30 works because it matches the source and destination addresses per the question and also matches SSH as the destination port, port 22.

Chapter 8

1. E. The question lists a command that enables the ACL for outbound packets. Routers do not apply ACL logic to packets created by that router, so the OSPF messages sent by the router will not drive ACL matching and will not match an ACE, therefore not incrementing ACE matching counters. All the incorrect answers imply that the router applied the ACL to outgoing OSPF packets created by the router, which is not true.

2. A and E. The DHCP messages per this question use

    - UDP

    - Source address 172.16.2.1 (server S1)

    - Source UDP port 67 (bootps)

    - Destination IP address 172.16.1.1 (the address of the router R1 interface with the **ip helper-address** command configured)

Two answers use the **ip** protocol keyword, so those ACEs match all DHCP messages, which use IP and UDP. Of those two answers, the one correct answer also matches the source address of the server's 172.16.2.1 IP address along with matching any destination address. The incorrect answer reverses the source and destination address fields and would match packets sent to the server rather than those coming from the server.

Of the three ACEs that refer to the **udp** protocol keyword, one lists the wrong source port keyword (**bootpc**, which implies port 68, instead of keyword **bootps**, which implies port 67). Another ACE lists the incorrect destination IP address (0.0.0.0). The one correct answer among those three matches the UDP protocol source address 172.16.2.1, source port bootps, and any destination address.

3. A. IOS supports enabling a standard ACL to filter inbound attempts to Telnet and SSH into the router. The enabled standard ACL checks the source IP address of the incoming packets. However, because IOS applies the filters for packets that attempt to log in to the router, it uses a different command and mode to enable the ACL: the **access-class** *name/number* **in** command in vty mode as listed in the correct answer.

4. B. In this scenario, the packets have these important protocol facts:

   ■ Protocol: IP followed by TCP

   ■ Source addresses: Subnet 172.16.1.0/24

   ■ Source port: dynamic (above 49,151)

   ■ Destination address: 172.16.12.1

   ■ Destination port: 22 (SSH well-known port)

   Given these facts, the two ACEs that match with the **udp** keyword will not match the packets. Of the other two, both match the details listed above. IOS uses first-match logic when processing ACLs, so the router will match the packets with the ACE at line 20.

5. C. Cisco IOS has long supported one IP ACL, per interface, per direction (in or out). For example, the **ip access-group acl_01 out** and **ip access-group acl_02 in** commands can coexist on an interface. However, if at that point you also configured the **ip access-group acl_03 out** command, it would replace the **ip access-group 1 out** command as the only outbound IP ACL on the interface.

6. B. IOS supports a command to resequence an ACL's sequence numbers, defining the starting and increment numbers. Using 50 as the starting number, with 20 as the increment, will renumber the first four ACEs to 50, 70, 90, and 110. Of the three commands that use the term **resequence** and the parameters **50 20**, the correct answer is the only one with the correct syntax and mode. There is no **resequence** subcommand in ACL mode.

   The other two incorrect answers would change the ACL to use the correct sequence numbers but would require several more commands to accomplish the task rather than the single command needed for the correct answer.

Chapter 9

1. B. A vulnerability is a weakness that can be exploited. Attack is not correct because it is a threat that is taking place. The term *exploit* refers to a tool that can be used to exploit a specific vulnerability.

2. D. When a vulnerability can be exploited, a threat is possible.

3. A and B. Attackers usually spoof the source IP address in packets they send in order to disguise themselves and make the actual IP address owner into a victim of the attack. MAC addresses can also be spoofed in ARP replies to confuse other hosts and routers on the local network. Destination IP addresses are not normally spoofed because packets used in the attack would go to unknown or nonexistent hosts. Finally, ARP address is not correct because it is not a legitimate term.

4. D. A denial-of-service attack is likely occurring because the attacker is trying to exhaust the target's TCP connection table with embryonic or incomplete TCP connections.

5. C. In a reflection attack, the goal is to force one host (the reflector) to reflect the packets toward a victim. Therefore, the spoofed source address contains the address of the victim and not the reflector.

6. A and C. Once an attacker is in position in a man-in-the-middle attack, traffic between hosts can be passively inspected and actively modified. This type of attack does not lend itself to inducing buffer overflows or using sweeps and scans.

7. B. In a brute-force attack, an attacker's software tries every combination of letters, numbers, and special characters to eventually find a string that matches a user's password.

8. D. The Cisco ISE platform provides the AAA services needed for authentication, authorization, and accounting. DHCP does not perform AAA but leases IP addresses to hosts instead. DNS resolves hostnames to IP addresses. SNMP is used for network management functions.

9. C. Physical access control is a necessary element of a security program that keeps sensitive locations like data centers and network closets locked and inaccessible, except to authorized personnel.

Chapter 10

1. B. If both commands are configured, IOS accepts only the password as configured in the **enable secret** command

2. A. The **service password-encryption** command encrypts passwords on a router or switch that would otherwise be shown in clear text. While a great idea in concept, the algorithm can be easily broken using websites found on the Internet. Cisco long ago provided replacements for commands that store passwords as clear text, instead using hashes—commands like **enable secret** and **username secret**. These commands are preferred in part because they avoid the issues of clear-text passwords and easily decrypted passwords.

3. B. The **enable secret** command stores an MD5 hash of the password. It is unaffected by the **service password-encryption** command. The router does not unhash the value back to the clear-text password. Instead, when the user types a clear-text password, the router also hashes that password and compares that hashed value with the hashed value as listed in the configuration.

4. B. The **username secret** command in the question stem shows a type of 8. Type 8 refers to the SHA256 hash type, configured with the **algorithm-type sha256** parameters. The other incorrect answers mention type 9 (Scrypt) and type 5 (MD5). Also, the one answer that omits the algorithm type has a different default based on whether using IOS (MD5) or IOS XE (Scrypt). So that answer would result in either type 5 or type 9, but not type 8.

5. B. Traditional and next-generation firewalls can check TCP and UDP port numbers, but next-generation firewalls are generally characterized as being able to also check application data beyond the Transport layer header. An NGFW would look into the application data, identifying messages that contain data structures used by Telnet, instead of matching with port numbers. This matching can catch attacks that seek to use port numbers that the firewall allows while using those ports to send data from applications that do not normally use those ports.

For the other answers, a traditional firewall would likely match based on destination port 23, which is the well-known port for Telnet. IP protocol number has nothing to do with Telnet.

6. A and D. Both traditional and next-generation IPSs (NGIPSs) use a signature database, with each signature listing details of what fields would be in a series of messages to identify those messages as part of some exploit. They both also generate events for review by the security team.

NGIPS devices add features that go beyond using a signature database, including gathering contextual information from hosts, like the OS used, currently running apps, open ports, and so on, so that the NGIPS does not have to log events if the hosts could not possibly be affected. Additionally, an NGIPS can use a list of reputation scores about IP addresses, domain names, and URIs of known bad actors, filtering traffic for sources that have a configured poor reputation level.

Chapter 11

1. B. The setting for the maximum number of MAC addresses has a default of 1, so the **switchport port-security maximum** command does not have to be configured. With sticky learning, you do not need to predefine the specific MAC addresses either. However, you must enable port security, which requires the **switchport port-security** interface subcommand.

2. B and D. First, about the sticky parameter: this command causes the switch to learn the source MAC and to add it to a **switchport port-security mac-address** *address* interface subcommand. However, port security adds that command to the running-config file; the network engineer must also issue a **copy running-config startup-config** EXEC command to save that configuration.

About the other correct answer, users can connect a switch to the end of the cable, with multiple devices connected to that switch. That happens in real networks when users decide they need more ports at their desk. However, the default setting of **switchport port-security maximum 1** means that a frame from the second unique source MAC address would cause a violation, and with the default violation action, to err-disable the port.

For the other incorrect answer, the configuration does not prevent unknown MAC addresses from accessing the port because the configuration does not predefine any MAC address.

3. B and C. IOS adds MAC addresses configured by the port security feature as static MAC addresses, so they do not show up in the output of the **show mac address-table dynamic** command. **show mac address-table port-security** is not a valid command.

4. B. The question states that the port security status is secure-shutdown. This state is used only by the shutdown port security mode, and when used, it means that the interface has been placed into an err-disabled state. Those facts explain why the correct answer is correct, and two of the incorrect answers are incorrect.

    The incorrect answer that mentions the violation counter is incorrect because in shut-down mode, the violation counter no longer increments after the switch places the interface into secure-shutdown mode.

5. B and C. First, about the two incorrect answers: In restrict mode, the arrival of a frame that violates the port security policy does not cause the switch to put the interface into err-disabled state. It does cause the switch to discard any frames that violate the policy, but it leaves the interface up and does not discard frames that do not violate the security policy, like the second frame that arrives.

    Regarding the two correct answers, a port in port security restrict does cause the switch to issue log messages for a violating frame, send SNMP traps about that same event (if SNMP is configured), and increment the counter of violating frames.

Chapter 12

1. A and C. DHCP Snooping must be implemented on a device that performs Layer 2 switching. The DHCP Snooping function needs to examine DHCP messages that flow between devices within the same broadcast domain (VLAN). Layer 2 switches, as well as multilayer switches, perform that function. Because a router performs only Layer 3 forwarding (that is, routing) and does not forward messages between devices in the same VLAN, a router does not provide a good platform to implement DHCP Snooping (and is not even a feature of Cisco IOS on routers). End-user devices would be a poor choice as a platform for DHCP Snooping because they would not receive all the DHCP messages, nor would they be able to prevent frames from flowing should an attack occur.

2. B and C. Switch ports connected to IT-controlled devices from which DHCP server messages may be received should be trusted by the DHCP Snooping function. Those devices include IT-controlled DHCP servers and IT-controlled routers and switches. All devices that are expected to be DHCP client devices (like PCs) are then treated as untrusted, because DHCP Snooping cannot know beforehand from which ports a DHCP-based attack will be launched. In this case, the ports connected to all three PCs will be treated as untrusted by DHCP Snooping.

C

3. C and D. Because of a default setting of untrusted, the switch does not need any configuration commands to cause a port to be untrusted. Of the two (incorrect) answers that relate to the trust state, **no ip dhcp snooping trust**, in interface config mode, would revert from a trust configuration state to an untrusted state. The other answer, **ip dhcp snooping untrusted**, is not a valid command.

The two correct answers list a pair of configuration commands that both must be included to enable DHCP Snooping (**ip dhcp snooping**) and to specify the VLAN list on which DHCP Snooping should operate (**ip dhcp snooping vlan 5**).

4. A. All the answers list commands with correct syntax that are useful for DHCP Snooping. However, the correct answer, **no ip dhcp snooping information option**, disables DHCP Snooping's feature of adding DHCP Option 82 fields to DHCP messages. This setting is useful if the switch does not act as a DHCP relay agent. The opposite setting (without the **no** to begin the command) works when the multilayer switch acts as a DHCP relay agent.

5. B. DAI always uses a core function that examines incoming ARP messages, specifically the ARP message sender hardware and sender IP address fields, versus tables of data in the switch about correct pairs of MAC and IP addresses. DAI on a switch can use DHCP Snooping's binding table as the table of data with valid MAC/IP address pairs, or use the logic in configured ARP ACLs. The question stem states that DAI uses DHCP Snooping, so the correct answer notes that the switch will compare the ARP message's sender hardware address to the switch's DHCP Snooping binding table.

One incorrect answer mentions a comparison of the message's ARP sender MAC (hardware) address with the message's Ethernet source MAC address. DAI can perform that check, but that feature can be configured to be enabled or disabled, so DAI would not always perform this comparison. The other incorrect answers list logic never performed by DAI.

6. B and D. Because of a default setting of untrusted, the switch must be configured so DAI trusts that one port. To add that configuration, the switch needs the **ip arp inspection trust** command in interface config mode. The similar (incorrect) answer of **no ip arp inspection untrust** is not a valid command.

To enable DAI for operation on a VLAN, the configuration needs one command: the **ip arp inspection vlan 6** command. This command both enables DAI and does so specifically for VLAN 6 alone. The answer **ip arp inspection** shows a command that would be rejected by the switch as needing more parameters.

7. C and D. With DAI, you can set a limit on the number of received ARP messages with a default burst interval of 1 second, or you can configure the burst interval. Once configured, DAI allows the configured number of ARP messages over the burst interval number of seconds. With the two correct answers, one shows 16 ARP messages, with a 4-second interval, for an average of 4 per second. The other correct answer shows a limit of 4, with the default burst interval of 1 second, for an average of 4. The two incorrect answers result in averages of 2 per second and 5 per second.

Chapter 13

1. D. By default, all message levels are logged to the console on a Cisco device. To do so, IOS uses logging level 7 (debugging), which causes IOS to send severity level 7, and levels below 7, to the console. All the incorrect answers list levels below level 7.

2. C. The **logging trap 4** command limits those messages sent to a syslog server (configured with the **logging host** *ip-address* command) to levels 4 and below, thus 0 through 4.

3. A. NTP uses protocol messages between clients and servers so that the clients can adjust their time-of-day clock to match the server. NTP is totally unrelated to interface speeds for Ethernet and serial interfaces. It also does not count CPU cycles, instead relying on messages from the NTP server. Also, the client defines the IP address of the server and does not have to be in the same subnet.

4. C. The **ntp server 10.1.1.1** command tells the router to be both an NTP server and client. However, the router first acts as an NTP client to synchronize its time with NTP server 10.1.1.1. Once synchronized, R1 knows the time to supply and can act as an NTP server.

5. E and F. CDP discovers information about neighbors. The **show cdp command** gives you several options that display more or less information, depending on the parameters used.

6. E and F. LLDP lists the neighbors' enabled capabilities in the output of the **show lldp neighbors** command, and both the enabled and possible (system) capabilities in the output of the **show lldp entry** *hostname* command.

Chapter 14

1. B and E. RFC 1918 identifies private network numbers. It includes Class A network 10.0.0.0, Class B networks 172.16.0.0 through 172.31.0.0, and Class C networks 192.168.0.0 through 192.168.255.0.

2. C. With static NAT for source addresses (inside source NAT), the NAT router uses static entries defined by the **ip nat inside source** command. Because the question mentions translation for inside addresses, the command needs the **inside** keyword. Other NAT features not discussed in the chapter use the **outside** keyword.

As for the other two answers, they both suggest triggering dynamic NAT table entries, which do not occur with static NAT.

3. A. With dynamic NAT, the entries are created due to the first packet flow from the inside network. Packets entering an outside interface do not trigger the creation of a NAT table entry. Dynamic NAT does not predefine NAT table entries, so the two answers that list configuration commands are incorrect.

4. A. The **ip nat inside source list alice pool barney** command enables inside source NAT. That means the router monitors packets that enter interfaces enabled for NAT with the **ip nat inside** interface subcommand. The router must also match and permit the packet with the referenced ACL (in this case, Alice) to trigger the translation. Those facts support the one correct answer.

One incorrect answer suggests that the ACL should deny packets instead of permitting them to trigger NAT. Instead, the ACL should permit the packet.

Two incorrect answers mention the NAT pool. When performing NAT and changing the source address, NAT uses an address from a defined pool (in this case, Barney). The packet that arrives in the inside interface does not list an address from the NAT pool at that point (before translation by NAT). Instead, the NAT pool includes public IP addresses representing the inside host. Those public addresses do not need to match anything in the NAT configuration.

5. A and C. The configuration lacks the **overload** keyword in the **ip nat inside source** command. Without this keyword, the router would perform dynamic NAT but not PAT, so it could not support more than one TCP or UDP connection or flow per inside global IP address. Also, each NAT outside interface needs the **ip nat outside** interface subcommand. The configuration lists interface G0/0/1 as its link connected to the Internet, with a public address, and it is missing this configuration command.

6. B. Regarding the correct answer: The last line in the output mentions that the pool has seven addresses, with all seven allocated, with the misses counter close to 1000—meaning that the router rejected roughly 1000 new flows because of insufficient space in the NAT pool. For the incorrect answers, NAT allows standard and extended ACLs, so NAT can use standard ACL 1. You can rule out the other two incorrect answers because the root cause, per the correct answer, can be found in the command output.

Chapter 15

1. A, B, and E. QoS tools manage bandwidth, delay, jitter, and loss.

2. B and C. The IP Precedence (IPP) and Differentiated Services Code Point (DSCP) fields exist in the IP header and would flow from source host to destination host. The Class of Service (CoS) field exists in the 802.1Q header, so it would be used only on trunks, and it would be stripped of the incoming data-link header by any router in the path. The MPLS EXP bits exist as the packet crosses the MPLS network only.

3. A, B, and C. In general, matching a packet with DiffServ relies on a comparison to something inside the message itself. The 802.1p CoS field exists in the data-link header on VLAN trunks; the IP DSCP field exists in the IP header; and extended ACLs check fields in message headers. The SNMP Location variable does not flow inside individual packets but is a value that can be requested from a device.

4. B and C. Low Latency Queuing (LLQ) applies priority queue scheduling, always taking the next packet from the LLQ if a packet is in that queue. To prevent queue starvation of the other queues, IOS also applies policing to the LLQ. However, applying shaping to an LLQ slows the traffic, which makes no sense with the presence of a policing function already. The answer that refers to round-robin scheduling is incorrect because LLQ instead uses priority queue scheduling.

5. A and D. With a shaper enabled on R1 at a rate of 200 Mbps while R1 attempts to send 300 Mbps out that interface, R1 begins queuing packets. R1 then allows data transmission, so the transmission rate is 200 Mbps over time.

As for the policing function on ISP1, with a configured rate of 250 Mbps, the policer will measure the rate and see that the incoming rate (200 Mbps because of R1's shaping) does not exceed the policing rate.

6. C and D. Drop management relies on the behavior of TCP, in that TCP connections slow down sending packets due to the TCP congestion window calculation. Voice traffic uses UDP, and the question states that queue 1 uses UDP. So, queues 2 and 3 are reasonable candidates for using a congestion management tool.

Chapter 16

1. D. With this design but no FHRP, host A can send packets off-subnet as long as connectivity exists from host A to R1. Similarly, host B can send packets off-subnet as long as host B has connectivity to router R2. Both routers can attach to the same LAN subnet and ignore each other concerning their roles as default routers because they do not use an FHRP option. When either router fails, the hosts using the failed router as the default router have no means to fail over.

2. C. The use of an FHRP in this design purposefully allows either router to fail and still support off-subnet traffic from all hosts in the subnet. Both routers can attach to the same LAN subnet per IPv4 addressing rules.

3. C. HSRP uses a virtual IP address. The virtual IP address comes from the same subnet as the routers' LAN interfaces but is a different IP address than the router addresses configured with the **ip address** interface subcommand. As a result, the hosts will not point to 10.1.19.1 or 10.1.19.2 as their default gateway in this design. The other wrong answer lists an idea of using the Domain Name System (DNS) to direct hosts to the right default router. Although an interesting idea, it is not a part of any of the three FHRP protocols.

4. B. Two answers mention load balancing the traffic hosts send in the subnet. Those hosts send traffic based on their default router setting, with HSRP creating redundancy for that function across routers R1, R2, and R3. HSRP provides active/standby load balancing, so all traffic flows through the currently active router (R2). Those facts identify one correct and one incorrect answer.

   As for the answer about ARP Requests, only the active router replies to the ARP Request. The standby routers sit silently, other than sending HSRP messages in anticipation of taking over as active one day.

   As for the answer about the virtual MAC, the end of the virtual MAC uses the three-digit hex equivalent of the decimal HSRP group number. The question lists a decimal HSRP group number of 16. Converted to hex, that gives you 10, or as a three-digit hex number, 010. So the correct virtual MAC address, 0000.0C9F.F010, ends in 010, not 016.

5. A and C. The answers to this question come in pairs, with one correct and one incorrect. In one pair, the answers ask if the VIP (virtual IP address) may be 10.1.1.3 or if it must be 10.1.1.3. R3's IP address, per the question stem, is 10.1.1.3. VRRP allows use of an interface IP address as the VIP but does not require it. (Note that HSRP and GLBP do not allow the use of an interface IP address as the VIP.) So, the answer stating that the VIP may be 10.1.1.3 is correct.

The pair of answers mentioning the multicast address used by VRRP requires you to recall the address. VRRP uses 224.0.0.18 (the correct answer), HSRPv1 uses 224.0.0.2 (the incorrect answer), and HSRPv2 uses 224.0.0.102.

6. D. GLBP makes each router in the group active, meaning each can act as the default router by using a unique GLBP virtual MAC address per router. All endpoint hosts have the same default router setting as normal. One GLBP router (the AVG) sends an ARP Reply in reaction to ARP Requests for the VIP IP address. The AVG's ARP Reply messages list different routers' virtual MAC addresses so that some hosts forward packets to one router and some to others.

As for the incorrect answers, the answer about using a different VIP per router in the same group is not allowed. Also, using a separate GLBP group per router means that the routers are not providing redundancy to each other.

Finally, one incorrect answer suggests using a VIP that is the same as one of the routers' interface IP addresses, which is not allowed with GLBP.

Chapter 17

1. B. SNMPv1 and SNMPv2c use community strings to authenticate Get and Set messages from an NMS. The agent defines a read-only community and can define a read-write community as well. Get requests, which read information, will be accepted if the NMS sends either the read-only or the read-write community with those requests.

2. A and C. SNMP agents reside on a device being managed. When an event happens about which the device wants to inform the SNMP manager, the agent sends either an SNMP Trap or SNMP Inform to the SNMP manager. The SNMP manager normally sends an SNMP Get Request message to an agent to retrieve MIB variables or an SNMP Set Request to change an MIB variable on the agent. The agent responds with a Get Reply message.

3. A. GetNext allows for an improvement in efficiency for retrieving lists of MIB variables. However, SNMP Version 1 defines Get and GetNext, making both answers incorrect. GetBulk, which further improves efficiency of retrieving lists of variables, was added with SNMP Version 2, making that answer correct. Inform, also defined by SNMP Version 2, does not retrieve MIB variable data.

4. A. FTP uses both a control connection and a data connection. The FTP client initiates the control connection. However, in active mode, the FTP server initiates the data connection.

5. B and D. TFTP supports fewer functions than FTP as a protocol. For instance, the client cannot change the current directory on the server, add directories, remove directories, or list the files in the directory. Both TFTP and FTP support the ability to transfer files in either direction.

6. B and C. The **show** *filesystem***:** EXEC command lists all files in the filesystem, whether in the root directory of the filesystem or in subdirectories. It returns a potentially long list of file and directory names. The **dir** EXEC command lists the files and directories in the filesystem and directory per the present working directory (**pwd**) command. In this case, it is set to the root of the file system, bootflash:. As a result, the **dir** command lists all files in the root of the file system, and directory names, but not files held within those directories.

Chapter 18

1. B and D. The access layer switches connect to the endpoint devices, whether end-user devices or servers. Then, from the access to the distribution layer, each access layer connects to two distribution switches typically, but with no direct connections between access layer switches, creating a mesh (but a partial mesh). A two-tier design, called a collapsed core, does not use core switches.

2. A and C. The access layer switches, not the distribution layer switches, connect to the endpoint devices, whether end-user devices or servers. Then, from the access to the distribution layer, each access layer connects to two distribution switches typically, but with no direct connections between access layer switches, creating a mesh (but a partial mesh). A three-tier design, also called a core design, does use core switches, with a partial mesh of links between the distribution and core switches. Each distribution switch connects to multiple core switches but often does not connect directly to other distribution switches.

3. D. The access layer uses access switches, which connect to endpoint devices. A single access switch with its endpoint devices looks like a star topology, with a centralized node connected to each other node.

   A full mesh connects each node to every other node, with a partial mesh being any subset of a full mesh. Hybrid topologies refer to more complex topologies, including subsets that use a star, full mesh, or partial mesh design.

4. B and C. The three answers with *CAT* refer to UTP cabling standards defined by TIA and ANSI. The answers with *OM*, meaning Optical Multimode, refer to ISO standards for multimode fiber. The question asks about 1000BASE-T, a standard that calls for UTP cabling, making the two answers that begin with *OM* incorrect.

   Of the three answers that begin with *CAT*, the 1000BASE-T standard requires CAT 5E cable quality, or better, to support distances up to 100 meters. That makes CAT 5E and CAT 6 correct among the available answers.

5. A and C. With a SOHO LAN, one integrated device typically supplies all the necessary functions, including routing, switching, wireless access point (AP), and firewall. The AP uses standalone mode, without a wireless LAN controller (WLC), and without a need to encapsulate frames in CAPWAP.

6. A. PoE switch ports begin with power detection (PD) to determine whether the attached device needs to receive power. The question stem tells us that the power detection process has been completed, and the device needs power.

   The PoE switch port begins power classification, first with a Layer 1 process, followed by a Layer 2 process, which dictates how much power the switch supplies. The first phase, the Layer 1 process, has the switch supply a standard low-voltage signal (which identifies the correct answer). It can then use CDP or LLDP messages to classify the power further, often after the device has powered up with enough function to reply to CDP/LLDP messages. The switch does not apply power based on any configured setting until after completing the Layer 1 power detection phase.

7. B and D. Universal Power over Ethernet (UPoE) and the enhanced UPoE Plus (UPoE+) supply power over all four cable pairs. Note that 1000BASE-T and faster UTP-based Ethernet standards often require four pairs, whereas earlier/slower standards did not,

and UPoE/UPoE+ take advantage of the existence of four pairs to supply power over all four pairs. Power over Ethernet (PoE) and PoE+ use two pairs for power and therefore work with Ethernet standards like 10BASE-T and 100BASE-T that use two pairs only.

Chapter 19

1. B and C. A Metro Ethernet E-Tree service uses a rooted point-to-multipoint Ethernet Virtual Connection (EVC), which means that one site connected to the service (the root) can communicate directly with each of the remote (leaf) sites. However, the leaf sites cannot send frames directly to each other; they can only send frames to the root site. Topology designs that allow a subset of all pairs in the group to communicate directly are called a partial mesh, or hub and spoke, or in some cases, a multipoint or point-to-multipoint topology.

    Of the incorrect answers, the *full mesh* term refers to topology designs in which each pair in the group can send data directly to each other, which is typical of a MetroE E-LAN service. The term *point-to-point* refers to topologies with only two nodes in the design, and they can send directly to each other, typical of a MetroE E-Line service.

2. A. Metro Ethernet uses Ethernet access links of various types. Time-division multiplexing (TDM) links, such as serial links, and even higher-speed links like T3 and E3, do not use Ethernet protocols and are less likely to be used. MPLS is a WAN technology that creates a Layer 3 service.

    Two answers refer to Ethernet standards usable as the physical access link for a Metro Ethernet service. However, 100BASE-T supports cable lengths of only 100 meters, so it is less likely to be used as a Metro Ethernet access link than 100BASE-LX10, which supports lengths of 10 km.

3. A and D. An E-LAN service is one in which the Metro Ethernet service acts as if the WAN were a single Ethernet switch so that each device can communicate directly with every other device. As a result, the routers sit in the same subnet. With one headquarters router and ten remote sites, each router will have ten OSPF neighbors.

4. B and C. A Layer 3 MPLS VPN creates an IP service with a different subnet on each access link. With one headquarters router and 10 remote sites, 11 access links exist, so 11 subnets are used.

    Each enterprise (CE) router has an OSPF neighbor relationship with the MPLS provider edge (PE) router, but the CE routers do not have OSPF neighbor relationships. As a result, each remote site router would have only one OSPF neighbor relationship.

5. D. Architecturally, MPLS allows for a wide variety of access technologies. They include TDM (serial links), Frame Relay, ATM, Metro Ethernet, and traditional Internet access technologies such as DSL and cable.

6. A and B. The term *remote access VPN* refers to a VPN for which one endpoint is a user device, such as a phone, tablet, or PC, with the other as a VPN concentrator, often a firewall or router. The VPN concentrator configuration dictates the protocol the VPN client should use, typically either TLS or IPsec.

Of the incorrect answers, site-to-site VPNs use GRE along with IPsec. FTPS refers to FTP Secure, which uses TLS to secure FTP sessions.

Chapter 20

1. A, B, and E. The hypervisor will virtualize each VM's RAM, CPU, NICs, and storage. The hypervisor itself is not virtualized but rather does the work of virtualizing other resources. Also, as virtual machines, the VMs do not use power, so the system does not have a concept of virtualized power.

2. D. Hypervisors create a virtual equivalent of Ethernet switching and cabling between the VMs and the physical NICs. The VMs use a virtual NIC (vNIC). The hypervisor uses a virtual switch (vSwitch), which includes the concept of a link between a vSwitch port and each VM's vNIC. The vSwitch also connects to both physical NICs. The switch configuration creates VLANs and trunks as needed.

3. B. Platform as a Service (PaaS) supplies one or more virtual machines (VMs) that have a working operating system (OS) as well as a predefined set of software development tools.

    As for the wrong answers, Software as a Service (SaaS) supplies a predefined software application but typically cannot install your applications later. Infrastructure as a Service (IaaS) delivers one or more working VMs, optionally with an OS installed. It could be used for software development, but the developer would have to install a variety of development tools, making IaaS less useful for development than a PaaS service. Finally, cloud services offer Server Load Balancing as a Service (SLBaaS). Still, it is not a general service in which customers get access to VMs to install their applications.

4. A. Infrastructure as a Service (IaaS) supplies one or more working virtual machines (VMs), optionally with an OS installed, where you can customize the systems by installing your own applications.

    Software as a Service (SaaS) supplies a predefined software application, but typically you cannot install your own applications later. Platform as a Service (PaaS) allows you to install your application because PaaS does supply one or more VMs. However, PaaS acts as a software development environment, with VMs that include various useful tools for software development. Finally, cloud services offer Server Load Balancing as a Service (SLBaaS). Still, it is not a general service in which customers get access to VMs to install their applications.

5. A. Both Internet options allow for easier migration because public cloud providers typically provide easy access over the Internet. An intercloud exchange is a purpose-built WAN service connecting enterprises and most public cloud providers, making the migration process more manageable.

    The one correct answer—the one that creates the most migration problems—is to use a private WAN connection to one cloud provider. While useful in other ways, migrating using this strategy would require installing a new private WAN connection to the new cloud provider.

6. A and C. Private WAN options use technologies like Ethernet WAN and MPLS, which keep data private and include QoS services. An intercloud exchange is a purpose-built

WAN service that connects enterprises and most public cloud providers using the same kinds of private WAN technology with those same benefits.

For the two incorrect answers, both use the Internet, so both cannot provide QoS services. The Internet VPN option does encrypt the data to keep it private.

Chapter 21

1. A. The *data plane* includes all networking device actions related to the receipt, processing, and forwarding of each message, as in the case described in the question. The term *table plane* is not used in networking. The *management plane* and *control plane* are not concerned with the per-message forwarding actions.

2. C. The *control plane* includes all networking device actions that create the information used by the data plane when processing messages. The control plane includes functions like IP routing protocols and Spanning Tree Protocol (STP).

    The term *table plane* is not used in networking. The *management plane* and *data plane* are not concerned with collecting the information that the data plane then uses.

3. C. Although many variations of SDN architectures exist, they typically use a centralized controller. That controller may centralize some or even all control plane functions in the controller. However, the data plane function of receiving messages, matching them based on header fields, taking actions (like making a forwarding decision), and forwarding the message still happens on the network elements (switches) and not on the controller.

    For the incorrect answers, the control plane functions may all happen on the controller, or some may happen on the controller, and some on the switches. The northbound and southbound interfaces are API interfaces on the controller, not on the switches.

4. A. The OpenDaylight Controller uses an Open SDN model with an OpenFlow southbound interface as defined by the Open Networking Foundation (ONF). The ONF SDN model centralizes most control plane functions. The APIC model for data centers partially centralizes control plane functions. The Cisco 9800 Series controller runs a distributed control plane.

5. C and D. ACI uses a spine-leaf topology. With a single-site topology, leaf switches must connect to all spine switches, and leaf switches must not connect to other leaf switches. Additionally, a leaf switch connects to some endpoints, with the endpoints being spread across the ports on all the leaf switches. (In some designs, two or more leaf switches connect to the same endpoints for redundancy and more capacity.)

6. A and D. Controller-based networks use a controller that communicates with each network device using a southbound interface (an API and protocol). By gathering network information into one central device, the controller can then allow for different operational models. The models often let the operator think in terms of enabling features in the network, rather than thinking about the particulars of each device and command on each device. The controller then configures the specific commands, resulting in more consistent device configuration.

    For the incorrect answers, both the old and new models use forwarding tables on each device. Also, controllers do not add to or remove from the programmatic interfaces on each device, some of which existed before controllers, but rather supply useful and powerful northbound APIs.

Chapter 22

1. C. The Cisco SD-Access underlay consists of the network devices and connections, along with configuration that allows IP connectivity between the Cisco SD-Access nodes, for the purpose of supporting overlay VXLAN tunnels. The fabric includes both the underlay and overlay, while VXLAN refers to the protocol used to create the tunnels used by the overlay.

2. B. The overlay includes the control plane and data plane features to locate the endpoints, decide to which fabric node a VXLAN tunnel should connect, direct the frames into the tunnel, and perform VXLAN tunnel encapsulation and de-encapsulation. The Cisco SD-Access underlay exists as network devices, links, and a separate IP network to provide connectivity between nodes to support the VXLAN tunnels.

   The fabric includes both the underlay and overlay, while VXLAN refers to the protocol used to create the tunnels used by the overlay.

3. D. The Cisco SD-Access overlay creates VXLAN tunnels between fabric edge nodes. Edge nodes then create a data plane by forwarding frames sent by endpoints over the VXLAN tunnels. LISP plays a role in the overlay as the control plane, which learns the identifiers of each endpoint, matching the endpoint to the fabric node that can teach the endpoint, so that the overlay knows where to create VXLAN tunnels.

   For the other incorrect answers, note that while GRE is a tunneling protocol, Cisco SD-Access uses VXLAN for tunneling, and not GRE. Finally, OSPF acts as a control plane routing protocol, rather than a data plane protocol for Cisco SD-Access.

4. A and D. As with any Cisco SD-Access feature, the configuration model is to configure the feature using Cisco Catalyst Center, with Cisco Catalyst Center using southbound APIs to communicate the intent to the devices. The methods to configure the feature using Cisco Catalyst Center include using the GUI or using the northbound REST-based API.

   Of the incorrect answers, you would not normally configure any of the Cisco SD-Access devices directly. Also, while Cisco Catalyst Center can use NETCONF as a southbound protocol to communicate with the Cisco SD-Access fabric nodes, it does not use NETCONF as a northbound API for configuration of features.

5. B, C, and D. Cisco Catalyst Center manages traditional network devices with traditional protocols like Telnet, SSH, and SNMP. Cisco Catalyst Center can also use NETCONF and RESTCONF if supported by the device. Note that while useful tools, Ansible and Puppet are not used by Cisco Catalyst Center.

6. A and D. Traditional network management platforms can do a large number of functions related to managing traditional networks and network devices, including the items listed in the two correct answers. However, when using Cisco's Prime Infrastructure as a traditional network management platform for comparison, it does not support Cisco SD-Access configuration, nor does it find the end-to-end path between two endpoints and analyze the ACLs in the path. Note that the two incorrect answers reference features available in Cisco Catalyst Center.

7.   B. Narrow AI is designed for specific tasks, while Generative AI has the capability to learn, make decisions, and potentially mimic human cognition through experiences.

Chapter 23

1.   B and D. The six primary required features of REST-based APIs include three features mentioned in the answers: a client/server architecture, stateless operation, and notation of whether each object is cacheable. Two items from these three REST attributes are the correct answers. Of the incorrect answers, stateful operation is the opposite of the REST-based API feature of stateless operation. For the other incorrect answer, although many REST-based APIs happen to use HTTP, REST APIs do not have to use HTTP.

2.   B and D. In the CRUD software development acronym, the matching terms (create, read, update, delete) match one or more HTTP verbs. While the HTTP verbs can sometimes be used for multiple CRUD actions, the following are the general rules: create performed by HTTP POST; read by HTTP GET; update by HTTP PATCH, PUT (and sometimes POST); delete by HTTP DELETE.

3.   C. The URI for a REST API call uses a format of protocol://hostname/ resource?parameters. The API documentation details the resource part of the URI, as well as any optional parameters. For instance, in this case, the resource section is /dna/ intent/api/v1/network-device. Additionally, the API documentation for this resource details optional parameters in the query field as listed after the ? in the URI.

4.   A and D. Of the four answers, two happen to be most commonly used to format and serialize data returned from a REST API: JSON and XML. For the incorrect answers, JavaScript is a programming language that first defined JSON as a data serialization language. YAML is a data serialization/modeling language and can be found most often in configuration management tools like Ansible.

5.   A and D. JSON defines variables as key:value pairs, with the key on the left of the colon (:) and always enclosed in double quotation marks, with the value on the right. The value can be a simple value or an object or array with additional complexity. The number of objects is defined by the number of matched curly brackets ({ and }), so this example shows a single JSON object.

  The one JSON object shown here includes one key and one :, so it has a single key:value pair (making one answer correct). The value in that key:value pair itself is a JSON array (a list in Python) that lists numbers 1, 2, and 3. The fact that the list is enclosed in square brackets defines it as a JSON array.

6.   C and D. To interpret this JSON data, first look for the innermost pairing of either curly brackets { }, which denote one object, or square brackets [ ], which indicate one array. In this case, the content within the inner pair of curly brackets { } shows one JSON object.

  Inside that one object, four key:value pairs exist, with the key before each colon and the value after each colon. That means "type" is a key, while "ACCESS" and "10.10.22.66" are values.

If you examine the outer pair of curly brackets that begin and end the JSON data, that pair also defines an object. That object has one key of "response" (making that answer incorrect). The "response" key then has a value equal to the entire inner object.

Chapter 24

1. C. Devices with the same role in an enterprise should have a similar configuration. When engineers make unique changes on individual devices—different changes from those made in the majority of devices with that same role—those devices' configurations become different than the intended ideal configuration for every device with that role. This effect is known as configuration drift. Configuration management tools can monitor a device's configuration versus a file that shows the intended ideal configuration for devices in that role, noting when the device configuration drifts away from that ideal configuration.

2. A and B. The version control system, applied to the centralized text files that contain the device configurations, automatically tracks changes. That means the system can see which user edited the file, when, and exactly what change was made, with the ability to make comparisons between different versions of the files.

   The two incorrect answers list useful features of a configuration management tool, but those answers list features typically found in the configuration management tool itself rather than in the version control tool.

3. D. Configuration monitoring (a generic description) refers to a process of checking the device's actual configuration versus the configuration management system's intended configuration for the device. If the actual configuration has moved away from the intended configuration—that is, if configuration drift has occurred—configuration monitoring can either reconfigure the device or notify the engineering staff.

   For the other answers, two refer to features of the associated version control software typically used along with the configuration management tool. Version control software will track the identity of each user who changes files and track the differences in files over time. The other incorrect answer is a useful feature of many configuration management tools, in which the tool verifies that the configuration will be accepted when attempted (or not). However, that useful feature is not part of what is called configuration monitoring

4. A and C. Both Ansible and Terraform can use a push model. The Ansible control node decides when to configure a device based on the instructions in a playbook. Although Ansible uses a push model by default, it can also use a pull model with a program called Ansible-pull.

5. B and C. These files go by the names *Ansible Playbook* and *Terraform Configuration*.

NUMERICS

2.4-GHz band   The frequency range between 2.400 and 2.4835 GHz that is used for wireless LAN communication.

2.5GBase-T   One of two Ethernet physical layer standards called multigigabit Ethernet (the other being 5.0GBase-T), first defined in IEEE addendum 802.3bz, which defines a 2.5 Gbps data rate over Cat 5E UTP cabling at distances of 100 meters.

3G/4G Internet   An Internet access technology that uses wireless radio signals to communicate through mobile phone towers, most often used by mobile phones, tablets, and some other mobile devices.

5-GHz band   The frequency range between 5.150 and 5.825 GHz that is used for wireless LAN communication.

5.0GBase-T   One of two Ethernet physical layer standards called multigigabit Ethernet (the other being 2.5GBase-T), first defined in IEEE addendum 802.3bz, which defines a 2.5 Gbps data rate over Cat 5E UTP cabling at distances of 100 meters.

6-GHz band   The frequency range between 5.925 and 7.125 GHz that is used for wireless LAN communication.

10BASE-T   An Ethernet physical layer standard, first defined directly in the 802.3 standard as the first UTP-based Ethernet physical layer standard. It uses two twisted-pair UTP cabling and supports 10 Mbps data rates.

10GBASE-SR   An Ethernet physical layer standard that uses optical multimode (OM) cabling, first defined in IEEE addendum 802.3ae, which defines a 10 Gbps data rate.

10GBase-T   An Ethernet physical layer standard, introduced as IEEE addendum 802.3an, supporting 10 Gbps data rates over four-pair UTP cabling.

40GBase-T   An Ethernet physical layer standard, introduced in IEEE addendum 802.3ba, supporting 40 Gbps data rates over four-pair UTP cabling.

100BASE-T   An Ethernet physical layer standard, introduced as IEEE addendum 802.3u, supporting 100 Mbps data rates over two-pair UTP cabling.

1000BASE-SX   An Ethernet physical layer standard that uses optical multimode (OM) cabling, first defined in IEEE addendum 802.3z, which defines a 1 Gbps data rate.

1000BASE-T   An Ethernet physical layer standard, introduced as IEEE addendum 802.3ab, supporting 1000 Mbps (1 Gbps) data rates over four-pair UTP cabling.

A

AAA   Authentication, authorization, and accounting. Authentication confirms the identity of the user or device. Authorization determines what the user or device is allowed to do. Accounting records information about access attempts, including inappropriate requests.

AAA server   *See* authentication, authorization, and accounting (AAA) server.

access control entry (ACE)   One configuration line with a permit or deny action in an access control list (ACL).

access interface   A LAN network design term that refers to a switch interface connected to end-user devices, configured so that it does not use VLAN trunking.

access layer   In a campus LAN design, the switches that connect directly to endpoint devices (servers, user devices), and also connect into the distribution layer switches.

access link   In campus LAN design, a link that connects an access switch to endpoint devices and wireless access points.

access link (WAN)   A physical link between a service provider and its customer that provides access to the SP's network from that customer site.

access point (AP)   A device that provides wireless service for clients within its coverage area or cell, with the AP connecting to both the wireless LAN and the wired Ethernet LAN.

accounting   In security, the recording of access attempts. *See also* AAA.

ACI   *See* Application Centric Infrastructure (ACI).

ACL   Access control list. A list configured on a router to control packet flow through the router, such as to prevent packets with a certain IP address from leaving a particular interface on the router.

ACL persistence   A feature of IOS XE (but not IOS) by which a router initialization event (power off/on or reload) does not cause reassigning ACL sequence numbers. The feature can be enabled (default, meaning no resequencing) or disabled.

ACL resequencing   The process of renumbering the sequence numbers of ACL commands, either for all ACLs at router initialization (power off/on or reload) or by using a command to renumber individual ACLs.

ACL sequence number   A number assigned to each ACL ACE when configured, either automatically or as typed in the configuration command, which allows easier deletion of individual ACEs.

ad hoc wireless network   *See* independent basic service set (IBSS).

administrative distance   In Cisco routers, a means for one router to choose between multiple routes to reach the same subnet when those routes are learned by different routing protocols. The lower the administrative distance, the more preferred the source of the routing information.

agent-based architecture   With configuration management tools, an architecture that uses a software agent inside the device being managed as part of the functions to manage the configuration.

agentless architecture   With configuration management tools, an architecture that does not need a software agent inside the device being managed as part of the functions to manage the configuration, instead using other mainstream methods like SSH and NETCONF.

AI Ops   Artificial Intelligence for IT Operations. Refers to the application of artificial intelligence and machine learning techniques to automate and enhance various aspects of IT operations, including monitoring, troubleshooting, and incident management, to improve efficiency and reliability in managing complex IT environments.

amplification attack   A reflection attack that leverages a service on the reflector to generate and reflect huge volumes of reply traffic to the victim.

Ansible   A popular configuration management application, which can be used with or without a server, using a push model to move configurations into devices, with strong capabilities to manage network device configurations.

APIC   *See* Application Policy Infrastructure Controller.

Application Centric Infrastructure (ACI)   Cisco's data center SDN solution, the concepts of defining policies that the APIC controller then pushes to the switches in the network using the OpFlex protocol, with the partially distributed control plane in each switch building the forwarding table entries to support the policies learned from the controller. It also supports a GUI, a CLI, and APIs.

Application Policy Infrastructure Controller (APIC)   The software that plays the role of controller, controlling the flows that the switches create to define where frames are forwarded, in a Cisco data center that uses the Application Centric Infrastructure (ACI) approach, switches, and software.

application programming interface (API)   A software mechanism that enables software components to communicate with each other.

application-specific integrated circuit (ASIC)   An integrated circuit (computer chip) designed for a specific purpose or application, often used to implement the functions of a networking device rather than running a software process as part of the device's OS that runs on a general-purpose processor.

ARP reply   An ARP message used to supply information about the sending (origin) host's hardware (Ethernet) and IP addresses as listed in the origin hardware and origin IP address fields. Typically sent in reaction to receipt of an ARP request message.

Artificial Intelligence (AI)   Refers to computer systems or software that can perform tasks typically requiring human intelligence, such as learning from data, making decisions, and solving problems.

ASIC   *See* application-specific integrated circuit.

association   A negotiated relationship between a wireless station and an access point.

association request   An 802.11 frame that a wireless client sends to an AP to request an association with it.

association response   An 802.11 frame that a wireless access point sends to a wireless client in reply to an association request.

authentication   In security, the verification of the identity of a person or a process. *See also* AAA.

authentication, authorization, and accounting (AAA) server   A server that holds security information and provides services related to user login, particularly authentication (is the user who he says he is), authorization (once authenticated, what do we allow the user to do), and accounting (tracking the user).

authorization   In security, the determination of the rights allowed for a particular user or device. *See also* AAA.

autonomous AP   A wireless AP operating in a standalone mode, such that it can provide a fully functional BSS and connect to the DS.

B

band   A contiguous range of frequencies.

bandwidth   The speed at which bits can be sent and received over a link.

basic service set (BSS)   Wireless service provided by one AP to one or more associated clients.

basic service set identifier (BSSID)   A unique MAC address that is used to identify the AP that is providing a BSS.

beacon   An 802.11 frame that an AP broadcasts at regular intervals to advertise the existence of an SSID. Separate beacons are transmitted for each SSID on each channel being used.

brute-force attack   An attack where a malicious user runs software that tries every possible combination of letters, numbers, and special characters to guess a user's password. Attacks of this scale are usually run offline, where more computing resources and time are available.

buffer overflow attack   An attack meant to exploit a vulnerability in processing inbound traffic such that the target system's buffers overflow; the target system can end up crashing or inadvertently running malicious code injected by the attacker.

C

cacheable   For resources that might be repeatedly requested over time, an attribute that means that the requesting host can keep in storage (cache) a copy of the resource for a specified amount of time.

CAPWAP   A standards-based tunneling protocol that defines communication between a light-weight AP and a wireless LAN controller.

CAT 5E   An unshielded twisted-pair (UTP) cable quality standard from the TIA and ANSI. It supports 1000BASE-T (and slower) UTP Ethernet at distances of 100 meters. It also supports multigig Ethernet standards at 100-meter distances.

CAT 6A   An unshielded twisted-pair (UTP) cable quality standard from the TIA and ANSI. It is the lowest UTP cable category that formally supports 10GBase-T UTP Ethernet at distances of 100 meters.

CDP   Cisco Discovery Protocol. A media- and protocol-independent device-discovery protocol that runs on most Cisco-manufactured equipment, including routers, access servers, and switches. Using CDP, a device can advertise its existence to other devices and receive information about other devices on the same LAN or on the remote side of a WAN.

cell   The area of wireless coverage provided by an AP; also known as the basic service area.

centralized control plane   An approach to architecting network protocols and products that places the control plane functions into a centralized function rather than distributing the function across the networking devices.

centralized WLC deployment   A wireless network design that places a WLC centrally within a network topology.

channel   An arbitrary index that points to a specific frequency within a band.

Chat Ops   A collaboration model that integrates chat tools with automated workflows and tools, allowing teams to manage and execute tasks directly within chat interfaces, enhancing communication, visibility, and efficiency in operations and development workflows.

CIDR   Classless interdomain routing. An RFC-standard tool for global IP address range assignment. CIDR reduces the size of Internet routers' IP routing tables, helping deal with the rapid growth of the Internet. The term *classless* refers to the fact that the summarized groups of networks represent a group of addresses that do not conform to IPv4 classful (Class A, B, and C) grouping rules.

Cisco AnyConnect Secure Mobility Client   Cisco software product used as client software on user devices to create a client VPN. Commonly referred to as the Cisco VPN client.

Cisco Catalyst 8000V   A virtual router platform designed for cloud and virtualized environments, offering high-performance, scalable, and secure routing capabilities with flexibility and agility.

Cisco Catalyst Center   Cisco software, delivered by Cisco on a physical or virtual appliance, that acts as a network management application as well as being the control for Cisco's Software-Defined Access (Cisco SD-Access) offering.

Cisco Prime Infrastructure (PI)   Graphical user interface (GUI) software that utilizes SNMP and can be used to manage your Cisco network devices. The term *Cisco Prime* is an umbrella term that encompasses many different individual software products.

Cisco SD-Access   Cisco's intent-based networking (IBN) offering for enterprise networks.

Cisco Secure Client (including AnyConnect)   Cisco software product used as client software on user devices to create a client VPN. Formerly called Cisco AnyConnect Secure Mobility Client, and sometimes referred to as the Cisco VPN client.

Class of Service (CoS)   The informal term for the 3-bit field in the 802.IQ header intended for marking and classifying Ethernet frames for the purposes of applying QoS actions. Another term for Priority Code Point (PCP).

classification   The process of examining various fields in networking messages in an effort to identify which messages fit into certain predetermined groups (classes).

cloud-based AP   A wireless AP operating much like an autonomous AP, but having management and control functions present in the Internet cloud.

cloud-based WLC deployment   A wireless network design that places a WLC centrally within a network topology, as a virtual machine in the private cloud portion of a data center.

Cloud Management   Involves administering, monitoring, and optimizing cloud resources and services to ensure efficient utilization, performance, security, and compliance across cloud environments.

cloud services catalog   A listing of the services available in a cloud computing service.

code integrity   A software security term that refers to how likely that the software (code) being used is the software supplied by the vendor, unchanged, with no viruses or other changes made to the software.

collapsed core design   A campus LAN design in which the design does not use a separate set of core switches in addition to the distribution switches—in effect collapsing the core into the distribution switches.

Common ACL   A feature of IOS XE (but not IOS) that supports enabling two ACLs on a single interface and direction.

configuration drift   A phenomenon that begins with the idea that devices with similar roles can and should have a similar standard configuration, so when one device's configuration is changed to be different, its configuration is considered to have moved away (drifted) from the standard configuration for a device in that role.

configuration management   A component of network management focused on creating, changing, removing, and monitoring device configuration.

configuration management tool   A class of application that manages data about the configuration of servers, network devices, and other computing nodes, providing consistent means of describing the configurations, moving the configurations into the devices, noticing unintended changes to the configurations, and troubleshooting by easily identifying changes to the configuration files over time.

configuration monitoring   With configuration management tools like Ansible, a process of comparing over time a device's on-device configuration (running-config) versus the text file showing the ideal device configuration listed in the tool's centralized configuration repository. If different, the process can either change the device's configuration or report the issue.

configuration provisioning   With configuration management tools like Ansible, the process of configuring a device to match the configuration as held in the configuration management tool.

configuration template   With configuration management tools like Ansible, a file with variables, for the purpose of having the tool substitute different variable values to create the configuration for a device.

connected mode   The operational mode used by a FlexConnect AP when the path back to its controller is up and working. In this mode, all wireless traffic flows over the CAPWAP tunnel to and from the controller.

connection establishment   The process by which a connection-oriented protocol creates a connection. With TCP, a connection is established by a three-way transmission of TCP segments.

container   One instance of a running application started from a container image and controlled by a container engine on a server.

container image   One file that holds and embeds all files related to an application: all related executable files, required software libraries, and other files such as operating environment variables. Container virtualization systems then allow treating the application as a single file for movement, starting, stopping, and monitoring the container.

control plane   Functions in networking devices and controllers that directly control how devices perform data plane forwarding, but excluding the data plane processes that work to forward each message in the network.

controller-based networking   A style of building computer networks that use a controller that centralizes some features and provides application programming interfaces (APIs) that allow for software interactions between applications and the controller (northbound APIs) and between the controller and the network devices (southbound APIs).

controller-less wireless deployment   A wireless design based on an embedded wireless controller (EWC), where the WLC function is co-located with an AP, rather than a discrete physical controller.

core   In computer architecture, an individual processing unit that can execute instructions of a CPU; modern server processors typically have multiple cores, each capable of concurrent execution of instructions.

core design   A campus LAN design that connects each access switch to distribution switches, and distribution switches into core switches, to provide a path between all LAN devices.

core layer   In a campus LAN design, the switches that connect the distribution layer switches, and to each other, to provide connectivity between the various distribution layer switches.

CRUD   In software development, an acronym that refers to the four most common actions taken by a program: Create, Read, Update, and Delete.

D

data plane   Functions in networking devices that are part of the process of receiving a message, processing the message, and forwarding the message.

data serialization language   A language that includes syntax and rules that provides a means to describe the variables inside applications in a text format, for the purpose of sending that text between applications over a network or storing the data models in a file.

Declarative Model   A method of describing IT automation that defines or declares the intended configuration, with the expectation that the automation software monitors the devices' configurations and changes them if they drift away from the intended (declared) configuration.

declarative policy model   A term that describes the approach in an intent-based network (IBN) in which the engineer chooses settings that describe the intended network behavior (the declared policy) but does not command the network with specific configuration commands for each protocol (as would be the case with an imperative policy model).

delay   In QoS, the amount of time it takes for a message to cross a network. Delay can refer to one-way delay (the time required for the message to be sent from the source host to the destination host) or two-way delay (the delay from the source to the destination host and then back again).

denial-of-service (DoS) attack   An attack that tries to deplete a system resource so that systems and services crash or become unavailable.

deny   An action taken with an ACL that implies that the packet is discarded.

DevNet   Cisco's community and resource site for software developers, open to all, with many great learning resources; https://developer.cisco.com.

DHCP attack   Any attack that takes advantage of DHCP protocol messages.

DHCP Snooping   A switch security feature in which the switch examines incoming DHCP messages and chooses to filter messages that are abnormal and therefore might be part of a DHCP attack.

DHCP Snooping binding table   When using DHCP Snooping, a table that the switch dynamically builds by analyzing the DHCP messages that flow through the switch. DHCP Snooping can use the table for part of its filtering logic, with other features, such as Dynamic ARP Inspection and IP Source Guard also using the table.

dictionary attack   An attack where a malicious user runs software that attempts to guess a user's password by trying words from a dictionary or word list.

dictionary variable   In applications, a single variable whose value is a list of other variables with values, known as key:value pairs.

Differentiated Services (DiffServ)   An approach to QoS, originally defined in RFC 2475, that uses a model of applying QoS per classification, with planning of which applications and other traffic types are assigned to each class, with each class given different QoS per-hop behaviors at each networking device in the path.

Differentiated Services Code Point (DSCP)   A field existing as the first 6 bits of the ToS byte, as defined by RFC 2474, which redefined the original IP RFC's definition for the IP header ToS byte. The field is used to mark a value in the header for the purpose of performing later QoS actions on the packet.

distributed control plane   An approach to architecting network protocols and products that places some control plane functions into each networking device rather than centralizing the control plane functions in one or a few devices. An example is the use of routing protocols on each router which then work together so that each router learns Layer 3 routes.

distributed denial-of-service (DDoS) attack   A DoS attack that is distributed across many hosts under centralized control of an attacker, all targeting the same victim.

distributed WLC deployment   A wireless design based on distributing multiple controllers within the network. Each of the controllers commonly supports a relatively small number of users.

distribution layer   In a campus LAN design, the switches that connect to access layer switches as the most efficient means to provide connectivity from the access layer into the other parts of the LAN.

distribution link   In campus LAN design, a link that connects a distribution switch to an access switch.

distribution system (DS)   The wired Ethernet that connects to an AP and transports traffic between a wired and wireless network.

DNS   Domain Name System. An application layer protocol used throughout the Internet for translating hostnames into their associated IP addresses.

DNS server   An application acting as a server for the purpose of providing name resolution services per the Domain Name System (DNS) protocol and worldwide system.

domain-specific language   A generic term that refers to an attribute of different languages within computing, for languages created for a specific purpose (domain) rather than a general-purpose language like Python or JavaScript.

Dynamic ARP Inspection (DAI)   A security feature in which a LAN switch filters a subset of incoming ARP messages on untrusted ports, based on a comparison of ARP, Ethernet, and IP header fields to data gathered in the IP DHCP Snooping binding table and found in any configured ARP ACLs.

E

egress tunnel router (ETR)   With LISP, a node at the end of a tunnel that receives an encapsulated message and then de-encapsulates the message.

E-LAN   A specific carrier/Metro Ethernet service defined by MEF (MEF.net) that provides a service much like a LAN, with two or more customer sites connected to one E-LAN service in a full mesh so that each device in the E-LAN can send Ethernet frames directly to every other device.

E-Line   A specific carrier/metro Ethernet service defined by MEF (MEF.net) that provides a point-to-point topology between two customer devices, much as if the two devices were connected using an Ethernet crossover cable.

embedded wireless controller (EWC)   A WLC function that is co-located within an AP.

embedded wireless controller (EWC) deployment   A wireless network design that places a WLC in the access layer, co-located with a LAN switch stack, near the APs it controls.

enable secret   A reference to the password configured on the **enable secret** *pass-value* command, which defines the password required to reach enable (privileged) mode.

error detection   The process of discovering whether a data-link level frame was changed during transmission. This process typically uses a Frame Check Sequence (FCS) field in the data-link trailer.

error disabled (err-disable)   An interface state on LAN switches that can be the result of one of many security violations.

error recovery   The process of noticing when some transmitted data was not successfully received and resending the data until it is successfully received.

Ethernet access link   A WAN access link (a physical link between a service provider and its customer) that happens to use Ethernet.

Ethernet WAN   A general and informal term for any WAN service that uses Ethernet links as the access link between the customer and the service provider.

exploit   A means of taking advantage of a vulnerability to compromise something.

extended access list   A list of IOS **access-list** global configuration commands that can match multiple parts of an IP packet, including the source and destination IP address and TCP/UDP ports, for the purpose of deciding which packets to discard and which to allow through the router.

extended service set (ESS)   Multiple APs that are connected by a common switched infrastructure.

extended service set identifier (ESSID)   The SSID used consistently throughout an ESS.

F

fabric   In SDA, the combination of overlay and underlay that together provide all features to deliver data across the network with the desired features and attributes.

fabric edge node   In SDA, a switch that connects to endpoint devices.

fiber Internet   A general term for any Internet access technology that happens to use fiber-optic cabling. It often uses Ethernet protocols on the fiber link.

firewall   A device that forwards packets between the less secure and more secure parts of the network, applying rules that determine which packets are allowed to pass and which are not.

flash memory   A type of read/write permanent memory that retains its contents even with no power applied to the memory and that uses no moving parts, making the memory less likely to fail over time.

FlexConnect mode   An AP mode tailored for remote sites. Wireless traffic flows to and from a controller if the AP's CAPWAP tunnel is up, or is locally switched if the tunnel is down.

flow control   The process of regulating the amount of data sent by a sending computer toward a receiving computer. Several flow control mechanisms exist, including TCP flow control, which uses windowing.

FTP   File Transfer Protocol. An application protocol, part of the TCP/IP protocol stack, used to transfer files between network nodes. FTP is defined in RFC 959.

FTP control connection   A TCP connection initiated by an FTP client to an FTP server for the purpose of sending FTP commands that direct the activities of the connection.

FTP data connection   A TCP connection created by an FTP client and server for the purpose of transferring data.

FTPS   FTP Secure. Common term for FTP over TLS.

full mesh   From a topology perspective, any topology that has two or more devices, with each device being able to send frames to every other device.

G

Generative AI   Also Strong AI; encompasses artificial intelligence systems capable of learning, reasoning, and making decisions similar to human cognition, often with the capability to create new content, ideas, or solutions beyond its initial training data.

Git   An open-source version control application, widely popular for version control in software development and for other uses, like managing network device configurations.

GitHub   A web-based platform for version control and collaboration, facilitating hosting, sharing, and managing of software projects using the Git version control system.

GLBP active virtual forwarder (AVF)   A role implemented by all routers in a GLBP group, listening for frames sent to a unique virtual MAC address, so it can act as one of several active default routers in the group.

GLBP active virtual gateway (AVG)   A role implemented by one router in a GLBP group, replying to ARP requests on behalf of the group's VIP, so that load balancing occurs.

gratuitous ARP   An ARP Reply not sent as a reaction to an ARP request message, but rather as a general announcement informing other hosts of the values of the sending (origin) host's addresses.

H

host (context: DC)   In a virtualized server environment, the term used to refer to one physical server that is running a hypervisor to create multiple virtual machines.

HSRP preemption   A configuration setting that dictates whether an HSRP router, when it initializes with HSRP, can immediately take over the HSRP active role (preemption) if it has a higher priority than the currently active router.

HSRP priority   A configuration setting from 0 through 255 that impacts the choice of HSRP active state, with the highest priority router chosen as active.

HTTP   Hypertext Transfer Protocol. The protocol used by web browsers and web servers to transfer files, such as text and graphic files.

HTTP/1.0   A version of the HTTP protocol, published as an RFC in the mid 1990s. It uses TCP, expects URLs that begin with http, implying a default well-known server port of 80. It allows the use of secure HTTP as well.

HTTP/1.1   A version of the HTTP protocol, published as an RFC in the mid 1990s. It uses TCP, expects URLs that begin with http, implying a default well-known server port of 80. It allows the use of secure HTTP as well.

HTTP/2.0   A version of the HTTP protocol, published as an RFC in the mid 2010s. The protocol improved HTTP application processes to increase overall performance in the end-user experience. It supports using Secure HTTP (with TLS) or not.

HTTP/3.0   A radically different HTTP version published as an RFC in 2022 and created by Google. It improved HTTP application processes plus changed the transport layer protocols, both to increase overall performance in the end-user experience. It uses the QUIC transport layer, which uses UDP (not TCP) and always includes TLS.

hub and spoke   From a topology perspective, any topology that has a device that can send messages to all other devices (the hub), with one or more spoke devices that can send messages only to the hub. Also called point-to-multipoint.

hypervisor   Software that runs on server hardware to create the foundations of a virtualized server environment primarily by allocating server hardware components like CPU core/threads, RAM, disk, and network to the VMs running on the server.

I

Imperative Model   A method of describing IT automation as a series of tasks, akin to a script or program, with the expectation that running the script will configure the devices to have the desired configuration.

imperative policy model   A term that describes the approach in traditional networks in which the engineer chooses configuration settings for each control and data plane protocol (the imperative commands) that dictate specifically how the devices act. This model acts in contrast to the newer declarative policy model and intent-based networking (IBN).

independent basic service set (IBSS)   An impromptu wireless network formed between two or more devices without an AP or a BSS; also known as an ad hoc network.

Infrastructure as Code (IAC)   A practice that involves managing and provisioning computing infrastructure through machine-readable definition files, enabling automation, consistency, and scalability in infrastructure deployment and management processes.

Infrastructure as a Service (IaaS)   A cloud service in which the service consists of a virtual machine that has defined computing resources (CPUs, RAM, disk, and network) and may or may not be provided with an installed OS.

infrastructure mode   The operating mode of an AP that is providing a BSS for wireless clients.

inside global   For packets sent to and from a host that resides inside the trusted part of a network that uses NAT, a term referring to the IP address used in the headers of those packets when those packets traverse the global (public) Internet.

inside local   For packets sent to and from a host that resides inside the trusted part of a network that uses NAT, a term referring to the IP address used in the headers of those packets when those packets traverse the enterprise (private) part of the network.

intent-based networking (IBN)   An approach to networking in which the system gives the operator the means to express business intent, with the networking system then determining what should be done by the network, activating the appropriate configuration, and monitoring (assuring) the results.

intrusion prevention system (IPS)   A security function that examines more complex traffic patterns against a list of both known attack signatures and general characteristics of how attacks can be carried out, rating each perceived threat, and reacting to prevent the more significant threats. *See also* IPS.

IOS File System (IFS)   A file system created by a Cisco device that uses IOS.

IOS image   A file that contains the IOS.

IP Precedence (IPP)   In the original definition of the IP header's Type of Service (ToS) byte, the first 3 bits of the ToS byte, used for marking IP packets for the purpose of applying QoS actions.

IPS   *See* intrusion prevention system.

IPsec   The term referring to the IP Security protocols, which is an architecture for providing encryption and authentication services, usually when creating VPN services through an IP network.

IPsec transport mode   The process of encrypting the data of the original IP packet when using IPsec, while using the original packet's IP header, plus VPN headers, to encapsulate the encrypted data. Typically used with remote access IPsec VPNs.

IPsec tunnel mode   The process of encrypting the entire original IP packet when using IPsec, which requires a new IP header, plus VPN headers, to encapsulate the encrypted original packet. Typically used with site-to-site IPsec VPNs.

J

Jinja2   A text-based language used to define templates, with text plus variables; used by Ansible for templates.

jitter   The variation in delay experienced by successive packets in a single application flow.

JSON (JavaScript Object Notation)   A popular data serialization language, originally used with the JavaScript programming language, and popular for use with REST APIs.

JSON array   A part of a set of JSON text that begins and ends with a matched set of square brackets that contain a list of values.

JSON object   A part of a set of JSON text that begins and ends with a matched set of curly brackets that contain a set of key:value pairs.

K–L

key:value pair   In software, one variable name (key) and its value, separated by a colon in some languages and data serialization languages.

Large Language Models (LLM)   Advanced artificial intelligence systems capable of understanding and generating human-like text based on extensive training on vast amounts of textual data.

leaf   In an ACI network design, a switch that connects to spine switches and to endpoints, but not to other leaf switches, so that the leaf can forward frames from an endpoint to a spine, which then delivers the frame to some other leaf switch.

LISP   Locator/ID Separation Protocol. A protocol, defined in RFC 6830, that separates the concepts and numbers used to identify an endpoint (the endpoint identifier) versus identifying the location of the endpoint (routing locator).

list variable   In applications, a single variable whose value is a list of values, rather than a simple value.

LLDP   Link Layer Discovery Protocol. An IEEE standard protocol (IEEE 802.1AB) that defines messages, encapsulated directly in Ethernet frames so they do not rely on a working IPv4 or IPv6 network, for the purpose of giving devices a means of announcing basic device information to other devices on the LAN. It is a standardized protocol similar to Cisco Discovery Protocol (CDP).

LLDP-MED   A group of endpoint-focused LLDP TLVs, defined as a group TIA standard TIA-1057. It includes TLVs to communicate voice and data VLANs to phones and to manage power levels with PoE.

local username   A username (with matching password), configured on a router or switch. It is considered local because it exists on the router or switch, and not on a remote server.

log message   A message generated by any computer, but including Cisco routers and switches, for which the device OS wants to notify the owner or administrator of the device about some event.

loss   A reference to packets in a network that are sent but do not reach the destination host.

M

malware   Malicious software.

Management Information Base (MIB)   The data structures defined by SNMP to define a hierarchy (tree) structure with variables at the leaves of the tree, so that SNMP messages can reference the variables.

management plane   Functions in networking devices and controllers that control the devices themselves but that do not impact the forwarding behavior of the devices like control plane protocols do.

man-in-the-middle attack   An attack where an attacker manages to position a machine on the network such that it is able to intercept traffic passing between target hosts.

marking   The process of changing one of a small set of fields in various network protocol headers, including the IP header's DSCP field, for the purpose of later classifying a message based on that marked value.

MD5 hash   A specific mathematical algorithm intended for use in various security protocols. In the context of Cisco routers and switches, the devices store the MD5 hash of certain passwords, rather than the passwords themselves, in an effort to make the device more secure.

Media Access Control (MAC) layer   The lower of the two sublayers of the data-link layer defined by the IEEE. Synonymous with IEEE 802.3 for Ethernet LANs.

Meraki Dashboard   A centralized cloud-based management platform that provides intuitive control and monitoring of Meraki networking devices, offering streamlined configuration, real-time analytics, and seamless network administration.

mesh network   A network of APs used to cover a large area without the need for wired Ethernet cabling; client traffic is bridged from AP to AP over a backhaul network.

Metro Ethernet   The original term used for WAN service that used Ethernet links as the access link between the customer and the service provider.

MIB   *See* Management Information Base.

mitigation technique   A method to counteract or prevent threats and malicious activity.

MPLS   *See* Multiprotocol Label Switching.

MPLS VPN   A WAN service that uses MPLS technology, with many customers connecting to the same MPLS network, but with the VPN features keeping each customer's traffic separate from others.

MTU   Maximum transmission unit. The maximum packet size, in bytes, that a particular interface can handle.

multifactor authentication   A technique that uses more than one type of credential to authenticate users.

Multigig Ethernet   The common name for the 2.5GBase-T and 5.0GBase-T Ethernet standards, which, when released simultaneously, represented an option for UTP Ethernet at speeds of multiple gigabits between the then-defined standard speeds of 1 Gbps and 10 Gbps.

Multiprotocol BGP (MPBGP)   A particular set of BGP extensions that allows BGP to support multiple address families, which when used to create an MPLS VPN service gives the SP the method to advertise the IPv4 routes of many customers while keeping those route advertisements logically separated.

Multiprotocol Label Switching (MPLS)   A WAN technology used to create an IP-based service for customers, with the service provider's internal network performing forwarding based on an MPLS label rather than the destination IP address.

N

named access list   An ACL that identifies the various statements in the ACL based on a name rather than a number.

Narrow AI   Also Weak AI. Refers to artificial intelligence designed and trained for specific tasks or a limited range of activities, lacking broad cognitive capabilities and adaptability beyond its predefined scope.

NAT   Network Address Translation. A mechanism for reducing the need for globally unique IP addresses. NAT allows an organization with addresses that are not globally unique to connect to the Internet, by translating those addresses into public addresses in the globally routable address space.

NAT overload   Another term for Port Address Translation (PAT). One of several methods of configuring NAT, in this case translating TCP and UDP flows based on port numbers in addition to using one or only a few inside global addresses.

NBI   *See* northbound API.

Network Management System (NMS)   A software platform that enables centralized monitoring, configuration, and administration of network infrastructure and devices to ensure optimal performance, security, and reliability.

Network Time Protocol (NTP)   A protocol used to synchronize time-of-day clocks so that multiple devices use the same time of day, which allows log messages to be more easily matched based on their timestamps.

Next-generation firewall (NGFW)   A firewall device with advanced features, including the ability to run many related security features in the same firewall device (IPS, malware detection, VPN termination), along with deep packet inspection with Application Visibility and Control (AVC) and the ability to perform URL filtering versus data collected about the reliability and risk associated with every domain name.

Next-generation IPS (NGIPS)   An IPS device with advanced features, including the capability to go beyond a comparison to known attack signatures to also look at contextual data, including the vulnerabilities in the current network, the capability to monitor for new zero-day threats, with frequent updates of signatures from the Cisco Talos security research group.

NMS   *See* Network Management System (NMS).

nonoverlapping channels   Successive channel numbers in a band that each have a frequency range that is narrow enough to not overlap the next channel above or below.

northbound API   In the area of SDN, a reference to the APIs that a controller supports that gives outside programs access to the services of the controller; for instance, to supply information about the network or to program flows into the network. Also called a northbound interface.

northbound interface (NBI)   Another term for northbound API. *See also* northbound API.

NTP client   Any device that attempts to use the Network Time Protocol (NTP) to synchronize its time by adjusting the local device's time based on NTP messages received from a server.

NTP client/server mode   A mode of operation with the Network Time Protocol (NTP) in which the device acts as both an NTP client, synchronizing its time with some servers, and as an NTP server, supplying time information to clients.

NTP server   Any device that uses Network Time Protocol (NTP) to help synchronize time-of-day clocks for other devices by telling other devices its current time.

NTP synchronization   The process with the Network Time Protocol (NTP) by which different devices send messages, exchanging the devices' current time-of-day clock information and other data, so that some devices adjust their clocks to the point that the time-of-day clocks list the same time (often accurate to at least the same second).

O

on-demand self-service   One of the five key attributes of a cloud computing service as defined by NIST, referring to the fact that the consumer of the server can request the service, with the service being created without any significant delay and without waiting on human intervention.

on-premises   An alternate term for private cloud. *See also* private cloud.

OpenFlow   The open standard for Software-Defined Networking (SDN) as defined by the Open Networking Foundation (ONF), which defines the OpenFlow protocol as well as the concept of an abstracted OpenFlow virtual switch.

Optical Multimode (OM)   The term used to refer to multimode fiber-optic cabling in various cabling standards.

ordered data transfer   A networking function, included in TCP, in which the protocol defines how the sending host should number the data transmitted, defines how the receiving device should attempt to reorder the data if it arrives out of order, and specifies to discard the data if it cannot be delivered in order.

outside global   With source NAT, the one address used by the host that resides outside the enterprise, which NAT does not change, so there is no need for a contrasting term.

overlay   In SDA, the combination of VXLAN tunnels between fabric edge nodes as a data plane for forwarding frames, plus LISP for the control plane for the discovery and registration of endpoint identifiers.

P

partial mesh   A network topology in which more than two devices could physically communicate, but by choice, only a subset of the pairs of devices connected to the network is allowed to communicate directly.

passive scanning   A technique used by a wireless client when it attempts to discover nearby APs by listening for their beacon frames.

password guessing   An attack where a malicious user simply makes repeated attempts to guess a user's password.

per-hop behavior (PHB)   The general term used to describe the set of QoS actions a device can apply to a message from the time it enters a networking device until the device forwards the message. PHBs include classification, marking, queuing, shaping, policing, and congestion avoidance.

pharming   An attack that compromises name services to silently redirect users toward a malicious site.

phishing   An attack technique that sends specially crafted emails to victims in the hope that the users will follow links to malicious websites.

Platform as a Service (PaaS)   A cloud service intended for software developers as a development platform, with a variety of tools useful to developers already installed so that developers can focus on developing software rather than on creating a good development environment.

PoE   Power over Ethernet. Both a generalized term for any of the standards that supply power over an Ethernet link, as well as a specific PoE standard as defined in the IEEE 802.3af amendment to the 802.3 standard.

point of presence (PoP)   A term used for a service provider's (SP) perspective to refer to a service provider's installation that is purposefully located relatively near to customers, with several spread around major cities, so that the distance from each customer site to one of the SP's PoPs is short.

point-to-point   From a topology perspective, any topology that has two and only two devices that can send messages directly to each other.

point-to-point bridge   An AP configured to bridge a wired network to a companion bridge at the far end of a line-of-sight path.

policing   A QoS tool that monitors the bit rate of the messages passing some point in the processing of a networking device, so that if the bit rate exceeds the policing rate for a period of time, the policer can discard excess packets to lower the rate.

policing rate   The bit rate at which a policer compares the bit rate of packets passing through a policing function, for the purpose of taking a different action against packets that conform (are under) to the rate versus those that exceed (go over) the rate.

port   (Multiple definitions) (1) In TCP and UDP, a number that is used to uniquely identify the application process that either sent (source port) or should receive (destination port) data. (2) In LAN switching, another term for switch interface.

Port Address Translation (PAT)   A NAT feature in which one inside global IP address supports over 65,000 concurrent TCP and UDP connections.

port number   A field in a TCP or UDP header that identifies the application that either sent (source port) or should receive (destination port) the data inside the data segment.

port security   A Cisco switch feature in which the switch watches Ethernet frames that come in an interface (a port), tracks the source MAC addresses of all such frames, and takes a security action if the number of different such MAC addresses is exceeded.

Power classification   With Power over Ethernet (PoE), the process by which a switch, once it detects a device wants power, discovers the amount of power as defined by a standardized set of power classes.

Power detection   With Power over Ethernet (PoE), the process by which a switch discovers if the connected device wants to receive power over the link or not.

Power over Ethernet (PoE)   Both a generalized term for any of the standards that supply power over an Ethernet link and a specific PoE standard as defined in the IEEE 802.3af amendment to the 802.3 standard.

Power over Ethernet Plus (PoE+)   A specific PoE standard as defined in the IEEE 802.3at amendment to the 802.3 standard, which uses two wire pairs to supply power with a maximum of 30 watts as supplied by the PSE.

power sourcing equipment (PSE)   With any Power over Ethernet standard, a term that refers to the device supplying the power over the cable, which is then used by the powered device (PD) on the other end of the cable.

powered device (PD)   With any Power over Ethernet standard, a term that refers to the device that receives or draws its power over the Ethernet cable, with the power being supplied by the power sourcing equipment (PSE) on the other end of the cable.

priority queue   In Cisco queuing systems, another term for a low latency queue (LLQ).

private cloud   A cloud computing service in which a company provides its own IT services to internal customers inside the same company but by following the practices defined as cloud computing.

private IP network   Any of the IPv4 Class A, B, or C networks as defined by RFC 1918, intended for use inside a company but not used as public IP networks.

probe request   A technique used by a wireless client to discover nearby APs by actively requesting a response.

provider   A plug-in that enables communication and interaction between Terraform and specific infrastructure platforms or services, facilitating the management and provisioning of resources within those environments through Terraform configuration files.

provider edge (PE)   A term used by service providers, both generally and also specifically in MPLS VPN networks, to refer to the SP device in a point of presence (PoP) that connects to the customer's network and therefore sits at the edge of the SP's network.

public cloud   A cloud computing service in which the cloud provider is a different company than the cloud consumer.

pull model   With configuration management tools, a practice by which an agent representing the device requests configuration data from the centralized configuration management tool, in effect pulling the configuration to the device.

push model   With configuration management tools, a practice by which the centralized configuration management tool software initiates the movement of configuration from that node to the device that will be configured, in effect pushing the configuration to the device.

Q–R

Quality of Service (QoS)   The performance of a message, or the messages sent by an application, in regard to the bandwidth, delay, jitter, or loss characteristics experienced by the message(s).

queuing   The process by which networking devices hold packets in memory while waiting on some constrained resource; for example, when waiting for the outgoing interface to become available when too many packets arrive in a short period of time.

QUIC   The name (not an acronym) for a transport layer protocol that improves overall performance of transferring objects over a network, in comparison to TCP. It uses UDP and integrates TLS into its connection setup tasks.

RADIUS   A security protocol often used for user authentication, including being used as part of the IEEE 802.lx messages between an 802.lx authenticator (typically a LAN switch) and a AAA server.

RAM   Random-access memory. A type of volatile memory that can be read and written by a microprocessor.

rapid elasticity   One of the five key attributes of a cloud computing service as defined by NIST, referring to the fact that the cloud service reacts to requests for new services quickly, and it expands (is elastic) to the point of appearing to be a limitless resource.

read-only community   An SNMP community (a value that acts as a password), defined on an SNMP agent, which then must be supplied by any SNMP manager that sends the agent any messages asking to learn the value of a variable (like SNMP Get and GetNext requests).

read-write community   An SNMP community (a value that acts as a password), defined on an SNMP agent, which then must be supplied by any SNMP manager that sends the agent any messages asking to set the value of a variable (like SNMP Set requests).

reassociation request   An 802.11 frame that a roaming wireless client sends to an AP to request that its existing association be moved to a new AP.

reconnaissance attack   An attack crafted to discover as much information about a target organization as possible; the attack can involve domain discovery, ping sweeps, port scans, and so on.

recursive DNS server   A DNS server that, when asked for information it does not have, performs a repetitive (recursive) process to ask other DNS servers in sequence, hoping to find the DNS server that knows the information.

reflection attack   An attack that uses spoofed source addresses so that a destination machine will reflect return traffic to the attack's target; the destination machine is known as the reflector.

remote access VPN   A VPN for which one endpoint is a user device, such as a phone, tablet, or PC, typically created dynamically, and often using TLS. Also called a client VPN.

repeater   A device that repeats or retransmits signals it receives, effectively expanding the wireless coverage area.

Representational State Transfer (REST)   A type of API that allows two programs that reside on separate computers to communicate, with a set of six primary API attributes as defined early in this century by its creator, Roy Fielding. The attributes include client/server architecture, stateless operation, cachability, uniform interfaces, layered, and code-on-demand.

resource pooling   One of the five key attributes of a cloud computing service as defined by NIST, referring to the fact that the cloud provider treats its resources as a large group (pool) of resources that its cloud management systems then allocate dynamically based on self-service requests by its customers.

REST   *See* Representational State Transfer.

REST API   Any API that uses the rules of Representational State Transfer (REST).

roaming   The process a wireless client uses to move from one AP to another as it changes location.

round robin   A queue scheduling algorithm in which the scheduling algorithm services one queue, then the next, then the next, and so on, working through the queues in sequence.

S

SBI   *See* Southbound API.

scalable group tag (SGT)   In SDA, a value assigned to the users in the same security group.

Secure HTTP (HTTP over TLS)   The IETF standard that defines how to use TLS to add security features such as server authentication and message encryption to HTTP/2 and earlier versions of HTTP.

segment (Multiple definitions) (1) In TCP, a term used to describe a TCP header and its encapsulated data (also called an L4PDU). (2) Also in TCP, the set of bytes formed when TCP breaks a large chunk of data given to it by the application layer into smaller pieces that fit into TCP segments. (3) In Ethernet, either a single Ethernet cable or a single collision domain (no matter how many cables are used).

sender hardware address In both an ARP request and reply message, the field intended to be used to list the sender (origin) device's hardware address, typically an Ethernet LAN address.

sender IP address In both an ARP request and reply message, the field intended to be used to list the sender (origin) device's IP address.

sender protocol address In both an ARP request and a reply message, the formal term the field intended to be used to list the sender (origin) device's network layer address.

service provider (SP) A company that provides a service to multiple customers. Used most often to refer to providers of private WAN services and Internet services. *See also* Internet service provider.

Service Set Identifier (SSID) A text string that is used to identify a wireless network.

shaping A QoS tool that monitors the bit rate of the messages exiting networking devices, so that if the bit rate exceeds the shaping rate for a period of time, the shaper can queue the packets, effectively slowing down the sending rate to match the shaping rate.

shaping rate The bit rate at which a shaper compares the bit rate of packets passing through the shaping function, so that when the rate is exceeded, the shaper enables the queuing of packets, resulting in slowing the bit rate of the collective packets that pass through the shaper, so the rate of bits getting through the shaper does not exceed the shaping rate.

shared key A reference to a security key whose value is known (shared) by both the sender and receiver.

Simple Network Management Protocol (SNMP) An Internet standard protocol for managing devices on IP networks. It is used mostly in network management systems to monitor network-attached devices for conditions that warrant administrative attention.

site-to-site VPN The mechanism that allows all devices at two different sites to communicate securely over some unsecure network like the Internet, by having one device at each site perform encryption/decryption and forwarding for all the packets sent between the sites.

sliding windows For protocols such as TCP that allow the receiving device to dictate the amount of data the sender can send before receiving an acknowledgment—a concept called a *window*—a reference to the fact that the mechanism to grant future windows is typically just a number that grows upward slowly after each acknowledgment, sliding upward.

SNMP *See* Simple Network Management Protocol.

SNMP agent Software that resides on the managed device and processes the SNMP messages sent by the Network Management Station (NMS).

SNMP community   A simple password mechanism in SNMP in which either the SNMP agent or manager defines a community string (password), and the other device must send that same password value in SNMP messages, or the messages are ignored. *See also* read-only community, read-write community, and notification community.

SNMP Get   Message used by SNMP to read from variables in the MIB.

SNMP Inform   An unsolicited SNMP message like a Trap message, except that the protocol requires that the Inform message needs to be acknowledged by the SNMP manager.

SNMP manager   Typically a Network Management System (NMS), with this term specifically referring to the use of SNMP and the typical role of the manager, which retrieves status information with SNMP Get requests, sets variables with the SNMP Set requests, and receives unsolicited notifications from SNMP agents by listening for SNMP Trap and Notify messages.

SNMP Set   SNMP message to set the value in variables of the MIB. These messages are the key to an administrator configuring the managed device using SNMP.

SNMP Trap   An unsolicited SNMP message generated by the managed device, and sent to the SNMP manager, to give information to the manager about some event or because a measurement threshold has been passed.

SNMPv2c   A variation of the second version of SNMP. SNMP Version 2 did not originally support communities; the term *SNMPv2c* refers to SNMP version 2 with support added for SNMP communities (which were part of SNMPvl).

SNMPv3   The third version of SNMP, with the notable addition of several security features as compared to SNMPv2c, specifically message integrity, authentication, and encryption.

social engineering   Attacks that leverage human trust and social behaviors to divulge sensitive information.

Software as a Service (SaaS)   A cloud service in which the service consists of access to working software, without the need to be concerned about the details of installing and maintaining the software or the servers on which it runs.

Software-Defined Access   Cisco's intent-based networking (IBN) offering for enterprise networks.

Software-Defined Networking (SDN)   A branch of networking that emerged in the marketplace in the 2010s characterized by the use of a centralized software controller that takes over varying amounts of the control plane processing formerly done inside networking devices, with the controller directing the networking elements as to what forwarding table entries to put into their forwarding tables.

SOHO   A classification of a business site with a relatively small number of devices, sometimes in an employee office in their home.

Source NAT   The type of Network Address Translation (NAT) used most commonly in networks (as compared to destination NAT), in which the source IP address of packets entering an inside interface is translated.

southbound API   In the area of SDN, a reference to the APIs used between a controller and the network elements for the purpose of learning information from the elements and for programming (controlling) the forwarding behavior of the elements. Also called a southbound interface.

southbound interface   Another term for southbound API. *See also* southbound API.

spear phishing   Phishing that begins with research about a related group of people so that the attack uses messaging that appears more legitimate by using those researched facts.

spine   In an ACI network design for a single site, a switch that connects to leaf switches only, for the purpose of receiving frames from one leaf switch and then forwarding the frame to some other leaf switch.

split-MAC architecture   A wireless AP strategy based around the idea that normal AP functions are split or divided between a wireless LAN controller and lightweight APs.

spoofing attack   A type of attack in which parameters such as IP and MAC addresses are spoofed with fake values to disguise the sender.

standalone mode   The operational mode used by a FlexConnect AP when the path back to its controller is down and not working. In this mode, all wireless traffic is switched locally, preserving local connectivity while the AP is isolated from its controller.

standard access list   A list of IOS global configuration commands that can match only a packet's source IP address for the purpose of deciding which packets to discard and which to allow through the router.

star topology   A network topology in which endpoints on a network are connected to a common central device by point-to-point links.

stateless   A protocol or process that does not use information stored from previous transactions to perform the current transaction.

station (STA)   An 802.11 client device that is associated with a BSS.

syslog server   A server application that collects syslog messages from many devices over the network and provides a user interface so that IT administrators can view the log messages to troubleshoot problems.

T

TCAM   *See* ternary content-addressable memory.

ternary content-addressable memory (TCAM)   A type of physical memory, either in a separate integrated circuit or built into an ASIC, that can store tables and then be searched against a key, such that the search time happens quickly and does not increase as the size of the table increases. TCAMs are used extensively in higher-performance networking devices as the means to store and search forwarding tables in Ethernet switches and higher-performance routers.

Terraform   An open-source infrastructure as code tool used for provisioning and managing cloud, on-premises, and hybrid infrastructure resources through declarative configuration files.

TFTP Trivial File Transfer Protocol. An application protocol that allows files to be transferred from one computer to another over a network, but with only a few features, making the software require little storage space.

threat An actual potential to use an exploit to take advantage of a vulnerability.

Transport Layer Security (TLS) A security standard that replaced the older Secure Sockets Layer (SSL) protocol, providing functions such as authentication, confidentiality, and message integrity over reliable in-order data streams like TCP.

trojan horse Malware that is hidden and packaged inside other legitimate software.

trusted port With both the DHCP Snooping and Dynamic ARP Inspection (DAI) switch features, the concept and configuration setting that tells the switch to allow all incoming messages of that respective type, rather than to consider the incoming messages (DHCP and ARP, respectively) for filtering.

two-tier design *See* collapsed core design.

U

underlay In SDA, the network devices and links that create basic IP connectivity to support the creation of VXLAN tunnels for the overlay.

Unified Computing System (UCS) The Cisco brand name for its server hardware products.

Universal Power over Ethernet (UPoE) A specific PoE standard as defined in the IEEE 802.3bt amendment to the 802.3 standard, which uses four wire pairs to supply power with a maximum of 60 watts as supplied by the PSE.

Universal Power over Ethernet Plus (UPoE+) A specific PoE standard as defined in the IEEE 802.3bt amendment to the 802.3 standard, which uses four wire pairs to supply power with a maximum of 100 watts as supplied by the PSE.

untrusted port With both the DHCP Snooping and Dynamic ARP Inspection (DAI) switch features, the concept and configuration setting that tells the switch to analyze each incoming message of that respective type (DHCP and ARP) and apply some rules to decide whether to discard the message.

UPoE *See* Universal Power over Ethernet (UPoE).

URI Uniform Resource Identifier. The formal and correct term for the formatted text used to refer to objects in an IP network. This text is commonly called a URL or a web address. For example, http://www.certskills.com/config-labs is a URI that identifies the protocol (HTTP), hostname (www.certskills.com), and web page (config-labs).

URI parameters *See* URI query (parameters).

URI path (resource) In a URI, the part that follows the first /, up to the query field (which begins with a ?), which identifies the resource in the context of a server.

URI query (parameters) In a URI, the part that follows the first ?, which provides a place to list variable names and values as parameters.

URI resource   *See* URI path (resource).

username secret   A reference to the password configured on the **username** *name* **secret** *pass-value* command, which defines a username and an encoded password, used to build a local username/password list on the router or switch.

UTP Cable Category   A set of standards from the TIA and ANSI that defines the electrical characteristics of UTP cabling under various tests. Ethernet standards then refer to these UTP cable categories to define the minimum category needed to support the Ethernet standard at stated distances.

V

violation mode   In port security, a configuration setting that defines the specific set of actions to take on a port when a port security violation occurs. The modes are shutdown, restrict, and protect.

virtual CPU (vCPU)   In a virtualized server environment, a CPU (processor) core or thread allocated to a virtual machine (VM) by the hypervisor.

Virtual IP address (VIP)   Used with first hop redundancy protocols, an address, referenced by hosts as their default router, that can move between multiple routers to support failover of the default router function from one router to another.

virtual machine   An instance of an operating system, running on server hardware that uses a hypervisor to allocate a subset of the server hardware (CPU, RAM, disk, and network) to that VM.

virtual NIC (vNIC)   In a virtualized server environment, a network interface card (NIC) used by a virtual machine, which then connects to some virtual switch (vSwitch) running on that same host, which in turn connects to a physical NIC on the host.

virtual private network (VPN)   A set of security protocols that, when implemented by two devices on either side of an unsecure network such as the Internet, can allow the devices to send data securely. VPNs provide privacy, device authentication, anti-replay services, and data integrity services.

Virtual routing and forwarding (VRF)   Virtual routing and forwarding instance. A feature of routers and Layer 3 switches that makes one router act as multiple routers by assigning interfaces and routing protocol neighbors to specific VRFs, with related routes landing in the associated VRF-unique routing table.

virtual switch (vSwitch)   A software-only virtual switch inside one host (one hardware server), to provide switching features to the virtual machines running on that host.

virus   Malware that injects itself into other applications and then propagates through user intervention.

VPN   *See* virtual private network.

VPN client   Software that resides on a PC, often a laptop, so that the host can implement the protocols required to be an endpoint of a VPN.

vty ACL An IP ACL enabled for inbound SSH and Telnet connections to a router or for outbound requests per the **ssh** and **telnet** commands issued by a user who is already connected to the router using SSH or Telnet.

vulnerability A weakness that can be used to compromise security.

VXLAN Virtual Extensible LAN. A flexible encapsulation protocol used for creating tunnels (overlays).

W

watering hole attack An attack where a site frequently visited by a group of users is compromised; when the target users visit the site, they will be infected with malware, but other users will not.

web server Software, running on a computer, that stores web pages and sends those web pages to web clients (web browsers) that request the web pages.

whaling Spear phishing that targets high-profile individuals.

wildcard mask The mask used in Cisco IOS ACL commands and OSPF and EIGRP **network** commands.

wireless LAN controller (WLC) A device that cooperates with wireless lightweight access points (LWAP) to create a wireless LAN by performing some control functions for each LWAP and forwarding data between each LWAP and the wired LAN.

workgroup bridge (WGB) An AP that is configured to bridge between a wired device and a wireless network. The WGB acts as a wireless client.

worm Malware that propagates from one system to another, infecting as it goes, all autonomously.

write community *See* read-write community.

X–Y–Z

XML (eXtensible Markup Language) A markup language that helps enable dynamic web pages; also useful as a data serialization language.

YAML (YAML Ain't Markup Language) A data serialization language that can be easily read by humans; used by Ansible.

Zero Touch Provisioning (ZTP) An automated deployment process that enables the remote configuration and setup of network devices without requiring manual intervention, allowing for seamless and efficient network deployment at scale.

Index

D

H

half-duplex mode, 7–8

hash function

  algorithm, 209

  enable secret command, 207–208

  MD5 (Message Digest 5), 207, 209

HCL (HashiCorp Configuration Language), 564

header fields

  IPv4, 109

  TCP (Transmission Control Protocol), 95

  UDP (User Datagram Protocol), 104

hold timer

  CDP (Cisco Discovery Protocol), 287

  HSRP (Hot Standby Router Protocol), 358

host mobility, 498

HSRP (Hot Standby Router Protocol), 356

  active/standby model, 356, 359

  failover, 357–358

  Hello message, 358

  Hold timer, 358

  interface tracking, 359–360

  load balancing, 359

  preemption, 360–361, 652

  priority, 357, 652

  similarities with VRRP, 362

  standby state, 357

  versions, 361–362

  VIP (virtual IP address), 357

HTTP (Hypertext Transfer Protocol), 104, 652

  GET response, 108

  how an app is chosen to receive data, 109

request and response, 534

and REST APIs, 533

transferring files, 108–109

verbs, 534

versions

  HTTP 1.0 and 1.1, 110

  HTTP 3.0, 111–112

  HTTP/2 and TLS, 110–111

HTTP/3, adjusting ACLs for, 154–155

hub and spoke topology, 652

human vulnerabilities, 195–196

  pharming, 195

  phishing, 195

  social engineering, 195

  spear phishing, 195

  watering hole attack, 195

  whaling, 195

hybrid topology, 403

hypervisor, 442, 444, 461, 652

I

IaaS (Infrastructure as a Service), 451–452, 653

IAC (infrastructure as code), 653

IANA (Internet Assigned Numbers Authority), 97

IBN (intent-based networking), 483, 486–488, 653

IBSS (independent basic service set), 13–14, 653

ICMP (Internet Control Message Protocol), message filtering, 164–165

IEEE 802.11, 7–8, 18–19

IEEE 802.3, 6

IFS (IOS File System), 653

Imperative Model, 652

J

K

O

P

S

Register your product at **ciscopress.com/register**
to unlock additional benefits:

- Save 35%* on your next purchase with an exclusive discount code

- Find companion files, errata, and product updates if available

- Sign up to receive special offers on new editions and related titles

Get more when you shop at **ciscopress.com**:

- Everyday discounts on books, eBooks, video courses, and more

- Free U.S. shipping on all orders

- Multi-format eBooks to read on your preferred device

- Print and eBook Best Value Packs

Cisco Press